BEFORE I GET OLD
THE STORY OF THE WHO

Dave Marsh

Plexus, London

All rights reserved including the right
of reproduction in whole or in part in any form
This edition first published in 2015
Copyright © 2015, 1983 by Duke & Duchess Ventures, Inc.
Published by Plexus Publishing Limited
The Studio, Hillgate Place
18-20 Balham Hill
London SW12 9ER
www.plexusbooks.com

British Library Cataloguing in Publication Data
A catalogue record for this book is available from the British Library

ISBN-13: 978-0-85965-524-8

Cover photo: Trinifold
Cover design by Coco Balderrama
Printed in Great Britain by Bell & Bain Ltd, Glasgow.

ACKNOWLEDGMENTS

The research materials for this book included more than six hundred newspaper and magazine clippings on the Who and related aspects of their career. The majority of these were collected by Wayne King, whose assistance there, as well as his general insight and friendship, made him absolutely indispensable to the creation of *Before I Get Old*. Debbie Geller also did a devoted job of research on photographs, as well as feeding me her ideas. I thank them both publicly, as I have not done sufficiently in private.

Chris Chappel negotiated me through many of the trickier bits of research in London, as well as keeping me posted on everyday developments with the band from 1977 through 1982. More than anything, Chris's sense of humor, good timing, friendship (and his flat in Clapham) got me through my first long stint abroad. Malu Halasa was also a lifesaver in making many arrangements during this period.

A number of my colleagues in the press were willing to share time, notes, and concepts. Steve Turner was especially generous, allowing me to use the transcript of his fine interview with Pete Meaden and helping me locate all sorts of material about mod that this Yank would never otherwise have uncovered. I also thank Roy Carr, Chris Charlesworth, Vic Garbarini and John Swenson.

John Landau has stopped writing, but not thinking, and he'll find herein many lines stolen from our conversations.

Jeep Holland initiated my Who fanaticism many years ago and sustained it with tips, theories and middle-of-the-night badgering. Bob London offered insights into rock & roll psyches that often rescued me.

Frank and June Barsalona, besides being simply good friends, have been kind enough to share many Who anecdotes and perceptions over the years. Frank's role in the story is told in the text, but June's insights, about England in particular, were equally useful.

I would like to thank all those who participated in interviews for the book, particularly Irene and the late Harry Daltrey and Cliff and Betty Townshend. Peter Rudge, Peter Blake, Mike McInnerney and Billy Nicholls spent several hours each with me, contributing much that doesn't show up directly and a great deal of what's between the lines.

The grandest interviews of all were with Irish Jack Lyons, the truest Who fan of them all, as well as the first. Jack kindly shared with me his eloquent reminiscences of the early days of Whomania, both verbal and written, and I would have been lost without them. I am also indebted to the entire Lyons family, especially to Maura Lyons, for their hospitality and friendship.

Peter Hogan nobly waded through a manuscript more messy than it ought to have been and yanked from it something of which I'm a good deal more proud than when he began. Hogan's insights about the Who, Meher Baba and the turmoil of publishing were often essential in just keeping me afloat. Peter also managed to make me feel like something other than a surfer in Brighton, for which he deserves to miss out on a couple of incarnations, if anyone is listening. Merrilee Heifetz, of Writers House, steered us through some tricky passages, and Bob Miller, at St. Martin's Press, provided consistent enthusiasm and stimulation, as well as valuable editorial comments.

The real shepherd of *Before I Get Old* was my friend and agent, Sandra Choron, who was nothing less than a rock when I needed one, a goad when she had to be, and the best person I know upon whom to try out ideas, tantrums and blarney. Sandy's selflessness and professionalism are more than appreciated; her willingness to combat a headstrong and relentless author are literally the only reason this volume ever got finished.

The most patient people in the world are my family, Barbara, Sasha, and Kristen Carr. For being kind enough to live with a bulky manuscript and a total grouch for the better part of two years, I bless them individually and collectively. And promise not to do it again, until the next time.

Lastly, the Who have been, over the years, very generous with their time and conversation. Their willingness to allow me access to their families in the course of my research is especially appreciated. I owe Pete Townshend a special debt of gratitude for going out on the limb when I first cooked up this harebrained scheme. As a musician, interview subject, and friend, Pete tops the bill. I hope I haven't added too much to his burden.

For Jeep, Obie, Wayne and Chris—
four who are more than all right.

*The compensation of a very early success
is a conviction that life is a romantic matter.
In the best sense, one stays young. When the
primary objects of love and money could be
taken for granted, and a shaky eminence had
lost its fascination, I had fair years to waste,
years that I can't honestly regret, in seeking
the eternal Carnival by the Sea.*
                    —F. Scott Fitzgerald
                    Early Success

All men are bored with other men's lives.
                    —Pete Townshend
                    "Pure and Easy"

INTRODUCTION

Before *I Get Old* is the product of an obsession that began the first time I ever heard the Who. It was the winter of 1965. I was fourteen, desperate for fifteen, and the old radio that sat upon my bedroom dresser was blaring Top 40.

Rock & roll had been my passion since the first time I had heard Elvis Presley, at age six. By 1965 I was engulfed in it: the exhilarating fantasy/reality of the Beach Boys, the sweet innocence of the Crystals, the romantic pangs of Smokey Robinson and the Miracles, the heart-stopping paranoia of the Righteous Brothers, the nasty blues of the Animals, the pure excitement of Jackie Wilson, the innocence of the Four Seasons, the dignity of Chuck Berry, the danger of Wilson Pickett, the dance fanaticism of James Brown, the mysterious sounds that came from Gene Pitney, Del Shannon, and Roy Orbison. In this context the Beatles and the Rolling Stones were more a fulfillment than a surprise. Certainly, the quality of the music was nothing new; I could never remember a time when rock & roll wasn't great. Those singers and their songs meant more to me than anything else I knew—books, movies, baseball stars or most other people, for that matter. In a world of fakes, rock & roll was real and true.

The fresh blast of "I Can't Explain" was a clean kill. It transfixed me as I stood fearful that it would end. Guitars cracked like whips; drums pounded like heads against walls. The vocal was a snarl of pain and confusion, perfectly suited to my own teenage tribulations. It took my breath away and left me reeling and dizzy.

In two minutes and five seconds the Who distilled the promise of all the other rock & roll I'd ever heard. It was vicious, raw and bruising, but somehow what it seemed to say was that if you could only be as strong as this music, that strength would armor you enough to get through the world. At the time, getting through seemed a highly dubious proposition. So I was hooked.

Almost twenty years on, "I Can't Explain" still seems a sufficient reason for writing this book. Just about everything that the Who had to say is implied in it—and that's not a sign that they didn't have much to say but of how much they compacted into that short song. For those of us still hanging on to visions and dreams, the Who have a special place in rock history, as in our hearts.

What I've written is not a biography. There are many facts, dates and names herein, but there could have been many more if that was what the job required. Instead, I hope that *Before I Get Old* functions as a species of history, the tale not just of a rock band but of its times, reflecting the concerns and changes felt not only by the musicians but by the audience, too.

There's no remotely major event in the Who's career that isn't covered here. There are many good stories that weren't told, though, because they took the story in a direction away from the heart of the matter. On the other hand, there is a great deal of information and analysis contained in the book which is parallel or peripheral to the Who: about pirate radio, skiffle music, the rock business, drugs and religion, for instance.

These digressions are important, because without them, the Who's story doesn't make sense. Unlike the Beatles or Elvis (or in a pinch, the Rolling Stones), the Who do not have a purely self-contained history. The move from the French crew cut to *Quadrophenia* is part of a long and complex process. Woodstock acquires more meaning through knowledge about package tours, workingmen's social clubs in west London, the mod clubs of Soho. Such famous and obscure situations themselves acquire a different flavor when set against the unraveling spiral of the Who's career.

At the start and at the finish, this is the story of the Who and the world in which that band lived and played. Trying to regain the exact spirit of those times is futile, I know. As Doris Lessing has written, recapturing the atmosphere of an era is much the same as trying to recapture the quality of a dream. "No communication possible, unless someone else had the same dream, and that you have to take on trust."

What I'm trusting here is that the reader also has some inkling of how much rock meant to its audiences in the heyday of the Who—of how much some of it still means. Those who know only the cynicism into which popular culture is sunk may find portions of this narrative naïve. I can only insist that many of us genuinely shared a dream in those days, that together we imagined that it was possible to create an open and democratic culture. And that the center of that dream was rock & roll.

For those who did share the dream, the digressions will make more sense. But perhaps even for these readers, the additional material—allusive as it must be—will seem redundant. I don't think so. We take too much for granted about our own times, and this is dangerous. Already we've abandoned the care and treatment of the history of our hope to those who wish to narrow or deny it: to say, for instance, that the anti-war demonstrations made Vietnam worse rather than better, or that rock & roll was never more than pretentious when it tried to surpass its commercial limitations. These are lies, and the only way to combat them is to insist on seeing what happened in its proper context.

For millions of rock fans, our hopes of creating a culture that abandoned voyeurism for involvement centered around the Who, a band that was honest with itself and with us as no other entertainers were willing to be. In consequence, I have tried to be equally open and honest in assessing and in spelling out the story of what happened to the Who and its audience. In my version of this story there is no happy ending. That doesn't mean that I have not looked for one or that I don't wish it were otherwise. But it would violate my love for the Who and destroy what's genuinely moving about the story if I were to duck the facts.

But however critical *Before I Get Old* may be of the Who, there is no way to deny the best music that the band created. The integrity, power and intelligence that animate those records, the compelling emotions evoked by their best music, the way that our lives were enriched by both are no illusion. After all these months of laboring at telling the story, it's hard to say when I will be able to listen to the Who purely for pleasure again. But I know that I will and that when that time comes my faith will be rewarded.

That's why the Who deserve this sort of extended treatment. In terms of record sales and public acclaim, much of what they did remains uncelebrated; given how fascinating they are as people, none of them is nearly famous enough. As people, the Who were frail—as we all are. As musicians, they were gifted—as we only hope to be. As a band, linked forever by history, they were an inspiration—and you and I may hope we are never cursed with such a burden. In the end, these are the things that are worth remembering. For me, they are unforgettable.

Dave Marsh
April 14, 1983

1

It was the time of the big mod cult, and there was nobody to represent it. We saw the opening and they accepted us. It was a good time. . . . But where has that old sense of urgency gone now? Where's the excitement?
— Roger Daltrey

In the winter of 1960, Jack Lyons left Cork for London. He immediately moved in with his mother's sister Nan, her husband, Jack Cole, and their daughter, Janice, at 22 Kelmscott Gardens, Shepherd's Bush. For a time he simply hung around the neighborhood and the Coles' upstairs flat acclimating himself, but after a couple of weeks Lyons found a job at the nearby London Electricity Board. Because he was still underage, Jack also attended the Hammersmith Day College each Tuesday.

Jack was short, skinny and a born chatterbox. He'd grown up only five miles from Blarney Castle, and one might have been forgiven the presumption that he had slept a fortnight with his tongue wrapped around its famous stone. Not that Jack's gift of gab was not accompanied by a certain eloquence and perceptivity. But this did him little good in London, either at work or at school, since all of his diatribes and expostulations were delivered with the thickest of Irish accents, a rendering of syllables all but unintelligible to the unwilling cockney ear. The result was a constant round of explanations and restatements, none to much avail, since Jack's thinking was as Irish as his speech: His thought, while bright and loquacious, began with the middle of the tale and ended at the start.

Sharp as he was, Jack quickly began to adjust to the English accent and its accompanying mannerisms, acquiring a kind of protective coloration, although this was never totally effective, since he never gained much regard for syllogistic logic and since his cockney was never more than a veil over the pure Irishness of his true accent. Along the way Jack also acquired a phobia about his Irishness, began almost to loathe his heritage, became bitterly self-conscious about his origins, uttered silent prayers in hopes of deliverance from them. In consequence, his convivial nature became encased in a loner's shell. Though he studiously copied the cool trendiness of the heavy boys in the Bush, Jack never quite felt that he fitted in.

Thus it was that Jack was unaccompanied when he entered the church hall, Boseley's, one night in late 1962. Lyons had drifted there for reasons he could never remember. Maybe his cousin had recommended it as a possible place to meet people; perhaps he was simply looking for something to do. It was a weekend night, and he was wearing skintight trousers, a sharp white mac, winklepicker boots and a then-stylish Robin Hood's hat—an outfit that might have been impressive for the day, had Boseley's contained anyone worth impressing. The ballroom held only about twenty-five people, few of whom were dancing, for someone had overwaxed the floor, and to chance out upon it was to ask for a tumble. Since he didn't see anyone approaching suitability as a partner, in any event, Jack didn't plan to stay long.

But his gaze fell upon the bandstand and the guitarist at stage left, half-hidden behind a jumbo acoustic. The sight of him riveted Jack, forced him to edge nearer. "I wanted to get a proper look," he said, "'cause it made my bloody night, it did. When I got close up to him, I could see he was wearing my true face—the face I always wanted. In him I could see me, if you know what I mean. See, I reckoned everything would have been perfect if I had a nose like this geezer, 'cause then people wouldn't take the piss out of me when I spoke with my seesaw Irish accent. They'd be too busy looking at my bleedin' nose."

This guitarist was playing with a quintet called the Detours. Dressed in collarless maroon jackets and white shirts with bow ties, they were fairly typical Young Entertainers. Their singer, a straight-backed, immobile lad, was an archetype of the Cliff Richard crooners then infesting the isle, making Elvis moves with the danger lobotomized from nuance or memory. The Detours' repertoire was built around the rather bland hits of the period; their playing made the music seem even blander.

Nonetheless, the guitar player (or at least his nose) was fascinating. After the show, Jack hung around for a word with him.

The guitarist was called Peter Townshend. He and the rest of the band, whose leader seemed to be the electric guitarist, Roger Daltrey, came from the nearby neighborhoods of Ealing and Acton, slightly more upscale than the downtrodden Bush. Five nights a week the Detours came together to play in pubs and clubs. In the daylight, all of them worked, save Townshend, who was attending art college.

Jack gleaned this much from the conversation that took place, though he was transfixed by Townshend's remarkable instrument, his beak. This was a genuinely fabulous device, for while it was neither bent nor crooked and was, for the most part, a proper Anglo-Saxon nose with nothing ethnic about it, beginning reasonably enough at the bridge with a gentle curve, it blossomed just below the eyes, swooping preposterously until its central stem seemed a mere trestle for the vast, vacant nostrils that mushroomed across Townshend's mug. It isn't known whether Jack mentioned the precise object of his fascination to Townshend, though the length of their conversation argues against it.

Jack forever after traced being stage-struck to this encounter, yet he did nothing toward becoming a performer as a result of it, and he soon lost sight of the group. He simply went back to the mailroom of the Electricity Board— with a thought planted in the back of his mind.

In the natural course of things, Jack began to frequent the Goldhawk Road Social Club. The Goldhawk was not a pub, nor was it your average workingman's club. Like any urban area laced with immigrants and possessed of an open-air market, Shepherd's Bush developed its share of hard cases, so that a club like the Goldhawk, which in another area might have been merely a place for the local yobs to catch a couple of pints away from the ball and chain of home life, was tinged with hints of danger. On weekends, especially, the garden was often the site of punch-ups and worse. This is not to say that most of the clientele were of the criminal persuasion, though it's true that a good many of them were working toward it. And the others, the relative innocents such as Jack, had a rather roughhouse idea of fun themselves.

It was in clubs like the Goldhawk, in similar working-class districts all over London, that the mods began to come into their own. There had been modernists in the East End since the late fifties, identifiable by their strut and the rather extreme cut of their suits. But by the beginning of 1963 what was once modernist had become mod and moved clear across town to the western working-class areas.

Mod might have been only another of the postwar style crazes that rise and fall with such regularity in England: It had its own clothing, its own rituals and eventually its own music, which is all most such cults need. But mod was something more than a marketing mechanism or an excuse for teen tribalism. At least among the hardcore who developed it, mod was a philosophy, articulated in the chrome of a motor scooter's proliferated head lamps, the flare of a pair of trousers, the choice of just the right bright shade of a Fred Perry knit shirt, the length of the vent in a sports jacket. The aim was a style both flamboyant and cool—that is, proclaiming a poise that did not need to prove itself. The result was an undercurrent of tension—the violence always implicit but rarely acted out.

Mod was a signal of a new kind of working-class rebellion, not only against bosses but also against the mods' own parents and elder brothers—against the entire pattern of conformism and conservatism in British life. Where tradition called for steady saving, honoring rank and tradition, a chipper attitude and an acceptance of limits, the mod's response was a penchant for consumption— snubbing one's superiors and all that was old, a cynical outlook and a refusal to stay in one's place. But this was an idea spelled out only in the width of one's lapels (and in the fact that one did not save, but spent whatever it cost to have them altered as often as necessary). It was never openly voiced. Mods were sophisticated and slick, rebels with a cause, an assault that burrowed from within, asserting not just their own dignity but also the absolute ludicrousness of stuffy conformism. If mod was a statement of the affluence many found in Prime Minister Macmillan's you've-never-had-it-so-good policies, it was also a mockery of those things. In its myriad shifts of detail—styles radically altering not just from month to month but from week to week and even from one end of the weekend to the other—mod contained not just an implicit critique but an almost conscious satire of the modernist philosophy of planned obsolescence.

Such shifts of style also enforced a rigid code among the members of the cult. "Mods believed in discipline," said Jack. "The whole mod thing was an army. The best thing about it was you had to be working to keep up with the changing fashions."

But mods didn't find jobs in order to build careers, and they never kept one because it had a future. They were the original exponents of the punk-as-clerk; they got jobs either because they paid well or because they offered some opportunity to swagger. On payday, mods spent. Mods worked in order to have clothes and scooters, amphetamines (purple hearts, or leapers, as they were also known) and more clothes, chic American soul records, chewing gum, some more clothes and what it cost to tailor them. Food, drink and girls hardly mattered. The look and the ability to support it were the end in themselves.

"When the fashion really got moving," said Jack in the unpublished memoir of the period which he later wrote, "it reached a stage where it took any one of us up to about three weeks to save up for a bit of gear that probably wouldn't have seen its way through a month of fashion. That's how much we cared about how we looked. We hated being out of fashion with each other. I mean, you felt like a worm turning up in something leading mods and faces had already stopped wearing."

Because mod fashion was virtually Ivy League, especially in the early days, the image of the mod clerk who dressed better than his boss is accurate. But antipathy for bosses went further than a corridor snicker. The best-dressed mods were liable to be those whose Fred Perry shirts had fallen off the back of a lorry or who spent money earned off the books in one of a variety of petty but indictable enterprises. Yet all mods lived by a certain code, and for those reluctant or inept at coming up with enough loot to obtain the proper gear, the answer might be staying in some weekends, lest one turn up in public less than acceptably turned out.

This was not the mod scene that was marketed to teenagers after the holiday outbreaks at Clacton and Margate and Brighton in 1964. But it is a fair picture of those who latched onto the style before the media made it notorious. And those were the sort of guys (female mods came later) who hung about the Goldhawk Road Social Club.

The Goldhawk wasn't a regular music venue. But on weekends, part of its attraction was live bands. The first band that Jack remembers seeing there was Screaming Lord Sutch and the Savages, Britain's answer to Screamin' Jay Hawkins in that Sutch (who was actually a plebeian from Northolt and, offstage, dispersed with even the veneer of a proper upper-class accent) began his show by rising from a coffin and played a sort of Anglified rhythm & blues. Sutch was a dreadful singer, but his bands included many soon-to-be-important musicians (notably Nicky Hopkins and Jimmy Page), and the musical style, if not the sound itself, was correct for mod tastes, which ran to blues and soul and the West Indian bluebeat (soon to be called ska and then to mutate further into reggae).

There was no mod music, just music that mods liked. Unlike the British style cults of a decade later, mod fashion didn't build itself around bands. Instead, a group of rock bands did its best to play music that would appeal to mods. It was the time of the British beat boom, the Rolling Stones bringing the movement into London in the wake of the Beatles and the Merseybeats. From the start, mods liked the Stones (though they eventually were written off as being beatniks), and in one way or another all the groups later identified with mod used variants of the Stones' approach to R&B.

For some of west London's young groups, the Goldhawk was a fairly important venue. It paid reasonably well, and the crowd were taste-makers. Go down well at the Goldhawk, and word would surely spread.

In any event, it was at the Goldhawk that Jack once more encountered the Detours. It was Townshend's nose that enabled him to recognize them; in every other way the group had changed radically. Daltrey, the short, feisty guitarist, had dumped the upright front man of Boseley's and now personally replaced him. This left Townshend as the only guitarist, accompanied by bassist John Entwistle and drummer Doug Sandom. The resulting trio-plus-vocalist was about as stripped down as a band could become, but the Detours played with so much furious energy that listeners were, if anything, overcompensated.

The Detours were also dressing better. They weren't mod—at least not quite, not while the stolid bassist and the streetwise drummer, who looked a decade older than the rest, were around. But at least their corny suits and bow ties had been exchanged for more stylish leather jackets.

More importantly, the music that they now played was blues, rhythm & blues and that new American variant, Tamla-Motown soul. Even though musical tastes within the mod cult hadn't yet been codified into obligatory loves and hates (though Gene Vincent struck Jack as "the epiphany of un-mod," hundreds of mods turned out for his stage shows), the Detours were playing what mods wanted to hear. They stripped down the sinuous, finger-popping rhythms of the breathy, danceable Motown records, like Marvin Gaye's "I Heard It Through the Grapevine" or Martha and the Vandellas' "Heat Wave" to their raw essence, adding an edge of pace and drive that was the perfect accompaniment for the mods' aggressive, amphetamined cool.

Playing pubs and clubs, the Detours had become more and more professional (though Townshend remained in school and the others kept their jobs). Their keynote song of the period was perfect for the hardboys at the Goldhawk: Mose

Allison's "Parchman Farm", originally a white Mississippian's fantasy of black prison life, complete with chain gang—but in the Detours' hands (and coming out of Daltrey's mouth), transcending its feeling of black exotica and becoming a complaint, an angry shout of defiance, a strutting assertion of the coolness of criminal potentiality, a resonance of effect made greater by the proximity of the Bush to the sprawling London jail complex, Wormwood Scrubs.

From the mods the Detours took everything—not just a suggestion of musical direction, but clothing, dance steps, a preference in pills (leapers) and drink (brandy and ginger) and their swaggering demeanor. Because they lacked the pretty face all the other British bands deemed necessary, the Detours were even more attractive in this macho scene. In due course the Detours acquired a Friday night residency at the Goldhawk, a vantage point from which Jack and his mates watched as they changed their name to the Who and their fortunes rose.

The Who was a name that the Goldhawk boys loved. "What a fucking name," Jack said. "No one liked it, but by the end of the first week no one could think of anything more suitable. It was anonymous—it was like a self-destructive pyramid. You said it, and the other person said it back in question: 'The Who, mate.' 'The Who?' 'Yes, you cunt—the Who.' We used to fucking love that. It put the Bush boys above everyone else."

As the Who's reputation spread across London, the Goldhawk crowd traveled with them, not only "up west" to the Marquee and the Scene, but as far off as St. Mary's Hall, Putney, where, opening for bands with bigger reputations, bands who had already cracked the charts, like Manfred Mann, they would sometimes wipe the headliner right off the stage and would be asked back to play as headliners themselves, because they'd proved they could pack the joint alone. They brought their audience with them. Jack—Irish Jack, he was dubbed one drunken night—led the pack; he was not only their original fan, having spotted them first, if ever so briefly, but the most passionate of them all.

Early in 1965, after acquiring a new, more mod drummer, Keith Moon, the band got a record deal, and Townshend began to write songs, which Jack and the Goldhawk mob loved even more, not only because his numbers reworked many of the rhythm & blues changes but also because they had lyrics that zeroed in on mod emotions. Townshend, it turned out, was the perfect person to articulate the frustration and anxiety that Irish Jack and his mates felt but could never express.

The records took the Who farther afield, to the provinces and the pop charts. But because of what those songs—"I Can't Explain," "Anyway, Anyhow, Anywhere," "My Generation"—had to say, the mods never felt alienated from their national success. In those records the Who had packaged the Goldhawk experience and sieved out its core, and the nation exploded in response. The role models for the stuttering renegade of "My Generation" not only weren't complaining, they were rejoicing, for mod was now moving out to conquer Britain. It was the headiest of moments, and everyone—Irish Jack included—was exhilarated beyond all hope of recovery.

And yet the increasing media attention, the opening of tacky tourist traps on the mods' main shopping street, Carnaby Street, in Soho, the influx of younger and younger kids wearing mod regalia, the distortions in the press and the eagerness of unallied bands and promoters to latch onto the trend were not only spoiling it, they were tearing apart the unspoken bonds of the original mods. No longer a philosophy, mod was now just a gesture, a way of signifying a certain immoderate hipness. No longer a threat, mod was just a fad, a means of attracting attention. And slowly but surely, the original rituals faded and new ones rose up in their place; old friends drifted away, and only a few remained in the familiar haunts; the old cohesion left the scene as all and everything about it split up. The Who went its way as a moderately famous pop band; the mods of the Goldhawk went theirs, as workers or thieves or some combination of both. Finally, Jack went back to Ireland. By the fall of 1966 it was all over.

Yet there was that moment when mod had been all-conquering, when the Who had spoken to Britain and Britain had roared back its allegiance; when the Goldhawk lads had swaggered in the East End (and even "up west") because the Who was *their* band and because those hits were not only the product of the labor of their mates but had somehow been crucially formed in an experience that the Goldhawk gang had shared. It was the winter of 1965 when the time and the tunes had been synchronized.

On Mondays, Hammersmith Palais held Off the Record Night. The hall was completely lit up with spotlights and packed with four hundred mods, faces from all over western London, come to listen to the latest smooth Tamla sounds —Marvin Gaye's "Grapevine," the Temptations' "Don't Look Back," the Miracles' swaying "I've Gotta Dance to Keep From Crying"—and to dance the block, but most of all to bask in the presence of so many like themselves. In those hours, loners discovered community, and somehow, those Who singles said it all for them. "I believed in them," Jack said. "I was willing to ditch Roman Catholicism for a greater religion, called the Who, and a Jack I'd never known before, someone who'd been trying to get out for so long." And this Jack was not alone; he was as connected as a man could be. When Peter Townshend, three years later, said that such moments were "the closest to patriotism I've ever felt," Jack and the mods who were there understood him perfectly.

For the exhibitionist in every mod, any chance to dance was a triumph, but for a brave few, the climax of Off the Record Night at the Palais topped everything. It was an amateur mime contest in which any gang of daydreamers could enact its performance fantasy, be it cool soul choreography or raw British beat.

"Me and my mates took it so seriously," Irish Jack said. "It was a fantastic feeling up there on that stage, almost like the real thing, if you know what I mean. Me and Martin Gaish and Peter Campbell and Lee Gaish used to always go up as the Who. Fuck me, who else?

"The butterflies in our stomachs before we got on stage, that was the best part of it. Once you went up as the Who, you couldn't fucking break up laughing at yourself halfway through the song like some of them did. The Who weren't a joke; they were for fucking real, and so were we."

Usually, the mock Who went on last. They were the best prepared: Lee Gaish had once caught a pair of Moon's cracked drumsticks, which Keith was even then throwing out to the crowd as they were ruined. Martin Gaish had talked Roger Daltrey out of a battered, old tambourine. These totems were the genuine articles, and though Peter Campbell and Irish Jack (as Entwistle and Townshend, respectively) never managed to get hold of Who guitars (since even the busted fragments were too preciously expensive to he discarded cavalierly), the magic of this instrumental nearness transferred itself to the group. "Blimey," said Jack, "you should have seen the compère's eyes when old Martin would start bashing that mike stand like Roger used to. The poor bloke used to look like there wouldn't be no mike stand left by the time Martin finished with it.

"Up on that Palais stage it really didn't matter that you didn't have a guitar hanging around your neck. The atmosphere was enough, especially with the record blaring out behind you.

"Honestly, you should've seen the way people looked when they saw Campbell running his fingers up and down the neck of his imaginary bass guitar. Campbell, see, wouldn't be playing the neck the ordinary way like most bass players. He used to have his hand coming up over the neck instead of the usual down-under way. That's how Entwistle played, see.

"I had to be Townshend. It was me what got these four mates of mine to do this mime in the first place. To them, I was coherent; to me, I was fucking Jekyll and Hyde! I was totally schizophrenic with a mountain of anxiety for mod acceptance going on inside me. No one did—except me.

"Anyway, there we are, just walked on the stage after the introduction. The compère looks over at us from his pulpit; he's got the record ready. This moment is magic up here. I give him one of me I-don't-care looks, and he turns the volume button. You can hear the speakers crackle just before the needle hits the first groove.

" . . . here come the opening chords. I feel like I'm going to go through the floor. Lee Gaish is twirling a drumstick, he's bouncing the other off the air. Martin's thumping the mike stand with the tambourine. *'Got a feeling inside . . . certain kind.'* Campbell looks into the crowd; he won't smile for anyone.

"I'm pounding up and down the stage, twiddling amp knobs which are supposed to be six feet in the air. I almost forget I haven't got a guitar around my neck. I stare into the front rows and some hard geezers are giving me back that look: 'Want bother?'

"But I can take any cunt while I'm up on this stage. I look back at those blokes, and the next thing, WHAM! I flash my arm around like a windmill blade, and as the chorus line comes up, I shout into the sea of Palais faces: 'I CAN'T EXPLAIN!' "

All through the winter of 1943–44, Nazi bombs fell on London, so many, so destructively, that nearly forty years later Irene Daltrey's voice trembled and shuddered, once more quivering with the terror of it. "I can hear them bombs falling now," she said. "Oh, it was a terrible sight, the fire of London. Everywhere you looked was blazing, everywhere. We lived in Percy Road, in the Bush. Every house was burning. It started on a Saturday evening and carried on through the night."

In late February, the house next door to 15 Percy Road, where Irene and her husband, Harry, had lived for several years, took a direct hit and was demolished. Twenty people were killed. Miraculously, the Daltreys escaped, but adding to Irene's terror was the fact that she was better than eight months pregnant. She should not have been.

The Daltreys had been married at twenty-three, in 1936, after several years' courtship. Harry had been working in the offices of Armitage Shanks, the water closet manufacturer, since leaving school at fourteen. Both Harry and Irene were lifelong residents of the Shepherd's Bush area.

Nine months after the marriage, Irene Daltrey lost a kidney to disease. "In them days, there were no kidney machines; it was really serious. And they said to me, 'You'll never be able to have a baby with one kidney.' And that really broke my heart, 'cause I had four sisters and they were all having children, except me."

Several months later she again fell ill. This time it was polio and polyneuritis;

for a while she was paralyzed. Irene never completely recovered the use of her hands, though she regained most of her mobility after a long stretch in a wheelchair.

When the war broke out, Harry was drafted. But several times he was granted up to three months compassionate leave and continued to be based in England until after D-Day.

"On one of those leaves," Mrs. Daltrey remembered, "he came home. I was thirty-two then, and I got pregnant. Then the air raids started." Then came the hit next door; the Daltreys' house was "messed up," but no one was injured, and it remained habitable. "This is only a week before the baby was due, so I was so scared of the air raids. I slept in the tube shelter, in the underground. Every night I'd take the blankets down. And it was while I was laying there, trying to sleep in this underground, that I came in labor.

"I wasn't afraid to have the baby, havin' this one kidney. I was more afraid when the ambulance men came down to the tube shelter to take me to the hospital. I was more afraid of the air raids, 'cause I could hear them. I could hear the planes coming over, and the doodlebugs—oh, it was dreadful.

"I was taken at nine o'clock. He would have been a leap year's baby, but I said, 'Oh, please don't let him come until March first.' They said, 'Why?' I said, 'Because it's my mother's birthday. Anyway, he came just before two o'clock in the morning; he just got into the first of March." She named him Roger Harry Daltrey.

Irene Daltrey came through the delivery with flying colors; she would have two more children, in the next four years. But her biggest fear was not for herself. "I really thought he'd be disfigured or harmed in some way by that bomb scare I had. But he came out of it all right, didn't he?"

When Roger was three months old, Harry was sent overseas. Irene and the baby were evacuated to a farm in Scotland. "I could hardly walk, and I couldn't use me hands much. So they evacuated us. And it was right on a farm, and the nearest shop about ten miles. We had no neighbors, and we didn't have any water—we had to walk about ten minutes to get water in a bucket. We had no light; we had oil. We had no cooking, only an open fire. A whole year I was there. All the snow—it was terrible."

City-bred, Irene Daltrey clearly had no taste for the crofter's life. She was worried about the baby, too. "I didn't think he would survive, because every day he had boiled potatoes. We had to go to bed when it got dark because the people who had let the room to us really couldn't afford the oil."

At the end of the war, in the summer of 1945, Harry Daltrey was mustered out of the army and the family was reunited back in the Bush. Soon after, the first of Roger's sisters, Gillian, was born. The youngest daughter, Carol, was born in late 1947.

At work, Harry Daltrey moved up a bit, eventually becoming office manager. By 1955 the family had saved enough to move to the much nicer, though still nearby, neighborhood of Acton.

Roger was a bright boy. At the time, the channeling of students within the

English state school system was begun with the eleven-plus examinations, taken when the students were only a few months past their eleventh birthdays. This test was crucial to a student's future. Those who exhibited little or no potential, according to the results, were shunted off to the secondary moderns, schools where the students are trained with an eye to getting jobs, mostly unskilled or semiskilled labor. (In contemporary Britain this can often mean being trained to join the ranks of the semipermanently unemployed.) Grammar schools, where those who did well on the eleven-pluses were sent, place much more emphasis on academics. While the line drawn by the eleven-plus exams wasn't as extreme as that created by the O- and A-level examinations taken a few years later, the distinction between doing well and doing poorly was understood by everyone involved in the process as an important harbinger of the future.

Taking his eleven-plus exams at Victoria Primary School in Shepherd's Bush, Roger Daltrey was placed at the very top of the class. But since the family had now moved to Bedford Park, he was assigned to Acton County Grammar, an all-boys school that drew most of its population from the more upscale communities of Chiswick, Acton and Ealing.

"He was very interested in school," Harry Daltrey recalled. "He got good reports, he was very interested in his P.T. [physical training], the choir. And then he was chosen to go to Acton Grammar. . . ."

"And he lost it," said Irene, still irked and half mournful. "He didn't have any interest in school once that little gang got together."

"Maybe it was the change of neighborhood," suggested Harry, "because at the time, we moved from Shepherd's Bush, which is more of a rougher type of area, and this [Bedford Park] is a much nicer area, really. And I don't really think Roger enjoyed that, because he lost all of his pals. At any rate, he carried on at school. His first year's report wasn't too bad, but gradually I could see that he didn't have the interest in his schooling that he should have had."

"I just could not identify," Roger said. He heard the more precise accents of his new schoolmates and was immediately threatened. To his cockney ear, the local schoolboys sounded posh, upper-class and mincing. "I thought, this is what the school's gonna do to me. . . .They were totally foreign to me. They didn't even know what playing in the street was." So he and a gang of ten others "who felt the same way" became one of Acton Grammar's antipodal cliques: near-Teddy boys, rough-edged and rebellious. "We were the worst lot at school," said Roger. Others remember it the same way.

All his life Roger would retain a sense of where he came from: Percy Road, in the grimy, semi-industrial Bush, with its small, narrow houses and its side streets ulcerated from neglect. He would never be able to identify with Acton, at least not with tidy, tree-lined Bedford Park, with its sturdy brick houses and well-groomed gardens. The difference is only between one end of the working class and the other, but for the Daltreys and others who made it, that difference was a leap across a chasm. Roger refused to jump.

In later years Roger has said, "If you come from the streets, you've got how many ways out? You can either work in a factory and become an ordinary geezer.

Or if you've got any spark of wanting to be a total individual, you can become one of four things—a footballer, a boxer, a criminal or a pop singer. I guess that's why I'll still be rockin' in my wheelchair. Rock and roll was my saviour."

More to the point is what Daltrey told Pete Hamill in 1982: "Rock & roll saved my life. A lot of my mates, the fellas I grew up with, ended in jail. After I took my eleven-plus exams, I was sent to Acton. I had good grades. But where I came from, I didn't know people like I met at Acton County. I thought everybody talked like *me*—until I got *there*. . . . I loved rock & roll because *they* hated it."

In mid-May of 1945 the bombs stopped falling, even in western Germany. On May 9 the Nazis had surrendered. Now, ten days later, the Royal Air Force's elite band, the Squadronaires, were playing martial music to accompany a morale-boosting speech by Air Wing Commander Tedder.

The Occupation troops were probably pleased to see the Squadronaires, since they were Britain's leading dance band. At clubs and bases all over British-held Europe, and before D-Day at bases back home, they played the kind of muscular swing arrangements popularized by Benny Goodman. Led by pianist Ronnie Aldrich, the Squadronaires were so hot that they were said to be favorites even among the American troops.

In the midst of Tedder's speech a motorcycle messenger was heard approaching the bandstand. The crowd tensed with expectation of some momentous news about to be dispatched to the Air Wing Commander. But rather than going to the speaker's platform, the messenger swung his cycle around and made a beeline for the bandstand. Skidding to a halt, leg thrust out in the motorcyclist's classic stance of urgency, he sought out the Squadronaires' alto saxophonist, Cliff Townshend. Spotting him, he hollered out, "Cliff! It's a boy!"

Cliff and his wife, a singer whose maiden name was Betty Dennis, named their son Peter Dennis Blandford Townshend. The date was May 19, 1945.

Both the Townshends were in the entertainment corps of the RAF. When they met, they were stationed in London, he with the Squadronaires, she doing canned programs to be broadcast to the troops in Italy and North Africa as featured vocalist with the Sydney Torch Orchestra. They were working with the best of Britain's variety show performers: Bebe Daniels, Lesley Douglas, Ben Lyon, Ann Shelton.

"It was through Lesley Douglas that I met Cliff," Betty remembered. "Lesley was on this show as an artist, and he heard me sing. He made a mental note of it and kept me in his mind. He had a band Cliff was in which used to tour around doing concerts all over the country. They had a girl singer at the time called Bette Roberts, and Bette Roberts was sick one day and couldn't do a concert somewhere—I think it was Bristol. Lesley Douglas phoned me and asked if I would do it. I did and met Cliff."

Cliff Townshend's star was already rising. Before the war, he had played trad jazz (the British term for Dixieland) in small combos in Soho and around

London, where he'd been raised. The emergence of swing virtually coincided with the start of the war in Europe, so playing in larger bands was a natural progression as well as a duty.

"Betty's a very good singer," Cliff said. "I used to think I was good at the time, and I never would have married her if I thought she was rotten, I can honestly tell you that. I couldn't have done; I was so enthusiastic at the time, it had to be somebody good."

Both Cliff and Betty had some musical experience in their family background. Betty's father had been in the Black and White Minstrels as a boy, never becoming a professional but continuing to sing on weekends all his life. Cliff's mother had been a soubrette (a singer/comedienne); his father played flute and piccolo and was a straight man in a music hall duo, as well.

After the war, the Squadronaires became Cliff's job. Mustered out in 1946, the members of the group decided to stay together as a cooperative and quickly became one of Britain's most well-regarded acts.

The Townshends made their first civilian quarters in the same neighborhood near Ealing Common where they now live. The house on Woodgrange Avenue, where Peter grew up, is an attractive middle-class brick home with spacious rooms and an upstairs flat that could be let for additional income. The atmosphere is miles from the dinge of Shepherd's Bush, though the neighborhoods are in fact quite near.

Young Peter spent a good deal of his first three years living with his maternal grandparents. Ostensibly, this is because both his parents worked and because Cliff, particularly, spent a good deal of time on the road, touring around the country on one-night stands with the band. However, it is also possible that the Townshends were separated for other reasons in this period. Certainly, their relationship was exceptionally volatile from the start—not surprisingly, since both had quick tempers and liked to drink.

In the summers, the Townshends could all be together. The Squadronaires took long engagements—up to eighteen weeks—at seaside resorts or on the offshore islands. The first of these was in the summer of 1946 at Clacton.

As Peter grew older, these visits became more frequent. Betty recalled, "Everywhere we could possibly take Peter, we took him. So Peter was there, in front of the stand, watching the rehearsals and always trying to sneak in round the back when he should be in bed. Watching the band, jumping, playing the drums. Oh, he loved music right from the word go."

"The days of the Squadronaires were really the important ones," said Cliff. "All our friends would be round our house with their wives. Betty and I would have a party at least once a week. Pete was only about four."

"All our friends were musicians," added Betty. "All our company were musicians. He had a musical background—not only from his family. It was environment."

After a few years, as the big band craze faded into the bland pop daze of the early fifties, the summer season shrank to fifteen weeks and the Clacton runs ended. The Squadronaires then spent thirteen summers in a row playing on the Isle of Man. "Because Peter was an only child at that time, we used to take a pal of his, Jimpy [Graham Beard], with us to keep him company. They were great buddies," said Betty, who can only remember this companion's first name: Jimpy.

It was at Man that Peter Townshend first encountered the musical style that would become his obsession. "I remember taking them to see Bill Haley in *Rock Around the Clock*," Betty said. "Well, they wanted to see it the next day and the next day and in the end we were giving them the money or getting passes for them. They were seeing this film daily—practically every rainy day, anyway. Peter really absolutely adored music, and when this Bill Haley and rock & roll thing started, he was right into it. He was very little; he was ten. And he loved it."

In this love he had an unlikely ally: his father. Where many aspiring rock & rollers found themselves immediately thrust into a generational battle over their liking for what was considered culturally barbaric, Cliff and Betty Townshend seem to have been consistently supportive. This isn't surprising. Most parents did not like rock & roll because they were unaware of its roots in American popular and folk music. But Cliff Townshend knew those roots very well, because the Squadronaires' form of jazz was also derived from rock's black antecedents. Cliff said he especially liked rock because it recognized the economic realities that forced the music back into small combos and also because it got people dancing again (which they had largely ceased to do after the advent of bebop).

So Cliff sympathized with and supported his son's enthusiasm for rock & roll, and thus Peter was spared the usual traumas of the time over musical taste. Not that his childhood was complacent and idyllic.

Peter felt inferior to an incredible degree, largely because of the size of his nose. (If the Townshend hooter seemed unaccountably large to Irish Jack when Peter was in his late teens, imagine how it must have looked on a ten-year-old.) As it happens, both Cliff and Betty Townshend have large features, and Betty has a particularly prominent nose. On an adult face, however, such a nose may simply be one strong characteristic among others. A kid hasn't yet grown into his features, and a bulky schnozz seems destined to perpetually disfigure the bearer.

Ironically, Cliff's life was partly dominated by a long relationship with pianist Ronnie Aldrich, the best-known of the Squadronaires. According to Pete, Aldrich "was always a bit of a red herring to my dad. They both started together and went to the same school and all this." Ronnie Aldrich had become a solo star with dozens of albums of mood music to his credit. Cliff, while a respected professional name, never succeeded on that level. But the spice of this conflict was that Ronnie Aldrich had a huge nose, as bent and unlikely in its way as Peter's.

In his cups, clumsily trying to assuage his son's insecurities (and perhaps his own misgivings) about the Nose, Cliff would deliver a spiel that Peter later remembered like this: "Look at Ronnie, look at Ronnie. He's the leader of a famous orchestra, he's got a beautiful wife, a beautiful house, a lovely car. What more can you want? He makes music all his life, he's a respected man. What more can you want in life? He's got a big nose, Peter."

Obviously, such succor was the opposite of help. Peter's obsession with his disfigurement was blown out of all proportion, convincing him not only that he had the world's largest nose but also that because of it he was condemned to the depths of eternal ugliness. "This seemed to be the biggest thing in my life: my fucking nose, man," said Peter when he was twenty-three.

There were other traumas to suffer. Peter had been an only child, but then, just as he turned twelve, his mother became pregnant. Before he was fifteen, he had two brothers, Paul and Simon. The advent of the new siblings at such a volatile stage in Peter's life, especially since these children must have occupied much of his mother's time while his father remained on the road a good deal, must have made those years exceptionally difficult for Peter.

Contributing to the general level of anxiety in his existence were the continuing battles between Cliff and Betty, who never found one another particularly easy to live with. All the Townshends seem to fly off the handle easily—a trait that comes from their mother, thinks Paul. "Many a time have dinners gone flying across the kitchen, through the window.

"If you're brought up in an environment where everything's getting smashed and there's arguments all the time, it rubs off on you," he continued. Certainly, it rubbed off on Peter, who even in his early teens already struck many as arrogant and hostile, too quick to fight. It's hard to imagine a more miserable adolescence than this: a smart kid who fears that he's ugly, with irascible parents and newborn siblings.

Fortunately, violence wasn't Peter Townshend's only outlet. When he was twelve, his grandmother Dennis favored him with a guitar, "a cheap Spanish thing," his mother calls it, but nonetheless an instrument of his own. Cliff, who had played some guitar himself, taught Peter rudimentary chords. But Peter didn't focus on guitar for long; instead, he got a banjo, a better instrument for the traditional jazz then in vogue. His aspirations weren't necessarily musical, anyway. He was more interested in graphic art and in writing and journalism.

It goes without saying that Peter did splendidly on his eleven-plus exams, whereupon he was sent off to Acton County Grammar.

3

In 1955, rock & roll hit Britain full force. Spearheaded by Elvis, with a phalanx of lieutenants including Jerry Lee Lewis, Eddie Cochran, Gene Vincent, Buddy Holly and the rhythm & blues singers Little Richard, Chuck Berry and Fats Domino, rock & roll proved as permanent an obsession in England as in America.

Rock & roll and rhythm & blues captured the imagination of many kids in England, partially because they were American Things, at a time when American Things were admired as expressions of affluence and cultural liberty. But there was precious little indigenous rock in England at this time. Initial British forays into the field misinterpreted the potential of the market, and the result was a series of odious, mannered "teen idols", cute boys who were more good-looking than talented and whose pallid songs were meant essentially as swooning exercises for young girls. The first British rock singer was Tommy Steele, whose version of Guy Mitchell's "Singin' the Blues" was closer to Pat Boone than Elvis. Steele and his cheery cockney presentation were soon absorbed into the more "adult" field of cabaret, where he enjoyed decades of popularity.

Larry Parnes ("Mr. Parnes, Shillings and Pence," as he became known) was one of the promoters behind Steele, and he soon created a virtual factory that ground out a succession of pretty but vacuous, artificially surnamed teen idols: Marty Wilde, Billy Fury, Dickie Pride, Johnny Gentle, Nelson Keene, Davy Jones, Vince Eager and Johnny Goode. Parnes kept his performers on wages, an exploitative system guaranteed to snuff ambition, and he controlled completely their recordings and performances on stage and TV. Although one or two of the Parnes stable (most notably Billy Fury and Georgie Fame) were genuinely talented rock performers, the rest were even more obnoxiously inconsequential than their American counterparts, Fabian and Frankie Avalon. But Parnes had sufficient control over live bookings (with his package tours of several stars from his company) to stifle whatever genuine undercurrent of musical rebellion rock & roll had stirred.

The inevitable response came with skiffle. The term originally applied to a kind of jug band music popular in Chicago during the twenties. Trad groups picked up on it as a lark, music to be played during the interval between sets at the jazz clubs that cropped up around London's West End entertainment district during the fifties. But skiffle had one extremely salient advantage for kids: It used a variety of homemade instruments, crude guitars, washboards, the legendary "tea chest" or "washtub" bass, even combs as kazoos. Drawing on a repertoire of simple, often humorous folk and blues tunes, almost all of them easily reduced to three chords and a basic 4/4 beat, skiffle was perfect for a grass-roots uprising. Besides being musically rudimentary, it required very small investment in equipment, and its very crudeness and lack of sophistication kept it out of the clutches of entrepreneurs like Parnes.

Late in 1956, Lonnie Donegan's "Rock Island Line" kicked off the real skiffle boom, and in neighborhoods all over England, young boys formed groups to play and sing for parties and friends, perhaps collecting a pound or two at a church outing or family gathering, but mostly bashing away for the sheer joy of it. (Skiffle seems to have been a virtually all-male phenomenon, probably because the needs of adolescent girls were better filled by Parnes's teen idols.) But with the exception of Donegan—who made both "Rock Island Line" and "Does Your Chewing Gum Lose Its Flavor (On the Bedpost Overnight)" international hits—skiffle developed few important recordings and no significant stars. The skiffle boom is remembered fondly today because it was the first flowering of the remarkable musical talents of postwar British youth. In sound and spirit, it had all the innocence of a fresh start.

Roger Daltrey was eleven in 1955, when rock & roll hit, and twelve when skiffle erupted in 1956. He was immediately taken over. "From the time I heard Elvis Presley and Lonnie Donegan, I didn't want to be anything else," he has said. And in the true spirit of skiffle's do-it-yourself amateurism, he set about making himself a homemade guitar.

"He came round with a great block of wood," Harry Daltrey remembered. "I said, 'What are you going to do with that, son?' He said, 'I'm going to make a guitar.' I said, 'Not with my tools.' He said, 'Yes.' Lo and behold, he carved this guitar out of a lump of wood.

"He had an uncle here who had a great liking for music. He took it down to his uncle's shop to have it painted and French polished, and it did look wonderful.

"I couldn't play worth a damn, but I really felt like something," said Roger.

That summer, the Daltreys made a holiday visit to Brighton, on the English seashore. "One night Harry and I were strolling along, and we saw a big crowd on the beach," said Irene. "We really thought someone had been drowned. So I thought, me being nosey, you know, we'd have a look. And it was only Roger, playing his guitar and singing all the old rock & roll songs. He had all the teenagers dancing. 'Course, the police moved him on, but oh, did we have a laugh that night!"

Later, during the same Brighton holiday, Roger informed his parents that he had acquired his first job, playing guitar in a pub. "But you're not of age," his mother said.

"Oh, they don't know that," Roger replied, unfazed.

Roger had belonged to the Boys' Brigade (similar to the American Boy Scouts) in his preteen years, where he had blown a silver trumpet for his squad; he had also sung in the church services the family attended, but he refused to join the choir, despite his grandmother's prodding. It wasn't just music he loved. It was rock & roll.

What he liked about it was obvious enough. Rock was fast, hard, tough and self-assertive, and it promised itself to all who heard it as a means of shattering convention and stuffiness, which, to teenagers, can seem like a promise of salvation.

Undoubtedly, Roger's major problem was a deep need to prove himself physically. For in an environment where physical strength counted a great deal, Roger was exceptionally short.

Neither Harry nor Irene Daltrey is very tall, and Roger inherited their stature. Full grown, he stands only about five-feet-five or six, and throughout his youth, he was steadily shorter than most of his mates. So he became extremely combative—at first, maybe, from a necessity to defend himself such as any small kid faces when confronted by bullies. Then Roger found that he was good with his fists and that there was a reputation to he gained by being ready to use them.

"Where I used to live, you had to be a hard nut," Roger said. "If anybody offered you outside for a punch-up, you had to go, and you had to have a good fight."

So Roger joined his gang of "near Teddy boys": schoolyard toughs wearing badass clothes, smoking, swearing, leering—the image that both in England and America spelled juvenile delinquent. It's unlikely that Daltrey and his friends ever adopted (or could have afforded) the full Ted uniform, complete with Edwardian drape coat, but they slicked back their hair and grew it long and swaggered enough to make the point. And they were ready to prove it, by combat if necessary.

Roger is, in fact, quick-witted, but he never appears to be as bright as he is, because of his yobbo accent and his lack of diplomacy. There wasn't much advantage in displaying one's intellect directly, either in Shepherd's Bush or in the circles in which Roger traveled at Acton Grammar. Pragmatic cleverness was an admirable necessity, but smartness for its own sake was little valued. That Roger was intelligent is demonstrated by his eleven-plus scores. That he was determined not to use that intelligence conventionally is proven by the shambles he made of his grammar school career.

"I was hoping, if he picked up his studies, he'd go on to university," said Irene. "It didn't work out that way. He came home from school and said the headmaster was always pickin' on him. We went up to see the headmaster to find out why, and he said, 'Well, Mrs. Daltrey, when you've got five hundred boys here and they're all in navy blue raincoats and you see one boy turn up in a white mac, it's so outstanding. That's Roger.'"

The Daltreys discovered that every morning, as soon as Roger left their house neatly dressed in his uniform, complete with cap and tie, he'd skip around the corner and modify his looks. "I thought he went out so smart," said Irene, outraged twenty years later. "As soon as he's around the corner, his cap went in his pocket, his tie's in his pocket. It was all behind my back you see."

Roger's grades went steadily downhill. He never got into any major scrapes with the law, but the school authorities kept the heat on his back over grades as well as deportment. "You know, I was a school rebel," Roger said. "Whatever, they said do, I didn't do. I was totally anti-everything. I was a right bastard, a right hard nut. I just totally closed the doors to ever wanting to know what they had to teach me. Rock & roll was the only thing I wanted to get into."

Together with some of his friends, he formed a band called the Detours.

In 1956, when he started Acton County Grammar School, Peter Townshend was no rock & roll fan. Although he had an early enthusiasm for Bill Haley's music, Haley had become passé when Elvis appeared, and Peter couldn't figure out Elvis at all. Presley looked too thuggish for a Townshend role model, and his music, like "Love Me Tender," was too maudlin to take seriously. Townshend liked the Evenly Brothers and Ricky Nelson (particularly Nelson's guitarist, James Burton), but as far as Britain went, "rock was unglamorous in its early days. The stars were homosexual or suspected of it. Jazz had respectability."

The jazz he favored wasn't the kind that his father and the Squadronaires played, though. Pete was a big trad fan. "I loved the kind of music [my father] hated, traditional jazz played by Scotsmen with plastic reeds, reverberant guitar music played by original three-chord East Enders. What I called practice must have disturbed him many a time, both physically and mentally."

One of the first people who Peter met at Acton County Grammar was John Entwistle, also a trad fan and a fair enough trumpet player to be the only kid at Acton Grammar asked to join the Middlesex Youth Orchestra, London's all-star school boy band. (Entwistle was switched to French horn because the Youth Orchestra was overpopulated with trumpeters.)

John Alec Entwistle was born on October 9, 1944, in Chiswick, just around the corner from Acton, to Herbert and Maud "Queenie" Entwistle. "I was born during the Blitz, and bombs were dropping every day," he said. Soon afterwards, his parents were divorced and John and his mother lived with his grandparents during most of his schoolboy years.

Growing up in a place and era in which broken homes and being an only child were uncommon, John grew reserved, at least outside his home. (His mother still maintains that he is raucous and loud.) Entwistle wasn't particularly shy; he just didn't see any reason to show too much of himself to strangers.

John early displayed his musicianly interests by standing up in a movie theatre to sing along with Al Jolson songs. He was three, and soon his grandfather took him along to the neighborhood workingman's club, where young John stood on a chair and sang while his grandfather passed the hat. The songs were Jolson standards like "Mammy" and "Climb Upon My Knee, Sonny Boy." One night John fell off his chair, leaving a scar on his face which lasted well into adulthood.

There was always music in Entwistle's life. His mother played piano, his father trumpet. When John was seven, his mother decided that his time to learn piano had come and sent him off to a music teacher "who was really ancient. She had this room full of cats, and fingers like spoons. It was really revolting, and I couldn't stand the smell. She'd sit and write out a report in this little book after every lesson saying how badly I was doing. The whole thing was extremely unpleasant, so when I got to the age of eleven, I convinced my mother that I could teach myself the piano. I told her that since I could read music, I could quite easily go out and buy sheet music and learn from that. She swallowed it, so I managed to switch to trumpet."

Entwistle's attachment to the trumpet can, of course, be traced to his father, who had already taught him several scales on the instrument. Trumpet was also the featured instrument in most trad arrangements. Hearing a holiday camp band playing "In a Persian Market" was also decisive in steering him toward the horn. "It was very piercing and gave me a nice feeling in the chest," he explained.

Because the school orchestra was also overendowed with trumpet students, they gave him a tenor horn "covered in cellophane tape." When he made the Middlesex Youth Orchestra, the school found enough funds to buy him a new horn.

Outside of class, Entwistle played in trad bands. "I never particularly liked jazz," he admitted, "but it is the thing you play with trumpet, you know." Entwistle went through a succession of after-school trad groups. In one of the first, the Confederates, he was matched with Peter Townshend, on banjo. The other members of the group were Chris Sherwin, on drums, and Phil Rhodes, on clarinet. They practiced much more than they played publicly, in the tradition of all schoolyard groups.

The Confederates' only live appearances were at the Congo Club, a teen center operated by Acton's Congregational church. (Although Townshend's family lived in Ealing and Entwistle's in Chiswick, Acton was just around the corner; in compact London, districts often only run a few hundred yards in any given direction.)

"The Congo wasn't just a place where we got together and entertained the troops, as it were," said Peter. "There was a lot of violence and sex and stuff going on." None of this was very high-level, certainly none of it was as risky as the sort of experiences that Roger Daltrey was having with his gang. But in the late fifties and early sixties, in a teen climate essentially unencumbered by drugs, racial antagonisms or even the factionalized clothing cults that have since reigned, the making out and fistfights of the Congo Club were exotic and fascinating.

"You'd go down to the club and sit around and maybe ask somebody to jive. All the girls seemed to be like five years older than the boys," Townshend remembered a decade later. "You wore a suit and that kind of scene."

Entwistle has described the Confederates as "pretty bad." Townshend says they played "stuff like 'Marching Through Georgia' and 'Farewell Blues.' " Typically, the personnel fluctuated a great deal: Townshend, Entwistle, Sherwin and Rhodes were the core members, but others came and went. At one point there were no less than three banjo players, luckily, according to John: "Pete was just learning to play banjo then, but with three in the band, nobody could tell how he was playing."

The Confederates proper played the Congo Club only once, but the gig left an indelible impression on Peter Townshend: "We stood up there—with about five people in the room—and I really blushed. It was the only time in my whole life that I've been nervous on a stage."

The Confederates, or one of their interim incarnations, did do a little busking (street playing) on the side. One night, during Christmas season, they were playing carols in a local pub when Entwistle's mother and stepfather came in. Queenie Entwistle remembers everyone being amused, but John was mortified: "My stepfather gave me five minutes to get out. He didn't want his evening's drinking disturbed by a rather loud and not very good trad band."

Eventually, Entwistle left the Confederates to join a larger, more prosperous trad group. Not insignificantly, the Confederates broke up over a row between Townshend and Chris Sherwin. It began as a fistfight, but Peter finally hit the drummer over the head with his book bag, giving Sherwin a concussion. The result was that Townshend was ostracized by most of his friends for the better part of a year.

Townshend stumbled through high school with a raging temper and an incurable inferiority complex. He felt that a great many of the other kids at school were laughing at him. "If I had said to myself, when I was a kid, 'One of these days you'll go through a whole day without once thinking that your nose is the biggest in the world, man,' I'd have laughed."

This led to a perhaps inevitable conflict with his parents. Parents aren't usually terribly useful to insecure teenagers, but then, it takes a very secure teenager indeed to understand this during adolescence. "My mother was no help," Peter said. "She seemed to think that anybody who wasn't beautiful couldn't be any good. She was gorgeous, of course. My father was very good-looking, too. How they spawned me, I'll never know. Dad was kind to me about the nose but in an unintentionally devastating manner. He used to say things like, 'Don't worry, Arthur Miller married Marilyn Monroe, didn't he?' I didn't want to look like Arthur Miller; I wanted to look like James Dean."

It was during his ostracism from the Confederates crowd that Peter became a guitarist. Trad was sinking as far as teen taste went, though it would still clutter up the British charts for a few more years. But by late 1958, rock & roll had made two tremendously serious intrusions on young Peter Townshend's consciousness.

England had lacked a teen idol who could produce music as authentically exciting as Elvis's or any of the other American stars. In Cliff Richard and the Shadows, it found a perfect object of obsession. Richard spat out rock & roll songs with the suave confidence of Gene Vincent, and he was not above crooning ballads as mawkish as Elvis's. His band, the Shadows, particularly guitarist Hank Marvin, had true panache. Though Cliff quickly discarded his rocking approach in favor of blander pop and became mostly an idol of rapt female listeners, even this development fit the Elvis model. The Shadows continued to make fine instrumental music all through the sixties. Between them, Cliff Richard and the Shadows rekindled the British rock & roll flame. (It was especially important to have a major home-grown talent in a country that was beginning to feel overwhelmed in too many ways by American popular culture.)

The other significant factor in young Peter Townshend's musical education was the emergence, through 1957 and 1958, of a remarkable string of hits by Chuck Berry: "Sweet Little Sixteen," "Johnny B. Goode" and "School Days." These powerful songs, shouted by Berry over his own stinging guitar lines, were gemlike narratives of American teen life, which struck universal chords in the rock audience. "I don't think it was until I heard Chuck Berry that I realized what you could do with words—how unimportant the music was, 'cause Chuck Berry always used the same song," said Townshend many years later.

With the impetus of Chuck Berry and Hank Marvin behind him, Peter Townshend once more took up the guitar. He had, in fact, switched to banjo not only because the latter instrument was more fashionable, but because the guitar his grandmother had given him was so crude that it came apart as he tried to play it, finally being reduced to just the D, G and B strings. (The few chords Townshend knew were built around those shapes.) So his guitar development was stunted for a time, then taken in an odd direction by his banjo work.

Betty Townshend ran an antiques shop on Ealing Common. One day during Peter's ostracism, a decent guitar, made in Czechoslovakia, turned up. It was acoustic but had a small pickup, and Peter took it home for three pounds (about eight dollars) and learned to play it. He soon discovered that as the result of those abortive early experiences, he could play quite well.

The Townshend household wasn't dominated by music. They had no piano, nor even a proper stereo setup for many years. Perhaps all that gear was a busman's holiday for Cliff and Betty; with three sons, they may have simply had more important debts to incur. Cliff practiced his sax and clarinet in a back room; Peter stumbled through his guitar licks in his bedroom, like any other aspirant.

Meantime, John Entwistle had been totally taken with Duane Eddy, whose chain of instrumental hits, most notably the first, "Rebel-'Rouser," began in mid-1958 as well. At first he tried to adapt the trumpet to rock & roll by using an American football helmet as a mute, trying for the flavor of a saxophone. It didn't work very well. "I just wanted to be louder," he recalled. I really got very irritated when people could turn up their guitar amps and play louder than me. So I decided that I was going to play guitar."

For a variety of reasons, John Entwistle was not destined to become a conventional guitarist. First, he had big hands with thick fingers which did not make manipulating six strings—some of them wire-thin—terribly easy. Then there was the Duane Eddy influence. Entwistle listened to others: the Shadows, Eddie Cochran, Buddy Holly. But "me first influence and probably me last was Duane Eddy. Much of his stuff was very bass-influenced, and you could play most of it on bass." And bass had only four strings, all of them thick.

The bass guitar was a relatively new instrument, invented in the early fifties to function electrically as a substitute for the standup or double bass, which was being overwhelmed by the new electric guitars. In fact, the changeover to strings-with-pickup changed the characteristic sound of the bass even more than the electrification of guitar had changed its sonic qualities. Indeed, the new bass was a *bass guitar*, but hardly anyone realized much of the instrument's potential. John Entwistle was one of the first to explore it.

"I did want to be a lead guitarist," he confessed. "The role of the lead guitarist was the most glamorous to me. I wanted to make solo spots in a group. And you don't go from being a front man [which he had been as a trumpeter] to a back man.

"But I always preferred the sound of the bass—it excited me the most. And you can play the bass easier than guitar, initially. If you want to play it well, it's a lot harder. You have to make up your own style, because it is a brand-new instrument."

In fact, it was so new that there were only two brands you could buy in England in 1959. Entwistle remembered that all the bassists he knew idolized Jet Harris, the Shadows' bassist, even though he wasn't a particularly exceptional player, because Harris had a Fender Precision, imported from the States. Not that there were that many bassists around in the first place; the knowledge that bassists were always in demand, unlike guitarists, of which there was a steady oversupply, was another factor in Entwistle's choice. "It's very easy to join a group playing bass. It's easy to go 'dum-dum' all the time. The only thing to differentiate a good bass player is the amount of riffs he knows or the way he can write the bass part as he goes along or the speed with which he can play."

The bass, with its solid, stable, unwavering sound, was the personification of John Entwistle. Late in his third year at Acton County Grammar, when he was sixteen, he met Alison Wise, fourteen and also from Chiswick. They remained together for the next twenty years as sweethearts and spouses. Of all the rock musicians of his era, John Entwistle was the most constant in his tastes, preferences and personality.

Now he set about building himself an instrument. There was no way the

Entwistle family budget could accommodate the purchase of such an exotic instrument as a bass guitar, and Britain's system of hire purchase (installment credit) was not yet widely available for such items, as it would be only a couple of years later.

Entwistle acquired a piece of mahogany and had a carpenter carve it in the shape of a Fender Precision body. The neck was square, and he took it to a local guitar-maker to have it fretted. Unfortunately, the Scale of Entwistle's bass was based on Fender's neck, but the frets were based on Hofner's smaller violin-shaped bass, leaving about eight inches of unfretted wood at the top of the neck.

Queenie Entwistle remembers John making this guitar "on his grandmother's best dining room table." Placing the pickup and wiring it, then painting the body, John managed to mar and permanently damage the surface of the table, much to his grandmother's dismay. Still, this bass served John for some time, at least giving him time to learn the basic technique. Then he left it lying across an armchair overnight and "turned it into a four-string harp."

Fenton-Weill, a guitar manufacturer with a factory in Chiswick, made oddly shaped but serviceable guitars. For a fiver (about twelve dollars), Entwistle convinced someone who worked for Fenton-Weill to smuggle out a body for his next instrument. A second factory hand put on all the other parts. Peter remembered this bass sounding "pretty good." John swore it was "diabolical."

With Entwistle on bass and Townshend on guitar, Peter's exile from Acton County Grammar's rock band clique was ended. Together, Townshend and Entwistle formed a succession of bands, first the Aristocrats, then the Scorpions, with their mates Mick Brown and Pete Wilson. Again, these groups woodshedded more than they performed publicly, though the Scorpions had another crack at the Congo Club.

The group played mostly Shadows material, with some American rock numbers influenced in selection by a pair of television Shows, "Oh Boy" and "Drumbeat," which featured performers like Little Richard, Eddie Cochran, Gene Vincent and Jerry Lee Lewis, the same sort of rockabilly and rhythm & blues that was inspiring teenage musicians from Belfast to Southend.

For Roger Daltrey, Acton County Grammar remained a drag. It wasn't just that he refused to wear the proper uniform, or even his inability to act the nice young schoolboy. Roger was getting out and about more now, and school was keeping him from the faster, more adult activity he preferred.

A portion of that activity—the most productive portion—centered around the Detours. This was one group not formed for sport or to play free at youth clubs. The Detours *worked*: company outings, weddings, bar mitzvahs—whatever a teenage band could scare up. Chances are, the money mattered as much as the music. Of the original Detours, only Roger seems to have had eyes for pop stardom as a way up and out of the working class.

The group rehearsed at the house of Reg Bowen, the rhythm guitarist. Roger was on lead. There was a singer, a drummer, a bassist, or floating members who filled those roles—no one seems to remember the early days of this all-too-typical teen combo very clearly.

By 1959, Roger was serious enough about his music to convince his father to buy him a professional's guitar, an Epiphone. Perhaps Harry Daltrey thought that this could also help to keep his son on the straight and narrow for a time. If so, it didn't work. Before the year was out, Roger was expelled from Acton County Grammar. The ostensible cause of expulsion was smoking, but that was a formality. The real problem was accumulated grievances—on both sides. "The headmaster said, 'I can't see the point of keeping him, Mr. Daltrey,'" Harry remembered. "He said, 'He's just got music, music, music, that's all there is.'"

Irene recalls: "The headmaster said, as he had no interest in school, he'd advise him to leave. So he left. And he started his sheet-metal work."

Roger Daltrey wasn't going to be a layabout; his parents wouldn't have allowed it, and anyway, he already had sophisticated tastes and desires which required an income. So he found a job in a sheet-metal shop in Shepherd's Bush working with a welding torch all day. After work he'd rehearse or play gigs with the Detours.

"I used to get up at eight o'clock, work in the factory until six o'clock at night, and then the group from seven till midnight, it was that every day of the week," said Roger. A slight exaggeration. Harry Daltrey remembered that Roger's foreman used to let him off early quite frequently in order to have more time for his band and that Roger was often late arriving in the morning, too. "I went down to see [the foreman], and he said to me, 'Can you do anything with your boy, Mr. Daltrey?' I said, 'Lord, no.' He said, 'Neither can I.'" Telling the story, Harry threw back his head and roared with laughter.

Twenty years earlier, however, the situation might not have seemed so amusing to him. Sheet-metal workers were unionized and made good wages; it would be a mistake for Roger to jeopardize his future for the sake of a rock & roll band. But there was no dissuading him. "Music, music seemed to be his game," said Harry.

Roger was aware of the two young musicians just a year behind him at Acton Grammar, at least aware enough to describe Townshend as looking like "a nose on a stick." And they were aware of him, too. "He was big bad Roger, the leader of the Teddy boys," said John. Whether Roger knew that Peter and John played music is unknown. Certainly, Entwistle and Townshend knew about the Detours. "Of all the bands at school, the Detours were the best," Peter said. "Roger was the best guitarist, a very basic guitar player but very confident and very fluid in a way. He could learn something, parrot fashion, then make it very fluid."

In any event, it was Daltrey who made the first move, when he saw Entwistle—"this great big geezer with a homemade bass that looked like a football boot with a neck sticking out of it"—coming down the street one day. His approach was direct: "I hear you play bass guitar."

"Yeah," replied Entwistle. ("After all, I was holding it under my arm. It was pretty obvious," he said later.)

"Do you want to try in my group?"

"I'm already in a group."

"Well, mine's earning money." Thus enticed, Entwistle went along and sat in on a couple of weeks' rehearsals at Reg Bowen's house. At that point Roger again approached him to find out if he was still interested, "now that you've heard us." Entwistle agreed to become a Detour, though it meant leaving the Scorpions and Townshend.

By then the Detours had two rhythm guitarists augmenting their basic lineup of lead guitar, bass, drums and singer Colin Dawson. The second rhythm guitarist was around because he had a Vox amp, an impressive piece of equipment in those days. But the complement of musicians peeled back pretty quickly. First the Vox-owner drowned; the group inherited his amp by confiscation. Then Entwistle began proposing that Reg Bowen was musically inadequate. He wanted to bounce Reg and hire his old friend Peter Townshend. Finally, Roger and the others agreed.

"The greatest bloody triumph of my school days was when Roger asked me if I could play guitar," said Townshend to Jay Cocks of *Time* twenty years later. "If he had ever said, 'Come out in the playground and I'll fight you,' I would have been down in one punch. Music was the only way I could ever win." For his part, Daltrey seemed to have no qualms. At least for the moment, neither Townshend nor Entwistle was a threat to his leadership.

In those early days, the Detours had a large and varied repertoire: trad jazz, rock hits, instrumentals like the Tornadoes' "Telstar," pop ballads like Andy Williams' "Can't Get Used to Losing You"—anything a random drunk requested. Entwistle played some trumpet, Daltrey trombone, Townshend a bit of banjo; almost everybody sang something. Nor was the group's style—to the extent it had one—especially "street": Colin Dawson used to show up on stage in a yachting blazer. No one had especially long hair, and the band wore corny uniforms, blazer jackets and neat trousers with shiny black shoes.

Sacking Reg Bowen, of course, also meant finding a new place to rehearse. Sometimes the boys were permitted to use the flat above Cliff and Betty Townshend's. Peter's parents were naturally sympathetic, being musicians themselves, but eventually, the disorganization and racket grew too much even for them. So the band resorted to subterfuge.

"At the time, we used to go out to whist trials, playing cards," said Mrs. Daltrey. "And we used to go out about half-past seven. Well, we didn't know it, but as soon as our backs was turned, there was Peter Townshend, John Entwistle and the rest, waiting around the corner. And as soon as our back was turned, they came in the house, made Roger's two sisters go to bed, put everything in my bedroom back against the wall. 'Course, the old drums were going, and the neighbors complained: 'Oh, the noise at your house last night!' I said, 'But we were out last night; there shouldn't have been any noise.' They used to practice here, and I never knew anything about it."

Occasionally, they could scrape together enough cash to rehearse at a proper rehearsal hall. One summer's day Roger Daltrey was lingering around such a hall when he ran into an older musician who happened to be as short as he was. Ever gregarious, Daltrey piped up, " 'Oo you waitin' for, mate?'

"Oh, I gotta see some guys about playing in their band," replied the older fellow, Doug Sandom by name.

"What d'ya play?" asked Daltrey.

"I play drums."

"Would you like to sit in with us? 'Cause our drummer's going on holiday."

"Sure I'd like to."

"Well, the best thing to do is, if you meet us next week, come hear us, listen to us, and maybe if our drummer don't mind, second half, you'll sit in, get used to us." Daltrey made it seem a much bigger deal than it was. The drummer wasn't leaving for a fortnight, and the Detours' repertoire was hardly so unusual that it would take that long for a new musician to be fitted in.

But maybe Daltrey wanted to impress. Doug Sandom had a small reputation. He was a good ten years older than the other Detours, was married and worked as a bricklayer. Sandom had played around the local circuit as a freelancer, never joining a band full time but building a name and connections. "I used to put myself about, used to sit in with this band, and that band. It's great experience, getting to know different people. I thought it was, you know," Sandom explained.

Most importantly, Sandom was a fine musician, "ten times better than we were," according to Entwistle. (Everyone else seemed to agree.) Getting him into the Detours would be a real coup and perhaps could help the band get some better jobs, since Sandom had contacts all around the west London pub circuit, where the money was. It could even be that the shrewd and ambitious Daltrey was not just passing the time of day when he chanced to stroll up to Sandom that afternoon.

In any event, when the Detours' original drummer returned from his holiday, he was given the axe, and Doug Sandom replaced him. It was no big deal. The Detours had no real following to upset with the departure of an "original" member, and anyway, musicians came and went from bands much more freely in those unstructured times. "I used to dream I was the best player in the groups I was with—but they always kicked me out," remembered Townshend. It's a typical lament of the day.

With Doug Sandom in the fold, the Detours assumed a set lineup: Sandom on drums, Entwistle on bass, Daltrey on lead guitar, Townshend on rhythm guitar and Dawson on lead vocals. They began adding dates at pubs and workingmen's clubs to their round of weddings and bar mitzvahs, and by the end of 1961, the Detours had acquired a small reputation around west London. That's when Irish Jack first saw them.

"We were just doing Top Ten hits and playing for about ten cents a night," Daltrey remembered. "At the time, the whole thing about groups was a joke."

*You could play in Acton all
your life and never get anywhere.
We played in Shepherd's Bush.*
                    —Roger Daltrey

P eter Townshend and John Entwistle graduated from Acton County
Grammar in the spring of 1961. Both did well on their examinations and
were offered opportunities to continue studying music or art. They were
sixteen years old, best friends, bandmates again, virtually equals in every way.
But there are many other issues that determine the decisions taken at such
crucial moments.

"I had a choice when I left school of either going to art school or music
school," Entwistle said. "But there was some trouble from my family about the
music thing, and I didn't particularly want to go to art school." The trouble
concerned money. One imagines that everyone in the Entwistle household
was sensible of the difference between John bringing in another pay check
and the expenditures without income that studying required. In fact, although
music students at Acton County Grammar were expected to provide their own
horns, the trumpet Entwistle had been using belonged to the school, since the
family could not afford one.

So Entwistle went to the local youth employment officer to ask him what
he had that was "easy, without too much work." The tax office was proposed,
strangely enough, since that was where Queenie Entwistle worked. John got
the job and began a checkered career with the Inland Revenue Service (IRS).

"At least I was starting to earn money," he said. "I stayed there for about
two-and-a-half years. But all the time, I was playing in a band about five or six
nights a week."

Entwistle's initial assignment was to work at the front counter of the office answering the tax queries of people who came in to question their tax bills.

"In those days, I used to get to sing 'I Saw Her Standing There' and 'Twist and Shout,' because Roger couldn't sing them, he couldn't get up there. But it started getting a bit impossible," Entwistle remembered. "We started getting five requests a night to do 'Twist and Shout,' and I used to end up going to the tax office in the morning with no voice at all." He was transferred to the filing department as a clerk, a posting he liked much better because it gave him a chance to occasionally sneak behind some cabinets for a quick snooze. (Queenie Entwistle says that when John finally did leave the IRS, it was one step ahead of being bounced for his napping on the job.)

Entwistle's day job was nothing unusual within the Detours. The band was still semiprofessional, at best. "If I hadn't got into rock & roll, I would have ended up as a French horn player with leather elbows on my jacket, playing sessions or something," Entwistle said many years later. The Detours must have seemed just a modernized version of such an avocation not only to John but also to the sheet-metal worker Daltrey, the bricklayer Sandom and to Colin Dawson, who worked as a manufacturer's representative for a Danish bacon company.

Peter Townshend had the same choices as Entwistle when he left Acton County: music school, art school, a job. The Townshends were not nearly wealthy enough for Peter to do nothing, but there was no question about continuing his education. "It was probably the horrible noise I used to make on my first electric guitar that made my father suggest that I go to art school and concentrate on the graphic rather than musical areas of education," Peter said. What's more important is that it was taken for granted that if Peter had the talent and grades, he would continue his schooling.

In the fall of 1961, he enrolled at Ealing Art School. This automatically distanced Peter from the rest of his band. For Sandom and Daltrey, who worked as laborers, Townshend's attending art school was the source of a rarely (or barely) articulated resentment of long standing. Sandom thought that art school had made Townshend a kind of snob. And Daltrey believed that Townshend's whiplash temper was caused by Peter never having had a laboring job. "He's never known what kids really have to do. He did rough it a bit in art school—if you call that roughing it."

The fact that the band's two strongest personalities formed an immediate antagonism toward one another had the most powerful consequences on its future. Rather than a creative alliance, as the Beatles had with John Lennon and Paul McCartney and the Rolling Stones with Keith Richard and Mick Jagger, the Detours' style took shape around the mutual antagonism of the sneering collegiate Townshend and the roughneck laborer Daltrey. The band developed a style and personality which was the collective expression of the resulting tension.

Temper played a big role in the Detours. Entwistle was taciturn, Sandom cool and, because of his relative maturity, virtually a diplomat, despite a feisty nature. Roger Daltrey, however, wanted to run the show, and he was willing to enforce his will by any means necessary. "When the band started," he said, "I was a shit singer. They didn't need a singer in those days, they needed somebody who could fight, and that was me." So Roger laid down the rules and "would punctuate his decisions with punches," as Entwistle put it.

Townshend's fists were no match for Daltrey's, but his verbal invective more than made up for it. These weren't casual struggles, they were for life and death, Townshend's sneering, oblique thrusts parried and challenged by Roger's growling, direct assaults over and over, in different ways, for the next twenty years. Like a centrifuge, they flung their passions so furiously that rather than being ripped apart, they were held together, often against what seemed to be everyone's will.

One of the principal benefits of having Peter Townshend join the Detours was the active support and enthusiasm of his mother. Betty Townshend must have had remarkable energy in those days. She raised her teenaged son, his toddler brother, Paul, and the third boy, Simon, who had been born in 1961. In addition, she ran her antique shop on Ealing Common. Now she added duties as the Detours' booking agent and van driver.

"I used to pick them up from Acton County and drive them out to Richmond," Betty remembered. In fact, she got the band a whole series of auditions. The first of these was at the Castle Hill Hotel in Richmond, a suburb farther west, but the gig there apparently didn't last long, because the wage wasn't sufficient to justify the drive. Nevertheless, the equipment would be loaded by the band into Betty's little yellow van, which she had acquired to haul antiques around, and then, crowded out by their gear, the group would make its way to the show by train. If the train was too out-of-the-way, the musicians would ride in back, sitting or lying on top of the amplifiers.

"They couldn't get any work," Betty continued. "Cliff didn't want to know. I used to know a bloke who used to run pub nights, and so I phoned this bloke, and he said, 'No, I don't want to know. But there is a bloke called Bob Druce at Rayford, and he's always looking for bands.' So I called this Bob Druce. I said, 'They're very good.' He said, 'How do you know they're very good?' I said, 'Because I've been a musician all my life, a singer and a musician, and my husband's a musician. And if I didn't think they were good, you don't think I'd be phoning you?' Of course, I thought they were wonderful; that's why I couldn't understand why they couldn't get jobs."

Bob Druce, who ran Commercial Entertainments Limited, booked weekly dances at a string of pubs, most with halls attached, and at a few licensed clubs. The most notable venues he controlled were the White Hart Hotel in Acton next door to the police station; the Goldhawk Road Social Club in Shepherd's Bush; the Oldfield Hotel in Greenford; and the Glenlyn Ballroom in Forest Hill. Druce managed and served as agent for a clutch of groups, the best-known of which was a country-oriented outfit, the Bel-Airs.

The Detours had their audition at the Oldfield Hotel during the interval between sets at a Bel-Airs gig. The Bel-Airs played mainly country music and drew a boisterous crowd. The Detours were still in their versatile period. According to Doug Sandom, Roger was extremely nervous, Peter "white as a sheet."

Sandom goes on, "When we went for auditions, they were nervous— really *nervous*. I used to talk to 'em and make 'em better. 'Leave it out. What you talkin' about? It's easy. If we get the work, we get it; if we don't, we go somewhere else.' I used to talk to 'em into it, you know. Because I had a lot of experience. I'd been *about*." Indeed, when Betty couldn't do the driving, it was Doug who rented a van (usually at the cost of most of the night's wage) and did the driving.

At the Oldfield audition, the Detours played only three or four numbers. Then the emcee came out and asked the crowd if they'd like to have the new band back. When the crowd responded enthusiastically, the group had passed its audition.

Doug Sandom, who had worked for Druce before, liked him but says that Druce was a "Mr. Ten Percent. He used to give us a wage packet at the end of the week. And he'd take ten percent."

In fact, Druce took two percentages, first as booking agent and then as "manager," although he never did anything resembling career direction for the group. Both fees came off the top. Druce signed the Detours to an "exclusive contract" with Commercial Entertainments, but the contract didn't mean much, since three of the band members were underage and their parents hadn't countersigned. All the contract really meant was that the group agreed to pay Druce his percentage and to work all of the jobs listed on the sheet he gave to them at the first of the month. On its own, the band was free to find other work, playing weddings and other social events.

Betty Townshend found the best of these at Douglas House, playing on Sunday afternoons for American GIs. "Lesley Douglas got that for them," she said. "I phoned Lesley and said, 'Peter will be phoning you. We're trying to let them do it on their own now.' I had had enough by then, and I had Paul then, plus the baby and a German au pair girl."

The Douglas House gig was a marvelous opportunity. It involved only two hours' work, from 1:00 to 3:00 P.M. each Sunday, yet paid the astonishing fee of £75 (about $200 in those days). This was about two or three times what the other well-known local bands made playing for a full night in pubs. And it was many times more than beginners like the Detours could have hoped to make anywhere else.

With this additional income, the Detours could afford to buy a van of their own. So they bought a battered old heap, or rather, Bob Druce did. He took the payments out of the group's weekly wage. The van was painted maroon and black, and "Detours" was painted on the side, with a white arrow pointing straight down. On the back, there were footprints in red and a chimney with a witch's hat welded to the roof, designed to distract attention from the dents.

The driver was Daltrey, although he had only a learner's permit. He drove fast and recklessly. On one trip Roger slammed the van into a bridge abutment, and although no one was hurt, the van's passenger-side door was permanently disabled.

No one had minded taking the train when Peter's mother had driven, but the new van was theirs, and everyone, or as many as possible, would crowd into the back, sitting on top of the stacked equipment. Since Roger often had a girl along, the vehicle could become ludicrously crowded.

By late 1962, the Detours were making good money. "We used to drag 'em in, I tell you," said Sandom. "There were nights in those places you couldn't move." Playing four to six nights a week, in halls that usually charged two shillings (about thirty cents) at the door, the Detours each managed to take home about twelve pounds (around thirty-five dollars) per week after commissions and expenses. Although that might not seem like much, it may well have equaled everyone's pay from their day jobs.

The Detours were, in Sandom's words, "the scruffiest band goin'," and in the pre-Rolling Stones music world, neatness was of some consequence. Eventually, Bob Druce said, "You'll have to smarten up. If I'm gonna give you work, you'll smarten up." So Townshend designed suits: collarless maroon jackets, white shirts, bow ties and shiny black shoes. "But that didn't last long," admitted Sandom. "Whenever we could, we had them off and had our jeans on." Finally, Daltrey loaned the uniforms to another band who never returned them, probably because they were never asked to.

For the most part, the Detours were too busy to see many of the other bands on Druce's circuit; these included, in addition to the Bel-Airs, the Riversiders, the Corvettes, the Beachcombers, Macabre and the Federals. From time to time the Detours were asked to open for the star bands that Druce booked into larger halls, such as St. Mary's in Putney and the Glenlyn Ballroom in Forest Hill. Serving as the opening act for such rockers as Shane Fenton and the Fentones and Cliff Bennett and the Rebel Rousers reinforced Daltrey's idea that the Detours' future was in rock, not the more versatile styles the band had been playing.

This ensured a conflict with Colin Dawson, who wanted to emulate Cliff Richard's watered-down version of Elvis at his most banal. Dawson's dapper, adult mannerisms, so reminiscent of cabaret and antithetical to the rock idea, were doomed, anyway. But Colin's departure from the Detours was hastened by his illusion that they were his backing group, an idea he could have maintained only by avoiding spending much time with the others. Dawson didn't, especially after he became engaged.

Townshend says that the basic problem was that Colin was "such an opposite of Roger, who by then really was the balls in the band and ran things the way he wanted them." But Sandom maintains that other tensions were at work.

"It was the same old thing that was going on in bands all the time. Niggling," said Sandom. "You know? Niggly, niggly, niggly, have a go about him while he's not there. This happens all the time in bands. Oh, God! It's terrible.

"[Dawson] didn't fit. I mean, Peter hated to see a singer like he was. He'd just stand there and wiggle his bum. Peter always used to say that: 'Look at him standin' there, wigglin' his arse.' It just didn't go down. Peter didn't like that. He'd rather see somebody jump about or at least play a guitar while singing. He had to go, you know what I mean? He was fated to go. I liked him; myself, I liked him."

Dawson was initially replaced by a singer named Gabby who had been vocalist with the Bel-Airs, whom the Detours had now overtaken as the top band on the Druce circuit. Gabby's specialty was singing country songs, especially those of Johnny Cash, and that was important for the Sunday shows at Douglas House, because Cash was the idol of many of the American GIs. But Roger Daltrey split the vocal chores with Gabby, and he gradually developed into the band's dominant singer while sticking with his guitar chores.

"The biggest change in us was when we met Johnny Kidd and the Pirates," Sandom said. "We played with 'em at St. Mary's Hall. That was when we started in on that sort of music, rhythm & blues, you know. That was more or less why we landed up a four-piece. It was great, y'know; that was really the time when I was enjoying myself. Really great."

Johnny Kidd and the Pirates were probably the best—or at least the most authentic—rock group that Britain produced prior to the emergence of the Beatles. Kidd's image was not as manipulated as the Larry Parnes groups, although he did wear an eye patch and the group did have gimmicky pirate costumes. The only important original song that Kidd produced, "Shakin' All Over," has a classic sensuality and insouciance that sums up the group's appeal.

The real appeal in the act was the Pirates. They were only a trio, but guitarist Mick Green's heart must have been pure, because his guitar playing had the strength of ten. A great many of England's up-and-coming generation of guitarists virtually worshipped at Mick Green's feet, for he not only had a brilliant, savage solo attack, he was one of the most inventive rhythm players in rock up to that time. In essence, Green fused the rawness of Link Wray's rumble and the almost mathematical elegance of Scotty Moore, coming up with a style that was pure rock & roll and which must have been even more impressive onstage than it was on record, because Green did most of his tricks live, with no overdubbing. Both Peter Townshend and John Entwistle were deeply impressed and influenced by his playing.

The Pirates' instrumental attack was stripped to its fundamentals—guitar, bass and drums—which gave enormous latitude to each of the players. For obvious reasons, each of the Detours found this an attractive format, and so Gabby was bounced out of the band. Roger Daltrey gave up guitar, influenced by split fingers from his sheet-metal job, with Townshend theoretically switching to lead playing.

But Townshend remained basically a rhythm guitarist, and his limitations forced John Entwistle into adopting a more assertive role than any other bassist up to that time. "The Who sound came from us playing as a three-piece band and trying to sound like more," said Entwistle to *Time* in 1979. "I play standard bass, but I combine it with long runs where I take over the lead while Pete bashes out chords." It was some time during early 1963 when this formula began to evolve.

The personnel change had a number of important consequences for the Detours. First, it strengthened John Entwistle's hand. "I wanted to play a lead instrument," he said; the new lineup gave him a chance to do that, on bass, and also made the group more cohesive by giving its most diffident member a powerful role. Secondly, the trio-plus-vocalist approach locked the group into rock & roll. Playing rock exclusively was a necessity for survival in that period immediately following the emergence of the Beatles, when all other forms of pop were quickly derided as disposable, irrelevant and outmoded.

The lack of a conventional lead vocalist prevented the Detours from sounding quite like anyone else. The other quartets who were important in early sixties English rock—the Beatles and Kinks, for instance—had vocalists who doubled as instrumentalists and whose abilities included singing ballads. It was absurd to think that Roger Daltrey, who was nobody's idea of a subtle song stylist, could do anything of the sort.

So Daltrey retained control of the band's material, which now leaned heavily on Beatles songs, Motown rarities like Eddie Holland's "Leaving Here," and older rock & roll numbers, a repertoire not distant from the Beatles' own Liverpudlian songbook. The Detours were encouraged when they got the chance to serve as opening act for Liverpool bands like the Undertakers; they simply blew such relative lightweights off the stage. Most of the so-called Mersey bands picked up on the marketable cuteness and vocal harmony aspect of the Beatles. But the Detours' inability to perform tight harmonies and its instrumental trio setup sent the group straight to the rocking core. Although they continued to pound out what should have been cover versions, they succeeded only in deviating from what they wanted to copy. When this didn't work, it was probably disastrous, but when it did, it was thrilling.

The Detours' originality was an advantage in the long run, because the new generation of British bands was increasingly required to come up with either self-written material or fairly obscure cover songs.

The band wasn't fully professional yet. The members still had their day jobs, and they still played some homemade instruments and used a PA system they had made themselves. "In them days it was all psychological warfare," said Daltrey. "So we hit on the idea of having the biggest cabinets you've ever seen in your life, yet inside, we'd have this little twelve-inch speaker in the bottom. . . . People used to come and see us and say, "Gah, they must be good, look at the size of their gear."

But the Detours didn't remain semipro because they wanted to. They were impeded by the lack of an original songwriter. Daltrey and Sandom never showed any interest or ability in composing. Entwistle felt hampered by all his music studies. "Knowing which chords I should go to next hindered me when I was writing a song," John explained. "I couldn't do anything out of the ordinary."

That left Townshend. But he wasn't especially confident about the idea of becoming a pop composer, either. By mid-1963, he had written only a couple of tentative numbers. None of them were exceptional, but one, "It Was You," led to the Detours' first recording experience.

Cliff Townshend was friendly with Barry Gray, the musical director of "Thunderbirds", a kids' TV program. Gray also liked to experiment with electric music, and he had a studio in the basement of his house for that purpose. There, Cliff arranged for the Detours to record "It Was You," a light harmony number in the Mersey style, one Sunday evening, with Gray acting as engineer. Though nothing came of the experience, the song was later recorded both by the Fourmost, as a B-side, and by an American group, the Naturals. The Detours also occasionally included "It Was You" in their shows, and according to Peter, "it was quite well received" in the pubs.

But Townshend didn't do much other writing for a while, instead focusing on his guitar playing. Maybe this was because he was less than encouraged by the initial results. More likely, it was because playing guitar (but not writing songs) was one of the hipper things to do at art school.

5

*The one thing we've always had is
an instinct, mainly from Pete. He came
from a musician's family. Because he
wasn't working class, he could stand back
from the whole mod thing in the sixties
and look at it objectively.*

—Roger Daltrey

In the fall of 1961, Ealing Art College was Pete Townshend's salvation. Here Townshend found the game played by an entirely different set of rules, ones under which he could compete quite well. And he breathed a sigh of relief. "Art college was where I sort of grew up. I had been going to a silly boys' school, with silly girls running around and all the silly childish games that people play . . . and I walked into a thing where all that counted was what really mattered. It was pretty staggering."

At Ealing, Townshend joined the Committee for Nuclear Disarmament (CND) and the Young Communist League, but more importantly, he learned how to succeed socially. "I couldn't believe that all those rules—that you had to be good-looking and smartly dressed, that you had to be intelligent and mustn't ever pick your nose, that you had to always have something to say and you had to be big and you had to be strong—none of those unwritten rules applied in art college. Incredibly beautiful women would talk to you without needing to see your credentials. It took me about a year to get over that."

The British art school system, although called a college program, was actually a part of the government's vocational education system. Peter Blake, the pop artist who would later become the designer of album covers for both the Beatles and the Who, began art school in the late forties. "If you failed your initial examination, then a year later you could take an examination for technical school," he said. "This is where you would go to learn bricklaying, technical things. But if you passed for technical school and you wanted to go to art school, you could do that." In consequence, art schools tended to attract a great many students who were bright, lacked academic aptitude or discipline but hadn't the patience to learn a trade.

Nevertheless, a great many of the students at colleges like Ealing Art School were studying graphic or commercial design of one sort or another or preparing for jobs in the advertising world, perhaps, or for one of the allied trades— photography or printing, for instance. There were also students with serious painterly ambition, however, and the instructors were often quite serious artists in their own right. At one time or other almost all of the best-known British painters of the fifties and sixties taught in art schools at this level. At Ealing, Townshend studied for a time under the expatriate American R. B. Kitaj.

According to Richard Barnes, who studied with Townshend at Ealing, shared a flat with him and plays a floating role in his musical history, art school was "where what used to be called commercial art became graphics and merged with fine art to become pop art." The interchange among disciplines and the breakdown of distinctions between "serious" subjects and frivolous ones was an important part of the art school ferment that produced a number of Britain's best and best-known musicians. At Ealing simultaneously with Townshend were Ron Wood, of the Faces and the Rolling Stones; Freddie Mercury, of Queen; and Roger Ruskin Spear of the Bonzo Dog Doo Dah Band. John Lennon, Ray Davies, Eric Clapton, Keith Richard, Ian Dury, Bryan Ferry and many other British pop stars also studied in art schools during the late fifties and sixties.

Ealing's program was especially fertile. Its new head tutor, Roy Ascot, based his educational theories on cybernetics, the synergistic concept of melding a variety of disciplines formerly held separate within the academy. Thus, Ealing students explored printmaking and sculpture alongside automation and auto-destruction. Although cybernetics, which literally means the theoretical study of electrical, mechanical and biological control systems, is a term derived from computer mathematics, Ascot's application was appropriate. It connected such process studies to the grand, confusing pattern of contemporary art and was a perfect term for a view of art that included both abstract and representational painting as well as conceptual and minimalist performance ideas. (For instance, Townshend once was assigned to deal with school as a legless man would have and wound up spending a term pushing himself around on a homemade cart. In another instance, he was taught a separate phonetic alphabet as part of a language developed with fellow students.) All of this work was designed to break down the conventional distinctions between art and nonart. As Ascot said, "Art is more than just 'old apples on tables.' "

As a vocational training institution, Ealing Art School was a failure, as was the entire British art school system, since it churned out far more students than there were jobs. But simply by having such a powerful impact upon the development of rock & roll, which was to become Britain's most important form of mass cultural expression over the next two decades, the art schools served their purpose.

It's tempting to suggest that art school had more impact on those musicians through its exposure of a bohemian sensibility than through what was learned in class. But that is not borne out by the development of British popular music in the next few years, especially the hard rock of such bands as the Beatles, the Kinks, the Rolling Stones and the Who, all of them led by art school alumni. Townshend, like Lennon and perhaps Davies, displayed a thorough familiarity with contemporary artistic theory, which can easily be seen in his immediate application of ideas derived from Blake's pop art paintings (notably, "The First Real Target" and "Self Portrait," in which the painter showed himself wearing a couple of dozen medals and badges, including one of Elvis Presley) and in his use of the auto-destructive technique he picked up at a lecture by the Austrian Gustav Metzke. Metzke exhibited photographs of paintings he had dipped in acid, showing the various stages of erosion as a weird form of beauty. "Metzke had another idea of putting up statues with weak foundations so that they'd fall down inside a year," said Townshend, who also recalled a lecture in which a double bass was destroyed.

Richard Barnes remembered lectures by such adventurous artists as the Americans Larry Rivers and Robert Brownjohn and by the radical playwright David Mercer. From these lectures and from his general art school experiences, Townshend picked up ideas about technical and conceptual aspects of performance and recording technique and about audience-performer interaction which would deeply affect all the rest of his work.

"There would be lessons where you sort of listened to jazz. Or listened to classical music. Or explored minimalism. We had jazz musicians, film writers, playwrights as well as artists like Jackson Pollock and Larry Rivers and people like that to come and lecture," Townshend told Pete Hamill in 1982. "It was a clearinghouse, and music was something that was very much considered to be okay. And not something that you only did after hours. It was part of life. You could sit in a classroom with people painting *and* playing. I used to do it."

None of this necessarily diminishes the social aspect of Townshend's art school experience. But it is important not to forget how much impact the idea that art and pop music were connected had on him. This juxtaposition led Pete and others to the concept that distinctions between pop culture and high art might not be particularly germane or useful any longer. These ideas were what Townshend struggled with throughout his career, and he was first directly exposed to them at Ealing Art School.

Townshend's art school social life was approached as self-consciously as a work of art. "I soon decided that I was going to get nowhere as an introvert and that I'd become an extrovert. . . ." he told Richard Barnes. Pete had been at Ealing for some weeks before he screwed up the courage, one afternoon in the commons room, to ask to borrow another student's guitar. Townshend might have been seeking nothing more than a way to kill some time, but he was clearly a superior player among the student population. Only a few years before, John Lennon had been regarded as a weirdo renegade among

Liverpool's art students because of his infatuation with American pop music. Now, because the Beatles had made rock and R&B fashionable even among sophisticated, trendy London art students, Townshend's guitar playing skills were a socially marketable commodity at Ealing.

The next day, the commons room episode made Townshend his first art school friend. Tom Wright was an American from Alabama studying in the school's photography section. Wright was taken with Townshend's collection of "fancy guitar licks" and asked Peter to teach him the knack at his flat across from the school on Sunnyside Road.

Townshend has since claimed that Wright was the first person to speak to him at school. Their friendship lasted over the next two decades. It was a good match. Townshend had extensive musical ability and a thirst for acceptance and rebellion (not necessarily mutually exclusive desires among students). Wright had a massive collection of American blues, R&B and jazz albums and a hipster's drawl and dry wit. For Townshend, who had never even had a record player of his own, the sounds were revelatory.

"I got my introduction to blues and a lot of other stuff, too," he said. "Mose Allison, Ray Charles, Jimmy Smith, Jimmy Reed, John Lee Hooker, a lot of great music, all in one year. By 1961–1962, I'd already started to develop a bit of knowledge of what lay behind rock music. . . . The guy who really influenced the sound I did was John Lee Hooker. That really impressed me. Although I was listening to a lot of jazz and playing jazz at the time, I preferred Hooker."

Elsewhere, Townshend has cited Jimmy Reed as his biggest influence among bluesmen, but the point is the same and just as surprising in either case. Reed and Hooker are the most primitive urban bluesmen, with their rough, chanted vocals and foot-stomping rhythms and the skeletal melodies that tend to remain static over the whole of their repertoire. But both Hooker and Reed had a sheer power of performance that must have made them especially attractive to Townshend. Their crudeness not only made their approach enticingly exotic but also *available* in a way that a more fully developed style might not be. That is, Townshend could more easily use such simple ideas than more carefully crafted ones whose originators had realized more of their potential.

Tom Wright also gave Pete Townshend his first taste of marijuana, a commodity virtually unknown in Britain at the time (among white Britons, at least: Indians and West Indians obviously knew considerably more about grass). "I was never really adventurous either in school or in the world," Townshend has said in explanation of marijuana's impact on him. "My guitar was an escape valve in many ways. Pot came as a pleasant door-opener in a world where I seemed to be left behind. Smoking pot at art school put me in a dangerous but exciting position.

"I suppose, too, that it gave me something that I had never had among friends and family—a secret. The fatal attraction of a drug that everybody in society deemed almost poisonous to the mind and yet proved to be almost harmless in use was incredible." For Townshend, over the next five years, pot smoking became inseparable from making (or even listening to) music. At the time, one of the major functions of pot smoking was to throw Townshend together with a group of very unconventional students, leading him to question the relative social stability in which he'd been raised and supporting his ego by marking him as eccentric rather than just weird. For someone as emotionally fragile as Peter Townshend, such distinctions were a matter of life and death.

The impact of pot smoking on Tom Wright was more direct and much less pleasant. Caught with some weed, he was ordered deported. Preparing a hasty exit, he proposed that Peter take over both his Sunnyside Road flat and his record collection.

It was a lifesaving offer, for Townshend was already on the outs with his parents, and he and Barnes were looking for a place to share. Pete and his mother were going through a series of rows, which characterized their relationship and which were intensified by Betty's expectation that her son become a serious commercial artist, not a layabout musician. Pete was too much a dreamer, too preoccupied with his band, which Betty liked much less now that the Detours were less "versatile" and more rock & roll oriented.

Pete was mystified by his family. "I spent a lot of time with them when other kids' parents were at work, and I spent a lot of time *away* from them when other kids had parents," he told Jann Wenner. "That was the way it came together. They were always out for long periods. But they were always home for long periods, too." This was especially true of Cliff, who did some touring right through the early sixties. Betty was home, but with two younger sons and the antiques shop and the household to run, she was preoccupied. Pete, with his late-night noise and layabed habits, got on her nerves and kept her awake, not only with his guitar but with the reel-to-reel tape recorder he'd acquired after he and classmate Dick Seamen ran into an eccentric but inventive jazz pianist and tape collagist, Andy "Thunderclap" Newman.

The tape experiments were especially attractive as a musical method for Townshend because he never learned how to read music. "My father was famous for his fast reading," Peter said. "He could play anything off the cuff. They used to use him on difficult electronic music, classical passages, because he could look at it and play it. He's able to do that under any circumstances, but I suppose I'm at the other end of the extreme. He used to say to me, 'Look, the only tip I can give you is that you learn to read music,' and naturally, it's the only musical tip I never took.

"If I ever had learned to read music, I don't know whether I would have gotten as hung up on tape recording, and if I wasn't as hung up on tape recording as I was, I don't think I would have learned to write." But Peter wasn't writing yet; he was simply toying with the effects possible on tape recorders. These experiments, which often kept him up all night making loud, weird noises, may have been the last straw for his mother.

By some lights, Pete had very little to complain about. He was not what anyone would call oversupervised. "Nobody ever stopped me playing guitar," he has acknowledged, "and nobody ever stopped me smoking pot, although they advised me against it. They didn't stop me from doing anything I wanted to do. I had my first fuck in the drawing room of my mother's house."

"Peter was always falling out with his mother and moving out," said Sandom. "Or not particularly falling out with her—maybe it just wasn't the thing to live at home."

At any rate, Pete and Barnes now moved into Wright's old flat and began a full-time life of student bohemia, with other students around at all hours, listening to records, singing or playing guitar, smoking pot or making out, spinning tales and theories. The Sunnyside Road flat had been a natural gathering center when Wright lived there; Barnes and Pete did their best to keep it that way.

In his Who memoir, *The Who: Maximum R&B*, Richard Barnes lists the contents of their windfall record collection: ". . . all of Jimmy Reed's albums, all of Chuck Berry's, all of James Brown's, Bo Diddley, John Lee Hooker, Snooks Eaglin, Mose Allison, all of Jimmy Smith's, Muddy Waters, Lightnin' Hopkins, Howlin' Wolf, Slim Harpo, Buddy Guy, Big Bill Broonzy, Sonny Terry and Brownie McGhee, Joe Turner, Nina Simone, Booker T., Little Richard, Jerry Lee Lewis, Carl Perkins, the Isley Brothers, Fats Domino, the Coasters, Ray Charles, Jimmy McGriff, Brother Jack McDuff, John Patton, Bobby Bland, the Drifters, the Miracles, the Shirelles, the Impressions and many jazz albums including Charlie Parker, Mingus, Coltrane, Miles Davis, Milt Jackson, West Montgomery, Jimmy Guiffre, Dave Brubeck, plus albums by Jonathan Winters, Mort Sahl, Shelley Berman and particularly Lord Buckley. There were also about thirty classical albums."

This would be an outstanding record collection even today, when most of the performers listed above are regarded as legends and masters. For 1962, the collection was not only astonishing in its scope and consistent excellence, but it also served as a kind of treasure trove of unknown mysteries. Even in America most of these performers were known only for one or two hit singles, if at all. The concept of a whole collection of such music wasn't unknown, but it was pretty much the exclusive province of blacks and certain white Southerners.

It was these records that really changed Townshend's mind about music. "I heard rhythm & blues and it was all over," he told Jann Wenner in 1968. "The first record I remember was 'Green Onions,' by Booker T. . . . It was Steve Cropper who really turned me on to aggressive guitar playing." (Of course, "Green Onions" was a major mod record, too. But the song was never a pop hit on the British charts, and it's unlikely that it would have had such impact on Townshend if he had heard it *only* at the Goldhawk Club. Chances are, Booker T. and the MGs, and their guitarist, Cropper, were Pete's most important musical link between school and the band during this period.)

According to Barnes, Townshend's social life was severely circumscribed because of his work with the Detours, which kept him busy on so many evenings that he was forced to forgo a great many of the parties and dances. Pete would leave for his gig at around 5:30 in the afternoon and return around midnight. While the same crowd might still be at the flat when he came home (and while a few art school mates would sometimes come along to the Detours' shows), Pete was obviously left out of whatever went on while he was away.

Townshend's social contacts were also limited by another problem, an absolute inability to keep his stories straight. A symptomatic example is contained in the quote above, in which he claims to have heard Jackson Pollock lecture at Ealing. Pollock died in 1956.

During his art school years, Townshend was undone in his first love affair by this trait. He had fallen in love with a girl some years his senior who was involved in a serious relationship with a jazz musician who played in West End clubs (Ronnie Scott's and the like). When the jazzman split, Townshend was left with his big chance, but he blew it by spinning a yarn about how he'd seen Parker (also dead several years) playing in a club.

Though some of this tendency to fabricate stories and lie may rest with Townshend's immaturity, with his desperation stemming from what he still considered his physical disfigurement or simply with a memory whose fantasies are more vivid than its realities, the fact that there is a string of doubling over and contradiction in Townshend's public statements is unignorable. It's as if he never sufficiently recovered from his adolescent trauma to realize that his later achievements were impressive by themselves. To this day, when hit records and millions of pounds ensure his stature, Townshend seemingly can't stop himself from gilding the lily.

It was another Townshend girlfriend who turned him on to Bob Dylan, sometime in 1963, by playing him Dylan's first two albums (the self-titled debut and *The Freewheelin' Bob Dylan*). Townshend was immediately fascinated by Dylan's cracked pseudo-hillbilly voice, his wonderful command of the humor and passion in the American folk music repertoire and his ability to weave stories and philosophies into his lyrics. This fascination continued for several years and would prove instrumental in converting Townshend from mere guitarist to song writer.

It was also at Ealing that Townshend first met Karen Astley, a student in the dress design course. Although they didn't date until later, it's said that Townshend was immediately captivated by her. (What neither Peter nor Karen knew then was that Karen's father, Edwin Astley, had often been the opening act for the Squadronaires when they played in the Astleys' home town, Manchester. The Astleys had moved to London so that Edwin could pursue a career scoring television programs for the BBC.)

Barnes and Townshend remained in the Sunnyside Road flat for about a year. But early in 1964, they were forced to move. Somewhere along the line, they acquired a dingy but well-outfitted converted ambulance, with "Yardbirds" scrawled across the back in lipstick. For about three weeks Barnes and Townshend lived in this van, sleeping in bedrolls. Then they decided to take the flat above Pete's parents.

The upstairs flat had two rooms. The larger one was converted into a replica of the Sunnyside Road flat, strewn with albums, clothing, mattresses, ashtrays and Barnes' painting and silkscreening gear. In the other, Peter planned to build a recording studio. A classmate, Des Donnellan, laid an inch of concrete on the floor to soundproof it.

"They tried to soundproof it," recalled Paul Townshend, who was then eight years old. "They had egg boxes everywhere on the walls, and they knocked a hole in one wall to put in a window. And they didn't put the window in; they didn't get round to that. Then the cement made the ceiling start to bow in downstairs. There was a blazing row, and my mom and dad kicked 'em out.

"The next day, their ambulance turned up—they used to have that ambulance, with flowers all over it. They moved it all to a flat down by Marble Arch, because they'd got a record contract by then, got a bit of money. So they moved into this flat in Marble Arch, with mattresses all over the floor."

6

Gather 'round you swingers and
friends, Help me forget my hurt again . . .
I gotta dance to keep from crying
—Smokey Robinson and the Miracles,
"I Gotta Dance to Keep From Crying"

The Beatles changed everything for bands like the Detours. It wasn't just that the Beatles were relatively poor boys who made good; pop music stardom had been one of the few legitimate vehicles to wealth for the unpropertied at least since Al Jolson, and almost every singer who cropped up in the wake of Elvis Presley came from one level of poverty or another. And it wasn't just that the Beatles played rock & roll and played it well, either, because there were plenty of other hot rock musicians around, both in England and America, from Del Shannon and Roy Orbison to Johnny Kidd and Billy Fury.

But none of these performers challenged the status quo. All that Elvis (and the pop singers who came before him and succeeded him) had managed to do was jump the gap between unskilled labor and the middle class by acquiring a trade. Though this made a significant difference in the lives of the singers themselves, and while the rock & roll singers, particularly, served as a radicalizing social force in other ways, no one had constituted a serious challenge to business as usual.

The Beatles were fundamentally disruptive. They revived rock & roll at its most leering, sneering potency, and they did so deliberately, in the face of an already known antipathy to such music and stage behavior on the part of public moralists and the music industry. The difference between Elvis Presley and John Lennon is the difference between an outlaw and a rebel.

The Beatles' very existence was a refutation of the idea that pop was nothing but frivolity. Their irreducible insolence and contempt for convention suggested the power of rock, both as music and as image, and their rapid-fire humor and imperturbable cool did the same for rhythm & blues. As a result, they attracted whole new groups of people to pop and brought forth from the closet many who had always loved such "trash."

Within the record business, the Beatles were the spearhead of equally significant changes—from easily manipulated singers who needed a supply of musicians, songwriters, producers and managers, to self-contained bands who played and wrote their own material, kept a firm grip on other aspects of their presentation to the public and had goals other than early retirement or a career in "adult" media such as cabaret, nightclubs or the movies.

For bands like the Detours, the changes were radical and immediate. It was no longer enough to be "versatile," adaptable followers of trends started (or imposed) from above. Now a group needed to be able to project a personality and style of its own and to tinker with established "rules" and concepts. There were many more bands around, as the Beatles inspired thousands of kids to emulate them. The more experienced groups had an advantage only if they could cope with the increased level of ambition introduced by the Beatles.

In west London this competitive situation was trebly intensified. The success of the Beatles had stirred further the activity on the local R&B scene, which had begun building when Chris Barber's trad band first imported American blues singers (Big Bill Broonzy, Muddy Waters) in the mid-fifties. A couple of years later, Alexis Korner and Cyril Davies left Barber's band to form Blues Incorporated, which played London jazz clubs. But their blues was too raw and electric for Soho jazz smoothies, and in early 1962 Korner and Davies helped found a new venue, the Ealing Club, located in a tea shop basement not far from where Pete Townshend grew up.

The Ealing Club quickly became a center for young blues and R&B-oriented musicians in the area, including Mick Jagger, Brian Jones, and all the other Rolling Stones (Charlie Watts played in Blues Inc.); Paul Jones and the rest of Manfred Mann; Mick Avory, later of the Kinks; Jack Bruce and Ginger Baker; Graham Bond; John Mayall; Long John Baldry and many others.

That summer, R&B made a major move into Soho with the opening of the Flamingo and its more soul-oriented sound. The headliner there was Georgie Fame and the Blue Flames. Also, that summer, Blues Inc. began a weekly residency at an Oxford Street jazz club, the Marquee; filling in for them one night that July was another new group, the Rolling Stones.

Meantime, the Beatles had hit the charts, and the concept of native British groups playing American-originated music began to skyrocket. By early 1963, Manfred Mann, Downliners Sect, the Yardbirds, Chris Farlowe and the Thunderbirds, Ronnie Jones and the Nightimers, the Graham Bond Organisation, Zoot Money's Big Roll Band and the Pretty Things were all playing Chicago-style American blues or some of the lighter soul sounds or a combination of the two. More clubs cropped up all around Soho and west London, most notably Giorgio Gomelsky's Crawdaddy Club, at Richmond athletic ground, where the Stones began a residency late that summer.

The London blues and rhythm & blues scene wasn't a big deal in the press; even the weekly music papers, *New Musical Express* and *Melody Maker*, still had their eyes up north. Typically, they were tuned in to the explosion that had already happened when another, ultimately far more devastating one was building up right under their noses. In the end, this lack of press attention worked to the scene's benefit; although it was highly competitive, it wasn't plagued with enterprising Brian Epstein clones (not yet) or record company gimmickmongers, who had focused their attention on the so-called Tottenham sound of lame Londoners, the Dave Clark Five, and Brian Poole and the Tremeloes.

The Detours spent most of 1962 working their way up the rungs of Druce's Commercial Entertainments ladder, becoming the most important group on his circuit. Now the Detours played five nights a week, minimum, their only rehearsals a half-hour onstage at the start of the evening before the crowd came in.

In the main, the stars for whom they served as opening act were rockers or Mersey groups or pop bands like the Hollies, from Manchester, or Lulu and the Lovers, from Glasgow.

Still, the Detours' following built up: the Goldhawk, the Glenlyn Ballroom, the Railway Hotel, the Trade Union Hall in Watford, the Assembly Room in Carpenders Park. Irish Jack remembered the band's first appearance at the Goldhawk: "I nearly collapsed when I saw my old mate up there, with his nose as long as ever. I could hardly believe it. . . . Mind you, I had to admire the way the group had improved. They were twice as loud as Boseley's, and the small geezer what used to play lead guitar had become the singer, 'cause the old one had left.

"Another thing I liked," Jack said, "was that they'd slung away their soppy old suits and had these leather Beatle jackets instead." According to Barnes, these were knee-length light tan leather waistcoats, collarless like the jackets the Beatles wore on their first album covers, but also sleeveless and buttonless. They were designed by Townshend; choosing them was one of the few battles he had won.

Roger and Peter were now arguing frequently, according to all accounts. "We were always known for squabblin', even back then," said Sandom, "because we used to have rehearsals where Roger was always smashing Peter in the nose." (Pete denied this. He said Roger never hit him until 1974.)

Sandom and Entwistle were fairly placid sorts, willing to get along, although Entwistle had a tough streak, activated when prodded too far, and Sandom had his own limits. But Daltrey and Townshend were a classic mismatch. Neither ever backed down.

"What's amazing is that [Pete] was a terrible fighter," said Sandom. "What it was, he had such a complex about his nose that he wanted to be nasty to them before they were nasty to him. He felt, 'Well, I'll get it in first.' I mean, so what, you've got a big nose?

"You couldn't help but like him, but Peter could be a pig, a pig of a man. He had a nasty thing about him—he could be so *sarcastic*, it was unbelievable. He could do things that you'd think, 'God, Pete, what are you *doing*?'

"Peter used to have goes at John, about his playing. But he used to have goes at anybody about anything. That's just how it went. John would never say a word."

Daltrey wasn't much different. "Roger used to have a go at Peter," Sandom went on. "He'd have a go at John, but John wouldn't argue. But you could argue with Pete, and that was why Roger was always punchin' him out. I've never seen Pete throw a punch—and he'd have a bleedin' nose. 'You all right, Peter?' 'Yeah, I'll be all right.' " (Townshend said Sandom was "gilding the lily," describing Doug's stories as "fairy tales" and "lies.")

Yet there was a sense in which Daltrey and Townshend were complete allies—in their ambition to make the Detours succeed. "Roger pulled it forward," in Sandom's opinion. "I think he spoke about it more. Peter thought a lot and put his thoughts into Roger's mind, and Roger put 'em out. They thought pretty well the same."

Neither Townshend nor Daltrey could have achieved any lasting success on his own. Daltrey's vision was too limited; he was not nearly articulate enough to survive the changes of the sixties. Townshend was too cerebral. He could never have put over the concepts he learned in art school and the instincts he nurtured so carefully in later years without someone like Daltrey to stand in front. Sandom's analysis is not only correct, it strikes to the essence of why Daltrey and Townshend remained partners for more than twenty years despite frequent antagonisms.

A distance began to develop, not between Daltrey and Townshend but between Doug Sandom's aspirations and those of the younger boys. In the beginning, Doug's value was not only that of a steady timekeeper, but that he possessed a measure of maturity. "He seemed to be a sensible guy to me, and whenever I knew Doug was with them, I felt quite a bit easier," said Harry Daltrey. "I felt, well, he'll steady them up. And I think he did, really."

Sandom puts it another way. After a time, he says, age became a "barrier, because I think I thought differently—I was bit more sensible in a way." Sandom was earning about twelve pounds (about thirty-five dollars) a week in the band, a substantial supplement to his income. He says he never imagined making more than "a nice little living" from music. To him, Townshend and Daltrey's dreams and schemes must have seemed wildly naïve and immature.

But it was a time of dreamers and schemers, a time when thinking big paid the biggest rewards.

The Detours were by no means already playing to a mostly mod following in 1962. Even the Goldhawk Social Club, which had latterly become such a symbolic mod institution, was (according to its most famous member, Irish Jack) "probably more rockers than mods. And you had guys in there who weren't mods or rockers. They were loners." The Goldhawk was a school for hardboys. In Jack's words, it was "packed with guys who were just after coming out of nick [jail]. They were the men to avoid: Norman Foreman, Georgie Harding, Percy Chaplin. They were Daltrey's mates."

But then, the Detours were not really mods themselves. Townshend was an art student, and though he had some inclination to the kind of style fetishism mod represented (as did Roger), he was closer to being a beat, a little scruffy and too casual. Doug was a rocker in almost everyone's opinion, including his own. John was more ambiguous, but both Jack and Sandom saw him as a rocker, and certainly his penchant for black and / or leather gear suggests this.

"John and I was a little bit rockified," Sandom said. "And the other two were mods. But John would never admit it. He'd say, 'No, I'm a mod.' And then when we was talking together, he'd say, 'No, not really. I'm a rocker.' Because John didn't like to upset anybody. He was the boy who was quiet, who wouldn't upset anybody."

In fact, one word alone described John Entwistle perfectly. First and last, he was a *musician*. He didn't really care about much else but playing. Being in the band altered his idea of *what* he should play and *how* he should play it—for instance, the gesture, if that's what it was, of fretting overhand rather than conventionally. But playing was what the Detours were about to John. The others could squabble about where they were going and what it all meant.

Because so many of their evenings were occupied with playing, the Detours themselves did not have a clear picture of what was going on locally. It was up to friends such as Barnes to fill them in on acts they had never seen but who were making a reputation on the circuit, which is how they first heard of the Rolling Stones and the Yardbirds, for instance. But if the Detours were to experience such music themselves, it was most likely going to be as an opening act.

Early in 1963 the Detours were hired to serve as the opening band for the Rolling Stones at St. Mary's Ballroom in Putney. St. Mary's was all the way south of the river and tough enough that it was one of the few places where John Entwistle did not allow Alison, ordinarily a fixture at all the band's shows. The local bands were Manfred Mann and the Mark Leeman Five, who hardly played R&B at all. But it drew a strong mod crowd and it paid well.

As opening act, the Detours did a fifteen-minute set to begin the evening; they were followed by the headliners, who played around thirty minutes, certainly never more than an hour. Then the Detours would be brought back on for a final set, somewhat longer than the first. In the interval, a disc jockey spun records, current hits and the imported bluebeat (from Jamaica) and R&B (from the States) that were beginning to catch on.

The Rolling Stones had only been together a couple of months, but they were already creating a sensation. Mick Jagger wasn't yet a great singer; he was still too obviously aping inspirations like Marvin Gaye and Chuck Berry. But Bill Wyman and Charlie Watts had proved themselves an exciting, flawless rhythm combo, and the guitarists, Keith Richard and Brian Jones, weren't just great players, they were exciting to look at, too. And Jagger more than made up for his vocal limitations with his complete showmanship. His entire body seemed elastic, his lips and legs pure rubber, able to be contorted into any bizarre or erotic configuration he chose.

For Townshend, the Stones were "a revelation . . . I was amazed that they were so scruffy, so organic, and they were still stars." After the show, Townshend was taken into the stars' dressing room by Glyn Johns, a singer with a band called the Presidents who was friendly with both bands. It is a measure of the esteem and awe he immediately felt for the Stones that even in the early 1980s, Townshend could remember the cool cordiality of Mick Jagger's greeting, Brian Jones's enthusiasm for the Detours, and the cool arrogance and nonchalance with which Keith Richard snubbed him.

The Detours, like a lot of other bands, were dabbling with blues and R&B. But the Detours were basically copyists, and they did not take the romance of the blues, its angst and folklore, to heart. They certainly did not do what the Rolling Stones did, which was play the blues and R&B material exclusively and unapologetically.

The Stones' influence showed up immediately and decisively in the Detours' subsequent performances. The trail began the very next night, when Townshend decided to use a Keith Richard gimmick in which Keith would pull his arm back and then slash it through the strings. It was a gesture in keeping with Richard's compact, laconic style, and Townshend simply exaggerated it, by pulling his arm far above his head and then bringing it down rapidly to thunder through the strings. Sometimes Townshend would rev up, whirling his arm in the air, windmill style, half a dozen times before coming down to strike the strings. The effect, coupled with his stork-like build and his beak, earned him a nickname: the Bird Man.

"I thought I was copying Keith," Townshend remembered several years later. "So when we did a gig with the Stones later, I didn't do it all night, and I watched him, and he didn't do it all night, either. 'Swing me what?' he said. He must have got into it as a warming up thing that night, but he didn't remember.

"There's a lot we pinched from the Stones," Townshend added. "We pinched absolutely nothing from the Beatles, funnily enough, but the Stones were like a local band to us. I saw some of their first gigs, at Richmond, and all the girls I was going out with at the time were in love with one or another of them. I was just a Rolling Stones substitute."

The biggest change that seeing the Stones encouraged was a switch in repertoire, from R&B and pop to straight R&B and electric blues. The Detours now played Howlin' Wolf's "Smokestack Lightnin' " and "Spoonful," Jimmy Reed's "Big Boss Man" and Muddy Waters's "I Just Want to Make Love to You," along with James Brown numbers like "Please, Please, Please" and "I Don't Mind." Strong stuff, but skeletal. It took imagination to flesh it out.

Turning to the blues also meant turning away from copying records. "Because so many of the songs sounded more or less exactly the same," said Roger, referring to the fact that many blues numbers are built around very simple keys and chords with very little melodic development or rhythmic variety, "we had to use our imagination to build them up. Blues taught us to use musical freedom. Playing pop before, you just copied a record and that was it. If we got near to the record, we were happy. But blues was a completely different thing altogether. We'd play one verse for twenty minutes and make up half the lyrics."

Another way to cope was by turning up the volume. "We used to get told off for being too loud," said Sandom. "We used to get people complaining way across the road. We'd buy these old speakers and Roger would make up these cabinets. It was pretty heavy gear for the sort of bands that was going about at that time. We was noted as being a loud band."

Although Daltrey has always attributed the large cabinets to the group's psychological campaign, Entwistle points out that the Detours were "the first band to use large amounts of equipment" because "we decided to be loud, to have a lot of impact. And to do that, we had to have four times as much equipment as anybody else. We only had two melodic instruments, my bass and Pete's guitar. So I devised a way of playing with a very trebly sound, as if my bass were a rhythm guitar. To get this effect, I half pluck and half tap the strings. This gets more notes in without blurring. So when Pete was doing chord work, I could get in a melodic line from the bass side. But to do this we needed one-hundred-watt amplifiers with four cabinets each."

That much power was a while coming, but over at Marshall's music shop in west Ealing, the technological capability was being developed. Jim Marshall was another key figure on the west London music scene, a drum shop proprietor who gave a lot of musicians their start, was willing to loan or sell on credit to struggling players and generally encouraged beginners and journeymen alike. "One day Jim's son came in and said, 'I'm going to invent this amp separate from the cabinet,' " recalled Speedy Keen, then an aspiring percussionist who hung out in the shop. "I remember everybody used to pick up the first prototype, and the transformer was so big, it was impossible to carry. I remember it taking months to work out how to balance this thing out, but it was a great idea."

According to Townshend, Entwistle was the first person to play through Marshall amplifiers. "We played some part in the development of the Marshalls, you know," Townshend said. "We used to hang out around the shop, which was quite near where I used to live. Anyway, once John had a Marshall, he was so loud, I had to get one." The result was a roar like thunder, an astonishing noise, not so much celebratory (as the deafening big bands of the forties had been) as assaultive and angry, as if the frustration of trying to find their own voice had driven the Detours to drastic measures. (Which, of course, it had.)

That's not to say that the band totally abandoned its pop attitudes. Doug Sandom remembers being hassled by Townshend when his wife came along to gigs. "Peter would come up to me and say, 'Take your ring off, no one must know you're married,' and all that rubbish. That used to get my wife's back up!" Townshend denied it, saying that Doug used to get upset if Pete told anyone that the drummer was really a married man.

According to Entwistle, the band did not play a full set of blues until one night when Bob Druce asked them to fill in for another group on short notice. The band then decided that they should be allowed to play whatever they wished, as they were doing Druce a favor in the first place. So the Detours cranked out an all-blues set, and when it went over as well as their usual shows, decided to stick with blues full time.

Daltrey, however, said that the decision to play R&B exclusively wasn't so simple. "We lost all the fans we had at the time by playing the blues," he claimed. "It took about six months for them all to come back, but when they did, we found that we had three times as many fans as we'd had six months before."

The result was a change so drastic that the band wasn't particularly panicked when one of them, watching the television show "Thank Your Lucky Stars," spotted a nine-piece Irish band also called the Detours. The London-based Detours would have to find a new name. This may even have been seen as an opportunity by some of the band, since they were also in the process of acquiring a new image and a new audience.

They held a meeting after a gig one night in an attempt to come up with something suitable. They drew a blank, and then they did feel a bit panicky. As Daltrey drove them home, they mulled it over, and when they reached Pete's place, Townshend suggested that everyone come up to continue the discussion. Richard Barnes was also there, wide awake though it was past midnight, and he joined in the search.

Barnes and Townshend immediately did what any art students of the day would have done in order to inspire creative thinking–they rolled and lit joints. The rest of the band demurred, probably because none of them had yet dared try the stuff. The natural result was that the conversation grew lopsided as Barnes arid Townshend ran through a whole series of what seemed to them hilarious names, including No One and the Group.

Many of the suggestions were specifically designed to curb the antics of the emcee at the Oldfield Tavern, an older gent named Lou who liked to make jokes of his announcements. Finally, Barnes hit on the Who, since it provided such a perfect opportunity for conundrum and also had a pop punch. Townshend disagreed. He wanted to call the band the Hair, since it was hair that was the major issue of the day, letters to editors all over the land decrying the moral decadence implicit in letting young men grow their locks out over the tips of their ears and perhaps down the backs of their necks.

However, the Hair did not seem to be a name with much potential for longevity—it could be outdated in about six minutes if Paul McCartney chose to get a crew cut. And anyhow, the Detours didn't have especially long hair.

Townshend responded by suggesting calling the group the Hair and the Who. Barnes reminded him that they were trying to name a rock band, not a surrealist pub. Eventually, they gave up and the others went home, Barnes seeing them out the door with the suggestion that they call themselves British European Airways.

The next morning, Daltrey turned up quite early to take Townshend by

Marshall's music shop to forage for equipment. "It's the Who, innit?" he said to Barnes, and so the decision was made.

The name change solidified the band's support at the Goldhawk. "Some blokes actually went and bought their own harmonicas, and they'd bring them down the Goldhawk, get the key right off Daltrey and start playing along under the stage," recalled Irish Jack. "I'd never seen anything like it happen before. Even after playing a couple of hours, the Detours would still be up onstage when it was all over, showing blokes how to tune a guitar and telling them how to start their own group off. I reckon they was more than a group, mate, they was a fucking music co-op.

"The Detours were cut and dried for blokes like us in the Goldhawk. They weren't a soppy light-hearted outfit churning out pop songs for some silly bird with an engagement ring on her finger. They were like us. That's why we respected them so much. They weren't above us because they could play instruments and pull birds better than we could. They drank in the bar with everyone and bought us drinks, as well. They were like a sort of community band. They were *our* band."

In its circuitous route across London, mod had still not surfaced in the media by 1963, although a perceptive fashion reporter or two had noticed that certain young men were beginning to regularly frequent Soho shops like John Stephen's His Clothes, previously the domain of gays and blacks, not straight boys with jobs. The key moment at which the Goldhawk or any other particular institution changed its colors was unclear, even to the participants. "One minute we were just ordinary blokes in the Goldhawk; the next thing we was all bleedin' mods," as Jack put it. "It seemed to happen overnight, like an electric current being switched on."

But mod did not move out of the London region for several months. This is extremely important, because the Goldhawk brand of mod was founded as an elite institution.

"It's the anonymity that's peculiar to the mod thing, the secretiveness," said Townshend. "I could only ever feel like a mod when I was off the stage and could mingle with the crowd." In that sense, early mod was a true cult with almost religious overtones, not a pop subculture like the style fads that succeeded it over the next twenty-odd years.

But when Richard Barnes says that mods "hated commercialism," he does not mean that they rejected the consumer society, as hippies would later do. "The mods weren't in any way revolutionary," said Frank Roddam, director of the film *Quadrophenia*. "They worked and spent their money on pills and clothes and music. They weren't saying, 'let's change the work system'; they weren't interested in change but in getting the best from what was there. . . ."

That meant being first to possess something, and first to discard it, as well. When an item grew too popular—when not just "everyone" but only too many knew about it or understood its value—one should already have moved on. Without exclusivity, possessions lost their romance. And without the romance of possession, the kind of discipline and character necessary to keep working rote, meaningless jobs was also pointless. Which left mod with a central contradiction.

"Mods believed in discipline—martial-like," said Irish Jack. "The best thing about it was you had to have a job." But five minutes later he could tell a story about how the mods went each Sunday evening to the Crawdaddy Club in Richmond, a wealthy suburb that they considered enemy territory. In such situations the mod still felt his working-class inferiority eating at him because of the knowledge that while the people in Richmond might be intellectual phonies and poseurs, they also did not have to labor with their backs five days a week for a chance to disport themselves on the weekends.

And even the highest-paying jobs weren't necessarily enough. "It was expensive being a mod," Entwistle pointed out. "Everything was custom-made—if your trousers had center vents and suddenly side vents were in, you had to have them."

"In England, we were the first generation after the war to have a lot of money," said Daltrey. "Rationing was in effect until the late fifties." Roger is speaking only of relative affluence, the kind that time payments and easy credit can handle, not an affluence that leads to a life of leisure and irresponsibility. Mods ultimately came to despise the bohemian Rolling Stones as much as rockers because they were appalled at the idea of consciously choosing the squalor from which the typical mod was escaping with his finery. Dirt, cold, lousy food, poverty—there was nothing romantic about these things for mods who *knew* them or the nearness of them.

Yet they must go to Richmond and the Crawdaddy, because that club was "classy, and that's what mods were all about," as Jack put it. So they went to the lair of their class enemy, often cheating or intimidating their way past the ticket-takers in order to prove their cool. "We had that swagger," said Jack. "But we hated the price we had to pay for it."

In Britain, the first order of stability was tradition, and the first tenet of tradition was respect for property. Mods made property fetishistic in the extreme, but without respecting it. It was important precisely because it was temporary. And this was a cultural conundrum. Mod wasn't exactly individualistic; in fact, the idea of a mod without mates to impress is a contradiction in terms. But if mod was a collective social movement, it was a society of loners in which every man stood for himself. And it was never more that than in those months before Clacton and Margate, when mod was still (in the parlance of the music business) "bubbling under," about to explode but still an undercurrent.

Externally, mod was superfunctional. "It was fashionable, it was clean and it was groovy," said Townshend. "You could be a bank clerk, it was acceptable. You got them on your ground. They thought, 'Well, there's a smart young lad.' "

But Townshend also saw the other side of the coin. "We made the establishment uptight, we made our parents uptight and our employers uptight, because although they didn't like the way we dressed, they couldn't accuse us of not being smart. We had short hair and were clean and tidy."

The Who were known primarily, as Sandom puts it, as a "bloke's band," which figures, because mod was largely a male movement. (Barnes thinks this was probably because of the amphetamines that cut into their users' sex drive.) The Who had more girls than most mods—except for Entwistle, always faithful to Alison, and Sandom, who was married—but not nearly so many as a more "typical" pop group. Although Sandom can remember being chased down Chiswick High Road by young girls on one or two occasions (always to his wife's annoyance), the Who were basically too aggressive to attract many girls. Anyway, they lacked a stereotypically pretty face: Even Roger was no teenybopper's heartthrob.

As far as the hardcore mod cult of the Goldhawk days goes, it certainly isn't true (as Daltrey and Entwistle have said) that the Who were too old to be mods. Irish Jack was a year older than Daltrey, which made him older than anyone associated with the Who, save Sandom, and Jack wasn't one of the older members of the Goldhawk Club. But age was not the major factor anyhow; style was the essence, and that would have been true whether or not mod had arrived. As Townshend has said, "We were one of the English bands who grew up in that Beatle maniacal era when image was almost as important as sound, probably more important."

There was already a tension building in the band, as some wanted to push forward and some wanted not so much to hold back as to consolidate the gains already made. "Some of us said, 'The reason people come to hear us is to hear pop entries.' And the others wanted to *educate* the audiences to accept something a bit farther out," said Townshend. "I wanted like a kind of desperation to try for wilder techniques and wilder statements than what we were doing. This led to each of us in the group being split inside himself, half for it and half against it."

7

*I don't think any band worth its oats ever
picked up a guitar because it wanted wealth
and fame. It wasn't why we wanted to play.
We wanted to play because we were into
the music and into the fact that the only
reality that existed was in losing yourself
in people's reaction to you.*
                        —Peter Townshend

Doug Sandom had a sister who worked in a hardware factory in the grungy backstreets of Shepherd's Bush. The place was actually a brass foundry where doorknobs and the like were made. It was run by an eccentric character called Helmut Gorden, a middle-aged, balding, somewhat stout Jewish immigrant with a fairly heavy Eastern European accent.

Like many other businessmen in late 1963, Helmut Gorden envied Brian Epstein, the entrepreneur who had taken the Beatles out of Liverpool to conquer the world. Although Gorden did not particularly like the kind of beat music that the Beatles played—his own favorite was the Irish vocal group the Bachelors—he considered Epstein's feat worth emulating. In Gorden's eyes (and in those of many others) it was Epstein who had made the Beatles, by converting them from a ragged rock band into smartly dressed young entertainers. Although this was a very dangerous misimpression, it seemed accurate enough for Gorden to proceed as if it were gospel.

Gorden was not an especially convivial fellow; he still lived with his mother and probably wasn't much on fraternizing with his employees. But he did get to know Doug Sandom and his wife and sometimes visited them at their flat. "I knew him," Sandom said. "He meant nothing to me. He didn't know nothing about music."

Gorden pestered Sandom about seeing the Who, and eventually Doug invited him along to see a show at one of their prime local venues, the White Hart Tavern, in Acton. Whether Gorden made clear his intentions about seeking a group to manage and in which to invest, Sandom doesn't recall. But Sandom does remember Gorden's reaction to the show. "He come in and seen all those little kids going mad, and pound notes started flying round in his eyes, you know. He thought, 'Oh, lots of money.' Because he was a right businessman."

Gorden made his interest known to the band after the show. "He was talking about, he was gonna get us making records. That was his strategy. As soon as he mentioned we were gonna make a record, well, money didn't mean a thing, then."

Gorden drew up papers, then called a meeting at Sandom's house. There they signed, with the three younger boys then going to their parents for cosignatures. As long as Roger and John kept their jobs, their parents were happy to have them assisted by a money man. As Sandom said, "They couldn't write on it quick enough. We didn't even read the thing."

But Townshend's parents, with more show business savvy, refused to sign. (Since Pete was still under twenty-one, this made the pact of dubious legality.)

Helmut Gorden, like the good businessman he was, had a thoroughly worked out plan for making stars of "my little diamonds," as he called them. He had compiled a list of music business names, and while they were mostly the sort of Denmark Street types who had been rendered obsolescent by the arrival of the Beatles, a few still had some clout. Gorden also agreed to buy the band a new van, new clothes and some new equipment.

The Who was still playing Bob Druce's circuit, which nominally meant that they were managed by him. But Druce must have known better than to push a contract with a band that was mostly underage and whose career he had never tried to direct. Still, Druce would have liked to continue handling the Who, who had more potential than any of his other acts.

After their set at the Oldfield one night, he got old Lou, the compère, to take the band into the bar. "And he took us into the bar and he was tellin' us what he could do for us. And we sat there, it was pitiful really, lettin' him go through with it. We let him go on and on and on. Then he said, 'We want you to sign a contract,' And then someone turned round and said, 'Too late, mate, we've already signed up.' It was pathetic, really. We should have told him in the first place," said Sandom.

Fortunately, Druce did not want to lose the top band on his circuit, and Gorden had no immediate alternative that could keep the band working, so both parties were kept reasonably happy. (A year or two later, Gorden and Druce worked together booking and promoting a band called Episode Six, which featured future members of Deep Purple.)

For the band's new equipment van, Daltrey chose a Commer diesel, used but smartly outfitted. It had but one fault: a complete lack of pickup, so bad that it had to be pushed up especially steep hills. This van eventually conked out on the M1 Motorway while the band was returning from a gig at Brighton; Gorden came out to rescue the band, taking photos so he could boast of his aid.

Gorden's first coup was arranging a contract with the Harold Davidson Agency for gigs outside the Druce circuit. Davidson was an old-style agent, but he still worked with some of the newer groups. It was also during this period that the Who began to prove their local drawing power. They had obtained a steady booking opening and closing for Chris Farlowe at Watford's Trade Union hall, which held about a thousand people. After a couple of weeks it was noted that the crowd filled the place for the Who but that most left before Farlowe's set. The Who were promoted to headliner status, though they did not get an opening act, meaning that they had to do all three sets themselves. It was also at this stage that their residency at the Railway Tavern, booked by Richard Barnes, began, and they soon ran attendance there from about sixty to over six hundred (all mods). Those kinds of local numbers were sure to impress a national booking agent like Davidson.

But Davidson abided by business-as-usual procedures, which worked against a young, unrecorded band at the expense of established stars. Gorden decided he didn't like the way the agency did business and bolted Davidson after only a few weeks. He then arranged another audition, with a representative of the Arthur Howes Agency. Again the band was signed up.

Gorden got his hair cut at a shop near Marble Arch by a local character called Jack the Barber. In the chair, Gorden would, of course, narrate his most recent adventures. A good deal of what he had to say toward the end of 1963 concerned his new enterprise as Epstein's successor.

Jack the Barber had another customer, Pete Meaden, who was an occasionally employed freelance publicist and promotion man in the record business. At about this time, Meaden had just ended an association with Andrew Loog Oldham and the Rolling Stones.

According to Meaden, one of his haircut chats went something like this: "There's a friend of mine called Helmut Gorden, and he has this band – you're in the pop business, aren't you?" asked Jack.

"Yeah, I know the Stones," replied Meaden. "I knock around with them. I lived with the Stones, as a matter of fact, with Mick and Keith for a while. Yeah, why?"

"Well, they're a good band. Do you reckon you could manage them?"

"Well, I expect so."

Meaden needed work. He had recently been turned away from a Stones reception by their new publicist, spurned as "a pillheaded mod." In revenge, Meaden vowed that he would create a mod sensation. (Of course, it was not altogether uncharitable or inaccurate to call Meaden "a pillheaded mod," since he viewed mod as a new religion and the chief sacrament of this religion was Drynamil, the legendary purple hearts, or amphetamines, to which Meaden was already a slave.)

As he spoke with Jack the Barber, Meaden thought: "Now, could this be the band that I could make into the mod trip? Could this be my focus, my focal point for this good life, which needs a focal point?"

He visited Helmut Gorden in Shepherd's Bush, and Gorden offered Meaden fifty pounds (about $140) to invest in promoting the group.

"I mean, I was known as the low-budget man," Meaden said, "so I thought,

'Great, man, here we go, another low-budget number.' Fifty quid I got this time, to make a supergroup out of. I spent it on clothes, of course, 'cause togs are the only things that keep a mod together. It's like he's a bag of protoplasm, smashed out of his head on the street. With his togs and a few pills inside him, he's God. He's as much God as you or I, he's as heavy as you want him to be."

Meaden's decision to reshape the Who was made without ever seeing them. Their initial encounter left a strong impression on each side. "He was English but talked like an American radio disc jockey, really fast and slick," wrote Barnes. "He called everybody 'Baby.' . . . Meaden never stopped for breath. He was like somebody you'd see in films, only he was this side of the screen, standing in front of you."

Meaden remembered what the band members were wearing: "Pierre Cardin leather jackets, they had cropped hair at the back and Beatle cuts at the front and they were into John Lee Hooker, early blues style. Roger was playing the harmonica, which I liked. I didn't do any more than say, 'Listen, fellers, if you wanna come along with me, I've got the plan for making you a mastergroup.' Mastergroup, mind you, not a supergroup, a mastergroup."

The band had to be impressed by the way Meaden looked, for even though he never made much money and lived in his crowded little office in Monmouth Street in Soho with just a sleeping bag, a chair and an ironing board to go with his telephone and filing cabinet, he was never less than immaculately turned out, his clothes always new and sharp.

But the group must have questioned Meaden's pillheadedness. Though the Who were surrounded by drugs, and though Townshend was a heavy pot smoker who dabbled with speed, the band wasn't yet really inculcated in the drug scene. Daltrey couldn't do much more than have a couple of drinks, because anything stronger hurt his throat, and Entwistle and Sandom were basically straight.

Meaden undeniably looked hip. He talked hipper, and his connection to the Stones, however peripheral, made it official. Daltrey recalled his advice: "Look, you know, there's a million groups looking like the Rolling Stones. Cut your hair, get their [the mods'] gear, be what they want, be how they are."

Gorden's attempt to make of them something they weren't was uncool. (He once told Barnes that he wished he could shave their heads and dress them in kilts.) But Meaden's changes violated nothing, certainly not the band's "integrity," for that concept hadn't yet been applied to rock groups.

"In 1964, when you put a group together, half of the thought went into the music and the other half went into what you looked like," Townshend said. "The Rolling Stones were scraggy beatniks who pissed against walls. The Beatles were moptops. The Who were grooved to the mod revolution, whatever that means."

Mod was about to bust out. You could smell it in the very air of the west London clubs, in the larger crowds at the gigs, in the Carnaby Street clothing shops just a bit more crowded each Saturday, in a few more smiles at each slangy reference to pills.

The Who went for Meaden's plan, and he was thrilled. "They were, in fact, the faces that I'd dreamed of, who'd galvanize this movement that I liked," he told Ray Connolly of the *Evening Standard*.

At the Oldfield, Townshend sometimes placed his amp on an unused piano at the back of the stage. When he switched to Rickenbacker guitars in late 1963, he began placing the amp at the same height as the guitar's single-coil pickup, causing electroacoustic feedback.

"The Yardbirds, funnily enough, were the reason I hit upon it," Townshend told Paul Nelson in 1968. "When I was at school, I lived with this guy who used to go and see Eric Clapton. And he would come back saying, 'Look, you've got to do this! Eric Clapton does this great thing where he goes *ba-ba-ba-bam* on the guitar for hours and hours and everyone goes crazy and lights flash on and off and its great, it's great.' So I used to go *ba-ba-ba-bam* and attempt to do this from what I'd heard from him. Luckily enough, the influence, which could have been very obvious and direct if I'd actually gone to see Clapton, was very effective coming secondhand.

"I used to play at this place where I put my amp on the piano, so the speaker was right opposite my guitar. One day, I was hitting this note and I was going *ba-ba-bam* and the amplifier was going *ur-ur-ur-ur* on its own. I said to myself, 'That's fun. I'll fool around with that.' And I started to pretend I was an airplane. Everyone went completely crazy.

"I started to use it, I started to control it. I regulated the guitar so that the middle pickup was preamped on the inside with a battery and raised right onto the strings so that it would feed back as soon as I switched it on. And I could control it and go through all kinds of things."

Entwistle and Townshend soon after started stacking their amplifiers, with their huge four-by-twelve speaker cabinets. (Townshend at first used to place his amp on a chair to locate the feedback.) "An electric guitar is really a guitar and a microphone," said Roger. "Pete used the microphone part instead of the fretboard. He wasn't interested in the technical qualities—he'd use it in a completely different way than [Jeff] Beck or [Jimi] Hendrix. He'd just *bang* it."

There were so many brilliant young guitarists around London at the time (Beck, Jimmy Page, Brian Jones, Keith Richard, Ritchie Blackmore, Dave Davies and, of course, Clapton) that Townshend felt frustrated by his own limitations. "I was very frustrated because I couldn't do all that flash stuff, so I just started getting into expressing myself physically. In those days I was very much a solid chord man; I wasn't into a featured guitar type thing. I mean, I never had any Eric Clapton or Jeff Beck type fans. Never. I had kids that dug me because I was crazy or because I was totally outrageous, not because I could play really well—in the accepted way of playing well."

But the accepted way of playing well was being redefined. The electric guitar was only invented in the 1930s, and the solid body electric guitar, which Townshend and almost all other sixties rock guitarists played, is younger than that. The electrical quality of the new guitars suggested all sorts of tonal possibilities: No longer was one restricted to conventionally plucking or strumming the strings or even to the basic notes of Western musical tradition. Feedback (the noise resulting when a loop is created between the source of the sound and the speaker that transmitted it) was a new, legitimate and exciting methodology in those days. A rock & roll quarrel soon arose about who invented it. Townshend, Dave Davies of the Kinks and Jeff Beck (then of the Tridents, soon to join the Yardbirds) have all staked their claims.

"I think possibly the truth is that it was happening in a lot of places at once, as the level went up and as people started to use bigger amps—and we were all using semi-acoustic instruments. It started to happen quite naturally. But I think the development of it was something like the word being around on the streets. Then Lennon used it at the beginning of that record 'I Feel Fine,' and then it became really quite common." Pete said.

However, Townshend certainly did more with distortion than any of his London peers. He was already experimenting with the technique by the time Meaden turned up. Irish Jack recalled Townshend at the Goldhawk, leaning back into the amps to achieve his effects. "He'd sing about four high notes and then go back to the amp and twiddle knobs," said Jack. "The only time you would see a guitarist at the amps in those days, remember, was like between numbers, and then the singer'd be looking at 'em like, 'C'mon, man!' But with the Who it was a regular part of the show."

Doug Sandom was unhappy. His wife hated the Who (particularly Peter Townshend). Doug himself was being given a hard time by the band (particularly Peter Townshend). For one thing, he wasn't especially happy playing blues. Nor was he thrilled about playing for mods, though he recalls the excitement of going to Brighton, in that summer after the first mods-versus-rockers riots at Clacton and Margate and the other seaside resorts. And Sandom wasn't fond of the drugs—pills and pot—that everyone else had begun to ingest.

"I couldn't understand it, and they could. I said, 'When I want it, I'll do it, but I don't feel that I need it,' " said Sandom. "But I'll tell you something—we played at Eel Pie Island, it was a students dance, typical students. And Peter, in the interval, went out to the little bridge that goes over to the shore, he stood out there and he was smokin'. And I'll tell you what—it did do things for him. When he went back, he was brilliant, you know, great!"

But these differences were only symbolic of the basic division between Sandom and the rest of the band. He was of an earlier generation that expected far less of pop music, and he was wary of Townshend's quest for experimentation and Daltrey's consuming ambition. "They all wanted to get on *badly*, you know. And if anybody woulda said, 'Right, you gotta go out and shoot your mother tomorrow, or else you won't get on,' they'd *do* it. That's how it was," Sandom said. To Doug, the band was a nice supplement to his bricklayer's wage, but music wasn't worth risking a steady job or his family's security. "At one point, my life just ended up as one big argument," said Sandom.

Still, it was unlikely that Sandom would have been thrown out of the group. According to Doug, John Entwistle has told him of a meeting called by Gorden (whom Sandom had introduced to the band!) at which the manager "said that me image wasn't right. They had a meeting, and this Gorden said, 'Doug'll never change his image, he's gotta go.' " But the band resisted making a move for three or four months.

In the spring of 1964, an audition was arranged with Chris Parmeinter, a well-respected A&R man with Fontana Records (who had also signed the Pretty Things, among others). The audition was held in the afternoon at a club that Gorden frequented, the Zanzibar, on Edgware Road. The band ran through some of its basic repertoire, and Parmeinter liked what he heard, especially the Bo Diddley song "Here 'Tis." But he had serious reservations about Sandom's drumming.

"As soon as I walked in that place, the guy was on me," Sandom said. "There was an old kit up on the stage and I'm bringing my stuff in. I said to him, 'Where do I put this stuff?' He said, 'Oh, no, you're not using that.' So I said, 'Leave it out. I must use me own gear.' He said, 'No. I say you're using this.' He was really on me back before we'd even started. And he was on me all the time, really niggling, you know?"

Perhaps Parmeinter had been put up to this by Gorden. Maybe he simply didn't like the idea of a drummer so much older than the rest of the group, a big factor in those image-mad days. Or then again, perhaps he simply wanted to use a session drummer if he ever got around to recording the group— that practice was common enough in those years. Whatever the case, Sandom (ordinarily a fairly mild-mannered guy with a slow fuse) felt the full pressure of the situation turned on him.

The audition completed, Parmeinter told the group he liked them very much, but "if you want to make a record, you'll have to get the drumming sorted out."

According to Barnes, Townshend then turned to Sandom and said, "Get it together. What's wrong with you? If you don't get it together, then you're out of the group."

Sandom doesn't pretend to recall the exact words, but he remembers their force and meaning. "Peter jumped on me. [Parmeinter] was really pickin' holes. Stupid little things, you know what I mean? It was unbelievable. I shouldn't have let him beat me, but I did. And I flew up afterwards—not to Parmeinter, but to Peter. I said, 'I'm finished with this band. I'm finished *now*.'

"So they said, 'You can't do that. We've got work.' I said, 'Alright, then, I'll work for a month, and when that month's up, I'm finished.' "

Sandom's decision shocked Daltrey and Entwistle. Everyone was used to Townshend's mouth; Doug shouldn't have taken it so seriously. If he'd wanted to stay, they'd have been willing to back him all the way.

But Sandom knew that he didn't fit into the band that was forming around Meaden's ideas and that even if he had been comfortable musically and socially, his image was too adult. So he played out the month's bookings and then split.

But when it came time for him to leave, Townshend again approached him. "Peter said to me, 'Look, I've got somebody to take your place, but he's got no kit. Would you lend us your kit?' So I said, 'Yeah, all right.' Silly me. I lent it, and in the end, I had to go and get it back myself." It was the last conversation between Doug Sandom and Peter Townshend for fourteen years.

Necessary though it may have been, Doug Sandom's departure proved a setback to Gorden and Meaden's aspirations for the group. There was little point in making a Who record while the group's membership was still in flux.

Whoever the drummer was that Townshend had in mind to borrow Doug's kit, he didn't last longer than the month. Neither did several other drummers recruited from Marshall's or recommended by Druce or by other groups on the circuit (so-called session drummers). Several auditions turned up no one suitable (although one who tried out, Mitch Mitchell, played amazingly well three years later in the Jimi Hendrix Experience).

The problem dragged on for two or three months. Gorden tried to force a solution by dragging in a drummer who had been in the Fourmost. But he had a rocker haircut and glasses, and the band adamantly refused him, even though Gorden offered to get him new clothes and plastic surgery. (Sandom believes that Gorden had engineered his removal from the group in favor of this drummer.)

Timing was of the essence in the short-term pop business of the early sixties; groups had lost shots at fame because of smaller difficulties than this one. Delaying Meaden's conversion plans was dangerous. Mod could go out as swiftly as it had come in. Yet the Who had little choice but to carry on with their gigs. They kept their regular schedule: the Railway Hotel on Tuesdays, the Oldfield Tavern on Thursdays, the Goldhawk on Fridays, headlining a ballroom or opening a concert on Saturdays, filling in odd gigs on the few nights left over. Entwistle was still at the IRS. Daltrey still trudged to work three or four days a week as an apprentice sheet-metal cutter. Townshend hung on in art school, though he socialized more than he went to class.

It was on a Thursday in April, as the band was slogging through another gig with yet another session drummer, that a drunken kid from the audience approached the bandstand to inform the players that his mate could play far better than the guy they had. As this was quite clearly a possibility, the Who invited the friend to climb up on stage and take his chances.

"So he brought up this little gingerbread man," Entwistle said. "Dyed ginger hair, a brown shirt, brown tie, brown suit, brown shoes. He looked just like a little gingerbread man. He got up on the kit, and we said, 'Can you play "Road Runner?" ' 'cause we hadn't come across a drummer that could play 'Road Runner' with us. And he played it, and we thought, 'Oh this is the fellow.' He played it perfectly."

Not only did the gingerbread drummer play perfectly, he played with extraordinary power and recklessness. "He broke the session drummer's bass drum pedal that he'd had for twenty years and mucked up the hi-hat as well," remembered Entwistle.

After the show, the gingerbread drummer told them he'd been playing with a surf band, the Beachcombers, on the Bob Druce circuit for several months. He was from Wembley, and his name was Keith Moon.

At the tag end of the night, Moon was sitting at the bar when Pete Townshend walked in. "You," he snapped. "Come 'ere."

"Yes?" said Moon meekly, approaching him. "Yes?"

Behind Townshend, Daltrey entered and elbowed the guitarist out of the way. "What're you doing next Monday?" asked the singer.

"Nothing. . . . Well, I work in the daytime."

"You'll have to give up work."

"All right. I'll pack it in, then."

"There's this gig on Monday. If you want to come, we'll pick you up in the van."

Many years later, Moon recalled this event with a mixture of glee and insecurity. "They said they'd come by at seven. And that was it. Nobody ever said, 'You're in.' They just said, 'What're you doing Monday?' "

Keith Moon was the only member of the band who was born after the war. He was born on August 23, 1947, to Alfred and Kitty Moon. Alfred was a motor mechanic; Kitty worked as a domestic. Keith was their first child, but the Moons later had a pair of girls, Linda and Lesley.

Keith attended Barham Primary School, where, according to his mother, "he was mischievous all right, but never to the point where he needed a good hiding. . . . On open nights at his primary school I used to go expecting the worst, but the teachers would always say that he never gave them any trouble." She says that even then, however, Keith was a "loner" and that he bored easily.

Moon was an active kid, taking up boxing for a while and getting his picture into the newspaper. "It looked like a spectacular knockout, but in fact, my opponent had just tripped, fallen over backwards and knocked himself out." That kind of serendipity characterized his entire life.

Although Moon once claimed that his only musical background came from his father tuning engines, he actually demonstrated his musical aptitude quite early. When he was around twelve, he joined the local branch of the Sea Cadets, a paramilitary extension of the Boy Scout concept, apparently quite popular in the neighborhood because of some army housing nearby. "Most of the guys in it went into the navy," said Keith. "I joined the band and played the bugle, which led to the trumpet."

His mother, however, says that his big ambition was to play drums: "That's what he really wanted. . . . As soon as Keith came in contact with the drums, that was all he seemed keen on. Of course, we all thought it was a passing fad, like everything else, but he stuck with it and got better and better. All of his energy went into it. Daft, really."

In 1957, Moon was sent to the Alperton Secondary School. This would indicate that he had not done well on his eleven-plus exams, an impression supported by the comments on a 1959 midterm report card reprinted in *The*

Who: Maximum R&B. His highest grades were *B*s in English, English literature and math, his lowest were *D*s in history and art—a poor record but far from a hopeless one. More revealing are the comments of his teachers. "Retarded artistically," wrote the art tutor. "Idiotic in other respects." "Tries to get by by putting on an act," said the history teacher. "Keen at times, but goonery seems to come before anything," wrote the physical training instructor.

Most important, in the long run, was the comment of his music teacher. "Great ability," he wrote, "but must guard against tendency to 'show off.' " But Keith could not help his exhibitionism; whether or not he was unduly influenced by the Goons (a popular broadcast comedy team that featured Spike Milligan and Peter Sellers and helped shape the humor of most other English rock musicians of the era, especially the Beatles), Keith already had discovered a real genius for making others laugh, for deflating all manner of pomposity and for exposing hypocrisy and conceit. Somehow, Keith was blessed with a nature that made him difficult, if not impossible, to embarrass, which left him free to do and say things denied to others. Kitty Moon told Barnes that when Keith was seven and his class had an outdoor dancing display in which her son was supposed to skip around a ring of other children, he got carried away and instead skipped around the entire schoolyard. He did not do this for any reason except for a natural love of attention and a deep-rooted desire to see others smile at him.

The root of Keith's antics remained hidden. Was he a spoiled child who just couldn't imagine not being the center of everyone's attention? Or was he coping with a secret set of anxieties, terrified lest anyone discover who he *really* was? Moon was fascinating to observe, but where he developed his personality remains a mystery to everyone who knew him.

Moon started playing drums on a proper kit in 1960, when he was fourteen. "A friend of mine had a set and a record player in Wembley. I used to pop over to his place and play to records. Then my mate's mum decided his hair was too long and that he ought to concentrate more on his job, so I bought the drums." Moon had a job already, delivering newspapers (one of his customers was Leslie Hornby, the future Twiggy, who allegedly had a crush on him), but it was his dad who paid for the drums.

"They were seventeen pounds [fifty dollars], and it was a really old, old kit. I just bashed about in the garage. Then I started playing with a jazz band."

Moon left school at fifteen and went through a series of bands and an extensive set of jobs. The bands had "ridiculous names": the Mighty Avengers, the Adequates, the Escorts. These bands played the same kind of schoolboy shows and music that Pete and John's pre-Detours groups had: Shane Fenton and Johnny Kidd hits, Shadows instrumentals, "Spanish Harlem" and whatever else was in the hit parade.

As for jobs, "I think the first time I really got bitten by any sort of ambition was when I was about fifteen," Moon said. "I saw all my friends were getting jobs in banks, and I got a job as a salesman. I knew then there was no way I was going to stay in that kind of business.

"I could earn more on the weekend playing drums in some local bands. When I first dropped out of school, I was getting four quid [about ten dollars] a week, and I was earning that just playing at weddings and parties with a local rock band. So I decided to stay in the music business."

Moon needed to supplement his income, so he took a series of day jobs, about none of which he seems to have been very serious (although his mother claims that he showed interest in becoming an electrician). By his own count, Moon had about twenty-three different jobs between 1962 and the first part of 1964. "I'd usually get the sack, because if I had a gig on Friday, I wouldn't bother to go to work."

Pressure from his parents and a need for a few more coppers each week kept Moon from giving up on regular jobs altogether. But sometimes he couldn't restrain himself, even in the midst of a job interview. "I would go into an office and apply for a job that I knew absolutely nothing about," he said. "But I'd answer all the questions right, have all the correct qualifications and really impress the boss. In fact, he'd just be on the point of offering me the job when I'd develop this terrible mannerism." Here Moon pulled a grotesque and twisted face, as if he were having an attack.

"Of course, the chap wouldn't know what to do. I'd pretend nothing had happened, and just when he thought I *was*, in fact, perfectly normal, I'd do *this*." He pulled another face, more gruesome than the last.

"The poor, unfortunate man would be thrown into terrible confusion." Then Moon would depart, having made an impression, if not a fortune.

Moon was given to telling tall tales about his private past, so the authenticity of such stories may be doubtful. But according to Ray Tolliday, an erstwhile journalist and publicist who worked at one of the day jobs with Moon, "he would lay on top of the filing cabinet in the office so he could terrorize the clerks on Monday morning as they came staggering in, wiping sleep from their eyes." And many of Moon's best stories, over the years, only seemed too good to be true. For certain, however, Keith Moon's employment record was checkered by the spring of 1964.

Moon joined the Beachcombers in 1963. The other Beachcombers were "young apprentices in their late teens," according to Moon biographer Ivan Waterman. They fastened their sights on what was then the only interesting alternative to Merseybeat and R&B, surf music.

"At that time, we were subject to nothing but American R&B," Moon explained. "England was subject to all of American rock & roll. It wasn't subject, however, to surf music. I'd listen to one or two tracks from the Beach Boys albums, Dick Dale, the Rip Chords. I liked that. I used to have a guy import all that stuff for me. I was very much of an odd man."

Moon loved several things about surf music. All of the songs were about sun, fun, girls, waves and good times—exactly the sort of life no one in England lived or could hope to. Implicit in the vision of the surf songs was a land of opportunity, romance, wealth and leisure.

"It was very difficult to relate to a surfing song in the middle of London, but perhaps my imagination was wilder, because I used to love it," said Moon. "[We] used to love the songs just for dreams that we saw. . . . That whole fantasy. I bought it heart and soul."

Moon was also enraptured with songs like Brian Wilson's "Don't Worry Baby." Wilson was the poet of the surf scene, the auteur of Southern California adolescence. Occasionally, that is, he took time out from celebrating the scene to have a look at its anxieties and insecurities. The greatest of these celebrations (one of the greatest rock records ever made) was "Don't Worry Baby." It was Moon's favorite song, and it was a hit in the spring and summer of 1964, just about the time when Moon was joining the Who.

One suspects that the lyric of "Don't Worry Baby" provides a clue to Moon's personality. It is the story of a teenage drag racer who gets in trouble for "bragging 'bout my car" and spends a sleepless night mulling over his fears, assuaged only by the attentions of his girlfriend, who tells him, "Don't worry baby/Everything will be all right." In this unbelievably sentimental and self-pitying story, it is possible that Keith found an analogy for all of his own anxieties, for his need to put up a front of bravado no matter how insecure and out of place he might be feeling. (And this does *not* place too much psychological weight on a mere pop song, not for a fan and *certainly* not for Keith Moon, who was a true-believer rock fan, who always used the music as a statement of principles and philosophy, a justification and self-sufficient explanation of who and what he was.)

Moon's insecurity nevertheless remains inexplicable. He was not only blessed with great musical talent and the most amazing sense of humor of anyone in his generation, but he was also exceptionally good-looking, with a baby face that drove girls wild. Irish Jack remembered him as "Keef, a really arrogant little geezer with a cheeky turn-of-phrase which always seemed to get him into further trouble. But he was a big hit with all the local girls, 'cause he was easily the best-looking bloke on the band circuit which played the Goldhawk."

There was certainly no touching Moon musically. One attraction of the surf records, certainly, was that the drummer on most of them was the great Hollywood session man Hal Blaine. Blaine had found a way to combine big-band finesse and flamboyance with rock & roll groove and power. Moon always doted on big-band players, too. "Gene Krupa, Jo Jones, Buddy Rich . . . to me, they were the *best*. I'd see a big band with a double bass drum setup, twirling the sticks, all the theatrics. They're the people I really dug, growing up."

Moon also liked theatre and theatrical music, even listing Liberace among his favorites. "I've always liked bands and people who've been extrovert the way they perform," he said. "So rock & roll was then a natural, with gold lamé and all the flash." But Moon found even rock somewhat inhibiting. "I'm a total extrovert," he said. "I love to be involved. I don't like this great big kit in front of me and the audience. I envy the guitarist, who can go over and get that much closer to the audience. I can't do that; I have to sit at the back, so I acted in a different way and started to draw attention to the drums in a different way, by acrobatics and all the tricks."

This had a telling, nearly revolutionary effect, even in those days. "Everyone looked up to him, even when he was in the Beachcombers," said Jack. "Keith was already flailing his arms around and blowing up his cheeks. At least half a dozen different drummers copied him and that inimitable style he had of crooking his hand down under till the drumsticks pointed at the skins vertically." (This gesture was adapted from Krupa's drumstick twirling routines.)

Sometime after joining the Druce circuit, Moon "decided my talent was wasted in a tight-knit harmony band" and set his sights on the band then called the Detours. "We were working the same circuit, and people used to come up to us and say, 'You're not as good as the Detours, they're a smashing band,'" Moon told Chris Charlesworth of *Melody Maker*. "After a couple of months of this, I was fed up of people saying it, and I decided to have a look at them.

"They were outrageous. All the groups at that time were smart, but onstage the Detours had stage things made of leather, which were terrible. Pete looked very sullen. They were a bit frightening, and I was scared of them. Obviously, they had been playing together a few years, and that showed, as well.

"So when I heard their drummer had left, I laid plans to insinuate myself into the group," Moon told Jerry Hopkins of *Rolling Stone*.

What emerges from these accounts (delivered several years later and riddled with Moon's talent for making myth of his biography) is a clear sense that Keith was making a move at the Oldfield that night. He had not shown up casually, by any means, but had deliberately gone over to audition. Perhaps he dressed as he did simply to attract attention; perhaps that was just his look that week.

Auditioning for the Who was a chance to take a step up. Moon was a fan of the group and had followed them around and studied them a bit. He must have known that he could fit in perfectly, but he also may have been terrified by the band's image. Keith was more shy than most people imagined.

"He was very excited," said his mother, who accompanied him that evening. "I think I told him not to put his hopes too high. I mean, you couldn't take it that seriously. They were just another group trying to make it. To me and my husband, it was like trying to win the pools."

Moon told Charlesworth that he asked the manager of the club—old Lou again—to introduce him and that he then asked the session drummer if it would be all right if he sat in. Of his looks, Keith said, "I was horrible. I looked a right state." He told Hopkins that he'd taken several drinks "to get me courage up," and that after breaking the bass drum pedal and two skins, "I figured, that was it. I was scared to death."

The rest of the band were stunned. They'd never heard anyone quite like Moon. If they did not respond with immediate enthusiasm, it is likely because they were too cool to show how tremendously impressed they really were—and too amazed to know just how to voice their enthusiasm.

"They asked me over for a drink, but they didn't say much. They didn't ask me to join the group but said they were having a rehearsal at some West Indian Club," Moon told Charlesworth. "Nobody said I had joined the group, but I went along."

Moon often referred to his lack of a formal offer to join the band, claiming that he never was even told that he was a full member. But John Entwistle told Barnes that it was Moon who was reluctant: He played with both the Beachcombers and the Who for two weeks after his "audition" because he wasn't sure he wanted to be associated with a group with such a "nasty reputation" (Entwistle's phrase).

The rest of the Who were sure that Moon understood he was in if be wanted to be, but Moon was so insecure that he let it gnaw at him (or else he was too intimidated to ask for a firm decision). In any event, after his fortnight of double duty, everyone must have realized what was fairly obvious after the first rendition of "Road Runner": Keith Moon belonged in this band; he played as if born to its rhythms and passions. "A natural psychopathic drummer," as Nik Cohn called him.

Replacing Sandom with Moon meant a complete psychological destabilization of the Who. Not only was the new member exceptionally volatile, so were all of the old ones, with the exception of Entwistle, who was too passive to make peace in the way that Sandom sometimes had. Moon's arrival turned the Who into the world's least likely (and least promising) group therapy session.

"We used to fight regularly," Moon said. "I left the band about three weeks after I joined. I only left for about three or four days, though. John and I used to have fights. . . . It wasn't very serious, it was more of an emotional spur-of-the-moment thing. In the early days, when you're getting to know everybody and have to work closely, you're bound to run into objections. Some people get over them and some don't. We did."

That's an exaggeration. Daltrey and Townshend were now locked in outright combat for control of the group, Roger prevailing because he could literally beat Peter up, but Peter's art school ideas becoming ever more important as the music scene shifted in that direction. Entwistle brooded because Moon was much more difficult to play with. Keith was not a timekeeper like Sandom; he was a beginning-to-end soloist. That made the role of the bassist, who in conventional groups works off the beat set down by the drummer, especially difficult. Moon was unreliable; he didn't always show up on time for gigs. Townshend was known to egg Moon on in his antics, and both of them, drunk or pilled up (Keith quickly became as passionate about speed as Townshend, if not Meaden), were capable of almost anything, from slamming doors in others' faces to leering, obscene comedic improvisation.

Well, the Who was a band made up of teenagers (Moon was still only seventeen). But Gorden was no source of control, since the band had no respect for him. The Who's wildness, their extreme lack of conventional show business courtesy, was just what had attracted Pete Meaden to them. So there was nothing to stop them from becoming even more exhibitionistic and wild.

The musical changes were as difficult as any others. When Entwistle, of all people, lost his temper with Keith, their playing together was always the cause. "I think if you listen to my bass parts on their own, they sound unbelievably disjointed, but when you play them with the other instruments on the track, they fit. That's what comes from playing with Keith," said Entwistle. "I mean, if you play Keith's drums alone, it sounds like an avalanche. But once you put it in with the track, it's okay.

"Keith must be the hardest drummer in the world to play with, mainly because he tries to hit nearly every drum at once. And if you try and fit in with one of his beats, you have to play like him, hippity-bippity, all over the place. It's really difficult; he doesn't play a hi-hat, either, so you've got no sort of backbeat going. I just try and fit in the bass runs with what the drummer is doing on the tom-toms and bass drum. I have to look at them all the time, so the audience gets forgotten."

Meanwhile, Moon's style was pushing him to the front. "The drummer was always at the back and very rarely noticed," Moon said. "He was the least photographed, the least interviewed. When I started twirling the sticks and standing up and those kind of things, nobody else did that kind of thing in rock."

No one would doubt that Entwistle was correct in saying that "when Keith joined, we started developing what was really the Who style."

"What's interesting in our group is that the roles are reversed," Townshend said. "John's the lead guitar player, and although I'm not the bass player, he does produce a hell of a lot of the lead work." Even more extraordinary was that *Moon* played so many parts that amounted to leads. With only two melodic instruments, there was plenty of space to fill, and Keith occupied it with cocky assurance and hammerlike strokes, crashing to the fore, even amidst the incredible racket being made by the new amp stacks that Townshend and Entwistle were developing.

The drums Moon brought to the group initially were woefully inadequate. Entwistle remembers his surprise when the new drummer showed up at his first gig with several yards of stout rope, which he proceeded to use to lash his kit down. The others didn't understand why until they heard how Keith could *really* play.

Moon proved to be as revolutionary in enlarging the size of the drum kit as Townshend and Entwistle were in enlarging the quantity of guitarists' amplification. He added a second bass drum and hordes of tom-toms and cymbals and hit everything full force, constantly. Soon, other drummers copied him until oversized kits became the standard in rock.

Ray Tolliday said that when be first went to see Moon's new group (of which he'd never heard), he made the trip "with some foreboding. Then, when they came on and started playing, I was rooted to the spot. I had never seen anything like it in my life. Pete was doing his legendary Birdman act. Roger looked like he was making love to the microphone. John seemed bored. And much to my amazement, Keith was playing the best rock & roll drums I had ever heard. I was in a state of shock for the rest of the night."

Speedy Keen was equally amazed by the Who: "They did everything everybody else wanted to do. . . . What was even more important was that it was exciting, because you never knew what was going to happen. They were the best band around." As a drummer himself, he was especially fascinated by Moon: "I've never seen anyone like him, ever. I've seen people that have bursts of energy, fifteen- or twenty-minute solos. But never anybody that attacked the drums like he did—and retained that attitude from the start to the end. . . . Everyone used to say, 'He's very strange. He's got the cymbals miles from the drum kit.' Everyone else had them right there, because it was all sort of trad." Moon positioned his equipment differently, of course, because he *played* differently. He needed full extension when he crashed into a cymbal to obtain the effects he heard in his head.

And so, just as the addition of Moon spurred the group into unending psychodrama, it also pushed them decisively into their own musical style. "The music of the Who can only be called rock & roll," wrote Jann Wenner in 1968. "It is neither derivative of folk music nor the blues; the primary influence is rock & roll itself." The primary reason was Keith Moon.

Moon wasn't immediately accepted, though, especially by the hardcore fans at places like the Goldhawk. "It was all very well for Keith to be popular with the Goldhawk crowd while he was with the Beachcombers," said Irish Jack. "But as word got round that he had actually joined the Who, most of the Goldhawk crowd were a bit wary of this new guy who had replaced Doug Sandom."

Moon wasn't from west London but from Wembley, farther north. "And that made him an outsider in the eyes of many of the Goldhawk mods, 'cause the rest of the Who were born and bred in west London," Jack remarked. But their wariness lasted only a couple of weeks. "As soon as it became obvious that he *was* the only drummer for a band like the Who, Keith became a true son of Shepherd's Bush, only he was still as bloody arrogant as ever—only worse! I think the Who went to his head as time went on."

The archetypal mod was male, sixteen years old, rode a scooter, swallowed pep pills by the hundred, thought of women as a completely inferior race, was obsessed by cool and dug it. He was also one hundred percent hung up on himself, on his clothes and hair and image; in every way, he was a miserable, narcissistic little runt.

—*Nik Cohn*

"We gotta get some clothes together," Meaden told the band. "And you gotta do this certain sound of music, which I'm calling new wave R&B, which is like a [mixture of] R&B, funk, fast soul, fast grooving off the walls, 'cause that's what you have to do when you're high, you know. And I wanna call you not the Who, not the Detours, but the High Numbers. High Numbers because we're all into pills, into a bit of pot, into doing these things, and when we're hip, we gotta dress hip and we're gonna be called the High Numbers."

To Meaden, the name the Who was "too ethereal, too abstract, too airy-fairy to connect. Now if it was called the World Health Organization, that's good, but I wanted a name that was adaptable, that was going to sustain the length of time, which is going to be more than just a six months or a year name."

This rationalization probably didn't make much more sense then than it does today, but Meaden was the mod expert, so no one put up much of a struggle. Not that anyone was crazy about the new name, either. Liking the name wasn't the issue. Making the charts was the idea.

Now Meaden began the really important part of his job, the retooling of the High Numbers' clothing. He decided that Roger should dress up as a "face," the others as "tickets." The terms denoted two levels of modism. As Townshend once explained, "There were like two terms that were used—*faces* and *tickets*. And faces were the leaders—they were very hard to find, very few. Tickets were the masses."

To this end, Meaden dressed Roger Daltrey in a white jacket, black trousers and two-tone shoes. Townshend suited up in an Ivy League jacket with side vents five inches long. Entwistle and Moon were outfitted in Levi's and striped jackets. Everybody except Daltrey (who already had one) went to Jack the Barber for the shortish French crew cuts.

Only John Entwistle rebelled. "I don't want to dress like a little ticket," he said. He even balked at the haircut, combing it forward the moment he left Jack the Barber's. (Typical Entwistle: He'd never insult a barber to his face.) But as the plan evolved and the rest of the band were outfitted as faces, too, with mod suits of their own, Entwistle's rebellion cooled. Could be he just resented anyone having more expensive gear than his own.

Townshend responded most enthusiastically to Meaden's ideas. On the other hand, Daltrey, who probably looked the most mod of them all, had reservations about being so blatantly retailored. He didn't want to look a fool in front of his friends. In any event, it was Townshend—under the supervision of Meaden, closely followed by Keith Moon—who led the High Numbers' assault upon the mod clubs of Soho.

Soho was "the place where you'd go after the Goldhawk on Friday or Saturday night," said Irish Jack. "Take the tube to Piccadilly and go straight to the three clubs [Scene, Flamingo and Marquee] to look for pills."

Of the three clubs, the Flamingo, as the province of black U.S. soldiers, was perhaps the most exotic, but the Scene was by far the most dangerous. "The very air suggested a police raid at any minute," said Jack. The room was downstairs in a little building in one of Soho's endless cul-de-sacs, Ham Yard. There was padding on the walls and cushions strewn upon the floor, an early, amphetamine version of the crash pad ambiance of the psychedelic sixties. But this was London in 1964, when the Scene was the "high altar of mod," a dodgy joint where pills were easy to get. Proprietor Ronan O'Rahilly was also the outlaw entrepreneur behind the pirate radio ship Radio Caroline. The crowd included the best-dressed mods in the entire city, and the Scene's disc jockey, a wraithlike soul music obsessive named Guy Stevens, was the hottest in the land. (Stevens ran Sue Records and leased for U.K. release many relatively obscure U.S. soul, blues and R&B discs, giving him early access to many hits. In the seventies, he became the producer of Mott the Hoople and the Clash.)

"Most of the mods that hung around the door of the Flamingo and the Scene would either be foaming at the mouth on a come-down or else seeing everything in triplicate," said Irish Jack. "That's what pills done. . . . There was always pills inside; it saved a lot of bother with the law out on the street. We used to buy these French blues [blue-colored amphetamines made in France]. They were a shilling each, and after about ten, they'd last you through to about five the next morning. The only thing was, they made you chew up packets of Wrigley's spearmint, and by the time the Flamingo finished, about five or six [A.M.], your mouth would have blisters and your jaws would really ache from the chewing." After the clubs closed, the mods of the western suburbs would congregate near Piccadilly Circus tube station again to nervously wait for the first train home.

"All I knew was I had to get [the band] established in the West End in a way that they would be recognized by the hardcore cult center, which was the mods that used to hang out in the Scene Club, you know," said Meaden. "You can't get any more authentic than that. So I had to give them the golden seal of authenticity. If they could turn on these kids, then they could turn on the world. And so that's what the next move was." The records Meaden recalled from this period were Tony Clarke's "Ain't Love Good, Ain't Love Proud," Smokey Robinson and the Miracles' "I Gotta Dance to Keep From Crying," Major Lance's "Monkey Time" and "Um, Um, Um, Um, Um" and the Impressions' "It's All Right," "Talking About My Baby" and "I'm So Proud," which he termed "eminently danceable by people who were not emotionally involved with other people." This was Meaden's new wave R&B: Motown, light soul, beautiful harmonies and tight, tough, danceable rhythms. The sound was spruced up, too modern and commercial even for many of the R&B fans, but perfect for mods and modism, which Meaden defined, in his most successful aphorism, as "an euphemism for clean living under difficult circumstances.

"That's what mod living is all about," he continued, remembering the weekends at the Scene and the Flamingo. "It's a continuous party, sustain it for as long as you can without doing too much damage to your body. You mustn't damage yourself too much, but take it right out on the rim."

Mod made itself nationally infamous beginning on March 26 and 27, 1964, the bleakest, coldest Easter weekend in eighty years, and nowhere drearier than at Clacton, a small resort town on the eastern seacoast which was favored by cockney kids. There, several hundred mods fought rockers on the beaches and in the streets, traumatizing the national press and inconveniencing more mature holidayers.

As a riot, Clacton was overrated. Damages were not great, few were hurt, and much of the tension was caused not by mods battling rockers so much as by the overreaction of the authorities and the media. Neither was Clacton a great clash between two warring teenage subcultures. If anything, modism was less of a factor than the fact that the mods generally came from London, while the rockers were more likely to be locals.

But as the beginning of a youth movement, Clacton was perfect. The exaggerated media attention it received set new role models for kids from Newcastle to Portsmouth, gave them a new vocabulary, a new set of ideals. It made these kids more aware of mod than any amount of positive hype could have. Overnight, mod became a media byword; there is no better proof than the continuing series of mods-versus-rockers battles at seaside resorts including Brighton, Great Yarmouth, Margate, and even up north, near Blackpool, on succeeding bank holidays for the next three years. It was a shortcut to turning mod into an artificial craze, with its own magazines, clothing, scooters—you name it.

But mod was unlike any other style craze, even the equally roughneck Teddy boy phenomenon that had erupted following rock & roll's British emergence. It wasn't manageable. Even though its obsession with clothing made it seem consumerist, that term misses the point.

In order to mass-market mod, however, more and more fetish objects had to be developed. Since pure mod was based not just on being one step ahead but on *staying* there, the exploitation drove the originals into a frenzy of ritualized activity. Style details began shifting even more rapidly than before. The mass-marketing cheapened it, but mod remained as much a philosophy expressed through consumerism as mere consumerism itself. Townshend took this to heart. "One of the things which has impressed me most in life was the mod movement in England, which was an incredible youthful thing," Pete said. "It was an army, a powerful, aggressive army with transport."

The Goldhawk and the other west London clubs remained the ideal workshops for studying trends. Townshend was a particularly devoted student.

"The band was working too hard for me to get really involved, but sometimes I'd jump offstage between sets and just disappear, though it was hard [since I was] in a group. But there were times when I was able to disappear, and in retrospect, those were the moments I treasure most."

"As soon as the interval came along in the Goldhawk, the Who would head straight for the bar," said Irish Jack. "But some nights Townshend would come out onto the dance floor; he'd have been watching things move from the stage. There'd be a disc jockey in the corner who spun the very latest imported pure Motown R&B.

"Townshend would start off with a few steps and practically take up a quarter of the floor. Then he'd go back onstage after the interval and try out a few steps *you* had just improvised. Then you'd go and see the Who the following Tuesday night . . . and Townshend would have *your* steps off perfectly."

Gangly Townshend was a surprisingly fluid dancer. He made an assiduous study of how mods walked and talked, the way they slouched and stuffed a hand in a jacket pocket when leaning in a doorway, the way they moved across a dance floor. Soon he could perfectly mimic them.

Townshend was well aware of his dual identity as both a mod icon and an outsider. Remembering the Who playing at Brighton in that riotous summer, he said, "I saw about two thousand mod kids, and there were three rockers up against a wall. They'd [the rockers] obviously just come into it, thinking that they were going to a party and they were really scared as hell, and the mods were throwing bottles at them.

"Those people who were kicking rockers in on the front would then come in and listen to our music. So I knew then that I had what felt like a certain kind of power. There were all the tough guys looking at me, waiting to hear what I was about to say."

This could make Townshend feel a bit of a fraud, not only because he wasn't a mod, but because he didn't necessarily want to be one. He still felt like an art student. "I had to learn how to be a mod," he said. "Like in those days, a scooter was a big status symbol. But I used to have an old American car—that was my symbol. But I used to have to lie to the little mod chicks I pulled and tell them I had a Vespa GS. . . . If I told them I had a '58 Cadillac, which to me was a dream, they would have thought I was a rocker."

On the other hand, art school also helped Townshend justify poaching on the mods' turf. "I was trained in graphic design," he said to Roy Carr, "to be an ideas man, to think up something new and different, like let's give a lemon away with the next album."

Townshend was obsessed with maintaining a complete, consistent, unassailable front—not only for himself but for the group, too. This idea came from his modern art studies.

"The thing that struck me about so many people who came to talk at college was that they were characters," he told Pete Hamill. "When you looked at people like Andy Warhol or Larry Rivers, they all had their look and they knew how they had to behave, and it was almost as if that was as important as their work. Everybody had his act together before he addressed the public. And so, when the band started, I used to say, 'Listen, we should look right, we should have an image, we should walk in a particular way, should talk in a particular way. We should look different from other people. After a concert is over, if we go to talk to people, we should maintain a facade.' "

Over the coming years, Townshend would retain this idea as a first principle and do his best to make sure that the Who lived up to its every detail, not always successfully but quite thoroughly.

Helmut Gorden arranged numerous auditions for the High Numbers. Because the auditions and other business meetings were held in the afternoon, the band members soon used up all their leave time at their jobs. When they complained, Gorden offered them contracts: They would be guaranteed a wage of twenty pounds (about fifty-five dollars) per week, a very good salary. Because they were all under twenty-one, the parents had to ratify the contracts. Cliff and Betty Townshend again refused, but the others agreed.

It was time for Pete Townshend to leave art school. He was still attending some classes, but ever more sporadically and with less interest in actually becoming a graphic artist.

Pete says that he sought advice from Robin Ray, head of the Ealing graphics department: "Look, I'm really worried about it," Peter said. "What should I do? Stick in college, in case the band doesn't work out?"

"How much are you making in this band?" asked Ray.

"Sometimes I make, well, about thirty pounds [eighty-five dollars] a week."

Robin Ray looked at Townshend, not an exceptionally gifted graphics student, with disbelief. Then he snapped his fingers. "Leave," he said.

According to Betty Townshend, she and Cliff were outraged that Pete wanted to quit his studies. Pete told her that art college students didn't earn degrees, anyway; if they were to find work at all, they'd do it with their portfolios, not diplomas.

"Peter said, 'What's the point, mum? It's not going to get me a job.' He named how many had got through. He said the principal had given them a lecture the day before and said, 'Now, boys, you're all on your own now. You've all done well and blah, blah, blah. I just hope that some of you manage to get a job of some kind.'

"I said to Pete, 'What do you mean, hopes that some of you get a job?' Pete said, 'That's what he said.' I said, 'I don't believe you.' I got in the car and went straight up and saw this principal, and I said, 'Is this true? Did you lecture yesterday and in fact say these words to these students?'

"He said, 'Yes, I have to be open and straight about it. If they are prepared to go to Denmark or one of the Scandinavian countries, they might find an opening there. But in this country there are too many students passing out with graphic design.'

"I said, 'Why take them in the first place if you know this is happening?' I was shouting at the man in the college, you know. And of course, [I] came back and had another shout at Peter."

In the end, it hardly mattered. The High Numbers were about to make a record, and this was vastly more important to Pete than compiling a better portfolio.

With the explosion of mod, Chris Parmeinter was more eager than ever to record the High Numbers. A contract was signed with Fontana Records, the label for which Parmeinter worked, calling for one guaranteed single but giving the company an option to demand more if and when the first was successful.

Sometime in June, Parmeinter arranged a session at Fontana's recording studio. The band was to do four songs under the supervision of Jack Bavistock (who also worked with the Merseybeats), although the eventual releases were credited to "producers" Pete Meaden and Chris Parmeinter.

Parmeinter was eager to cut two of the High Numbers' R&B covers, "Leavin' Here," which was a minor Tamla hit for Eddie Holland in the States that year, and Bo Diddley's "Here 'Tis," originally a B-side that never charted in either America or Britain. Of the two, their "Leaving Here" was tougher and more raucous. The song was also more appropriate for the High Numbers because its lyric was a mod fable. The singer "seen it all in a dream last night." (At least he did in the original. Roger never quite got the words straightened out.) Now he's telling what will happen if his mates don't stop abusing their girlfriends: The ladies will pack up and leave town, forcing the fellas back on their own resources. Pounded out and shouted, "Leaving Here" is a marvelous paranoid fantasy, a modernist teenage rewrite of "The Pied Piper of Hamelin." The High Numbers version is a bit awkward, since the lyric is not quite enough of a chant to let Daltrey bowl it over and he is not quite fluid enough to get past the sticky spots. But the playing (especially Entwistle's) is powerful and shows a solid grasp of the band's ability to convert hard R&B to rock.

The surviving take of "Here 'Tis" is much more effective. Although Bo Diddley is famous for his guitar style, with its shave-and-a-haircut beat, the rhythm in his songs was also carried by Jerome Green's maracas, and it is the maracas' beat—incessant and uninterrupted—on which Moon picks up, Townshend and Entwistle playing with and against his accents. Moon gets off a classic, powerhouse roll just before Daltrey's concluding harp solo, but the truly remarkable aspects are the way Townshend's best guitar licks serve as supplementary cymbal splashes, and the high profile bass, which underpins everything.

The maracas' rhythm actually makes "Here 'Tis" relatively light, perfect for harmony singing, and the High Numbers' backing vocals are surprisingly precise, especially given the crudeness of "Leaving Here." (Fontana may have brought in studio singers for the harmonies, though.)

Daltrey's vocal is coarse and guttural but extremely effective and confident, an assured performance (especially when matched against Keith Relf's vocal in the Yardbirds' version of the song, which also pales against this one instrumentally). In fact, this may be Roger's best performance on a blues standard until "Young Man Blues," several years down the line.

But "Leaving Here" and "Here 'Tis" were never released. For a group to be really effective in the 1964 marketplace, it needed original material (or so it was felt), and for the High Numbers, Meaden, particularly, wanted a clear statement of mod principles.

Thus Meaden decided to write the songs for the recording session himself. The week before the session, he went up to Guy Stevens' flat. For a fee, Stevens would tape any song in his extensive record collection (which was later a primary source for Townshend, too). Meaden settled on two recent soul records, Slim Harpo's "Got Love If You Want It," which he quickly altered to become "I'm the Face," and the B-side of the Showmen hit "It Will Stand," a song called "Country Fool," which took a bit longer to rework into "Zoot Suit."

"I'd been thinking about the record for some time," Meaden said. "On the night before the session, I'd written down the words. I got the melody down, and I'd given the records to Pete to listen to. I heard the melody, and the night before the session, I dreamed up the lyrics, and I wrote them all down. I wrote them down on speed, you know, on Drynamil, on good old purple hearts, which really does clear out your mind."

Empties the mind might be a more accurate assessment. Meaden's lyrics were mod agitprop, cataloging details of the mod styles. ("I'm the snappiest dresser, right down to my inch-wide tie," sings Daltrey in "Zoot Suit.") "I'm the Face" is a vehicle for Daltrey to brag of his prowess as an ace face. But the boasts finally seem idle, since he has nothing to talk about and too little music—aside from a neat zoom bass riff—to work against. In the end, "I'm the Face" simply can't compare to "Here 'Tis," much less to the Yardbirds' version of "Got Love If You Want It." (Not that any of these was a match for Slim Harpo.)

"Zoot Suit" is more intriguing because of its fast, jazzy guitar and light drums. The vocals, in which Daltrey's lead is continually answered by the band, Mersey style, makes it seem more pop than R&B. It is hard to believe that the music here has much to do with the Showmen, a very slick soul band. Aside from Townshend's guitar, which is a pretty good example of single-string work for the period, the highlight once more is Daltrey's singing, this time influenced by Paul McCartney, but in a gruff register. Again, Meaden's lyrics slide into monomania. Imagine Daltrey singing, "The main thing, is, unless you're a fool/You know, you gotta know, yeah, you gotta be cool."

What's even stranger about "Zoot Suit" and "I'm the Face" is the way they're mixed, as if to downplay Moon. Although the band already had a fairly revolutionary style, it could not be heard on the single finally released, which featured "I'm the Face" as the A-side and "Zoot Suit" as the flip.

"I'm the Face"/"Zoot Suit" was released on July 3, 1964. Fontana pressed 1,000 copies, of which Meaden bought, according to which source one believes, between 50 and 250. John Entwistle's grandmother also bought a couple dozen.) Then Meaden went into his PR act, which was not entirely ineffective, resulting in a story in the music paper *Disc* and one in *Fabulous*, the latter featuring the immortal line "They're up-to-dates with a difference—they're even ahead of themselves." The single was also reviewed in *Melody Maker*'s "Blind Date" column, in which, each week, various successful musicians were asked to comment on a few of the week's new 45s. The Merseybeats were featured that week, and they didn't think much of the High Numbers (as one might have predicted, given the Merseybeats' name and their rocker outlook). "I doubt if it will be a hit," opined John Banks, and the others were no more charitable. The record was also reviewed in another magazine, *Boyfriend*, which, as the name implies, was aimed at young girls. "The lyrics . . . are not at all romantic," the reviewer said. "They're more we're-talking-your-language type story line, the appeal lying in the authentic expressions. . . . This disc is already going down well in the centre of London's mod world, the Scene Club. . . ." It would not be surprising to discover that Meaden had written this "review" himself.

"I'm the Face" wasn't a hit, primarily because it wasn't good enough; it's tempting to speculate on the potential result of releasing "Leaving Here" or "Here 'Tis." The summer of 1964 was a particularly fertile time for rock & roll, the Beatles riding high with "A Hard Day's Night," the Stones challenging them with "It's All Over Now" (an R&B cover version) and such other classics as the Animals' "House of the Rising Sun" (based on an ancient blues number) and Manfred Mann's "Do Wah Diddy Diddy" also competing for chart space and media attention. Many of the hits of the period (and all of those mentioned) were far superior to the High Numbers single. And every one of the hits had more promotional clout behind it.

That's not to say that Fontana didn't try. After the August bank holiday riots, they even began plugging "Zoot Suit" in an attempt to kick up some action, which indicates that they did support the record. But the High Numbers weren't associated with a powerful manager (or even a canny one), nor were they blessed with enough capital to make the kind of extra promotional effort (or payoffs) necessary to receive massive airplay on the pirate stations. And the pirates were the key to Britain's pop explosion.

The first pirate radio ship, Radio Caroline, began broadcasting on March 27, 1964 (the weekend of the Clacton riot). For the previous forty years, the state-owned British Broadcasting Corporation (BBC) had controlled the nation's only electronic mass communications system, licensing receivers for the public good. The policy of the BBC Light Programme (its only pop music service) was to offer something for everyone, from teenagers to housewives to senior citizens, which meant a motley lineup including some semi-serious drama, spot news, comedy and a bit of music. Most of the music was indigenous music hall pop or show tunes. Very little of it was rock & roll.

A central reason for the BBC's stodginess was the British Musicians' Union restriction on broadcasting "needle time," which restricted the Light Programme to eighty-two hours of prerecorded music per week. That meant *any* prerecorded music, even if a band came into the studio Tuesday for a show to be broadcast on Saturday.

Although the needle time restrictions were designed to protect the jobs of "live" musicians, needle time effectively placed both the union and the broadcasting system in opposition to the most effective new musical technology. This was a stumbling block to the rise, in Britain, of rock music, which was conceived and concocted with electric instruments, originated primarily in the recording studio (rather than on stage) and depended almost entirely on records for its initial response. Only Radio Luxembourg and the U.S. Armed Forces Network leaked much rock onto England's airwaves.

It was Ronan O'Rahilly, the proprietor of the Scene Club, who decided that the appropriate remedy was to broadcast from ships anchored just off the statutory three-mile limit in international waters and equipped with transmitters powerful enough to blanket London and most of southern England.

There was nothing illegal about this—yet—so the business offices of England's first commercial radio station (the BBC accepts no advertising) could be safely located in Soho. With much ballyhoo, Radio Caroline went on the air with its exact replica of American Top 40–super-lunged deejays, station identification jingles, pop records, moronic commercials and spot news presented without so much as a nod to stuffy "culture".

In May, Radio Caroline was joined by Radio Atlanta (in July they merged to become Caroline South and Caroline North, blanketing the nation). By the end of the year, the Carolines had been joined by Radio London, an even more powerful station, and as many as fifteen smaller pirates. The effect on the recording business was immediate: 61,300,000 singles were sold in England in 1963. In 1964 the number rose to 72,800,000. (And remember, the 1963 figure incorporates the first successes of the Beatles.)

The record business should have been on the side of the broadcasting establishment, since its over-the-air royalty system was based on needle time. In fact, some old-line companies did express concern about "overexposure" of their product. And the pirates, relieved of their statutory obligation to pay royalties, certainly weren't going to volunteer payments.

Nevertheless, plenty of smaller labels (the so-called independents) welcomed the opportunity to break the hegemony of the BBC, which favored the more staid product of the majors (Decca, the EMI group, etc.). Caroline, like Radio Luxembourg and some other European stations, sold airtime: thirty plays per week cost £100 ($280). It was the independents who most often made use of this opportunity. The power of the majors wasn't broken, but it was weakened in important ways.

Companies like Fontana (owned by one of the majors, Philips) were not as free to pay off the pirates as the more free-wheeling smaller labels. Without pirate support, the High Numbers single was doomed; if there was any natural constituency for the disc, it was the aspiring young mods who had sprouted up in the wake of Clacton. And such mods listened to Caroline, period.

The single's failure to sell depressed everyone, especially since it was clear that Fontana had no interest in a follow-up. This brought the band's situation with Helmut Gorden to its worst state. They were now disillusioned with (or at least, less naïve about) the glamour of the record business, while Gorden was convinced that the band's major problem was its failure to follow his orders.

Although Gorden had done some very good things for the group, not only by connecting them with Meaden and with Fontana but also by providing some money to upgrade their gear, he refused to be a backstage manager. He wanted the kind of shaping role—and attention—that Brian Epstein received in his management of the Beatles.

Gorden and the group seem never to have liked each other personally. They regarded him, in Daltrey's phrase, as "a cash register," and while he may have referred to them as "little diamonds," there wasn't much question that he felt that these gems needed lots of polishing.

Gorden sealed his fate with the group late in the summer, when he announced that he was having a garden party at his house. He wished the group to play for the guests, he said, many of whom would be the sort of "influential" people who could speed the band's career along. But neither he nor his guests was willing to endure a racket. Therefore, the band was to bring its guitars but leave its amplifiers at home.

Infuriated as they were by this demand, there was no way for the High Numbers to fight back. They didn't play the party, but Gorden still had a contract; he held the purse strings, and he was even the basis of their relationship with Peter Meaden.

*Behind every band is some sort of mentor
figure, some Svengali. This is the thing that
can't be provided without love, care and
full-time attention.*

—Pete Townshend

From the street, the Railway Tavern, located near the Harrow and
Wealdstone tube station in northern London, didn't look much different
from many of the other pubs and taverns nearby. It was a large white
building presenting a blank face to the world.

When Richard Barnes began promoting rock shows at the Railway in early
1964, he removed all of the lightbulbs, save two, and painted those pink,
casting a dull reddish glow around the darkened room. And he turned up
all the radiators to guarantee a hot, sweaty atmosphere year round. Because
Barnes also had a keen sense of which bands to book (including the High
Numbers every Tuesday), he was able to consistently cram 500 to 1,000
customers into a room rated for only 180.

The overcrowding kept Barnes and the club's half-dozen bouncers alert for
any sign of visitors from the local council or the brewery that actually owned
the pub; neither body would have approved of the amassed mods or of the
noises and decorations that attracted them. So when a dapperly dressed man
pulled up in a Volkswagen Beetle one Tuesday night in late July 1964, Barnes
alerted the bouncers and stepped to the entrance himself.

The man approached the doorway and stopped. Inside the murky club, the
heat was stifling. Even on the threshold, the noise was deafening. "Is it always
like this?" asked the stranger. "Not always," muttered Barnes. True. There were
only about seven hundred people inside tonight. The man continued to stare
about him, casing the joint. "What's the name of the group?" he inquired.

"The High Numbers," Barnes told him. "Ah, I'm looking for a band for a film I'm producing," said the newcomer. Barnes gladly showed him through the crowd to the garden, where Peter Meaden, the band's ostensible manager, was lurking.

The dapper little man was fitted out in a custom-tailored grey suit, posh enough for a mod but not quite so radical. He told Meaden that his name was Kit Lambert. According to the Meaden version of their encounter, he said he was "looking for a band to put in his club. So I gave him the hard sell. 'This is absolutely where it's at. You cannot fail on this, squire,' I said. 'If you'll just listen to me, you can make a lot of money out of this as a promoter, if you'll believe me, because they are of the people, they are the hippest numbers in town, there's no one quite like them. Just look at the queue down there.' And so I hard-selled myself right out of a band."

Christopher "Kit" Lambert was an upper-class Englishman. His father, Constant Lambert, a man of mercurial temperament and ambiguous sexuality, was an important figure in the British classical music community in the 1930s and 1940s and up until his death in 1951. Constant Lambert was one of the first critics in England to write favorably of Franz Liszt. He was a noted composer and conductor in his own right, and he traveled in those public school and university circles that later produced Kim Philby and similarly ambivalent figures of English espionage.

Kit Lambert was born in 1938, and he worshipped his untamable father, who had preceded him at Lancing College, an important public (that is, elite) school, and then at Trinity College at Oxford University. Yet Kit never displayed the discipline or talent required to follow in father's footsteps. When he received his degree, he enlisted in the army and immediately became, by his own reckoning, the "worst officer in the whole corps." Discharged, he joined an anthropological expedition to the Amazon Jungle, with apparently hilarious consequences. Then he came home, and through an attachment to theatre and a gift for the nomenclature, if not the nuts and bolts, of logistics, drifted into the movie business as an assistant director.

At Shepperton film studios, Lambert began working with another assistant director, Chris Stamp, on such films as *The L-Shaped Room*, *Of Human Bondage* and *I Could Go On Singing*. Chris was five years younger, the son of an East End tugboatman, a street fighter who dropped out of grammar school and drifted into show business on the heels of his brother Terence, the actor.

"Kit was an utter maniac who lived off nervous energy and the sound of his own voice, who was so tense it hurt, who hardly ever went to sleep," wrote Nik Cohn. "Chris, by contrast, was the voice of sanity, very cool and hard. Together they fitted like Laurel and Hardy." They shared two significant traits: a taste for hard, flashy living, and a burning ambition to make enough money to afford to act it out. Though Lambert was as openly gay as he could afford to be and Stamp chased skirts, they were perfect for one another, a matched set.

Sometime after they first met, Lambert and Stamp decided to share a flat near Baker Street in central London. (Lambert had class but not much cash.) Then they conceived the idea of making a really good pop film—like the ones that Richard Lester and John Boorman were just then churning out with the Beatles and the Dave Clark Five. Stamp got hold of an old friend of his from Plaistow Grammar School, Mike Shaw, who was working as a lighting director in a theatre in Bristol. Stamp convinced Shaw to come to London to help them find an unknown group to star in the film.

They split the town up into territories. Shaw had a scooter, and he would run around town taking down information on gigs from posters pasted on walls and hoardings or picking up news of local groups from the neighborhood newspapers. Then he and Lambert would divvy up the opportunities and go to the gigs, staying only a few minutes at losers, lingering a bit longer if an act seemed promising. In the beginning, around Easter time, Stamp would reconnoiter with the others, but after a couple of months, their funds began to dry up, and rather than eat into the money they had salted away for the film making, Chris took a job as an assistant director on *Young Cassidy*, which John Ford was shooting in Dublin. That's where Stamp was when Lambert phoned to tell him about the High Numbers.

Lambert asked Stamp to come to London for the weekend to confirm his judgment that the High Numbers were ideal. Stamp arrived just in time to see the last fifteen minutes of the band's set at the Trade Union Hall in Watford.

"Seeing the other bands was sort of a good rehearsal for us," said Mike Shaw, who also saw them for the first time that weekend. "Once we saw the Who, we realized how good they were and how different compared to everyone else."

"We couldn't even see them properly," Stamp told Nik Cohn. "There was this fantastic crush between us and the stage, and all we could see were bodies, all we could hear was a great, dirty noise. Still, we sensed this amazing excitement all around us, and we knew that it had to be wild."

Lambert and Stamp then arranged for the High Numbers to do an audition for them at a school in Holland Park (right next to the Bush) that Sunday afternoon. Lambert didn't turn up. "That was his forte, to be late or never to arrive," said Shaw. "The first meeting that he arranged with them, and I had to go and say, 'I'm sorry but Mr. Lambert won't be able to make it.' "

The audition went off, anyway. Stamp and Shaw were given a full-blown performance. "It was the first time I'd seen them play," Shaw said, "and it was startling, it really was—for that period, for that time. I mean, the whole band just gave off this kind of—I don't know what you'd call it, this power. It was just impressive; this huge, empty hall and the little tiny speakers and it was such a sound. They were louder than anybody; it was deafening."

No one has ever determined the nature of Lambert's and Stamp's proposed pop music movie. If it was like any of Lambert's future ideas, that was probably because it was never detailed. More than likely, it was just a money-making scheme, since both budding impresarios were desperate to get rich.

Lambert and Stamp were seeking an unknown group because they hadn't much choice. They hadn't the money to work with even a semiestablished group nor sufficient credentials to persuade an influential manager to lend them one of his up-and-coming talents.

Stamp and Shaw soon learned of the band's hatred of Gorden and their disappointment that the single had flopped. They took Gorden's contract with the group to a famous music business attorney, David Jacobs (who represented Brian Epstein and the Beatles). It didn't take an expert to see that a contract with underaged kids, one of whose parents hadn't countersigned, wasn't worth very much. Helmut Gorden was finished without much of a struggle (although Doug Sandom, whose exit from the Detours Gorden engineered, said he was asked to give an affidavit in Gorden's defense some months later; Sandom refused). Now Lambert and Stamp began managing the band themselves. Lambert had entrepreneurial propensities himself; in a way, he was no less struck by Brian Epstein's success than Helmut Gorden, though Kit was a good deal more shrewd about the nature and meaning of Epstein's triumph. Stamp was quite willing to go along. So they took over.

"Really, the main problem was with Pete Meaden," Shaw recalled. "He'd been closer to the band, he'd been involved with them more than Gorden—I mean, Gorden had just signed them up and put them on the road. Peter had changed their name and written a couple of songs for them and molded them into mods, with all the American gear that the mods were getting into. So he was a big influence on them. That was the main problem: getting rid of him, in effect."

Had Meaden been a bit less obsessed, or at least more subdued, Lambert and Stamp probably would have been eager to continue his relationship with the band. But Meaden *was* a pillhead, chalky mouthed and incoherent from speed most of the time, and his mumbling was maddening. The band remained loyal to Meaden for a while, but they dropped him when it became clear that they couldn't have him and Lambert and Stamp, too. (Meaden was only Gorden's hired hand—he had no contractual rights.)

"Roger and I went and had a drink in a pub in Brewer Street," Meaden said. "I bought him a drink, and he said, 'Well, listen, man, we're gonna get paid twenty quid [about fifty dollars] a week, now, plus our cars. Why don't you go and have a talk with Kit?' He came straight out with it. There was nothing more to say about it, except Kit got in touch with me and said, 'Let's have lunch.'

"Kit took me into the Number Four restaurant, in Frith Street. I had steak and kidney pie or something and Kit said, 'How much do you want?' I said, 'I don't know how much I want, Kit. I don't know what sort of value you put on it.'

"I was frightened out of my life, because I'd made a monster. I knew it was a monster. And he said, 'I'll give you a hundred and fifty pounds [$420] for them.' I learned later that I was supposed to accept five thousand pounds [$14,000]. But I just said, 'Yeah, that's all right. That'll do. Thanks a lot.'

"He said, 'I can't pay you right away. I'll pay you in lump sums, as much as I can.' Which was abusing the right of what he should have done. Still, at least he didn't just rip them off me."

According to Shaw, Meaden didn't leave quite so placidly. "When we took them to a couple of rehearsals, he came along with a couple of heavy friends, supposedly to beat Kit up. But of course it didn't happen. They just stood around and looked menacing. And eventually, Peter disappeared off that scene, went on to other things."

To the High Numbers, Lambert and Stamp seemed heaven-sent. Kit and Chris were just a bit older than the band but so smooth, they assumed immediate authority. "We were very smart dressers," Mike Shaw said. "The Italian suits, the short jackets." They weren't mods, but the kind of suave hipsters from which mod had developed were men very much like these.

In the eyes of the High Numbers, their new managers had as much money as suss. According to one account, Lambert and Stamp were earning about £5,000 pounds each per year, a livable middle-class wage but no more than that. They'd also saved £13,000 ($36,400) to invest in their film. (Lambert probably had some income from his father's estate, in addition to his wages.)

If Lambert and Stamp were expert at anything at all, it was putting up a front. Irish Jack, who met Kit when he visited the Goldhawk, said he had "the atmosphere of a man who knew what he was about. I couldn't believe he could be connected with the music business—never mind being the new manager of the High Numbers. He had this way of putting himself across. When I heard him talk, I thought he was one of the Queen's messengers. You could hear every word he said. He could cut anyone down to size as well, 'cause he had a tongue like a whip."

In order to legally manage the band, whose members were still under twenty-one, Lambert and Stamp had to offer them a contract that "sort of" (Stamp's phrase) guaranteed the boys a wage of £1,000 ($2,800) each per year. They also had to obtain written parental consent, a process made more onerous since everyone but Pete was still living at home (and Pete was still in the flat above his parents).

The chief obstacles were the Townshends and the Daltreys. "The first time we saw Kit Lambert," Harry Daltrey recalled, "was when he came round one Sunday afternoon to sign Roger's contract. He was quite a nice chap. Kit seemed confident that he was going to make something of them."

Irene Daltrey was much more dubious. "The age of consent was twenty-one in them days," she said. "And he wasn't twenty-one and he only had nine months to go to finish his apprenticeship as a sheet-metal worker when Kit Lambert came here. I didn't want to [sign]. Harry didn't know what to do.

"Roger flew up in the air. 'You won't grumble if you ever see me on *telly*-vision,' he said. So I said, 'Well, I'll sign on one condition, that you keep your union card going.' Because if [the music] didn't turn out a success, he could go back. And that's how we gave in."

There was one other complication for Roger Daltrey. He had gotten his girlfriend, Jackie, whom he'd met at St. Mary's Hall, pregnant, and they were about to be married. Although Doug Sandom, who knew the couple, said that it was a "never-on" marriage, which couldn't have lasted under any circumstances, Irene Daltrey says that Kit Lambert was the instrumental factor in eventually breaking it up once the wedding took place.

" 'Cause in those days, if you remember, even the Beatles didn't like people to know if they were married. Kit didn't like that, and eventually he said, 'You'll have to leave your wife and get a flat.' So Roger left; he started going [away] weekends, and then he started not going home at all."

Chances are that Roger's marriage wasn't destined to work, but certainly, the ludicrous pressure of those years for pop stars to remain unmarried must have scuttled it sooner than it otherwise might have been.

Moon and Entwistle's parents had no objections to the contract. John was still working at the IRS. Keith's prospects as a musician were far better than any others he had. But Cliff and Betty Townshend weren't only more cautious about their son's future, they were show business-wise.

"Kit told us he thought there was a great potential and that he was in it for the money," said Betty Townshend. "He said, 'I'm going to make them famous, and I'm going to make a lot of money.' " That was certainly true. The management agreement that Lambert presented gave him and Stamp (as New Action Limited) 40 percent of the band's earnings. That is, Kit and Chris would earn 20 percent each, presuming an even split. The band would split the remaining 60 percent four ways, giving them 15 percent each.

To Cliff Townshend, who had been around, this seemed fair. "They were completely unknown. Fair enough, if they're going to put the money in." But he balked at other details of the contract.

"They produced a contract, and I actually read it. Pete was a very young fellow, and I read it through and came to one part that said, '. . . and a percentage of all personal writing.' I went and got a pen and drew through that line and Peter said, 'Dad, what are you trying to do? This is good. They're all honest, and we're going to do good with these fellows.'

"I said, 'Not that, no.' And they agreed to do it without. What [Pete] did afterwards, when he was twenty-one, is his own business. But before that period, I crossed it out."

Cliff Townshend thus saved his son from one of the most typical abuses of the music industry: the signing away of up to 100 percent of a songwriter's rightful income from his work. This can amount to as much as a performer/ writer will ever realize from sales of his recordings alone, and in Peter Townshend's case could potentially have saved him hundreds of thousands of dollars, as he later learned the hard way.

Once he had the entire band signed up, Lambert began to turn on his entrepreneurial genius. He had a genuine flair for unusual promotions and a complete ignorance of standard music practice (the questionable clauses in the contract had been drawn by an industry-sharp attorney). He never feared failure.

The film project wasn't exactly shelved, it just withered away. "The film was always there; they wanted to do it," said Shaw. "But they got so swept up once they took over the management and everything started to roll.

"They didn't think about records for a while. Their main thing was developing the act, getting the act together, because Kit and Chris, being in films or theatre, saw the promotional end differently than perhaps someone who'd been in the business awhile. That was one of their mainstays, the visual. It was all impressive."

Lambert's first promotional idea was to make a 16-millimeter promotional film of the stage act, shot at gigs at the Railway and the Scene, using not only footage of the band but also shots of kids dancing, leaning on scooters outside or lounging against Soho walls and hanging out in front of Carnaby Street shops. The film was crudely made, with handheld camera (Kit) and lights (Mike Shaw), and the sound, taped in mono, was even cruder. But it showed the band's flair, and Lambert used it in various ways: to impress the proprietors of clubs where the band might play; to introduce the band at gigs; eventually, to give a sample of his product to booking agents and record company executives.

It was the perfect moment for such an approach. "The summer of 1964 really brought out the mod image," as Irish Jack said, and half of England seemed to be looking for pink Sta-Prest Levi's, blue plastic macs, shoes by Raoul, college scarves (like the one Lambert affected) or Hong Kong nylon socks. Lambert and Stamp had no intention of abandoning the mod image that Meaden had left behind, though they did plan to remodel it quite a bit.

Chris Stamp began seeking a way to break the band into the East End. He approached promoters in Leytonstone, Wanstead and Stratford directly, using the reviews of the single and the promo film. Because the High Numbers' gigs on the Bob Druce circuit were falling off, they had to find a way to compensate. Replacement jobs were in short supply, though. Within a couple of months, Stamp would be forced to take another film job, this time as an assistant on Anthony Mann's *The Heroes of Telemark*, filming in Norway.

Lambert decided to promote East End shows on his own. He found two halls, the Greenwich Town Hall, with a capacity of about one thousand, and the slightly smaller Red Lion pub in Lewisham. Both areas had very strong mod contingents, but neither had ever heard a word about the High Numbers. Lambert promoted about three shows at each spot under the rubric: "The High Numbers: The Worst in Family Entertainment." This slogan was possibly chosen because it cleared up any possible confusion with a Bingo night but more likely picked because it fitted Kit's sense of the absurd. For whatever reason, these gigs were financial flops, and the group retreated back to home turf.

At this point, Lambert and Stamp were operating from a flat in Eaton Square, in ritzy Belgravia. "Talk about flash!" remembered Irish Jack. "They used to leave everything lying around. When you went in, you'd think a bomb had hit the place. The whole flat would be littered with sheets of business paper, an army of sour milk bottles and two or three rented typewriters.

"Kit had this Shell map of London on the wall, and he had it covered all over with drawing pins and red and blue circles where the Who was going to play in different clubs. The place looked more like Churchill's bloody war room."

If there was a decidedly militaristic cast to Lambert's approach, it was a mad hatter's version of military. His attempt to reduce everything to logistical order invariably wound up creating a state of chaos and disarray. Lambert loved the feeling of giving orders and making grandiose plans, but he had a bit of trouble with details.

Lambert was profligate and flamboyant in both his personal and business behavior. "One day Kit's shirt began to stink a bit under the armpits," Irish Jack recalled. "Chris said something about it and Kit spoke a bit of Oxford and took off the shirt.

"But instead of bunging it in the wash-bag like we thought he would, he just rolled it up into a ball and stuck it in the wastepaper basket. Then he went into the bedroom and pulled out this great big Victorian drawer, and there's a whole drawer full of fucking shirts, brand-new, every one of them. He took out this striped one, and it was even still inside the plastic wrapper with the pins in it."

"Any money Kit got, he'd rush off to the gambling casino and try to win some money to pay for whatever next week," said Shaw. "In the first year, it was the money that Chris sent back from the film he was working on that kept us going. But Kit said the best time to borrow money is when you owe some, because they'll lend it to you to get the rest back. That was one of his maxims."

Irrational as much of his behavior undoubtedly was, it would be a mistake not to see Lambert as dead serious. He wanted and needed to make a giant pop success—and a small fortune—to prove himself to his father's memory and for his own satisfaction.

"Kit spent many hours meditating," said Shaw. "You couldn't talk to him, he'd really be concentrating on something, working things out, and he'd come up with these ideas. I mean, Chris came up with ideas, too, you know; he had quite a flair, as well. Between them, they'd come up with the final idea, and we'd put it into action."

One is nonetheless confident that the most outrageous and grandiose or ridiculous schemes came from Kit. There was, for instance, the plot that was briefly afoot in which the group were to record with the blind pianist, Russ Conway. That fell through. "But Kit and Chris would try any scam to get some money," said Shaw.

The High Numbers were now ruled by a kind of mass neurosis. Given their ages, this might have been a band whose members were fumbling toward adulthood and maturity. But in pop music, the last thing one wanted in 1964 was a star who was visibly maturing. Growing up was supposed to be the kiss of death. Nobody involved with the High Numbers (including the musicians) envisioned a career lasting into middle age. Least of all Kit Lambert.

"He was an opposite of traditional managers," said Simon Napier-Bell, former TV producer and rock group manager. "Most of them said to their musicians, 'Dress nicely and behave well, boys.' Kit directed them to do the opposite: to shoot their mouths off and look scruffy."

Nor were Lambert and Stamp especially businesslike or efficient, as even they recognized. ("We don't get deals because we're the best negotiators," said Chris Stamp at the height of their success. "We're probably the worst.")

"As solemn management, [the situation's] always been farcical," wrote Nik Cohn. "Lambert is neurotic, Townshend is neurotic, Keith Moon is neurotic. Almost everyone involved is a maniac, almost everyone is extremely bright, and for years, hardly a week [has] gone by without some kind of major trauma."

One of the few ventures Lambert and Stamp inherited from Helmut Gorden was a national package tour that played Sunday concerts in provincial cities from Glasgow to Brighton and featured various headliners, including the Beatles, P. J. Proby, Tom Jones, Marianne Faithfull and Lulu and the Luvvers.

By now, Mike Shaw had been named production manager, which meant "looking after the band on the road, getting them to the gigs, making travel arrangements plus doing the lighting." The lighting was to be the group's first real theatrical coup, and to prepare for it, Lambert booked rehearsal time at a cinema, the Wandsworth Granada, south of the Thames. Not even the Beatles did their own concert lighting, but Lambert, Shaw and Stamp had enough theatrical experience to work out simple but effective cues that even provincial theatres could handle. (At the same time, Lambert took the lads to Max Factor in Bond Street for theatrical makeup lessons and to Carnaby Street for stage clothes, some of which were also used for everyday wear, since the band needed to maintain a constant image.)

"When we went into those theatres, I wrote out some lighting cues and we got some spectacular lighting. A lot of bands never realized you could go to a lighting man and tell him what lights you wanted on. For our two numbers, there'd be lights flashing off and on, good changing colors, blackouts and everything. Suddenly, the whole stage was blowing up sound-wise and the lights were going," said Shaw.

Lambert finally got the band a van that could hold both the musicians and their gear plus whoever was along for the ride and which would also go uphill at a steady pace. Roger still insisted on driving, and he was still likely to have a girl with him in the front seat. But at least the band was getting around in some kind of decent style.

The package shows weren't especially challenging, since the band was allowed to do only two songs. Pushing their luck, the High Numbers often stretched their second number out for ten minutes.

Worse yet was their stint backing pop vocalist Val McCallum, whose specialty was a rinky-dink version of "Let the Good Times Roll." Moon so hated playing her songs that he finally bought a five-inch toy cymbal and hit it— *ding!*—at what he considered appropriate moments. She fired them before the tour was complete.

The tour's highlight was opening for the Beatles in Blackpool's Opera House. Although Pete Townshend once sneered that "the Beatles are no more mod than Elvis Presley," there's no doubt that the chance to appear on a Beatles bill was an important occasion for the High Numbers. The glimmer of association with the world's most famous and popular band was invaluable, especially in 1964, when all other rock band audiences were essentially subsets of Beatles fans. Anyway, the Beatles music remained terrific, their songwriting superb, and even if they dressed like Liverpudlian moppets rather than sharp Shepherd's Bush mods, they were *the* standard-bearers of rock.

After the Blackpool show, the Beatles made a safe escape, but the High Numbers, who still moved their own equipment, were in the act of loading their van when a horde of Beatlemaniacs approached, screaming, tearing their hair and rending their garments at the sight of a pop group. Any pop group. Townshend always blamed this incident on Lambert's slight resemblance to Brian Epstein, but it's hardly likely that anyone mistook Roger for Paul McCartney, and he's the one who lost a sleeve off his jacket. (The others had the collars of their madras jackets ripped off.)

Lambert encouraged comparisons with Epstein. Though he was more realistic about it than Helmut Gorden, Kit was also fascinated and obsessed with the success of the Liverpool shopkeeper, and he meant to match it, both in terms of his group's success and through his own sense of cool. (Epstein's public unflappability was his most noted characteristic.) Irish Jack remembers Lambert grabbing his sleeve one evening and pulling Jack over to the young mod whom Kit was cruising. "Who do I look like, Jack? Tell him who I look like," Kit insisted.

Jack knew what Lambert wanted to hear. "Brian Epstein," he said. Kit beamed.

Lambert could never have been satisfied with mere physical resemblance. He needed to prove himself Epstein's equal—or his superior, for Lambert had an upper-class Londoner's disdain for all that was provincial and commercial, and Epstein was the personification of provincial commercialization.

At the very least, he had the ideal partner and the perfect vehicle. As Keith Moon put it, "Kit and Chris! They were as incongruous a team as we were. You got Chris on one hand, 'Oh well, fuck it, just whack 'im inna 'head, 'it 'im inna balls an' all.' And Kit says, 'Well, I don't agree, Chris. The thing is, the whole thing needs to be thought out in damned fine detail.'

"These people were perfect for us because there's me, bouncing about, full of pills, full of everything I could get me hands on. And there's Pete, very serious, never laughed, always cool, a grass head. I was working at about ten times the speed Pete was. And Kit and Chris were like the epitome of what we were."

At times, it used to go in every other direction than the one we wanted it to go in. We knew where we wanted to go, but we didn't know how to get there.
— *Keith Moon*

In mid-August 1964, Columbia Records released Bob Dylan's *Another Side of Bob Dylan*, the singer's fourth record and his most striking departure from the folk-protest tradition.

Pete Townshend bought *Another Side* as soon as he saw it, and he spent the next few weeks engrossed in its subtleties, the ferocious anger and deep compassion, the acidic humor and stark fury of Dylan's writing. The ebb and flow of his cracked voice winding through his strange meters and unlikely rhymes fascinated Townshend. Pete especially loved "All I Really Want to Do," an almost dadaist love song, chains of negatives strung together with a moaning, almost yodeling sing-song vocal and bleated harmonica punctuation of the simple guitar strum. "All I Really Want to Do" was not rock—it was far from blues—but it was contemporary and startling and it inspired Townshend in important ways.

"You can't deny that Dylan's music marked a new dimension in rock & roll," Townshend told Cameron Crowe. "He opened the door for rock to say bigger and better things. . . . I think rock became more idealistic. It became the music of the adolescent and a vehicle for the denunciation of whatever we didn't believe in. If there was something a bit dodgy, we knew that pretty soon there'd be a song about it, and through that music, we'd know what we felt to be right and what we felt to be wrong. It was like an affirmation."

Before Dylan, rock had been capable of only certain kinds of affirmation, and those expressions were themselves limited in their seriousness by their linkage to "teenage pop." The unspoken assumption was that none of the agonies expressed in Eddie Cochran's "Summertime Blues," the Coasters' "Yakety Yak" and "Charlie Brown" and Chuck Berry's "School Days" and "Almost Grown" were serious, because they would be outgrown. This was true even of those few rock (or more often, rhythm & blues) songs that tackled economic subjects: Barrett Strong's "Money" is a kind of joke, the Silhouettes' "Get a Job" an overt one. The serious sociological bent of many gospel-schooled soul singers (especially Curtis Mayfield of the Impressions, whose "Keep on Pushing" was a hit in the Summer of 1964) was tempered because the message was hidden beneath a veneer of romance.

Dylan suggested a context in which rock singers not only could establish their seriousness, but one in which the standard adolescent assertion that something is terribly wrong in the adult world could be developed as an implicit critique of society. That context was pop itself, which in Dylan's wake became a forum for statements of discontent of all kinds: from "Norwegian Wood," John Lennon's coded defiance of sexual conventions, to the Rolling Stones' outright hostility to bourgeois values in "Get Off of My Cloud," "(I Can't Get No) Satisfaction," "Mother's Little Helper," "19th Nervous Breakdown" and "Play with Fire." (Dylan's career had changed direction partly because of his encounters with British rock during his 1964 tour there.)

These songs confirmed each listener's intuition not just once but a thousand times. Part of the pop process—by which a hit record is disseminated through the tremendously public mechanisms of radio broadcasts and record players, leaking across store counters, out bedroom windows, rumbling from schoolyard transistors—ensured that each of these songs united the singer and an individual listener in their common perception and also brought together each separate listener with all the others who bought the record (and thus, the message).

So the next eighteen months became a time of unprecedented communion in pop. In 1965 alone, there were such hits as Sam Cooke's "A Change Is Gonna Come," the Animals' "It's My Life" and "We Gotta Get Out of This Place," the Impressions' "People Get Ready," the Beatles' "Help" and "I'm Down," Dylan's "Positively 4th Street" and "Like a Rolling Stone," the Stones' "Satisfaction"— not to mention "My Generation."

Not all of these were "protest songs" in the propagandistic sense. Very few of them worked off newspaper headlines or displayed explicit class anger or political outrage. But the rock audience—galvanized by the Beatles, radicalized by Dylan—accepted these songs as common statements of principle and belief. So rock came into its own as a self-conscious social force.

Pete Townshend's response to "All I Really Want to Do" was not only appropriate but typical. He picked up guitar and pen and for the first time began to write songs in earnest. Dylan liberated him from the need to write self-consciously "teen" songs—and allowed him to write even more self-conscious songs about adolescents struggling toward maturity: coded versions of his own dilemma.

"I felt that the only way I was ever, ever, ever going to make myself felt was through writing," Townshend said. "So I really got obsessed with writing rock songs, and I probably concentrated far more on that than on any other single thing in life. I just used to go back after gigs and write and write and write all the time."

Townshend told Crowe that it was only when he began to write that he "really came together in one piece for the first time. Even in the early years of the band, I suffered that frustration of searching for my niche. That's why my first songs were so screwed up and inarticulate."

In fact, Townshend's first few songs were heard by no one except his flatmates. It was not only predictable insecurity that kept Pete from playing his first songs to the band but a deep need for secrecy.

"I have always been aware of a barrier that Pete throws up around himself," Ray Tolliday wrote. "As if he distrusts or is afraid of any intimacies or burdens that relationships involve. He is very much a loner, a self-supporting type who creates and exists from within and has no need to draw on outside people or influences."

This couldn't be less true. Townshend created barriers because he was (and is) desperately insecure; his need for affirmation is virtually never-ending and his ability to withstand rejection extremely limited. One of the results is that he often thinks he's skulking when his behavior is transparent. Another is that he is often a poor judge of character, frequently trusting exactly the people whose "yeses" are most damaging and engaging in long-term friendships that are frightfully parasitical.

That aspect of his personality was central to his relationship with Kit Lambert. Lambert won Townshend forever by his response to the demo of "It Was You." Kit bought Pete a pair of high quality Revox tape decks, flexible and accurate enough to accommodate and accelerate Pete's composing experiments. "It was a great outlet for him, once he got a Revox and started putting some songs down," said Mike Shaw. "It all came out." And it was the beginning of a deep feeling of indebtedness from Townshend to his manager, a loyalty that went beyond any contractual bonds and which later survived even business betrayals.

More and more, Pete showed his songs to Kit first. Lambert could be counted on to be enthusiastic, to quickly spot flaws in conception, and he always spurred Pete toward clearer, more succinct or more radical ways of saying what he felt. "Kit actually had something, you know," Townshend told Barnes. "He had a great grasp of musical terms and was able to make a critique." It was a perfect editor-writer relationship.

"The thing was, Townshend was intellectual and Lambert wasn't exactly intellectual but he had the jargon," wrote Nik Cohn. If Townshend wanted to theorize, Daltrey, Moon or Entwistle would have looked at him blankly, but in Lambert, Pete finally felt he'd found someone who could take his college bull session ideas and prod them toward reality.

Unfortunately, the extent of Townshend and Lambert's friendship was severely circumscribed by Kit's homosexuality. When Stamp went off to Norway for *Heroes of Telemark*, Kit convinced Pete to move into the spare room of the Belgravia flat. Townshend did, but not without qualms. It didn't help that Kit daily stumbled down to breakfast with yet another poor young fellow who had had to be rescued from being stranded without shelter the night before.

Lambert used the opportunity of living with Townshend to groom him for stardom, introducing Pete to a range of restaurants and social situations that were beyond the purview of Pete's middle-class upbringing. Kit thought Pete's pot-smoking art college pretensions a waste of time, merely minor-league decadence.

Townshend has denied that there was ever anything sexual between him or any of the other band members and Lambert. Which makes sense: An affair could jeopardize all Kit's hopes for the band. One can imagine that Pete and Kit's joint living arrangement caused some talk at the time, however.

Roger Daltrey might have led the gab. Daltrey was a walking definition of macho; part of what made him appealing onstage was his rooster strut, but he carried that hard-guy attitude all the time. While Townshend spent time in Belgravia learning how to properly sip the proper vintages and listening to baroque music and other classics, Daltrey was sleeping in the back of the equipment van. As Moon and Entwistle became more pillheaded and susceptible to Townshend's artiness and Lambert's outrageousness, the rift deepened to become Daltrey versus the entire band.

As the summer of 1964 ended, the material circumstances of the band had not changed much. When the string of Sunday concerts was played out, Lambert insisted on changing the name of the band again—reverting to the Who. "It was simple formula," Lambert told Cohn. "The Who was easy to remember, made good conversation fuel, provided ready-made gags for the disc jockeys. It was so corny it had to be good."

But the band was still playing the same circuit, including the Goldhawk and the Railway, with an occasional excursion to mod reservations like Brighton.

With a record out (even a flop), the Who had a certain amount of west London clout. That's probably how Barnes got his job at the Railway, and it's certainly the reason that the Who were allowed to modify that pub's stage, making it longer and higher than the original so they would have room for their increasing number of amplifiers and their ever-wilder stage antics.

Moon was now a crazy man behind his growing mountain of gear, puffing out his cheeks, tossing sticks overhead and catching them in time (more or less) for the next beat, flailing his arms, standing up and pounding, sweat pouring down over his cherubic face. Daltrey was a figure of great malevolence, leering and strutting from one end of the stage to the other, whipping his mike cord, not above leaping into the crowd, mike in hand, to put his voice right in a patron's face.

Daltrey and Moon were at least consistent on stage and off: Roger was a cocky, assertive tough guy, and Moon was almost uncontrollably maniacal in every situation. But onstage, the normally diffident Townshend, shy and vulnerable in his private life, became even more raging and lunatic than his cohorts.

"Sometimes I'd hold my guitar like a machine gun and move it along the audience, mowing them down one by one," Townshend told Cohn. "It was a very real, very violent thing, and by the time that I got to the end of the line, they'd be cowering and doubled up and trying to hide."

Audiences were probably more intrigued than frightened by Townshend's antics, which included really violent episodes of arm-windmilling; huge leaps into the air, at the apex of which Pete would jackknife his legs in a powerful kick; frantic duckwalks across the stage, à la Chuck Berry; wild gesticulations with mike stand and guitar; and a variety of horrible facial expressions.

Privately, Townshend controlled his anger pretty well, except for his sarcastic tongue. But onstage, he was the most demonstrative instrumentalist in sixties rock. Even Pete felt alienated from the character he assumed as a performer. "I don't really feel the showmanship side of my contribution to the Who's stage show is fundamentally a part of my personality. It's something that automatically happens," he said.

Had Townshend been involved in any other aspect of show business, from the circus to the symphony, his demeanor could be dismissed as *schtick*, a gimmick designed to attract attention to an otherwise limited and frustrated performer. But rock musicians are expected to make every move a reflection of a personal struggle with their work and the world—expected to do this, in the end, not only by their fans but by themselves. (When Townshend later began feeling *his* gestures were *schtick*, he felt as though he was betraying himself and tried to quit.)

For Townshend, playing guitar is "very physical. The way you feel, the way you move and the way you move your body, everything is a big part of it. Sometimes to actually pull a string up by the right amount, you have to give it some momentum. So for me, all that macho stuff became an expression.

"My whole absurdly demonstrative stage act was worked out to turn myself into a body instead of a face. What I wanted to do was to distract attention from my nose to my body and make people look at my body instead of my face—turn my body into a machine. But by the time I was into visual things like that, I'd forgotten all about my nose and a big ego trip."

John Entwistle saw other reasons. "No one understands [Pete] very well," he said. "[He's] a moody person. One day you'll say something and he'll jump down your throat, and the next he's extremely amiable. He's quick-tempered and believes in saying what he thinks, whoever he's with.

"Sometimes, if a show's not going well, Pete will try to carry it off by a sudden urgent display of thundering and arm-swinging—and other times he just won't care a damn how it goes. He gets very angry with his equipment."

Maybe Pete was socially and technically frustrated, but whatever their source, his tirades fit right into the Who. "We were all pillheads," said Daltrey. "We were probably the most aggressive group that's ever happened in England."

"Stage fights were fairly common," said Moon. "One of us would always turn up late—usually me. We just generally didn't get on all that well. We used to take it out onstage—we used to avoid each other offstage. The only time we got together was onstage, so all the pent-up aggression would come out then. Sometimes it used to get to a flash point, where instead of being directed toward the audience, we would turn it back on ourselves."

There was no one to control the rows and bickering, which on occasion could even result in onstage punch-ups. Certainly Lambert or Stamp could not curb them, since Kit believed more wholeheartedly in outrage than anything and Stamp was a seasoned street-brawler. And because each band member, in his own way, was terribly insecure, every time Roger got a girl Pete fancied, or Moon got attention at Entwistle's expense, or Townshend mouthed off in ways that were opaque and annoying to everyone else, each onstage mistake and offstage slight was taken personally and responded to in kind. The result was a wild west atmosphere that was great to watch but must have been hell to live through.

The music they created was largely the product of their competition. "I think the whole thing was that the guitar just became a piece of hardware which was something to be used to assert myself. . . . It was a tough group to do that in. I mean, Roger has a very, very powerful stage presence, and Keith was just amazing," said Pete. "Apart from being a dynamite drummer, he was also very, very pretty. And John was just the straight quiet bass player. It was a bit to work against, and I had to use every trick in the book."

Even Entwistle felt frustrated. He recalled having acquired his first "proper bass setup" with an eighteen-inch speaker. "I had a big cabinet with curtain material on the front, and because we thought it was too heavy, we used to hang the eighteen-inch speaker on a nail every time we'd go to a concert, and when I played a bottom E, it would fall off the nail. So we'd have to stop halfway through the number and hang it back on the nail. The first time I could ever play my E string properly was after I'd been playing bass for about three years. I was just playing on the first three strings [until then]."

That wasn't John's biggest problem. "It's really still funny to this day when we do a song with John doing a blinding bass run, making Alvin Lee look like he plays in slow motion, and I'm just standing there plucking away and they wonder how I do it," said Townshend. "John doesn't demand attention. For years, nobody even noticed John was there." And while many of the things that drove the others nuts hardly disturbed John, the lack of credit for his musical contribution sent him up the wall.

So everyone was furious about something almost all the time. The result was an absolutely murderous show that scared the competition off. "There were a lot of bands at that time who used to try to copy us. They could get the sound nearly the same, but they couldn't understand why we sounded like that," said Entwistle. "The thing was, at the back of our minds, we trained ourselves to think everyone else was below us. I never would have been able to walk out on stage if I didn't think I was the best bass player in England. We were determined that we were going to make it, and we told each other—very often."

Status conscious as they were, however, the Who were not only hyper-aware of those beneath them but also of those above them in the rock hierarchy. "There's a thing that we call the Stones walk-on," Townshend once said. "You have to walk on and pretend that you're a Rolling Stone. The Stones are a bigger group than us; so we go on pretending we're the Stones.

"Kit Lambert said, 'I've noticed, Pete, that when you do the Stones walk-on, you're always much better than when you walk on ordinarily. You've got to run on; you've got to feel like you want to get on the stage.' So now we stand off the stage and it's like waiting for the green flag. We run on and run all over the place like a dog defining his territory and then we plug in and play."

This combination of insecurities and arrogances (defining each individual and the band collectively) created one of rock's first strong anti-pop images. "As a group, we are self-consciously aware of our image," Townshend once wrote. "We've never lost that feeling of our early days, when image was almost as important as sound. It's somehow intrinsic in the mood of the band. When we stand together on a stage or in a studio, we feel that image take over and become bigger than any single one of us."

The Who's image deliberately evaded many of the "requirements" of contemporary pop. The group's only pretty face (Moon's) was hidden behind the drums; its aggression was delivered full-force and without respite; its undercurrent of sexual tension was more likely to alienate than attract innocent young girls. In fact, the entire approach of the Who was designed to make its audience either terribly uncomfortable or, alternatively, almost smug in its assurance that this, and only this, was the currently fashionable mode of behavior. In that sense, the Who were the first genuinely avant-garde rock band.

The Railway Tavern had a relatively low ceiling, and when the Who's stage extension raised them, Townshend and Entwistle, both six-footers, were practically playing in the rafters.

"I was trying to control the feedback one night," Pete explained. "I had a whistle on the guitar and I couldn't shake it off, and I was banging the guitar around and the neck hit the ceiling, And because I look as if I'm doing everything so positively on the stage, I did it again. And it sounded great. It was going *boing-boing*—and it was a big visual thing."

In that night's second set, Townshend was challenged by some art school friends in the front ranks of the crowd to bang his axe against the ceiling again. When he did, the guitar broke, "the neck dangling straight up at the ceiling."

"There were a few laughs, mainly negative reaction; everyone was waiting for me to kind of sob over my guitar, going, 'Yeah, yeah, that'll teach you to jump around like a lunatic, that'll teach you to be flash,' " Townshend recalls. "I had no recourse but to completely look as though I meant to do it, so I smashed the guitar and jumped all over the bits. It gave me a fantastic buzz.

"Luckily, I'd brought a spare guitar, the twelve-string. I picked it up and carried on as though nothing had happened. The next day, the place was packed."

It wasn't nearly that simple. Immediately after the first guitar-breaking gig,

Daltrey had a go at Townshend backstage, arguing that he should not have completed the destruction job, that the guitar could have been repaired. John Entwistle, as a musician's musician, was properly horrified at Pete's lack of respect for his axe, and Kit Lambert also opposed it (but only because it was too expensive a move).

But the next week at the Railway, the crowd was waiting for another destruction job. When they didn't get it, they left, and Moon grew so cross about that, he kicked his kit to pieces, even though only the band, the crew and a handful of lingering customers were still there. The stragglers passed on word of Moon's demonstration, though, and the third week, an even larger crowd had even higher expectations. This time, both Townshend and Moon destroyed their gear. (Keith's could be repaired; Pete's couldn't, partly because Rickenbackers had weak necks, partly because he got carried away and smashed big pieces into little bits.)

After that, destruction became a semi-regular part of the act, and Townshend began to connect his guitar-bashing with the auto-destructive performances given by his "hero," Gustave Metzke, at Ealing. (Metzke became a fan of the band and wound up trying to persuade them to destroy their equipment at an academic seminar.)

For Townshend, academic auto-destruction was fairly ineffectual. "When it actually came to being done, it was always presented so badly; people would half-wittedly smash something and it would always turn round, so the people who were against it would always be more powerful than the people that were doing it.

"Someone would come up and say, 'Well, *why* did you do it?' And the thing about auto-destruction is that it has no purpose, no reason at all. There is no reason why you allow these things to happen, why you build a building that will fall down. . . . I've always thought that high-class, high-powered auto-destructive art—glossy pop destruction—was far, far better than the terrible, messy, dirty disorganized destruction that other people were involved in."

But in the Railway Tavern incident (and the crowd's response to it), Townshend offered auto-destruction a meaningful context: the fury of rock & roll's attempt to exorcise the world of all its impurities. In this sense, guitar-smashing was not just an exercise, it was the climactic moment of what the Who's stage presentation was all about—probably the only appropriate one conceivable.

Not that it was entirely an elevated concept. "I think I justified it in terms of being noticed," Townshend said once in a frank moment. "And fuck it, I wasn't going to stand on the stage and play rock & roll if it was just for the music; because that's not what rock & roll is, anyway. It might be what the blues is, but rock & roll is something else again."

Keith Moon saw another dimension in the wreckage. "When Pete smashed his guitar, it was because he was pissed off. When I smashed me drums, it was because I was pissed off. We were frustrated. You're working as hard as you can to get that song across, to get that audience by the balls, to make it an event.

When you've done all that, when you've worked your balls off and you've given the audience everything you can give and they don't give anything back, that's when the fucking instruments go."

But what's perhaps most curious about the Who's auto-destruction (especially in light of the interpretations suggested by both Moon and Townshend) is that the cue to *keep on* smashing came from the crowd, which perceived this as some sort of "valid statement" weeks before the group did. It was the fans who gave the event meaning, by choosing to interpret Townshend's original broken instrument not just as a part of the show but as a part that could and *should* be repeated. In the end, the Who was given little choice but to keep the auto-destruction in its arsenal. All of Townshend's rationalizations (intriguing and insightful as many of them are) are after the fact. As with the Who's appropriation of mod fashion, the interchange between audience and band was two-way—and not all of the smart parts originated with the performers.

Townshend was at least bright enough to draw the right lesson from the experience. "I had discovered that every artist needs a platform," he told Pete Hamill. "And no artist is given a platform. He has to claim it. He has to demand it. He can make his claim, but nobody's going to let him on it unless he's interesting. Or novel. Or fucking crazy."

11

Whereas Eddie Cochran's audiences probably took him completely at face value, ours react to us once removed. When we smash up our equipment onstage, for instance, they know that it isn't spontaneous, and oddly enough, they get more excited by it because they know it's a ritual.
—Pete Townshend

"From the start," wrote Nik Cohn, "Kit and Chris spent like madmen. They had no knowledge of management whatsoever, but they made up for it in sheer style and bravado. . . .Within three months, Kit and Chris had gone neck-deep in debt."

If Lambert and Stamp had had as much money as the Who imagined (or only as much as they themselves claimed), maybe their debts would have been inconsequential, but the Who's rate of necessary and unnecessary expenditure (rampant) and its rate of income (negligible) could have bankrupted a principality.

Equipment-smashing was the worst problem. Moon's gear could usually be fixed in time for the next gig; drums are built to be bashed. But guitars are more delicate. Soon even Marshall's, the only shop in town that could be counted on to loan a musician equipment, became hostile. When Townshend went to them, asking to borrow a guitar to replace one he'd smashed, they turned him down flat.

"So I just grabbed a Rickenbacker off the wall and ran out," Townshend told Barnes. "Eventually, they sent me hire purchase [installment credit] papers for it." After that, Townshend limited his breakage—and still wound up making simultaneous payments on as many as eight guitars. At least nobody could repossess them.

"We'd do a show and get a hundred quid [$280]," said Moon, "but a guitar would be a hundred and fifty pounds and a drum set a hundred pounds [$420

114

and $280 respectively]. The debt got up to thirty or forty thousand pounds [$84,000 or $112,000] and probably a lot more."

The act was now too expensive to be supported only by the London club circuit. There was no choice but to acquire a foothold in Soho, London's entertainment and theatrical district and the spot where you went to get discovered by record companies and the media. Meaden had already given the High Numbers some notoriety in those precincts, but the band's name had changed, and its record had flopped. Besides, the Scene, the 100 Club, the Flamingo and Le Discotheque all featured records, not live bands.

Ziggy Jackson was one of London's more prominent jazz promoters. His club, the Marquee, had long been ensconced in Oxford Street, but as the trad boom faded, he moved deeper into Soho's sleazy bowels, to Wardour Street. There his promotions shifted toward slick jazz and hard R&B.

Toward the end of 1964, hip London's musical tastes went through another shift, turning away from raw Chicago blues (exemplified by Howlin' Wolf, who played the Marquee that winter) toward the more elegant and cosmopolitan soul sound represented by Motown (or Tamla, as it was called in Britain). In addition to Wolf, among the bands appearing at the Marquee that winter were sedate jazzmen Humphrey Lyttelton and Johnny Dankworth, who played drawing-room jazz, nothing raucous or funky, and such pop-R&B groups as the Moody Blues (on the verge of a hit with "Go Now"), John Baldry's Hoochie Koochie Men (whose floating membership included Rod Stewart), and the T-Bones (organ-based soul with Gary Farr and Keith Emerson). Tuesday was the night when the Marquee still featured trad jazz, and Tuesday was a dud.

Lambert and Stamp approached Ziggy Jackson, proposing to take over the club on Tuesdays, guaranteeing Jackson a fee and turning a profit themselves only if they were able to pack the place. It was the kind of move in which Lambert and Stamp later specialized: nervy and unorthodox, but shrewd if you had the right product and knew how to promote it.

The Marquee was the most respectable R&B-oriented club in Soho. It was the only one that did not stay open all night (it closed at eleven), and it was cheaper to enter. At the other clubs, speed and grass were openly dealt. At the Marquee, the back wall was painted with a giant warning: "SPEED KILLS."

Jackson agreed to Lambert and Stamp's deal; he had little or nothing to lose. "We got a regular Tuesday night residency, which was a big coup for us," Townshend said. "The first night, there were maybe fifty people, the next night two hundred and after that we were packing it."

Before moving into the band's first big-time residency, Lambert decided that he needed a slogan. He came up with "Maximum R&B."

Lambert seems to have chosen the slogan because it gave him more to work with than the brief "The Who." But Maximum R&B was not a name without implications. "We were playing a lot of Bo Diddley, Chuck Berry, Elmore James, B. B. King," said Moon. "And they are maximum R&B. You can't get any better. Most of the songs we played were their songs. . . . Of course, any song we did get hold of we weren't playing straight from the record. We 'Who'd' it, so that what came out was the Who, not a copy."

At a time when almost every other band—even the Stones—was hewing close to the structure of the original blues and R&B models, "Maximum R&B" suggested that the Who not only knew what to play but had a new way of playing it. Which was absolutely correct.

What made "Maximum R&B" an even more effective slogan was the poster Lambert commissioned to go with it. Designed by a professional graphic artist, it featured a picture of Townshend, his right arm upraised, ready to crash down in windmill stroke upon his huge Rickenbacker. Produced in monochrome, this picture encapsulates pure rock energy, and its profile of Townshend, his nose pushing the border of the picture into blackness, made him seem absolutely predatory, a true Bird Man delivering a rock & roll salute.

This image became a logo for the group. Lambert not only used it for a poster but featured elements of it in his publicity handouts and on the free tickets he handed out to the Goldhawk mods.

The mods were the key to Kit's and Chris's strategy. The Bush crowd provided a hardcore following for the Who wherever they played. Building from this base, the Who's shows at the Marquee became spectacularly successful. "The first time, we got the regular following from the scene," said Shaw. "We spent days giving out free tickets [for the second week], and we got a hundred people in, rising in a month to over a thousand, breaking the record that Manfred Mann had held until then."

The Marquee was a relatively long journey for west London mods, especially on a Tuesday evening, when most had work or school the next day. But Kit soon thought up a scheme that made the proposition more attractive. He formed a kind of Who fan club, the 100 Faces. The members were all kids who went from gig to gig with the Who whenever they could, anyway. Lambert now organized them by allowing them certain privileges (ease of admission and so forth) in return for which they were to go out and proselytize for the Who.

"He had about four or five of us who were regulars handing out these leaflets and stuff for him," remembered Irish Jack, who was one of the 100 Faces, of course. "Honest, old Lambert was so precise about everything, we were like bloody frontline shock troops or something.

"Lambert would stand about in the foyer [of the Marquee] looking like the ace face, and I think he must've imagined he was back in the army, 'cause he'd have about eight hundred of these Who posters under his arm, and the first person he thought sounded cockney, he'd automatically assume they was from the Bush, and he'd grab their arm and stick about two hundred of these 'Maximum R&B' posters into their hand, and he'd even sound like bleedin' Monty: 'Oxford Street. Quickly . . .' Then he'd give them a pass to get in after they came back."

Jack was around for the first night at the Marquee, and he says the crowd could have numbered no more than twenty, thirty at the outside. "The Marquee began to fill up slowly, and then it suddenly all seemed to happen one night. We used to get up there early for the posters and handouts. Everything seemed quiet as usual around half-past seven. Then suddenly, by about eight, there was this fucking wave of mods everywhere.

"I couldn't believe it. It was as if they all decided to come this one particular night. They were from all over London. What struck me as funny in an odd way was how much us lot from the Goldhawk were at a loss for words when we saw this great throng queuing up to see four blokes that we had always taken for granted down the Goldhawk and the first few weeks in the Marquee. See, we'd always known them as mates, and it was weird in a way when you looked at the length of the queue. It was like seeing a member of your own family becoming more and more famous. A lot of the geezers felt as if they'd lost the Who in one sense. I don't think us lot from the Bush ever thought we'd have to share the Who.

"After that first night, the place was besieged. We made sure we got rid of our posters before they locked the doors."

The band had some of the same reactions. "It happened so fast it was amazing," said Daltrey. "You had the feeling anything could happen. We were the kids' group."

What were the Who, especially to the hardcore mods who went to see them precisely because of what they stood for? Certainly, they were not faces themselves. "[They] wore stuff that was five months out of date, as far as we were concerned," David Bowie (then a south London mod called David Jones) told *NME* many years later. "But we liked them 'cause they were kind of like us. They were our band."

And Townshend himself has admitted, "though we were on a stage, we were still tickets—watchers rather than leaders. Because we could look down from the stage and see instantly who the faces were. We could see what they were wearing and what their dances were and instantly copy them. And in the end, the faces started to think we were inventing things . . . and they'd take a lot of leads from us."

It's extremely unlikely that the true faces—the hardest of the guys who hung about the Goldhawk—even went to the Marquee. Nick Jones, a teenager who often got into the Marquee on Tuesdays because his father, Max, was a well-known *Melody Maker* critic, remembered his sole visit to the Goldhawk: "It scared the shit out of me. The Marquee seemed to be a younger following, but the Goldhawk was another thing, really very sharp-looking guys who all looked as if they were twice my age, the real faces, the guys who actually had day jobs and spent every penny on mohair, tonic, made-to-measure suits, Italian shoes, into the Lambretta. Hardboys, you know, not above carrying some steel. It was too hard for me; I really felt like a very young kid there."

The Marquee shows began just when the mod world was expanding in the wake of the bank holiday beach clashes and pirate radio. In the process, mod became less exclusive, and a good deal of its style and ritual changed. If the Who were five months behind Bowie's ultra-hip coterie, they might have been a solid year ahead of the newer tickets on the scene.

"What the Mods taught us in the band was how to lead by following," Townshend once told *Rolling Stone*. "I mean, you'd look in the dance floor and see some bloke stop dancing the dance of the week and for some reason feel like doing some silly sort of step. And you'd notice some of the blokes around him looking out of the corners of their eyes and thinking, 'Is this the latest?' And on their own, without acknowledging the first fellow, a few of 'em would start dancing that way.

"And we'd be watching. By the time they looked up on the stage again, *we'd* be doing that dance, and they'd think the original one had been imitating *us*. And next week they'd come back and look to us for dances."

Absorbing information from the crowd was a key to the Who's pickup of mod iconography in the first place, just as it was instrumental in the group's development of feedback and auto-destruction.

The new mods were no less frustrated and aggressive than the early ones and sometimes a good bit less particular about how they expressed it. This was especially true of those who had acquired serious pillhead habits without the funds to support them. It led to a lot of larceny and, because Soho was also one of London's biggest homosexual cruising areas, considerable male prostitution. (Girls were only a little more prominent in post-Clacton mod than they had been in the early days.)

For Townshend, rock & roll was "the only real bridge between real events and getting events into perspective" within this tightly circumscribed scene. "I'd see someone beating up on somebody else," he said, "and then an hour later he'd come into the club and say what a great guitarist I was. That really turned my head around, because I knew if I wasn't holding a guitar, I'd probably be the guy he was kicking shit out of."

"We were a cult within a cult," Townshend told another interviewer. "There's a great feeling of affirmation when the audience knows they're sharing in the success; they're making the success happen, as well. So you become incredibly close. The two or three thousand people who regularly attended the Marquee residency—I think I know them all by their first names." And even though they were working at a time when all rock bands were expected to cause riots, the Who never had to rely on screaming girls or gimmicks to create a rallying spirit. The mods came prepared to demonstrate. "There were occasions, of course, when we incited a crowd to get up and do something, but only when it looked as if it was going that way," Townshend admitted. "[But] the Stones had to get that kind of thing going for them, because their sound was fucked, to be cruel to the Stones."

The Who, of course, had better methods of overcoming their musical limitations: distortion, volume and destruction added up to the biggest distraction of all—distraction within the music. It was a total act by now. "We didn't go out of our way to be nasty," said Moon. "We were naturally nasty."

"I couldn't think of anything to contribute," said Roger. "So I scratched the speaker column with my fingernail. It made the best row of all."

The Marquee shows had exactly the effect that Kit Lambert and Chris Stamp had hoped for. Even a seasoned Who observer like Irish Jack was impressed. "It was like a sort of West End revue," he said. "Everything was concentrated on the stage; there weren't no bar in the Marquee then. If you wanted a drink, you had to wait until the interval and go up to the Ship [the pub on the corner].

"They even had these cinema seats going round the edge of the stage, about five rows deep. That's what really gave it the revue feeling. I mean, the Marquee wasn't personal. You wasn't exactly miles away from the stage, either. You was right on top of the bloody thing, and when that wall of sound came at you, it was fucking great. I think what really made the Marquee work for me was Townshend and his guitar. We never knew what he might do next. What a tension builder."

But it wasn't only Townshend—he was basically doing a more refined and powerful version of what he had done in the pubs. It was also the atmosphere, the Motown material, the increasing rapport of the musicians, the whole mood of mod that was bubbling in the streets outside.

Jack remembered the shows vividly. "A geezer in a mohair suit would walk up to the microphone with his hands in his jacket pockets and make a really professional announcement. Then suddenly the Who would come storming onto the stage, and the noise from the crowd would come up like thunder. There weren't no screaming from soppy birds—it was blokes making all that noise.

"The heat would get really close as the crowd pressed in. I used to take a last look at the closeup 'nose card' [a 100 Faces card with Pete's picture] I had in me inside pocket. Then I'd look back at the wall of Marshall speakers draped in Union Jacks—and Christ! The next thing, the whole place would go up in the air, as the speakers shook with 'Heat Wave.'

"Those standing in the very front would have to move back from the edge of the stage, 'cause the way Daltrey started, you'd think he was going to whack some cunt who might be standing too close. That was one thing the Who done—they fucking made you step back a bit.

"The place would get stuffy with the stink of sweat, and the condensation would run off the walls. But you just didn't care that there weren't no more room for dancing when you looked up and saw the madness in Moon's eyes as he waved his drumsticks about in the air like a lunatic. Daltrey, his golden hair soaked in sweat, bashing the skin out of a new tambourine off the mike stand, his harmonica blazing rhythm & blues down the microphone and out into the system. Entwistle steady as a rock. How he used to do it I never knew, with all that tension building up around him. Sometimes I think Entwistle created *more* bloody tension by remaining calm. He didn't do nothing, but you still couldn't take your eyes off him.

"Then that mad geezer Townshend, his right arm spinning like a windmill blade gone daft. That Rickenbacker used to go through the face of the cabinets like a sledgehammer through a sheet of aeroboard. When it was over, you felt empty, spent. Then you noticed that your fucking clothes was wringing wet."

If that's how an old hand like Irish Jack took the Marquee events, imagine the effect on mods still struggling to perfect their style. A typical case is Nick

Jones. Jones was an aspiring rock drummer, about seventeen, and he still felt awkward around girls—all this by his own account. He was living an essentially middle-class, fairly sheltered existence at his parents' home in north London. Nick Jones could not have been more perfectly targeted for mod's leap into mass culture. For him, the Who epitomized mod.

In fact, Jones was so enthralled by the Who that (through his father) he persuaded *Melody Maker* to let him review the Who's Marquee shows. This was another coup for the Who. *Melody Maker* was Britain's oldest, largest, most conservative music-oriented paper, begun in the jazz age and part of the huge IPC publishing conglomerate. (When Nick Jones went to work there, in mid-1965, he was immediately told to get a haircut.)

Melody Maker was essentially a tabloid voice of the established music industry. It covered the rise of rock with reluctant enthusiasm (with the result that IPC inaugurated a new all-rock weekly, *Disc*). It was virtually unheard of for *Melody Maker* to run a review of a band as unknown and unrecorded as the Who, much less for it to print the kind of rave written by Nick Jones.

"The Who . . . should be billed not only as 'Maximum R&B' but as 'Far-out R&B,' " said the notice, which was buried in the fine print of the January 9, 1965, issue. He mentioned two numbers, "Heat Wave," the Martha and the Vandellas' hit that the Who did as an extended rave-up; and "You Can't Sit Down," a dance-rock hit by the Philadelphia group the Dovells, which jazz guitarist Phil Upchurch had converted into a funky instrumental improvisation. It was "You Can't Sit Down" that particularly caught Jones's attention: "This performance demonstrated the weird and effective techniques of guitarist Paul [*sic*] Townshend, who expertly uses speaker feedback to accompany many of his solos.

"The Who, spurred by a most exhilarating drummer and a tireless vocalist, must surely be one of the trend-setting groups of 1965."

In essence, that was it—about 250 quick words but the most important piece of publicity that the little band from Shepherd's Bush had yet received. And it was not altogether true that *Melody Maker* was going out on a gigantic limb by running the piece. A week after that issue appeared on the newsstands, on January 15, 1965, the Who released their first single.

When the band started off in 1964–65, I really thought we were just gonna explode. I thought I was gonna die. . . . I never ate; it was all dope, dope, dope and horrible vibes of aggression and bitterness.

Out of that we were saying: "We are the mirror for the desperation and bitterness and frustration and misery of the misunderstood adolescents; people in the vacuum."

—Pete Townshend

As the Who established its West End credentials, Kit Lambert began moving on another front, approaching record companies for auditions. The band had its demo tapes of live shows, it had the Fontana single (though that label was no longer interested in them) and it had the rough film footage Lambert had cobbled together. All of the major companies were pursued without much luck. Their West End success was too new and underground to make the Who a must signing, and the fact that their earlier single had died counted heavily against them.

Lambert and Stamp secured only one audition, with EMI, the largest label in Britain and the home of the Beatles. The supervisor of the session, held at Abbey Road Studios, was John Burgess.

This audition took place some time in the autumn; Burgess's letter formally rejecting the group's "white labels" (demonstration discs) is dated October 22, 1964.

"I have listened again and again to the High Numbers' white labels, taken from our test session and still cannot decide whether or not they have anything to offer," Burgess wrote. "You may, of course, in the meantime, have signed with another company, in which case, I wish you all the luck in the world. If you have not, I will be very interested to hear any other tapes you may have, featuring the group."

"We went away very discouraged," Townshend remembered, "because we thought, well, if we're a great group, why don't they just take us on?"

The answer was the changing reality of the record business. "Listen, you are a great group, and we'd love to take you on," Burgess told them. "But since the Beatles, we're only taking on groups that can write their own material."

Before the Beatles, A&R men like Burgess had been in control of the recording process, selecting not just the singers and musicians but also the songs (which were submitted by professional, nonperforming songwriters). But the Beatles were self-contained—writers, singers and musicians all in one package. When they hit, the A&R man's control was dismantled. By late 1964, smart British A&R men began to realize the implications of the new situation, understanding that they no longer knew what the pop market wanted but that the best young musicians *did* know. So they began to insist on original material.

The Who hadn't developed any original material for several reasons. Many of the clubs where the Who played would not have considered booking a band that was playing only—or even primarily—its own songs. Mods wanted original arrangements, not original songs.

Additionally, the Who had modeled itself after the Rolling Stones, not the Beatles, and the Stones, even at this period, were performing only a smattering of their own numbers. Indeed, to an extent it's a myth that the British Invasion bands produced a pack of great songwriters. This was true of the Beatles (Lennon and McCartney), the Rolling Stones (Mick Jagger and Keith Richard) and the Kinks (Ray Davies). But it was by no means true of the Animals, the Yardbirds and Manfred Mann, who based their repertoires on a combination of blues standards, old rock hits, recent soul material and whatever was sent their way by the writers in America's Tin Pan Alley. And it is these six acts, together with the Who, who represent the most important artistic contribution of the so-called British Invasion of 1964-66.

That doesn't mean that Burgess's analysis was wrong; in fact, it only makes it more perspicacious. The difference between the Beatles, the Rolling Stones and the Kinks (and, ultimately, the Who) and the Animals, the Yardbirds and Manfred Mann may be expressed in many ways: in degrees of influence, commercial success, career longevity or sheer creative vision. But the root of those differences lies in the fact that the former, more significant groups developed songwriting skills. Eric Burdon of the Animals, for instance, was a far better R&B singer than Mick Jagger. But once Burdon was cut off from a supply of strong material (which happened to be just the same moment when he tried and failed to create his own songs), his career collapsed. The Yardbirds had three of rock's greatest guitarists in their lineup at one point or another (Eric Clapton, Jeff Beck, Jimmy Page), yet because they never developed a songwriter, they were doomed to fragmentation: Whatever musical vision the band members shared was never clearly expressed.

It is certainly the Yardbirds' experience that provides the most interesting parallels and contrasts with the Who's, not only because they began on the same circuit but also because both were bands whose music was a product of a genuinely collaborative process, without a single dominant figure. The difference, again, is that the Who developed a dominant member while the

Yardbirds did not. But what makes the Who different from all of these bands is that the essence of the Who's dilemma has always been the unresolved tension between the rock band as a genuine democracy and the necessity for a single vision to dominate (if only so that collective imperatives could be more clearly expressed).

It boiled down to a contest for control of the group between Roger Daltrey and Pete Townshend. Up to this point, Daltrey had remained the group's principal leader, through sheer force of personality. Daltrey's greatest asset was a natural instinct for structuring live performances, but if the Who remained only a stage act, its career was all but over. In order to make the jump to recording, the band needed songs and vision. Only Pete Townshend could supply them.

Most rock bands are begun with one member in control from the beginning. Not so with the Who. In the beginning, it was Daltrey's band. But even at the start, that was more true socially than it was musically. When Roger abandoned guitar to become the singer and the band acquired Moon, perhaps the most distinctive instrumentalist in rock at this time, Roger's centrality was further diminished. But Moon had no singing skills, nor was he a writer; his talent was entirely for the drum kit. Entwistle, locked in his preconceptions, was not assertive enough to adopt a leadership role, even though he had all the necessary musical (and, ultimately, compositional) skills.

That left Townshend, too ungainly to serve as the band's onstage frontman, too undiplomatic to run the show from behind the scenes but with tremendous focus in his songwriting and as it turned out, with a real genius for exploring themes of identity. When the band needed a songwriter, the job fell to the only person to whom it could have fallen—but to a person who was constitutionally ill-equipped for leadership.

"I think what a lot of people probably don't realize about working in a group is that you've got a basis for learning all of life's hardest lessons very rapidly," Townshend said. "In other words, you say, 'I think we should do such and such a thing,' and everybody says, 'Nonsense, we're going to do such and such a thing.' The first thing you realize is that if you want to do what you want to do, you've got a choice. Either you're going to fight like hell to get it done—convince the people you're working with that it's right or demonstrate that it's right—or alternatively, you can run away and do it on your own.

"In a group, you learn the art of compromise, you learn the art of diplomacy. I think most of all you learn the art of caring about other people's opinions." Even in a group as individualistic and contentiously egotistical as the Who, such lessons were absorbed, though generally not without a great many bruises.

Townshend's assumption of a role for which the Who had no natural member led him through the extraordinary frustration of having his own insights and ideas voiced by another, who would inevitably alter them, for good or ill. Yet it is a major mistake to jump to the conclusion expressed by critic Simon Frith that "Townshend has *always* been a fake. . . . The most articulate musician ever got his musical kicks making Roger Daltrey play dumb; the most together man in the business took his equipment apart with a smirk. Basic and honest, huh!!"

In fact, Daltrey isn't faking Townshend—he's interpreting him. Townshend isn't playing basic and honest—he's complex and deceitful from the start. Basic and honest are qualities added to the mix not by the writer but by the singer. As for that smirk that crossed his face as he brought his guitar down for its hundredth bashing of an amp—was it directed at himself, his audience or, perhaps, the equipment itself? Or all three?

What's going on here is one of the most important processes in all of popular art, the completion of an individual artist's vision by his collaborators (much as a fine cinematographer, good actors and intelligent writers complement a director's vision, which could not be fully realized without them, but without which, the others would remain essentially technicians). Ironically, Frith expressed this perspective perfectly in the very same review in which he took Townshend to task: "The wonderful lie on which the Who is based is that Roger Daltrey is Pete Townshend. Daltrey may be making the noises, but the voice we hear is Townshend's. No other group carries such tension."

This is the Who's glory. They balanced the tension between individual vision and collective achievement without ever bothering to conceal the stress it caused—and this became part and parcel of their image, a key to what they sold for twenty years and, in its way, an apotheosis of mod itself. For what was mod except the ultimate instance of individuality acquiring its deepest meaning from interaction with others?

This doesn't mean that anyone found the situation easy to live with. As Townshend summarized it, "I took the band over when they asked me to write for them in 1964 . . . and used them as a mouthpiece, hitting out at anyone who tried to have a say in what the group (mainly Roger) said and then grumbling when they didn't appreciate my dictatorship. . . ."

Townshend tells only half the story. The rest is encapsulated by Moon: "There was no one of us that dictated policy. Policy was always group policy. It had to be, because we always disagreed."

The method in which Townshend chose to present his new material, on which he'd been working intently since August, was unorthodox. "Since the band began, I have written songs at home in my studio and served them up to the group as completed single tracks, with all instruments either played already or at least indicated," he said. "For the musician that can't read music—can't really communicate, anyway—the only way to get across what you want is to play it."

That's how most rock music is communicated: orally, in interchange among band members. Rock compositions are traditionally written down on paper only after they are recorded, in one form or another, and then only for copyright purposes. This is true not only because most rock musicians can't read music but also because conventional western music notation does not have an adequate vocabulary for the range of sounds, inflections and effects which may be required in a rock number.

In consequence, rock musicians don't study scores. They learn from records. All that Townshend did was present his own material in the same way that he would have presented a song by Mose Allison or Eddie Cochran: as a recorded prototype on which the group could expand.

As written texts, the songs were more important for their lyrics. These were probably the single place where this shy, stubborn, often deceitful young man could truly reveal himself, since he always had the advantage, in his songs, of stressing that he was writing about a "character" not himself. And so the songs came in a sudden, shocking rush, which surprised no one more than Pete Townshend himself.

Superficially, Townshend's first songs were still love songs. But they had other dimensions. "I really like my first few songs, because they were an incredible surprise," Townshend claimed. "Through writing, I discovered how to free my subconscious, in a way." And he told another interviewer: "I find writing fairly much an unconscious thing. It doesn't involve that much effort, so I don't need much stimulation. I don't really look around for it. And if I like something, usually I like it pretty much at face value."

But even though Townshend wrote easily and naturally, he was ultimately writing to solve a specific set of problems; not simply to get a hit record (which was an important and valid goal) but also because the Who had become the standard-bearers of mod. Their original material ought to be something that attempted to deal with or define some new dimensions of the movement. As historian Greg Shaw wrote, "That angry feedback was all right for capturing mod's hostility, but what of the great sense of aloneness and uncertainty that were also part of the young rebel's life?"

When he began to write, Townshend focused fairly narrowly on lyrics. The result was that he found himself, for the first time, preoccupied with attempting to make explicit what had been inchoate before. The first successful song he wrote was called "I Can't Explain," and although it is superficially just a lyric about a boy who can't find words to express his infatuation, Townshend soon discovered that it was much more.

"I suppose in a way it's a moon-and-June song," he said. "I thought later, 'Yeah, it's got nothing to do with love at all, it's got to do with a whole lot of other things.' But that was only in retrospect.

"I discovered then that I had this ability to just sit down and scribble things out and think that I was writing consciously. But the real meaning was coming from somewhere else that I had absolutely no control over. Like odd things would give me an incredible surprise. I suppose I was surprised by how obviously observant I was without ever really being conscious of it."

"[I] thought it ["I Can't Explain"] was about a boy who can't explain to a girl that he's falling in love with her," Townshend told Cameron Crowe. "But two weeks later, I looked at the lyrics and they meant something completely different. I began to see just what an outpouring that song really was.

"At that point, I became the greatest rock critic in the world. I was two people—someone who sat down and wrote a song for a particular purpose, and then somebody who looked at it and saw something totally different.

"Then I realized, of course, that's why Bob Dylan doesn't know what to say when people ask him about one of his songs—because he doesn't fucking know what it's all about. I know, because I'm on the outside reacting to it, and whatever it means to me is it. But he doesn't. How could he? All he did was write it."

You could chalk this up to Townshend's essentially divided personality; you could view it as a lesson learned from mods, who taught all of the members of the Who the importance of performers closely observing their audience. You'd be more accurate if you said that Townshend took from all these influences, and probably a lot more, to become the most incisive commentator on pop affairs of his generation. But one thing is certain: If Kit Lambert and Chris Stamp had not found the Who a recording contract very quickly thereafter, none of it would have counted much. "I Can't Explain"—like any rock song—was not just a composition. To come to life, it needed to be performed and distributed.

Kit Lambert loved chaos. He thought it the ideal creative atmosphere. So he turned the Eaton Square flat into a genuine madhouse.

"One feature of the group's headquarters . . . was an accountant slowly going demented as the bills piled up and the money didn't," wrote Moon's friend Ray Tolliday, soon to become a Who/New Action assistant himself.

"The office-cum-flat generally looked as though Oscar Madison lived there, and droves of people drifted in and out, reporting parking tickets and stolen gear. Chris Stamp's East End accent grew so affected that in the end, nobody could understand him, and he threatened to go and make films in Red China for nothing. People sat through the night sticking felt pop-art cutouts onto T-shirts with offensive-smelling glue . . . while Lambert hung onto sanity with the help of Wagner and the occasional shock of setting his bed and himself on fire."

"Kit and Chris were really hard-working wheelers and dealers in those days. It was incredible, really," said Townshend. What was most incredible in those late months of 1964 was keeping the organization together at all.

"If we'd gone down then," Daltrey claimed, "we would have faced a debt of sixty thousand pounds [$168,000]. We were getting fifty quid [$140] a night, and Pete was smashing guitars worth two hundred pounds [$560] and amps worth twice that. It took us three years to pay off those debts."

At the time, it seemed very likely that the bills would never be paid and that the whole operation would simply blow up in Lambert's face. Naturally, their savior turned out to be a lowly and unlikely character.

Kit went through legions of assistants, secretaries, receptionists. Few could cope with his "work methods"; Irish Jack remembers one actually quitting because she could no longer endure Daltrey cursing on the telephone. But Kit did find an invaluable aide in a woman named Anya Butler.

Anya Butler's best friend was married to Shel Talmy, an American record producer who had recently emigrated to England. One of Talmy's first signings was the Kinks, and his first two singles with them, "You Really Got Me" and "All Day and All of the Night," were both international smashes toward the end of 1964.

The Kinks and the Who knew each other, although the Kinks were from much farther north, in Muswell Hill. The Kinks played the same ballroom circuit as the Who, and the Who actually opened for them on the Sunday concert tour. "They were a bit before us," Townshend said. "I remember first seeing them and thinking how ridiculous they looked in their silly caps, red coats and kinky boots, they were so old-fashioned. 'You Really Got Me' was a great record, though."

The Kinks' ruffled shirts and red hunting coats were nowhere near as hip as the Who's garb. But the Kinks had unignorable musical virtues. Even though Davies's early songs were simply built around slight variations of the basic "Louie Louie" riff, the group was probably the first to sing with genuinely cockney accents. And the Kinks' "Louie Louie" variations were special, the guitar more raunchy than any previous version, distorted and dirty, and Ray Davies's vocals absolutely leering in their sensuality.

Moon described the Kinks as "one of the major influences on us. There's a lot of the Kinks' style in the Who . . . the chords. We used to nick a lot of things from bands around, and when Pete wrote ['I Can't Explain'], there was a lot of Ray Davies in there."

John Entwistle went further. "Townshend wrote 'I Can't Explain' as an answer to 'You Really Got Me,' " he told Roy Carr. Even Townshend has allowed that it's "kind of a lift off the feeling the Kinks had in 'You Really Got Me.' "

No one's ever mentioned whether Townshend was consciously trying to get Shel Talmy's attention. In any event, "I Can't Explain" is pure "Louie Louie," even more brash and arrogant than the Kinks, Davies's leer replaced with Daltrey's sneer. If Townshend was looking to catch Talmy's ear, he did a hell of a good job.

It was left up to Mike Shaw to actually play the "I Can't Explain" demo to Shel Talmy—over the telephone. "He liked it," said Shaw. "And then it all got going from there."

Shel Talmy was born in Chicago and grew up elsewhere in Illinois. He moved to Los Angeles to attend UCLA, graduated and went looking for work in show business, first landing a job as a network TV page, then became a recording engineer as a result of hanging around recording studios. Talmy sometimes worked with Nik Venet, the Capitol Records A&R man who had signed the Beach Boys and produced their early records. Venet and Talmy became close enough so that when Talmy decided to go to England, Venet told him who to approach at Decca Records' London office and gave him a batch of acetates that he permitted Talmy to claim as his own work, though Venet had actually cut them himself. Since the acetates included songs by the Beach Boys and Lou Rawls, Talmy was quickly hired as a Decca house producer. He spent the next few months making records with the likes of the Orchids (a Liverpudlian girl group) and Helmut Gorden's favorites, the Bachelors.

Ray Davies wrote a song ("I Got a Feeling") for the Orchids, and in late 1963 Talmy began working with Davies's band, then called the Ravens. When the

Kinks' records hit the charts, Talmy's immediate future was secured. He took an office in Soho's Greek Street, which is where Anya Butler and Mike Shaw contacted him.

"Kit, at that time, I believe, came straight out of some sort of theatre situation," Talmy told *Record World* in 1974. "The Who was his first venture into the pop business. He was looking for a deal for the group. Annie said she'd like me to see them, so I went down to some hall in Shepherd's Bush or thereabouts."

"They were the first band I'd heard in England who sounded like an American rock & roll band," Talmy said. "Funky. They were loud, raw, but they had balls. At that point in time, that was the most difficult thing to find, a really ballsy band. I loved them the moment I heard them, and I said, 'Let's do it.' "

It wasn't quite that simple. Talmy loathed Lambert, and the feeling was mutual. From Talmy's point of view, "Lambert . . . was obviously unsure of himself, a trend followed by virtually any manager." But personality aside, the deal that Talmy made with the Who was virtually guaranteed to cause trouble.

"Kit made the first deal he'd ever made in show business, a deal which was really pathetic, like one-half percent or something," said Townshend. The deal wasn't quite that awful, but it was bad enough: 2½ per cent of the retail price, quite low even by 1964 standards. (A more typical royalty was 4 to 6 percent.)

The basic reason that it was so low was that the Who were not signed to a record label—they were signed to Shel Talmy's production company, which would place their finished master tapes with a label. Talmy would make his money on the difference between the record label's royalty and what he had to pay the group. At that 2½ percent rate, he would probably rake off at least an amount equivalent to the Who's share, and without four band members and two managers to split it with.

Talmy hoped to build the kind of entrepreneurial empire such contemporary producers as Phil Spector and Jerry Leiber and Mike Stoller had created. He would have full creative autonomy, a much larger than usual share of profits and a substantial power base, with leverage over both the companies (which needed the producer's creative skills) and the acts (which needed the producer's access to manufacturing and distribution). From this point of view, it was the producer's responsibility to make the records, and his was the credit due when they were hits.

It's extremely difficult to judge such business practices from the vantage point of twenty years later. In terms of the development of the record business, that's an eon. In 1964, almost no one thought of long-term careers for rock groups. As Entwistle once said, "When we started, you had to release a single every three months to stay in the public eye. Whichever came first, your marriage or your twenty-first birthday, was the end of it all."

Probably, Lambert and Stamp simply hoped to pick up the action by getting any kind of record success so that they could cash in with follow-up hits, profitable tours and, inevitably, the Movie. In the British rock business, this was the conventional career pattern in those years. Unfortunately, it had disastrous

Above: *"Call Me Lightning." The Who, 1967. Left to right: John Entwistle, Keith Moon, Roger Daltrey, Pete Townshend.* (Tom Wright/Pete Townshend).

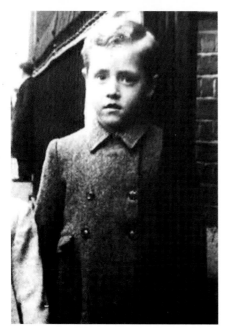

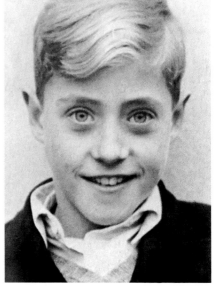

Top left: *One of the first photographs of baby Pete Townshend on the shoulders of his dad, Cliff,* and right *as a toddler, Pete travelled everywhere with his singer mum and saxophonist dad.* (Pete Townshend/Betty Townshend).

Bottom left: *As a toddler, Roger Daltrey lived with his mum and dad in Shepherd's Bush,* and right *aged nine years, Roger was already top of his class at Victoria Primary School. His musical talent was discovered by his mum when he was thirteen.* (Irene Daltrey).

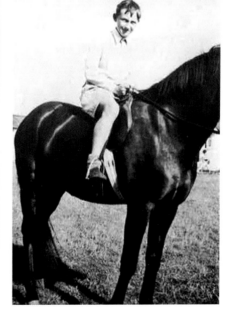

Top left: *Baby Keith Moon in his first studio photograph* and right *Keith as a page boy. Even at an early age Keith had a deep-rooted desire to make others smile at him. His musical talent was demonstrated when he first played the bugle in the Sea Cadets.* (Mrs. Moon).

Bottom left: *John Entwistle aged about five on holiday at the seaside. His musical interests were displayed by the age of three and* right *by the age of seven, John had already started to learn the piano.* ('Queenie' Johns).

Top: *The Detours on stage, 1963. Left to right: Pete Townshend, John Entwistle, Colin Dawson, Doug Sandom, Roger Daltrey.* (Trinifold). Bottom: *The Detours changed their name to the Who. The original line-up: John, Doug Sandom, Roger and Pete.* (Irene Daltrey).

Above: *Creating the "Shepherd's Bush" sound. John (left) worked in the Tax Office during the day and Pete (right) went to Art School, but they both played in the band five or six nights a week.* (Trinifold).

Top: *Enter mod publicist Pete Meaden and exit Doug Sandom. "When we're hip, we gotta dress hip and we're gonna be called the High Numbers."* (Trinifold). Bottom: *The High Numbers at the Scene Club, July, 1964. "The very air suggested a police raid at any minute."* (T. Spenser/Colorific).

Above: *The High Numbers, as mods, pose for publicity photographs.* (*Fabulous* Magazine).

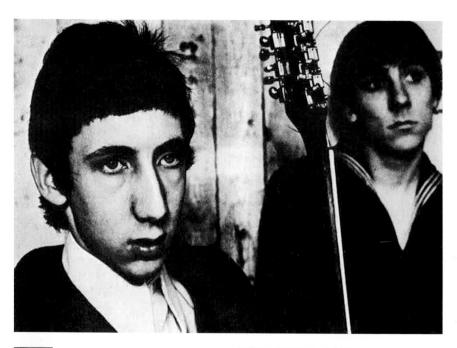

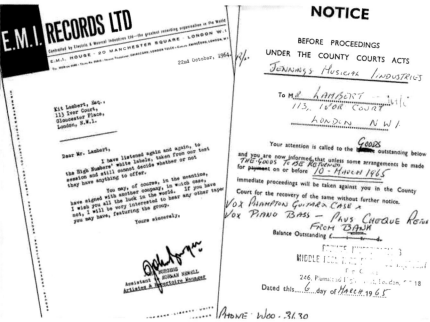

Top: *"Nobody ever said 'You're in'. They just said 'What're you doing Monday?'."*—*Keith Moon.* (Trinifold). Bottom: *The High Numbers' rejection letter from EMI Records.*

Top: *The Marquee poster, commissioned by Kit Lambert, became a logo for the group.* "We were playing a lot of Bo Diddley, Chuck Berry, Elmore James, B.B. King. And they are maximum R & B."—Keith Moon. (Trinifold). Bottom: *The Who appear on television's 'Ready, Steady, Go!' on New Year's Eve, 1965, shortly after the release of their album* My Generation. (Popperfoto).

Above and opposite: *The Pop Art Sound. Kit Lambert called them "the first Pop Art band". The Who stood firmly for Pop Art, which meant how they behaved and dressed both on and offstage. "We don't change offstage; we live Pop Art."*—Pete Townshend. (Trinifold).

Top: *Pete with his art school girlfriend, Karen Astley in 1966.* (Chris Morphet). Bottom: *Destruction became a regular part of the act.* "*Someone would come up and say, 'Well, why did you do it?' And the thing about auto-destruction is that it has no purpose, no reason at all.*"—Pete Townshend. (Trinifold).

Above: *By 1966 the group was designing its own performance wardrobe with graphic inventiveness. "[Mod] was about fashion, but that doesn't mean it was superficial. Fashion, in a sense, is a description of events after the fact. And the mods had a great taste in music."* —Pete Townshend. (Trinifold).

Top: *The Who recording a promotional film for "I'm A Boy", London, 1966.* (Pictorial Press). Bottom: *Pete Townshend with one of his managers, Chris Stamp. "Kit and Chris were just a bit older than the band, but so smooth they assumed immediate authority. They were the kind of suave hipsters from which mod had developed."* (Chris Morphet).

Above: *John and Pete with "Ready, Steady, Go!" television presenter Cathy McGowan, 1966.* (Trinifold).

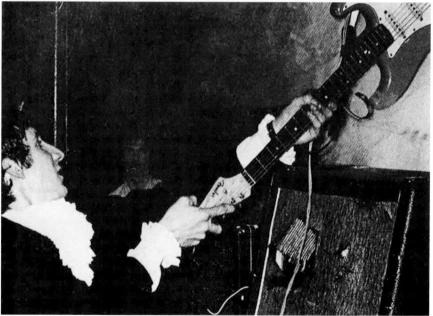

Top and bottom: *"When Pete smashed his guitar it was because he was pissed off. When I smashed me drums, it was because I was pissed off. We were frustrated. You're working as hard as you can to get that song across, to get the audience by the balls, to make it an event. When you've done all that, when you've worked your balls off and given the audience all you can give and they don't give anything back, that's when the fucking instruments go."—Keith Moon.* (Pete Townshend/ Chris Morphet).

long-term financial consequences for every act caught up in it, including the Beatles and the Rolling Stones.

All of this is hindsight. No one caught up in the pressures of the time could have predicted that a band like the Who was embarking on a twenty-year career. It is *not* unfair, however, to say that Lambert and Stamp made a deal that was poor even by contemporary standards. But had you told this to them or the band, they might well have scoffed. What lay ahead was only success— all that was needed was the right record, and the Who was ready to make it. And they were right. Success was next on the agenda.

Talmy and the Who went into Pye Studios in London in January 1965. The number was basically worked out before they got to Pye, though Talmy told *Record World* that when he first heard "I Can't Explain," "It lasted about a minute and thirty seconds. I rearranged the whole thing and added a couple of choruses . . . the Ivy League was on backing vocals."

It wasn't only the Ivy League (a pop singing trio) that Talmy planned to use to supplement the group. Entwistle told Roy Carr that when the group arrived at Pye, they found themselves "outnumbered" by session people. "Talmy didn't like our backing vocals, so he dragged in the Ivy League. Likewise, he was a little unsure of Townshend's ability as a lead guitarist—hence Jimmy Page."

Though he was only a couple of years older than Townshend, Page was already a legendary British rock guitarist. Pete recalled, "I first saw Jimmy Page when I was fourteen or fifteen and he was already in a professional band at sixteen, earning thirty pounds a week, playing really fast stuff."

Page was an anonymous force in many of the best British records of the period—including the early Kinks hits, according to some sources. "Talmy kept Jimmy Page permanently on hold, just in case a group guitarist didn't cut the mustard," Roy Carr wrote. "Likewise, he often kept a drummer and other spare parts in reserve." (Entwistle adds: "I'm quite certain that if Talmy could have pulled it off, he'd have brought in Clem Cattini to play drums instead of Moon.")

Townshend summarized the situation: "Shel Talmy . . . was a great believer in making groups who were nothing into stars. He was also a great believer in pretending the group didn't exist when they were in a recording studio. Despite the fact that . . . our first few records are among our best, they were the least fun to make."

As far as Pete was concerned, Talmy made the Who "part of a machine—a pop-record-churning-out type machine, a big package. At the same time, I don't want to belittle [Talmy] too much, because he's part of the old school."

At the time, it was quite common for rock bands to use session men such as Page in place of the actual group members for recordings. The choice was usually the prerogative of the record producer. Townshend had leverage, however. To acquire the ringing tone that made his version of the "Louie Louie" riff so much more expansive than the Kinks', the proper equipment was needed. Jimmy Page did not have a twelve-string Rickenbacker, and Pete was not about to loan his. So Townshend did the solos, with Page strumming along as rhythm guitarist.

Page and Talmy had their revenge on the B-side, which was a song Talmy wrote called "Bald Headed Woman." (The Kinks also recorded this song on one of their albums; in those days it was not unusual for a producer to attempt to earn some extra royalty money by placing a song he'd written on the B-side of a potential hit.) "Bald Headed Woman" was harmonica-driven blues (the harmonica part may have been contributed by Paul Jones of Manfred Mann), but it had an unusual guitar riff that required a fuzztone effects box, which Townshend didn't own. Jimmy Page had one, so he ended up playing lead guitar on a Who single after all.

Talmy's engineer was Glyn Johns. Johns, a couple of years older than Daltrey, had been friendly with the Who since their Detours days (when Glyn had been a sometime singer and band manager with a group called the Presidents). Glyn started engineering in 1959, working on some records by Marty Wilde, one of Larry Parnes's more successful protégés, but he came into his own at the beginning of British beat, recording sides by the Rolling Stones and Georgie Fame. (It was Glyn who introduced Townshend to the Stones.)

By 1965, Johns had established himself as Britain's premier recording engineer because he was one of the few technicians who grasped the technical objectives of rock recording. Johns could be extremely haughty, but Shel Talmy found him entirely compatible and used him whenever possible on all his sessions.

"Shel Talmy's forte was definitely finding artists and selecting material, and as far as producing a record's concerned, he had a pretty good method, too," Johns said. "I don't think he was brilliant as a producer, [but] within a year of arriving in England, he'd picked a lot of really successful acts and made some great records."

Johns said that the Who sessions were initially fairly free of tension. "The band were unusual to record, because they were loud. No recording technique had been developed to record anything that loud. It wasn't just Moon, it was everything. You just had to think again, really."

Townshend perhaps found Talmy too passive (he later claimed that Talmy "was just sitting there and Glyn Johns, the engineer, was doing all the work"), or perhaps he was surprised that the sessions went by so quickly. "We got an hour to do a single," he remarked some years later. "I know it sounds daft now, but that's the way everybody used to work in those days." Nevertheless, the series of records that the Who made with Shel Talmy are technically among the best that the group ever did, and they have a distinct, original sound.

When Talmy first saw the group, they were still doing cover material, mostly blues and R&B numbers (such as "I'm a Man"). Daltrey says they decided to make "I Can't Explain" their first single because it was the only original song that they had. "What I thought we had to do was get away from covers and into their own songs," Talmy said. "I wanted them to have their own sound and not copy everybody else. Even at that point, the big bread was in America and not in England, and I was intent on getting records that were going to sell in America and not in England. I wanted to sell records in England, but the big bucks were in America."

Given their unique lineup, there was little chance of the Who "sounding like everybody else." Talmy really meant that he wanted to impose *his* sound on them, making records that resembled his other hits as much as possible. This is one reason that Townshend's charge that Talmy was passive doesn't make sense.

In any event, the music they made was thoroughly amazing. It established the Who not only as a group capable of making hits but as one that had the potential to redefine some of the most fundamental rock concepts.

"I Can't Explain" is a slight song with a lyric on the edge of moony adolescent cliché, but as a recorded performance, it remains one of the outstanding documents of rock & roll. The sound is sharp, percussive, electric as a live wire. Voices ricochet off rim shots, bass lines throb beneath guitar static. Roles are reversed: Moon's drums take short, shotgun solos, functioning similarly to conventional lead guitar. Townshend's guitar punches out its notes as if he's playing drum fills.

Daltrey *slurs* the vocals, in striking contrast to both the taut accents of the instruments and the precise punctuation of the Ivy League's chorus. Through this slur, often unintelligible, Daltrey transforms the character of the lyric from a moonstruck kid to a glaring, hostile mod whose inarticulate state is a source of rage and frustration.

In their *New Musical Express* "Who Consumer Guide," Roy Carr and Charles Shaar-Murray describe "I Can't Explain" as "a natural fusion of the Kinks' original heavy metal riff with the block[ed] harmonies of California's sunkist Beach Boys." If that were all it were, "I Can't Explain" would be an amusing, intriguing record. What made it more was not Townshend's writing, which was fine, or Daltrey's vocal, which made of the writing an entirely different and deeper thing, but the playing of Keith Moon.

"Moon was incredible," Talmy said. "He could do things with drums that probably haven't been done since. He was a great drummer. Complete nutcase, but a great drummer."

That's an utterly accurate assessment, which needs to be modified only by adding that Moon's nuttiness was intertwined completely with his brilliance as a musician, the same panache and fearless front which allowed him to pull off so many unlikely stunts carrying through into his cool, precise but dementedly imaginative playing. Listen to the end of the second verse of "I Can't Explain": "I know what it means/But . . ." Daltrey sings, and he pauses, the music fades away and in a twinkling come six sharp shots "hard as two cracks from a rifle," Greil Marcus wrote of them) before Daltrey finishes the line.

What Moon adds here is what he would always add: suspense. He was not only a drummer with amazing rhythmic ability and endless imagination, he understood each song that the Who played and got inside it, peeling and prying until he cracked it open. If Daltrey's vocal takes Townshend's lyrics to a higher level, Moon's drumming does the same for his music. The solo you remember in this record is not Townshend's, which is a rather humorous, trashy comment on all "Louie Louie" solos, but the solo Moon *seizes*, the one he plays throughout the entire song, bursting through at every seam in the song's structure. This isn't vanity or egotism. Moon doesn't clutter the song, he simply propels it into a new dimension and in the process invents an entirely new approach to rock & roll drumming.

"I Can't Explain" was not only a breakthrough record, an extremely unusual and immensely powerful song; it was an exceptional expression of the mod ethos, not because Townshend was reaching for some kind of statement but because he was acting one out. As John Swenson wrote, it expressed "a wonder at life and a frustration at the inability to rationalize and understand that wonder." That is a fair summary of the mod outlook—and one of the central themes of Pete Townshend's writing for the next twenty years.

13

*I don't see any career ahead. That's why
I like it—it makes you feel young, feeding
on insecurity. If you are insecure, you are
secure in your insecurity. I still don't
know what I'm going to do.*

—Pete Townshend

Having made such a remarkable recording, Talmy now had to go out and sell it, something he apparently hadn't tried to do beforehand. Talmy went not to English Decca, with whom he had a relationship, but to Decca's American subsidiary, a completely different entity with no foothold in the renewed rock market.

"I went out to sell the first single because nobody else was doing it, so I figured to do it myself," Talmy said. "I took them into Decca-America. The youngest guy there was sixty-three. 'I don't understand this' [they said]. I said, 'I don't care if you understand it or not, do you think you can sell it?' So they took a gamble."

American Decca was the record's principal backer, Talmy said, "but of course we had a deal with Decca over here, who didn't like it, because they had to put the record out here under the American deal." In England the Who were released on Brunswick, which was the label English Decca used for American acts. U.K. Decca was unhappy, because if this native group (or recording) were really any good, then the hometown label should have snapped it up.

"If I recall correctly, there was originally very little enthusiasm within the English Decca group for 'I Can't Explain,' " Tony Hall, Decca's promotion manager, told *Record World*. "It was just another of some twenty releases that particular week. I remember Kit's frustrations vividly. I think he came into my office and made me promise to really 'live' with the record over the weekend and to give him an honest opinion on the Monday. This I did, and I came in on the Monday morning convinced that with sufficient exposure, this was a smash hit. I then rushed into every department at Decca and managed to get them equally excited."

Now Lambert and Stamp really went to work. Even Talmy had to admit that "Kit and Chris did a very good job here." "I Can't Explain" was released on January 15, 1965, only a few days after it was recorded. (That same day, John Entwistle finally quit his job with Inland Revenue, making him the last band member to leave his day job.) The song entered the charts that week at number 47 (of Britain's Top 50) but quickly dropped off after peaking at number 25.

The song had strong sales in parts of London but lacked radio and TV exposure. Of the two, radio was probably more important, at least at first, because it went on all day and all night, at least on the pirate channels. "When a single of ours got on the pirates playing list, it sold copies," Townshend said.

Pirate radio was not exactly pop paradise: The station identification jingles and too many of the commercials were copied directly from the most brash and garish clichés of American Top 40 radio, and far from being deeply committed to rock music, the stations programmed for a mainstream audience.

"The pirate radio system wasn't really perfect. The format methods used by all of them were easy to rig, and one could buy time for any record on the air," Townshend wrote several years later. He was referring not only to practices of payola but to the habit (not uncommon in Europe) of labels and promoters actually buying time on a station to play a disc. Chart-rigging was a matter of knowing both which palms to grease and which shops were surveyed for sales figures. A few purchases in the right stores were better than bribery.

"The most endearing thing about pirate radio was the fact that you could mark all the stations on the dial of your radio (at one time there were about six you could hear clearly in London) and turn off bloody Ken Dodd and listen to a good down-home Who record if you fancied. When the Who record finished and the new station played Ken Dodd, you could switch him off yet again and possibly even find the Who again somewhere," Pete wrote. Such diversity, however commercially effective, was a complete contradiction of the tight state control that prevailed in almost all areas of European cultural life. Even though it reflected only marketplace values, pirate radio was too radical a concept to last, though it was also too liberating for its effect to vanish. At the beginning of 1965, outlaw stations were at the peak of their power, possibly the most influential factor in the marketing of British pop.

British TV was also undergoing a pop explosion, spearheaded by ITV's "Ready! Steady! Go!" and featuring such other pop-oriented programs as "Beat Room," "That's For Me," "Thank Your Lucky Stars" and the BBC's then-new "RSG" challenger, "Top of the Pops."

By far the most important of these was "Ready! Steady! Go!" which ITV had premiered in August 1963. "RSG" was designed as the sixties answer to the best British pop show of the fifties, Jack Good's "Oh Boy." It was blessed with a unique staff: producer Vicki Wickham, director Michael Lindsay-Hogg and host Cathy McGowan (who split her chores with a succession of male sidekicks), all of them quite young, all serious about their pop music tastes.

"We'd stick to a very rigid booking formula of only using artists we liked," Vicki Wickham said. "Now that I think about it, this was incredibly pretentious of us—but it worked and made 'Ready! Steady! Go!' the unique pop art show it was, shaped the careers of a heap of acts." Among those who got their start on "RSG" were the Rolling Stones, Dusty Springfield, the Animals, the Kinks, the Moody Blues and, a bit later, Jimi Hendrix. Additionally, the show also featured a great deal of American rhythm & blues and soul, including Stevie Wonder, James Brown and Ike and Tina Turner. As a result, it became a mod must— when the show came on, at 6:07 P.M., using a hit such as Manfred Mann's "5-4-3-2-1" for its opening theme, the weekend had officially begun.

"I was walking down Brewer Street [in Soho] about six months after the show started and saw Pete Meaden with a pile of the High Numbers' new single, 'I'm the Face,' under his arm," Wickham remembered. "We stopped and chatted and he told me how the record was going to be a hit, and I told him I didn't think so and that I really didn't like it 'cause I thought the group was just trying to cash in on the mod-rocker trend and it was dated already and that in my opinion he should forget about the High Numbers and find another group."

Lambert and Stamp took a more prudent approach, for once. They didn't just send "RSG" the Who record and tell them that the group was great, they invited Wickham and Lindsay-Hogg to join the mod elite Tuesday evening at the Marquee. Wickham had already heard (and liked) "I Can't Explain," and she was happy to join the 600 sweaty souls who packed the Marquee. (The "RSG" crew, interestingly enough, had originally guessed that the Who was an American group, since the record had been released through Brunswick.) In due course, Vicki Wickham became a Marquee regular and the Who were booked for "RSG."

Meanwhile, Lambert and Stamp took their Who promo film, made for £350 (around $975) and sold it to "That's for Me" for £25 ($70). Then they arranged the group's first live TV appearance, on "Beat Room." The group would simply come out and mime to its record, but Lambert and Stamp were confident that if the Who were presented visually, they'd sell.

John Entwistle remembered that first live television experience vividly. "We went all the way through a camera rehearsal, did a run-through and everything, but I only got shown in one long shot at the very end," recalled the ordinarily taciturn bassist. "So I picked up my bag and walked out of the studio, closely followed by my manager, who was pleading with me to come back. I did, we did the show and it turned out exactly the same—except the camera didn't pull back enough for that final long shot. I wasn't in it at all." Entwistle said he vowed then that he would never let it happen again; and though he never has walked out, it's been close a few times.

For Roger Daltrey, on the other hand, making TV appearances was certifiable evidence that the Who was on the cusp of making it really big. "That's why 'I Can't Explain' was so good. It gave people listening all over the country an idea who we were, it was different—not completely original but a different sound. And it gave us the chance to get our ugly mugs on the box."

But neither "That's for Me" nor "Beat Room" had enough clout to establish a hit; and the record still meant nothing in the provinces. Thus, the "Ready! Steady! Go!" booking came just when the band's fortunes needed a boost. As Nik Cohn wrote, "If 'I Can't Explain' had flopped, the entire Who crusade would very likely have collapsed before it had even got properly started."

Lambert racked his brain to ensure the band's success on "RSG." Finally, he decided to recruit the 100 Faces for an assault on the ITV studio in Wembley.

"He got as many of these people as he could to go to the show, and we bought them all scarves," said Mike Shaw.

"On the day of the show," Wickham said, "suddenly hundreds of Who fans started appearing and besieging the building, all firmly equipped with Who scarves and pop art jerseys and all looking like leftovers from St. Trinians. Somehow, they all squeezed in the studio, and the show was a phenomenal success."

Lambert had coached the kids on what to do, Shaw said. "They'd all been sort of primed that as soon as the Who finished their number, they'd throw all these scarves up in the air, anywhere—throw them at the group, throw them at the cameras, throw them everywhere, cause a rumpus, go mad. And that's what they did. It shook everyone.

"It was a live show, so it's well alive. All through the program, they're cool and polite, and all of a sudden, there's this mad crowd throwing things at everybody."

The following week's *New Musical Express* chart (dated March 7, 1965) showed "I Can't Explain" once again, this time at number 23. The record had captured the imagination of mod-infatuated kids across the country—and without sacrificing the group's power base in London.

"When the record hit the charts," claimed Nik Cohn, "Kit lost his cool completely, went berserk and ran wildly around the streets screaming: 'We've cracked it, you bastards, we've cracked it!' " An apocryphal story, no doubt, but it surely captures the emotions felt by not only Lambert but Stamp and the band, too.

The incident did a bit of good for "Ready! Steady! Go!" as well, giving it genuine cachet as the one place in broadcasting where *anything* could be expected to happen.

"Of all the groups on 'Ready! Steady! Go!' the Who most typified what the show was all about," said Wickham. " 'RSG' was instant pop music. It was every trend before it happened, and things came and went super fast. It was about youth and their dreams and aspirations and had nothing to do with thinking about tomorrow. . . . The Who was all of that."

"That was rock television at its best," Townshend wrote, referring to the "insanity and abandon" of the program. "Most of the time was spent fighting to get American artists on the show. It was the only one in the world I've ever seen that managed a balance between either side of the ocean."

As the place where mod met its broadest audience, "Ready, Steady, Go!" needed the standard-bearers of the scene. So the Who became semi-regulars on a national show just at a time when London was beginning to outgrow mod.

One of the reasons that the Who loved to play "RSG" so much was the incredible chances that Lindsay-Hogg took in directing it. "Michael would do incredible things with the lights and the direction on them, using some of the first and fastest intercutting between four cameras ever used on English TV— and the best, 'cause it fitted in so perfectly with the excitement and energy of the group," said Wickham.

"When I started showing off a bit, the directors would notice," said Moon. "There were two great directors, Michael Lindsay-Hogg and Mike Mansfield, and they started getting the camera on the drums. 'Ready! Steady! Go!' and 'Top of the Pops' really treated the band as a whole. . . . Most of the TV in those days was only a couple of cameras, one trained on the front of the singer and the other getting a side shot of the singer, and they never bothered with the rest of the group. They were always there as part of the furniture.

"It wasn't until Townshend started smashing guitars and I started smashing up the drums that the producers of the shows began to realize that there was more than the singer in a band. They'd actually line up a camera for the drums, which was a first. People started to actually notice the drummer."

Well, that one was pretty hard to ignore.

The journey up the charts of "I Can't Explain" was anything but smooth— herky-jerky would be a better description for its fitful passage to the Top 10. At any number of points, the record might have stalled, but Lambert and Stamp refused to slack off. Their big break came when the Who were asked to fill in as a last-minute replacement in "Tip for the Top," a segment of "Top of the Pops." (It is not insignificant that no one can seem to recall the band they replaced.)

"Top of the Pops" was based primarily on music that was already in the BBC sales charts (and thus played on the radio, and thus familiar). It cut a much broader swath through the marketplace than "RSG," and that was its aim. For selling records, this was more ideal than the elite format of "RSG," though the show wasn't nearly as much fun.

"In those days," Townshend remembered, "it was sent out live from Manchester; the studio was a converted church. In those days, we had to mime to our record, thus, it was a cinch. No worries about throats or atmosphere or getting in tune, just about what color pants to wear or what silly outfit to put on to attract the camera's attention.

"Keith would get about eighty percent of the camera time simply because the director was convinced that it was a drummer-led group. Every time the camera swung to me, I would swing my arm like a maniac, and as soon as I did, the camera would go off."

The "Tip for the Top" spot was always effective. After the Who's appearance, "I Can't Explain" climbed the chart to number 8.

"I Can't Explain" sold 104,000 copies. That represented a gross (from retailers) of £35,000 (over $96,000). Of this amount, Decca got £16,000 ($45,000) as distributor and taxes took another £5,000 ($14,000). The Who, who were on a 2½ percent royalty, received just £1,000 ($2,800). And remember, Lambert and Stamp were entitled to the first £400—40 percent, or about $1,000—under their management agreement, leaving the band to split the remainder, or about 150 pounds ($400) per man. (Pete got slightly more than the other musicians, as songwriter of the A-side.) At this point, of course, Lambert and Stamp's percentage was insignificant compared to how much they had invested without recouping. They tried to correct the recording deal by renegotiating, a three-week battle that saw the band's royalty rise to a much more respectable 4 percent.

At least "I Can't Explain" kicked up national interest in the Who's stage act. Lambert and Stamp negotiated a deal with the Malcolm Rose Agency, which got the Who on a short package tour of Scotland; Kit put together a set of appearances at the Brighton Aquarium, and unlike his earlier promotions, these turned a profit and enhanced the band's mod mystique. Mod was fading in west London because it had become too pop, but the rest of the country was only beginning to catch on. For provincials, the shining symbol of mod— more than Lambrettas, Levi's or Carnaby Street itself—became the Who.

The Who now began to work in the press to reinforce and alter their image. There was a danger that they might become overidentified with mod. When that style faded, it could drag the group down with it. Townshend and Entwistle have both said that they expected to be in the charts for no more than one year but even then they knew it would have been stupid to sacrifice the group's potential to the mod cause.

Through the spring, the Who played live gigs and worked TV shows such as "Gadzooks!" and "Disc A Go Go." Their fortunes took a striking upturn when Paul McCartney told an interviewer, "The Who are the most exciting thing around."

By early summer, they were able to command a percentage of the gate as well as a guarantee. A typical engagement would be arranged for a £200 ($560) guarantee versus 60 percent of the gate. If the Who drew, say, 900 kids at 10 shillings ($1.40) each, they would then be paid £270 ($750)—presuming that they received an honest count from the promoter.

To thwart such potential chicanery (which many of that period's relatively fly-by-night promoters took for granted), the Who stationed road manager Mike Shaw at the door with a clicker counter. In this area, the band's touring tactics were quite sophisticated. It was all but unheard of to take such precautions in percentage bookings. Shaw also kept a detailed notebook in which he wrote down the location of each gig, its technical requirements, the money earned (or lost), crowd preferences and the relative enthusiasm of their response to the Who. "We built up a dossier of all the gigs in Britain," said Shaw, "so that we knew which ones to get rebooked at and which ones not to bother with." Partly as a result, the band drifted away from package shows, with their inherently frustrating ten minutes per act and comparatively low wages, toward one-nighters in which the band had more time to make its point and which paid more money.

Every penny was needed, because the "auto-destructive" stage show was running the group deeper and deeper into debt. "That was in the days when Pete was smashing cabinets," remembered Cyrano Langston, one of the group's earliest roadies. " 'I Can't Explain' had got them plenty of work—probably four or five nights a week. I'd get home from a gig somewhere up north—and I was working on my own for a good bit of the time when I was a roadie with them—and I'd get back about three or four in the morning. After packing the gear and driving the van home, I'd literally have to go straight to Marshall's, replace all the broken speakers and then drive to another gig somewhere else."

The destruction had to be real. "You can fake the amplifier quite easily," Townshend told Paul Nelson. "I mean, you can have a crap old amplifier on the stage, but then everyone knows its a crap old amplifier and what's the point of going up to an old cardboard box and kicking it around the stage? Somebody throws a cardboard box, and you say, 'Right, audience, now this cardboard box is really an amplifier.' And they go, 'Big deal.'

"The fact is that you've got to get the amplifier that they know the sound is coming out of. They wait for you. They say, 'That's the amplifier that the sound is coming out of. When will they kick *that*?' And when you kick it, then they're happy. Until you do, they're not. Also, you know, if you change the guitar at the end of the act, everyone gets very mad. You can't put on a special guitar for [the last number]."

While Townshend drove his guitar into his Union Jack-covered amplifiers every night, generally knocking them over, he smashed guitars much less frequently, since the amps were sturdier and simpler to repair. (Rickenbackers were quite fragile—that's why they broke in the first place.)

Kit Lambert had to learn the hard way. That summer, Ziggy Jackson of the Marquee promoted a pop music festival at Reading at which the Who were among the headliners. Kit invited reporter Virginia Ironside of the *Daily Mirror* to the gig, promising her a guitar-smashing story.

Townshend was reluctant to smash a guitar that afternoon, since he had no spare. But Lambert told him to go ahead. "I'll pay for it," he said.

The Who came to the conclusion of their short set. Townshend raised his guitar over his head and brought it crashing down, splintering it thoroughly. Unfortunately, Lambert and Ironside were still in the bar and missed it.

Lambert went back to the dressing room to hear the news. "You mean you really broke it?" he shrieked. Pete convinced him by showing him a guitar case filled with shards and fragments.

"You've smashed it to bits!" Lambert moaned.

"But that's what you told me to do," Townshend said, all innocence and bitterness. "It's what I've been doing."

"You're crazy!" Lambert shouted. "We can't afford this!"

Just then another voice piped up. "Oh, by the way, Kit," said Keith Moon with perfect nonchalance. "I've smashed me drums up, too."

But Lambert could not back off from his philosophy, which reigned behind everything the Who's management did. This was a mixture of equal parts bravado and camp, placing a great deal of emphasis on putting up a front, on the appearance of success.

Thus, no matter what the condition of the group's bank statements, Townshend continued to live in Belgravia, as did Lambert and Stamp. Everyone spent almost as heavily on clothing as on equipment. "The Who were incredibly exciting onstage, they were spendthrift and big-mouthed, they were just magnificent," wrote Nik Cohn. "Also, even though they were nobody's idea of handsome, they had glamour." Lambert said he wanted the band to be "choirboys committing mayhem," which required a very precise look. In addition, he was preparing to jettison mod, on the theory that the Who needed to be fashion trend-setters, not followers.

The financial pressures should have stymied them. At one point, Lambert and Stamp were kiting checks on three banks at once, even bouncing checks at gambling casinos, a very risky business. Often Lambert would take £100 to the Casanova Club, his favorite gambling spot, to see if he could turn it into £300. Sometimes he succeeded; more often he failed. Long before debt restructuring became commonplace for industry and third world governments, Lambert was using the idea to finance the Who's operations.

Sometimes his bluff went to ludicrous lengths. Simon Napier-Bell was filming a special that spring, "Ready! Steady! Go! Goes to Woburn Abbey." "Vicki Wickham said she'd heard this band called the Who. I phoned Kit and his partner, Chris Stamp, and there was an incredibly comic conversation in which he did a big-time thing of: 'Well, we're not sure we could do it, you know. We'd want fifty pounds [$140]. I said I had two hundred pounds [$560] in the budget, and they could have that for the appearance.

"We laughed about his hard-to-get attitude a lot later," continued Bell, who grew close to Lambert. "Lambert and Stamp said they were desperate for the part and would have done it for free, anyway."

To pull off this act, Lambert needed allies. He did not have any of the natural resources the personal manager of a recording star is expected to command. He was signed to Talmy's production company, but Talmy despised him. American Decca was three thousand miles away, and the Who's singles had not done well enough in the States to justify any financial commitments, anyhow. Brunswick, which should have been thrilled to be working with a Top 10 band, still felt saddled with the group.

That left the press. This included broadcasters like Vicki Wickham and Cathy McGowan of "RSG," Alan Freeman of the BBC's "Top of the Pops" (and occasional magazine articles) and Nick Jones of *Melody Maker*. As time went on and the rock critic began to evolve from the fan magazine journalist—while the Who were themselves evolving from pop band into something else—the band would encounter many sympathetic writers. Just then, though, their biggest advantage was the nature of the British pop press. The Who soon became seen as spokesmen for the entire younger generation, mostly because Townshend had a gift for pontification.

In 1965 there were three important British music weeklies. *Melody Maker*, the oldest and most established, was founded in the 1920s. It contained the most staid, comprehensive and responsible coverage. *New Musical Express*, which published the nation's most influential music charts, beginning about 1952, was a bit more progressive than *Melody Maker*. It focused more exclusively on pop. *NME* generally complemented *MM* more than they competed, probably because both were owned by the huge Fleet Street conglomerate, IPC, which also published *Disc Weekly* (later, *Disc* and *Music Echo*), the most teeny-bopper-oriented of the weeklies. All of these were tabloids, came out on Thursdays and had almost as much influence as radio.

A few glossy magazines were also crucial to image-building. The most significant were the mod-oriented *Rave* and *Fabulous*, designed to cash in on teen tastes not just in music but also in fashion, cosmetics and the like.

None of these magazines criticized the music intelligently; not one of them yet had any sort of analysis of why so many people responded so passionately to rock and its accoutrements. The operative presumption seemed to be that pop was a fad, something still destined to be outgrown and forgotten (or at any rate, put aside) when people reached "maturity." All the music papers were possessed of Fleet Street's disregard (not to say contempt) for fact. That doesn't mean that they favored introspection to reportage—they certainly didn't—but that they preferred good copy, no matter how outlandish, to the truth. The most sensational rubbish could be fed these publications either by a musician or by a correspondent, and it would be published without question—unless it was boring.

As younger writers found work on these papers and magazines, less disdain for the music was expressed between the lines. Someone like Nick Jones at least understood the importance of Moon's drumming, Townshend's experimentation with feedback and destruction, the Who's general appeal to the mod generation. On the other hand, nobody was around to instruct the new breed of writers in the importance of factual accuracy. The result was ludicrously fanciful writing but also a marvelous opportunity for people as imaginatively duplicitous as Townshend and Lambert. They could spin any fantasy and see it spring to life on the page, act out any scenario before a gullible reporter and see it written up with a straight face, offer any philosophical bullshit and see it lapped up, grist for the mill.

A classic example is the story that *Melody Maker* ran in its August 28, 1965, issue. Written from information compiled by Nick Jones and titled "The Price of Pop Art" (with the subhead: "Item One: £100 A Week for Clothes . . ."), the story purported to describe the expenditures of the group in a typical week of gigs, "spending what to most pop fans is a small fortune every week to maintain this image."

In this story, Townshend claimed to "own nine guitars, all on HP. Five of these cost one hundred and seventy pounds [$475] each, four of which are already smashed to bits." That might have been true, as might the other musical expenditures he listed (though even they were high). But it is unlikely that he actually bought a new £20 ($55) jacket every week. Nor could Moon have conceivably spent £100 ($280) per month on drumsticks. Nor was it "usual . . . for two or three of the boys to go to London's Carnaby Street and spend two hundred pounds in one visit" each month. (Nor can the argument be made that no one was meant to take such stories seriously—people *did* take stories about the bands that moved and inspired them seriously.)

The only reality that these articles served was to keep the journalist knee-deep in interesting copy, to keep the magazine filled for the publisher and the advertisers and to keep the audience in artificial awe of the income and expenditures of pop stars. And, of course, to enhance exactly those qualities that Nik Cohn used to define the Who: newness, reckless wealth, braggadocio, glamour. The net effect was to ensure that Townshend's analysis of the situation was and remained the truth: "If you're in a group, you can behave like a kid—and not only get away with it, but be encouraged.

"In the early days of the Who, we were tagged with gimmicks, and subsequently, it made me very gimmick-conscious," Townshend told Roy Carr of *NME* ten years later. Once the tall tales and confabulations have been defined as gimmicks, something fundamental has changed in the way in which the rock performer sees himself—and in the way in which he is seen by his audience and, ultimately, by the press.

By reducing his aspirations and achievements to one-dimensional qualities, by denying his boldest desires and most pressing fears, pumping up his wealth and concealing the fact that he was not making much more than glorified wages, the rock star betrayed not his fans or some abstract standard of journalistic evidence-gathering but his own long-term self-interest. By accepting deceit and cheating as a standard part of the pop process, the pop star set himself up to be eventually betrayed and deceived and swindled. Sooner or later everything would turn on him—even the press itself. As Townshend said, "There's nothing wrong with the press manufacturing things. We were slightly press manufactured, we were slightly manufactured by 'Ready! Steady! Go!' . . . You do get a bit press controlled. However, bands learn the knack of manipulating the press, and then the press suddenly decide they're not going to be manipulated anymore." As long as everyone was willing to accept those cynical terms there was no problem. But the time was not far off when those terms would change, and for the British bands who'd grown up in the old system, this presented many confusing situations, especially since they were then liable to be called to account for their deceptions.

So the press and the Who used one another. It would be silly to pretend that there were no long-range consequences, but it would be equally stupid to ignore the fact that in the spring and summer of 1965 the system worked enormously in favor of the Who, allowing them the space in which to stake out a public image.

If there was one publication that was as useful to the Who as "Ready! Steady! Go!" or the pirate broadcasters, it was *Fabulous*, which was smack in the middle of the post-Clacton commercialization of mod, selling hip images to the provinces. That did not necessarily mean that their writers were comfortable when confronted with hardcore mod, as Nancy Lewis found out on her first assignment to cover the Who—at the Goldhawk on a Friday night, no comfortable place for a woman.

"Chris Stamp sorta came up and said, 'Hi, I'm Kit's partner.' He was very boring and talked about this film he had just finished doing in Norway with Kirk Douglas," Lewis told John Swenson. "I just wanted to go home. Then the group came off and I did a very stimulating interview with them, asking: 'What are your likes and dislikes?' They were very nice and very young and did the interview totally straight. I had heard that Townshend was supposed to be strange, but not much had been written about them, so I didn't know enough to be scared."

Lewis certainly must have seen or heard something that made an impression. In her story she predicted that within six months the group would break up. "I didn't do it maliciously," she said. "They didn't seem to like each other very much and they were such different people, I just could never see them lasting."

The Who instinctively understood the need to establish distinct personae in post-Beatles rock (a lesson learned by too few bands). Their individual quirks were only effective if they added up to one fascinating whole, and the Who were fortunate that even Entwistle, the most normal musician in the bunch, seemed exotic in this context; since there was but one of him, he provided a background against which the eccentricity of the others could be judged.

"In interviews," wrote Nik Cohn, "Pete would be endlessly arrogant; Roger would pick his nose; John would refuse to say a word; Keith would rant on about getting rich. . . . Apart from John, all of them were variously ambitious, hard, tricky and, by most standards, outrageous."

But that was only part of it—each member's personality (or at least the public perception of it) was reinforced by the snide, disparaging comments the others made about him. "On most of our interviews, I don't say anything simply because Pete does all the flattering," Entwistle said. "How are we supposed to say anything? Pete writes and makes the demo discs of our new records, so obviously he answers that one [about new records]."

Both Moon and Daltrey were matter-of-fact about inter-group animosity. "We really have absolutely nothing in common apart from music," said Keith, and Daltrey agreed. "We're not mates at all," Roger said, although he seemed to think that this in part accounted for the positive musical results.

The nastiest of all was Pete Townshend. About Entwistle, he remained pretty charitable, but then, Entwistle was no challenge to Pete's dominance. Of Moon, Pete said, "He used to be a lot of fun. Unfortunately, he's turning into a little old man. It's a shame. He used to be young and unaffected by pop music, but now he is obsessed with money. I still like him, and I don't really care what he thinks of me."

Townshend at least said that Moon was the "only drummer in England" who he was interested in playing with. About Daltrey, he was unremittingly vicious. "Roger is not a very good singer at all in my opinion," Townshend told *Disc*. "He has got a good act, but I think he expects a backing group more than an integrated group. I don't think he will ever understand that he will never have the Who as a backing group."

At this stage the Who was one long series of faction fights. All the others were down on Daltrey, because Roger never really picked up on amphetamines at a time when Townshend and Moon couldn't gobble enough of the stuff. Roger and John were both driven somewhat crazy by Moon's undisciplined playing. Townshend's arrogance was held in contempt by Moon and Entwistle.

If the pop music world at that time could be compared to a neighborhood, then the Who were the one family in every block who simply cannot keep their squabbles private, who make a mess that dangles out of the windows and into the yard and who unashamedly tangle with one another publicly in ways that mortify the neighbors. The Beatles might have argued among themselves as much as the Who, but they were discreet. The Stones were scruffier by far, but their very essence was never losing their cool. The Who battled it out right in public.

Keith Altham, then working for *Fabulous* and known (with a straight face) as *Fab*'s Keith, described the Who as "the first of the emergent rock & roll football teams"—along with the Yardbirds and the Animals. "They were not geared for making young girls wet their knickers," said Altham, noting that in 1965 the normal pop band's audience was 80 percent female. "The great asset to the guys was that we all considered ourselves to be *far* better-looking than Pete Townshend."

But *Fabulous*, like most teen-oriented magazines of the day, was heavily oriented to girls, and so Altham's principal assignment with the Who was to cover Keith Moon, "the only one who fit the pop 'Identikit.' All the teen magazines wanted to do the pretty one, and he was the one who kinda looked like Paul McCartney's kid brother."

Altham had already seen the band at the Marquee, "and watched with considerable trepidation while this maniac whirled his guitar around about six inches from my nose and appeared intent upon committing a sort of version of the Texas Chainsaw Massacre with an electric guitar upon the audience.

"I suppose I was intrigued," he continued, "though I wasn't particularly impressed with the music. I just thought they were too crazy to miss." So he set up an interview with Keith, around the corner from the house in Wembley, where Keith still lived with his parents. Moon never turned up, despite an increasingly hysterical series of telephoned excuses. "Needless to say, I was considerably mortified with him," Altham said, but he needed the copy, so he set up an interview with Moon for the next Friday evening.

"So I went to 'Ready! Steady! Go!' and sat at a table in the canteen," Altham remembered with a shudder of glee. "Moon finally emerged from the backstage area looking somewhat dishevelled, with an Adidas sports bag in his hand.

"He marched into the room with that sort of manic gleam in his eye, banged the bag down on the table, said, 'Keef? I'm Keef,' and proceeded to dig into the bag and bring out an *axe*, which he banged down on the table."

Altham stared at the axe. He took a deep breath, screwed up his courage and asked: "What's that for?"

"That's for Roger," said Moon lethally. "You 'aven't seen 'im, 'ave you?"

The chief characteristic of fashion is to impose and suddenly to accept as a new rule or norm what was, until a minute before, an exception or whim, then to abandon it again after it has become a commonplace, everybody's "thing."
　　　　　—Renato Poggioli,
　　　The Theory of the Avant-Garde

[Mod] was about fashion, but that doesn't mean it was superficial. Fashion, in a sense, is a description of events after the fact. And the mods had great taste in music.
　　　　　—Pete Townshend

Among the reasons that the Who made such attractive copy for the pop magazines was its constant graphic inventiveness. By mid-1965, the group was designing its own performance wardrobe. Townshend had been draping his amplifiers with a Union Jack, but it was in the spring that John Entwistle came up with the idea of having a jacket tailored from flag cloth. Pete got one, too.

Entwistle was the band's least likely fashion pioneer, but he set off another craze when he began decorating jackets with old military insignia and medals that he bought at flea markets.

Keith Moon effected target T-shirts—ordinary cotton T-shirts with bull's-eye targets painted on the front. Daltrey wore white pullover sweaters with designs stuck on with electrician's tape—basic geometric shapes (arrows, circles, squares, diamonds, triangles) in black and white which were easy to change for every single show.

Townshend was living (alone) in a flat in Chesham Place, Belgravia, for what was even then the astonishingly low rent of twelve pounds (about thirty-five dollars) a week. He had decorated the place with pages torn from a book on pop art which he'd swiped from the Ealing Art School library. Among these was Peter Blake's painting *Female Wrestler* which was as emblazoned with medals as Entwistle's jackets.

Kit Lambert retained his high-brow aesthete's disdain for Townshend's bohemianism, but he was fond of pop art, since it was camp, full of jokes and artifice, exactly the qualities that attracted him first to films and then to rock music. Late at night he and Townshend would discuss the concept of the Who as it ought to be, and Kit began to describe the Who as "the first pop art band." Now it was up to Townshend to define the term, not necessarily an easy task. Like any contemporary artistic movement, pop art was less a unified style than it was a confluence of certain tendencies and concepts on the part of a number of artists.

Pop was a basically American style, even though many of its most important figures were British, because it was a response to the world of technology and commercialization—and not just a response, but a whole-hearted (if humorous) embrace of that world, at least to the extent of acknowledging that it's the only one we have.

Pop artists worked with images derived from advertising, with the labels from commercial products, with comic strips, with badges and china and cigarette packages, with soup cans, the faces of movie stars, neon, cardboard boxes, beer cans, baseballs, hot rods, historical figures, flags, TV sets, money, motorcycles and rock & roll stars. No image was too clichéd, and even though the worst of it (Andy Warhol) was reactionary and sloppy and soullessly mechanistic, the best artists associated with pop (Robert Rauschenberg, Richard Hamilton, Peter Blake, Jasper Johns, Claes Oldenburg, James Rosenquist, Red Grooms, Jim Dine) displayed all the affection, egalitarianism, wit and deliberate accessibility that progressive generations of artists had discarded in their search for a method of properly conveying their alienation from an increasingly mechanized and dehumanized culture. Confronted with a world so terrible that it faced the ultimate absurdity of imminent atomic self-destruction, the pop artists were forced to work "in the gap between art and life," to use Rauschenberg's expression, for only there might any hope reside—for either art *or* life.

What Jasper Johns unveiled with his 1955 painting *Flag*, a huge rendering of the stars and stripes, was only a more self-conscious equivalent of the point that Chuck Berry and Elvis Presley were making in recording studios at the very same moment. This is not to say that rock & roll and pop art are in other ways equivalent. But as responses to the terrible time in which they were created, they are very much alike. And in this, too: Neither was afraid to omit or include anything, each was willing to reach beyond the established categories of "dignified" images and sounds. For the American painter Thomas Hess, the only art worth seeing (and the only music worth hearing) was "difficult, serious, remote, aristocratic," but the pop painters (just as pop musicians) stood this precept on its head, creating worthwhile work that was easy on the eye and ear, humorous, accessible, democratic. In this way, pop art (proceeding from an elitist tradition) and pop music (proceeding from the status of trash) groped toward one another.

More than anything, pop art and the new rock music of the sixties shared a creative, affirmative, imaginative response to the new technology. How does the painter paint in a society where the dominant symbols have been created and disseminated by advertising hucksters, often expropriating recent avant-garde techniques? How does the musician compose when what's being heard is not the instrument or the orchestra but the noise that the instrument and/or orchestra makes, many times removed, on a piece of black plastic with a context of its own? Just by raising such questions, pop gave itself more access to the society as a whole than art had had in many decades—and more leverage upon that society. And in its performances—the "happenings"—it brought high art closer to show biz than anyone had dared in more than a century. This is what John Russell refers to as the "element of exorcism" in pop, and it functions as effectively in a Who 45 as in an Oldenburg sculpture, as provocatively in a recording like Dylan's "I Want You" as in one of Roy Lichtenstein's comic book paintings—and *more* powerfully in the Beatles' "She's Leaving Home" than in all of Andy Warhol put together. Thus were barriers—between art objects and everyday stuff, between the theory of avant-garde viewers and unaesthetic masses, between high culture and low, between respectability and trash—not simply eradicated but demolished.

They came together not in a middle ground of mediocrity but in a space born of the greatest compassion, courage and collective goodwill. Neither would last there long before retreating to their original niches, but for a few months or years, there was in our culture a window in which could be seen a new kind of cultural possibility, liberating rather than ensnaring, blurring distinctions rather than emphasizing them. (The fact that most pundits of both "art" and "entertainment" continue to make false distinctions between them does not refute the point. It only explains why these pundits are forever bewildered at their own lack of effect not only upon the world but even upon the artists and entertainers about whom they comment.)

Pete Townshend was more sensitive to these trends than almost any other musician, not just because he had been an art student (as we've seen, there were many of those in rock bands), but because he was the rock musician most concerned with sound *as* sound, the one most involved with expanding the concept of pop music to include elements of chance and noise (although this made him more similar to Pollock and the other action painters who had introduced similar elements into high art).

Many of Townshend's earlier experiments—the feedback, the guitar-smashing, some aspects of his costuming and, most clearly, the idea of draping the flags over his amplifier—were obviously derived from pop artists, particularly Jasper Johns and Peter Blake. (A pair of Blake paintings from 1961, *The First Real Target* and his *Self Portrait* of that year, have the quality of bizarre mock-ups of later Who paraphernalia.)

Much of Townshend's theorizing was filibuster—Lambert himself barely understood it, except to say that the theories would do for the press. When Townshend said, "We stand for pop art clothes, pop art music and pop art behavior . . . we don't change offstage; we live pop art," was he speaking for anyone except himself? *Including* himself? What *was* pop art behavior? No one asked.

But Townshend could also be acute. "We play pop art with standard group equipment," he told *Melody Maker*. "I get jet plane sounds, morse code signals, howling wind effects." And he quite correctly cited a number of recent records as "near pop art," including the Shangri-Las' "Remember (Walkin' in the Sand)" and "Leader of the Pack" and Twinkle's "Terry."

Pop art was a sensation in the papers, since it was the first important figurative movement in years and derived so many of its most famous and successful images from everyday objects. It might be difficult for a Sunday magazine writer to explain *why* an Andy Warhol lithograph of a Campbell's soup can was an important artistic statement (for one thing, it wasn't, even though it was an important artistic *gesture*). At least the writer didn't have to worry about describing and explaining the soup can label.

So, as the Who traveled around the country, Townshend spent a lot of time discoursing upon pop art and its musical applications. "If we hadn't have done it, it might have taken another year to catch on," he said in another *Melody Maker* interview. "The number of journalists I had to explain it to, especially on local papers."

But converting the Who from modism to pop art was Lambert's idea. For the rest of the band, pop art was probably only what Moon termed it, "just a way of dressing up the music, putting it across." Only Townshend and Lambert understood the impact they might have with the concept.

"From valueless objects—a guitar, a microphone, a hackneyed pop tune, we extract a new value," Townshend told the *Observer* Sunday magazine. "We take objects with one function and give them another. And the auto-destructive element . . . adds immediacy to it all."

There remained the task of recording a second single. As late as March 20, 1965, the band was still thinking R&B. Townshend told *Melody Maker* that week that the follow-up single might be another of his originals, "You Don't Have to Jerk," since "the group all digs the jerk." Pete also named the group's favorite performers as Bobby Bland, James Brown and everybody at Tamla-Motown but especially Marvin Gaye. Townshend said the single was "moving up" the American charts (an outrageous fabrication) and that the band was to begin recording its album the following week.

It's not clear how much work was done toward an LP at this time. Daltrey was desperately unhappy with "I Can't Explain," worried that the band's image was too pop. (That's pretty strange, since the Who were at that time one of the most cult-oriented acts in the history of pop music.) Roger wanted to cut a James Brown song as the band's follow-up single.

The Who did at least one LP session, at IBC Studios on March 19. A few weeks later, *Beat Instrumental* said that the Who's first album would include such songs as Martha and the Vandellas' "Heat Wave" and "Motoring," James Brown's "I Don't Mind," and Bo Diddley's "I'm a Man," plus one Townshend original, "You're Going to Know Me." *Beat Instrumental* criticized the album, without hearing it, as unoriginal, and according to Barnes, this is the reason that the album was scrapped.

Townshend did have some original songs that he was considering for the second single, which was no less important than the first. At this time, albums were often conceived as luxuries, tossed off much more casually than singles. Everyone's attention focussed on 45s because that was where most of the sales—and all of the airplay—were.

Pete was living in Ebury Street, still in Belgravia, just around the corner from Kit and Chris. Townshend has described his living quarters as squalid, but Nick Jones (who had grown up in similarly middle-class circumstances) was impressed by the place, or at least its technology. "His stereo hooked into four-by-twelve Marshalls," Jones recalled. "He was getting more and more into the technology—all his ideas of taping and home demoing were all congealing at that point."

One night, in this flat, a stoned Townshend was reclining on a mattress listening intently to the bleats and blasts from Charlie Parker's alto sax. At the peak of his rapture, Pete scribbled three words on a scrap of paper: *anyway, anyhow, anywhere*. "You used to do that when you were stoned out of your head. You look at it the next day and say, 'What the fuck was I talking about?' " Townshend said. "Those three words were what I wrote to describe the way Charlie Parker plays. I just felt the guy was so free when he was playing. He was a soul without a body, riding, flying on the music."

Townshend decided to write a song around the phrase, but "the freedom suggested by the title became restricted by the aggression of our tightly defined image when I came to write the words. I knocked out the song, and it was much more of a conscious thing. I already looked back at 'Can't Explain,' and I started to think, 'Yeah, this one's gonna be about a punk kid.' "

Roger had other ideas. If the Who couldn't cover R&B songs, Daltrey wanted to make sure that the words he sang at least reflected his own attitude. According to Barnes, Daltrey and Townshend stayed up all night before the session rewriting the lyrics. "Anyway, Anyhow, Anywhere" is the only Who composition credited to both Daltrey and Townshend. As a result, said Pete, "It is the most excitingly pigheaded of our songs. It's blatant, proud and—dare I say it—sassy."

It was Kit Lambert who insisted on the rehearsals. He understood that it would be better for the band to be prepared going into the session, and he wanted to come up with something so devastating that it would be past any attempt by Shel Talmy to take control over the group's music.

"Kit realized that we had to be seen before people would begin to buy our records," John said. " 'Anyway, Anyhow, Anywhere' was his way of taking a shortcut. The intention was to encapsulate the Who's entire stage act on just one side of a single—to illustrate the arrogance of the mod movement and then, through the feedback, the smashing of the instruments.

"We recorded it at IBC Studios in next to no time. After doing the basic backing track, we set up Townshend's stack and let him do the various whooshing, smashing, morse code and feedback effects as overdubs. It was as simple as that."

Shel Talmy told *Record World* that he believed "Anyway" was the "first ever record with feedback recorded on it," which is demonstrably untrue: "I Feel Fine," the Beatles' single released in November 1964, opens with a short burst of feedback from John Lennon's guitar.

Nevertheless, the concept of using feedback and the process of recording it seemed to overwhelm everyone's impressions of the session. "Pete was playing around with it as an idea," said Talmy, "and we had to work out some technique in the studio to get it down on tape. The equipment at that time was not nearly as good as it is now. . . . I had messed around with various ways of recording stuff when I was engineering in L.A., so I set up the mikes the way I thought they would work, and it worked perfectly the first time."

When Talmy sent them the tapes, Decca returned the master, thinking it was defective. Once that was straightened out, Lambert pressured Brunswick to understand and promote this exceptionally difficult pop disc. In America, "Anyway" didn't even make the Hot 100.

"The first time [I heard it] I didn't like it at all, 'cause it was very unusual for its time," Nancy Lewis (of *Fabulous*) said. "I remember there were things like explosive noises and feedback and things on it which were totally foreign elements then." Unfortunately, pop music is primarily a music of first impressions, and Lewis wasn't alone—or entirely mistaken. "Anyway" was just what it seemed, a record that was primarily a vehicle for a gimmick (feedback), full of interesting (or at least arresting) parts that did not add up to a whole. Moon was brilliant, as usual, session piano player Nicky Hopkins dueling with him wonderfully through the first half of the song; and Townshend got off some accurate impressions of jet planes and morse code in his feedback solo at the bridge. But Daltrey's boasting lyrics and his blustering, raspy vocal were fairly ordinary, Entwistle could barely be heard and the song lacked the basic passion of "I Can't Explain."

"Anyway, Anyhow, Anywhere" entered the British charts on May 27, a week after it was issued, and stayed there for twelve weeks, lingering long into the summer, largely on the basis of being adopted as an unofficial, temporary "RSG" theme tune. But the record peaked quickly, at number 10, and never threatened to rise again, as "I Can't Explain" had done. (It sold less, too: only 88,000 copies.)

"Anyway, Anyhow, Anywhere" was simply not strong enough to compete with such memorable hits as the Animals' "Bring It on Home to Me," the Beatles' "Ticket to Ride," the Byrds' "Mr. Tambourine Man," Elvis Presley's "Crying in the Chapel," the Stones' "The Last Time," "Here Comes the Night," by Them, the Yardbirds' "For Your Love," the Supremes' "Stop! In the Name of Love," or even the Kinks' "Set Me Free." Few of these records (all hits during the period when "Anyway" was on the charts) were as ambitious as the Who's single, but all of them were more listenable on their own terms.

"The fantastic thing about the three-minute single is that it stands alone," said Townshend. "It's a simple statement. That's why I felt, perhaps wrongly, that pop art was so close to rock & roll—the fact that you could get a baked bean can, frame it and it would say something—something about tins, something about the companies that sold it, about advertising, about eating."

But in fact, you couldn't do that. Warhol's soup cans are cynical statements about the artist's intellectual sloppiness and his conviction that most men are marks. As Townshend knew, the great pop artists achieved their effects by subtly altering the stereotypes they pilfered from popular culture, by subverting—not celebrating—the gimmick.

"Anyway, Anyhow, Anywhere" had no subtlety at all; there was no mystery about it. If the appeal of "I Can't Explain" was that it was only superficially a love song, the downfall of its successor was that it was only superficial.

"Kit Lambert described 'Anyway, Anyhow, Anywhere' to reporters as 'a pop art record containing pop art music,' " Townshend ruefully reminisced. " 'The sounds of war and chaos and frustration expressed musically without the use of sound effects.' A bored and then cynical Nik Cohn . . . said calmly, 'That's impressionism, not pop art.' "

"I repeated what Kit had briefed me to say, mumbling something about Peter Blake and Roy Lichtenstein and went red. Completely out of order when your record is screaming in the background."

"Anyway, Anyhow, Anywhere" received much airplay on all the pirate stations, and of course, its use as the "Ready, Steady, Go!" theme helped keep it alive. But most of the attention paid to it was in print.

On June 5, a week after "Anyway" was issued, *Melody Maker* ran a screaming headline: "EVERY SO OFTEN A GROUP IS POISED ON THE BRINK OF A BREAKTHROUGH. WORD HAS IT IT'S . . . THE WHO." The story, which was skimpy on fact but long on pumping up the product, went on to say, "This is no note-perfect, 'showbiz' group singing in harmony and playing clean guitar runs. . . . There's sadism in their character and in their music."

The Who were using the press as craftily as possible to distance themselves from the mods while remaining mod icons. Townshend now challenged mod. "We found out that mods were just as conformist and reactionary as anyone else," Pete said. "We announced that we were ex-mods and that we were finished with all that label stuff." (This was in an interview filled with discussion of the Who's new pop art label, of course.)

But the Who kept their mod credentials, too, largely because Daltrey remained loyal. Still resident at the Marquee, still providing the theme song for "Ready! Steady! Go!", still wearing mod fashions and (no doubt) still pinching graphic and dance ideas off their mod followers, the Who didn't—couldn't— escape mod completely.

Townshend also found other ways to stir up controversy. For instance, he became one of the first pop musicians to admit using drugs. "Drugs don't harm you," he told *Rave*. "I know. I take them. I'm not saying I use opium or heroin, but hashish is harmless, and everyone takes it. . . . Drink is far more harmful to the body. Spirits give you ulcers. My dad's got one through whiskey."

In the same interview, Townshend said, "Having to conform and go to church and be baptized is all wrong. I shall not have my children baptized and I don't care if they are banned from certain schools and that. I don't agree with doing things because everyone else does."

Though he'd later be embarrassed by "all those things I used to say when I was nineteen," Townshend obviously believed every word that came out of his own mouth, at least at the moment of its emission. And his preaching of religious nonconformism is fairly ironic in light of the answer he gave to an *NME* interrogation about his favorite styles of music: "Anything that's currently recognized as being liked." He never changed *that* attitude.

But Townshend's controversial comments, whatever else they were, proved effective. Journalist Alan Freeman, writing in a pop magazine, referred to the band as "the most criticized since the Rolling Stones." The idea of a pop musician with outspoken opinions was still novel. But it wasn't only Townshend's mouth that caused trouble for the Who—they were even more widely berated for their stage act. As Freeman commented, "It's a funny thing about England that the ordinary bloke in the street can see violence done to the human body in all sorts of ways . . . without ever feeling that it concerns him. But . . . a bit of property is smashed up, he goes potty and cries out about senseless destruction."

The Who were pioneering a kind of pop culture Luddism, although ultimately in a spirit that was the opposite of the Luddites, who were a group of early nineteenth-century textile workers who demolished new weaving machines because they believed (correctly) that their jobs would be eliminated by them. The Who were *celebrating* planned obsolescence, the joyous knowledge that any machine could be interchangeably replaced with another of the same kind.

In America (or even Japan), such "news" could be shrugged off—it was the overt basis of society. But in England, where some feudal customs had survived, where tradition must always be paid obeisance, the Who were regarded as wild revolutionaries. One did not destroy goods, especially such expensive goods as electric guitars.

It says a great deal about the mentality with which the Who were dealing that those most outraged and befuddled were often journalists and other musicians, and that mugging guitars remained alive as an issue for three years and more. As late as 1968, Townshend complained: "People come up to me and say, 'How can you break a guitar?' And some fool in the Bee Gees said, 'You wouldn't break a Stradivarius, would you?' The answer is, 'Of course I wouldn't break a Stradivarius,' but a Gibson guitar that came off a production line—fuck it! I can get a better one tomorrow."

Nik Cohn defined the difference between the violence of the Who and that of their imitators (such as the Move): "The point about the Who's violence, the reason why it doesn't feel squalid, is that it carries such surprise and precision. Unlike the hard rock groups that have followed them . . . they don't go in for slow mutilation, wrestling a song to the ground and then bludgeoning it and tearing it, stomping all over it until it has been mashed beyond all recognition. Instead, their brutality is fast and total, like a one-punch knockout or a clean kill in a bullfight. On its own terms, it carries elegance, rage, humor and, yes, beauty."

Townshend knew exactly how to exploit the teapot tempest over the Who's instrumental destruction. "My personal motivation on stage is simple," he would tell gullible interviewers. "It consists of a hatred of every kind of pop music and a hate of everything our group has done. You are getting higher and higher but chopping away at your own legs. I prefer to be in this position." Since most of his interviewers didn't know that Townshend was only paraphrasing every avant-garde artist since Artaud, his statements seemed provocative and shocking.

Townshend was only laughing up one sleeve. There was a dimension of belief in what he said (that's partly how he got away with it). Reminiscing a decade later, he told Michael Brooks of *Guitar Player*, "From the very beginning, my favorite quote that I've ever said in an interview was like, 'We never let the music get in the way of our stage act.' I mean, in a lot of ways that's true, because *stage act* means that we are committed to one another and the audience, and *music* means we are committed to the way we play, it means that we are committed to our limitations." Ten years on, Townshend had perfected the art of being interviewed, not only by saying what was memorable and outrageous but by offering his own interpretations, which were usually tangential and often irrelevant but never failed to mesmerize.

Townshend had adopted the persona of Lord High Rock & Roller. He was a born spokesman, a pundit *maudit*. His personal ambition, he told *NME*, was "just not to let what happens get me down." This bleak belief that pop was not entirely the sunny side of life had deep and natural appeal for the young breed of pop journalist, the guy who may have been ashamed of the slavering magazine he worked for but was quite fond of the music about which he wrote.

"Pete was always intense, and there were things he cared passionately about, and he tried to inject some of that feeling and indeed, some of that anger, into his interviews," said Keith Altham. "It was an angry situation, I felt, with Pete."

That summer, Kit Lambert's film of the band was shown on French television, after which the band filmed a live "Ready! Steady! Go!" with the Yardbirds using actual Parisian locations. "The show was done from a discotheque and went surprisingly well, as none of us spoke French and none of the French crew spoke English," recalled Vicki Wickham. "At the end of the show, the Yardbirds and the Who finished playing and ran through the club out into the streets with the cameras following them. The show was going out live in both France and England and the time came for the finale and the cameras duly followed, recording the event—into the street go the Who, into the alley and all stop and immediately pee against the wall!"

The Who's ability to get away with such antics is not easily explained.

Around the same time, the Rolling Stones had been arrested and fined for pissing against the wall of a gas station on a dark highway on a weekend night with no one around. Perhaps, as in so many other areas, the Who were able to piggyback on the scandals created by those who'd come before them. Townshend's anti-clericalism was overshadowed by Lennon's "We're bigger than Jesus," and his announcement that he took drugs was eclipsed by Paul McCartney's endorsement of pot and acid. But other musicians, some of lesser stature, made less provocative remarks and were harassed, especially by the narcotics squad.

The Who surely didn't escape because they were all talk and no action. In the *NME* survey, Moon listed his favorite food as "French blues," and the entire band was now as pillheaded as Pete Meaden had ever dreamed of being. (Daltrey only dabbled, then stopped altogether, largely because amphetamines made his throat sore.) Brandy—with or without ginger ale—also loomed large in the Who's larder.

Of course, as the band became more drug-obsessed, its playing became more energetic but less precise; its enthusiasms were high but not sustained; its discipline grew lax. Roger Daltrey, who took the job of being in a band most seriously, looked upon the doping and boozing with a dubious eye and did his best to talk or beat the others out of their recalcitrant ways.

"In the old days," said Entwistle, "we used to play up north and dash back in the furniture van to play in Tottenham. We were complete pillheads, and we'd often still be playing when the other group went on.

"Then we got to drunken playing, and I'd often forget I'd done a gig. Moon would pass out before a gig, sober up just before we went on, play like a maniac and go back on the bottle as soon as we finished."

With Daltrey sober and the others wrecked, they inevitably went for one another's throats. And once again, these fights were no secret. "If there was back-biting going on," said Altham, "most of it went on in front of the people involved. In other bands there would be little cliques. The one thing that made the Who work, more than anything else, was that it was a totally honest relationship.

"You'd go backstage and see Keith being throttled by Roger or Keith throwing cymbals at Pete. I mean, it just all happened. And when that adrenalin was running after a gig that wasn't as good as they knew it should be, if you knew anything at all about the Who, you didn't go *near* that dressing room for twenty minutes. Until they sorted out in their own minds what was right and wrong with the performance that night. Because they *cared* about it—much more so than a lot of other bands. And that caused a lot of fights, too.

"It would have ruined most relationships to see the kind of R-A-G-E that was being vented on each other backstage. You'd think, 'This band cannot possibly ever go onstage again after this kind of abuse'—Roger hitting Keith or John hitting Pete or whatever. But it was over, it had been sorted out, it was all out in the open and *gone*, I think. And if there was any spite, most of it got used up and thrown out, and it was clean."

15

Perhaps you cannot hang an event on the wall, only a picture. But this is a problem for the picture more than it is for events.
—*Harold Rosenberg,*
The Tradition of the New

The Who now began to seriously rethink its music. Townshend and Lambert wanted desperately to make some kind of statement, have some sort of public impact, to vindicate themselves in their own eyes, to do something genuinely worthwhile; to prove a point to their fathers; to certify their own deeply harbored (but rarely revealed, even to one another) conceptions of themselves as artists. Townshend and Lambert may not have had exactly identical goals—Townshend wanted to take a giant step toward making pop music respectable, Lambert wanted to prove his superiority to form in general. But they were close enough to be inseparable on major issues. The others had goals, too. At the least, everyone wanted to make some real money, which hadn't been seen yet.

The power play within the Who continued. Roger Daltrey fought a rear-guard action to preserve the Who for mod and R&B. Townshend tried to tug the group into line behind his version of pop avant-gardism, original material and stoned mannerisms.

Work on their album was abandoned. "WHO MAKE DRASTIC POLICY CHANGES," read the banner headline in *Melody Maker*'s July 17 issue. "The Who are having serious doubts about the state of R&B," said Kit Lambert. "Now the LP material will consist of hard pop. They've finished with 'Smokestack Lightnin'.' "

The "main contents" of the Who album would now be original songs by Townshend *and Daltrey*. The story said that the Who would take a holiday, regroup on July 26 and begin rehearsals for the album.

In fact, the album project now went on the back burner because the need for a third single was more pressing. "Anyway, Anyhow, Anywhere" had about run its course in Britain; it had never been alive in America. Especially in the States, the Who needed a certified winner their third time out—they were running short of chances.

The leading contender for the next single was a slow talking blues based on a Jimmy Reed melody. Townshend had written the lyric for the song, called "My Generation," in the back of a car "without thinking." He was returning from a meeting in which Kit Lambert exhorted him to "make a statement!"

Townshend assembled the music on his tape recorders. The resulting demo "sounded like . . . Jimmy Reed at ten years old suffering from nervous indigestion," Townshend claimed.

The only person who saw much in it was Chris Stamp, who was convinced that "My Generation" was the song to take the Who over the top. And it was basically Stamp's enthusiasm that made Lambert encourage Townshend to do another demo of the number. "Make it beefier," Lambert suggested.

So Townshend went back and turned his talking blues into a chunky, chugging blues. (This demo may be heard as a flexidisc insert in the Richard Barnes book, *The Who: Maximum R&B*.) This version of "My Generation" resembles nothing so much as the heavy metal version of the song included on the later album *Live at Leeds*. It is thunderous, somewhat lumbering but a good deal more exciting than the song could have been as a talking blues.

Roger Daltrey still didn't like the song, probably because he was still resisting Townshend's control of the group's material. " 'My Generation' was a heavy block," said Stamp. "It really took a lot of persuading to get it going. It took me at least two months to persuade Roger and everybody that they should record it."

Meantime, the band toured. While doing some dates in Sweden in early September, Daltrey reached his limit. According to Moon, Roger flipped out about the others taking pills, vowing that he would no longer play with "junkies." Yet, by the time the band got back home, Roger was ready to proceed. But the others weren't so sure they wanted to continue with him.

Nevertheless, they began working on "My Generation," cutting demos with the full band at a small studio located behind the Marquee. According to Entwistle, the first two versions of the song recorded with Lambert were straight. "Then we decided to incorporate a bass solo, but so as to get the right effect, I had to buy a Danelectro bass, because it has little thin strings that produce a very twangy sound."

The Danelectro was made in America. "It had wire-wound strings that sounded like a piano's but had this raspy, distorted, trebly sound," said Entwistle. Unfortunately, the Danelectro's thin strings broke easily, and there were no replacements available in London. Entwistle broke one string during his first crack at the bass solo and had to buy another Danelectro (for £60—about $170). He broke another set of strings on the fourth run-through, bought a third guitar, and finally made it through the fifth Lambert-produced demo of the song with strings intact.

"Kit made suggestion after suggestion to improve the song," Townshend said. "He later said that it was because he was unsure of it." According to Townshend, the most significant alterations were the introduction of the song's two upward key changes (allegedly pinched from the Kinks) and the idea of using a vocal stutter on key words in the chorus: "F-f-fade away," "c-c-cold," "g-g-generation." "From then on we knew we had it," said Townshend.

But Roger Daltrey still resisted the song, especially the stutter. This wasn't because he was worried about mocking stutterers. As Roger knew, the stutter was introduced because the "My Generation" character was supposed to be a mod blocked on pills—and amphetamine abusers stammered like mad.

Roger fought the song because he fought what the song implied: Townshend's victory as the group's leader. Once Daltrey was won over, he *became* the nasty little pillhead in the song. Then it was simply a matter of taking the prearranged song to Shel Talmy.

The recording session was swift and sure. "I knew it would be a hit as sure as I was sitting in my seat," said Glyn Johns. "There was absolutely no doubt in my mind."

"[We] were so into what was going on . . . that I knew immediately when we started doing that thing that it was going to be a number one record," said Talmy. "It was one of those things that sounded like a natural to me. We were all sky high by the time we were finished, because it had everything."

What was obvious to Johns and Talmy wasn't nearly so clear to the band, which had reached such a point of frustration and intramural hostility that it was seriously considering breaking up. At a show in Denmark, Daltrey tipped a box of Moon's pills down a toilet. When Keith complained, Roger punched the drummer flat.

At this point, Moon, Townshend and Entwistle concluded that they'd had enough of Daltrey's beatings and bullyings. "He was a dynamo," said Pete. "If he punched you, it fucking hurt." And thrashings were still Roger's preferred mode of argument.

So the others laid new plans for themselves. John and Keith would form their own group; Pete was to link up with Paddy, Klaus and Gibson, a trio managed by Brian Epstein. At least that was one thought.

Roger was as disgusted with the others as they were with him. Part of the problem was his rationality versus their profligacy. "It's great, Moon being a funny man when you're really rich and can afford it," said Roger. "But then, if we were gonna get anywhere, we still had lots of responsibilities."

Mike Shaw, then the band's road manager, saw several linked issues dividing the group. "That was one of the worst periods, because there were a lot of pills going around and there was a lot of jealousy in the group as to who was the leader of the band," he said.

"All three turned against Roger because he was always telling them off for playing too loud. Which was true, they played outrageously loud and he couldn't sing above it. As he said, his voice was his instrument and he could only take it so far. He saw himself as the group's front man, and if he couldn't sing, they couldn't give a good performance and that's what he wanted to do.

"It was three against one. From there it reached the point where Roger was gonna leave."

From Daltrey's point of view, the issues were even more complex. The disagreement between him and Moon was basic. Keith wanted the band to play Beach Boys car-and-surf songs. Keith also wanted to be the band's lead singer, in complete disregard of the fact that he was one of the worst vocalists ever to draw breath.

But all of the other difficulties stemmed from the drug situation. "Once I got off the pill thing," said Daltrey, "I realized how much the band had deteriorated through playing on speed. Musically, it really took a downturn."

"We were very, very, very into leapers, uppers—John, Keith and I," said Pete. "Roger never, ever was. I think he occasionally had one or two, but he didn't really like the sensation. It affected his voice; that was one problem.

"Anyway, the three of us just loved it, getting really sort of spaced out and playing. So we'd gabble on about anything. If Keith wanted to play surfing music, John and I would just go, 'Yeah, sure! Anything!' Because we were just so up on being up, never disagreeing about anything."

Stamp and Lambert were eager to see Roger go. "We really fancied Pete's voice, anyway," Stamp told Richard Barnes. "He didn't have as strong a voice, but it was an interesting voice. And we were going to form another group around Roger to keep everyone happy. Roger could do all of these R&B things that he always wanted to do, because a lot of the arguments were about the fact that we kept shoving Pete's stuff in. . . ."

Lambert was more ambivalent—he was distressed by the feuding and wanted more than anything simply to end it. Disbanding the Who meant starting from scratch, no matter what the new configuration. One afternoon, Pete and Kit took a long walk through Hyde Park to consider what would happen once the band split. But they weren't plotting against Daltrey, as Lambert's later actions proved.

Kit and Chris surely understood, as Townshend later acknowledged, that the differences were very deep, "not just in musical things." The confrontation stemmed from the bedrock of the group's relationships; it was based on the fact that there was only one steady axis of friendship in the band—between Entwistle and Moon. As a result, there were constant combinations of cliques and political maneuverings.

"I used to clutch at moments when I could feel like a member of the gang. So if Keith and John wanted to play fucking surf music, I would, too," said Pete.

Roger couldn't be so malleable. In a way, this was because the group was more important to him than to the others. ("In those days, I didn't ever feel that it was my life's work, as it were," Pete said.) Roger wasn't an exceptional vocalist. He would have a hard time latching on with another group (at least, with another group as good as this one). His alternative to music was hot, sweaty sheet-metal work.

"I thought if I lost the band I was dead," said Daltrey. "If I didn't stick with the Who, I would be a sheet-metal worker for the rest of my life." So a couple of days after he'd been chucked out, Roger swallowed his pride and went to Lambert.

At a meeting with the others arranged by Kit, Daltrey took the blame. "I was a bastard, a real cunt," he said. "But there again, I sat down and thought, 'Well, the biggest thing in my life is the group.' And I literally changed. Anything they ever did from then on never bothered me. I let them play their Beach Boys. It went down okay, but it didn't last five minutes."

Townshend described the meeting as "sort of humiliating. We told Roger, 'You know, whatever the band as a whole want to do, you're going to go along with. No more tantrums, no more outbursts, no more using aggression to get your point across.'

"Roger said, 'From now on, I'll be Peaceful Perce,' and he did it. It was a lesson to all of us, if you like, that there is no need to always get your way. That the most important thing is to just stay together."

This realization spelled a major difference between the Who and other groups of the period, many of whom reached a similar stage of disagreement and split up for good. As Townshend has pointed out, it's significant that it was Roger who was mature enough to settle the issue. He could no longer lead the Who—but he could keep it together.

To say that Daltrey rejoined the band on terms dictated by the others and that these terms favored Townshend's creative dominance is far different from saying that Townshend had "won." Clearly, Pete now had carte blanche to write the Who's songs. But the terms on which Roger rejoined applied to all the members. If all decisions were group decisions, then there could be no true leader. By agreeing to these terms (even implicitly), Townshend made a commitment to limit his ambitions to the horizons perceived by the group as a whole. So Townshend also guaranteed himself frustration.

The terms ("Whatever the band as a whole want to do, you're going to go along with") provided a perfect means for Townshend to evade responsibility. As late as 1971, therefore, Pete could still maintain that his responsibility for the Who's creative affairs was no greater than Lambert's or Moon's.

There was room for a certain amount of democracy in the small creative units around which rock was formed; there was even more need for equality in a band like the Who, in which the vocalist was *not* the writer (and in which the writer was not even necessarily the dominant instrumentalist). But the Who was stuck with only the illusion of democracy. Townshend had achieved the dream state of the tyrant, the reality of control without its consequences. He could blame any failure of his music upon the failure of the group to execute or understand his intentions. Having accepted that "the most important thing is just to stay together," he was cut off from meaningful rebellion when the group's concepts radically departed from his own. Yet at the same time, the Who was primarily Pete Townshend's vehicle—his songs dictated what the group played and, to a great extent, how.

Yet there wasn't really much choice, except to stick it out. The Who had to stay together, because "My Generation" had exploded on Britain's charts and airwaves. It was the hit for which the band had prayed and dreamed and worked all along, the one that made them not just a success but a legend.

"My Generation" was released on November 5, 1965. It entered the *New Musical Express* chart at number 16, then vaulted to 3, before peaking at number 2. Townshend had indeed made a statement, and the world responded in all sorts of ways. The BBC initially banned the disc on the grounds that Daltrey's vocal was insulting to stammerers, but (as often, with BBC censorship) ample sales and heavy airplay from the pirate competitors caused the ban to be rescinded.

On the other side, the Rolling Stones' Brian Jones proclaimed the Who "the only young group doing something new both visually and musically." "Originality usually means success," Jones added. "My Generation" sold 300,000 copies.

"My Generation" had such impact because it was not just an original record but an authentically revolutionary one. While the Beatles and the Rolling Stones had disrupted pop and rock conventions, the Who were the first to apply to everyday pop the principle articulated by John Cage, that music is nothing more than consciously organized noise.

The record opened like the logical successor to "I Can't Explain" and "Anyway, Anyhow, Anywhere," with power chords and rustling drums. But this time, the music was underpinned by heavy, overmodulated bass, perhaps the most prominently recorded electric bass in rock up to that time. But there was nothing lumbering about Entwistle's playing—it was agile and limber, ready to spring into any open space and seize it for its own while at the same time providing the necessary definition of time to keep the record on balance.

The voices in the background, chanting "Talkin' 'bout my gen-er-a-tion," were (for the first time) the Who's own. They added a crisply percussive effect, abetted by popping fingers and handclaps. Above them, Daltrey spat out an angry vocal that turned the mod protests of the lyric into epithets and imprecations. Daltrey did not whine, he snarled, proclaiming himself above the very fray he described. When he snapped, "Hope I die before I get old," what chilled you to the marrow was that he had considered what the words meant, and that the music backed up every syllable.

What was most revolutionary about "My Generation" was the feedback, and what was most insurrectionary about the feedback was its inevitability. The feedback suggests a complete breakdown in the structure of this pop song (and in consequence, all pop songs). The Beatles, the Kinks, the Who themselves had all used feedback as a gimmick separate from the basic flow of the music. In "My Generation" feedback is for the first time an integral part of a rock composition—without it, the song would feel incomplete.

For years, Pete Townshend (because he wrote the song and had its best moment for himself) has been plagued by "My Generation." Where did it come from? What was its meaning? Did he really plan to die before he got old? Publicly and privately, Townshend has wrestled with these questions, tortured himself with them, tried to take them as a joke, tried to bear down and come to a conclusion about them, tried to dismiss them and embrace them. He has never gotten to the bottom of the subject, mostly because those questions are beyond answers.

Which is one way of saying that Townshend never had control over "My Generation" because the song was an expression of an historical process that operates quite independently of individual will—and it was Townshend's good fortune to have been an open channel for it.

"To me, the success of any truly great rock song is related to the fact that people who couldn't really communicate in normal ways can quite easily communicate through the mutual enjoyment of rock music," said Townshend. "And that was simply because for them, it was infinitely more charismatic than anything else around at that time." That is an oversimplification—it was equally important that rock was so despised that it was open to all sorts of banished or disreputable voices and that it was cheap enough to produce that it was available to working-class and poor people. But the germ of Townshend's idea—that rock functions best as a mouthpiece for those who have no other cultural voice—is entirely right. And the desperate passion with which so many greeted rock's articulation of their anger and anxiety was an unmistakable indication that Townshend's idea was correct. People were moved by rock as by little else.

"I've never really felt like anybody's hero," Pete once told an interviewer. "That part of my dream never came true. But I have felt like a lot of people's voice." And this is so, even if "My Generation" (the Townshend song that established his stature as a generation's voice) began as nothing more than "some pilled-up mod dancing around trying to explain to you why he's such a groovy guy but can't because he's so stoned he can hardly talk."

John Swenson defined the situation perfectly: "Pete had his creative outlet, and he hammered it home, sensing what the audience was like across the footlights and playing his guts out for them."

"My Generation" is the flip side of 1965's other great rock anthem, the Rolling Stones' "(I Can't Get No) Satisfaction." Both songs convey the same message, but in the style of true bohemians, the Stones personalized their discontent, while the Who, like true populists, transformed individual alienation into a statement of Everyman angst. Taken together, "Satisfaction" and "My Generation" measure a moment: a time when the rock generation was becoming aware of itself and its potential.

Rock & roll had begun as nothing more than a series of inspired moments. But once records like "Satisfaction" and "My Generation" gave the genre their kind of interpretive, almost analytical leverage, the linkages among pop moments became much less random; pop became part of a process of history whose important moments were defined not only by themselves but also by their relationship to what had preceded them and by the nature of a pop idiom that understood and exploited those links.

So it isn't surprising that for years Townshend has wavered about his most famous song and its most famous line: "Hope I die before I get old." From time to time, he has tried to deny the power and validity of "My Generation." But always he has returned to it, to its central truths about his generation's (and his own) aspirations and achievements. For as he wrote in 1971, "We did mean it. We didn't care about ourselves or our future. We didn't even really care about one another. We were hoping to screw the system, screw the older generation, screw the hippies, screw the rockers, screw the record business, screw the Beatles and screw ourselves. We've been most successful on the last account. I think that speaks for a lot of the groups in the sixties.

"We didn't really want to end up yabbering in pop papers about our hang-ups, we wanted to die in plane crashes or get torn to pieces by a crowd of screaming girls."

16

Before the Who got big, I wanted them to get bigger and bigger until a number one record and then wrap dynamite round their heads and blow themselves up on TV. It's just been one of those things.
—Pete Townshend

"My Generation" had only been in the shops about two weeks before *Melody Maker* got wind of the band's latest internal squabbling and ran the story on the front page of its November 20 issue.

"THE WHO SPLIT MYSTERY," said the headline, and the story read, in part: "This is the first time the Who have hit the Top 10, and rumors circling the pop world this week suggested that it would be the last. Wild tales in London's in-clubs flashed the news that twenty-year-old Roger Daltrey would be leaving the group." The story maintained that Boz Burrell of Boz's People would be replacing Daltrey, a rumor that Burrell, later a member of Bad Company and King Crimson, indignantly denied, vowing never to become a part of such a gimmick-ridden enterprise as the Who. (Burrell did play bass on a Pete Townshend solo record in 1977, however.)

"This is absolute c-c-crap!" Chris Stamp told *Melody Maker*. "I've never heard such a lot of rubbish. Does anybody in their right mind think the Who would split at a time like this?" But Stamp didn't deny the band's differences (he hardly could have—every existing clipping of the period discussed them).

The story concluded with further denials from Stamp and a notice that the band was still recording its first album, which was to feature a track called "Lies."

Just that week, the Who played the London Students Glad Rag Ball, a charity show at the huge Wembley Arena. In the midst of their performance, Roger stormed off the stage, refusing to return until the house microphone and public address system were replaced with the Who's own equipment. It was installed, and after a delay, the Who resumed. But the display was accurately interpreted as evidence that no matter what the band or their managers might claim, the Who had not solved their internal dissension.

Meantime, the group was rehearsing in preparation for its first album. The reasons an album wasn't cut before the late fall of 1965 are easy to see: Until the tussle between Daltrey and Townshend was resolved, it wasn't clear just what material would be recorded, and once Townshend "won," the band needed time to work up the batch of songs he had written. The band also wanted to protect itself lest Talmy get up to his old tricks and try to banish them from playing on their own LP.

The conflict with Talmy had become intense and troublesome. The band mostly just stayed out of Talmy's way, but he and Kit Lambert were at each other's throats in the studio. According to Pete Townshend, the entire recording time for the album was only about six or seven hours, but it must have seemed longer.

It wasn't just a personality conflict. Kit felt that he understood the group well enough to produce them, and he constantly interfered, without much diplomacy. Both Talmy and Glyn Johns thought Lambert's ideas amateurish and bumbling.

"Glyn used to side with Talmy, who was paying his wages," said Townshend. "Kit never forgave him and Glyn never forgave Kit and it caused problems years later." Or to put it in Glyn Johns's terms, "I didn't like Kit Lambert and he didn't like me. It was a very mutual sort of thing." "From my point of view, that first album was just miserable," concluded Townshend.

Shel Talmy never perceived any problem between himself and the group. "We never had any trouble in the studio at all," he told *Record World*. "All the things people have said about how difficult they can be I personally have never experienced. They were one of the easiest groups I've ever recorded. We worked hard, and we came up with good things."

Talmy seemed oblivious to the way that he eroded the confidence of the band by bringing session musicians into the singles sessions, preferring instead to consider the coolness between himself and the Who the result of the "influence, possibly the undue influence" of the managers, principally Kit Lambert. "I think many of his decisions were totally erroneous, based on a deviated sense of responsibility," Talmy said of his nemesis. "We came very close to coming to blows at one point." Talmy—a partially sighted man with a powerful determination to do things his way—was no less volatile than every other personality associated with the Who.

The album was recorded in a single session at IBC Studios after the week of rehearsals with Lambert, who "shaped the songs, got rid of the lousy verses and coached Roger's vocals," according to Pete. The most time-consuming part of preproduction was sifting through Townshend's songs, "of which I had thousands," seeking those that were "fairly commercial." This task also fell to Lambert. "Then we went in," said Townshend, "laid it on a plate and Shel Talmy gave us our sound."

Daltrey has said that the Who missed recording a whole stage of their development, skipping over the R&B period completely and thus giving a distorted picture of what the band's stage show was like at the time. Like many rock musicians, Daltrey believed that the one irreducible purpose of record making must be recapturing a group's live sound—even though this contradicts the aesthetic function of electric recording, which is to liberate the musician from worrying about recreating anything.

In any event, the debut album, titled *My Generation* and released in December 1965, doesn't ignore R&B. It devotes three songs—about a quarter of its contents—to covers of R&B standards: James Brown's "I Don't Mind" and "Please, Please, Please" and Bo Diddley's "I'm a Man," properly raved up by the instruments and absurdly overemoted by Daltrey. These numbers make a convincing argument for the Who as a group that could prosper only by *abandoning* R&B, since it's easy to think of a half-dozen British groups much more competent and interesting in their approach to such material. (Whether the Who were a great R&B band on stage is quite beside the point; they were not able to transfer their live excitement to vinyl.)

Nevertheless, Daltrey (who had *never* liked a Who single) was the only band member who publicly supported the album after its release. Entwistle was noncommittal, and Townshend and Moon both attacked it. Townshend complained that Moon's drumming drowned out the vocals, which is pretty strange if he meant it, because Daltrey's performance is by far the weakest on the record and Moon's is one of the great sustained debuts of rock history. Which makes it less surprising—given the continuing tension between those two—that Moon leaped straight into Daltrey's face, telling *New Musical Express*: "Roger . . . hates me . . . because I told him he can't sing. . . . I don't like half our records, and Roger is the reason. It's not true to say we do not like the LP. There are some old tracks which we did not want released, but Pete has written some great songs for the album." The "old tracks" were the R&B material (left over from the suspended sessions earlier in the year). And the inclusion of R&B at all was at Daltrey's demand.

To be fair to Daltrey, however, it must be said that it wasn't unusual for great English bands to have weak vocalists: Mick Jagger's performances are easily the least impressive element of early Rolling Stones albums, for instance. And if Lambert and Stamp had seriously considered making Townshend the full-time lead singer, his vocal on "A Legal Matter," while not without charm, suggests that he wasn't then good enough to pull it off.

"In England, albums were what you got for Christmas, singles were what you bought for prestige," Townshend wrote. "We believed only in singles, in the Top Ten records and pirate radio." Albums were bonuses, a chance to experiment a little bit and to pick up a few extra sales, but they could not approach singles in commercial importance, especially since there was no regular radio or TV broadcast of rock album tracks. That meant that the general public only *ever* heard a band's singles; albums were for fans only.

Artistically speaking, a rock band's albums nevertheless tend to be its most revealing and important work. And the Who are no exception. Whatever complaints one may have about details, *My Generation* is a great rock album and one of the most influential ever recorded. It would have this stature even if all it offered was the first full-scale performance by Keith Moon, but *My Generation* has far more: Townshend's songs are uniformly intelligent and witty in a Dylanesque manner. They show a thorough understanding of rock and pop forms and a willingness to explode them. Townshend's guitar playing is very nearly a match for Moon's drumming—fast, incisive and occasionally as explosive as the percussion in which it is engulfed. And the group playing of Townshend, Moon, Entwistle and occasionally Nicky Hopkins is equally revelatory.

"[The] Who reverse . . . the traditional artistic process," Geoffrey Stokes once wrote. "They struggle not to bring order to chaos but to smash reality into splinters." The key to this demolition of order is Keith Moon. The entire structure of *My Generation* is predicated on Moon's playing, with its busy, nonstop action, its powerhouse assortment of rolls and embellishments on the basic beat.

It was Greil Marcus who best defined Moon's achievement: "Right from the beginning . . . Moon trashed the limits that the best of his contemporaries— Charlie Watts, Hal Blame, Kenny Buttrey—instinctively respected. There seemed no conscious arrogance or musical ambition involved: Moon simply didn't recognize those limits. He didn't hear them, so he didn't play them. . . . The connection [between Moon and his influences] is there, but it is not remotely implicit. There's an inexplicable leap, a missing link, involved— and it's the presence of that missing link that proves Moon's greatness. His triumphs can be described, they can be analyzed, but they can't be traced. Like all rock & roll originals, Moon sounded as if he came out of nowhere to take over the world."

Every song on the album is built on a similar musical pattern, and it is not established by the guitar but by the drums. As Marcus wrote, "Townshend takes his cues from Moon, most often coming down on Moon's licks to emphasize them, when previously the rules of rock & roll had always dictated that it be the other way around. Even so, Townshend's most spectacular early solo, in 'The Kids Are Alright' . . . takes off from patterns Moon establishes early in the song—and which he extends in front of Townshend—before hurling the band out of the instrumental break with one of the most sublime drum rolls in all of rock. . . ."

Moon is outstanding on every track on the album, but he reaches special heights on "My Generation," "The Kids Are Alright," "The Ox" (in which he simply eclipses every surf drummer in history on a song that is nothing so much as an Anglo "Wipe Out"), "The Good's Gone" (a virtual duel with Nicky Hopkins) and "It's Not True," on which he proves his ability to play straight-ahead rock drums as well as anyone of his generation.

Moon was never a funky drummer—it's even hard to say that he *swings* in any conventionally understood sense, something that clearly can be said of the much more limited Charlie Watts—yet it's no accident that jazz drummers like Elvin Jones and Tony Williams have sung Keith's praises. What he did was propel the music, give it a drive and lift that can't be measured in ordinary terms but must be heard and understood on its own.

The best Who ensemble playing comes on "My Generation," of course, but "The Ox," which appears to be a studio jam session built around Moon's surf drumming and, to a lesser extent, Townshend's variations on Link Wray's "Rumble," is also worthy of some comment for the way that the band members interact not only with each other but also with pianist Nicky Hopkins.

Hopkins is probably the most important session musician in British rock history. Getting his start with Screaming Lord Sutch and then Cyril Davies, he wound up playing on records by everyone from the Beatles and the Rolling Stones on down. *My Generation* is one of his most impressive performances, since his task is to add melodic color without dampening the band's murderously skeletal attack. He does this competently throughout the record, brilliantly on "The Good's Gone," and if anything salvages the blues performances, it is his work. On the blues numbers, Hopkins essentially mediates between Moon's nonstop solo and the droning, zooming guitar and bass, providing an elastic center off which everyone can work. When he briefly lays out, you can hear how silly the song would sound without him; the music may be built around Moon, but it is held together by the piano. Yet with Hopkins present, it is finally clear how sympathetic to one another (especially to one another's competitiveness) Moon, Entwistle and Townshend really are.

Entwistle's role is to supply a drone in unison with Townshend, occasionally to burst forward with a solo passage (definitively in "My Generation") with an emphasis on chords and sustain. Like most of the era's rock band bassists, Entwistle wasn't recorded very distinctly. Yet he underpins the sound, adding a toughness of tone without which Townshend's guitar would be a great deal less effective and at the same time providing a rhythmic footing much truer than anything Moon usually cared to establish.

Townshend uses a number of guitar-playing guises. For the most part, he, too, drones away underneath the tug of war created between the voice and drums or piano and drums. Less often, but still frequently, Townshend goes into his Bird Man act, swooping through the strings so that they actually ring. When necessary, he plays the kind of lead rhythm figures made popular by the Beatles. Of course, there are also a few songs ("My Generation," "Out in the Street," "The Ox," "I'm a Man") where Townshend unleashes his feedback effects. Overall, though, Townshend seems willing to simply function as a rhythm guitarist.

For the most part, the original songs on *My Generation* are merely musical shells, hollow cores into which almost any kind of rock could have been poured. Part of Townshend's intelligence as a rock songwriter was to compose for his band; the genius of his demos is not only that the Who copied many of them so exactly but that the resulting records sound so *right*. Townshend's song structures, when they are successful, are always barely disciplined enough to allow recordings to function without losing sight of rock's essential wildness.

For Townshend, complexity of musical structure was something to be appreciated, but the essence of the matter was to get the idea across. And surprisingly often, that idea was extremely personal—perhaps even confessional. " 'A Legal Matter' is about a guy on the run from a chick about to pin him down for breach of contract," wrote Townshend. "What this song was screaming from behind lines like 'It's a legal matter, baby, marrying's no fun/ It's a legal matter, baby, you got me on the run' was, 'I'm lonely, I'm hungry and the bed needs making.' I wanted a maid, I suppose."

In this sense, the idea that *My Generation* is some great mod statement is clearly nonsense. Songs like "A Legal Matter," "La La La Lies" and "Much Too Much" are as personal as anything Pete Townshend ever wrote. There is no conceivable sense in which lines like these, from "Much Too Much," could possibly be any sort of generational statement:

There was a time
I could give all I had to you,
But my enthusiasm waned
And I can't bear the pain
Of doing what I don't want to do

Unless, of course, we are dealing with a generation in desperate need of a spanking. (Townshend may have been creating a persona here, setting up a character who was spoiled and insensitive. But I don't think so.)

That's not to say that there aren't some attempts at the kind of spokesmanship critics often assign to Townshend; "My Generation" and "The Kids Are Alright" certainly qualify. But in general, Greg Shaw probably came closer to defining Townshend's theme when he wrote that each song here is "basically about one thing—finding self-image through the release of frustration-born tension. Tension and its release was the whole essence of the Who, both thematically and musically."

Townshend had an even more narrow fixation: the illusion of identity. "From his group's name on down, Townshend's real concern has always been not youth or rebellion but identity—identity as something to be searched for or escaped, but above all as something you can never be sure of," as Shaw put it. And it is in this regard that *My Generation* is an album that typified the dilemma of Townshend's audience. "My Generation," with its befuddled mod protagonist asserting himself against an enemy who clearly couldn't be bothered listening to his pillhead prattle, is only the most outstanding example. In "La La La Lies" the singer berates a friend who has been fibbing about who the vocalist really is. In "It's Not True" the protagonist attempts to defend himself against rumors and distortions—but he is only able to do this by negation, by asserting who he is *not*. In "The Kids Are Alright" a mod must immerse himself in the dancing, brawling crowd in order to recapture his sense of identity. The reason the guy in "A Legal Matter" doesn't want to marry is, in the end, because he's terrified of discovering who he really is (boring, middle-class and conventional; Townshend is one of rock's truest bohemians).

So it makes sense that the only one of the blues songs in which Townshend sounds genuinely involved, the only one to which he contributes anything as wild and excited as the solos in his own songs, is "I'm a Man," Bo Diddley's great and silly assertion of manhood and one whose first boast ("I'm a man now/I made twenty-one") is destined forever to impress teenagers and bemuse adults.

Townshend was far from a complete original: "A Legal Matter," the best of the original songs after "My Generation," borrows some of its hallucinatory humor from Dylan (especially "Motorpsycho Nightmare," Dylan's elaborate traveling salesman joke from the *Another Side* LP), and debts to Lennon and McCartney, Jagger and Richard and, most of all, Chuck Berry abound on the album. But Townshend did immediately establish a personal songwriting identity, and it was from the beginning one of the clearest and most forceful in rock. The way he delivered himself was quite clearly keyed into the way others were feeling: somewhat snotty, proudly youthful (but insecure and inexperienced, nevertheless), frustrated and angry, sexually sophisticated (but naïve in some ways), the very model of the modern mod gentleman—unless that was just appearance, too. *My Generation* isn't a mod statement, but the influence of mod is all over it.

My Generation was an enormously influential album. Moon's playing and Townshend's feedback effects are only the most obvious reasons. In addition, there's the record's basic sound.

My Generation wasn't state of the art in audio fidelity; it wasn't even recorded in stereo. But in those days, rock records were not necessarily in the forefront of hi-fi. If *My Generation* lacked the powerful brightness of contemporary Motown singles, it unquestionably had a raw power altogether absent from most other British or American productions of that period. And the crudity of the sound had its purpose in demarcating the Who as a rock & roll group, not as a pop band. As Townshend said, "the actual poorness of the recorded sound is a kind of trademark with us. The roughness of the recording has got to do with the roughness of the music."

John Swenson is correct when he notes that "without modern recording techniques, the Who invented a sound that has influenced virtually every other major hard rock group to come after them." The very brittleness and thinness of the sound—just as likely the result of haste and frustration as of planning—inspired other bands to go for less polished recordings. Whatever its flaws, *My Generation* is indisputably a great record because the impact of its sound is complete, and sonic impact is of the essence in rock & roll.

The question of credit for this production style (if that's what it is) immediately arose as the next Who tempest. The band had developed a breakthrough rock style, and beyond production, it is largely this that made the record so revolutionary. But *My Generation* is also consistent with some elements of other Shel Talmy productions—particularly its clarity and musical rawness.

Since the Who were clearly going to be a big and influential group, the question of credit became doubly important, and it probably made a split between Talmy and the group inevitable. For his part, Talmy had specific and domineering ideas about the producer's role in rock. "I think the role of the producer should be the same as the artist," he told Alan Betrock. "That is, it is a real role, and one has to be a part of the group—the whole thing should not be a giant ego trip for the band. The producer must be a tangible aspect and catalyst who oversees the whole project from beginning to end." In that sense, Talmy was not truly the Who's creative producer. At least, not if the stories of Kit Lambert's preproduction work are true. To the extent that the history of rock record production is a story of increasing control by the performer of his own work, even history argues against Talmy playing an indispensable (much less central) role with the Who.

It should also be remembered, as Betrock adds, that Talmy "was one of the few British producers who preferred to sacrifice slickness for rawness. While most U.K. record makers strove for a professionally bland sound, Talmy believed that the British sound was 'too precise, too perfect and as a result, lacking in feeling.' " *My Generation* is an album that demolishes such production criteria. So Talmy clearly contributed something of value to the Who; few of the records they made without him sound anything at all like the records they made with him. It's not a question of better or worse—just different.

Nevertheless, Talmy's insistence on being the dominant partner in the relationship forced a split, an inevitability compounded by the rotten record deal to which he'd signed the Who. Even after the post-"I Can't Explain" renegotiation, they were still receiving a substandard 4 percent royalty.

In January 1966, Chris Stamp flew to America (piggybacking on a ticket his brother, Terence, had been sent by the producers of *The Collector*, a film in which he was to star). But Chris Stamp wasn't looking for a meeting with American Decca—he went to New York because Sir Edward Lewis, head of the British Decca group, happened to be there. Stamp contacted Lewis in Manhattan in an attempt to get him to use his leverage with Talmy to renegotiate or obtain a release from the producer's contract. But this attempt was fruitless.

Brunswick was well pleased with Who sales, but in America, Decca hadn't been able to break the band any further than the lowest reaches of the charts: Even "My Generation" never climbed past number 74, and neither the album nor "Anyway, Anyhow, Anywhere" charted at all. There was very little incentive for U.S. Decca (to which the band was legally obligated) to do what Stamp wanted, which was essentially either to give the Who a complete release or to buy out Talmy and do things New Action's way. For at that point, Talmy was the one with the American track record (thanks to his hits with the Kinks). Therefore, he was the one Decca chose to keep happy.

However, while in New York, Stamp did go to see Atlantic Records and received an offer of a £10,000 ($28,000) advance against a 10 percent royalty, which more than doubled their percentage with Talmy. Since Lambert and Stamp had already spent their entire savings, this deal was especially attractive. Stamp phoned Lambert in London and told him, "Break the contract!"

New Action had retained a new lawyer, Edward Oldman, a veteran British show business attorney. "He was the first one to say to us, 'You can break the contract,' " Stamp said, and with their new lawyer, Stamp and Lambert set out to do just that.

Talmy said he "received a letter in the post saying something to the effect that my services were no longer required. 'We consider this contract terminated. . . .' " Talmy must have had some inkling of what was about to happen; he has acknowledged that "when the letter came, it wasn't a total surprise, as I had already made a decision as to what I thought of Lambert."

But Talmy refused to deal, so the Who's only alternative was to smoke him out.

Townshend had written a new song, "Substitute," based on a riff lifted from Robb Storme's "Where Is My Girl," a record that he'd heard during a *Melody Maker* "Blind Date" session. (The "Blind Date" feature in *Melody Maker* was a weekly record review column in which new singles were played for a pop star who didn't know whose music he was hearing but who was expected to comment during and after the playing. "They say terrible things about their best mates' latest, and it all makes the pop scene even snottier and more competitive," commented Townshend.) Townshend has said that "Substitute" was "written as a spoof of [the Rolling Stones'] '19th Nervous Breakdown,' " which (if true) means that Townshend wrote the song very shortly before it was recorded, since "19th Nervous Breakdown" was released in early February and "Substitute" was issued by March 4.

"On the demo, I sang with an affected Jagger-like accent," said Townshend, "which Kit obviously liked, as he suggested the song as the follow-up to 'My Generation.' " Since Glyn Johns had taken Talmy's side in the dispute—he had little choice, since Talmy was one of his most important clients—there was scant reason to record at IBC Studio. Instead, the group went to Olympic, off Baker Street in central London. The track was produced by Pete Townshend (although it was first released as "a New Action production").

After "My Generation," "Substitute" is by far the most exciting of the early Who singles. That riff—based on what was to become Townshend's favorite chord progression, D-A-D-G, with the open D used as a constant drone—was truly electrifying, and its force was doubled by the nonstop reiteration of Entwistle's bass. As Roy Carr and Charles Shaar-Murray noted, " 'Substitute' was the first time when Townshend proved he could build up the same amount of aggressive intensity on a twelve-string acoustic jumbo as he had previously achieved on a succession of rather battered Rickenbackers." Moon did his usual wild man act, although he was later to deny any memory of doing the session and in fact panicked when he first heard "Substitute" on the radio, certain that the Who was finally eliminating him and had already begun recording with someone else. Only constant assurances from the rest of the band convinced him it was really his playing. At any rate, as Townshend later pointed out, this memory lapse is a pretty good indication of how far gone on pills and booze Moon was even in those early days. He had taken to pop stardom like a lovable pup, drinking and doping his way through endless nights and never letting up, already acquiring a reputation in the press as the rock & roll delinquent.

Lyrically, "Substitute" is one of the most complicated and intriguing extensions of Townshend's identity crisis theme. It works off the same affirmation-by-negation scheme as "A Legal Matter," as the singer denies a whole series of qualities:

> I'm a substitute for another guy,
> I look pretty tall, but my heels are high,
> The simple things you see are all complicated,
> I look pretty young, but I'm just back-dated

In terms of vocal interplay, this is by far the best song that the Who had produced, Daltrey sounding convincing and the responding group vocals crisp and precise. This is one song that delivers on every element of the Who's promise; the unleashed explosiveness of the music is more than a match for the tension of the singer's befuddled self-image.

"Substitute" was an ideal follow-up to "My Generation," sustaining the group's image while extending its sound. But the band needed a record label again. To their rescue came Robert Stigwood, their booking agent, who had just formed a label called Reaction, destined to be one of the most significant record companies in England over the next few years. (In addition to the Who, Reaction also issued records by Jimi Hendrix, Cream and the Bee Gees—the latter pair also managed by Stigwood.) The Reaction agreement was short-term but crucial to the band's plans, since it was unlikely that any established label would agree to release anything by a band about to be swept up in litigation. But Stigwood's distribution contract with Polydor allowed him to take the risk, and his friendship with Lambert and Stamp ensured his willingness.

Stigwood, who was just then sharing office space with Lambert and Stamp, signed the group before "Substitute" was recorded. "We went in and played through the thing, and we went up and heard the playbacks and they sounded all right, mixed it, and Robert Stigwood came in and listened to the vocals and said, 'Sounds all right.' [He] didn't really know much of what was going on at the time," said Townshend.

According to Chris Stamp, the Who chose the song "Circles" (also known as "Instant Party") as the initial B-side of "Substitute" for political reasons. " 'Cause then Shel Talmy had to [enjoin] the record. And by stopping that record, he had to go to court. He had to face us." If this was really the cornerstone of the Who's legal strategy, it was a fairly absurd one.

"Circles" had been originally scheduled as the Who's follow-up to "My Generation" on Brunswick, and that label had listed it in its February release schedule. But on February 12, a front-page story in *Melody Maker* announced that the band had decided that "Circles" . . . has just not worked out." This story added that "Substitute" would replace it as the follow-up release, Kit Lambert calling the new song "better than 'My Generation.' " But Lambert and Stamp couldn't have been all that eager to be sued: Most (though not all) of the singles called the song "Instant Party," even though the number was nothing but a rerecorded version of "Circles." (For production quality, Talmy's version—which is also longer—gets the nod.)

Talmy immediately moved for a High Court injunction against Reaction's release of "Instant Party," not on the grounds that the Who were contracted exclusively to him—that was a whole separate lawsuit—but on the contention that there was a copyright inherent in the recorded version of a musical composition. As Pete Townshend once tried to explain, "If you're a record producer and you produce a song with a group and you make a creative contribution, then you own that sound—there's a copyright in that sound, that arrangement." This wasn't a bad piece of legal theorizing (although it took copyright law another decade to begin to recognize it), but then Talmy should have had good legal strategy, since he had retained Quintin Hogg, a former Tory cabinet minister who was one of England's most famous litigation attorneys.

By March 11, a week after Reaction issued "Substitute"/"Instant Party," Talmy had obtained an injunction preventing Polydor from continuing to distribute the B-side. Reaction then sent the Graham Bond Organisation into the studio to cut an instrumental, "Waltz for a Pig," which replaced "Instant Party" as the new B-side. For the occasion, Bond's group was rechristened the Who Orchestra.

Meanwhile, Talmy and Brunswick rushed out his version of "Circles" as the B-side of "A Legal Matter," yanked out of the album for single release. Perhaps out of spite (or because he figured he could cash in on the preexisting publicity "Substitute" gathered), Talmy also called his B-side "Instant Party."

This controversy would make a lot more sense historically if a more significant song had been involved. But "Circles" (or "Instant Party" or whatever one cares to call it) is one of the slighter Townshend songs of the period, notable primarily for John Entwistle's braying French horn (his recorded debut on that instrument).

Legal points are not won and lost on artistic issues, though. Talmy's case was strong enough for his side to obtain an injunction; furthermore, he got it without settling the central issue. This was an advantage to him, since he had more financial and legal resources than the Who and could afford to wait them out, and because the central issue—the legality and fairness of the contract—was one he hoped to avoid.

The group, on the other hand, was pressured not only because it needed money but also because it had been almost six months since the release of "My Generation." They needed another hit to sustain their career and image. More than once, lawsuits such as this one had stalled promising careers.

The two sides were attacking each other with real animosity. Even years later their comments about one another were venomous. "Kit Lambert is insane," Talmy told Alan Betrock. "He should be locked up."

Lambert and Stamp were properly embarrassed by the deal that they'd made with Talmy. "Although we didn't think it was such a bad deal at the time, we then learned about other deals," Stamp told Barnes. "Then we thought, 'Oh, fucking hell.' " Pete Townshend may have been most bitter of all, because he felt that Talmy had treated the Who (especially himself) as nothing more than a dispensable pop group who were in the studio to take orders from their producer/boss.

All of this came into focus at the hearing on the High Court injunction. Talmy argued his theory before the judge saying "things like, 'And then on bar thirty-six I suggested to the lead guitarist that he play a diminuendo, forget the adagio and play thirty-six bars modulating to the key of E flat,' which was a total bullshit—he used to fall asleep at the desk. Glyn Johns used to do everything," according to Townshend. If Talmy had given such instructions, they were pointless, since only Entwistle could read music.

That wasn't the way that Glyn saw it. "It was a very awkward situation," he said, "because I was very close to both sides of the argument. I mean, Shel was a good friend, and the Who, of course, were really good friends as well.

"I evaluated it to be the fact that they were breaking a contract with somebody; they actually were at fault as a result, and so, therefore, I took Shel's side and actually signed an affidavit in court to that effect.

"[The Who] were actually making claims that he didn't do anything. It's extraordinary—it turned out in the end that they tried to claim that I actually did the producing, and so, in fact, I was a witness against myself in a way."

Johns also admits that "in a way, I did do as much as he—but it doesn't alter the fact that he did find the band, he did bring them into the studio and he was the creative force with them initially, there's no question about it."

Townshend further resented "the fact that Shel's attitude was, 'You're just a load of punks and I made you, you should be happy you've got where you have because if it wasn't for me you'd be nowhere.' And the other thing was that he had a specific sound and it became inflexible." (Yet Townshend also says that "if it wasn't for him, I don't think the Who would have got off the ground," citing his recording of "I Can't Explain" as the key.)

Glyn Johns is also probably correct in saying that the root of the problem was the band's failure to break in America. "If they had broken in America, then everything would have been hunky-dory, they would never have had the disagreement, I'm sure." This is unlikely—the recording agreement with Talmy simply didn't provide the Who enough money, and eventually, they would have broken over it. But since Talmy himself admits that, financially, America was the whole ball game for rock bands, the Who had legitimate reason for disgruntlement there.

In any event, the legal situation hinged on none of this. When Quintin Hogg approached the judge to introduce the case, he said, "Your honor, this is the case of *Shel Talmy versus the Who*."

"The Who?"

"The Who, your honor."

"Ah, yes, I see, the World Health Organization."

"Right there," said Talmy, "I knew I had the case won." And so did the opposition. They made a deal—or the beginning of one—that afternoon on the courthouse steps.

In the meantime, the Who were winning the battle of the charts. "Substitute" came in at number 19 and eventually reached number 1 in the *New Musical Express* listings. "A Legal Matter" never got past number 32. By March 25, the injunction against Reaction's release of the alternate version of "Circles"/"Instant Party" had been lifted. Now all that was left was to sort out the nature of the break-up. Talmy clearly could no longer hope to work with the band; by then, he probably no longer wanted to.

At this time there were a number of behind-the-scenes machinations involving the Who's management. Lambert hoped to create a formal relationship with Brian Epstein. Andrew Loog Oldham, the Rolling Stones' manager/producer, had designs on managing the Who himself. And Oldham had told the Stones' American business manager, Allen Klein, that the Who were Britain's next big thing, thus kindling Klein's always disruptive interest.

Klein had begun his career as an accountant specializing in auditing record companies for performers, most of whom did not know that such a thing could be done. In the fly-by-night rock business of the early sixties, Klein was able to find hundreds of thousands of hidden dollars for clients such as Bobby Darin and Sam Cooke. As Klein learned the processes by which the industry functioned, he drove some of the hardest bargains in making recording agreements and in setting up music publishing companies. A good deal of this money stuck to Klein's fingers. At the time, he was the height of high-powered business advice in the American rock industry. Klein represented the Stones, through Andrew Oldham, as well as Herman's Hermits, the Animals and the Dave Clark Five, the acts represented by the British producer/entrepreneur Mickie Most. He made no secret of his desire to control the entire British rock scene, or at least the American development of it.

As a condition of settling with Lambert and Stamp, Shel Talmy insisted that the negotiations be handled by Klein. (Maybe this was a favor to Klein, or maybe it was simply Talmy's way of making sure his own interests were well-protected.) In consequence, that spring, Stamp (who had taken over complete responsibility for the band's American affairs, leaving Lambert free to wrestle with England and Europe), Townshend and their attorney, Edward Oldman, flew to New York to deal with Allen Klein on his yacht in New York Harbor.

According to Townshend, Oldman, "an austere, conservative, almost Edward Heath character . . . took two looks at Klein and said, 'We're leaving.' So we ate his caviar, had a look at the Statue of Liberty from his yacht, shat in his toilet and went back to England." (In fact, Klein paid for Townshend's first *two* visits to the States—the meetings were spread over a period during which the Who had a gig at Sheffield University. Klein paid for Townshend's airfare, first class, roundtrip, so that he could play the show and then rejoin the business discussions. Pete missed the gig, anyway. But his loathing for Klein remained genuine enough; he later wrote the song "Lazy Fat People," one of his most devastating bits of sarcasm, about Klein.)

Klein's major concern was not to find a deal advantageous to Shel Talmy but to insinuate himself into some kind of authoritative role with the Who. (Once there, as he had already demonstrated by ousting Oldham's partner, Eric Easton, Klein could be counted on to take over completely.) Lambert and Stamp quickly saw enough to pick up on the manner of his maneuvering and in what Stamp describes as "our first really sharp move" set out to trap the fox with his own bait.

They signed an agreement giving Klein the right to manage the Who but only if he were able to nail a deal together within twenty days. At the end of that period, if all parties hadn't signed, Lambert and Stamp were free to retain their management interest.

Kit and Chris then set to work complicating negotiations, which wasn't difficult, especially over transatlantic distances. "We just sort of started mad phone calls to him, you know what I mean, and mixed the whole thing up," said Stamp. "Just very clever bullshit. He never realized what was going on and ran out of time." Meanwhile, a settlement with Talmy was achieved.

This settlement was perhaps the least shrewd of all the business deals the Who were ever involved in (very few of which were shrewd at all). For the next five years, Talmy would receive an override of 5 percent on all Who recordings—which included the two biggest albums of the group's career, *Tommy* (1969) and *Who's Next* (1971). Superficially, the details of the settlement weren't that onerous: Talmy received a 5 percent royalty, and since the Who's renegotiation with Decca U.S. and their new contract with Polydor in England gave them a 10 percent fee, they were still ahead of the 2½ percent that Talmy's original contract had given them.

But these mathematics are short-sighted and primitive. In fact, each of the members of the Who received only one-fourth of the 5 percent (and this after management commissions of up to 40 percent)—that is, a royalty of 1.25 percent per musician. While this is better than the .75 percent each received under the original deal, it is grossly unjust when compared to Talmy's rake-off. The settlement insured that the Who would never receive anything approaching a fair share of the wealth generated by their recordings. (And the albums that made the most money for the Who are not records that Shel Talmy could conceivably have created.)

Lambert and Stamp's justification for such an extravagant settlement is obvious: "We were left with Shel Talmy on paper," as Stamp put it, "but we were not left with Shel Talmy in the studio." The Who probably had very little legal justification to break the original contract, and they didn't have the time or money for a lengthy litigation. And once again, it is essential to recall that nobody conceived of a pop band surviving at the top of the heap for five years, much less getting bigger as they went along. By the summer of 1966, the Beatles had been a worldwide phenomenon for three years, and already people were expecting them to fade.

Nevertheless, this settlement with Talmy had terrible economic consequences for the Who, and in a way the eccentric shape of their career (in which live performance was always emphasized above recordings, though the latter are more profitable for almost every other group in the business) may be traced to attitudes ingrained by the persistent, gnawing knowledge that so much of their proceeds would line Shel Talmy's pockets.

Lambert and Stamp did a better job of getting advances from the record companies. U.S. Decca paid out $50,000 against future royalties and promised not to sue. In England, Polydor advanced the group £50,000 ($140,000) for rights to U.K. and European releases. This gave the group a total of about £70,000 (almost $200,000) with which to pay off debts. Most of the money was eaten up right away.

The success of "Substitute," however, poked the group's price for concerts up past £300 ($850), previously considered the top price for anything except the Beatles and, occasionally, the Stones. The Who actually managed to squeeze as much as £500 ($1,400) out of some of their percentage deals, largely because they knew how to do advance promotion and because Mike Shaw's presence at the door assured them of a fairly accurate ticket count.

The group also played some package tours that summer, first going out with the Merseybeats, the Fortunes, the Graham Bond Organisation and Screaming Lord Sutch, then touring with the Spencer Davis Group, Mike Scarne and the Band of Angels. They also played the *NME* Poll Winners concert, with the Beatles, the Stones, the Spencer Davis Group, Herman's Hermits, the Alan Price Set, Cliff Richard, the Yardbirds, the Small Faces, Roy Orbison, the Walker Brothers and the Shadows. *NME* called the Who's set the most remarkable of the night.

The band made its biggest money playing in Europe, where they were even bigger than in England. (Richard Barnes suggests that this is because the Who's exceptionally visual act was extremely effective in non-English-speaking countries.) In Stockholm, they played a stadium and drew 11,000 kids that summer which was way out of proportion to their overall drawing power, a gloriously isolated triumph.

None of this relieved the debts very much. Keith Moon had been married to a seventeen-year-old model named Kim Kerrigan that March and became even more money-mad in consequence. He estimated that the band's unpaid bills had reached £30,000 to £40,000 (around $85,000 to $110,000). And they kept rising, not only because of the band's destructive stage show (by now, their road crew knew every trick of patching gear) but also because the group insisted upon living like full-fledged stars, regardless of the status of their bank accounts.

"The thing was that if they were doing well, had a good gig or a successful record, they expected the rock & roll rewards," said Stamp. "No point in having the hit record and not being able to buy the flash car. And there were these sort of celebrations just to make the hit record real. Although we really all owed fortunes—real fortunes. It was incredibly dicey."

In later years, Moon said that he never understood why so many people found the group's early days glamorous. "To me, it just means number 92 buses back to Ealing. We could just about afford bus fares in those days. I'll never know why people used to think we had a load of money." But of course, Moon knew precisely why people thought that: because the Who *spent* as though they had a great deal of cash, in the all-night clubs, on huge American cars (Townshend drove a Lincoln Continental convertible), on pills and booze and clothes and on replacing smashed-up equipment.

Money pressures were still dictating what the group attempted artistically. There's nothing entirely wrong with that—playing music is a job, as Daltrey knew all along. The Who should have been relatively independent of such desperation tactics; they'd had their chart success, followed it up with another. *Still* they searched for a gimmick.

17

Opera-goers today accept without indignation vocal emissions that would have been soundly and rightly denounced as bawling by eighteenth-century connoisseurs of bel canto.

But they will not, as a rule, accept the sounds of soul.

—Henry Pleasants,
The Great American Popular Singers

The convergence of American and British popular music trends in the sixties by no means reflects a continuous state of affairs, not even within the post-war rock & roll era (and ultimately, not even within the post-Beatles rock period). There were always a great many American acts who meant nothing in England, while some of the biggest hit-makers England produced (Cliff Richard, most notoriously) never dented the American consciousness. Even in the mid-to-late sixties, when British and American audiences almost always heard the same records—Motown, the Beatles, the Rolling Stones, Dylan, Cream, Hendrix, Sly and the Family Stone—there were still significant differences that reflected the separate development of the music industry in each country.

American rock & roll was born from sources in industrial-era folk forms (blues, rhythm & blues, gospel, country-western). Such music was almost always produced by groups despised for regional, ethnic, racial or, ultimately, class-based reasons: black and white Southerners, Holy Rollers, moonshining mountaineers, urban blacks, the working class in general. American industry had a tremendous investment in the continuing oppression of all these groups, but it could not deny or ignore their force as a market.

That didn't do the first generation of rock singers much good: The debacle of Elvis Presley's Hollywood years only exemplifies what happened to every rock singer who attempted to forge a career within the mainstream of show business. Most of these performers simply retreated (to honkytonks or the chitlin' circuit or the church). But they left a legacy that the more self-conscious second generation of rock singers could not ignore.

In both Britain and America, the second generation of white rock performers tended to be more middle-class, which made its dissatisfaction with the options provided by contemporary mainstream culture that much more bitter. For performers like John Lennon, Bob Dylan and Pete Townshend, Vegas and supper clubs, Hollywood movies and glittering television specials weren't a goal, they were a trap to avoid. Very few of the post-Beatles generation of performers courted "respectability"—at least not any kind of respectability that Col. Tom Parker or Larry Parnes would have understood. Instead, they stood for the self-respect of the performer and the audience, the refusal to be put off with cheap spectacle and a set of aspirations that simply confounded the traditional standards not only of show business but of Art, as well.

To the extent that the performers were aware of the effective cap that had been placed on their advancement, there was even a tradition of rebellion that rock & roll singers could tap into. American rock's stable base in various kinds of folk music (and American folk's historic associations with left-wing radicalism) gave it a base from which to create an anti-show-business alternative. Needless to say, this alternative was extremely limited; within a decade, the rock anti-establishment had become almost as greedy and decadent as the older form of show business. But in the meantime, structures were created under which rock stars worked with the greatest independence (and at the highest wages) of any group of performers (or workers) in the world.

In England, there was no tradition of counter-show-biz rebellion. Rock absorbed the old music hall practices. Because the country was culturally homogenous, (the growing West Indian population had not yet emerged as a market or as a political force), Britain's aesthetic traditions were limited to high culture (Art) and low or mass culture (entertainment). As in most Western nations, these were considered irrevocably opposed.

Within the century-old conventions of music hall tradition, rebellion was not a concept, much less an issue. Within the context of high art, rebellion was not only a possibility—in modernist terms, it was a necessity. But high art rebellion was the province of avant-gardism, which was in theory and in practice innately hostile to the mass culture of which rock was perhaps the most articulate (and certainly the angriest and least apologetic) part.

Susan Sontag uses rock as an example in "Notes on Camp" (1964), citing it as an instance of camp using "things which, from a 'serious' point of view, are either bad art or kitsch." The disdain is deliberate. High-brows might wish to annex the interpretation of rock (and other mass culture) but only to diminish its effective power.

Nevertheless, avant-gardism and camp were the only sensibilities that offered British rock artists a viable alternative for both their rebellion and their ambition. Nothing else suggested both a critique of society—including a critique of traditional forms of culture—and an embrace of a proletarian industrial form such as rock. This didn't prevent John Lennon's "studied pataphysical" and other borrowings from and dabblings with the surrealistic and conceptual avant-garde. It didn't stop Pete Townshend from expropriating concepts from pop art and auto-destruction. Nor did it deter Ray Davies from concocting satires on the *haut monde* and *demimonde* in the best bohemian tradition or the Rolling Stones from adopting a sooty, scruffy demeanor that was perhaps the quintessential avant-garde, life-as-art (or life-as-art-criticism) gesture.

To the extent that pop really was a shallow, manipulative commodity, cynically produced, exploitatively packaged, such perspectives were extremely useful. But rock showed every indication of being what Townshend claimed it was, a vehicle for "people who couldn't really communicate in normal ways"— by which he meant the culturally disenfranchised, not an elite.

In that sense, British rock's absorption in avant-gardism could only lead to nihilistic self-indulgence or complete self-loathing. Or both.

According to almost all high art theories, even Marxist ones, rock's content was completely determined by the fact that it was a product of capitalist industrial society. So even rock's content could never truly challenge the dominant ideology.

The content of rock contradicted such suppositions, but only those who actually listened before judging could know this. And in the end, the facts didn't make much difference. If the high art avant-garde was the only tradition in which rock artists could find a way toward rebellion once they'd left pure pop, then they were doomed. As the British critic-sociologist Simon Frith has written, "British rock, too, is built round a claim to rebellion, but for British rockers the problem is, from the beginning, to relate their self-proclaimed misunderstood artistic identity to the reality (and goal) of popularity. In the British theory, the most successful artist is the one who has no success at all. . . ."

The alternative was Britain's drab show business, which had hardly a fragment of Hollywood's glamour and which was dedicated to such corniness that it shunned any hint of sophistication. There wasn't any middle ground, and because Lennon, Townshend, Jagger, Davies and their peers were too perceptive to abandon rock (because they liked it, because it was effective beyond the dictates of any theory, because it made them rich), they were again forced back into the conventions of music hall.

A decade later, Townshend and Jagger were still apologizing for continuing with "only rock & roll." In short, they were so trapped by the central myth of show biz—that entertainment is meaningless fun—that they were unable to proceed, except as farce. (Of course, this philosophy also made it much easier to deny the responsibilities and accept the rewards accruing to star status.) Under the circumstances, it is a wonder that hypocrisy was staved off for so long, that even more performers weren't cheated out of everything by businessmen who *did* take the game seriously, that so few were driven mad by the supposed pointlessness of what they were driven to do.

But that doesn't mean that during the middle sixties many British rock musicians weren't hoping to use rock music as a vehicle to create social change, as a means of making important artistic statements in the most serious sense and as a way of dismantling everything corny and unhip in the entertainment business. It certainly doesn't mean that rock didn't succeed in attaining some portion of each of these goals. It just means that British rock performers were limited, not by any lack of quality in their work and definitely not by any lack of merit in rock as a form, but because society still regarded rock as a children's pastime.

In an early July 1965 issue of *Melody Maker*, Townshend boasted, "What we are trying to do in our music [is] protest against 'show biz' stuff, clear the hit parade of stodge." As more conservative entrepreneurs once more tried to horn in on the post-Beatles action with acts like Britain's Herman's Hermits and Freddie and the Dreamers and America's Every Mother's Son, Dino, Desi and Billy and the Cowsills, rock itself was indeed becoming stodgy. Because such music was indubitably safer than real rock, it got heavy airplay in both England and the United States—and the records sold. Yet short of creating something utterly unlistenable (a pointless gesture, since no one *would* listen), what kind of challenge to stodge could the Who mount?

What Townshend was seeking was a way past the artificial limitations imposed by the three-minute pop single. As Pete, among others, was beginning to see, the album was the ideal medium for recorded music—or at least the place where the next phase of pop expansion would take place. Bob Dylan's "Like a Rolling Stone" was 5:59, and it had already been a Top 10 hit on both sides of the Atlantic.

In May 1966, the Beach Boys released their first conceptually integrated album, *Pet Sounds*. It went only a little further than some of the Beach Boys' earlier surf and hot rod LPs in stringing together songs with lyrical, harmonic and melodic relationships, but it immediately stirred the thinking of everyone in rock. Surf music purists like Moon hated it, while other musicians, including Pete Townshend, were tremendously excited by the possibilities of the serious "concept" album. Yet no one was quite sure where to take the basic idea.

This situation was tailor-made for Kit Lambert, who became the dominant figure in the band's business life (since Chris was spending more and more time in America) and in its creative projects, as well (since Kit was anointed producer now that Shel Talmy was out of the way). Expanding beyond the limits of the pop single was the thrust of all Lambert's work for the next three years.

Meanwhile, the band members were still at war. Townshend had a go at Moon that spring when Keith showed up late at the Ricky Tick club in Newbury. Pete bashed the drummer in the head with his guitar. The group played with a stand-in drummer for a few gigs while Keith threatened to take John and form a new band. Townshend and Moon soon patched it up, but the row exemplified the constant conflict that remained within the band.

As for Townshend versus Daltrey, there was no end to that feud. Roger's sorties in the press, where he tried to pontificate like Pete, were hapless. "This beat generation is moving so fast people are running out of ideas," he told a reporter. "The people who invented electric guitars, whoever they were, will have to think of something new. The groups have exploited them to the full. Maybe we'll have to go back to violins. Still, we always were on the fiddle." Daltrey wound up making a corny joke out of a statement that had a kernel of truth.

Maybe Roger couldn't help it. As Townshend commented a few years later, "Roger feels that perhaps he's unsuccessful when it comes to creative things. It's got a lot to do with enjoying painting and writing compositions at school. I don't think Roger was ever like that, and I don't think today, because he's in a rock band and probably expected to come up with the odd song, that he's automatically going to be able to write. I mean, his talents are elsewhere. And it's not just standing holding a mike, it's in firing the Who, and he does it in a way nobody would ever understand. Nobody would believe it if they knew how it worked." In mid-1966, Daltrey was simply trying to hang on.

Just as the artistic situation played into the best part of Kit Lambert's talents, the band's personnel squabbles activated all of his worst ones. Lambert proceeded to do the one thing that personal management theory, sound business judgment and simple common sense would insist was a mistake: He took sides.

Lambert and Townshend needed each other; in a sense, each was the other's most important collaborator. Nothing Chris Stamp or Roger Daltrey could offer was nearly as important. "Kit had this enormous output and exuberance that Pete certainly plugged into," said Keith Altham. "I'm sure he encouraged and excited Pete into a whole lot of things. Pete would come up with the idea and Kit would get enthused and take the thing a step further and say, 'Fantastic. Let's hire the whole world.' And gradually the thing seemed to snowball and escalate. And from a fairly firm idea you suddenly had a huge global plan emerge from Kit.

"Pete must have had the initial ideas and Kit took 'em and magnified them and gave them back, and Pete thought, 'God, maybe that was a better idea than I thought.' "

Unfortunately, too much of Lambert's escalation of ideas was done in order to create from something reasonable the kind of overblown fantasy that epitomizes Camp. Camp is inevitably associated with gay subculture, and surely Kit's homosexuality was one reason why he overhyped everything. But another and equally (perhaps more) important reason was an inability to take rock as seriously as it deserved. Lambert never thought much of rock as music, and because of that, he never had the passion for detail that was essential to the producer of records by a group as adventurous as the Who.

That doesn't mean that Lambert didn't want the Who to be serious about what they did; as Sontag writes, "the essential element [of Camp] is seriousness, a seriousness that fails. Of course, not all seriousness that fails can be redeemed as Camp. Only that which has the proper mixture of the exaggerated, the fantastic, the passionate and the naïve." What the Camp sensibility requires is misguided ambition at which to sneer. "It seems unlikely that much of the traditional opera repertoire could be such satisfying Camp if the melodramatic absurdities of most opera plots had not been taken seriously by their composers," notes Sontag.

From the point of view of the naïve artist himself, the function of Camp is to place a low ceiling on the perceived (if not actual) value of his work. Camp is a laugh in the face of the artist who doesn't live up to the exaggerated sophistication of the contemporary aesthete. Like all avant-garde sensibilities, Camp's inherent hostility to intelligent mass culture—and necessarily, rock & roll music—is self-evident.

Yet for someone like Townshend, who was having a hard time taking his own work seriously (despite his instinct that what he was doing was well worth the effort), Lambert's Camp perspective was nevertheless productive: It spurred him on, past all bounds of modesty, because even if by these lights rock was fundamentally worthless, the only way to make anything at all out of it was to explode it and expose its ludicrous inadequacy as a form.

Rock might be changing, but the Who's next priority had to be another hit single. The lawsuit meant that nothing new was recorded until the end of the summer, and once "Substitute" dropped off the charts in mid-June, there was no new product for the next two months, a commercially risky situation. In mid-August, Brunswick finally released "The Kids Are Alright," backed with "The Ox," as a single, which annoyed Lambert, not so much because they released it without consulting the group as because Decca had promised to release "La La La Lies." The single made the charts, but not until the group released its next new song, and then only for two weeks.

The lawsuit was not the only reason for the delay. Townshend decided that the solution to the dilemma of rock's expanding potential was narrative, and with Lambert's encouragement, he set about writing a series of rock songs with a story line. Lambert was already referring to this as Pete's rock opera, but more teasingly than meaningfully.

Quads was the story of a family, in the year 1999, in a society where couples could select the sex of their children. This family has requested four girls but receives three daughters and a son. All four are nevertheless raised as females, with predictable attendant misery and black humor. "It goes on in later life where the three girls become a singing group, and I had amazing visions of Keith, John and I pretending to be the Beverly Sisters," Townshend reminisced in 1971. "There was a lot of comedy in it . . . but I think at the same time it was a heavily serious thing as well because it had these flashbacks to childhood which I was very into at the time." Without knowing more, it's hard to say just how deeply Townshend based *Quads* on his own life, but in its themes of rejection, identity crisis and oddity, one can easily recognize a pattern.

Pete apparently got no further with *Quads* than a single completed song. Taken out of context, the song is a truly miserable (and thus perfectly thrilling) exposition of tortured sexual misidentification. "I'm a Boy," as it's called, was released on August 26, hitting the charts September 1, and it remained there for thirteen weeks and hit number 1 on the BBC. (The B-side, "In the City," was written by Moon and Entwistle, who were also the only two who played on it, Daltrey and Townshend having been kept in the dark about the session. It is a Beach Boys pastiche with a nice bass figure, pathetic lead vocals and predictably dynamic percussion. The principal value of "In the City" is as evidence of just how deep the band's artistic warring went—although it might also have been useful in dissuading Moon of his vocal ambitions.)

"I'm a Boy" is not an especially successful narrative, but it is a nice piece of characterization, which turned out to be Townshend's real strength as a lyricist. It, too, is heavily influenced by the Beach Boys, with a massed choir of backing vocals at the beginning and end of the song. The lead vocal is a trade-off between Townshend as narrator and Daltrey, who incarnates the poor child. Moon and Townshend combat each other all the way through, chop for chop, riff for riff, while Entwistle has his best-recorded performance yet.

In the midst of the song's chart run, Kit Lambert announced that the Who would do a special "Ready! Steady! Go!" program. The show's usual format was to devote not more than two—usually only one—segments per group, but "RSG" agreed to devote sixteen minutes to the Who's new stage act—a show "based upon the 'Theatre of the Absurd' ideas that the Who have," said Lambert, who was filibustering as usual. "Theatre of the Absurd" merely seemed like the logical catch phrase to use after "pop art" and "auto-destruction," so he tossed it in.

The show aired on Friday, October 21; it was taped and shown in France, Switzerland, Germany and Sweden over the next two weeks. And on the twenty-eighth, the Who released its next recording, a five-song EP, *Ready, Steady, Who!* which was designed to give the appearance of a live recording though the music was in fact made in the studio. The songs included the Who's version of "Circles"; a new Townshend song, "Disguises"; a pair of Jan and Dean/Beach Boys numbers, "Barbara Ann" and "Bucket T"; and Neal Hefti's theme song for the TV show "Batman."

It was a last fling for super-pop, a final attempt to catch the glory of the mad mod moment that both the Who and "Ready! Steady! Go!" had promulgated. That time was now coming to an end, not at all prematurely. By the end of the year, "RSG" was finished. (That may have been one reason it agreed to break format and give the Who so much time.) And the era of pop music simplicity was ending with it. By the end of 1966, as Chris Charlesworth wrote, "Pop music was no longer aimed directly at young fans who screamed at their idols, and neither was it looked upon by its creators as a disposable commodity, good for a quick run on the charts and little else. Musical awareness, appreciation and talent were driving a cleft into pop music which would change the medium for all time."

Ready! Steady! Who! sounded almost nostalgic, even when it was released. It was a self-conscious attempt to regain an innocence and naïvete about rock and its environment that was swiftly becoming not only outmoded but impossible. "Bucket T" and "Barbara Ann" are almost desperate attempts to keep things light and "entertaining," and "Batman" was probably meant that way, too.

But it is "Batman" (which had been a hit in America that spring for the semi-surf instrumental group, the Marketts) which most decisively enters the new era, even if it's against everyone's will. "Batman," originally written by Neal Hefti as a big band arrangement, is a trivial pop melody on which the Who wreak absolute havoc; this is one of their most balanced performances of the period—Entwistle's bass carries the tune, Townshend and Moon weave chaos all around him. It is a throwaway performance, not two minutes long, yet it is hard to think of anything that more conclusively defines *why* rock had to change: The ominous growl of Entwistle's bass, the compulsive sting of Townshend's guitar licks, the ceaseless sizzle of Moon's kit demand more content than this flimsy structure can give them. *Demand* is the operative word.

This moment could have been a dead end for rock. It could have led the musicians of the sixties into the trap that buried their fifties forebears: the trap of Camp, in which gestures such as "Batman" and "Bucket T" and "Barbara Ann" and the occasional obscure old hit, like "Circles," became the complete substance of what was offered by performers and accepted by their audiences. In terms of pop mythology, it would have been understandable if "Batman" was the last gasp of a great but narrow talent and the Who had never had another hit.

But the Who were no longer bound by the old formulas. The proof of that is "Disguises," the one song here that is not just what it seems: in this case, a pastiche derived from the Beatles' *Revolver*-style pop. "Disguises" certainly owes a lot to the Beatles, for its harmonies, its off-center rhythm and even for the backwards-running tape effects that swirl around everything else. But the bizarre perspective of the lyrics is pure Townshend, a statement of mistaken identity to go with all his others:

Only today I saw you dressed as a flower bed,
Last week you had a wig on your head,
Misdirecting traffic in the street
And your shoes were too big for your feet
You were wearin' disguises

Here a debt to *Blonde on Blonde* Dylan (with his fascination with weird hats and wigs) is equally evident—but the context belongs to Townshend, not just its era, which is only a way of saying that the Who had arrived at a period even more suitable to its strange array of talents than mod had been. Rather than latching onto a style and exploiting it, this time the Who became natural leaders of the next stage of rock's development. "Disguises" wasn't the best song Townshend had written, but it was the most adventurous. For the moment, that meant everything.

18

*We still live in the Stone Age
as far as art is concerned.*
—*Pete Townshend*

Ready, Steady, Who! was a last fling in another sense: It was the final Who recording to carry no production credit. Beginning with the recording sessions for the group's second album, which began in early September, just after the release of "I'm a Boy," Kit Lambert had grown more and more involved, but it wasn't until the album was close to completion that he officially donned the role of producer. As Pete Townshend said, "Kit didn't slide naturally into the seat of producing the Who—he kind of arrived in the position of producing the Who because we desperately needed a producer." Pete couldn't keep the job—even though "I'm a Boy" and "Substitute" sounded superb—because of band politics.

The issue of record production and the function of the record producer—ideally and practically—is one of the key issues of the rock era. Initially, the producer was the record company A&R man, who was totally responsible for matching the pop performer with his song and his musicians, working out the arrangement, arranging all the pre- and post-production aspects of the record-making process. Gradually, certain A&R men began working independently of any single label. These independents—Jerry Leiber and Mike Stoller, Phil Spector, Berry Gordy—sometimes worked with established acts, sometimes with raw talent, sometimes under contract for a specific project at a specific label, sometimes creating tapes and peddling them. Many of them were nearly as dictatorial as the A&R men and as insensitive to the artist, but if they succeeded, they almost always exhibited a genuine sympathy for the marketplace and some marginal empathy for talent. Needless to say, these independents worked almost exclusively in rock and in rhythm & blues.

Britain moved more slowly, largely because the country's record industry was continuously dominated by the four major companies (EMI, Decca, Philips, Pye and their subsidiaries and licensees) and because the country hadn't any market as volatile and adventuresome as R&B. When the Beatles signed to EMI's Parlophone in 1962, they were assigned a producer, George Martin (who happened also to be their "discoverer"), who worked with them until the very end of their career. But other bands had other approaches (the Rolling Stones worked with their manager, Andrew Loog Oldham, for several years at the beginning of their career), and the manager/producer was a familiar figure in Britain through the mid-seventies. But only a few true independent producers made their mark in the British Invasion era. Most were outsiders, such as the Americans Shel Talmy and Jimmy Miller; even the most successful British independent, Mickie Most, had to go to South Africa to get his start. It was not until very late in the decade that Britain began to develop an outstanding crop of independent record producers, largely from its always excellent corps of recording engineers.

The role of the rock record producer varies from genre to genre, time to time, country to country. Theoretically, the producer is responsible for what transpires during the session itself: which of the available songs and musicians are used, what gets edited out, what's added. There's a tempting analogy here with the director's role in movie making, but it's a parallel that rarely holds up, since (while films are almost always the personal expression of the director) very few producers can be said to do anything more than create an environment in which the performer's vision is expressed. There are producers (Phil Spector, Mike Chapman, Giorgio Moroder) whose contributions often exceed those of the performers with whom they work, but these are the exceptions.

Usually, a producer is brought in either to make a specific technical contribution to the sound of a record or because he can make some kind of conceptual contribution (acting as either a musical or psychological catalyst).

Kit Lambert's evident disdain for studio technique made him a liability in many ways. Probably, Lambert should never have been more than the band's coproducer, working with a good engineer or perhaps Townshend himself. Townshend has gone so far as to say that "there was never any point when Kit knew more than I did about the mechanics of a recording studio." This seems to have concerned Townshend very little at some times and to have embarrassed him a great deal at others. Clearly, the Who's records with Lambert at the helm never sounded as good as they could have (or should have, compared to contemporary records by the Beatles and Rolling Stones, for instance—a comparison that's especially relevant because the Who had access to the same facilities and engineers that those bands did).

Glib as ever, Townshend was capable of explaining away the limitations of the group's sound. "We made records to sound tinny—recorded tinny to sound tinny," he claimed more than once. "It's no good recording things to sound hi-fi if they're gonna sound tinny. It was just a real clangy sound. But that early clangy Who sound was very much suited to the Dansette record player with the tin speaker and two-watt amplifier." But that's an excuse—as Townshend knew, the Who's major production problem was not tinniness but a muddy mix, without the crisp highs and well-defined bass others were delivering.

Some of his other defenses made a great deal more sense, however, though these had nothing at all to do with sound. "Working with Kit, we had a lot of . . . recorded image strength," Townshend told John Swenson. "He was very certain to make sure that the group's individual musical identities came across very strongly in the music." And to *Rolling Stone*'s Jonathan Cott, Pete said, "The production of our records has got nothing to do with sound. It's got to do with trying to keep Keith Moon on his fucking drum stool and keep him away from the booze. And through that period, it was to do with keeping me from fucking up on some kind of other dope. I'm very good now, I sit there waiting for each tape, but there was a whole period when Kit Lambert was just keeping us from really fighting. We're a dreadful group to record."

This may be the key to why Lambert got the job in the first place, since Townshend was a much more obvious selection to produce the group. But making Townshend the Who's producer, writer and guitarist (as well as its occasional lead singer) would have been tantamount to acknowledging that it was his band. That would probably have spelled breakup, since not only Daltrey but also Moon and Entwistle had their own ideas about what the Who was "really" all about. At least Daltrey would listen when Kit Lambert told him to sing "completely opposite" to the way he felt about a song. If Townshend had made any such suggestion, blood might have flowed.

Lambert did have a few musical contributions to make. Townshend has said that Kit "thoroughly produced" the Who, "altering things in composition and influencing me in certain directions." But he's also said that Lambert's work had been "marvelously preposterous and outrageous and at other times has been embarrassing for us. In other words, when it worked, it worked amazingly well, but when it failed, it was difficult to identify with."

Lambert's other contributions were more atmospheric. "Kit . . . knew the value of burning studio time," said Townshend. "He knew the value of saying, 'Right, there's too many takes, they're getting worse; everybody over the pub.' Pick everybody up and take them out and perhaps not go back into the studio all night. You'd go home feeling terrible, and you'd think, 'oh, we've had a terrible day and why did Kit take us out,' but the next day you go in and do that track straight away because you've built up to it overnight and you get this great recording. He knew about techniques like that; he knew human nature and he knew about the Who."

Kit managed to convince the band members that he had special insight into their character, and he kept the group mystified about himself: "Kit thoroughly understands the Who, but we don't understand him at all, which puts us in a very difficult position," as Townshend put it.

Kit Lambert's greatest contribution to the Who, however, was his unrelenting expansion and projection of Townshend's fantasies and ideas. "Kit's ambition was such that . . . it would rub off on the band and they'd think: 'Yeah! Why not?' " said Keith Altham.

The idea of doing a rock song narrative may have been Pete Townshend's, but there seems absolutely no doubt that rock opera was Kit's. "About a year after [I started writing] Kit Lambert started announcing to everyone that he thought I was a genius," said Townshend. "Kit often used to fantasize about doing something on a grand scale, even then. I think it was his idea to do the mini-opera on the [second] album. It was him pushing me to do things in a grander way. So even if I wasn't getting written about as a great writer, Kit Lambert was telling me I was a great writer. And I believed him, because I wanted to believe him."

Kit's concern was not with rock but with the stuffy atmosphere of opera itself; that was still his idea of what was culturally consequential. "We'd had lots of conversations about the hang-ups of opera, all the bullshit about queueing for tickets and the audience who all stood up and cheered together and then clapped before the end because they didn't know the piece enough. Kit hated all this. He wanted to take a group into Covent Garden, shit all over the stage and storm out again. He wanted to do this because he loved the opera and wanted to bring it back to its proper musical level," said Townshend.

Successful as their last few records had been, the Who were still enjoying what Chris Stamp called "profitless prosperity." The records were successful in Britain but a great deal less so in America, where the big recording money was. And whatever they made from recordings, a substantial chunk continued to go to Shel Talmy. Furthermore, the group's live performances weren't any more profitable—maybe less, since the destruction was an every-night necessity, and following the trend of "successful" rock groups of the period, the Who had now engaged a road crew to haul equipment and take care of non-playing business. This initial crew was a two-man effort: John "Wiggy" Wolff and Bobby Pridden. (Mike Shaw had been injured in an automobile accident that left him a paraplegic. He would return to work for Lambert and Stamp, but only in the office.)

Yet the Who's need for money increased. Daltrey was divorced, but he still had child support payments to make; Moon was married, with a baby due; Entwistle and Townshend were both engaged, to Alison Wise and Karen Astley, respectively. Roger was now past twenty-two, Pete and John both twenty-one, and even Keith had left his teens. As adults, the Who had expectations and responsibilities that went beyond the simple requirements of the band's beginnings.

Moon, in particular, was spending madly. Pilled up half the time, drunk the rest, he was already exhibiting every indication of the alcoholism and addictions that would plague him for the next ten years. "I had a house in Chelsea," he told Chris Charlesworth, "and it just got ridiculous. I could never get any peace. Regular every night at five-past-three, when the Speakeasy [the most important after-hours club of the period] shut, the telephone would go. Immediately, the cars would arrive outside the door. They'd all troop in, and it was always the same.... I used to dread going back there." Well, there were always other clubs to keep him away from the crowds at home, and Moon took full advantage of them.

In an attempt to alleviate some of the economic pressure, Lambert signed all four members of the band to a songwriting pact with Essex Music. (Townshend, now twenty-one, was free to make any deal he wanted without the benefit of his father's stuffy but eminently accurate advice.) Essex Music was a very established British firm; it would have been difficult to find a more reputable publisher. But the agreement also required that each member of the group contribute two songs to the Who's next album in order to earn an advance of £500 ($1,400) each.

This was ludicrous. The Who had just fought a long war internally to establish Townshend as the main supplier of the band's material. A major portion of the group's public image was tied up with the concept of Pete as the group's writer. The reason Townshend had become the writer in the first place was that nobody else had shown much ability or inclination in this area. Lambert's deal didn't make sense artistically or even commercially (since record sales were more important than songwriting royalties—since, indeed, songwriting royalties were ultimately a *function* of record sales).

He lucked out.

"Keith managed his two [songs], Roger managed one and I composed 'Whiskey Man' (which was all the ideas for tunes in my head all rolled into one) on a Vortexian stereo tape recorder," Entwistle said. "But we all more or less left it to Pete.

"I still had one more number to write, so I went out and got drunk down the Scotch Club with Bill Wyman, and we started talking about spiders and why they frighten people and that gave me an idea for a song."

But as the recording date approached, Entwistle still hadn't written the second song. Pete, on whom the burden of any writing shortfall would descend, was getting nervous, too. One day after rehearsal he asked John whether he'd written his second song.

"Sure," said Entwistle brazenly.

"What's it about?" asked Townshend innocently.

"It's about a spider—Boris the Spider," said Entwistle, using the first idea that came to mind.

"Great," said Pete. "How's it go?"

Entwistle hummed the first reasonably original tune he could think of, then rushed home to write the damn thing down before he forgot it, Townshend having insisted that it be worked up the very next afternoon.

"Boris the Spider" was the first great John Entwistle song, a rumbling, chunky rocker that featured a singer who contemplated an arachnid climbing his bedroom wall; thoroughly described in hilariously macabre detail, the bug is properly dealt with in the final verse. The song became the most requested number the Who ever did onstage, much to Townshend's chagrin, and it established Entwistle as a second writer to be reckoned with in the Who. Out of sheer good fortune, Lambert had made a terrible deal that wound up reinforcing the group's music and its image, as well.

Nevertheless, the inclusion of the Entwistle, Moon and Daltrey songs left *A Quick One*, released in December 1966, something of a hodge-podge. "Boris the Spider" was an excellent song, but "Whiskey Man" (a character study of a boozer who might have been Entwistle himself—or almost any other member of the Who and its entourage) was a shaggy dog story without enough music to support it. Daltrey's "See My Way" was a boast very much in keeping with Roger's aggressive spirit, and it had a nice Buddy Holly feeling (Moon playing a furious roll right out of "Peggy Sue"), but the song had a strange structure— only one verse and one chorus long—it didn't feel finished.

Moon's songs were another story. "I Need You" was a halfway decent lift of the basic Beatles harmonies, with rather obtuse lyrics. Keith's other song, "Cobwebs and Strange," was an instrumental showcase for drums and spurious brass band, revved up and raring to go. It had about as much to do with rock & roll as "Pop Goes the Weasel" (which it resembled), but it was funny and charming, anyhow.

The recording of "Cobwebs and Strange" seems to have provided one of the most memorable incidents of the entire session. "Our manager was completely nuts," Entwistle told John Swenson. "He had us marching in band formation around the studio because he wanted that going-away-and-coming-back sound. We were marching around this monitor speaker at one end of the studio which already had the bass guitar, drums and guitar track on it. Pete was leading, playing a recorder, me playing a tuba, Roger was playing bum notes on a trombone behind me and Keith had strapped on two cymbals. And every time we got to the other end of the studio, we realized we were out of time, because by the time we got to the other end of the studio we couldn't hear the backing track. If we'd worn cans [headphones] we would have gotten tangled up, so we had to finally track it standing still." So much for Kit Lambert's production methods.

"Cobwebs and Strange" was pure filler. Townshend added three new songs, "Run, Run, Run," "So Sad About Us" and "Don't Look Away," all rockers; "So Sad" was fairly innovative in its harmonies, but none of these songs was major. The album was further fleshed out with a cover version of the Martha and the Vandellas' hit "Heat Wave," which is probably the closest that the Who ever came to capturing the essence of their R&B attack on an official recording. Even with so much padding, however, the album was a good ten minutes short of a reasonable playing time. Lambert proposed a quick fix: Townshend should compose a mini-opera.

"But rock songs can't be ten minutes long," Townshend protested. "They're two-and-a-half minutes long. It's like a law." Lambert remained adamant. Finally, Townshend decided that Kit was right—especially since the album needed some kind of material that fit with the new trend toward "serious rock."

The album, initially announced for October release, was pushed back to November and then December while Townshend wrote. What he came up with was "A Quick One While He's Away," which Kit Lambert immediately dubbed "the first mini-opera," a succinct if not necessarily accurate description.

"A Quick One" has a plot that is halfway between a Gilbert and Sullivan operetta and a stag film. A lonely female lover despairs of the return of her beloved, who has been "gone for nearly a year" and is a day overdue. Her grief being well-known throughout the community, suitors flock to her door (ah, Penelope!). The most successful is Ivor the Engine Driver, an alleged crony of the wandering boyfriend. After her tryst with Ivor, we witness the return of the wayfaring lover (oh, Odysseus!), their reunion, her confession and his ultimate forgiveness.

To term this thin story farcical is almost too generous; the narrative is so scantily developed that (except for old Ivor) the characters don't even have names. In fact, "I'm a Boy" exhibited greater character development (and arguably, so did "Substitute," "Anyway, Anyhow, Anywhere," and a few of the songs from the first LP). Yet this isn't quite the issue; there are many operas in the standard repertoire based on equally flimsy material. It was the music that allowed Jon Landau, in a highly laudatory *Crawdaddy* review, to term the mini-opera "on the whole . . . the most successful utilization of a long cut yet recorded, surpassing the efforts of Love, the Doors, the Dead and even the Stones, in the level of imagination and creativity involved."

Structurally, "A Quick One" was much more complex than any of the similar experiments with longer rock tracks then being made ("The End" by the Doors, "Going Home" by the Stones, Love's "Revelation"). Landau discerned "nine different tunes and fragments employed at one point or another," and the label identified six separate pieces: "Her Man's Gone," rendered in close harmony; "Crying Town," featuring Daltrey at his most sardonic and the famous D-G-D-Am chord progression Townshend used for a later operatic experiment, as well as superb Beach Boys harmony; "We Have a Remedy," a more typically Townshend song, leering and tough; "Ivor the Engine Driver," sung by Entwistle over basic guitar/bass/drums accompaniment, moving midway from $^2/_4$ to $^4/_4$ with a resulting increase in intensity and threat to the woman's security; "Soon Be Home," a mock cowboy song in the Gene Autry/Roy Rogers tradition with clip-clop sound effects and what sounds like a saw whipping away in counterpoint to the acoustic guitar strums; "You Are Forgiven," which is the most Wholike of the songs, with a background chorus singing "cello, cello, cello" in place of the strings Lambert couldn't afford to hire. Townshend sings the male part and Daltrey contributes the female's apologetic confession as "A Quick One" ends in a brilliant burst of semi-operatic counterpoint, a coda of falsetto voices singing "you are forgiven" over and over again, set against another familiar set of chords later to become famous in another rock opera.

As an album, *A Quick One* is obviously inferior to *My Generation*; it contains no single song as outstanding as "My Generation," many of the non-Townshend contributions are inferior to those on the first LP (even in indulging Pete's consistent theme of role confusion and identity loss), and "A Quick One" itself is at best a facile realization of a half-baked idea. Yet Townshend was correct in saying that "now we've rehearsed carefully, are singing in harmony and unison and there is a kind of orderly disorder." Every individual guitar, bass and drum part on the record is sharp and intelligent, even in the trivial songs. The harmony vocals (not only in "A Quick One" but also in "So Sad About Us," "See My Way" and "Don't Look Away") are invariably fine—except in "Heat Wave," which perhaps indicates that the Who were better at sounding like a Church of England choir than a doo-wop group. It's hard not to imagine that, had Townshend written the whole thing himself (or had such uncollected tracks as "Substitute," "Disguises" and "I'm a Boy" been included), *A Quick One* might have been a masterpiece.

Whatever its shortcomings, *A Quick One*, which completely abandoned mod, moved the Who past the ranks of gimmicky pop groups, and began to foster an image as one of the most successfully adventurous groups on the rock scene.

A Quick One entered the British charts at number 4. Its immediate success reestablished the Who as one of the country's most important bands and signaled their permanent move out of the small clubs and into ballrooms and theatres.

The mini-opera wasn't entirely unprecedented: Some of the Shadow Morton-produced hits by the Shangri-Las had been heavily plotted and laden with the kind of musical and sound effects the Who used, and there was even the more minor but not necessarily uninfluential example of *Jan and Dean Meet Batman*, a non-hit masterpiece of chaos and comedy. But "A Quick One" was the first successful narrative song cycle by a band that already had had straight hit singles. In its wake, Townshend, always a source of good quotes, became accepted as a spokesman for the rock generation (including not necessarily just musicians but the audience, too). Bob Dylan might give gnomic replies to the simplest queries, Mick Jagger could be derisive or even abusive, the Beatles were likely to treat everything as a put-on. But Townshend could be counted upon to pontificate at length, to make a certain amount of sense, and he was much easier to find than the rest.

Townshend was outspoken about his drug use; he was now not only an acknowledged pot-smoker and pill-abuser but an admitted acidhead, too. "There was a time when I was desperately trying to get into trouble and no one would have anything to do with me," Townshend said in 1970. "I was going on television saying that I was a drug addict, and no one took any notice. . . ." Yet Townshend influenced other pop stars—even members of the Beatles and Rolling Stones—to come out in the open about their drug use.

Acid had a powerful impact on Townshend, as it did on most of those who used it. Among other things, it reconfirmed many of his feelings (derived from readings in science fiction and pop cosmology) about flying saucers and ESP and other psychic phenomena. "I kind of stopped working and got very obsessed with it and really did believe that it was something enormous and incredibly important, and [I] was involved also with some of the sentiments surrounding it, the sort of love and peace thing," Pete told Bruce Pollock. "During that period, I can only remember three songs that I wrote. Just pre my first acid trip, I wrote 'Relax,' which ended up on one of our albums; 'Pictures of Lily,' which was released as a single; and the other one I don't think anything happened to. And then afterward I wrote some very weird songs. I wrote a song called 'Faith in Something Bigger'; 'Happy Jack'; and what became the 'Underture to *Tommy*'; and 'Welcome,' from *Tommy*."

But Townshend's most passionate advocacy was for the concept of rock & roll as a new art form. "People still cannot accept that a rock song is an artistic event," he said sourly to Keith Altham. "They put on the record and say, 'Like where's the art?'

"But the art does not just lie in the record. It lies in the whole life of the composition, through the record production, what the record says, how people react, what people dance to the record and what the record does to the time. This is what art is, and it won't really be appreciated until you can look at the thing in retrospect.

"It matters not to us today that some of our 'works of art' took some poor bastard seventy years to paint. It's just a work of art, and the assistance he might have been given by tools or machinery pales into insignificance in time."

This obsession with the relativity of historical time became a persistent theme of Townshend's work and his public pronouncements. Thus did the incipient nostalgia of *Ready! Steady! Who!* incorporate itself as an element of the band's style. And why not? For by Townshend's own theory, in a medium as volatile as rock, where a trend could come and go in a matter of months, where yesterday's futurism is passé before the next dawn, where aging is even more bizarrely accelerated than in sports (athletes are aging at thirty, old at thirty-five, ancient by forty; rockers are middle-aged by their mid-twenties, suspect by thirty, decrepit thereafter, at least according to British thinking)— in this medium, moreover, where something as trivial as "Louie Louie" might turn out to he more influential and long-lived (and more meaningful and transcendent, too) than the pretensions of the Grateful Dead and other self-conscious "artists"—history had to be kept track of moment to moment, almost second by second, for it could alter its entire shape in a twinkling. Keeping the story straight was a lifetime's work.

"The real point is that almost everyone in pop—artists, managers, promoters, agents—have always treated their audience like so many clockwork morons, making a special point of conning them blind at all times," Townshend told Nik Cohn. "My only idea is that we should work hard, we should really involve ourselves and we should try anything to reach some kind of communication with our public."

That meant finding the largest possible public—and that meant America.

America is the beckoning dream.
Where, if you're English, you get
cheered for half an hour after your
act because they love your accent. . . .
The first trip to the States of any
major English act is always treated as a
group's next big step. They wave happily
from the top steps of a VC-10 and set
off to make their fortune. A couple of
months later, after the most gruelling
and exhausting work they have probably
ever done, they return triumphantly
home and start to tell lies. "It was great!"
"We made thousands!" It went terribly,
and they lost thousands.
                              —*Pete Townshend*

C hris Stamp had spent most of 1966 traveling back and forth to New York, first fighting off the Talmy lawsuit and the grasp of Allen Klein, and then trying to establish some sort of relationship with U.S. Decca— anything to establish an American beachhead for the Who.

"American Decca was sort of archaic," Stamp told Richard Barnes. "I mean, they didn't even know about Elvis Presley, let alone the Who. I realized that we would never break the Who with this company." Not quite fair: Decca had had a decent rock & roll roster in the fifties, including two of the better teen idols, Ricky Nelson and Johnny Burnette, and even one of rock's father figures, Bill Haley. Chris Charlesworth is probably closer to the mark when he characterizes the label as "unimaginative and complacent." For the Who, Decca made the best effort it knew how, but that wasn't good enough, mostly because of how different the post-Beatles record market really was.

The result, notes Charlesworth, was that the first few Who singles were "lost in the stampede. . . . There were no mods in America, and the teenage girls that screamed for the Dave Clark Five saw few aesthetic attractions in a blond thug, a scrawny guitarist with a big nose, a deadpan bass player and a bug-eyed drummer who was plainly off his rocker." It is hard to imagine just what American record company could have properly handled a British group whose appeal was primarily visual but which wasn't cute.

Yet where the Who were heard they were appreciated. Ellen Willis, a bohemian intellectual living on New York's Lower East Side, recalled hearing the Who's first singles. "It seemed an odd case of cultural lag that the Who hadn't caught on here," she wrote. "They were obviously superstar material, they were apparently making it big in England and 'Substitute' was a sure hit if I had ever heard one." But "Substitute" was buried by the confusion over the Talmy lawsuit; Atlantic stopped promoting it once they realized they would not have the band on a long-term basis. Anyway, Atlantic ran into radio resistance on the record, both because its sound was harder, more metallic than most U.S. hits of even that era, and because of the lyrics: "I look all white but my dad was black" was funny in England, but on American radio, it was controversial.

Others also responded enthusiastically to their glimpses of the Who. Pete Gidion, then Decca's Detroit promotion representative (and considerably younger than most Decca promo men), pushed the group hard from the beginning and with good results, actually getting "I Can't Explain" to number 1 in that crucial market. Gidion didn't do as well with "Anyway, Anyhow, Anywhere," but "My Generation" was a hit in Michigan, also getting airplay in San Francisco, San Diego and Boston. Decca was unable to spread the action to the rest of the country, but by the beginning of 1967, the Who had built an underground following in each of those towns.

The most effective promotion the Who received in the United States during this time was its periodic stints on the TV show "Shindig." Produced by Jack Good, who had invented British rock with "Oh Boy!" it focused heavily on British groups, often picking up clips from "Ready, Steady, Go!" or "Top of the Pops."

The Who made three appearances on the show, performing "I Can't Explain," "Daddy Rolling Stone" (the R&B tune that was the B-side of "Anyway, Anyhow, Anywhere") and finally, "Anyway, Anyhow, Anywhere" and "My Generation" from a special taping of the Richmond Jazz Festival.

"They did 'Generation,' and during the break, Daltrey took his mike stand and started bashing the drum set," Binky Philips, then a Brooklyn teenager, remembered. "Moon was going berserk! His hair was plastered to his head because it was so wet. When they showed Townshend, he looked furious—he'd play a few chords and every few seconds walk up to his amp and turn it up. It really looked impressive. He had a Union Jack jacket and was playing a Rickenbacker. At that time, that was the guitar to own. If you didn't have one, you were nothing. . . . I was just watching him, and all of a sudden he takes it off, holds it over his head and rams it into the speakers. I fell off my bed. . . .

"He was getting weird noises now by wrenching it around in the speaker, and when he pulled it out, the neck from the third fret up was gone. He looked at it and got furious—so he threw it over the amps into a curtain or something. You could see people standing next to his amps with their mouths open. Townshend stalked onstage with another Rickenbacker and finished the song. I wouldn't shut up the next day at school."

"The Who, there on TV in 1965, were more than just ahead of their time," wrote Greg Shaw, then a Northern California teenager. "Following the basically lame R&B reworkings of the other groups, they were like nothing any of us had been exposed to before, an inkling perhaps of the violence to which the younger generation would be driven in years to come."

The Who did not have much of a chance at mainstream Top 40 appeal, but there was another audience for rock by now: It was sometimes a bit older, considerably more male, composed of a surprising number of amateur musicians and future rock critics. (Binky Philips is now a guitarist; Greg Shaw wrote about rock until he formed his own record label.) This cult, like the others that would form around esoteric rock groups over the next few years, considered itself much more serious about popular music than the mainstream teen crowd, identified heavily with its idealism and its artistic potential and (while still only a fragment of rock's mass audience) was amazingly large, once businessmen learned how to cater to its tastes.

It would be inaccurate to completely identify the various rock music cults of the middle sixties with the underground, as the youth counterculture was called. Yet listeners with an early taste for the music of the most important "second wave" groups of the British Invasion—the Who, the Yardbirds, Cream—did tend to share the same interests (in politics, drugs, other media) as the counterculture.

"They aren't earnest or 'serious,' " Jon Landau wrote of the Who. "They aren't proselytizers, even when they proselytize. They're sharp, sarcastic, cynical but never weighed down with their own self-importance. They are a life force on a rock scene in which too many people are hiding behind facile slogan songs about how all the world needs is for everyone to love everyone else. . . ."

Although it is couched in terms highly critical of the underground rock sensibility, Landau's praise of the Who is a reflection of the band's stature within this burgeoning movement—there was no way to make sense of the Who in America unless one understood them as some kind of underground band. They surely weren't a pop group, and no one seemed quite sure what a mod was.

That doesn't mean that the Who—or Stamp and Lambert—immediately saw the difference. For the most part, the essential difference between the old and new rock audiences remained undefined or poorly articulated, even during the period when that difference was having a strong effect on mainstream pop culture.

That time had not yet come, and in the meantime, the goal was still a hit single. The problem wasn't just Decca's ineptitude—there was also the confusing discrepancy between Who records and the Who live. As John Swenson pointed out, "The biggest contradiction inherent in the Who was that their violently aggressive stage act sounded nothing like their records, which were precise, witty and very lyrical. . . . The point is that there was a lot more to the Who than the kids who came just to see them smash up instruments bargained for." Since the records couldn't (or at least didn't) spell out the connections, someone else had to.

That meant that Decca needed hip staff, people like Pete Gidion, who could appreciate the nuances of what the band was doing. "I had to get them to hire young guys—young commercial men to do our bidding," said Stamp. "We had a whole revolution within U.S. Decca."

If so, the revolt wasn't an especially effective one. Copies of some of the Who singles never reached the weekly trade papers (*Billboard*, *Cash Box*, *Record World*). Decca was also laggard in hiring the sort of independent promotion men who had the ear of programmers in crucial markets, able to acquire over- or under-the-table indebtedness that the company employees could not afford or risk.

One of the lessons that large record companies had to learn when dealing with rock & roll was that they were simply not competent to tinker with the music. It can be said of almost every important rock group of the sixties that its greatest successes, commercial as well as artistic, began when the record label relinquished its aesthetic control.

Decca tampered clumsily with the Who's work from the beginning. Both "Anyway, Anyhow, Anywhere" and "My Generation" were initially rejected because of the feedback that opens the former and closes the latter. Decca changed the cover of the group's first album and altered the title to read *The Who Sing My Generation*. (The Who did almost everything else to "My Generation," but it can hardly be said that they did anything so nice as *sing* it. It has been a favorite sport of Who fans for many years to try to think up more appropriate verbs: *The Who Scream My Generation* or *The Who Annihilate My Generation*.)

Worse, the American albums were both cursed with Decca's idea of proper liner notes. The back cover of *The Who Sing My Generation* was adorned with blurbs for other Decca albums "you'll be sure to enjoy": *Best Always* by Rick Nelson, *1-2-3* by Len Barry, *Somethin' Else* by the Kingston Trio and Brenda Lee's *Bye Bye Blues*. Daltrey and Entwistle's names were misspelled. The second album sleeve had thoroughly fictitious and inappropriate teeny-bopper notes and again misspelled Daltrey (leaving out the *e*). But Decca's flubbing of the spelling was only symptomatic of its carelessness about the Who.

"Scarcely twelve groups of the thousands performing all over Britain are making any real money," wrote *The Observer* in its 1968 profile of Lambert and Stamp. "Those that are have made it in America." And those that had made it in the States had toured there.

At least as important as a good record company was a good booking agency. Without hits, a group like the Who could hardly hope to be taken on by one of the big agencies such as William Morris or GAC, which were in any case more eager to handle movie and TV stars. For the Who, the agency to go with had to be Premier Talent, run by young Frank Barsalona.

Barsalona was already creating a legend in the rock world. He had grown up an insomniac on Staten Island, in a community so completely Italian-American that he was five before he figured out that not all elderly people spoke with accents. From late-night radio he conceived a passion for country music and developed an act as a child yodeler which was quite successful on the touring circuit. As his voice changed, he had to give up yodeling and instead went on to college and then took up acting at the Berghof School. While studying, Barsalona took a job with GAC just to make ends meet. He said he "hated agents and the thought of agencies . . . but I thought if I could be at an agency, I could be at the center point of everything that was happening. I could meet the important people and meet the important performers. . . . "

But once he was inside the agency, Barsalona realized he had underestimated the situation. To him, the other agents were "putzers," without enough vision to understand most of the opportunities available to their clients. This was especially true in the contemporary music department (where Barsalona, because of his youth, was assigned). "There were certain acts we had that I thought could be developed and I thought could last for a long while," Barsalona said. "I told my elders, and they said, 'Look kid, you've been in the business forty-three minutes, just cool it.' "

It was considered ludicrous that a rock performer could have a lengthy career. Although agents were encouraged to tell prospective clients and their managers that the agency would work to obtain film and TV deals for them, these promises were never taken seriously, since anyone vulgar enough to sing rock had already ruined his image as far as the mainstream show business moguls were concerned. (Elvis was a fluke, the Beatles an exception.) "If you were young and had a hit record, to them you had no talent, you were just lucky and manufactured. . . . There was no chance of growth for a new performer," Barsalona told Robert Stephen Spitz. "Rock was the asshole, it really was."

The general idea was that no rock performer's career lasted longer than eighteen months, so the dollars had to be sucked up quickly and indiscriminately. This meant that anything—from the huge package tours of Dick Clark and Irving Feld, which were like cattle drives, to the most tawdry forms of merchandising—was permissible. It meant working with the most fly-by-night promoters or for peanuts at the beck and call of influential disc jockeys who used the acts to promote their shows at high school record hops. In general, the agencies' philosophy squandered and ignored talent, putting the act out of business quickly and effectively.

Barsalona saw more potential; he keyed in on the incredible devotion that rock fans had, something he'd witnessed firsthand as the agent for the Beatles' first American tour. So he decided to take a chance on opening an agency concentrating solely on rock groups. Premier Talent, as it was called, wasn't taken especially seriously by the major agencies, even with such clients as Mitch Ryder, Little Anthony and the Imperials, Jay and the Americans, Del Shannon and Freddie Cannon. Nobody really wanted these people, because everyone presumed that the hits they'd had would fade away and that would be the end of them. (For most of these acts, that was pretty much the case.)

But, as he began working with less established acts, Barsalona used his original client list to build his real strength, a network of committed young promoters with whom he built relationships founded on a simple principle. If a promoter took a chance on a developing act, that act would stay with the promoter in that market once success was achieved. This allowed Barsalona to get gigs for some of his marginally successful performers who otherwise would not have been able to work at all. And for the first time, it gave the live performance end of the rock business a big incentive to create artists with the potential for long-lived careers.

When Barsalona applied this formula to British acts—beginning with the highly unlikely Herman's Hermits and Freddie and the Dreamers—he reaped rewards that revolutionized the rock concert business. Suddenly, it became clear that not only were rock audiences loyal, not only did the acts have some long-term potential, but that rock was a potential gold mine. After the Hermits and the Dreamers, Barsalona began working with somewhat more substantial British performers, such as the Animals. He became the most important agent in a business that was getting set to break wide open.

Stamp was desperate to get with Premier almost from the beginning of his campaign in the States. Atlantic approached Barsalona (who was quite friendly with the label's owners, Ahmet Ertegun and Jerry Wexler) during the period when they had "Substitute," but he turned them down. Stamp himself made several overtures, also rebuffed.

Barsalona kept saying no because he had first met Stamp and Lambert through Mickie Most and because they had been in the company of Allen Klein, who represented Most's acts in the States. Barsalona had already booked some of Most's bands, and he knew that he wanted no more of anybody who was affiliated with the blustering Klein. Because there was no real incentive to sign the Who, the possibility that they were associated with Klein was a strong enough reason to veto working with them.

At the time, Premier was a partnership, and co-owner Dick Freedberg had equal authority to sign acts, even though he was basically in charge of the financial side. While Barsalona was in California for a few days in the winter of 1965, Stamp persuaded Freedberg to sign the Who, and Barsalona was presented with a *fait accompli* when he got back to New York. (Because of musicians' union regulations, a booking agent cannot unilaterally drop an act once it is signed.)

"Great!" shouted the furious Barsalona. "*You* signed 'em. *You* book 'em!"

Stamp had achieved the impossible. The Who now had an incompetent American record company and a booking agent who hated them.

Things weren't looking so swell in England, either. By the end of 1966, with "Ready! Steady! Go!" gone from the air and mod sinking like a stone, the Who were having trouble getting live bookings. Over the next few months, their price for live appearances plummeted from £300 ($840) to £60 ($170) per gig.

Once mod sank, the Who were without a concrete image. They were neither pop, like the Hermits or Tremeloes, nor underground, like the two hot new acts Swinging London buzzed about, Cream, led by former Yardbird Eric Clapton, and the Jimi Hendrix Experience, led by the greatest guitarist anyone had ever heard (or even heard about). Cream was perhaps not that threatening to the Who—they had known of Clapton's ability for a long time. But Hendrix was another matter. According to the story that Townshend told in the film *Jimi*, when Hendrix first turned up in the London clubs, he and Clapton were so overawed that they went to the movies together as an excuse to talk it over. (Yet John Entwistle swears that Hendrix did the circuit of the London clubs studying other players in order to steal their licks.)

The underground groups, like Cream and Hendrix, were associated with two things at which the Who were never very proficient: the blues and psychedelic drugs. The new, stretched-out version of the blues was a long way from what Roger Daltrey had had in mind when he begged his mates to stay the course; it favored bands that did not have writers as skillful as Townshend. Nevertheless, it was the rage of London's underground for the next couple of years, and the fact that the Who weren't a blues-oriented act hurt their hip credentials.

Psychedelia was another matter. Of the group, only Townshend ever seemed very interested in LSD. Moon positively despised hippies. When he was offered flowers by the gentle new breed, he would smile, accept them and proceed to devour the bouquet. (One night, Moon was trapped in an American hotel room by perhaps a dozen hippies and grew so desperate that he called Entwistle and they staged a gory fight just to get rid of the visitors.)

If hippies were about peace and love, the Who were their antithesis. Their stage act remained violent—even after they began to discard the smash-up finale after their January 29, 1967, appearance at Brian Epstein's Saville Theatre. Only Townshend had significant psychedelic connections. Pete was spending a lot of time in the acid-drenched UFO Club (one mod remembered seeing Townshend there in beads listening to Pink Floyd and understanding then and there that an era had ended). He was also writing progressively more spaced-out songs and "operas." Townshend had moved to Soho's Wardour Street, where he lived in what he later described as his "hi-fi showroom" and spent most of his time either listening to music stoned on pot or creating bizarre effects with his array of tape decks. By February 1967, Townshend was telling *Disc* of an opera he'd written with twenty-five acts, a "sound experiment" sprawled over two discs about "a man whose wife dies and he leaves his home and travels and becomes involved in wars, revolutions and gets killed."

Binky Philips remembers hearing about another opera, this one about "a big white rabbit who ruled the world." One of the songs from that abortive opera was called "Happy Jack," and in late 1966 the Who recorded it as its next single.

"Happy Jack" is about a hermit who lives on the Isle of Man and is taunted by the children there. The lyric is basically a fairy tale, not surprisingly, given the links to Pete's childhood. The song broke no new ground, simply restating what the Who did well: soaring harmonies, enormously fat bass notes, thunderous drumming, Townshend riffing on his usual chords. You couldn't call it lightweight pop (not with Moon crashing all over the place), but it didn't exactly measure up as "underground," either.

The hippest thing about "Happy Jack" may be its conclusion. As the harmonies fade away, Townshend can be heard shouting, "I saw ya!" in a voice that's just repressing a giggle. "That was the day when Keith Moon decided to strong-arm his first vocal performance on the Who," Townshend explained many years later. "He decided that he was a singer of merit because 'Bucket T,' which was a spoof Beach Boys track we did on our *Ready, Steady, Who!* EP, was number one in Sweden and Keith was singing the lead in his squeaky voice. He went over to Sweden and did it [during the Who's tour there that winter], and Keith was swamped with screaming teenagers.

"So when he came back to record 'Happy Jack,' he was intent to take, if not the lead vocal, definitely the backing vocal. So we tried it over and over again and it was terrible. Finally, we put him in the control room in the studio. We practically had to tie him up, because he kept escaping and coming out and creeping around the back of all the equipment and popping up behind the mike at the very end. We did this six or seven times; the vocals were getting better, but he was fucking them up by appearing and making us laugh.

"In the end, Kit had to make him promise to lay on the floor in the control room down behind the glass so nobody could see him. So he lay there on the ground all the way through the number, and we're all watching to see whether he can make it. And just at the very last bars, his little head comes up and goes down again. And I shouted out, 'I saw ya!' "

Everyone in the Who was going through new stages of growing up. Roger had his hair straightened to make it look less mod and more hip (it looked awful, instead). Townshend was down at the UFO club with the acidheads and the New Left intellectuals. Moon and Entwistle were crawling around Blaisès, the Revolution, the Bag O'Nails and the Speakeasy, London's current crop of apolitical all-night musicians' drinking spots, as if Keith wasn't married (and the father of a daughter, Mandy, born in August 1966), nor Entwistle engaged.

"Happy Jack" was a major British hit, topping out at number 3 and enjoying an eleven-week run on the charts. But it confused the group's image still further, since it didn't fit into any of the current categories (and the "underground" was as rife with pigeonholes as pop had ever been).

Decca, meantime, sat idly, not even bothering to release "Happy Jack." Lambert and Stamp were desperate for a break. Despite the hit, the Who's English position had never been shakier; they needed an American hit worse than ever, because even without the equipment-smashing, the debts had piled up.

Frank Barsalona had a major problem. Murray the K, one of the most influential disc jockeys in America, did an annual stage show featuring several acts and himself as promoter and emcee, at the RKO Theatre at Fifty-eighth Street and Third Avenue in New York City. Since Murray was the fabled "fifth Beatle" and a disc jockey whose picks influenced every other deejay in North America, he had pretty much his choice of talent for the undercard. But booking a headliner sometimes required flexing some muscle. For his Easter 1967 show, Murray called Barsalona and told him that Mitch Ryder, the blue-eyed soul singer who had just left the Detroit Wheels and whom Barsalona handled, owed him a favor and that he could repay it by playing the Easter shows.

Ryder was desperate to avoid the shows, primarily because doing them was so strenuous. The RKO opened at 10:00 A.M. and the shows began shortly thereafter, five of them per day. Even though Ryder could be expected to be well-compensated, and even though he wouldn't have to perform for very long—twenty to thirty minutes—it meant gruelling, draining work. He told Barsalona that whatever it took, he wanted no part of the gig.

Frank tried. He shocked Murray with the price he was asking. Murray met it anyhow. Barsalona demanded that Ryder's dressing room and everything in it be painted in a certain shade of blue. Murray was apoplectic. But he bought it. Barsalona was desperate. What could he do to turn Murray off?

The Who (who'd been signed only a couple of days before) popped into his mind. Why not insist on saddling the show with the worst act in his stable? "Murray," Barsalona said, "there's one other requirement." Murray must have shuddered. "Mitch has a thing for an act in England called the Who. They must be on the show with him."

The disc jockey balked at this. "Those guys don't mean anything," Murray said. "They'll draw nothing. I've got tickets to sell." Barsalona was relieved. "I really don't think I can persuade Mitch to do it without them," he said, already adding a graceful note of regret to his voice and preparing to close the conversation.

But Murray the K was not without some resources of his own. "Didn't I just hear something about them?" he said quizzically.

"Well, yes," admitted Barsalona, seeing his advantage slip away. "They just signed with Brian Epstein's booking agency." Murray was pleased; Epstein was his friend. This could be worked out after all. Still he was shocked when Barsalona told him the Who's price for appearing at the bottom of the bill: 75 percent billing, $7,500 (£2,700) for the week of shows plus $1,500 (£550) for appearing on the TV special Murray was planning. But he agreed, undoubtedly reckoning that he could phone Epstein, talk the price down and still have done Epstein a favor. (Most acts of the Who's stature would have been happy to play the shows for free, just for Murray the K's endorsement.)

Anticipating just such a maneuver, Barsalona phoned Epstein in London the moment Murray the K left Premier's offices. Epstein told him that he didn't handle the booking business himself; Robert Stigwood, now his associate, did. Barsalona gave firm instructions to Stigwood; he was to accept not a penny less than $7,500 plus $1,500 for the TV show. Stigwood grew nervous; he was sure the band would be glad to play for just the exposure. Murray certainly didn't need to pay them; he didn't want to press too hard and blow the deal. "Just stick to the price," insisted Barsalona.

Two days later, Murray the K again called Barsalona. The contract for the Who should be drafted—but at a lower price, $5,000 (£1,800). Barsalona was outfoxed; he couldn't let the promoter know about his instructions to Stigwood (after all, Ryder was supposed to be insisting on the Who appearing, not on what they were getting paid). Now Ryder would have to headline. It was February 23, a month before the shows (billed as Murray the K's Fifth

Dimension, a sign of the incipient rise of psychedelia and Murray's switch from Top 40 AM to the new "underground" FM format) were to begin.

Frank Barsalona was despondent. He prided himself on being a master deal-maker and strategist. Now he had failed. Ryder, his top act, would be furious with him; this was the kind of thing you lost clients over. And the way his luck was running, the Who would probably wind up being one of the all-time dog acts, ruining his reputation with Murray and embarrassing him in the business. Barsalona was about as dejected as a man on the way to the biggest breakthrough of his career could be.

The Who arrived in New York on March 22, 1967. Only Townshend had ever been in America before. Accompanied by John "Wiggy" Wolff and Chris Stamp, they checked into the Drake Hotel on East Fifty-sixth Street. They hadn't brought much equipment with them, since they would already be taking a loss on the gigs without having to pay huge freight charges as well. This left some of the band—particularly John Entwistle—none too happy. Together with his roommate, Keith Moon, John decided to turn the New York sojourn into an orgy of room service caviar and lobster. They ordered tray after tray of food and champagne and brandy sent to their rooms. (The Who had only three hotel rooms: Moon and Entwistle shared one, Daltrey and Townshend another, Wolff and Stamp put up in the third.)

The shows started on Saturday, March 25 (running to April 2), but the first dress rehearsal was the next day, Thursday, March 23. The Who headed over to the theatre excited to be playing on a bill that included—in addition to Mitch Ryder—Wilson Pickett, the Blues Magoos, the Mandala, the Chicago Loop, Jim and Jean, Smokey Robinson and the Miracles, the Blues Project, Cream and a comedy group, the Hardly Worthit Players.

Chris Stamp was fairly frantic. "I was going out signing these bits of paper saying the Who would be the exclusive user of Vox, right. And I mean, I went to every maker of equipment in New York just to get the equipment shipped to the theatre." The Who had abandoned smash-ups in Britain, where the idea was already old hat and widely imitated. But they needed to return to auto-destruction in America in order to make maximum impact in the five- to eight-minute spot they were allowed. (Stamp also arranged for the band to get regular shots of amphetamines, ostensibly for stamina, and doses of penicillin, just in case.)

Barsalona went to the dress rehearsal fearfully. He would have avoided it altogether if he could have, but there were too many Premier acts involved to skip out completely. As luck would have it, the Who came on only a few moments after his arrival. Barsalona was sitting in the back of the darkened theatre with his wife, June (who was a former pop journalist herself). All around them, workmen were busy with last-minute preparations, ignoring the music.

The Who were wearing their stage clothes, including the jacket with battery-operated lights that Townshend had had made especially for the occasion. Barsalona groaned. He had never seen such an unkempt, outright ugly act. But when the group started to play, the Barsalonas exchanged glances.

The band wasn't playing badly at all; they were exciting. As they finished their opening number, "Happy Jack," and swung into "My Generation," beginning to get physically involved in the gut-stomping music even though it was only a dress rehearsal, Barsalona sat up straight in his seat. These guys were really *good*, he thought.

Just then, Townshend threw his guitar up into the air, way over his head. As it came down, he tried to catch it and missed. It crashed to the stage. "What a klutz," thought Barsalona. "Well, at least this isn't the show." Townshend tossed his guitar again. Again it crashed. Infuriated, he seized it and began smashing it against the floor.

Barsalona was horrified. What was this maniac up to? It got worse when Daltrey and then Moon began to bash their equipment about. Smoke bombs went off, and Townshend gave his amps a flying kick, toppling them.

Barsalona looked at June, who was as shocked as he was. Then he began to look wildly around the room, trying to find Chris Stamp. The manager should put a stop to this debacle, he thought. But he finally saw Stamp sitting coolly in the middle of the house, arms folded, chatting with Nancy Lewis, who was now his U.S. assistant. Slowly, it dawned on the booking agent that this was the Who's *act*! He rose to his feet, shouting and cheering. "They're great! They're brilliant!" he exclaimed. As if to confirm it, the blasé construction workers and stage hands stopped what they were doing to give the Who a hand.

There was no doubt in Frank Barsalona's mind that the show would be a triumph for the Who. He rushed backstage to celebrate with Murray (and, no doubt, to praise Mitch Ryder's good taste in obscure favorite acts). But Murray was irascible. "Yeah, yeah, they'll do fine," the bewigged "fifth Beatle" grumbled. "But what about this other piece of shit you've stuck me with?"

"You mean Mitch? You wanted Mitch, you begged for Mitch!"

"Not Mitch. That other crap group."

"What are you talking about?" Barsalona demanded.

"You know what I mean," snapped Murray. "That piece of shit, the Cream."

Barsalona was stunned; he'd seen them on the bill but had no idea he had anything to do with them. Murray told him the story: When he phoned Stigwood to arrange for the Who's appearance, he was told he had to take Cream as well. (That's what happened to the other $2,500 the Who were supposed to receive.) Barsalona immediately realized that Stigwood had been shrewd enough to perceive that Premier had some sort of leverage over Murray the K and that he could use this to Cream's advantage. (Stigwood not only booked that group, he also managed them.) So Stigwood simply shoved them down Murray's throat, too.

Between them, Frank Barsalona and Robert Stigwood transformed Murray the K's Fifth Dimension from an ordinary package show into one of the watershed performance events of the mid-sixties. Before the ten-day run was over, both the Who and Cream were the talk of New York's rock world. Their success with an audience of mostly high school kids confirmed the commercial potential of the British underground rock acts.

Of course, the Who did not achieve their success unaided. Stamp found that the Who fans were only too willing to show up for the first show at 10:00 A.M. and stay all through the day. He pushed them into the front row seats, turned them into an ad hoc version of the 100 Faces, got them back each day and made sure that the Who's ravers could not be ignored.

"I was totally flabbergasted," said Binky Philips, one of that crowd. "I've never seen anything so loud and brutal. They were the absolute epitome of flash. Townshend dressed in white, with pants up to his chest. Daltrey's hair was all puffed up—they were gorgeous.

"Townshend would throw his Stratocaster twenty feet up in the air and catch it. When he was tired, he would let it slam on the floor. Such a gas!

"Townshend was really smart. He did five shows a day for ten days and only broke five guitars. He would put them together again so they would look good, then go out and smash it again." Adding to the Who's hipness was their promo film, screened as the group thundered through "Happy Jack," which featured them sitting in a room being raided by cops and fighting back with custard pies and concluding with a Keystone Kops chase scene.

Al Kooper, already well-known as a session musician on Bob Dylan's "Like a Rolling Stone," appeared on the Murray the K bill with his group, the Blues Project. "I had read all about them in the imported English papers, so I knew what their trip was," he wrote in his memoir, *Backstage Passes*. "The first day, everyone in the cast stood in the wings to see what all the talk was about.

"Well, they launched into 'My Generation,' and you could feel it coming. Keith Moon flailed away on those clear plastic drums and it seemed like he had about twenty of 'em. It was the first time any of us had seen the typical English drum kit. There are usually six to eight tom-toms of various sizes, as compared to two or three in most American drum sets. [This drum set was 'typical' only of Moon and those he had influenced, of course.] And huge double bass drums, one of which said 'The' and the other, of course, 'WHO.' Moon just beat the shit out of them for fifteen minutes nonstop.

"Peter Townshend ('He's a God in England,' Eric Clapton said to me before they went on) leaped in the air, spinning his arms wildly and just being the most generally uninhibited guitar player ever seen in these parts. Roger Daltrey broke a total of eighteen microphones over the full run of the show. And John Entwistle would just lean up against his amp taking it all in.

"They reached the modulation part of the instrumental, and Townshend spun his guitar in the air, caught it and smashed it into a placebo amp. No cracks in his Strat, so he aimed for the mike stand. *Whackkkk!* Crack number one. Then the floor. *Whommmppp!* The guitar is in three or four pieces, and he's still got signal coming out of it! All of a sudden Moon kicks his entire drum kit over and the curtain rings down in a cloud of artificial smoke.

"Just then I realized my heart was beating three times its normal speed. I figure, as a critic of that show, my electrocardiogram was the best testimonial I could have offered."

Back at the hotel, chaos reigned. Stamp went wild when he learned about

Entwistle and Moon's room service charges, but the damage—$5,000 to $7,000 worth (£1,800 to £2,500)—was done. All the money the Who would earn from the Murray the K shows was spent within two or three days. The band checked out of the Drake and into the nearby but considerably less expensive Gorham. They didn't get to stay there long, either, because Moon noisily demolished his room. (He claimed this was because Entwistle was practicing his trumpet in the wee hours.) So they trudged wearily to a third hotel—except for Townshend, who put up on somebody's couch.

The Who was in constant trouble at the theatre, too, receiving daily lectures from the impresario. Murray the K was extremely devoted to presenting a "with-it" image, but he was, in fact, middle-aged and wore a long-hair wig, and this incited the contempt of the Shepherd's Bush mods in a way that only such huckstering hypocrisy could.

"He had what he called his personal microphone for doing the instructions with, and we were fairly irreverent towards it while we were smashing our instruments up five times a day," Townshend told Vic Garbarini. "When we ran out of microphones, his used to come in for a bit of bashing. And so we used to actually get daily lectures from him about abusing his personal microphone, which we thought was pretty funny.

"Then the last thing was when Wilson Pickett called a meeting, because we were using smoke bombs as well, and he felt that we were very unprofessional and that the smoke was affecting everybody else's act. Actually, I think he didn't like following us.

"But they were all on a different *planet*, basically. We didn't really know what was going on and we didn't take it very seriously. And when it got to the last day, we all put funny masks on and went in and sat and listened to [Murray] with these masks on. I remember he asked us to take them off, demanded we remove them." The masks stayed on.

Ironically, it was partly due to airplay on the Murray the K radio show that "Happy Jack" acquired enough credibility to become a legitimate U.S. Top 40 hit. (Barsalona also persuaded Decca to hire three independent promo men, a second major factor in tipping the scales.) "Happy Jack" got to number 24 and sold 300,000 copies—not a smash but a healthy start on cracking the American market. Decca now took the Who much more seriously and in May finally released the second album, with "Heat Wave" deleted and replaced by "Happy Jack" as the new title track.

The final day of the Murray the K show was Easter Sunday; it also happened to be the day that New York's hippies kicked off the Summer of Love with the first Human Be-In in Central Park. It was a symbolically appropriate juxtaposition, for the Murray the K show was the last of its kind. Rock was making decisive transition from the package shows to something less teen-oriented. The be-in was a version of the pop festival to come.

20

The Who exploded into fire
and light . . .
—Eric Burdon, "Monterey"

Kit Lambert and Chris Stamp had been laying plans for their own record label, Track Records, since the previous summer. They realized that the bulk of the clout and cash in the record business did not go to managers or even producers but to the corporations that made and distributed the records.

According to the figures they worked up before starting Track, the record company grossed up to 500 percent more profit than the performer on each Who record. The situation was worse in Britain than in some other countries (notably the United States), because in addition to their powerful distribution setups, the four major recording companies also operated virtually all of the record-pressing plants. As a result of what were effectively pressing and distribution monopolies, the major U.K. record labels were able to drive nasty, often unfair bargains with anyone who wanted to start a label of his own.

Lambert and Stamp went the long way around for their deal, first studying (according to what they told the *Observer*, at least) other manufactured goods—biscuits, for instance—of roughly the same size as a box of records, then analogously figuring out the real manufacturing costs of an LP. The process took about sixty days. When they'd arrived at a figure that satisfied them, Kit and Chris went to Polydor and proposed a partnership.

Even though they were already successfully releasing Who records in Britain and Europe, Polydor was reluctant to make a deal with two such unorthodox and often troublesome figures as Lambert and Stamp. As Stamp told the *Observer*, "We get [on] because we are lunatics and can stop the board meeting and say, 'Bollocks—do you want a hit product or don't you?' We're telling them that their next record is going to be a smash. And we know. They don't. That's why we get the deal."

Well, not exactly. No company likes being told it's stupid about marketing its product (even though this happens to be true in the case of most record companies). And Lambert and Stamp had no experience with acts other than the Who—finding some was the biggest question mark in their plan. Polydor was wavering when Lambert came up with one of his usual strokes of luck.

In September, Lambert had gone to the Scotch of St. James, a rock night club, to see a new act that Chas Chandler, formerly bassist with the Animals, had brought over from America. There was already a stir about this black guitar player named Jimi Hendrix, but Lambert had made eliciting a buzz from the London in-crowd his speciality. He didn't expect too much.

The guitarist immediately changed Lambert's mind. Hendrix had the kind of devastating power, electric stage presence and ruthless innovative genius that had made the Who stars. "Kit nearly knocked all the tables over in the Scotch and wanted Jimi to be on the new label he was launching," Chandler said. Chandler was already negotiating with Decca, but when they passed, he signed with Lambert. And it was Hendrix who convinced Polydor that Lambert's outlandish label concept was viable.

Still, it was not until March 23, 1967 (the very day of the Who's dress rehearsal in New York), that Track's first single, "Purple Haze," by Jimi Hendrix, was issued. (Hendrix had released "Hey Joe" on Polydor the previous December.)

It is strange (and perhaps significant in light of what later happened) that the Who were not given the honor of having Track's first release. They certainly had a right to expect it, since the label wouldn't have existed without them. But Track sought a thoroughly underground image, and Lambert and Stamp undoubtedly did not want their company to look like a mere offshoot of the Who. Furthermore, the Who's sales had leveled off, while Polydor was rabid to get more product from Hendrix, who was a superstar from his first release and whose stock was still soaring. Still, it was an unsettling statement of the priorities of the Who's managers.

Track was an immediate success for Lambert and Stamp. In its first nine months, it placed seven records in the British Top 10. Hendrix's first album alone grossed £3,500 ($9,800) per week for Lambert and Stamp, according to the *Observer*. They claimed net profits of £30,000 ($84,000) for the first year of releases by Hendrix, the Who, John's Children, the Crazy World of Arthur Brown, Marsha Hunt and American comedian Murray Roman.

The Who were promised a piece of the action. "The idea was they would be involved," said Mike Shaw. "They would all handle a certain section of music. Kit was classical, Roger was gonna look after R&B, Keith would handle surf music (and comedy—Roman was his idea), Pete was gonna bring in all new ideas, new music, new sounds. I don't remember what John was going to do. They were originally all supposed to be directors of the company, which they never were." In fact, the company allowed Lambert and Stamp to even take profits from the group's recordings over and above their already exorbitant managerial slice (30 percent, double the industry standard) and in some cases, such as Arthur Brown and later, Thunderclap Newman, from talent that Townshend discovered or developed.

(Townshend said that he never really expected to get shares in the firm, despite Kit's promise. Pete also claimed that the group wasn't interested in participating in Track's profits, although later events contradict him on this score.)

Additionally, Lambert, especially, became more distracted, less involved with the band's daily operations. Wiggy Wolff took over many of the day-to-day chores. Lambert continued as record producer and as planner of the group's future—at least for a time.

This doesn't mean that Lambert and Stamp didn't remain loyal to the Who.

But unlike Cream and Hendrix, the Who were not handled in a way that ensured that their image matured along with their music. For the rest of 1967, Lambert and Stamp would float rumors about plans for a Who TV show, a weekly comic, a pop art sweater, dolls, toffee crunch bars, breakable guitars and binoculars. This kind of exploitation was beginning to be seen for what it was, and the better represented underground acts avoided such crassly commercial associations.

But then, the Who took a stand for pop—even if it was for pop art or arty pop. It was easy to become confused on the business side. The penalty for the band's cheek and brashness, its sense of humor and refusal to remain sanctimonious as rock grew more and more "adult," was precisely this sort of misunderstanding. The pop press and the rock audience grew more sophisticated but still saw image-mongering as gross, without much sense of the nuance and subtlety that were the Who's greatest virtues. This led to a distorted impression of the band as go-for-the-bucks lightweights, especially in England. (This was so even though none of the plans were ever realized.) The distorted impression that such a frivolous group could not possibly create anything resembling art is a problem that obviously stems from a general misapprehension of what art is. Still, being treated as a toy by their business representatives did the Who no good.

Just after the Who's return from Germany, "Pictures of Lily"/"Doctor, Doctor," which had been recorded earlier in the year, was released as the band's first Track single. "Doctor, Doctor" was true to John Entwistle's pattern of producing witty, morbid, rumbling B-sides: It concerned hypochondria, featured a suitably breathless vocal and was generally hilarious.

"Pictures of Lily" was another Townshend tune, and it displayed characteristically tough sound and complexity of wit. Ira Robbins described it best: "Scathing guitar and a pulsing bridge create a tension between the taut and the casual, while soaring vocal harmonies and a brilliant descending chord line emphatically set the Who off from their competition." In other words, on the surface, "Pictures of Lily" was not much more than a run-through of the Who's basic approach as redefined on *A Quick One*. What made it more were the details: Daltrey's most confident lead vocal, Entwistle's French horn trills (pinched from Jack Nitzsche's "Lonely Surfer") and the vaguely dissonant guitar. Most of all, the single was by far the tightest Who production yet. " 'Pictures of Lily' just *jells* [sic] perfectly somehow," wrote Townshend, which about sums it up. With a more integrated sound, better balancing the Who's distinctive parts, "Pictures of Lily" came nearer to capturing the Who's onstage power than any single song since "My Generation," although it did so in a very different way.

"Lily" was a hit in England, reaching number 4, but in America, it stalled out at number 51, largely because many radio stations banned it for its lyric. "Merely a ditty about masturbation and the importance of it to a young man," Townshend commented when the dust settled. "I was really digging at my folks, who, when catching me at it, would talk in loud voices in the corridor outside my room. 'Why can't he do it with girls like *other* boys?' "

"Really, it's just a look back to that period in every boy's life when he has pin-ups," said Townshend at the time. "The idea was inspired by a picture my girlfriend had on her wall of an old vaudeville star, Lily Bayless. It was an old 1920s postcard, and someone had written on it, 'Here's another picture of Lily—hope you haven't got this one.' It made me think that everyone has a pin-up period. John Entwistle and I used to swop 'dirties' when we were kids at school—we used to get a kick out of buying a thousand pin-up pictures at a time from tawdry little newspaper shops."

Most significantly "Pictures of Lily" presented a clear direction for the band. Townshend even had a name for it: power pop.

"Power pop is what we play," he told an interviewer. "What the Small Faces used to play and the kind of pop the Beach Boys played in the days of 'Fun, Fun, Fun,' which I preferred."

As in so many of his theoretical interviews, however, Townshend's words quickly contradicted his actions. "There are too many groups involved in the same kind of scene as the Move, where every word has to mean something," he continued. "The Beach Boys are playing on this kind of ethereal level, where the public is expected to come to them and be taught.

"I believe pop music should be like the TV—something you can turn on or off and shouldn't disturb the mind. Eventually, these people are going to go too far and leave the rest of the world behind. It's very hard to like 'Strawberry Fields' for simply what it is. Some artists are becoming musically unapproachable." This from the innovator of feedback, the pop opera and the three-minute hit single about jacking off!

From time to time, Townshend's status as rock's most articulate spokesperson served only to remind one of how incoherent almost all of the competition was.

At home in England, the Who worked almost constantly, simply because that was the only way they could make enough money to pay their ever-voluminous portfolio of bills. They went on the road in Britain quite casually, since many gigs were near enough London not to require so much as a hotel room overnight. The only roadies were Wolff and Bob Pridden, but some of the band usually had drivers (Entwistle had originally hired Wiggy to drive for him). Townshend had become close to Speedy Keen and had put him on the payroll.

Keen looked up to Townshend. For one thing, Speedy (whose name came from motorcycling, not drugs) had a nose that was a match for the master's. For another, Townshend's hi-fi gear amazed him. "He had two four-by-twelve's up against each wall and a club amp driving it, and to sit and listen to music that loud and powerful, it was a bit too instant. That was the trouble." When Townshend moved to Wardour Street, Keen lived in for a while, being paid fifteen pounds (about forty dollars) a week as the driver of Townshend's huge Lincoln Continental convertible.

"We had a lot of things in common," Keen says now. "We liked really good cars, big cars with big engines. We liked high-energy music, and just the whole thing of how he set up his life was just phenomenal to me at that point, because of that sound system. He had instruments and all the things no one else had.

"But besides all that, he was much more positive. At that time, you couldn't get a long paper between us. We were close." Townshend encouraged Speedy to write songs and form groups, although at that point, not too much was coming of it.

However close they may have been, the driving led to squabbles. Keen remembered being evicted from a moving vehicle in the middle of a roundabout one night on the way back from a gig in Brighton. (Townshend said that he thought the least Keen could do for his wage was stay awake on the drive back home.) Townshend's relationship with Speedy was typical of a number of friendships from this period; the one with Barnes is another. His cronies were talented but not nearly successful enough to provide a challenge to Townshend's authority. On the other hand, none of them was the sort to shut up when Townshend grew too pompous or abusive (as he did often enough, a set of bad habits amply detailed in Barnes's book).

A set of contradictions was coming to define Pete's adult personality: genius, pretension, silliness, intellectuality, boldness, fear, generosity, jealousy. All mingled but without merging.

In early May, the Who received an invitation to play at the First Annual Monterey International Pop Festival, to be held in mid-June at the Monterey, California, fairgrounds, where a jazz festival was held annually.

The Monterey Pop Festival was the most prestigious rock event ever assembled—its significance might more easily be appreciated by considering whether a "prestigious" event involving rock music was even imaginable prior to the summer of 1967.

Monterey was designed to showcase the best rock and pop talent available, famous and unknown. The festival was headed by a stellar board of directors including Terry Melcher (producer of the Byrds, among others), Andrew

Oldham, Johnny Rivers, Smokey Robinson, Paul Simon, Art Garfunkel, agent/ manager Abe Somers and agent/promoter Alan Pariser, who had dreamed up the festival. John Phillips of the Mamas and the Papas and his manager and producer, Lou Adler, were the directors of the event, "advised" by Paul McCartney, Mick Jagger and Donovan.

The concerts were scheduled for June 16, 17 and 18 at the fairgrounds, which had seats for 7,500 people. Among the other acts appearing at Monterey were the Mamas and the Papas, Jefferson Airplane, the Blues Project, Simon and Garfunkel, Canned Heat, the Steve Miller Band, Otis Redding with the Mar-Keys and MGs, the Quicksilver Messenger Service, Al Kooper, the Association, the Byrds, Country Joe and the Fish, Lou Rawls, Buffalo Springfield, the Jimi Hendrix Experience, Big Brother and the Holding Company, Moby Grape, the Paupers, the Group With No Name, Beverly Martin (billed as "Beverly"), Ravi Shankar (given an entire afternoon to himself), Eric Burdon and the Animals, the Paul Butterfield Blues Band, the Electric Flag and Hugh Masekela.

This was extraordinarily impressive company for the Who to be keeping. While none of rock's trinity of creative leaders—Bob Dylan, the Beatles and the Rolling Stones—would appear, while rockers of the fifties were underrepresented (Chuck Berry having refused to appear free, as all the other acts were doing) and despite the absence of any soul performers, save Redding and (marginally) Rawls, Monterey was nonetheless the most effective statement of community the new rock scene had been able to assemble.

Like the other acts booked for the shows, the Who were paid only with round-trip, first-class airfares—for themselves but not for their equipment, which they again picked up on a catch-as-catch-can basis. They were slated to play Monterey on the final night, June 18, a Sunday. They actually landed a week early in Detroit and played a single show there, in Ann Arbor's Fifth Dimension, the smallest club the band ever worked in the States (it held about 250 people), and a couple of shows in Chicago before heading west. After the festival, they headlined two nights at San Francisco's Fillmore Auditorium, beginning a long and fruitful alliance with promoter Bill Graham.

The rock festival phenomenon that Monterey inaugurated developed from the be-ins that hippies from coast to coast had been staging in public parks for the past year or so. But the be-ins were free, while the festival charged. The festival also created an atmosphere where music was central, rather than incidental, as it had been at the be-ins. Festivals were anathema to rock's root strength, but they were the most profitable way to operate the rock business (even though many performers—including the Who—became and remained draws precisely because they were able to generate feelings of community in their audiences).

Sensitive to accusations of profit-mongering and saddled with an outdoor amphitheatre too small to enable them to pay competitive prices anyhow, Monterey's promoters made the first pop festival a nonprofit event at the instigation of the musicians themselves. In the end, the shows drew vast crowds—as many as 50,000 people on Saturday—and turned a substantial profit, paying back the original investors (a group that included Phillips, Paul Simon, Art Garfunkel, Terry Melcher and Johnny Rivers) and distributing $200,000 (over £70,000) to such charities as the Sam Cooke Memorial Scholarship Fund. (A festival bookkeeper embezzled $51,000 (£18,000) of the proceeds, leading to an investigation by the San Francisco based rock paper *Rolling Stone*, which came to the accurate conclusion that the festival was ultimately exploitative of both stars and fans.)

Monterey was significant because it demonstrated that so many rock fans could come together without a hint of the riots associated with fifties and early sixties teen events, for the cops had been cool enough to allow a certain amount of open pot-smoking. Most important, a genuine camaraderie had been expressed by many of the bands, the performers and listeners having taken one another seriously. Reputations were won and lost that weekend: Otis Redding found a whole new audience in what he called the love crowd; the Who and Hendrix were certified superstars when it was over; San Francisco rock came of age as Big Brother and the Holding Company, featuring Janis Joplin, and the Steve Miller Band walked away with lucrative major label record deals; the Group With No Name was ridiculed as the Group With No Talent, its potential finished; the Beach Boys lost all their hip credentials by reneging on an earlier commitment to play the festival; the Electric Flag were written off as the result of an unfortunately clumsy set. Those groups who did well at Monterey became virtually legendary, while those who did poorly either soon broke up (the Flag) or were never heard from again (the Group With No Name).

Superficially, at least, the atmosphere was not especially competitive. Brian Jones introduced Jimi Hendrix; Eric Burdon introduced the Who; Paul Simon stuck his neck out for the folk singer Beverly and the writer/singer Laura Nyro, two of the festival's least well-received acts. (Nyro was about the only performer whose career prospered after being panned at Monterey.) When their sets were finished or while they waited to go on, musicians sat in the audience to listen to other bands as fans themselves.

Some of this spirit may actually have been legitimate. What is barely reflected in most analyses of the event (or in the D.A. Pennebaker film *Monterey Pop*) is the amount of internecine bickering that riddled the event. Some of the San Francisco groups, particularly the Grateful Dead, were highly critical all along of what they considered the commercialism and huckstering surrounding the festival. Bill Graham's rival promoter, Chet Helms, set up free shows near the fairgrounds, where Bay Area bands played to the overflow crowd.

The British acts, coming from a more frankly competitive scene, felt the pressures especially powerfully. The Who were so panicked, that they rehearsed at their hotel room. They were expected to do about forty minutes at both Monterey and the Fillmore and may also have wanted to extend their act or open it up to older material that would be more familiar to the American audience.

Entwistle was furious with Kit Lambert because he had once again sent the Who to America without their own amplifiers. John was quite justified, too, since Marshall amplifiers (as used by Hendrix and, shortly thereafter, Cream) totally changed American concepts of sound reproduction. The Who were intimately involved in the development of Marshalls but looked like latecomers as a result of what John called Kit's "penny-pinching."

The most dramatic confrontation of the festival occurred Sunday night. The Grateful Dead and the Blues Project were the opening acts, lulling the audience with their placid acid jamming. Meantime, backstage, the Who and Jimi Hendrix were preparing for a battle of the bands. Their Saville Theatre shows in London had ignited a keen sense of rivalry between the two groups, so similar in concept and theatricality. Now Townshend heard that Hendrix planned not only to light his guitar on fire (as he had been doing from time to time) but was also going to smash it.

Townshend went into Hendrix's dressing room, closed the door and accused him of stealing the Who's act. Hendrix stared at the lanky Englishman, called him several kinds of honky, and told him to leave, which Townshend did. But Pete, who idolized Hendrix as the spirit of rock incarnate, was hurt. He was also pissed off—and with Townshend raging, the Who might very well be the greatest rock band in the world. They certainly took the stage that night with every intention of being the most unforgettable act of the weekend. Rather than being nervous, they were furious.

Eric Burdon introduced them. Knowing that most of the crowd had never heard of the Who, let alone seen what they did, he said, "I promise this group will destroy you in more ways than one." Then the Who jogged out, took their places and swung into an epic set.

This was a very different version of the Who from the one that had rocked the Goldhawk. Townshend wore a brocade jacket and a ruffled shirt; Entwistle a jacket with a dragon design; Daltrey a silk print cape, bell-bottom trousers and a flowing blouse. Only Moon, with his red shirt and impish cheeks seemed the same, but even he wore a Nehru jacket. Yet these were still Shepherd's Bush mods. And on this night, they spat in the eye of hippie pastoralism.

They started with "Summertime Blues," Eddie Cochran's rockabilly lament about teenage anguish, transformed by time and modern amplification into a raging protest about life beyond rock & roll. Then they switched to "A Quick One," ripping through the entire mini-opera, stunning the crowd with the complexity and diversity of the piece, by far the most ambitious number anyone had assayed during the entire weekend. They followed with "Happy Jack." ("We will take our repertoire from our American hits—all one of them," Moon had promised a British interviewer.) And then, "My Generation."

"My Generation" was too fast. It careened recklessly as Daltrey spat out the verses, but the band pounded home the tempo, anyhow. As they came to the end, the crowd was already stunned—outside of a few musicians, there couldn't have been more than a few hundred listeners who had any idea what was coming.

It began simply enough with Townshend rubbing the neck of his guitar against the mike stand. Smoke bombs started going off. Daltrey spun his microphone cord in ever-widening arcs, more like a lash than a lariat. Moon comically snapped drumsticks. Entwistle was as imperturbable as ever.

Smoke filled the air as Townshend tossed his guitar overhead, caught it, banged it hard against the floor, once, twice, a third time and then turned and, using it as a spear, attacked his amp stacks, crunching into them full force as festival producer Lou Adler and several stagehands attempted to hold them up. Townshend continued to beat and thrash and finally, as if revolted that his guitar was still intact (or pissed off at Adler), threw it over the amp toward the crew and staff backstage. Moon gave the crowd a big smile, continuing to play as the others walked offstage, then triggered a battery of smoke bombs and trashed his kit, leaving the stage a complete shambles.

Hendrix burned his guitar, but it didn't make much difference. The Who delivered a show that Jimi could match but never top. Nor could anyone else. "The destructiveness of the Who is consistent theatre deriving directly from the group's defiantly lower-class stance," wrote Robert Christgau in *Esquire*, echoing many of the early British reviewers of the band and for the same reasons. The Who had now arrived in America. When the festival ended, four names remained: Otis Redding, Jimi Hendrix, Janis Joplin and the Who.

The Who themselves weren't that happy with their playing. "We used Vox equipment and sounded dire," said Entwistle. "Then after we'd smashed it up, Jimi Hendrix came on, set fire to his guitar and completely upstaged us."

Townshend also felt that the Who had played poorly and been outdone. (He had painfully wrenched his back while attacking the amps, too.) He was much more enthusiastic about their two nights at Bill Graham's Fillmore Auditorium. "We played two forty-five-minute spots each night," he said. "It was like going back to the Marquee. It's a great pity that England doesn't take pop as seriously as those American guys do. The bloke who runs the Fillmore [Graham] really worried about what we thought of his place and whether the amps were okay. They had spent so much money on their electrification. They're really conscientious." Townshend thus began to sound a theme that became familiar in his British interviews over the next few years: the greater degree of seriousness with which he felt America took him and his work.

Townshend was pleased with most of the American groups he heard, particularly Country Joe and the Fish, the Blues Project and Moby Grape (though he did characterize the Grateful Dead as "terrible . . . one of the original ropeys!").

Roger Daltrey felt otherwise. "The Mothers of Invention and Moby Grape are marvelous, but the rest are a lot of rubbish. It's time somebody told the truth about the American scene. Really, most of the groups don't know where it's at. Their material is good. They have this environment which seems great for writing songs. But groups themselves are nothing on stage. Part of the trouble may be that people don't take groups seriously over there."

Townshend and Daltrey have had a history of seeing things in opposite terms, but rarely have they been this much opposed. Yet it is impossible to deny that both were correct to a degree. Daltrey was speaking of an industrious seriousness—Townshend of the music being taken seriously by listeners. Quite clearly, American bands had not figured out as many interesting ways to present themselves as their English counterparts; most of the San Francisco bands considered themselves too cool to do anything theatrical at all. Townshend put it most succinctly: "American bands don't understand about image; that's why you can't tell one from the other."

American bands (and what sometimes seemed like the entire city of San Francisco, if not the state of California) were into LSD and other psychedelics in a way that no one in England imagined. Townshend had taken his share of whatever was around the UFO Club; he even had access to acid from the Sandoz Laboratories in Switzerland, where it was originally synthesized. Yet dosing people (the despicable practice of lacing food and drink with psychedelics and giving them to the unprepared without warning) hadn't yet caught on in England.

Pete was sufficiently confident that Monterey was going to be an exceptional experience that he brought his fiancée, Karen Astley, with him, which turned out to be fortunate when he was dosed not with LSD but with the more potent STP, which San Francisco acid chemist Owsley was then pushing.

"We took some on the plane coming home, thinking it was acid. It turned out to be STP, something that I would never ever take. It was bloody terrible. I mean, you wouldn't believe it," Townshend said. "You know when they say under Japanese torture, sometimes, if it's horrible enough the person actually gets the feeling that they're leaving their body? In this case, I had to do just that, abandon my body.

"It was a hundred years. It was actually about a four-hour hump, whereas a normal acid hump is about twenty-five or thirty minutes . . . you have a hump and then plane off into a nice trip. Well, on this STP trip, the hump was about four to five hours, and it was on an airplane over the Atlantic. I said, 'Fuck this, I can't stand any more.' And I was free of the trip. And I was just like floating in midair looking at myself in a chair, for about an hour and a half. And then I would go back in again and it would be the same. And I was just like, zap, completely unconscious as far as the outside world was concerned. But I was very much alive, crawling alive.

"Eventually, it tailed off and then you get like, instead of a night's lovely planing out, nice colorful images, you get about a week of it and you get a week of trying to repiece your ego, remember who you were and what you are and stuff like that. So that made me decide to stop taking psychedelics."

This was a major change, and for a long time, Townshend didn't talk about it much, certainly not in public. He had been one of the first rock performers to acknowledge psychedelic drug use (pot as well as acid), and to back off now would be a complicated ideological process, tantamount to betraying the counterculture, perhaps even threatening to his career. Anyhow, Townshend wasn't "down on drugs"; he continued to smoke large quantities of grass because he was unable to enjoy listening to music without it.

The rest of the band was never as interested in acid as Townshend in the first place, and the lesson his experience offered seemed to prevent them from becoming deeply involved. "We went through just about everything," said Moon. "Not Roger, so much. He smoked, but that was it. The rest of us went through the same stages everybody goes through—the bloody drug corridor. Eventually, we stopped fucking about with the chemicals and started on the grape. Drinking suited the group a lot better."

Maybe. But at that Ann Arbor club show, one of the promoters was sent out to acquire crystal methedrine for the group to snort. And even after they were weaned, neither Pete nor Keith managed to kick drugs completely, though they tried many times over the next decade.

Kit Lambert was eager to get the Who back in the studio. There was no shortage of material; Townshend once estimated that between "My Generation" and "Pictures of Lily" (a period when the Who were working steadily but almost always near home), he created two to three hundred demos. Much of this material was still under consideration as possible future singles or album tracks.

The band had been scheduled to begin recording in mid-May. But John Entwistle, in a rare display of temper, broke his finger punching a dressing room wall after a gig in Stevenage. A week later, Keith strained his stomach muscles hurling his drums into the audience at a particularly stuffy Oxford University garden party that the Who had somehow been booked to play. (He was replaced on a couple of dates by Julian Covey, a friend of Daltrey's and by Chris Townson of Track's group John's Children.) So after their return from Monterey, they had accomplished nothing.

The Rolling Stones had not played at Monterey as a result of Mick Jagger and Keith Richard's arrest on drug charges the previous February, which made it difficult for them to leave Britain (or enter the States). On May 10, Brian Jones was arrested on similar charges, only a few minutes after Jagger and Richard were granted bail before the start of their trial. Quite clearly, the Stones were being harassed by the government, which (correctly) viewed them as the embodiment of the entire anti-traditional and anti-authoritarian youth movement.

On June 22, Jagger and Richard went on trial. On the twenty-seventh, they were convicted, and Jagger spent the night in Brixton jail while Richard was held at Wormwood Scrubs. On the twenty-ninth, Richard was sentenced to a year in prison, Jagger to ninety days.

Liberal London was outraged. The austere *Times* itself was moved to write its famous "Who Breaks a Butterfly on a Wheel?" editorial, protesting Jagger's sentence (though not Richard's). "There must remain a suspicion in this case that Mr. Jagger received a more severe sentence than would have been thought proper for any purely anonymous young man," concluded the editorial, which emphasized that British justice must be dispensed indiscriminately.

Townshend was angry. He proposed to Lambert, Moon and Daltrey that the Who record a pair of Rolling Stones songs they loved, "The Last Time" and

"Under My Thumb," and release them immediately as a "special jail release." All profits would go to the Stones' legal defense fund.

John Entwistle had been married on June 24 (to Alison Wise), and he was honeymooning on the *Queen Elizabeth* en route to the States. He was reached by ship-to-shore telephone (at 3:00 A.M.) and gave his go-ahead for Townshend to play bass and for the use of his name in the advertising.

By the thirtieth, the single was finished and in the shops, none too soon, since Jagger and Richard were released on £7,000 ($20,000) bail that afternoon. (Brian Jones suffered more extensively from the cops' harassment, though he never spent time in jail. On July 6, he was hospitalized in a state of nervous collapse.) But Radio Caroline was already playing the Who record, it was in the shops and Track had taken out newspaper advertisements reading: "SPECIAL ANNOUNCEMENT: The Who consider Mick Jagger & Keith Richard have been treated as scapegoats for the drug problem and as a protest against the savage sentences imposed upon them at Chichester yesterday, the Who are issuing today the first of a series of Jagger/Richard songs to keep their work before the public until they are again free to record themselves." This was serious stuff, although Keith Moon's claim that he had bought a hundred broom handles and some cardboard and made "Free Mick & Keith" signs for distribution to the courthouse crowd from his Bentley limousine shows just how much stock *he* put in anything smacking of politics.

The "jail release" single was not exploitation. The group pledged to make no money from it. (Jagger and Richard had their sentences overturned on July 31, relieving Townshend of sorting through their song catalog any further.) Yet it could hardly be said that it was typical for the hard-boiled Who to make such a gesture of solidarity, even with the tough-as-nails Stones.

Perhaps the gesture was the product of the rock & roll camaraderie engendered at Monterey. Or maybe Pete Townshend just wanted a chance to cop the Rolling Stones' act for a few minutes while his rivals were guaranteed to be offstage. Maybe this was the ultimate version of the Stones' walk-on. Yet it is all but impossible to imagine the Stones ever reciprocating. (Mick Jagger's comment on the Who single was classic: "Peter, you're a gentleman," he smirked.) There is tough and there is tender-tough. The Who belonged to the Humphrey Bogart school; the Stones were the real thing.

Between Entwistle's wedding and the jail release, the Who accomplished virtually nothing toward making a record during their spell at home. And by mid-July, it was time to return to America, this time for a ten-week tour with Herman's Hermits and the Blues Magoos.

Evil, in the eyes of the Anarchists,
lies in the principle of Authority.
　　　　　—*Peter Kropotkin,*
　　　　　at his trial in 1883

That Frank Barsalona put the Who on the Herman's Hermits package was a measure of his confidence in the band, for the Hermits had become Premier Talent's hottest act. Yet the move was also an act of desperation. Not even Premier, by far the most significant booking agency for rock acts, had enough successful hard rock or underground acts to create a tour around them. Adding the Blues Magoos, a New York group who had had a successful Top 40 hit with the watered-down psychedelia of "(We Ain't Got) Nothin' Yet," was the best Premier could do to ensure the hipness of the Hermits tour.

There was dissension in the Who camp about opening for the Hermits. Although the Hermits had had a long string of British hits (dating back to 1965), their image was purely teeny-bopper. No one took them seriously— fittingly enough, since nothing the Hermits did could be remotely construed as serious, and especially since they included in their repertoire some of the hoariest music hail clichés: "I'm Henry the VIII, I Am" and "Mrs. Brown You've Got a Lovely Daughter." Significantly, those songs weren't British hits. But in America, both made number 1.

Roger Daltrey was especially opposed to the tour. "It got us around America, but it did us no good at all. The audiences didn't mix."

Moon disagreed. "Backing up the Hermits was ideal," he told Jerry Hopkins of *Rolling Stone*. "We weren't on the line. If the place sold only a portion of what it could have sold, the disaster was never blamed on us, it was blamed on Herman's Hermits. We didn't have the responsibility. We had time to discover.

We found the good towns," which he said were New York, Chicago, Detroit, Los Angeles, San Francisco and Cleveland, a mix of media metropolises and blue-collar industrial cities, places with flash and power.

Even Daltrey felt that the Hermits tour had one benefit: It brought the group closer together. "We had no responsibilities; we weren't headlining and we could just roll up and do our bit in half an hour." With such a short set, even Roger could stay up through the night and sing the next day.

Yet the Who weren't very well served by the Hermits tour. True, the band needed the exposure, but the money wasn't great—for thirty dates, they grossed about $40,000 (almost £15,000), and there was never much chance of breaking even. Furthermore, the Hermits' audience tended to be extremely young and impatient with the wild antics of the Who.

Tom Wright, Townshend's old friend from art school, joined up as a roadie for the Hermits tour. Wright was an American and had a better idea of what to expect from the crowds, yet he was still surprised. "The kids yelled for Herman right through the set," he told Barnes. "A lot of times there was no clapping whatsoever, just dead silence. People in the front rows were just sitting there with their mouths open, stunned." To compensate, the Who would begin playing before the curtain rose. They didn't stop at all between numbers, lest the heckling drown them out or demoralize them. They played for twenty-five minutes, then smashed all the gear. (Stamp, still signing "everything I could get my hands on," wanted Townshend to fake it, but Townshend didn't like to bluff, and anyhow, he had to take out his hatred of the crowds somehow.)

Lambert and Stamp were in and out of America all summer, Chris to check up on how well John Wolff was handling business details and to scrounge equipment, Kit to try to squeeze in some recording time. The group had no new single after "Pictures of Lily" did its swan dive, but Atlantic reissued "Substitute" for the Hermits tour, in a version with censored lyrics. (The line "I look all white but my dad was black" was changed to "I try walking forward but my feet walk back.")

The group recorded and mixed six tracks during the tour. The bulk of the work was actually done during a three-day stay in New York just before the tour started (on July 14), at Talent Masters Studio on Forty-second street, owned by Chris Huston, a former member of the Undertakers, the rocker group the Who had opened for back in their Helmut Gorden days. (The Rascals' "Groovin'" and James Brown's "It's a Man's Man's Man's World" were also cut at Talent Masters.) Some mixing was done during a break in the West Coast leg of the tour, at Gold Star Studios (made famous by Phil Spector) in Los Angeles. This is where "I Can See For Miles," for one, was completed.

"The American tour was like it was in London when we first started to get really big," Townshend told Nick Jones of *Melody Maker*. "It's like starting all over again. We did three days of interviews and promotion before we played, and I think I was doing about twenty or thirty interviews per day—and each one had to be a little bit different. But America is important, and I think we handled it professionally and convincingly."

They were able to do so at least partly because they finally had brought their own Marshall amplifiers along with them. The equipment also included the custom kit Premier Drums had manufactured for Keith Moon. The infamous "Pictures of Lily" kit is probably the single most famous set of percussion instruments in rock history. It included three mounted toms, a pair of twenty-two-inch bass drums, three sixteen-inch floor toms, a hi-hat (locked half-closed) and three cymbals, a huge quantity of gear for its day. The most notorious aspect of the kit, however, was the bass drum shells, which sported a set of rectangular panels depicting reclining nudes (thus the association with "Lily") interspersed with Who logos and the legend, "KEITH MOON. PATENT BRITISH EXPLODING DRUMMER."

Moon played these drums through 1969, proving that whatever superficial destruction he might wreak, Keith basically took pretty good care of his gear. (Townshend claimed that Moon mostly wrecked drum heads, which are replaceable but expensive. "I mean, just a set of skins is about three hundred dollars [about £110], and after every show he'd just go bang, bang, bang, bang, through all his skins and then kick the whole thing over.") According to Moon, the "Lily" drum kit took six months to put together and was assembled by five people. All of the designs lit up under black light, which hardly made any difference, since the band never *played* under black light.

The Hermits tour became depressing, however, because the Who lived and traveled under fairly primitive conditions. Barsalona had not been able to eradicate the fly-by-night aspects of rock touring, and as a result, the Hermits-Who-Blues Magoos package played everywhere from modern arenas in big towns to decrepit high school football stadiums in medium-sized ones. Hotel accommodations were equally catch-as-catch-can.

The logistics of touring over a continent three thousand miles broad were brought home many times over. One show was in Vancouver, British Columbia, Canada, which meant that the Who needed their passports and visas to reenter the United States. Keith Moon had left his in New York. Nancy Lewis sent it on by air freight; the band's flight had to be diverted so it could be picked up. At the Vancouver show, Townshend smashed his guitar and then discovered it was the last one he had. Lewis again came to the rescue, going to Manny's music store on West Forty-eighth Street, where Townshend was already considered an important customer, and having a new guitar sent to Salt Lake City, site of the next gig. In the middle of August, the band ran out of smokebombs; U.S. Customs refused to let any others enter the country. They continued with smoke powder, the much less impressive American equivalent.

The bands traveled on a chartered plane with their names painted on the side. But the plane was so ramshackle that they often feared for their lives—and not without reason. En route to one gig, the engines of the aircraft cut out, and they made a crash landing on a foam-covered runway. "That was a bleedin' nightmare," said John. "Two blokes on the plane were out of their heads on acid. Actually, it was probably that incident that inspired Townshend to write 'Glow Girl.' "

Townshend has indicated as much. "I never regarded myself as a person afraid of traveling by air. When we did the Herman's Hermits tour in an old charter plane, I wrote so many songs about plane crashes, it was incredible." Two of those songs were "I Can't Reach You" and "Glow Girl." The first of these became a merely pleasant album track with surging harmonies and desperate lyrics. But "Glow Girl" was a key song in his development as a writer, not so much musically as because of its theme and story.

"I wrote it because we were taking off in a plane which I seriously thought was going to crash, and as I was going up, I was writing a list. I thought that if I was a chick and I was in a plane that was diving for the ground and I had my boyfriend next to me and we were on our honeymoon or we were about to get married, I know what I'd think of. I'd think about him and I'd think about what I am going to be missing," Townshend told Jann Wenner.

"So I went through this list, you know how women get screwed up about their purse. I just went through a big list of what was in this chick's purse—cigarettes, Tampax—a whole lyrical list and then holding his hand and what he felt and what he was gonna say to her.

"He is a romanticist. The man, he's trying to have some romantic and soaring last thoughts. Eventually, what happens is that they crash and they are reincarnated that very instant musically. What I wanted was the list, getting franticer and franticer, she's going through her handbag, ballpoint pen, cigarettes, book matches, lipstick and Excedrin and he's going, 'We will be this and we will do this and we will be together in heaven and don't worry, little one, you're safe with me,' and all this kind of bullshit.

"What happens is the Who do an incredible destruction as the plane hits the ground, with explosions, then this little tune comes out which goes, 'It's a girl, Mrs. Walker, it's a girl. It's a girl, Mrs. Walker, it's a girl.' That was supposed to be the end of the thing and you suss out that they've been reincarnated as this girl."

Others had their own ways of coping. Keith Moon (operating on the theory that "he has to be involved in some form of entertainment all the time," as Pete put it) found bliss in Georgia, the only state in the Union where the sale of firecrackers is legal. He took singular delight in all manner of explosives but became enormously enamored of the cherry bomb, one of the most powerful types.

A few days after the tour's Georgia stop, Townshend stopped by Moon's room and noticed that all the paint around his door was black; Moon had been stuffing the round, red little explosives into the keyhole. "I happened to ask if I could use the loo," Townshend recalled. "He just smiled and said, 'Sure.' I went in and there was no toilet—just a sort of S-bend coming out of the floor!"

"Christ!" Pete exclaimed. "What's happened?"

"Well," said Moon, droll as ever, "this cherry bomb was about to go off in my hand, so I threw it down the bog to put it out."

"Are they *that* powerful?"

Moon nodded, savoring the thought.

"How many of them have you got?"

"Five hundred," smiled the drummer and opened a chock-full suitcase to prove he wasn't fooling.

"Of course, from that moment on, we got thrown out of every hotel we ever stayed in," Townshend said. "It got to the point where they were asking five thousand dollars [£1,800] deposit to let us stay in even the shoddiest hotel."

To be completely fair, Moon's shenanigans were often instigated by Townshend, who was usually canny enough to slip off to bed before Moon (with assistance from the road crew) finished this task and the blame-laying began. Not that Moon wasn't capable of supreme acts of mischief on his own.

On his twentieth birthday, August 23, 1967, Moon declared that this anniversary was his twenty-first (largely because twenty-one was the legal drinking age in most states). Moon made sure a major fuss was made over this fictitious milestone in hopes of getting enough publicity to prevent his baby face from ever again being challenged by suspicious bartenders. (In Moon's estimation, there was no problem that fame couldn't cure.) Decca sent out drum-shaped cakes to key disc jockeys all over the country, and Premier Drums and Decca chipped in for a five-tier cake to be presented to Moon after that night's show, at Atwood Stadium, a high school football field, in Flint, Michigan. Nancy Lewis flew to Flint (about sixty miles north of Detroit) to organize the celebration.

The show was rocky. It didn't draw well (surprisingly, since Flint's WTRX was literally the first radio station in America to play "I Can't Explain" and since all of the band's other records had been aired in town), and everyone was a bit disgruntled as the party began. But nothing untoward happened until nearly midnight, when the Holiday Inn manager came into the room to tell the bands and their assembled guests that the record player was making too much noise, that they had booked the room until precisely midnight and could have it "not one minute longer" and that they were to lower the noise level *now*.

Moon took offense. "The first thing he did," Nancy Lewis said, "was pick up the cake and hurl it against the wall. A whole melee started to break loose; Herman [Peter Noone] was involved, too. They had a big cake fight right there. It was total chaos."

According to some accounts, Moon hurled the cake not at the wall but directly into the sanctimonious mug of the hotel manager, who, according to still other accounts, promptly sat down, telexed the entire international Holiday Inn chain banning the Who and the other bands for life, severally and individually, and then phoned the cops.

Whether this is exactly what happened is questionable: No version is consistent with the others in all its details, and Moon's own account, in the *Rolling Stone* interview with Jerry Hopkins, is by far the most preposterous. Nevertheless, Moon took it upon himself to split. He raced down the hallway and, according to which account one believes: grabbed a fire extinguisher and sprayed every car in the motel parking lot; locked himself in his hotel room and demolished it; leaped into the hotel's swimming pool—which was empty; stripped naked and tripped on a doorsill just as the sheriff arrived, knocking out two teeth.

When the dust cleared, most of the cars in the lot had no paint or were missing large blotches where the extinguisher foam had hit. Moon had to be rushed to the dentist to get emergency caps and was then jailed for the day. After his release, a second chartered plane flew him to Philadelphia and the next gig. The bill came to somewhere between $5,000, or £1,800 (according to Nancy Lewis), and $24,000, or £8,500 (Moon). Keith's figure is more believable if you also trust his story about driving a Lincoln Continental into the pool, which in this account was full to the brim.

All in all, it seems pretty cheap, considering how much fun it must have been for all but those who had to clean up. Probably the most bizarre aspect of the whole episode is the fact that it never even made the Flint *Journal*, the city's daily newspaper. (Frank Barsalona says he remembers being awakened around 3:00 A.M. with the news about the cars needing Earl Scheib—bad—but can't recall if somebody paid off the press.)

At any rate, Keith's twenty-first birthday party entered the annals of rock & roll lore, and he did his best thereafter to live up to the reputation it earned him. "Boom!" he told Hopkins. "There goes another room. What're you gonna do about it! Send us the bill. Fuck the expense. This is the attitude. . . . There was a time in Saskatoon in Canada. It was another Holiday Inn [unlikely; they really were barred] and I was bored.

"Now, when I get bored, I rebel. I said, 'Fuck it, fuck the lot o' ya.' And I took out me hatchet and chopped the hotel room to bits. The television. The chairs. The dresser. The cupboard doors. The bed. The lot of it." It did not occur to Hopkins to ask Moon exactly what a hatchet was doing in Keith's luggage, but then, Sea Cadets, like Boy Scouts, are undoubtedly taught to "be prepared" in any event.

"When we had our first hit," Roger Daltrey told the *Observer*, "we started earning what was then pretty good money. But after the first year we were sixty thousand pounds [$168,000] in debt. The next year, after working our balls off, we were forty thousand pounds [$112,000] down. The biggest choke of all came a year after that when we found we were back up to sixty thousand pounds again. Every accountant's meeting was ridiculous. We always owed so much money that we ended up rolling around the floor, laughing ourselves silly."

Daltrey didn't think that the antics of Moon and Townshend were very funny, since they kept the band buried in debt. John Entwistle wasn't smiling, either. He had to borrow $100 (£35) in order to fly home from the Hermits tour first class rather than coach.

Nothing much fazed Pete and Keith, both of whom seemed to adopt the attitude that the money wasn't real in the first place. As they understood, only a huge hit could bail the Who out of the hole it was in. Until such a hit turned up, there was no point in taking things too seriously. But sometimes even their nerves snapped. During a brief British tour in October, Pete and Roger again fought onstage.

Ironically, the day-to-day struggle to pay the bills worked against solvency.

Like any rock band, the Who had only one source of immediate revenue: live gigs. Record royalties trickled in over months and years; song publishing money was not a meaningful factor for anyone but Townshend and Entwistle. The Who had to work live as much as they could.

The shows took their toll. When Townshend was out all night or away in America, he was often too weary to write songs, and since his method of composing was so heavily involved with making demos, he was hampered by the absence of equipment, too. Furthermore, the pace was exhausting, not at all conducive to coming up with an overall scheme for an album—and all the most significant white rock hits of the period were concept LPs. Meanwhile, the Who barely found time to record at all.

The band arrived back in England on September 16. They had three solid weeks of recording booked. It was their first chance to do any concerted period of studio work since *A Quick One*. The most immediate task was finishing a single. By October 14, "I Can See For Miles" was released and on the charts, which was quick work indeed. The song had mostly been recorded the previous spring at CBS Studios in London, then mixed at the legendary Gold Star in Hollywood, which perhaps accounts for the Spectorian density of the sound.

"I Can See For Miles" had been around for a bit—it was probably written around the same time as "I'm a Boy," certainly before "Pictures of Lily." "But the demo was just so exciting and so good that for a long time we didn't dare make a single because it was blackmail," said Townshend. "I was more or less blackmailing Kit Lambert into doing better. So we always put it off until Kit was very sure of himself. One night he just turned around and said, 'Let's do "I Can See For Miles."'" I had the demo there, and we put it on and dug it again. He just seemed like he was going to do it, and he did it. He got it together."

Yet Townshend has also said that the reason the record was so good was that "I sat down and *made* it good from the beginning. The fact that I did a lot of work on arrangements doesn't really count. You know, you can do all kinds of incredible things to it, but you're never gonna get it, not unless the meat and potatoes are there."

"My Generation" is Townshend's greatest anthemic rock statement, but "I Can See For Miles" is quite simply the most exciting piece of music the Who ever recorded and, by a wide margin, their most effective recording. Its ambition is virtually limitless, and everything it seeks is achieved. Like so much of the Who's music, it is built around drones and crescendos, Townshend's guitar figure circling Moon's cymbal splashes. It starts out full bore, with a pulsating E chord, sustained beyond belief, then punctuated with a clattering shot by Moon. The effect is ominous and hallucinatory, and Daltrey drives it home:

I know you've deceived me
Now here's a surpr*izzzze*,
I know that you have
'Cause there's magic in my eyes

Daltrey hisses those syllables; he does not spit or shout as he usually does. And the result is chilling, a cold warning. With the exception of "Like a Rolling Stone," there is no other record in the world that starts so threateningly.

Part of what makes it so good are the sounds themselves: The drums have a spaciousness at the top end that is close to live percussion (and as far from every other Kit Lambert production as can be imagined); the guitar is all sustain and treble; the bass a hint, not a rumble (which is probably why Entwistle was never very fond of the record).

One reason for using Gold Star was its echo chamber, which, Townshend said, "must be the deepest, clearest sounding in the world." It lends Daltrey's voice a depth it had never before possessed; the result was a kind of charisma, something that could be listened to over and over. And there's still more to it—the charge Moon lays on during the chorus; the way Townshend and Moon trade off punctuating the lyrics on the two repetitions of the third verse (and the way that Moon uses the same accents in Townshend's solo); the way Daltrey makes the transition between verses with a slurred "Oh yeah" that's cool and mean and visionary; the final thundering coda, Daltrey proclaiming, "I can see for miles and miles," into infinity while Townshend revs up his guitar lick and Moon crashes into the fade. "My Generation" is a rock classic that defines its time; "I Can See For Miles" is a masterpiece that stands outside of time, sounding as fresh fifteen years later as it did the first time around.

Townshend's expectations of the song, which he *knew* beyond a doubt was his best work, were so great that he was crushed when "Miles" only stumbled into the British Top 10. "That was the real heartbreaker for me," he said. "It was the number we'd been saving, thinking that if the Who ever got into trouble, that would be the one that would pull us out. The Who did a marvelous performance on it; in my opinion, Kit did an incredible production; and we got a marvelous pressing of it. It reached number seventeen in the charts, and the day I saw it was about to go down without reaching any higher, I spat on the British record buyer. To me this was the ultimate Who record, and yet it didn't sell," Townshend told Ray Tolliday.

His reaction was strange. In *New Musical Express*, Britain's basic reference chart, "I Can See For Miles" reached number 10. But Townshend was so convinced that he had the market sussed perfectly that he would not have been satisfied with anything less than the top three, at minimum. That was what he wanted, what he thought the record deserved. And that was the kind of major hit the Who needed if they were to prosper in the highly competitive British singles world.

Anyway, if Townshend spat, he spat long-distance. The Who toured in support of the single, not in Britain but in North America. And this may have something to do with why the song, which reached number 9 in the *Billboard* chart, was perceived as a breakthrough in the United States while in Britain, with a virtually identical degree of success, it was seen as a flop.

The Who made considerable progress toward finishing their album during their three weeks of recording, but when they left for a U.S. tour with Eric Burdon and the Animals, the project was still in pieces.

The American tour was a three-week in-and-out job playing somewhat larger halls than the Hermits had but with an equally dismal chance of financial success, especially after $5,000 (£1,800) was stolen from one of the band's hotel rooms. As it turned out, the highlight of the trip was the beginning, in Los Angeles, where they played the Hollywood Bowl and appeared on "The Smothers Brothers Comedy Hour."

The Smothers Brothers had started out as folk music satirists but were adopted by the pop scene when their TV show hit (Tommy Smothers was an emcee at Monterey). The Who appeared on the program with Mickey Rooney and Bette Davis, who did what celebrity guest stars usually do on variety shows.

The program was taped in the evening, after an afternoon dress rehearsal. The Who's two songs, "I Can See For Miles" and "My Generation," complete with smash-up, with a brief comic introduction sandwiched between, went smoothly at the rehearsal. Between then and show time, Keith Moon went to work on the stagehand with twenty-dollar bills and frequent nips from a pocket flask of brandy. By air time, Keith had beguiled the crewman into loading his kit with ten times the standard dose of gunpowder.

"My Generation" went flawlessly when the cameras were rolling, the number studded with all the Who's special effects: smokebombs, windmilling arms and microphones, cracked amps, smashed mikes, tortured guitars. As Pete Townshend swung his axe in one last arc while standing just in front of the drum riser, Moon set off his drums.

The blast threw Moon off the riser and sent cymbal shrapnel slicing through his arm. Townshend's left ear took the full force of the explosion, which also fried his hair, a nearby camera and the studio's monitors.

Townshend shook his head, dazedly felt his hair, banged his ears to try to get rid of the ringing. Behind him, Moon held his injured arm gingerly with a lunatic's grin on his face.

From the wings, Tommy Smothers—one of the all-time deadpan faces—entered, acting nonplussed. His acoustic guitar was strapped around his neck. Spying him, Townshend forgot his own pain and grabbed the guitar, smacked it on the floor and put his foot through it. Backstage, Bette Davis fainted dead away into the arms of Mickey Rooney.

After seeing *that* show, anyone who didn't buy the single was either humorless—or dead.

Pete Townshend had developed an obsession with the fate of pirate radio. "It wasn't just the Who that were made by pirate radio," he said, "it was pirate radio that made the music scene in this country. It made the Beatles, it made the Stones, it made lots and lots and lots of people that were around at the time." But on August 15, 1967, the Marine Broadcasting Bill became law, and the reign of the pirates was effectively ended. A few ships continued to send out signals, but this was mostly a spiteful gesture. The pirates' force was spent.

Theoretically, they were replaced by the BBC's new pop music service, Radio One, which the musicians' union had sanctioned for increased needle time. In some ways, Radio One did a better job of representing the diversity and complexity of the developing pop scene. But Townshend loved the crassness of the pirates, with their screaming commercials, hyperthyroid disc jockeys and sanctimonious public service announcements, their attitude that broadcasting wasn't a social responsibility but a business, a device to sell goods. Pete's exposure to American radio, with its multitude of stations and its Top 40 system featuring disc jockeys ten times more lunatic and commercials far more brazen than anything the pirates ever dared, had further convinced him of radio's potential as a pop device. But he also knew that even American Top 40 was changing, the old shouters drying up and dying out as more and more listeners turned to the mellower, more "laid back" deejays and more progressive, less overtly exciting music of FM rock stations.

"Categories are defined in American broadcasting very clearly," Townshend wrote in 1971. "If one is a housewife, one listens to stations that play music that is a little like, say, Terry Wogan's show or Tony Brandon. If you're younger than twenty-nine, however, you listen to good old Rock and Roll.

"We will never be so money-oriented in this country as to have stereo FM radio playing Rock albums even before there is a demand. Unlike Americans, we don't understand the business theory of *creating* demands by allowing people to hear or see what it is they're going to buy." And he pointed out that "discussions, interviews, live concerts and specials" were much more rarely heard on American radio.

"Granted, FM rock radio has done a lot to change this, but slowly and surely the advertisers will get their clutches on the whole thing. They don't want breathing space for their listeners, they want a killing floor." The prophecy was precisely accurate.

From Townshend's point of view, neither Radio One nor U.S. FM was as perfect as the pirates and American Top 40 stations, which were living, breathing, unselfconscious examples of pop art. As John Swenson put it, American Top 40 "worked its commercials so effectively into the format of the medium that there were always smooth transitions. In some cases the commercials were the high point of the programming . . . [In] a hit parade that was repeated with such frequency, the songs themselves became, in a sense, self-commercials." To an extent, the blaring commercials of Top 40 dictated as well as followed the style of the hits. No one was ashamed of this state of affairs; no one thought to question it. All of the most important American rock performers—Bob Dylan, Creedence Clearwater Revival, Sly and the Family Stone—made hit singles as well as hit LPs. This was in stark contrast to the British situation, in which the LP and 45 markets were considered so intrinsically separate that a hit single was often not included on the group's succeeding album. (In America, as Townshend mentioned, some record labels—Motown, most notoriously—conceived of the albums as a device for repackaging a hit single or two with whatever banal filler was around.)

Out of this obsession Townshend came up with a concept for the band's third album. It should be a document not only of the Who's music but of the context in which that music was meant to be heard. It should have commercials, public service announcements and announcer blather as well as songs.

Like any great notion, this one did not spring to life full-grown. "It all started with this number I had written called 'Jaguar,' " Townshend said. "The number was a really powerful and loose thing, something like 'The Ox' from our first album, with Keith thrashing away like hell and us all pumping out 'Jag-u-ar' like the *Batman* theme tune. Of course, with Jaguar cars you have this suggestion of speed and power. At this time, we were working on new ideas for the album. As it stood, I could see that we just had an album of fairly good songs, but there was nothing really to differentiate it from our last LP. It needed something to make it stand out.

"We thought of using a powerful instrumental number that we'd made for Coca-Cola, and then I linked it up with the number 'Jaguar,' and then, of course, we thought, 'Why not do a whole side of adverts?' As things progressed, we realized the whole album could be built around this aspect of commercial advertising.

"At the same time, Radio London and the pirates were being outlawed. You don't realize how good something like the pirates are until they've gone. So, to give the album that ethereal flavor of a pirate radio station, we incorporated some 'groovy' jingles. And so, *The Who Sell Out.*"

At one stage, Chris Stamp was approaching potential advertisers to sell space on the album, but he gave up on this plan (it was Pete's idea) when only Coke seemed interested. The Who had done a commercial for the beverage company as part of a campaign in which it hired dozens of pop singers and groups (from Aretha Franklin and Ray Charles to the Beach Boys and the Troggs). Based on the "Batman" riff, it was a rumbling slice of rock and would have fitted well on the album.

Adding the jingles and advertisements made assembling the tapes extremely tricky, and the record was postponed throughout the autumn as Kit Lambert worked to pull all the details together while the band kept on touring. In Britain, *The Who Sell Out* wasn't released until November 1967. (It came out a month later in the States.)

The Who Sell Out was well worth the struggle and delay. As Richard Barnes wrote, "More than a year after the group had disowned pop art, they produced a truly pop art album." The material ranged from the sublime ("I Can See For Miles") to the trivial ("Cobwebs and Strange" recycled as a commercial for "Heinz Baked Beans"), from the acidly comic ("Mary Anne With the Shakey Hand") to the passionately romantic ("Our Love Was"). They rerecorded authentic jingles (Radio London's ad agency later sued for plagiarism) and narrative songs that functioned as commercials ("Odorono"). The entire first side was strung together as a montage, actually creating the illusion of a bizarre version of Radio London that played only music and jingles recorded by the Who.

On the second side, all seemed the same, starting with a Charles Atlas ad followed by Townshend's lovely "Can't Reach You" and Entwistle's "Medac," a spoof commercial narrative about acne. But "Medac" ran right into Townshend's protopsychedelic "Relax" (which sounds like nothing so much as early Pink Floyd). For the rest of the side, the concept disappeared.

The best contemporary analysis of this schizophrenia was Nik Cohn's review: "It's an approach I find naturally sympathetic," he wrote of the pop radio material, "being an obvious reaction against the fashionable psychedelphic solemnity, against the idea of pop as capital-letter Art, against everything that I most detest. . . .

"The trouble is that the idea hasn't been carried right the way through; it has only been half-heartedly sketched in. This, of course, is a traditional Who fault—Pete Townshend works something out, the group half completes it and then everyone sits back until another group walks in and steals the whole thing.

"In a way, it's an attractive fault, it shows a nice lack of intensity towards success. In this case, however, it's a disaster.

"What this album should really have been is a total ad explosion, incredibly fast, loud, brash and vulgar, stuffed full of the wildest jingles, insane commercials, snippets from your man Rosko [one of the more important pirate deejays], plus anything else that came to hand—a holocaust, an utter wipe-out, a monster rotor whirl of everything that pop and advertising really are."

While the best parts of *Sell Out* succeed because Townshend and the Who are genuinely—and affectionately—involved with what they satirize. Cohn (for all his anti-hipster posturing) in fact holds the pop scene in contempt. *Sell Out* is a let-down conceptually, not because it doesn't go far enough in its execution but because the concept is abandoned. While they keep it up, the Who strike a beautiful balance between the necessities of their music and the restrictions and requirements of its unlikely environment. (In a century, *The Who Sell Out* could seem like one of Townshend's less likely science fiction fantasies.)

What Cohn wanted—commercialism taken to an absurdist extreme—was fully delivered on the album cover. This featured four panels with photos by David Montgomery. In each, one of the band members portrayed one of the commercials from the album: the perpetually innocent-looking Moon with a giant tube of Medac acne ointment; Pete Townshend rolling on a stick of Odorono whose size is matched only by his beak; John Entwistle draped in a Tarzan costume holding a teddy bear and hugging a blonde, representing the Charles Atlas course; and poor Roger Daltrey dunked in a huge tub of one hundred catering-size tins of frigid Heinz baked beans (the photo session gave him a mild dose of pneumonia).

The most interesting question Cohn raises is why the Who abandoned the radio concept. He suggests one reason: to competently finish such a task would require "the kind of studio time that only the Beatles can fit in. The Who have been pretty hectic these last months, crossing and recrossing America, and just haven't had the breathing space they needed."

This implies that the Who scrapped their plan for a fully conceptual album because of a lack of material. But that isn't the case. In addition to "Jaguar" and the Coke commercial (both of which are as well done as most LP filler of the period), the out-takes included two Eddie Cochran songs, "Summertime Blues" and "My Way," complete with radio intros.

Chances are, the Cochran songs weren't used because their presence would have skewed the album too far away from Townshend's songwriting. As it was, the album opened with Speedy Keen's "Armenia City in the Sky" (although it sounded so much like a Townshend song that no one who hadn't scrutinized the credits could tell), and included two Entwistle tunes, "Medac" (U.S. title: "Spotted Henry") and "Silas Stingy." A second album with five non-Townshend writing credits could seriously jeopardize his reputation, and the inclusion of so many songs written by non-band members would have been highly unfashionable.

Yet a trove of Townshend originals of superior quality was available, if only the British bias against putting hit singles on albums could be overcome. "Substitute," "I'm a Boy" and "Pictures of Lily" had never appeared on an album, and while the first two were perhaps a bit dated, "Lily" belongs on *Sell Out* because of its sound as well as its theme.

In a way, this English rock tradition (which was so utterly different from the American) is admirable. Theoretically, it prevents record companies (or recording artists) from cynically slapping together a couple of hits, a B-side or two and some filler and calling it an album's worth of material. Yet, while rock is made track by track, it's heard differently in different contexts. Just as a single may sound great on a car radio and lousy at home, fantastic in a bar-room but horrible at the beach—so a song can actually mean different things as a single or on an album.

As more and more contemporary rock artists were learning, the important thing was to create unified statements, and that meant singles that worked from opening to close, album tracks that contributed to an overall image as well as standing on their own, albums that hung together regardless of the origin of their separate cuts.

Cohn is correct when he suggests that the Who's lack of follow-through displays "a nice lack of intensity towards success." But that impression wasn't intended; of the band, only Townshend could be said to be even ambivalent about success. The others lusted for it.

"We wanted to do *The Who Sell Out* just to make fun of ourselves to a certain degree," Townshend told Paul Nelson. "We wanted, as I said, to take away some of the gravity which seems to be weighing the group down in [America]. We wanted to change the fact that so many fans take us so seriously." But this was never a problem for the Who in England, where they needed to establish their seriousness. In the States, the Who were *saved* by seriousness, since (with the exception of "I Can See For Miles") they'd never had a Top 10 hit.

If escaping seriousness really was Townshend's aim, *The Who Sell Out* was a complete backfire. The album sold well (but not spectacularly), and its listeners were almost all the sort of underground audience who would take the group, the album's concept and even Top 40 radio seriously. For one thing, the teenaged listeners Townshend was concerned not to alienate didn't buy albums. For another, *The Who Sell Out* is ultimately a nostalgic in-joke: Who but a pop intellectual could appreciate such a thing?

One indication of *Sell Out*'s greatness is that even though its concept isn't sustained, it is utterly without filler—the filler had become an integral part of the way the album worked.

The chief reason for the greater consistency of *Sell Out* is the development of Pete Townshend's songwriting. And the chief change in that writing was an increased emphasis on narrative. "When I write today, I feel that it has to tell a little story," he said. "And I can't shake this. Like 'Odorono,' [which] I dug because it was a little story, and although I thought it's a good song, it was about something groovy—underarm perspiration. He rushes backstage to congratulate her and it looks like she's all set, not only for stardom but also for true love. And then, underarm perspiration cuts the whole thing. And you know, without getting too serious about it, because it's supposed to be very light, that's life. It really is. That really is life."

Several of *Sell Out*'s other songs also told stories: "Mary Anne With the Shakey Hand" and the brilliant "Tattoo," which extended Townshend's obsession with adolescence into a story about two boys who decide to have themselves tattooed and suffer the consequences.

Narrative also played a key role in Townshend's continuing attempt to create a workable rock opera. Yet it is significant that "Rael," the opera fragment that concludes *The Who Sell Out*, is the one piece here whose story can't be summarized. Paul Nelson, who wrote a rave review of the album for the Sunday *New York Times*, said, "The repetition of legend-simple verses . . . sets up mythological tensions as real pragmatism defeats Rael idealism." John Swenson wrote: "It's about 'overspill,' when the world's population becomes so great in years ahead that everyone is assigned to their one square foot of earth." Ira Robbins, editor of *Trouser Press* magazine, suggested that Rael might be an abbreviation for Israel and that the Red Chins might be the Red Chinese. Richard Barnes states assuredly that " 'Rael' was to be political, about the Red Chinese (The Red Chins)."

All of this is reasonable. Assenting to one interpretation does not necessarily contradict any of the others. In his book *The Story of Tommy*, Townshend states that the Red Chins were the Communist Chinese and says that the story was set in 1999 and that a portion of the plot concerned the Chinese crushing established religions as they conquered the world. Yet he acknowledges, "No one will ever know what it means; it has been squeezed up too tightly to make sense."

But this isn't playing fair; "Rael" is meant to be at least as lucid as "Happy Jack" or "Tattoo." The reason that no one—not even Townshend—can give a succinct summary of the plot is that there is no succinct story offered. There is less narrative here than in many of the shorter songs Townshend had written.

Pete's growth as a composer may have been even more impressive than his development as a lyricist. The change announced itself on *The Who Sell Out* in all sorts of ways: through the increasingly complex vocal structures, the much freer use of keyboards to supplement the band's basic instrumental lineup, the more focused use of repeated themes and drones and the greater compression and efficiency with which he manipulated the basic Who sound. The most perfect expression of all of this is "I Can See For Miles," but there's something of it in almost every track on the album, from the beautiful opening chorus of "Rael," which makes the Beach Boys' harmonies more glorious, to the spacious, enthralling organ work on "Armenia City in the Sky." Otherwise slight love songs, such as "Our Love Was" and "I Can't Reach You" become majestic, and Pete's great assurance even makes the psychedelic pretensions of "Relax" convincing—the music soars to unbelievably exhilarating heights. "Rael" flows smoothly; it's not all fragments, like "A Quick One," but an integrated suite.

Daltrey's singing had gained important assurance, Entwistle's writing had become consistently amusing, Moon's drumming still justified every bit of his cockiness. But it is Townshend whose work transforms the group's music from sporadically captivating to completely mesmerizing.

Townshend attributed much of his growth as a writer and arranger to finally learning to play piano, a skill amply reflected in the album's beautiful, intricate keyboard parts (most of which Pete played himself). But *The Who Sell Out* doesn't rank with rock's finest albums because it's the album Pete Townshend made the year he learned piano; what counts was that Townshend had incorporated his new musicality into an already formed aesthetic, which was grounded in the basic excitement of rock & roll. By applying this new technique, Townshend belied all his public rhetoric: He did take his music very seriously.

22

*I spent too much of my
adolescence attributing
everything I was capable of
to drugs and not to myself.*
—Pete Townshend

The progress made by the Who in 1967 was symbolized by the award the
group received from *Rolling Stone* magazine as Rock & Roll Group of
the Year—a sign of the prestige the Who now possessed in the States,
particularly since *Rolling Stone* was so parochial and patriotic about the
superiority of the San Francisco rock scene.

"We've found in America that we've accomplished in a very short time what
it took us three years to do in England," said Townshend. "In England, it wasn't
just automatic success. We didn't bring out a hit record and suddenly make it,
[and] America is the same case. We had to come here, be seen and make sure
people know we're here and they can't look away while we're around."

Yet there were vast differences between the image of the Who in the two
countries. "In England, we remain just a good pop group, now concerned with
writing and composing instead of carefully molding an image," said Townshend.
"In the United States, we are regarded as part of the British underground."

The American perception was more accurate, though not because the
underground was any less assiduous or crafty about image-mongering. The
Who belonged with the underground because it was one of rock's most
adventuresome groups. At home, they were viewed as a band with a history
of modism, pop art, frivolous singles with a few good ideas but never much
depth, a group that created its own bandwagons but nonetheless was largely
devoted to riding trends. In the States, the Who were introduced in a cultish
fashion. "During the early days, a Who album in the States was a rare thing,"

said Townshend. "Because we were not that easily obtainable, we and our records became exclusive, and everyone wanted to know more."

It was this advantage of being able to escape the unwanted portion of their history and be taken seriously—much more than the silly business about the so-called failure of "I Can See For Miles"—that really urged the Who to turn its back on Britain and work most of the time in the States. Not that there was much hope for the Who to make a profit back home.

"Being a smaller scene than the United States gives [the British rocker] an advantage in a way," Townshend wrote in 1971. "He stands to gain less if he makes it, but he stands a good chance of making it if he is good.

"No matter how good he is, though, the British scene cannot sustain him forever. . . . We have too much talent and not enough audience. . . . Make your name here, mates, but don't expect to make anything else. Whether it be your favorite British band going over there or your favorite American band coming over here, American audiences are paying the fare."

As an explanation of the international economics in rock, that analysis made strong pragmatic sense. But the Who, in particular, became obsessed with the differences between the two countries. They knew what was strong about Britain already. "Britain is a country where Elvis can remain a myth," wrote Townshend in that same article. "It's a country that loves Tom Paxton more than his own neighbors do. It's a country that knows more about the American blues heritage and its history than even some of the old bluesmen themselves. A country where you can play the good old Albert Hall and make your name even if no one has ever heard of you."

Ultimately, however, as Townshend confessed to *Melody Maker* in the fall of 1968, "The English scene for us, unfortunately, doesn't compare with America. . . . The States offers us more money, fans and excitement." This made a wicked kind of sense. In England, *The Who Sell Out* was a response to pirate radio—some decent music, not much else. In America, it was controversial. (WMCA-FM radio banned it because of the cover and internal vulgarity, while retailers were upset by the cover, which was the first in pop history not to list the song titles.) In Britain, the Who were mods, but mod was already passé. In America, as Roger Daltrey said, "The idea of a mod is somebody wearing a bull's-eye T-shirt," which meant that the Who had great panache as a result of their association with the style cult.

The greatest difference, perhaps, was in the response to guitar destruction. "In England, I used to get people asking me for my guitars and calling me terrible names because I smashed equipment up," Townshend said. "They said I wasn't worthy of having such expensive guitars just to wreck them, so why didn't I give them away.

"But in the States, it was the other way round. They thought it was a gas. They loved it. I became a kind of hero. I was presented with beautiful guitars— just to smash them up. It became ludicrous."

Another difference was the relative importance placed upon image, the intimacy that was expected between audience and performer and the degree of seriousness with which people listened and bands were expected to play. "English pop has got far too involved with this star-image bit," Pete said. "Groups arriving five minutes before they go on in their black-windowed limousines, doing a half-hour spot and then disappearing. Well, that's not the way to do it. And it's got to be changed." In America, as Townshend knew, it was already changing. At the hippie ballrooms in San Francisco and Detroit, Chicago and Philadelphia, he was able to mingle with crowds as he hadn't done since the Goldhawk and Marquee days.

In the late summer of 1968, Townshend attempted to define the difference between the hippies and the mods for Jann Wenner of *Rolling Stone*. "The acceptance of what one already has is the thing [for hippies]," he said. "Whereas the mod thing was the rejection of everything one already had. You didn't want to know about the fucking TV. . . . You didn't want to know about the politicians, you didn't want to know about the war. If there had been a draft, man, they would have just disappeared.

"Over here, it's imperfect, it's not a sterile situation. The groups themselves can't become powerful, because they can be weakened at so many points. They can be weakened by their education, by their spirituality, by their intelligence, by the sheer fact that Americans are more highly educated. The Englishmen I'm talking about probably left school when they were fourteen or fifteen. Some of them can't even read or write. But yet they were mods—you see something nearer, I suppose, in what it's like to be a Hell's Angel, but not as much flash, not as much gimmick, much less part of a huge machine."

What was arising in both Britain and the United States were assorted forms of what Robert Christgau calls "mass bohemianism," the contradiction in which production workers are expected to behave as leisure class consumers away from the job. But this took very different forms in the two countries, a fact that is expressive of their different-but-similar historical development. It can perhaps best be expressed through the following analogy: A group of British kids identically dressed, let's say, in sta-prest Levi's, desert boots and Fred Perry shirts, see in one another an image of community. A group of American kids all wearing the same clothes will see themselves as complete individualists because their shirts are different colors. And it was this difference in self-expression—the British always leaning toward creating some kind of group; the Americans always tending to pull groups apart—which the bands of the late 1960s and early 1970s were tending to manipulate.

This process had to be learned. Mostly, that meant that British bands had to understand what parts of America couldn't be taken for granted. "Everything we do for the States is what we do for England," explained Townshend. "But we know everything about England. We know what sort of records they want, what sort of television they want to see us on.

"But in the States, it's a different matter. We do television shows for the States which we never see. We record interviews for the States which we never hear. Other English groups have just done it without thinking, they've just shot up. Perhaps we have regarded success in the States as being far more important to us than any other English group." That may very well be the case, and if it is, it goes a long way toward explaining which groups lasted over the next decade (those who took America seriously) and which groups burned out or never made it at all (those who never learned to make distinctions between the two cultures).

The Who were able to exploit this differential better than any other rock band, except perhaps the Rolling Stones, who had the advantage of being part of the first wave of the British Invasion. The Who's strength was summed up by Nik Cohn, always their most apt critic. "They have it both ways," he wrote. "They're intelligent, musical. They do keep moving forward; but they're also flash and they come on with all the noise and nonsense of some backdated rock & roll group. They make good music, and they're still pop. That's almost a contradiction in terms, but somehow they make it."

One thing that had not changed was the constant need for new material. "Compositions come out so fast in rock because there's a demand created and contracts have to be fulfilled," said Townshend. "I mean, whoever put Beethoven under contract? Prince Charming may have asked him to do this and that, but there was none of this 'six records a year.' The pressures of the pop industry are part and parcel of it all."

That didn't mean that Townshend rejected the power and value of rock's commerciality and mass appeal. "It's the only fucking healthy thing about it!" he exclaimed. "The commercial market refuses to change at the speed musicians and composers might wish. It has its own pace, adjusted by the mass, which is to me absolutely the most important thing on earth. There are levers in the commercial market to be pulled, but if people buy a record, they were moved in some way to do so. . . . Huge musical personalities like Clapton and Hendrix can get the machine to do what they want, but it's still the machinery that does the work. What people find oppressive is the dependence on the system, but the commercial system comes halfway to pop but pop won't come halfway back. Anything that does is classed as bubblegum and chucked out. But some of the world's best music *is* bubblegum. . . . And the machine created the Cream. It *really* did." Thus Townshend came to terms with the stipulations of high art and avant-gardism while remaining true to his experience and self-interest.

In certain respects, Townshend was unable to live what he preached. After the relative failure of "I Can See For Miles," Townshend felt more than just a frustration with the British audience. He also felt that he'd "lost the knack of getting [the Who] in the singles market." But he was not yet prepared to abandon singles for the album market, nor to dissolve the group. (One of his visions was of John and Keith finally going off with Jimmy Page to form a band called Led Zeppelin while he became a soundtrack composer.)

As a result, even the band's plans for albums stumbled. "The trouble is our last few singles have taken us so long to make," said Entwistle. This was an especially difficult matter at a time when rock was changing so rapidly. The borders of both record production and what was acceptable to the marketplace were being expanded almost weekly. Meantime, the Who stalled and dabbled, made plans and did not complete them. "We finish them [the singles] and then we add fiddly little bits which take days. 'Happy Jack,' on the other hand, took us just half a day in the studio," John complained.

Townshend put it another way. "Kit Lambert was 'practicing' record production at the time," he said in *Record World*. "He used to take us all down to a studio called City of London Studios, which at the time was mono. . . . It was small and poorly equipped, but it had something that no other studio in Britain could offer at that time: an engineer who could understand what Kit was saying."

Working there cheaply enough to afford time to experiment, Lambert and the band formulated plans for their projected fourth album, to be released in mid-summer, around the time of the tennis championships at Wimbledon. *Who's For Tennis*, perhaps the worst pun in a history studded with poor ones, was to lead off with a single, "Glow Girl," Townshend's plane crash tune. A version was recorded in January 1968 complete with sound effects: a ripping, slashing Townshend guitar solo fading into sustained notes and feedback out of which emerges the reincarnation chorus: "It's a girl, Mrs. Walker, it's a girl."

"Glow Girl" was again much lighter and more melodic than the Who's thundering stage shows. In an early 1968 interview with Keith Altham of *New Musical Express*, Townshend said that the single might be only an American release. "We're working along the lines of a very slow ballad-type number, like 'Strangers in the Night,' with a wild guitar sound laid over the top, for England." If this project was ever seriously considered (and even if it wasn't), it ranks as one of the most bizarre fantasies in Lambert's and Townshend's history of concocting them. The Who could barely have held still long enough to have played a ballad, and the idea of Roger Daltrey singing a Sinatra-style melody, much less a Sinatra-like lyric, is completely absurd.

Townshend seemed to recognize this more clearly in the Altham interview when he vowed to "preach" on his next album, adding, "We want to produce it on the lines of 'You've Got to Have Faith in Something Bigger Than Yourselves' [the title of one of his worst acid-period songs]. But can you imagine Roger standing there singing something like that? No one will believe we are serious. Our problem is that we are Mickey Mouse figures still!"

They weren't doing too much to counteract the image. As rock grew more pretentious, the Who continued to think in terms of the pop band image they had begun with. There was no way they could eradicate their history as guitar-busting, pop-culture-championing, hotel-wrecking wild men, so they alternately wallowed in it and tried to push forward without much reference to the past. But there was no way that the new breed of self-serious pop listeners (which included critics, journalists, deejays and even other musicians) was able to incorporate the idea of an Important Rock Band that specialized in commercial jingles and pure rock & roll.

The Who's instincts were clear (and correct). Even though it was a weird step in terms of image-making, the other composition Townshend boasted about at this stage was "Little Billy," a commercial that he'd written (on request) for the American Cancer Society's teenage anti-smoking campaign. (The band also included it in their stage show.) "Little Billy" was a good song—but it was meant to burst the preconceptions of what a "serious" rock group did, and many missed the point. (Townshend also wrote a second anti-smoking tune, "Do You Want Kids, Kids," for the ACS.)

The band also continued to talk about doing a TV show. A WMCA fan's newsletter from their spring tour of America spoke of an "upcoming" BBC series—a "one-hour weekly pop music show with other artists filmed by the BBC mostly in America." The Who would do an original number each week and also appear in a three-minute weekly serial. Bob Dylan, the Monkees and Lulu were to be among the early guests. The BBC confirmed plans for the show through a press release from its American office, but the deal apparently fell through.

Trapped at home with a pop group image, Townshend couldn't help feeling that the best way out was to go cinematic. This had been Lambert's and Stamp's hope all along, and they were apparently prepared for a comic book success (sort of like a psychedelic era Kiss) if they couldn't create something as multi-dimensional as the Beatles. It is entirely possible that the Who could have gotten their TV program—and it's just as possible (likely, in fact) that having gotten it, they would have been ruined within a year, as the Monkees were. The rock culture was developing certain standards and values of its own, and these had to be reckoned with if a group aspired to any kind of longevity.

The record market was especially volatile. In Britain and in America, 1968 was the first year in which more albums than singles were sold. In America, albums now represented 80 percent of recording revenues. In Britain, 11 million more LPs were sold in 1968 than in 1967. The change reflected the increasing importance of underground rock and the ultimate economic importance of the hit record. Touring could take one only so far, but the potential impact of a record—which could go into homes in which nobody would even consider entering a rock hall—was almost limitless.

Yet over and over again, Townshend restated his impression that to the Who, "record success is secondary to what we've achieved on our personal appearances." In many ways, this was true; the band's records were adventuresome, but they hardly suggested the audacity of the stage show: The Who had never found a recorded equivalent of guitar-bashing. Perhaps they never would, for the very qualities of spontaneity, immediacy and collective spirit which their concerts represented were, by definition, beyond reproduction. Now they proposed to try to capture the essence of their sound on a live album to be recorded at their spring shows in New York at Bill Graham's new Fillmore East.

In late January, the Who were booked for a two-week tour of Australia with the Small Faces, Manfred Mann and John Walker of the Walker Brothers. Mod was huge in Australia, since it mediated perfectly the antipodean contradiction between New World rootlessness and individualism and Old World tradition and community.

The tour was a disaster from the very beginning. The long plane flight left all the musicians extremely fatigued; Ronnie Lane of the Faces remembered seeing three sunsets in the course of the journey. Lane recalled clearly the beginning of the catastrophe.

"We was really tired when we got there," he said. "We got off the plane, walked down the steps and there's the media waiting at the bottom of the stairs. And the first thing they said to us was, 'How do you feel now that the pound's been devalued?' [The devaluation had occurred in November 1967.] As if that meant anything to us—and it was supposed to.

"The whole thing was so bloody and horrible and pathetic. I think Pete Townshend hit this fellow and this is what got the tour off to a good bollocking in the press.

"And then, of course, the media slagged us. They made us look so demonic that we decided in the end that we might as well go and do some of these things. We started to live up to our name, which really wasn't very satisfying, 'cause we really wasn't that bad."

The antagonism of the press was bad enough. The hostility of the public—outside of the adoring mods, of course—was what pushed them over the edge. "It's sort of like the kind of thing you would think would happen in the Midwest in the thirties," said Lane. "Really, really sort of backward, redneck, stupid, thick, ignorant behavior on the side of the authorities. The kids used to come to see the Who and the Faces on their scooters and all that. They were really into it. They were really up on it, as well; they had all the stuff.

"They used to come and get harassed by the authorities just for existing. As if they were having punch-ups on the beaches, which they weren't."

Minor incidents piled up. Townshend phoned down for breakfast one morning at what he considered a reasonable hour and was laughed at by the desk. "This is Oz, mate. We get out of bed in the mornin' 'ere," he was told. Pissed off, he walked down the street to a grocery store, bought a huge box of corn flakes and a gallon of milk, fixed himself a meal in the sink in his room, ate a few bites and left the rest to solidify (dried cornflakes and milk are like concrete). Then he checked out. Another day, EMI, which released the Faces' records in Australia, gave singer Steve Marriott a portable record player. A speck of dust got on the needle, and he dropped it on the floor in contempt. Keith Moon gave the stereo a boot, and it was eventually tossed several stories out a window. To top it off, the concert promoter had thought of everything: facilities, amplifiers, backstage amenities—but he had not provided a proper public address system, dooming the sound to murkiness.

This was the dark side of the touring sport, when all went wrong and young men, not yet grown to responsibility, far from their homes, persecuted for looking and acting differently by xenophobic authorities, on schedules that put them out of synch with society, just went nuts out of unhappiness. There were occasions, as on Moon's birthday, when the destruction might be a good time gotten out of hand. There were other times when it was an act of revenge against an oppressor too vague to identify—or so it seemed. It happened sometimes in the States in smaller cities and towns; once in a while, there was even an inkling of it in England. But it was the essence of the tour in Australia.

After one domestic flight, a stewardess accused various members of both the Small Faces and the Who of harassing her and threatened to press charges and have them deported. The story was picked up in all the Australian papers. Suddenly, the bands really were villains. After the final concert, in Wellington, New Zealand, on January 29, the New Zealand *Truth* wrote: "We really don't want them back again. They are just unwashed, foul-smelling, booze-swilling no-hopers."

The feeling was mutual. Pete Townshend uttered a public vow never to return, a promise he has kept.

Off the road, at least, the Who were growing up. By the end of 1968, Keith Moon's marriage and fatherhood had been revealed, as had Roger Daltrey's divorce. Like Entwistle, Pete Townshend was married openly, to Karen Astley from Ealing Art College, on May 20, 1968, the day after he turned twenty-three. The Townshends bought a Georgian house in Twickenham, a London suburb, for £16,500 (around $46,000), then spent an additional £8,000 ($22,000) to furnish it and add a home studio complex. John Entwistle was still living in his Acton semi-detached, while Kim and Mandy Moon still shared the Chelsea flat with Keith and his motley assortment of all-hours-of-the-day-and-night guests. Roger Daltrey bought a 400-year-old cottage in Berkshire and learned to love the country life. Already Roger had met the woman who would become his second wife, Heather Taylor, during a tour of America.

Of the band members, Moon had changed the least, maybe because he was the youngest but more likely because he was completely irrepressible. Entwistle had a wife, and a son on the way, but he had always been so emotionally stable that the difference was nothing radical. Even Roger, since his peaceful reemergence after nearly being sacked, hadn't changed much.

But to Pete Townshend, adolescence and rock were to a great degree inseparable. "I think what's always been my problem is that I've always been *fascinated* by the period of adolescence," he told Greil Marcus in 1980. "And by the fact that rock's most *frenetic* attachments, the deepest connections, seem to happen during adolescence or just post-adolescence. Rock does evolve, and it does change . . . but to you as a listener, someone who needs both the music and the exchange of ideas—you always tend to listen in the same way. You expect—and you feel happiest when you get—an album that does for you what your first few albums did. You're always looking for that *first fuck*. Of course, you can never have that first fuck, but you're always looking for it. Occasionally, you get very close. Always chasing the same feeling, the same magic."

Townshend may not have been speaking for all rock fans (though he certainly spoke for many), but he was unquestionably speaking for himself. And since, for Townshend, rock is lifestyle and philosophy as much or more than music, he was also describing an attitude that affected his personal and business relationships. Like any celebrity, he was encouraged to remain willful and spoiled, not questioning too much. And in many cases, Pete took this to an extreme.

"I was bitter, cynical and angry most of the time," he has said of himself during this period. "But most of all I was really very stupid. It's taken a long, long time to actually learn to value the human beings around me." He recalled seeing some film footage taken on one of the group's U.S. tours. "I talk about the rest of the guys in the band as though they were cardboard cutouts. I say something like 'John doesn't give a shit, Roger's just a tough guy, Keith's just a comic' or something like that. I thought, that guy, that *cunt*, made it by being like that."

There were forces working to temper Townshend's anger and bitterness. He read the spaceship writings of George Adamski, who claimed that a race of spiritually exalted beings lived on another planet in our solar system. Townshend claimed to have actually seen the saucers. Adamski, he said later, "taught me to open my mind—in other words, he taught me faith." LSD had led Townshend through the usual array of theologies and pseudotheologies. He was bold enough to theorize quite openly among his friends about mysticism and the universe, sometimes even spouting about it in interviews.

Listening to him, his friend Mike McInnerney, then art director of *International Times*, an underground paper, told him that there was an intriguing correspondence between many of Townshend's ideas and those of an Indian spiritual master (or guru) that McInnerney followed, Meher Baba.

"I took one look at Mike and I thought, 'There's a good bloke, right?' " remembered Townshend. "If it hadn't been him telling me about it—I mean, he wasn't pushing it down my throat, he was just saying, 'Listen, stop talking for a minute and look at that. Take it or leave it.' So it was him, it was his quality, it was his personality. It was him and what he'd done and the fact that he was talking about Baba that impressed me to the point of picking up the book."

McInnerney claims much less credit. "I had an immediate strong feeling for Pete and felt that I would like to give him some books on Meher Baba. Baba has a way of grabbing you fundamentally and then hanging on. There was a lot of Baba activity in London at the time, and Pete just picked up on it."

Meher Baba was born in 1894 in Poona, India, southeast of Bombay, the son of Persian parents. Merwan Sheriar Irani, as he was born, was not exceptionally pious as a youth, but while in college he developed an attachment to Hazrat Babajan, a local spiritual teacher and Sadguru (Perfect Master). One day, she kissed Merwan in the center of his forehead, sending him into a cycle of deep contemplation during which he neither ate nor slept for many months while he realized his essential Godhood. Merwan then entered a long period of study with five Perfect Masters, one of whom, Sadguru Upasni Maharaj, threw a stone at him, hitting him squarely in the forehead in the same place as Babajan's kiss. In that instant, Merwan Irani realized his role as not just a Sadguru but as the Avatar of the Age: that is, the Original Enlightened Soul who returns—at periods of between 700 and 1,400 years—to give humanity a spiritual push and forcefully but compassionately show the path of spiritual reawakening.

Merwan did not reveal himself as Avatar for many years. In the meantime, he gathered about himself a group of disciples (the Mandali) and set out across India, teaching, meditating, and performing a variety of activities opaque to the normal mind. He was an ascetic—a vegetarian who handled no money— but he did not expect all of his disciples to display the same degree of devotion to form. In the Sufi tradition (ages older than Islam), he accepted adherents and supplicants of all faiths and lifestyles.

However, beginning on July 10, 1925, Meher Baba (as he was renamed by the Mandali; Meher Baba means "compassionate father") took a vow of silence. This was originally intended to be symbolic and temporary, but Baba spoke not a single word until he died (or "dropped the body," in spiritual parlance) in 1969. "You have had enough of my words. Now it is time to live by them," said Baba, who as Avatar was proclaimed the reincarnation of Christ, Buddha, Moses, Mohammed, Zoroaster and all the other great spiritual leaders. But he continued to meet with many people (including some in the West, on his various journeys to England, Europe and America) and to lecture by means of a handheld alphabet board or hand gestures interpreted by the Mandali.

It is not the purpose of this book to debate the merits of Baba's teachings (which are, however, quite consistent with other great spiritual teachings, although well adapted to modern language and custom). What's important is that Baba was (and remains) an extraordinarily powerful figure in the lives of many people, from oil executives to shop clerks. Since Baba himself was a musician before his silence, it is perhaps not surprising that several musicians of stature (including Ronnie Lane, Melanie Safka, Robbie Basho) became devotees. But the connection between Townshend and Meher Baba is by far the most famous and, somehow, seems the most fated. (When Baba was shown a copy of the *Observer* Sunday magazine cover story on the Who, just after Pete became aware of him, the Master immediately placed his thumb directly on Townshend's nose—which was only slightly smaller than his own.)

"As is normal with coming to Baba," wrote Townshend in a 1970 *Rolling Stone* article about his relationship with his guru, "I didn't have to make any decision. No sooner had the thought [of whether his teachings were 'for me' or not] entered my head than it left. It's just not that cut and dried. Baba has to be adjusted to over a few months, or maybe some older Baba-lovers would say a few lives, and it is never apparent at any given moment how real or genuine your own affections are."

One thing should immediately be made clear: In becoming a Baba-lover (as they are known), Townshend was not joining a personality cult (although like all spiritual orders, Baba's followers pledge love, devotion and surrender) or any army of the Saved united against a hostile outside world. "Baba only asked people for their love," wrote Townshend, "not their possessions or even their lives. Just their love." Baba-lovers don't wear eccentric garments (on the sensible ground that if this world is an illusion anyhow, it hardly matters how one is draped), nor do they follow many elaborate rituals. Baba refused to establish anything resembling a church, for fear that its hierarchy and bureaucracy would lead disciples away from the spirit of his teachings.

The simple values Baba taught—compassion, love, intense introspection—are discipline enough.

Loving Baba is not a panacea; it is a struggle. "A lot of people equate finding a spiritual master with discovering the escape clause in life," Townshend said. "Actually, it's just the opposite. All that happens is that for the first time in your life you acknowledge the fact that you've got problems instead of futilely trying to solve them. The problems become more acute, yet somehow less painful. Still, they don't get solved automatically. The only way in this lifetime that you can move something from A to B is to get up and fucking *move* it. There's no magic.

"What makes following Baba different to following anybody else is that you don't change at all. You don't look upon ego, in the mystical sense, as being an enemy. You look at it in proportion and you realize there is the thing which is driving you and it's eventually going to destroy itself." But up to the end, following those precepts is a constant challenge—"the only game that matters"—as Townshend immediately began to learn.

One of the few hard-and-fast laws laid down by Meher Baba was this: "Drugs are harmful mentally, spiritually and physically. . . . For a few sincere seekers, the use of hallucinogenic drugs may have instilled in them a state of longing that has brought them into my contact, but further injection would not only be harmful but have no purpose."

At first, this injunction gave Townshend little trouble. He didn't learn of Baba's existence until after the Monterey STP experience, when he made the decision against taking any more psychedelic drugs.

In the spring of 1968, Townshend came to California with the Who. While in San Diego, he visited with Rick Chapman, a San Francisco Baba-lover well known for plastering Haight-Ashbury and Berkeley with photos of Baba bearing his best-known teaching: "Don't worry. Be happy." (This is an abbreviation of the more complex: "Do your best, then leave the results to me and don't worry—be happy.")

As was his wont, Townshend was babbling to Chapman about his devotion to Meher Baba and his teachings while rolling a joint. Gently, Rick asked, "You aren't still smoking pot?"

"Sure," said Pete. "Why not?"

"Don't you know it's been ascertained that marijuana is hallucinogenic and therefore comes under Baba's guidelines?" said Chapman. Townshend was stunned. He stopped smoking, but he wasn't happy about it.

"When I first got into pot, I was involved in the environment more," he told John Tobler. "There was a newness about art college, having beautiful girls around for the first time in my life, having all that music around me for the first time, and it was such a great period, with the Beatles and all that exploding all over the place. So it was very exciting, but although pot was important to me, it wasn't the biggest thing. . . .

"Four years after, I'd gotten into that rut of listening to every record stoned, and it was just turning to sculpture in my head. . . . I was seeing the music rather than hearing it. It's hard to explain, but it was like symmetrical towers of sound. That's how I saw it."

"In fact, it is this single facet of pot-smoking that made it so invaluable to the musician," Townshend told an interviewer for the Meher Baba publication *The Glow*. "It has a way of separating jumbled musical sounds and enabling the listener to *see* what he is hearing in visual extravagances. When playing under the influence of pot, for example, it is very easy for the musician to forget his audience and live only for his music and his own enjoyment of it."

Townshend, always caught up in some form of attempted rapport with his audience, did not often play stoned, though he did many shows half-drunk. But he found he could not *listen* to music except while high. "I've got about two hundred and fifty albums now, and the only ones I like are the ones that I first heard when I was stoned . . . what I call the 'stoned ones,' the ones that had that 'stonedness' around them, that aura. I've got to learn to listen to music all over again, and I've got to learn to write all over again. . . . I've got to learn how to enjoy life all over again, without leaning on dope."

The worst betrayal he felt, Townshend said, was "that I found I could give it up just like that [snapped fingers]. When I realized that everything I'd been crediting to pot was nothing at all to do with it, the fact that I could write a song or play guitar or have a good time at a party or enjoy a satisfying sexual relationship. A lot of people would say that I learned through pot, but it was like a betrayal." All the more so because Townshend had been such an active pot proselytizer.

For a spiritual seeker, however, drugs were especially harmful because they upset the natural balance, creating an illusion within an illusion. While it's not true (as Townshend has also claimed, though not recently) that one is better off on alcohol, psychedelic drugs do give a particularly distorted view of both life and life's potential. This is the heart of the betrayal Townshend felt, for what he had experienced seemed so true that it was hard to accept its ultimate falsity. He actually came to the conclusion that "pot is possibly the most subtle evil of all, because of its subtlety and because the psychological dependence takes over . . . it's more spiritually based, where you can't enjoy the pleasures of the spirit or the soul."

As Townshend soon realized, reliance on drugs was a basic problem with the entire underground scene of the sixties, which despite all its pretensions to enlightenment was often without the basic human compassion at the core of true spirituality. The underground could be extremely sanctimonious and unforgiving about certain kinds of action or classes of people—especially about anyone or anything that challenged the assumptions that lay behind its hedonistic self-indulgence.

"Basically, everyone had this mood that something was happening . . . something was changing," Townshend said. "In essence, it did, but unfortunately, a lot of its impetus was carried off by the drug obsession. Everybody credited everything innovative and exciting to drugs. . . .

"Then, when things turned out to be meaningless and people had missed the bus, they quickly realized that they'd gambled everything on something that had run away. The same thing happened to rock. Rock got very excited and flew off ahead, leaving most of its audience behind. The Who went on to do what I feel were some very brave and courageous things, but in the end, the audience was a bit apathetic." In other words, the rock performance became a spectacle for the passive entertainment of an audience that was not only largely impassive but had deliberately incapacitated itself. Townshend was not used to such audiences; he needed interaction to feel alive and creative, he needed the feedback of an active, involved public to know he was getting through.

In some ways, "Little Billy" (and "Do You Want Kids, Kids") were the first tentative steps toward changing those attitudes. The lyrics of both songs are designed to steer kids away from one of the most damaging drugs of all, tobacco (even though Pete and everyone else in the Who chain-smoked). And "Little Billy," particularly, is a frightening song, as gruesome as any of Entwistle's tales.

Yet Townshend laid back on the drug issue for a while, maybe because he was still absorbing Baba's tenets. When Hugh Nolan of *Disc and Music Echo* came to interview Townshend in his new house, the reporter was stunned to find pictures of Baba everywhere—not just on the walls but even in Pete's car. Townshend gladly acknowledged his master: "Baba has made an incredible amount of difference to my life. Not so much outwardly—I still shout at cars which get in my way, I still talk too much and I still smash up guitars when I can't afford to. Baba is the Avatar of the Age—the Messiah. He can't do anything but good. He has completely and utterly changed my whole life and, through me, the group as a whole." The fact that this change could not be complete, since it had not yet affected Townshend (much less the Who) outwardly, begs the point. Townshend believed he was transformed, and the next period of his career is a rather forceful argument that he truly was.

What's rather surprising is that Townshend was reluctant to bring Baba's teachings—especially about drugs—into the interview. Apparently, he was fearful of the response.

"It was very unfashionable, because dope, acid in particular, was still a happening thing," Townshend said in *The Story of Tommy*. "It made people interested in spiritual things, they kept taking the tablets, as it were, interest just shifted all the time from one thing to another. If you like, they missed the stop . . . they'd keep coming in and out of the railway station but never get off the train." Townshend ultimately felt fortunate that his horrid STP trip had already dissuaded him from psychedelics. But for the pop star who had identified his musical tastes only three years before as "anything currently recognized as being liked," it was too much to buck convention so drastically.

On the other hand, there was, for the first time in Townshend's life, a stronger force than the desire to be accepted: his love for Meher Baba. "It's something inside where all you want is for the things that seem so simple and fundamental to your life to mean something more than they appear to mean," he said. Now he began to find it.

23

Musicians are like mathematicians— talented, knowing the techniques, practiced. We're not musicians. We're entertainers.
—Pete Townshend

The Who returned to America in mid-February 1968 for a projected three-week tour that was stretched out to nine, rebooked en route as new opportunities became available. Frank Barsalona had built up a circuit with stops at the Boston Tea Party, Detroit's Grande Ballroom, the Electric Factory in Philadelphia, the Kinetic Theatre in Chicago, the Fillmore in San Francisco and various other venues in Los Angeles and New York. The promoters were the equivalent of a cartel in that they respected one another's turf and kept exclusive—or fairly exclusive—bookings with acts they had first brought into a specific market. For the time being, the cartel was exceptionally effective because of its willingness to experiment and develop new talent.

Dates at these ballrooms, with their hip audiences and accoutrements (light shows, for instance), could be supplemented by occasional college gigs, which always paid well, or, in the summer, various outdoor concerts. There was also the remnant of the once-proliferating local teen club circuit; the larger facilities in what was left of it could accommodate some of the underground bands.

There were all sorts of developments that played into the growing stature of bands like the Who. (Their peers included Jimi Hendrix, Cream and the Jeff Beck Group. The Rolling Stones and the Beatles were still spending all their time in recording studios and courtrooms.) For instance, groupies. Roger Daltrey has said he had five or six girls a night on some stands during the band's 1968 and 1969 tours. But the groupies often provided much more than sex. "The old groupies made sure they built up a relationship with you apart from the fucking," Roger said. "They used to cook for you, travel with you, everything. They still wanted to score you up, but they also wanted to fuck you in order to give you a good time. And they also had a good time themselves, because they really had a thing about making love." In a rock scene where there was little opportunity for women, becoming a groupie was too often one of the few outlets a female fan might have. When the groupie concept began to get publicity and it became a trendy experience to screw a rock star, this sort of groupie disappeared. "The last ones I had, you felt as if you were just another notch on whatever they put their notches on, they were just fucking you to say they had done it." By then, Roger was about to be remarried, anyway.

The band's equipment, its care and transportation also became streamlined. On most of their 1968 tours, the Who worked with a three-man crew, always including Tom Wright and Bob Pridden, usually with a third, less experienced roadie to simply help with the physical labor. Wright was the road manager, primarily concerned with the logistics of travel and hotel reservations, finding the hall and taking care of the money—counting heads at the door when the band was being paid a percentage of the gate, for instance.

Pridden's job was taking care of the gear. "I got into the equipment scene and it all started escalating," Pridden said, "I was like a mad professor. I think we were one of the first bands to have a huge thousand-watt PA. . . . As the PAs grew and grew, I started to find myself being my own enemy. I was adding equipment and doing all kinds of things." To Pridden, he had to become "much more than a guy that knows his onions as far as leads and wires and gaffs and valves and whatever. You've also got to be a court jester. You've got to bring them up when they're down. . . . When the set's wrong, I know it's basically always my fault. We have a saying in the band, 'Bob unhappy, group extremely happy. Bob happy, group extremely unhappy.' "

One of Pridden's primary tasks, besides keeping Moon and Townshend amused when they started to go stir-crazy from an endless succession of Ramada (certainly not Holiday) Inns, was repairing the equipment. Townshend and Moon were still demolishing remarkable quantities of gear, and while Keith's was comparatively simple to repair, Pete's was always a worry. Townshend tried to work with Fenders, which are about the sturdiest guitar made, but if it happened to be a Rickenbacker he cracked, it might pop like a light bulb. Then he and Pridden would have to sit up all night piecing together splinters with the extremely powerful English glue Pete carried in his luggage. Finally, Pridden would do his best to rewire the guitar.

Moon's destruction less often took place at the shows than in hotel rooms. He just couldn't stop, and since the Who usually traveled a circuit of the same towns, after a time it became difficult to find hotels where the management was willing to suffer them.

"My nerves finally broke in the Gorham, which is the hotel in New York where all the groups stay," said Townshend. "My wife was with me at the time, and it was hard enough just to try and keep the hangers-on away. But we got ensconced in our room and tried to make it feel a bit like home. A couple of hours or so later, we got to sleep, only to be woken up by police cars outside and a lot of police running about.

"I thought that Tom might have been busted, because he was really heavily into dope, so I ran out and got the lift to the seventh floor, where his room was. Then I heard this huge, great explosion, which rocked the lift. Then the lift stopped, the doors opened and all I could see was thick smoke—so I got back in. Just as the doors were closing, I saw Moon walk past. He'd apparently picked the hotel manager's wife's room. Of course, we got thrown out of that and every other hotel in New York as a result. We still have difficulty finding a place to stay in New York."

Moon attributed the wreckage to boredom, the grungy aesthetics of most hotels and his wacky sense of humor. There was also a lot of immaturity involved. Keith still felt he had an image to maintain. After a while, wholesale destruction was no longer enough. He would create elaborate, almost artistic chaos. Once, he nailed all the furniture to the ceiling in the same order as it had been on the floor. Or he would unscrew cabinets and pry them apart. Or pour catsup in the bathtub and buy plastic limbs from joke shops to stick out of the "gore" and frighten the maid. Moon could even be philosophical about his destruction. "In my opinion, America would be far better off if they'd just give every aggressive person a drum kit or a guitar to smash about and let 'em get rid of all the frustration that way," he said.

From the point of view of the rest of the band—or at least Daltrey, Entwistle and the managers—the Who would have been better off if Moon had stuck to bashing his drum kit. Between low fees and high travel expenses, wrecked equipment and ruined hotel rooms, the Who continued to lose money on their touring. Entwistle said they were running at a constant loss of about £150,000 ($420,000) because of the destruction. The group had finally realized that short stints in the States were more trouble than they were worth.

"You have to tour for at least six weeks over there," said Daltrey, always the most cost-conscious of the group. "The first three weeks pays your fares and all the expenses. The fourth week pays for your road managers. The fifth pays for your manager. The sixth is profit for us." In the sixth week of the Who's first 1968 tour of America, Martin Luther King was assassinated in Memphis and there was rioting all over the country. One of the two New York dates was canceled, and the profit was lost.

Earlier, the group had spent a week in Los Angeles finishing "Call Me Lightning," which was released as a single just after the tour began in February. Although the B-side was another memorably mock-macabre Entwistle opus, "Dr. Jekyll & Mr. Hyde" (John's attempt to come to grips with rooming with Keith on the road), "Call Me Lightning" was too slight to make much impact on the charts. It peaked at number 40.

While in L.A., the group also made the official recordings of "Little Billy" and "Do You Want Kids, Kids," for the American Cancer Society. But the ACS didn't use them, because they considered "Little Billy" far too gruesome, its plot centering around an indolent, unlikable kid who nevertheless lives longer and more happily than his schoolmates because they smoke and he doesn't.

More curiously, Pete Townshend also recorded a commercial urging radio listeners to enlist in the U.S. Air Force. Keith Moon cut a special program for the Armed Forces Radio Network.

Nothing better symbolizes how far out of touch the Who often were with their own best interests than their recording of commercials for military recruitment. While Meher Baba did not preach pure pacifism, it is hard to see how Townshend reconciled his spiritual beliefs with encouraging Americans to join an Air Force that was daily dropping a nauseating tonnage of bombs and chemicals upon the innocent citizens of Vietnam. While he might have thought these spots harmless, the endorsements were not even in the best interests of the band itself, which was trying to appeal to a youthful constituency determined not to die in Asian swamps (or determined to get home and never go back if they were already there). It's as if the Who spent all that time in America without ever catching the TV news or reading a newspaper.

Townshend knew he was out of touch. "Pop audiences and pop musicians are geared to different time structures, they lead different lives entirely," he told *Rolling Stone*'s Jann Wenner. "The group is doing one gig out of a hundred gigs, whereas to the fan, this is a very important occasion. For the group, it's another gig and they're going to be on the road in another ten minutes. The fan is going to catch a section of something which as a whole is a complicated network."

But the lives of his listeners were also complex. A large part of any rock band's credibility was based on a sense of shared intimacy and values between audience and performer, and it is amazing that Pete Townshend, who basically represented everything decent, generous and spiritual in rock, could casually betray his fans by tacitly endorsing a war he had attacked in his own country.

Yet the Who survived this, partly because the military commercials were not widely reported until many years later, when the war was over and the rock audience had been trained in apolitical apathy. (Today, of course, Townshend is mortified that he ever did such a thing.)

This isn't quite the same as saying that Townshend was a hypocrite when he told Sandy Darlington of the San Francisco *Express Times* just a few weeks later that "the Who are more a group now, rather than a teenage phenomenon, they are a group of musicians and of human beings that know a lot about living and working together. . . . We suddenly realized this at the beginning of the tour when things were going pretty badly, and we said, 'What are we fucking doing here? What are we on tour for? How is it we can charter a plane which is costing six times what we're going to get for the show when we know damn well half the people will have gone home because we're seven hours late and still be conscientious about putting on a good performance?'

"And we realized that it's not because of professionalism or 'the show must go on.' It's because you *want* to get on the fucking stage, and it doesn't matter if you were a million miles away, you'd walk there just for the honor, just for the opportunity of getting on a stage and in front of an audience, however small, large, sympathetic or unsympathetic, exhibiting that you can operate with three other members as efficiently as we can. The fact that you can say, 'Look, we are four members of the human race and we get on well together and we operate as a unit.' It's something to be proud of."

Indeed it was. And it is unlikely that Townshend would have been nearly so cavalier about endorsing the Air Force at the end of his first 1968 tour of the United States as he was at the beginning, simply because among his constituency, at any rate, the war was the premier concern. And the Who—most popular in such industrial cities as Detroit, Cleveland and New York, where rebellious kids were *really* rebellious—could not have failed to learn this, because they experienced something of what it was like to be everyday Midwestern long-hairs themselves.

"When we first toured the States, we had short hair but got taken the piss out of for having 'long' hair," said Entwistle. "We had to lay all the ground for what's happening now, but we had to lay it the hard way. We had to take all the digs from Americans in airports. . . . Musicians starting now are starting with an advantage, because they've got the standard of musicians previous to them to latch on to."

This was even more true on this tour, when they traveled by bus. This was ostensibly to save money, although according to Townshend, it ended up costing every bit as much as if they'd flown. The bus was fully outfitted with beds "and all modern conveniences—like beer and Scotch and comics and numerous back copies of *Playboy*."

While they were in Los Angeles, Decca agreed to throw a press reception for the Who at the Beverly Hills Hilton. Unfortunately, the Who party was placed right next door to a gathering of Shriners, all wearing their red fezzes and swilling down booze at a pace equal to Moon and Townshend. As the group entered their banquet hail, one of the Shriners yelled out, "Keep America beautiful—cut your hair!" When various members of the Who and entourage shouted back, disparaging the Shriners' headgear, a nasty scene nearly erupted, quelled only by massive application of alcoholic spirits to all concerned. But the hostility was endemic. "Every time we walked into a hotel lobby, we had a fifty-fifty chance of getting in, even if our reservations were made ages ago," said Tom Wright. "We looked so bizarre."

At the end of the tour, in early April, the Who recorded their show at the Fillmore East, which Bill Graham had only recently opened on New York's Lower East Side. They also recorded a few weeks later at Fillmore West. They did sets that included "Substitute"; "Pictures of Lily"; "Summertime Blues"; a medley of "Tattoo" and Garnett Mimms' "Fortune Teller"; "Little Billy"; "I Can't Explain"; "Happy Jack"; a version of "Relax" vastly expanded from the one on *The Who Sell Out* (and realizing even more of the song's acid-rock potential); "I'm a Boy"; a transcendent "A Quick One," which concluded with Townshend blessing the audience ("You are *all* forgiven"); a pair of Eddie Cochran rockabilly numbers, "My Way" and "C'mon Everybody"; a violent and supercharged rendition of Johnny Kidd's "Shakin' All Over"; "Boris the Spider"; and the inevitable finale, "My Generation."

The tape of the Fillmore East concert is extraordinary, the sound very clear for the time, and the performance is outstanding, a remarkable burst of sustained energy that nevertheless has an amplitude of surges and ebbs all its own. Each of the extended numbers is a triumph: "Relax," in which Townshend introduces many of the musical motifs around which his next set of songs were built; "A Quick One," more serious, less farcical than the recording; "Generation," in a stunning version that opened up the recorded version without sacrificing any of its immediacy—or any of the inevitability of the smash-up finale. And the hard rock songs ("Summertime Blues," "Substitute," "My Way," "C'mon Everybody," "I Can't Explain," "Shakin' All Over," "My Generation") redefined rock's power and authority at a time when the bluster of British blues and the laid-back modalities of West Coast acid-rock were beginning to lose touch with the genre's original resources. In many ways, *The Who Live at Fillmore East* would have been convincing proof that the Who was the greatest live rock group in the world.

But once they'd scrutinized the tapes back home, the Who decided against releasing them as a live LP. The performance was perfect when it was experienced live or heard casually on tape. But subjected to the kind of minute analysis an album must inevitably receive, flaws leaped out: guitars in and out of tune, drumsticks in the air when they should have been pounding out the beat, vocals ragged (at one point in "Boris the Spider" Daltrey and Entwistle sing different verses simultaneously), guitarists whirling their arms overhead when they ought to have been striking chords. What was missing was the action, which magnetic tape could not hope to capture, missing the indispensable interaction between band and audience, which was the medium by which the Who and its fans broke through into spiritual communion.

But the Who must also have instinctively realized that it would be poor strategy to release a live LP just then. Like all of the rock bands of this period, the Who had never expected to have a history, much less that songs three and four years old would have continuing relevance or that the meaning and shape of their music could take on so many different forms over a period of time. A live album would inevitably be retrospective, and it could fix the Who's image in a deadly way. Whether or not they knew it then, it was a good idea for the Who not to fulfill their fans' expectations with a concert album.

The Who needed recorded product desperately—the kind of product that would enhance their reputation and image. They hadn't released anything at all in Britain since *The Who Sell Out* until June, when Track issued "Dogs," a Townshend fantasy about a workingman devoted to greyhound racing. If Pete had been disappointed with the reception given "I Can See For Miles," then "Dogs" must have pushed him into true despondence. The single stumbled up to number 25 on the charts and dived off after only five weeks, the worst showing for a Who disc since the Shel Talmy days.

"Dogs" didn't deserve much better. It was well-performed but totally trivial music warranting the epithets with which Roger labeled it: "A real self-indulgent wanking-off period which didn't work." In his most recent songs, Townshend's writing had become personal in all the wrong ways: "Call Me Lightning" and "Dogs" were just self-conscious, not revealing. They were contract music, put out to fill marketing demands, and had nothing to do with what the Who was really about.

"When this happens, a group generally splits up," Pete said after they were over the hump. "If a group goes along without accelerating its talents, it is inevitable that you either split up or go into cabaret." The Who weren't far from a genuine breakup. Keith Moon appeared on Jeff Beck's album *Truth* that summer (credited as "You Know Who") which was the ever-insecure Moon's way of making sure he had options in case the band was finished.

"We said, 'It can't be that simple,'" Townshend continued. "Why should we split up? The group were in a quandary. We still worshipped the two-and-a-half-minute rock single, but worshipping it and playing it are two different things. Musically, the Who were totally capable of making records like these, but by now we were doing things that just couldn't be captured on the pop single. We needed a bigger vehicle."

They also needed the kind of British hit that would lend them a new image in keeping with current trends, an American hit that would consolidate their commercial potential, and a new ending for the stage show, which would never be profitable as long as it required a smash-up.

Kit Lambert had an idea for a stage show. "He said he'd like us to do a new stage show which would be called 'The Ages of Man' or something," said Townshend to Paul Nelson. "Each one of us would write a song about a certain period of our life—or songs about certain periods of life—and then we would link them all together and perform them in an evening's entertainment. This would include lots of other songs from different periods, like 'My Generation' and 'I'm a Boy' and songs about people getting old and things. It was a very simple idea; just a one-shot."

It was also too corny to work. But Lambert continued to rant about rock opera, and Pete was now captivated by the idea. Since *Sgt. Pepper's*, the Pretty Things, with *S. F. Sorrow*, and the Small Faces, with their beautiful, quirky *Ogden's Nut Gone Flake*, had made albums with some elements of narrative intertwined with consistent musical themes. But no one had yet come up with a coherent narrative with specific musical themes tailored for a rock band.

Townshend also hoped to create a story that would symbolize the changes that rock and the underground culture were causing in society; to incorporate his devotion to Meher Baba as reflected in his views of spirituality; to find a perfect balance between the single and LP formats; and above all, to get together a recording that better realized the Who's onstage power. "If you slow down just a little bit and gear yourself to your audience, you can give them one hundred percent," he said. "If you do a slightly longer set on the stage, you can give all instead of having to cram a lot of unused energy into guitar-smashing, for example. Unchanneled or misdirected energy is incredible in pop music."

Pete had been exploring his opera ideas since early 1968. At one point, he wanted to write "a series of songs that flashed between my point of view of reality and the point of view of illusion as seen through the eyes of someone on the spiritual path, a young boy." This meant that all of the action would be described twice—first from the narrator's perspective, then from the seeker's. Predictably, that approach proved far too cumbersome, and this plan was scrapped (though the concept at the heart of it was retained).

Townshend also thought of writing the opera as a side project for Arthur Brown, a strange singer he'd met at the UFO Club. "I was convinced that he was the perfect foil for it; he was a great rock singer with an operatic range and all that. But I was hedging my bets. Kit kept pushing me back to the band."

There was also the concept of taking a string of rock singles and stringing them together to form a longer piece. "I felt strongly that we were being tied down too much to single records," wrote Townshend. "I felt that if I had to say everything on a record in three minutes maximum, then I wasn't ever really going to say very much, in spite of the fact that I respected the limitations. . . . I wanted to find a way to 'stretch' it a bit more, without making it pretentious or pompous and without making it sound too much like classical music.

"So what I finally decided to do was to take a series of rock singles, or 'cameos,' and put them back-to-back on an album. They wouldn't flow musically but would just be isolated singles—and they would tell a story when heard one after another. In other words, you could listen to any number on its own, or if you wanted you could listen to the whole thing as a continuous story." This idea was never entirely discarded, but the rhetoric shifted ever more to a piece of dramatic music—*rock opera*, in Kit Lambert's term.

Furthermore, the rock opera he created should not only be a record but also a stage piece. The Beatles and the Beach Boys, along with most other groups who were making concept albums, had abandoned all hope of performing such technically sophisticated music; it seemed inevitably bound to the recording studio and to be heard only in private. Townshend wanted to burst this limitation, operating on the sensible intuition that such music couldn't possibly capture the incredible energy generated at rock concerts.

In a nutshell, Townshend wanted it all. Describing one version to Paul Nelson, he referred to a story told in sections. Between the sections, a theme would be developing. "And it will contain everything: the way the songs are going, the way the music's going, the way the Who feel about the progress of the opera—everything. Until eventually, the thing turns into an anthem, which becomes what we hope we're going to be ending our shows with in the future."

It was obviously impossible to write such an elaborate piece during time stolen from tours or under the pressure of having to churn out more product for the charts. Townshend had a number of people to bounce ideas off: Richard Stanley, a film maker friend who shared a house with Pete and Karen for a while; Mike McInnerney; Richard Barnes; and even Roger Daltrey got an earful on the road. The key coconspirator, however, was Kit Lambert, whose enthusiasm and ability to inflate the flimsiest concept into a majestic theatrical

Top: *The first US tour, New York, 1967. D.J. 'Murray the K' holds the US flag.* (Trinifold).
Bottom: *"Some fool in the Bee Gees said, 'You wouldn't break a Stradivarius, would you?' The answer is, 'of course, I wouldn't break a Stradivarius' but a Gibson guitar that came off a production line—fuck it!"—Pete Townshend.* (Pictorial Press).

Above: *Pete backstage at the Saville Theatre, London, 1967. His jacket was made by Karen Astley.* (Chris Morphet).

Top: *Christ Stamp (left) and Kit Lambert (right). "Kit (an upper class Englishman) was an utter maniac who lived off nervous energy, Chris by contrast, (the son of an East End tugboat man) was the voice of sanity, very cool and hard."—Nik Cohn.* (Pictorial Press). Bottom: *Pete and John recording* The Who Sell Out, *1967.* (Trinifold).

Top and bottom: *The Who enjoy themselves at an Oxford May Ball, 1967. In the top photograph, left to right: John, Pete, Karen Astley and John 'Wiggy' Wolff.* Bottom: *Townshend performs, but debutantes don't like feedback.* (Chris Morphet).

Above: *Kit Lambert often used to breakfast at the Ritz. "With Stamp he shared a taste for hard, flashy living, and a burning ambition to make enough money to afford to act it out."—Nik Cohn.* (Colin Jones).

Top: *Keith Moon with his wife, Kim, their baby daughter, Mandy, and a baby fox. Married in 1965, Moon had kept his marriage a secret for three years.* (Trinifold). Bottom: *Pete Townshend and his girlfriend, Karen Astley, on a boat on the Thames.* (Chris Morphet).

Top: *Pete Townshend at home in his recording studio. Avatar Meher Baba, his spiritual Master and inspiration for* Tommy, *is on the wall in the background.* (Chris Morphet). Bottom: *Pete and Karen's wedding, May, 1968.* (Pete Townshend).

Top: *Karen and Pete's first baby daughter, Emma, is born at Queen Charlotte's hospital in London, 1969.* (Trinifold). Bottom: *Several months later. The Townshends at home with baby Emma—and Towser.* (Chris Morphet).

Top: *John Entwistle with his wife, Alison.* (Chris Morphet). Bottom: *John with Alison and their new baby son, Christopher Alexander John, London, 1972.* (Trinifold).

Top: *Promoting* Magic Bus, *1968.* (London Features International). Bottom: *December, 1968, the Who and others join the Rolling Stones to make* The Rolling Stones' Rock and Roll Circus, *a film that was never to be released. Left to right: Bill Wyman, Pete Townshend, Keith Moon, Charlie Watts and Brian Jones in background.* (Keystone).

Top: *Interacting with the audience, 1968. Note the "Pictures of Lily" drum kit.* (Chris Morphet).
Bottom: *Pete, Kit Lambert and Roger, during recording sessions for* Tommy, *1968.* "Tommy *is just like a grand opera. It's incredibly difficult to follow the story."—Kit Lambert. "We probably did as much talking as we did recording."—Roger Daltrey.* (Chris Morphet).

Above: *Townshend playing in mid-flight at Woodstock, August 16, 1969. "The worst gig we ever played."—Roger Daltrey.* (Trinifold).

Top: "Tommy *was a rock ritual. The Who enacted it on stage in a way that de-emphasised the plot, accenting the music and the gestures of the performance." The Who perform* Tommy *at the Royal Albert Hall, 1969.* (Trinifold). Bottom left: Tommy *at the Met in New York, June, 1970—there were standing ovations.* (Trinifold). Bottom right: *Pete recording demos in his home studio at Twickenham.* (Chris Morphet/Pete Townshend).

Above: Tommy, *Berkeley, 1970. Daltrey brought Townshend's rock opera to life. "It was as though I was just singing Who songs until the second time we played it on stage, and then I realised that I was becoming something else."—Roger Daltrey.* (David Olsen/Pete Townshend).

Above: *Townshend performs his famous leap at the opening of the new Rainbow rock theatre.* (Trinifold).

cataclysm was unmatched. Lambert took Townshend's fragmentary ideas and gave them back to him so embellished that Pete realized how good the kernels of his thinking were.

"It really is the most incredible thing that after two years of brainwashing himself into being a producer of singles for Top Ten radio play, Kit Lambert actually turned his brain inside out and came up with rock opera. Enigmatic paradox. But good thinking for a group who stopped getting hits," wrote Townshend.

It was also Kit Lambert who saved Townshend from his own—and the contemporary rock scene's—worst excesses. "At the time we were writing *Tommy*, the music business was very super-cynical. For example, at that time, the Moody Blues and people were doing ambitious works (from their point of view, anyway) and they were instantly getting labeled as pretentious, and at the same time, garbage was being pushed out into the charts. The Beatles and the Stones and people like that, the Small Faces, even—anybody that was any good was more or less becoming insignificant again," Townshend wrote. "They weren't new anymore, they weren't fresh and a lot of the new stuff that was coming out was really trash, there was a lot of psychedelic bullshit going about. . . .

"I wanted to hit everybody all at once. So I did, cautiously, put across a spiritual message because I did feel that I had learned a fantastic amount through my life and perhaps even through dope, which had led me to Baba, and I knew that Baba was something very special and I wanted that all to be wound up. But at the same time, I wanted *Tommy* to be rock & roll. . . . I even wanted it to appeal to kids. John Entwistle and I always used to talk a lot about that. . . . We just wanted it to appeal on every level, like a Sufi tale. . . . If you're a seeker, you get something from it, if you're well along the path, you get something from it."

Lambert was able to take Townshend's thinking and drag it away from pretension and this was one of the most valuable contributions anyone could have made to Townshend. Kit Lambert could never have taught Pete ambition, because that was outside the scope of his camp sensibility. But he could and did teach him a sense of proportion about his own intelligence.

As early as May 1968, Chris Welch of *Melody Maker* visited Pete in his flat and heard "Now I'm a Farmer," a song described as being "from the long-awaited Townshend opera, which he has been working on in different forms, on and off, for a couple of years."

"I'm working on an opera, which I did once before, and I am thinking of calling it *The Amazing Journey*," Townshend said. "I've completed some of it and I'd like to put it on an LP. The theme is about a deaf, dumb and blind boy who has dreams and sees himself as ruler of the cosmos."

Who's For Tennis and *Live at the Fillmore East* were never much more than interim projects designed to buy time. Once it became obvious that Pete wasn't able to complete writing such a massive and complex work in spare moments between gigs, the crunch came. Economics dictated that the Who must work steadily. The only answer was to do another extensive tour and then hole up until the task was completed.

Chris Stamp called it "one fucking huge great once-and-for-all gamble." But it was the only choice they really had.

At the end of June 1968, the Who flew back to America for another nine-week tour. They stayed there straight through the beginning of September, playing the same succession of ballrooms, clubs and concerts. The equipment destruction and hotel breakage were just as costly this time around, but the fees were a bit better. This time, said Tom Wright, "it always seemed to just about even out."

Press coverage picked up. *Time*, the weekly news magazine, ran a very favorable review of the show, and *Sell Out* even praised the smash-up. There was a new kind of paper growing in America, however, the so-called underground press, and it was there that Townshend did dozens of extensive interviews. In many of these, he explained his opera concepts (he was still writing and talking about the project in every spare moment). The underground journalists were not much like the Fleet Street professionals from the music weeklies that Townshend was used to coping with. These writers were younger, they were often fans and they were well informed about rock and related matters. Talking to such sympathetic reporters, Pete worked out more of the nuances of what he wanted to say.

The most important interview Townshend ever did was with *Rolling Stone* editor and owner Jann Wenner. *Rolling Stone* was not quite a part of the underground press scene; it shared few of the typical underground newspaper's radical political values and was designed from the beginning to be a competitive, professional publication, focusing almost exclusively on music and later dabbling in liberal Democratic politics. Wenner liked rock, and he loved hobnobbing with rock stars. But he was also one of the best interviewers in the American press, able to draw stars out of themselves, unafraid to ask obvious or embarrassing questions, relentless in his pursuit of certain truths. His interview with Townshend was probably his first great piece and certainly the most memorable of *Rolling Stone*'s first year or two.

Wenner recalled that the conversation began at 2:00 A.M. after the Who's late August Fillmore West show. Wenner had previously met Townshend at Monterey and at the San Francisco Cow Palace, when the Who had played there with Herman's Hermits in 1967. During the interview, they were hanging out as much as working.

Wenner remembered another strange interlude. "We'd been drinking orange juice," he wrote, "and in the middle of a long and wandering answer [Pete] asked if I had spiked his drink . . . when I asked him what he meant by 'spiked,' he said he felt as though he were beginning an LSD trip. I hadn't slipped him anything." Dosing people wasn't Wenner's style, but the full Townshend/Wenner interview does have an almost lysergic lucidity (and sometimes, incoherence) to it. They covered Townshend's entire life history, his relationship with the band, and many of his thoughts about rock and the rock scene. Early in the piece, Wenner asked Townshend about his experimental rock ideas. After a discussion of tape experiments, Townshend segued into the story of his opera.

"We've been talking about doing an opera," he said. "We've been talking about a whole lot of things, and what has basically happened is that we've condensed all of these ideas, all of this energy and all these gimmicks and whatever we've decided on for future albums, into one juicy package. The package I hope is going to be called *Deaf, Dumb and Blind Boy*. It's a story about a kid that's born deaf, dumb and blind and what happens to him throughout his life.

"The deaf, dumb and blind boy is played by the Who, the musical entity. He's represented musically, which begins the opera itself, and then there's a song describing the deaf, dumb and blind boy. But what it's really all about is the fact that because the boy is 'D, D & B,' he's seeing things basically as vibrations which we translate as music. That's really what we want to do: create this feeling that when you listen to the music you can actually become aware of the boy and aware of what he is all about, because we are creating him as we play."

"And the whole album is about his experience?" asked Wenner.

"Yes, it's a pretty far-out thing, actually," Townshend replied, beginning to soar into his spiel. "But it's very, very endearing to me because the thing is . . . inside, the boy sees things musically and in dreams and nothing has got any weight at all. He is touched from the outside and he feels his mother's touch, he feels his father's touch, but he just interprets them as music. His father gets pretty upset that his kid is deaf, dumb and blind. He wants a kid that will play football and God knows what.

"One night, he comes in and he's drunk and he sits over the kid's bed and he looks at him and he starts to talk to him and the kid just smiles up and his father is trying to get through to him, telling him about how the other dads have a kid that they can take to football and they can teach them to play football and all this kind of crap and he starts to say, 'Can you hear me?' The kid, of course, can't hear him. He's groovin' in this musical thing, this incredible musical thing, he'll be out of his mind. Then there's his father outside, outside of his body, and this song is going to be written by John. I hope John will write this song about the father who is really uptight.

"The kid won't respond, he just smiles. The father starts to hit him, and at this moment the whole thing becomes incredibly realistic. On one side you have the dreamy music of the boy wasting through his nothing life. And on the other you have the reality of the father outside, uptight, but now you've got blows, you've got communication. The father is hitting the kid; musically, then, I want the thing to break out, hand it over to Keith—'This is your scene, man, take it from here.'

"And the kid doesn't catch the violence. He just knows that some sensation is happening. He doesn't feel the pain, doesn't associate it with anything. He just accepts it.

"A similar situation happens later on in the opera, where the father starts to get the mother to take the kid away from home to an uncle. The uncle is a bit of a perv, you know. He plays with the kid's body while the kid is out. And at this particular time the child has heard his own name, his mother called him. And he managed to hear these words: 'Tommy.' He's really got this big thing about his name, whatever his name is going to be, you know, 'Tommy.' And he gets really hung up on his own name. He decides that this is the king and this is the goal. Tommy is the thing, man.

"He's going through this, and the uncle comes in and starts to go through a scene with the kid's body, you know, and the boy experiences sexual vibrations, you know, sexual experience, and again it's just basic music, it's interpreted as music and it is nothing more than music. It's got no association with sleaziness or with undercover or with any of the things normally associated with sex. None of the romance, none of the visual stimulus, none of the sound stimulus. Just basic touch. It's *meaningless*. Or not meaningless, you just don't react, you know. Slowly but surely the kid starts to get together, out of this simplicity, this incredible simplicity in his mind. He starts to realize that he can see and he can hear and he can speak; they are there and they are happening all the time. And that all the time he has been able to hear and see. All the time it's been there in front of him, for him to see.

"This is the difficult jump. It's going to be extremely difficult, but we want to try to do it musically. At this point, the theme, which has been the boy, starts to change. You start to realize that he is coming to the point where he is going to get over the top, he's going to get over his hang-ups. You're gonna stop monkeying around with songs about people being tinkered with and with father's getting uptight, with mother's getting precious and things, and you're gonna get down to the fact of what is going to happen to this kid.

"The music has got to explain what happens, that the boy elevates and finds something which is incredible. To us, it's nothing to be able to see and hear and speak, but to him, it's absolutely incredible and overwhelming; this is what we want to do musically. Lyrically, it's quite easy to do it; in fact, I've written it out several times. It makes great poetry, but so much depends on the music, so much. I'm hoping that we can do it. The lyrics are going to be okay, but every pitfall of what we're trying to say lies in the music, lies in the way we play the music, the way we interpret, the way things are going during the opera.

"The main characters are going to be the boy and his musical things. He's got a mother and a father and an uncle. There is a doctor involved who tries to do some psychiatric treatment on the kid which is only partly successful. The first two big events are when he hears his mother calling him and hears the word *Tommy*, and he devotes a whole part of his life to this one word. The second important event is when he sees himself in a mirror, suddenly seeing himself for the first time: He takes an immediate back step, bases his whole life around his own image. The whole thing then becomes incredibly introverted. The music and the lyrics become introverted, and he starts to talk about himself, starts to talk about his beauty. Not knowing, of course, that what he saw was him, but still regarding it as something which belonged to him, and of course it did all of the time, anyway."

This is a remarkably coherent picture of what the eventual album would be; narratively, it is often *more* coherent than the record. Townshend later complained that by telling the story at such length, in such an influential publication, he limited his options when he went back into the recording studio. But if anything, he placed an additional burden on himself in trying to live up to such a clear exposition of the *Tommy* story, not only here but also in other interviews of the time. It's also fascinating to know that Townshend already had so much of the tale in place. In any case, this interview, which ran a full eleven tabloid pages when first published, solidified Townshend's reputation as the most committed and passionate rock musician.

Before heading back to England, the Who also played a date in New York, at the Singer Bowl, on a bill with Jim Morrison and the Doors. Townshend was fascinated and appalled by Morrison's behavior—he punched one fan in the chest and impassively observed another roughed up by his bodyguards. At the show that night, there was incredible tension. The Who's smash-up wound up damaging some of the Doors' equipment, and the crowd surged forward in a general melee. One girl reached the stage and, trying to elude the stagehands, fell head first, badly cutting her face. The result of the damage (and observing Morrison) was another Townshend song, "Sally Simpson." As with everything else he'd written in the past couple of years, it found its way into the rock opera.

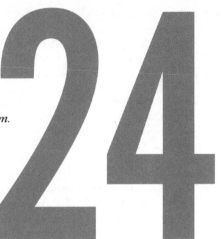

You can tell what is and what isn't rock & roll. To be the real thing, a song has to have an awareness of rock history. It has to have the beat, that undulating rhythm. Even while it feels like history, it has to say something new. And most important, it has to have crammed into it all the poignancy and excitement of youth, because that's what it's really all about.
—Pete Townshend

B ack in England, the Who began recording. The opera project had no name, or rather it had several: *Deaf, Dumb and Blind Boy*; *Amazing Journey*; *Journey into Space*; *The Brain Opera*; and *Omnibus* were all considered and used publicly. Nor did Pete have a firm story, despite the interviews, or even a certain name for the character. He liked Tommy because it was very British, very common, had associations with World War I (British soldiers were called Tommies, as American soldiers were called GIs), and because, he thought, "The middle syllable was *om*." (It isn't.)

Having so many fundamental loose ends meant that the Who couldn't simply walk into the studio and begin cutting. First a plot and a musical method had to be agreed upon. Although the group was for once willing to let Pete have things just the way he wanted them, he was not immediately prepared to take advantage of the opportunity.

He did have several numbers completed, including "Welcome," "We're Not Gonna Take It," "Sensation" and "Amazing Journey." Several of these had been written for other purposes: "Sensation" was about a girl he'd met in Australia; "We're Not Gonna Take It" was a general anti-fascist statement; "Welcome" was an expression of the peace Pete had found through Meher Baba. But it was "Amazing Journey," in many ways the most forced, the slightest, of these early tunes that Townshend called "the absolute beginning" of the opera. In it, he said, were the seeds of all one needed to know about the tale. Townshend wrote the song on piano (he was still learning at the time), but it was built around a guitar strumming the basic D-A-D progression on which *Tommy* is based. And the lyrics outline both the plot and some of the other levels of meaning Townshend hoped to convey.

Townshend had also created the kernels of several of *Tommy*'s other songs: "Sally Simpson" was inspired by the Jim Morrison incident; "It's A Boy" by "Glow Girl," picking up after the reincarnation of the plane crash victim (and with the sex of the baby reversed); "I'm Free" was another early expression of Townshend's emotions as a Baba-lover. Both "Underture" and "Sparks" grew out of guitar riffs Townshend had featured in "A Quick One" and "Rael," his mini-opera. ("Rael" also suggested a few of *Tommy*'s details: Its hero was also afflicted, though only with a lisp.)

"I tend to think in trains of thought for maybe up to two years," Pete told Bruce Pollock. "I'll start to write a song and I won't really know what it's got to do with, then two years from now I'll look back on it and know why I wrote it. I know when I put *Tommy* together I drew on all kinds of sources."

The slowness, Townshend once wrote, was necessary because "I wanted the story of *Tommy* to have several levels just as I wanted it to have a rock singles level and a bigger concept level. I wanted it to appeal as a fairy story to young people and to be intellectually entertaining. But I also wanted it to have a spiritual message, too."

Townshend's need to put the Who back on some kind of realistic commercial schedule and to make *Tommy* both watertight and multiply significant were in head-on collision. The Who had been a recording act for the better part of four years. In that time, they had made three albums. In their first four years, the Beatles, the Rolling Stones and Bob Dylan had each made seven albums. It is true that the Who started a bit later and that they were not expected to churn out quite so much product as artists in the early sixties. But they were undoubtedly working far too slowly for the market.

When it became obvious that the rock opera would still not be finished for Christmas, Track assembled *Direct Hits*, an LP of the Who's singles. Several of the songs had been British hits, including "Substitute," "I'm a Boy," "Pictures of Lily," and "I Can See For Miles." Of the others, "Bucket T" came from *Ready, Steady, Who!* "Mary Anne With the Shakey Hand" had appeared on *Sell Out* (as well as on the B-side of "I Can See For Miles"). Nothing else had ever appeared on EP or LP. *Direct Hits* gave an accurate overview of the Who's development in the first stage of its recording career.

Decca was even more eager than Track for a Who album. "Magic Bus", a song from the "Pictures of Lily" period Townshend had been saving, was only a moderate hit that summer (reaching number 25 in *Billboard*), but the Who's touring had made them a natural group for the album market. Because they hadn't had enough chart success in the States to justify an American greatest hits anthology, the group proposed putting together a singles collection to be called *The Who's Greatest Flops*. This could have included some of the material recorded with Talmy (which Track didn't control but Decca did) as well as such singles as "Pictures of Lily," "Substitute" and "Magic Bus," none of which had made it to most American ears. It would have been an even better overview of the band's work to date than *Direct Hits*, and because the material was so consistent and so strong, it would have satisfied the demand the live shows had created. (Greil Marcus, writing in *Rolling Stone*, even proposed that some of the material from the scrapped live LP could have been incorporated.)

Instead, Decca chose to assemble an album from whatever it had lying around. Often, this meant inferior masters or poor mixes (especially on "Disguises" and "Bucket T," from the *Ready, Steady, Who!* EP that had never been issued in the States). Worse, Decca chose much material that had already been included in Who albums, including the inferior "Run, Run, Run" from *Happy Jack* and the powerful but atypical "I Can't Reach You" and "Our Love Was, Is" from *Sell Out*. Rather than utilize "Substitute," "I Can't Explain," "My Generation," or some of the other songs familiar from Who concerts, the album included three Entwistle B-sides, "Dr. Jekyll & Mr. Hyde," "Someone's Coming" and "Doctor, Doctor," all good but quite irrelevant to the band's central appeal.

But the gravest error Decca made was in titling the album *Magic Bus—The Who on Tour*, implying that the album contained live recordings, which it did not. This impression was furthered by the cover photograph, which showed the group climbing aboard a touring coach.

"We were working on *Tommy*, and we kept telling them it would be ready next week, it would be ready next week, it would be ready next week," Townshend told Chris Van Ness. "And it never was. So in the end, in desperation, they got us to do this photo session, which they said was for a publicity handout, of us farting around with this absurd bus. They then got together a few old tapes and threw together [the album], which was a culmination of all the most terrible things American record companies ever get up to. Just exploitation. They didn't care about *Tommy* ever coming out; they just wanted to exploit the Who while the Who were big—though we weren't that big then, really—and make a few bucks, because who knows what may happen tomorrow. Plus the fact that they made it look like a live album. I mean that's the worst thing that's ever gone down."

Townshend was right, of course. Most English record companies had learned their lesson by late 1968. The new rock music was too complex and its audience's taste too volatile to be effectively managed by corporate minds (though this would change as the music became increasingly codified and younger, shrewder marketers entered the field). The most effective approach, the labels learned, was to give the performers their head. American labels were only beginning to come to this conclusion, largely through association with either folk-rock performers (such as Columbia, with Bob Dylan, the Byrds and Simon and Garfunkel) or the hippie bands of San Francisco (such as Warner Bros. with the Grateful Dead). Decca hadn't much relationship with rock groups at all, and so it isn't surprising that the company simply proceeded as if the situation was still the same as always, assembling each album as a hodgepodge designed to capture a market established elsewhere (in singles or on the stage or on TV), rather than as a medium unto itself.

Decca took a great deal of heat in the rock press for *Magic Bus*. Greil Marcus, in *Rolling Stone*, and Paul Williams, in the *San Francisco Express Times*, two of the best-known American rock critics, each wrote a scathing review of the album, attacking Decca not just for attempting to delude the public with the title and cover but also for its general stodginess and failure to promote the Who. "There are over a dozen fantastic cuts by the Who that have never been released on American LPs," griped Marcus. "We could have had a classic record." Both critics ended by expressing their faith that the Who would come up with a great album and their doubt that Decca would know what to do with it when they did.

The Who were by now familiar with working in the recording studio, especially at IBC, where engineer Damon Lyon-Shaw had also become an important part of the process. Kit Lambert's confidence had increased (especially after his production of "Fire" by the Crazy World of Arthur Brown—the singer Townshend had found at the UFO Club—became a worldwide number 1 hit that autumn). "Going into the studio was something to be sort of looked forward to and dreaded simultaneously," Townshend told Barnes.

The band was depressed by its slow progress but still hoped to push the record out for the all-important Christmas season (when as much as 25 percent of the year's records would be sold).

The progress was slow because Townshend still hadn't settled on plot points or even much of the song selection. Indeed, he was still writing, often with Kit Lambert pointing the way. "Some days, Pete would come in with only half a demo," said Daltrey. "We probably did as much talking as we did recording. We used to talk for hours, literally, sorting out arrangements and things."

For instance, it was Lambert who insisted that the piece have a formal overture. "This clues you in to a lot of the themes and gives a continuity to the individual tracks," Townshend pointed out. "You think you've heard them before because they've been stated in the overture. It gives more of a flow and strengthens the whole thing."

In early November, Chris Welch of *Melody Maker* came by IBC to do a story. Word was out that the Townshend opus was something special, and the few bits Welch heard reassured him that this was so. He described the band's working process: Lambert taking a back seat while Lyon-Shaw and Townshend worked in the control room to get the proper microphone balances and drum sounds, then Kit stepping forward to direct the band as Pete went into the studio to play piano or guitar. Lambert's concern, as always, was in capturing a specific performance, not in the details of how that performance sounded on tape. But then, as Pete said, "Kit was as much a producer in the writing as he was in the studio. Kit was much more involved in the overall concept of the thing—much more than people imagine. Not all that much, in fact, with the overall sound, although he did produce it and mix it and he did make us work at it. Still, the main thing was that he thought of the idea of rock opera."

More than anything, Lambert was the person Townshend turned to when he got stuck or when he just wanted someone to scheme with. "It was approached in exactly the way anti-intellectual rock people would hate," Pete said. "We went into it in depth before we worked out the plot; we worked out the sociological implications, the religious implications, the rock implications. We made sure every bit was . . . solid. When we'd done that, we went into the studio, got smashed out of our brains and made it. Then we listened, pruned and edited very carefully, then got smashed and did it all again. And somehow it came out as if we'd done it all in one breath."

This element of planned spontaneity is probably the hallmark of all great popular art, which is produced with great effort but maintains an almost casual surface. One of the advantages of *Tommy* being assembled piecemeal, with no clearly articulated strategy ("Nobody knew what it was all about or how the hell it was going to end," snorted Entwistle) was that it choked off any glimmerings of sanctimoniousness.

Yet the greatest advantage that Townshend was given—greater even than the gift of time that circumstances and the evolution of the industry had bestowed upon him—was the willingness of the group to let him be the leader, at least for this one project. "I mean, what other three musicians would have put up with all my bullshit in order to get this album out?" Townshend wondered once it was all over. "It's *my* whole trip, coming from Baba, and they just sat there, let it come out and then leapt upon it and gave it an extra boot."

Roger said: "He really *needed* the album to himself, because he's been talking about an opera for so long, people had obviously thought we were talking a lot of shit and we'd never get it done." And so they gave him the room to work—and quite inevitably, music making being the collaborative process it is, Townshend wound up coming right back to the band.

"He had been writing songs and fitting them together just like a jigsaw," said Moon. "Then, when we were in the studio and it was still in bits and pieces, Pete would say, 'Well, what do you think about this bit?' and John or someone would come up with an idea and then, gradually, it became a group effort."

"I had absolutely no idea what the story was, who the characters were or what they did," grumped Entwistle. "I can remember Townshend coming to see me and saying that he'd got a couple of main characters: one a kid called Tommy who was gonna go through all these *traumatic* (he always used that word) experiences with some chick who slips him acid and a homo uncle and a bully.

"He then asked me if I could write songs for the last two, because he felt that he couldn't write nearly as nasty as me. I wrote 'Fiddle About' that same evening; 'Cousin Kevin' I based on an old school chum. [But] it was only when we decided to make a double album that it became much easier to work out the story line. Before, when we put it all together, it just didn't seem to make any sense, so we cut off the ending, stuck 'Tommy's Holiday Camp' on and finished off with another bit of 'See Me Feel Me.' " ("Tommy's Holiday Camp" was Moon's idea, proposed when Townshend was bemoaning his inability to create a religious organization for his hero; Townshend wrote the song because he didn't trust Moon's ability to write a song to order but credited it to the drummer, anyhow.)

They were, in any event, several months away from having *Tommy* near enough to completion to even know him by that name, much less be able to figure out a vague plot outline. (When Welch visited, the Who were still recording *Deaf, Dumb and Blind Boy*.) Nor were they entirely free of obligations during this period. Anticipating that the record would be completed in time for Christmas, Lambert and Stamp had booked the band on its only English tour of the year, a two-week swing around the country with the Small Faces, the Crazy World of Arthur Brown (both of whom got equal billing, symbolic of what low stature the Who had in its own homeland) and the Mindbenders.

On December 12, they were booked to play the mini-opera "A Quick One" at Intertel Studios, in Wembley, for "The Rolling Stones' Rock & Roll Circus," a television special the Stones were planning which also featured Jimi Hendrix, Jethro Tull and John Lennon and Yoko Ono. The mini-opera turned out to be the hit of the show, as the Who performed with unequaled ferocity—the studio work had made their music more tightly knit than ever. They also saved the day when the Rolling Stones didn't manage to hit the stage until past 1:00 A.M. (a typical Stones stunt), leaving the crowd bored and restless. The Who donned seat-cushion covers, worn over their heads like bishops' mitres, and went out as a comedy act. The next day, a huge bouquet of flowers arrived at the Track offices bearing a handwritten message. "To the Who: Thank you for working so hard on the television show—really. Mick."

("The Rock & Roll Circus" never aired. "Allen Klein didn't think the Stones spot was good enough or something," Townshend said. "They were really a wee bit upside down. It was just before Brian [Jones] died and he was really unhappy and they were really unhappy and the music wasn't good." Later, Klein attempted to sell the entire program to the Who to be released as *their* "Rock & Roll Circus." But that idea never materialized.)

As the recording process dragged on through the winter and early spring, the Who had to keep doing weekend gigs. They worked at IBC from Monday until Thursday, then left on Friday to do the shows. These gave them a chance to test some of their new songs, which may have helped make *Tommy* such an effective stage piece; for once, the Who knew for certain which of their songs would go over with their listeners.

Having to stop recording after only four days each week must have contributed to the band's sense of frustration. Finally, despairing of Townshend ever coming up with a coherent outline of where they were going, Kit Lambert sat down, wrote a script (*Tommy, 1914-1984*) and had it printed up and professionally bound for presentation to the band. Around the same time, it was decided to make the record a double-disc set.

The rest of the band never quite outgrew their sense that the opera was a nebulous project. "I can't believe we spent six months doing it. That's studio time and that's talking about it, discussing it, arranging it, producing and writing it," said Moon. "Recording it and then saying we could do it better and recording it again. Six months, continuously in the studio." Rock groups just didn't work like that. Only the Beatles and perhaps the Beach Boys had ever spent this much time in the studio working on one project.

Lambert's enthusiasm was indispensable in keeping the group's spirits up at this stage of the affair. But that doesn't mean there weren't rows. "It was Kit Lambert giving me hell, and me giving Kit hell," said Daltrey.

Townshend and Lambert particularly disagreed about two issues. Lambert demanded a formal overture, and he wanted to overdub an orchestra, possibly also using outside vocal groups.

At first, Townshend was willing about the orchestrations—he told *Disc* in its November 30 issue that "this will be the first time the Who has ever, ever, EVER used outside orchestration of any kind"—but he remained adamant about the overture. Upon reflection, he reversed himself. The overture could be useful in establishing themes and images. But the orchestration and the outside vocalists were out of the question; they would violate the unity of the Who in the same way that Shel Talmy did. (Townshend's piano and organ and Entwistle's French horn were about the only extra instruments added to the band, and both instruments had been used by the Who previously.)

Another reason that *Tommy* remained unorchestrated was that Townshend didn't trust any other arranger to do it for him (although he did consider asking his father-in-law, Ted Astley). Townshend actually went so far as to write some orchestrations, he said, which "looked good on paper. But a guy comes along and says, 'You are going to know how this sounds only after you hire an orchestra.' Then he tells me that I've got to conduct the orchestra. I just didn't want to do it."

Lambert didn't think much of rock as music. He wanted to legitimize the Who's sound by taking it closer to European classical traditions. Instinctively, Townshend knew that this was the wrong move. So they made a *rock* record— the first Who album that could be described by that term, used to designate the softer complexity that had crept into rock & roll since the Beatles. "It was at the time very 'un-Wholike,' " as Moon said. "A lot of the songs were sort of soft. We never played like that." Oddly, however, in creating this rock opera, which was so unlike their onstage persona, the Who established themselves as the greatest concert attraction in rock.

"When you listen to the early stuff," Townshend acknowledged, "it's incredibly raucous, high energy, but this was fairly laid back and Kit Lambert deliberately mixed it like that, with the voices up front. The music was structured to allow the concept to breathe. . . . It has a quite deliberate blandness with no freneticism at all."

Entwistle was more explicit—and more pungent. "The drums always seemed to sound like biscuit tins," he said of Lambert's production. And Entwistle also accused Lambert of rushing the band ("We didn't get a chance to put on any of the overdubs that we'd planned"), though this was probably because the record had to be finished in time for a tour that had been booked (the previous autumn) to begin at the end of April 1969.

Tommy didn't sound very good by any professional standard; today it sounds positively dated and amateurish next to *The Who Sell Out*. Lambert was cutting corners—IBC was not Gold Star, nor even in the top rank of British studios—in order to spend less money and give the group more studio time. Kit was also far too unconcerned with the technical details of the sound.

Yet *Tommy* was meant to be—just about had to be—a rock milestone, and that meant that it should have been state of the art in every possible way. In terms of writing and performance, it generally was: Daltrey's vocals were brilliant without losing any of his rock edge, Moon's drumming was still unsurpassed, the complexity of the musical relationships in Townshend's songs could be touched only by Lennon and McCartney. But the dull, flat sound made the eventual LP seem much more one-dimensional and pretentious than the concept demanded. This was preventable, and it should not have been surprising that *Tommy* was essentially Lambert's swan song as the Who's producer.

In any event, Townshend was becoming as proficient as anyone around at record making. Early in the new year, he assembled a group around Andy Newman, the piano player he'd idolized in art school, and Speedy Keen, the former chauffeur and roommate who'd written "Armenia City in the Sky." Thunderclap Newman, as they were called, scored a worldwide hit with their first single, "Something in the Air," which Pete produced in his home studio. (The song had originally been put together the previous year for a Richard Stanley film.)

"Something in the Air" is a majestic piece of music, sweeping through Keen's fantasy of revolutionary Utopia with a hard-edged rock beat. The recording is a model of spaciousness, and the suggestions of orchestration are beautiful and expansive. It makes the pinched, muddy sound of *Tommy* that much more difficult to bear.

And yet, under the circumstances, maybe it would have been hard to do much better. Kit Lambert's greatest achievement was keeping the project going to completion, never succumbing to what must have been constant pressure to simply cut the sessions short and shove the album into the stores. The Who were primed for a breakthrough, and the obvious thing to do was capitalize on it as soon as possible. By holding out as long as he could and by keeping the band focused and disciplined, Kit Lambert did an heroic job.

"There's not a song there that hasn't been recorded twice and not one that hasn't been rewritten three or four times," Townshend said, "and not one that hasn't had two or three demos made for it. And yet there's still lumps missing, bits of double meaning, of failure . . . where the music is too big for the lyric, where the lyric isn't well enough supported musically, where both the lyric and the music fail and cancel each other out. It works on so many different levels, and with something this big you just can't control it."

For its time, *Tommy* was a triumph and a masterpiece. It was a real *rock* record that still conveyed a narrative, an ambitious interlocking of all the pieces on four sides of an album.

Tommy is a cohesive musical statement; it is truly state of the art as far as composition and construction are concerned. Any weakness in the writing is mostly due to the attempt to build a narrative; the expository songs ("1921," "Miracle Cure," "Do You Think It's Alright?") are the insubstantial ones. Of the major tracks on the album, only "Sally Simpson" doesn't work. Even within the album's slightest tracks, such as "1921," one may encounter lines as beautiful as

I had no reason to be over-optimistic
but somehow when you smile I can brave bad weather

The best writing here is Townshend's most subtle, and the arrangements are among his most efficient. *Tommy* is built around the simple chords stated at the beginning of the "Overture" and restated in succession through the full complement of the opera's instrumentation (acoustic and electric guitar, bass, drums, piano, organ, French horn and voice). The rhythms never stray from rock, not even on the awful choral version of "Tommy Can You Hear Me."

The sense of dynamism is enhanced because Townshend plays so much acoustic guitar (as well as integrating keyboards into the group's sound; previously, the Who had used them as an obtrusive overlay). Townshend had already shown how hard a hollow body guitar could rock on "Magic Bus," with its simple Bo Diddley strums, but "Pinball Wizard" makes even more imaginative use of the instrument.

In "Pinball Wizard," the acoustic guitar establishes a drone against which the electric guitar's chords crash and explode. The acoustic guitar is the one that propels the song, cutting through the percussion like a scythe. This track virtually redefines a whole area of rock in its own image, the one song on *Tommy* that realizes all of Townshend's hopes: musical, narrative and spiritual. (Townshend and Nik Cohn agree that Pete wrote the song partly because they were both zealous pinball players; Cohn had even written a novel, *Arfur*, about a fourteen-year-old pinball fanatic. The obsessive passion behind Tommy's pinball playing is also linked to Meher Baba's incorporation of game playing as part of his work.)

Moon, Entwistle and Townshend had all maintained the quality of their playing. Each was regarded as one of the most important figures in rock on his instrument prior to *Tommy*'s release, and on it each extended his scope— Townshend by branching out into some lovely keyboard work, Entwistle with his French horn playing and songwriting, Moon by displaying a much greater sense of nuance. But Roger Daltrey's singing on *Tommy* placed him in a new league. He could still bluster with the best of them, as the rock songs proved, but even more than Moon, Roger benefited from *Tommy*'s added dynamism. His first full-fledged vocal on the album, in "Amazing Journey," has a delicacy he had never before exhibited. By "Christmas," the opening track of side two, Daltrey is as commanding as any rock singer has ever been. In the course of the album, he *becomes* Tommy, not just supplying his voice but inhabiting the character, as well. This achievement is more remarkable because the lyrics offer so little characterization. Yet by the time Tommy, through Daltrey, informs his disciples, "Listening to you, I get the music," what we're hearing isn't just a pose. It's a full-fledged figure of classic folklore: Tommy incarnate.

Tommy cannot stand on its own as a collection of potential rock & roll hits, as Pete Townshend had originally hoped. The expository songs, those that primarily serve the purpose of moving the story along, squelch that idea: "Miracle Cure" and "1921" are probably the two worst songs that the Who ever recorded. On the other hand, the musical transitions effected by pieces such as "Overture," "Underture" and "Sparks" are brilliant, and even though these instrumentals are often understated, they gave a closer glimpse of the Who onstage than anything else the band had recorded.

"Christmas," "I'm Free," "Acid Queen" and "We're Not Gonna Take It," along with the two Entwistle numbers, "Fiddle About" and "Cousin Kevin," are qualified to stand alongside "Pinball Wizard" as self-contained rock music, though, and the length of that list suggests the absurdity of holding Townshend to his overstated ambition. There were many extraordinary rock albums released in 1969. Of them all, however, only the Beatles' *Abbey Road*, *Let It Bleed* by the Rolling Stones and *The Band* are as ambitious and fully realized as *Tommy*. Just as those albums served to introduce a new vocabulary of sounds, images and ideas into rock, so *Tommy* helped refresh not just the Who but the entire pop scene. Townshend, the rest of the band and many of the group's hardcore followers may not have liked everything that *Tommy* inspired—the bathetic pop operas of Andrew Lloyd Webber, the sententious art rock of groups such as Genesis and Jethro Tull—but there is no denying its influence. And to the extent that it confirmed rock's ability to make deeply imaginative fantasies come to life, *Tommy* was a celebration of rock, not a betrayal or denial of its spirit.

In the words of Meher Baba, "To penetrate into the essence of all being and significance and to release the fragrance of that inner attainment for the guidance and benefit of others, by expressing in the world of forms, truth, love, purity and beauty—this is the sole game which has any intrinsic and absolute worth. All other happenings, incidents and attainments can, in themselves, have no lasting importance."

"*Tommy* is just like grand opera," Kit Lambert once boasted. "It's incredibly difficult to follow the story." Pete Townshend didn't want it that way, any more than Richard Wagner or Giacomo Puccini had. It also must be said for all three composers that their audiences almost always knew more or less what the composers were driving at; and this was no less true in the Fillmore East in 1969 than it had been in a fastidious European concert hall a century before.

Music's deepest, most pertinent advantage over the other arts is its high degree of abstraction. Opera and all of its related forms, from operetta to the Broadway musical, must always compromise between the sense music makes on its own and the more linear logic required by dramatic narrative. Grand opera as a genre long ago decided the question in favor of music; Broadway has never come to a conclusion; operetta relegates everything to the trivialities of story. None of these bastard forms is ever entirely satisfactory, even though any may be glorious in part. In this respect, *Tommy* is nothing if not typical.

The *Tommy* package contained a libretto at a time when librettos were by no means common in rock or pop albums. But following along song by song as the recording plays, one still does not have much sense of just what's supposed to be happening. Because *Tommy* was not conceived as a stage production (as a product of an era when music was primarily disseminated electronically, it didn't need to be), there were no stage directions. Because Townshend had decided against outside singers and musicians, there was no cast; he and Daltrey assume almost all of the roles. The only narration, which is skeletal, is provided by the harmony vocals, but these mostly repeat key phrases ("Tommy can you hear me?") in the rock tradition.

"The characters react to each other only in single-line statements or cameos," wrote John Swenson. "Tommy's relationships cannot be portrayed in words, thus giving the music added importance." But the music cannot portray personality—only emotion and sensibility. The characters and the action need to be outlined verbally to obtain enough shape for the music to complete them.

Townshend was already trying to cram too much into the lyrics. "Each song has to capsule an event in the boy's life and also the feeling, and knit-up all the possibilities in all the other fields of action as well," he said. "All these things had to be tied up in advance and then referred back to. I can tell you it was quite difficult."

It was impossible. Almost inevitably, only Townshend—perhaps Lambert and, in some cases, one or two of the band members—knew the story that the lyrics or music meant to convey. Most often, no one outside the group could possibly have guessed.

Townshend, either knowing or sensing this, filled in as only he could, by doing literally hundreds—possibly a thousand—interviews, describing and explaining the *Tommy* story. Of course, since the action was sufficiently vague to confuse even Pete from time to time, his explanations were often contradictory, misleading or simply confusing. One of *Tommy*'s purposes was to disseminate the spiritual precepts of Meher Baba as all-too-imperfectly grasped by Townshend. Since those precepts were none too understandable to begin with, much of the opera was a muddle. This engendered further misunderstandings and additional rounds of clarification.

The middle action of *Tommy* isn't actually all that unclear. It's the beginning and end that are murky. This is where Townshend fails to provide proper transitional material. On the basis of most of the pre-*Tommy* interviews, what happened was that the boy had seen the murder of his mother's lover by his father, who was returning from the war (the "Overture" established that he was missing). In other versions, the father was murdered by the lover. Either way, the song never alludes to death, much less murder—much less who did what to whom.

Witnessing the crime and then being told that he hadn't so badly traumatizes Tommy that he cuts off all his senses, except touch. Deaf, dumb and blind, Tommy lives in his own world of imagination and spiritual harmony (portrayed in "Amazing Journey"). Needless to say, he can't be institutionalized.

The frustrations of dealing with such a catatonic child are portrayed in "Christmas" and in "Fiddle About," and the potential of such a child as a playground for perversion is depicted in "Cousin Kevin," "The Acid Queen," and "Fiddle About." Ostensibly, these songs were to establish that because he was unburdened by the everyday veil of illusion, Tommy suffered no harm at the hands of the sadist, the pusher and the child molester. Once more, this crucial information is omitted from the lyrics, which makes much less surprising the reaction of many uninitiated listeners that *Tommy* was "sick."

"Pinball Wizard" makes a bit more sense; at least it's clear that the "deaf, dumb and blind kid" must be Tommy, though there isn't a clue about why he plays the game. Immediately thereafter, in the sequence described in "There's a Doctor," "Go to the Mirror," "Tommy Can You Hear Me" and "Smash the Mirror," the action is at its most understandable. The father finds a doctor who believes he can cure the child; the treatment involves testing Tommy's senses, at which point it's discovered that he is fully functional but thoroughly unresponsive—the classic psychosomatic syndrome. (Tommy is the world's greatest hypochondriac.) Tommy responds only to his own image in the mirror which enrages his mother. She smashes the mirror, liberating Tommy, or at least his senses. (Whether freeing one's gross senses is truly "liberation" in the mystical sense is another question.)

At this crucial juncture, the musical transition is flubbed. Rather than an explosion of sound, totally demolishing Tommy's now-familiar dream world, we get the quite gentle, softly strummed introduction to "Sensation." Daltrey sings this song splendidly, but the drama needs something bolder. When the lyric reads, "I overwhelm as I approach you," one ought to be overwhelmed. (And in concert, one might be.)

"Sensation" leads to the album's finale, which is a jumble. One can easily see why the Who chose to make a double-disc set, for so much happens in such a brief space that they might have benefited from a third record. "Miracle Cure" is meant to establish that Tommy's cure has made him famous; "Sally Simpson" that he has acquired disciples, formed a kind of church and (apparently) that as a result of this form of hierarchical organization—which Baba frequently warned against—the worshippers are actually being led into perdition.

"I'm Free" presents Tommy's spiritual message at its purest, while "Welcome," besides being a lovely melody, establishes his hope of reaching all humanity. But as "Tommy's Holiday Camp" shows, the Tommy cult has already fallen into hucksterism.

"We're Not Gonna Take It," the album's last song, is its most compressed. It begins with Tommy instructing his followers. Once more, Townshend explained the song more lucidly in conversation. "He says, 'You can follow me by playing pinball and doing things my way.' But when he says, 'Here's Uncle Ernie with your very own machine,' it's like they're being led back to their very own life. All the time they demand more, and so he starts to get hard: 'Well, if you *really* want to know what to do, you've got to stop drinking, for a start. You've got to stop smoking pot.' And he starts to lay down hard, moral facts— like Jesus did—but nobody wants to know. (Baba actually gives the reasons: A stable, moral life is a good one because it doesn't hang you up.)"

The song isn't nearly so clear, because the information is presented in scrambled order: Tommy lays down the law, the disciples are led to the machines, and *then* comes the rebellion.

But Townshend also omits the album's true conclusion, which is Tommy singing the prayerlike lines he first offered to his own image in the mirror:

Listening to you I get the music,
Gazing at you I get the heat,
Following you I climb the mountain,
I get excitement at your feet

Townshend has criticized himself for writing these lines. "It's meant to be extremely serious and plaintive; but words fail so miserably to represent emotions unless you skirt around the outside, and I didn't do it enough there. . . . This one fails because it actually comes out and says it."

What's happening here? Tommy is no longer gazing into the mirror; that's been smashed. Still he repeats these words over and over as the opera fades away. But why and about whom?

I would suggest that Tommy sings them to his disciples. "The whole thing with Tommy was that in the last count he realizes that they're being conned, and so he hots things up so they'll rebel against him. It's like a sort of crucifixion thing: He sacrifices his own aura to them in order that they can go back to what they were doing before, because he realizes that that's the best thing they could be doing," Townshend said in 1975.

"When it came down to it, what I thought was so incredible about that was that here he was, he was still the same guy, he was still God-realized and all that, but this was now the pain, if you like, and the remoteness and the loneliness and the frustration, plus being God-realized. In other words, 'Now I've done it, but now I've got to have the patience and the love to drag the rest of humanity through it.'

"That's really what the whole end of it is—that despite the fact that he created this big achievement, he's not going to be complete or not going to be at rest until everybody is. And that that will never be.

"Deep down inside of every human being is this feeling that nothing is ever going to be complete, that the circle will never connect and that that in itself is the secret to infinity, the fact that the circle will never ever be completed is the knowledge of infinity. . . ."

Or in the words of the great hymn: "Will the circle be unbroken, by and by, Lord, by and by?" To this, Tommy answers no, and having said so, shows his compassion by fully embracing not only his own humanity but everyone's. Thus those final lines, sweetly sung to the backs of his departing believers.

Is this what *Tommy* "means"? Maybe. Certainly it is what it meant to Townshend after he'd struggled for nearly a decade with its sense and the sense that his audience made of it. *Tommy* also meant many other things, and from time to time Townshend has articulated these meanings, too.

For instance, *Tommy* partly stemmed from Pete's conviction that "practically every talented person spends most of his time hiding his talent—or freakiness. . . . Some hide it behind the aura of being a superstar in glittering show business. The reason is the remoteness it creates. . . ." This is certainly plausible, especially for a modernist sensibility: The statement applies equally well to Antonin Artaud and James Joyce and Jimi Hendrix and Alfred Hitchcock and—Peter Townshend.

But Townshend has also admitted that "even in *Tommy*, where I tried to take a stance *away* . . . it seemed to have a lot of familiar threads running through it, like family problems, the standard social problems, like the bullying cousin Kevin and the druggy things." In this special sense, *Tommy* is also a form of autobiography in which Peter Townshend describes what growing older, more mature, more aware has done to him.

At least once, Townshend has asserted that the opera "fell into place" when he began "thinking in spiritual terms rather than the frustrated adolescent terms I had been thinking up to that point." But this is clearly *not* true. Tommy may very well be the ultimate frustrated adolescent, closing himself off completely from the world of reality rather than face its true horror. That's a big part of his appeal: Consider the audience the opera reached and the ones it did not.

Just as fundamentalist Christians like Jerry Lee Lewis and Little Richard found their fullest expression by singing "devil music," Townshend understood himself, his music and his Lord only by embracing an awful contradiction. *Tommy*'s denouement does not offer a revelation about gurus; it offers insights about disciples. In the end, even the protagonist is a skeptic, with no fantasies left about his own godhood or anything else. So Tommy sings: "Listening to you, I get the music." And in this sense, Townshend's rock opera is as much a product of those nights at the Goldhawk, watching the audience and celebrating their moves from the stage, as it is of meditation and the study of Meher Baba's message.

Tommy is a hero in the deepest sense: a mythological hero. "The hero represents the gift of love, or again, grace—the latter epitomized, for example, in Arthur's effortless raising of the sword from the rock—or, in Hindu mythology, Rama's similar lifting of the bow. Both deeds indicate how heroic feats of critical importance are enacted at moments when there no longer exists a clear dividing line between will and act, or rather when, beyond all necessity to proceed according to any attitude of 'intentional' motivation whatever, performer and performance are one. This occurs when the performer himself is not even conscious that what he has done is heroic. Yet it is, perhaps, just because he is not, that he alone can have achieved his task." So wrote Dorothy Norman in *The Hero: Myth/Image/Symbol*.

Tommy is a myth that summarizes the most transcendent aspirations of the generation Townshend had been portraying since he began writing. That hardly negates Townshend's purpose. As the philosopher Friedrich Schelling has written, "The crisis through which the world and the history of the gods develop is not outside the poets; it takes place in the poets themselves, it *makes* their poems."

Tommy can be criticized for the flaws of its songs or the failures of its story, for being too schematic and failing as drama, for being too corny to succeed as that rigorous and cold formalism that is all that modernism wishes to recognize as "art." For being, in other words, dogmatic, unironic and sentimental. It is all of these, but it is also glorious and may move any listener prepared to accept it joyously to the core of his or her being. Undeniably, *Tommy* did this much more effectively on stage than on record, but then, there is a vast difference between being present at Mass and watching Mass performed on television. Ritual is a participatory form of magic.

"The latest incarnation of Oedipus, the continued romance of *Beauty and the Beast*, stands this afternoon on the corner of Forty-second Street and Fifth Avenue, waiting for the traffic light to change," wrote the great mythologist Joseph Campbell. With *Tommy*, the Who took the tradition of centuries, wrapped it in the cloth of rock & roll and sent it to center stage. Together, they became legends.

I don't understand a thing about Tommy *myself, but then, I don't understand everything about* Don Giovanni, *either.*
— *Rudolf Bing*

N o one was quite sure *Tommy* would come together perfectly, but the American tour booked for May 1969 couldn't be moved, and the album needed to be released to coincide with the tour, preferably with a single a bit in front of it to stir up excitement. So recording was wrapped up.

Early in the year, Townshend asked Mike McInnerney for some potential cover illustrations. (A number of drawings and illustrations were also required for the libretto.) An earlier rendering had been rejected, but McInnerney was the right choice. He and Pete were good friends, as were their wives. (Karen Townshend had designed the clothes for the McInnerneys' wedding, a real hippie bash, held in Hyde Park.) More important, McInnerney was a Baba-lover. His designs would help emphasize the spiritual dimension of the music.

"By the time Pete came to me, *Tommy* was pretty well finished," said McInnerney. "He brought me a number of cassettes, I remember, and they gave me the gist of the story, which wasn't too difficult for me to understand, because it was so obviously based on Baba's teachings. I tried to catch the sense of *Tommy*'s world—to give it a sense of unlimited space and some idea of what a deaf, dumb and blind boy's world was like, which is pretty hard to do in pictures.

"On the cover, I wanted to depict a kind of breaking out of a certain restricted plane into freedom." McInnerney's cover concept was a blue and white honeycombed web of clouds, with a few birds soaring, and on the left-hand side of the cover's fold-out triptych, a fist punching its way into the black void that surrounds the web. From within holes of the web, the members of the Who reach out. On the far left, are the credits (including "Avatar: Meher Baba," the first public acknowledgment of Townshend's faith); on the right, the words to "Amazing Journey." The cover of the album is folded so that the front reveals the honeycomb with the Who reaching out to the viewer, a symbol of the record's aim. The interior triptych shows a hand reaching to light, a light shining in a black void and finally, on the right, a hand reaching outward through a honeycomb web toward birds and leaves on the other side—here we are seeing things from Tommy's own point of view. The libretto illustrations concern specific incidents in the story (views of pinball machines, the holiday camp, Christmas). All in all, McInnerney's concepts were an extremely lucid representation of Townshend's ideas.

"Pete was so totally involved with getting the music together that he just left the ball in my court," McInnerney said. "I just went ahead and showed the drawings to Kit Lambert. Kit was great to work for. He had this idea that all artists work in garrets."

Once Lambert approved the artwork, the next step was to show it to Decca. "They looked like members of the CIA with their raincoats and crew cuts," McInnerney said of his meeting with the Americans. "But it was up to them if the cover would be done. There was a lot of doubt about the whole project— except in my mind and Pete's."

Decca wasn't thrilled with such an unorthodox approach, but it seemed more sensible than *The Who Sell Out*. Even though it barely depicted the band at all, this cover at least had the titles on the sleeve. Decca was more concerned with the music, anyhow, though certainly not concerned enough for Townshend.

"We told them that they were going to have a five-million-copy album on their hands and they refused to even listen," Pete said. "I mean, I was going up to people and shaking them by the lapels and saying, 'Look this album is going to sell more copies than any other fucking album in history, so get your fucking brains together.' " But Decca was too unconscious of the rock market to fully grasp the opportunity.

Decca did understand the American singles market, however, and when they heard "Pinball Wizard," the album was quickly accepted. With the daft "Dogs Part II" (credited to Keith Moon and Jason and Towser, Pete's and John's mutts) on the B-side, "Pinball Wizard" was released the first week in March. In Britain, where Track knew exactly how to promote, it made number 4 on the chart, lasting thirteen weeks, just overlapping the release of the album. In America, where Decca still had a promotion staff that (with the exception of a few such as Pete Gidion) could have screwed anything up, it made only number 19. But it was a high-impact nineteen, capitalizing on the recent turn of the rock audience from the AM to the FM radio band. (As record companies were learning, FM rock stations didn't sell singles, but they could immensely escalate sales of the much more profitable albums those singles were taken from.)

As a pop single, "Pinball Wizard" was even more perfect and surprising than it was as an album track. Slightly sped up and compressed, heard in vibrant mono (and a trebly mono at that, which compensated a bit for the dull production), it was an instant classic. It may not have sold all that well, since the 45s market still catered to housewife ballads and teenage pop (the number 1 records in this period were Tommy Roe's "Dizzy" and "Aquarius/Let the Sun Shine In" by the Fifth Dimension), but that didn't stop deejays from blasting it.

In England, amazingly enough, "Pinball Wizard" was controversial; this, the most straightforward song on *Tommy*, the most pop, the wittiest, was attacked as "distasteful" by the BBC disc jockey Tony Blackburn. "There is no excuse for the lyric," Blackburn said on the air. Apparently, Blackburn felt that the "deaf, dumb and blind kid" was being mocked—although even out of context, it's obvious that the singer is in awe of the Pinball Wizard's achievements. Nevertheless, not only Blackburn but the BBC in general were hostile to the song, labeling it "sick."

The cudgel was picked up by *New Musical Express*, too. In the long run, this was perhaps to the Who's advantage, since it made the single especially noteworthy. The single came into the chart at number 26, the first week out, and sold 2,500 copies during that period, both very respectable figures but by no means a sure thing. Track's real worry must have been that the "sick" theme would carry over to the album and then drag *Tommy* down in America, as well. Both "I Can See For Miles" and "Magic Bus" had been accused of being drug-oriented in the States.

Townshend turned the situation into an advantage by using the controversy as a chance to explain the opera. "For the average intelligent person, [sick] is what it was meant to be," Pete said. "The kid is having *terrible* things done to him, because that's life as it is. In fact, what I was out to show is that someone who has suffered terribly at the hands of society has the ability to turn all these experiences into a tremendous musical awareness. Sickness is in the mind of the listener, and I don't give a damn what people think."

The album was released on May 23. The attacks were less vociferous, probably because the album placed Tommy's affliction in perspective, though there were still some jabs at Entwistle's numbers.

The May release date was considerably behind schedule. Townshend worked up to the last minute, and some basic issues remained unresolved into the spring. In mid-March, for instance, the Who's fan club newsletter was still referring to the opera as *Deaf, Dumb and Blind Boy* (a news flash changed it to *Tommy*) and listed Mose Allison's "Young Man Blues" among the tracks. And in the March 22 issue of *New Musical Express* (which carried the chart showing "Pinball Wizard" at number 26), Townshend told Richard Greene that Tommy's loss of senses was "instilled by his parents. . . . *Gradually* he loses his senses because of the pressures put on him. . . ." But in the album, Tommy loses his senses immediately—there is no time lapse at all. Townshend was already in America by the time the album was mastered; he never heard the final sequence until the album came out. "There's so much I would change now," Townshend later moaned, "but we had to stop working on it. We'd been working on it a *long* time and we were sick of it. The last part of it was very rushed."

Playing the opera live was a revelation to the band. "I remember when

Keith and I went down to the rehearsal after finishing the album as we were about to go on tour," said Townshend. "We did one day's rehearsal, did the whole thing from start to finish and *that* was when we first realized we had something cohesive and playable.

"Keith and I went to a pub on the way back and sat there, both incredulous at how quickly it had come together. Roger had become something else, and we debated what would happen and how it would change everything. We knew we had something that was magic and that magic wasn't as clear on the album as it would be in a live performance."

The Who previewed *Tommy* for the London press the week before they left for the States. (The first public run-through of *Tommy* was at a concert in Dolton on April 22, 1969.) The press reception was held at Ronnie Scott's, the Soho jazz club from which Alexis Korner and Cyril Davies had been forced to flee many years ago for playing electric Chicago blues. Now the Who piled a huge, ominously humming wall of equipment at the back of its stage.

Townshend introduced the opera with a story synopsis; the band had learned by now that merely running through the songs wouldn't communicate the tale, even if listeners were equipped with librettos. Yet as Chris Welch of *Melody Maker* noted, many of those at Scott's lost the plot, anyway. Scott's is a small club, and the Who played the whole opera, straight through, over an hour of music without a break, at their usual blitzkrieg volume. Welch claimed that "scores of people [left] literally deaf" and that his own ears rang for twenty hours afterward.

"There were moments during *Tommy* when I had to clutch the table for support," he wrote. "I felt my stomach contracting and my head spinning. But we wanted more." *Disc* was more direct: "WHO'S TOMMY: A MASTERPIECE," screamed the front-page headline, which credited the opera with being "the first attempt to use pop as a truly dramatic medium."

The U.S. tour began May 9 at Detroit's Grande Ballroom. (Tom Wright was now the Grande's manager.) The tour was slated to last for two months. But except for a couple of days in late June and July (when they returned to fulfill a booking at London's Pop Proms), the Who were not to spend any time in England until late August.

Tommy was received with ravenous enthusiasm in the States; it was greeted as a distinct musical and social event, and there was little talk about whether it was "sick." From the beginning, it was a popular success; in the first two weeks it sold more than 200,000 copies, and by August 18 was awarded a gold record for sales of more than 500,000.

In America, the only controversy about *Tommy* was whether it was really an opera. This issue was also raised in Britain, but usually dismissively. Tony Palmer described the general attitude: "How could a layabout like this Pete Townshend possibly write an opera? Artists are *nice* people whose products live on in museums and libraries. It is against this kind of idiocy that Townshend and his opera are fighting an uphill battle."

These are the terms on which *Tommy* has been discussed in Britain ever since. As late as 1975, Ian McDonald wrote in *New Musical Express*: "An opera is a *dramatic* structure, a theatrical experience in three dimensions. And a theatrical experience requires depth and focus in the action and the characters. *Tommy* is schematic rather than dramatic. It's not a story, it's a parable. In classical terms, it's not a secular opera, it's a sacred cantata." (This point was also made by the New York *Times* opera critic Donal Henahan after the Who played the Metropolitan Opera House in 1970.)

But McDonald misses the point—the question isn't whether *Tommy* is an opera per se. (It obviously isn't, though it isn't a cantata, either.) The issue is whether Townshend had written (or the Who were performing) a new form, whether one wished to term it rock opera or rock cantata or spiritual situation comedy.

As even Townshend acknowledged, "It had no arias or anything, although it did have restated themes. But we didn't feel we had to justify the term in any way, because in rock you can say what you want and not have to justify it." The proof of Townshend's seriousness (and of the idea that *Tommy* is a truly hybrid form) is that he still spent all that time justifying, clarifying and explaining. If *Tommy* had been a hype, just a few pop songs slapped together around a juvenile story, Townshend wouldn't have spent so many months in 1969 and 1970 doing interviews in which he pored over every detail and possible interpretation of the damn thing. (To read these is to understand very clearly why, by the end of that time, the Who had had a surfeit of their "masterpiece.") In the end, as Townshend told Chris Welch in 1979, "We only called it an opera for a joke. It's a musical. . . . In a way, a new word needs to be coined."

Tommy received serious scrutiny from a number of classical critics in the States. After the group played a week at the Fillmore East in October, *Opera News* wrote respectfully, "As with medieval Indian music, their bodies expressed the sound of the music and to a certain degree their libretto. . . ." And while the reviewer said *Tommy* lacked the "originality of the Beatles," and complained that the Who were "three times as loud as *Hair*, ten times as loud as the *fff* in the 'Dies Irae' of the Verdi *Requiem*," the tone throughout was that this was an experiment and an experience well worth taking seriously. As *Time* commented, "For the young, *Tommy* strikes a responsive chord not as a living musical drama but as a hopeful sign that pop forms like rock may have the vocabulary and expressive scope to deal with important subjects on a broad symphonic and operatic range. Every troubled society or social group needs its own encouraging myths and fables. From that point of view, for the rock world *Tommy* is at least a start."

Donal Henahan of the *New York Times* asked the most provocative questions. "Unstaged, unacted and uncostumed, and minimally sung, *Tommy* actually represents one of the most successful attempts by aging pop performers [Townshend was 25] to move past the standard rock concert or even transfigure it, somewhat as the Beatles did in *Sgt. Pepper's*," he wrote. "But why muddy the waters with the hybrid term *rock-opera*? After all, hyphenated opera automatically invites a snicker—soap-opera and horse-opera come to mind—and *Tommy* deserves better than a snicker."

Inviting a snicker and then defying the snickerers is a rock tradition that began with Elvis Presley. In the sixties, with an unbounded sense of cultural opportunity and optimism abroad, it actually seemed urgent that the possibility of expanded form in rock not be left to *Hair* and *Jesus Christ Superstar*. The latter are attempts to exploit rock (feeble attempts, at that). *Tommy* is a development of the rock tradition as established by Presley and redefined by the Beatles.

Like any artist, Pete Townshend wanted his work to be heard as widely as possible. If he had not presented *Tommy* as "the rock opera," there was little chance that Henahan (or *Opera News* or *Time*) or any of their readers would have paid attention.

There was an inherent danger here, but it wasn't a question of whether *Tommy* worked as opera. Townshend expressed it perfectly: "In a way, I like *Tommy* and I like what it did, but I don't know whether it was a rock & roll album. That's what worries me the most. . . . I mean, anybody can write an opera." By opening the door to a merger with the tradition of high art, rock was also forced into an uneasy rapprochement with the *standards* of elitist culture. At its worst, this resulted in entire schools of pretentious art rock (exemplified by such groups as Emerson Lake and Palmer, with their bombastic electronic "classics") and a cult of "good music" (in which form is thought to equal content). These approaches reduced rock to the weary enterprise of recycling ideas discarded by previous generations of "serious" music's avant-gardists. Too many of the performers in the generation that followed (and was inspired by) *Tommy* felt rock needed to be justified by reference to some outside authority. For Townshend, *Tommy* was in this sense a kind of failure.

But that has more to do with *Tommy* as a composition and as a record (since recordings, rather than scores, are the formal means of communicating rock compositions). *Tommy* really came to life as a stage piece—with about a quarter of its songs excised. In rehearsals, the band discovered that the piece was more efficient if some of the songs were dropped, either because they were ineffective or too difficult to perform or simply because the show needed streamlining. Ultimately, one of the reasons *Tommy* had an extremely positive effect on rock was because it was a great stage piece (unlike *Sgt. Pepper's* or much of Frank Zappa's music).

During the lengthy tours that occupied almost all of their time in 1969 and 1970, the Who had to deal with both phenomena. "Overnight we became snob rock—the band that Jackie Onassis came to see and all that rubbish," said Entwistle. But also overnight, the Who became the most inspiring performance group in the world.

This was not the case in the early dates of their U.S. tour. Opening night, at Grande Ballroom, in a steaming hot room filled with 1,200 sweating souls packed to the walls of the grungy old dance palace, the Who went over as a hard rock group, period. They played their standard set of the time, opening with Entwistle's "Heaven and Hell," probably the most powerful song he ever wrote and certainly the best concert piece, followed by a couple of the early singles (usually "I Can't Explain" and "Substitute"), then the mini-opera and finally about forty-five minutes of *Tommy*. (The album ran just over an hour and a quarter.) They still finished with "My Generation," but the new material was so strong that Townshend no longer had to bust up his gear. (He continued to do so when the mood struck him.)

At the Grande, despite *Tommy*'s power, the reaction was intent but not transcendent. The album had not yet been released; people were *listening*. At the end of May, when the album had been out for only a week, they played four nights in Chicago at the Kinetic Theatre. "Halfway through the gig," Townshend recalled, "all of a sudden we realized that something was working. . . . Everybody all at the same time just stood up and stayed standing up. From that moment on, they would stand up around the same point. We were able to just come in, do it and not need to worry about what was going on."

The album had sunk in that quickly. Of course, there was also the fact that Daltrey was transformed by *Tommy*. "To me," he said, "it was as though I was just singing Who songs until the second time we played it on the stage, and then I realized that I was becoming something else."

Daltrey even looked different. Gone were his short mod hairstyles and frilly clothes. Now he wore his curly golden locks as tresses, swooping to his shoulders and framing a face from which blue eyes glared. Only *Tommy* seemed to gentle Roger. He wore a fringed suede jacket or vest, often open over his bare chest. Bronzed from hours in the sun, always fit as an athlete, Daltrey stood in the full heat of the white spots and defined a new kind of rock star: sensual, rugged but with the macho aspects eliminated. Never had he and Townshend worked in such sympathetic alliance. Standing alongside Pete, who was only a bit less gangly, with his beard and his white boiler suit and clunky work boots, Roger seemed beyond whatever petty animosity they had known in their years together.

Pete Townshend had written an opera that gave Roger Daltrey the opportunity to become the pop star he had dreamed of being. Daltrey had brought Townshend's opera to life. If this did not make them friends, nothing could. (And it didn't—not for long.)

Tommy was a rock ritual. The Who enacted it onstage in a way that deemphasized the plot, accenting the music and the gestures of performance. You no more needed to know the words to "See Me, Feel Me" or "Pinball Wizard" to understand what the Who were saying than you needed to know Latin to comprehend the Mass. You didn't even need to be a rock fan.

"*Tommy* was originally aimed at the rock business and maybe to cause an explosion within the rock business," Townshend wrote. "But the explosion in fact came from outside, from people of all ages and all types." He didn't say whether the reaction surpassed his expectations or confirmed his fears. Maybe it did a little of both. Townshend wanted his credibility as a rocker, but no less than John Lennon, he wanted to turn on the world.

Through 1969 and 1970, as the Who dragged the deaf, dumb and blind boy around America and Europe, they were the exemplars of Rock, the shining symbol of What Could Be. "As far as a peak in our career is concerned, I think that *Tommy* is just about equal to 'My Generation,' " said Townshend. "We are still talking about the same generation." True enough. But *Tommy* was speaking directly to a vast international audience which in many ways used the opera to symbolize its sense of power, spirituality and–ultimately–its intention to transform not only itself but the entire world. Once again, we are back to *Tommy* the symbolic hero.

By the end of June, the Who were exhausted. The round of gigs and hotel rooms, greasy food and constant plane flights, Townshend's unending series of interviewers with their ceaseless repetitions of the same old questions, Moon's stale pranks, Daltrey's hordes of women, Entwistle's fixation on the sound—all grew tiresome as nerves were rubbed thin. The constant work and travel left everyone drained, without energy, except during the shows, when the nightly invocation of *Tommy*'s magic would lift them once more.

The Who played *Tommy* in ballrooms and theatres and at a couple of colleges. The itinerary included no arenas and no stadiums, however. And the group continued to avoid the great rock phenomenon of 1969, the pop festival.

In the wake of Monterey, the festival had become the fashion among hippie promoters. Replacing the package show concept, in which a group of performers traveled to small knots of listeners, the festival put together a lump of performers in one place and let the audience come to them—in vast numbers. Crowds of 100,000 had turned up for festivals in Newport, California, and in Miami in 1968; the second Newport festival, in June 1969, drew 150,000, as did the Atlanta Pop Festival over Independence Day weekend. That same weekend, even the staid Newport Jazz Festival was overrun by a crowd of 78,000 who came to hear the rock and soul performers (Jeff Beck, Jethro Tull, James Brown, Sly and the Family Stone) who were booked for the first time at the usually sedate event.

The music was never the central attraction of the rock festivals; the crowd were the real stars, forcing the authorities—through their sheer numbers alone—to tolerate unconventional clothing and behavior, right down to semi-nudity and pot-smoking, creating a brief but exhilarating rush of community feeling.

Monterey had in some sense tapped into this spirit at a higher level, giving rise to an international musicians' community. But the pop festivals perverted this spirit. Although some hippie rhetoric about love and brotherhood was used, the festivals were money-making ventures. A group of headliners would be booked, at a total price that was less than what might have been paid to book the acts for separate concerts in that geographic region (but more than the acts could have made for so little work on their own). Less well-known acts played the festivals for very little money—they needed the exposure, and sometimes, as when Grand Funk became sensations after Atlanta, the festivals actually created new stars overnight.

The comfort and needs of the festival audience were afterthoughts. Sound systems were barely adequate to fill the open spaces with noise, much less music. Toilet and sanitation facilities were scant. If it rained, the audience sat in mud and discomfort for up to three days; if it was beautiful and sunny and hot, backs and faces became blistered. Outside of the promoter-controlled concession stands, there was no way to obtain food and drink. The acts who came on before the stars were often lame or incompetent, leaving the crowd to entertain itself.

The festival audience came to celebrate a spirit that eventually disintegrated in their faces, and strangest and nastiest of all, they were willing to pay up for the privilege and resented anyone who questioned their wisdom. This does not endorse the logic of the law-and-order Right, which wished to quell the festivals because they still represented a ghost of hope for the youth counterculture as a community. But licentious opportunity was finally the only justification for the festivals, even if the drug-taking and sex *were* decadent in the long run. Ultimately, the pop festival served to reestablish the old order of the entertainment business: Star time had come to the hippie generation.

The Who avoided the pop festivals. They didn't need the prestige a festival could confer; and the Who's dance card was already full, anyway. The band had an attitude about festivals, and it wasn't especially positive. Based on their experiences at the Goldhawk and even at Monterey, the Who knew a rock audience's real power to contribute to a performance. And they knew how to spot a ringer.

Frank Barsalona basically agreed. The Who were *the* prestige group in Premier Talent's client list now. He saw no reason to cheapen the group by adding them to a festival's foot-long roster of mediocrities, and there was little to gain by associating them with other rock groups of similar stature.

What Barsalona wanted the Who to do that summer was especially important. He had been the key adviser in the band's American touring strategy since they had won him over at the Murray the K show, assisting Chris Stamp in all of his negotiations and scheming. In the summer of 1969, the pressing business of Track Records—with the Who, Hendrix, Arthur Brown and Thunderclap Newman all riding hits—kept Lambert and Stamp in England. They had turned day-to-day management of the Who over to John Wolff, and this meant that Townshend made most decisions himself, in consultation with the other musicians. Pete was smart enough to know what he didn't know and that Frank Barsalona was the man to fill in many of the gaps.

There was one festival that Barsalona felt the Who ought to play: Woodstock, to be held near Bob Dylan's residence in upstate New York. Because of its proximity to the reclusive Dylan, Woodstock had the greatest mystique of any festival since Monterey. Barsalona had already booked a number of Premier Talent's acts—Joe Cocker; Jeff Beck; Alvin Lee's Ten Years After; Johnny Winter; Blood, Sweat and Tears—to appear there on the weekend of August 15-17. Now production coordinator John Morris was calling him, desperate for the Who as a headliner. Barsalona initially said no; the Who were scheduled to be back in England by then, and he knew they needed the rest. But Barsalona thought again as he looked over the lineup and as the word-of-mouth on the festival began to build (and as he began to see how eager Morris was, how willing to pay).

When the Who were in Manhattan on a day off, he arranged a dinner at his apartment on West Fifty-seventh Street. When Morris, Townshend and the booking agent sat down to dinner, Townshend was adamantly against playing Woodstock. But, Barsalona pointed out, even though the Who were scheduled to go back to England on August 1, they had to be in the States the weekend of Woodstock, anyhow. They were to play at Tanglewood, Massachusetts, the outdoor classical concert facility, on August 15.

Townshend said he was eager to break that engagement, too. Barsalona pointed out that Bill Graham, who was promoting rock shows at Tanglewood that summer, was the most important promoter in rock and that the Who had an especially good relationship with him; in fact, a good deal of their prestige and income had come from Graham's Fillmores East and West. Blowing Tanglewood might annoy Graham so much that he'd cancel the Who's week of shows at the Fillmore East, planned for October.

Morris offered to have a helicopter pick the Who up at Tanglewood, shuttle them straight to the festival and, the minute they came offstage, take them to Kennedy Airport for their flight back to Britain. Townshend said no. He was unshakable.

Barsalona said Woodstock would be too big to miss, and it wasn't sound business to fly all the way to America just to play Tanglewood. He argued and harangued through the night; the hours didn't make much difference to him, since he was an insomniac. But Townshend was beat. He curled up in a corner while Morris and Barsalona enthused to one another. Whenever his eyes closed, Frank would shake him awake. It was like some Keith Moon prank, only this time the issue was serious.

At 1:00 A.M. John Wolff arrived. He was even more firm than Pete. The Who was nearing physical collapse; Roger's voice could go at any time. They shouldn't really even do Tanglewood. The situation seemed well in hand, and Pete leaned against a wall, sprawled his legs, and tried to doze. Once more, Barsalona awakened him, keeping Townshend as alert as possible while Morris worked on Wiggy.

The sun came up and the harassment went on. It was a bizarre night. Nobody took any drugs; Barsalona didn't even drink. But nobody slept; Frank made sure of that. By 8:00 A.M., Townshend felt as frustrated as Cornwallis at Yorktown. He'd agree to anything to get some rest. "Okay. We'll do it. Just let me get to fucking bed."

"Wait," said Wolff. "How much?"

Morris was in a bind. He was strapped for cash, though no one knew it. He offered $10,000 (£4,100). Wolff sneered and Barsalona blanched. Graham was paying that much for Tanglewood. They haggled briefly and settled on $12,500 (£5,000).

Standard rock concert contracts call for a deposit of 50 percent of the fee for an engagement, and the Who's Woodstock deal was no exception. In those days, this clause was often honored only in the breach. The Who received only $1,300 (£550) up front for playing Woodstock. This made John Wolff wary, and with good reason. Promoters still stiffed acts, especially festival promoters with unexpectedly large crowd problems.

That's what Woodstock had. By midday on Saturday, August 16, when the Who arrived, about half a million people were crowding the fields before the stage. The New York Thruway was a parking lot for thousands of cars. The concert had been declared free, meaning that so many unticketed fans had shown up that there was no way to expel any of them. Woodstock was officially a national disaster area.

Quite aptly so. There was no violence, but violence wasn't the issue. Sanitation was. The toilet facilities were completely overwhelmed, as were supplies of food and drink. To make matters worse, the early hours of the weekend alternated between drizzle and downpour, so that the crowd was stuck deep in mud. Somehow, the atmosphere remained benign. Part of the reason might have been the huge quantity of pot and acid consumed, though if that's the case, then there is no need to make the argument that such drugs induce unenlightened passivity. The spiritually aware do not happily squat in mud without water or food or shelter.

The Who had no use for the rhetoric of hippie pastoralism that ruled at Woodstock. Daltrey was living in the country, but he was working his farm, not lying back and grooving. Townshend was one of the first rock stars to adopt an Eastern guru, but Meher Baba did not teach his disciples to withdraw from their everyday lives. They'd all paid enough dues to have rid themselves of any illusions about the nearness of glamour to squalor. Townshend was naturally in sympathy with some hippie goals; Daltrey paid them lip service; Entwistle ignored them; Moon actively hated them.

Backstage, Woodstock producer Michael Lang was hiding out in a trailer; he didn't want to be bothered with paying the acts. After all, it was now a "free festival." (Of course, the promoters had collected more than $1 million [£418,000] in advances on film rights, recording rights and ticket sales.) When the Who or any other group refused to go on without their money, they were threatened, told that an announcement would be made from the stage informing the crowd of the situation. No performer wanted this crowd hostile; even if they didn't get nasty on the spot, the repercussions could be permanent.

But John Wolff knew that there was no way the promoters could afford to antagonize the crowd, either. There were too many people out there— even an aggressive 1 percent could overwhelm the backstage area and either take control of the stage and other facilities or simply create so much havoc that Woodstock would be turned from a spectacle of the Aquarian Age into something a great deal darker. Wolff called Lang's bluff.

At 3:30 A.M. Sunday, just after Sly and the Family Stone left the stage after an orgasmic set, Joel Rosenman, one of the festival's principals, handed Wolff a certified check for $11,200 (£4,450). Moments later, the Who took the stage. "We were more arrogant than nervous before we went on," said Townshend. Pissed off is more like it. Backstage, everything from the Coca-Cola to the coffee was spiked with acid, and the band had been flat out tripping against its will for twelve hours. The fourteen-hour delay hadn't cheered them much, either, especially since Alison Entwistle and Karen Townshend (with infant Emma) were waiting back at the hotel in New York City without any word from their husbands.

When the Who took the stage, it was jammed with photographers and the camera crew from the movie Michael Wadleigh was making of the weekend's events. Townshend kicked the first cameraman he saw (it happened to be Wadleigh, though Pete didn't know it) into the photographers' pit, a good ten-foot drop. The others scattered like moneychangers from the temple.

The Who were playing "Pinball Wizard" when Abbie Hoffman, the Yippie *provocateur*, took the stage and seized a microphone. Hoffman was crazed on LSD and had decided that he must make a speech protesting the ten-year sentence of his crony, the Detroit White Panther Party leader John Sinclair, for charges of possessing two joints of marijuana. "I think this is a pile of shit while John Sinclair rots in prison," Hoffman shouted into the microphone.

That was as far as he got. Townshend put one of his Dr. Marten boots squarely into Hoffman's ass, swatted him with his Gibson SG and, as the Yippie fell into the photographers' pit, played on. Hoffman screamed unheard curses into the gale of the music, then ran over a hill and out of sight, clear back to Manhattan. Townshend later described kicking Abbie's ass as "the most political thing I ever did."

The Who played a ragged set, everybody fighting against the drugs, lack of sleep and their anger that they had been put into such an absurd position in the first place. But just as they were finishing, with "We're Not Gonna Take It," with Roger's last cries of "See me, feel me, touch me, heal me" echoing over the hills, the sun burst up over the horizon, dazzling the crowd. "It was just incredible," Townshend said. "I really felt we didn't deserve it, in a way." But even if it was a lousy show by the Who's high standards—Daltrey called it "the worst gig we ever played" —it was legendary in the morning.

The Who straggled back into Manhattan by helicopter about noon on Sunday. Alison Entwistle was just getting up when John walked in the door, a good eighteen hours late. When he told her what had happened, she refused to believe him.

Only two weeks after Woodstock, at the end of August, the Who made a triumphant homecoming at the Isle of Wight Festival. The band was at the top of the bill with Bob Dylan, who was making his first stage appearance anywhere in several years. The Who were probably the best-received act of the entire weekend. It was their first hour of genuine prestige in their native country.

In September, they rested, but by October, they were back in the States for their week at the Fillmore East, some other ballroom gigs and a few college dates. When they got back home in early November, there was a British tour and French TV appearances. After Christmas, they embarked on the most ambitious and ridiculous venture of the entire *Tommy* period: a tour of continental opera houses. This tour, credited to Lambert's imagination, was in fact put together by Peter Rudge, a bright young Cambridge graduate who had gotten his job by writing Kit a letter. Rudge had started out as an Arthur Brown roadie but quickly displayed enough moxie to be put in charge of much of the Who's affairs.

The logistics of producing a rock show in an opera house were complex. There were prohibitive union rules in some places, there was the natural hostility between high culture and hard rock, there was the pure politics of trying to move a rock band internationally. In London, for instance, the group couldn't get Covent Garden; they settled for playing the London Coliseum, which had presented opera as well as ballet. The group never toured any of the great Italian halls, either. (Italy is always a dodgy place for rock bands.) But during the last two weeks of January 1970, they did manage to hit the Théâtre des Champs Elysées in Paris; the Royal Theatre in Copenhagen; the state opera houses in Cologne, Hamburg and West Berlin; and the Concertgebouw in Amsterdam.

Meanwhile, Nat Weiss, the group's New York attorney, was attempting to arrange for a gig at the Metropolitan Opera House. Director Rudolf Bing at first turned him down, but Weiss finally persuaded Bing to listen to the *Tommy* LP, and he was impressed enough to give permission. (The Who still had to pay double union fees for bringing their own crew and equipment and were forced to take out insurance at larcenous rates.)

"It's an interesting scene," Peter Rudge said of the opera houses. "You see the rock people, all dressed loosely and smoking away, arriving at these places that usually only see dark suits or evening dress. The ushers don't really know what to make of it all—that's where you see the real generation gap." But the Met's ushers told the newspapers that the Who crowd was generally much better behaved than the opera regulars.

The Who played two concerts at the Met, both on the night of June 7, to sell-out houses of 4,000 per show. *Variety* estimated that the gross, at an average ticket price of $7.50 (£3) was $55,000 (£23,000), which means that the Who probably netted less than $10,000 (£4,000) for the two shows combined. But the dates provided the group much of their ink in the prestige press, they were considered a counterculture landmark and they were a perfect kick-off for the Who's summer tour of America.

The Metropolitan Opera House shows were also something more: They were the Who's first "last *Tommy* ever." In all, a triumph, right down to Pete Townshend's response to the crowd's call for an encore after the second show.

"Fuck off," he said.

Lots of air hostesses said, "I know you,
you're Tommy *the Who." It was that*
much a complete picture. "The Who
play Tommy." *Then* Tommy *got*
*even bigger than us: "*Tommy
*and the Who." Then "*Tommy."
*"*Tommy *comes to town." I've*
seen that on posters.
                    —Pete Townshend

For the Who, *Tommy* changed everything. It wasn't just a matter of more fame, more wealth, more prestige. At no point previously had anyone in the band ever considered the Who a permanent proposition. Conceivably, they would finally clear up their debts, have a couple of profitable years, then fade away, some joining other bands, some leaving show business. Townshend imagined himself writing film scores, Daltrey was ready to be a real yeoman farmer. And while Entwistle and Moon could only have been musicians, they certainly didn't expect to spend their whole careers with the Who.

After *Tommy*, the Who's future was certain. Anything the band chose to do would be listened to respectfully; everything it did would be profitable—record companies and promoters were willing to pay very high guarantees. (Decca Records favorably renegotiated the Who's contract, following the common record business practice when an unexpected plateau has been reached.)

If the individuals in the Who wished to try other musical projects, the opportunity was available. Within the year, John Entwistle, who wrote many more songs than the Who could record, was at work on his first solo album. If the band wished to make films—which Lambert and Townshend were particularly eager to try—funding could be arranged. MCA/Universal, the film company that now owned Decca Records, had an option on the film rights to *Tommy*, and other studios were also interested. The band's debts were resolved; if Keith wanted to smash his hotel room every night of the year, he could afford it. It wasn't until the end of 1970 that the Who were informed that they were millionaires, but for months before that, they had known they were getting close.

The reactions of the band members to their wealth were predictable. The more conservative Daltrey and Entwistle saved, living well but within their means. Moon spent everything he could get his hands on; he bought a pyramid-shaped home in Chertsey for £65,000 ($155,000), a pub in Oxfordshire and uncounted cars and gadgets. He ran up ludicrous bar bills and worked himself as close to bankruptcy as possible.

Townshend felt "embarrassed" to have grown so wealthy from "trying to put out spiritual ideas." He poured much of his money into creating a Meher Baba center, donated a great deal more to other charities and spent for himself and his family in much the same style as Roger and John: not lavishly but not parsimoniously, either.

Everyone was married now; all had children. But there was no contentment. Acquiring and maintaining their wealth kept the band on the road more than anyone—their wives, especially—would have preferred. And when the men did come home, they were out of synch with domestic realities: making the beds, keeping to a schedule, going to the bank, making all the myriad decisions that for most of us *are* life.

For some, the transition was almost impossible. Keith found life off the road excruciatingly boring. He attempted to carry on as if his life were one long tour. He became a notorious character in the British tabloid press: "Moon the Loon," the rock madman who was liable to do anything from stalling his hovercraft on the train tracks, delaying an entire line of British Rail for an afternoon, to barging into London Bierkellers (along with co-conspirator Viv Stanshall) decked out in full Nazi uniform.

If Moon was not the funniest man in show business, he was unquestionably the funniest in rock. But he was also deeply unhappy. Often he missed the band, which never socialized when not touring. And his marriage was always on the brink, a product of the fact that he and Kim were so young when they had been married (he had been nineteen, she seventeen) and the fact that when they moved to Chertsey, Kim's mother, Joan, and her younger brother, not yet in his teens, lived with them.

Keith got on well with his in-laws, but having them in the house provided a major excuse for his increasingly frequent binges. He drank constantly, took pills obsessively, was loud at all hours, absent as much as he could be and from time to time even showed up at the house with a girl on his arm. He was subject to unpardonable, irreparable fits of rage.

In short, so badly did Keith Moon need to feel wanted that he was liable to do almost anything to get attention and just as likely to respond suspiciously if he got it. Keith's personality had been arrested at a particularly juvenile stage—whether by rock or by some other trauma—which accounts for his penchant for publicly disrobing, for wearing costumes, for his inability to get through an evening without at some point becoming (and remaining) the center of attention. He was boyishly proud of his ability to ingest quantities of drugs and survive, not so much because he needed to drink and take pills (Moon was manic from birth) as because taking so much impressed others. Townshend's generosity was quiet and compassionate. Keith's was flamboyant and a bit desperate, although it was no less well-intentioned. Although he was the mainspring of the band's style and knew it, Keith remained, even at this stage, unsure of his position—in the band and in life.

The seventies were laced with tragedy for Moon; he simply never learned to cope. The decade even began badly, when, on January 4, he, Kim, "Legs" Larry Smith (of the Bonzo Dog Doo Dah Band) and Smith's girlfriend set out in Moon's chauffeured Rolls-Royce for a discotheque in Hertfordshire. Moon had agreed to grace its opening night. As they pulled into the drive, they were met by a crowd of jeering skinheads (a style cult formed around the nastier remnants of mod, devoted to hooliganism and racism). The skinheads put their faces to the car's windows and threatened the occupants.

The chauffeur, Neil Boland, who doubled as Moon's bodyguard, got out of the car to deal with the problem. As he did, Moon climbed into the front seat. What happened next was never clearly explained, because it all happened so quickly. The skinheads pressured Boland and he fell; as he did, the car went into gear and rolled forward. The front wheels crushed Neil Boland's skull. He died on the way to the hospital.

Though the coroner ruled the death accidental, Moon admitted being behind the wheel and that he had been drinking. Keith sank into an alcoholic depression for the next three months. He was shaken out of it only when the Who went back on the road in America, back to the fantasy world in which Keith Moon was needed.

The real question confronting the Who was how to follow up the success of *Tommy*. The group had to release records that sustained and extended their commercial success, and they needed to establish that the Who wasn't just a traveling rock opera company. There was a danger from the beginning that *Tommy* would so completely eclipse the group that the band's other virtues would be sucked into the undertow. This was especially problematic because the Who had never solved the frustrating problem of capturing its live sound on record.

It would have been foolish and risky to consider another rock opera at this point. Even a successful one would stereotype the band. "It would have been a bore to go through it again," said Townshend. "That follow-up terminology is bearable on a three-minute single, but when you're dealing with seventy minutes of work that took nearly nineteen months to get together and nearly a year of solid recording, I just don't think we could last it out again."

One possibility was making a movie. "We got really excited immediately after *Tommy*, 'cause the natural thing to do was make a movie," Townshend said. "Our management originally was involved in the making of deals, but I don't know; it just never seemed to happen. It was just as if it was never meant to be; all the deals fell through.

"Eventually, a year passed and I said, 'Look, it's been too long now; I don't want to be involved in a movie. We've got to go out and do something else.' And this really upset Kit Lambert. He'd just made a deal—probably the sixth or seventh in a row—and my outburst kind of killed the film stone dead." (The deal was with Joseph Strick, who had directed a film version of James Joyce's *Ulysses* in 1967 and one of Henry Miller's *Tropic of Cancer* in 1969. The Who decided against the film when Strick turned to them too often for ideas.)

The rest of the Who were content to become successful professional entertainers, but Townshend needed more. That's not to say that the others were less talented or ambitious; they understood their needs in a very different way. What Pete required was challenge, adventure, goals—constant insecurity. The others wanted the opposite, a chance to build some kind of foundation, an end to nagging worries.

Townshend had a commitment to the idealism in rock, which seemed to him closer in its essence to what he had found in Meher Baba and in his other spiritual investigations than any other form of culture. Rock had an innocence with which it wielded its new-found power, even though some of what was associated with it was all too obviously maligned (Altamont and the Manson murders were reflections of rock culture, too).

"I felt that where the Who was at was very much a reflection of what's happening to rock & roll as a whole," Townshend told Chris Van Ness. "And I felt that we were beginning to cliché ourselves in so many different ways and that we really needed to shake ourselves up fantastically if we were going to stay in a position of being a band that was really saying what was needed to be said.

"I felt that the stream of rock was splitting up, the way it did a while back when the Chuck Berrys went one way and the pop scene went the other way. I mean, it was a dreadful pop scene, but Chuck Berry's still there, waving the banner desperately for that time and place. But all it does is tell you about the fifties. It doesn't tell you about today."

Townshend felt that there was a genuine danger that the Who could be trapped into an equally deadening self-parody, that they would come to represent the spirit of the sixties not as an active principle but as a dead letter. The rest of the band were much more content to play out their roles and let history determine itself.

Ironically, it was *Tommy*'s long run on the charts that gave the Who the time to maneuver for a proper follow-up. Their extensive touring plus the release of a number of its tracks as singles (none especially successful, but all keeping *Tommy* in the air) kept the opera on the charts in both Britain and America through the end of 1969. On *Billboard*'s album chart, *Tommy* originally rose to number 7 during July 1969. After the Assembled Multitude hit with its bland version of "Overture" (which got into the Top 20 by August) and the Who's next album, *Live at Leeds*, hit the Top 10 (around the same time), *Tommy* revived. *Live at Leeds* was released at the end of May and stayed in the Top 10 through the end of September. *Tommy* reentered the chart on July 18, and by mid-September it had surpassed the original release (thanks, in part, to a new Decca promotion campaign), topping out at number 4. For a month, from the end of August to the end of September, the Who had two albums simultaneously in the Top 10.

Live at Leeds had been recorded at a special concert at Leeds University on February 14, 1970. The Who had recorded all the shows on their autumn 1969 American tour, but when they got them back to England, Townshend refused to wade through eighty hours of the same material, claiming it would leave him "brainwashed." (He said he burned the tapes "in a huge bonfire.") The group slated the Leeds show and one in Hull, especially to be recorded by Pye's mobile studio. The Hull tape was ruined by equipment malfunction.

The live album wasn't the first new material the Who released after *Tommy*. That honor went to a single, "The Seeker," which the group had recorded (without Kit Lambert, although he was still given the production credit) earlier in the new year. Between them, the single and the album define the horns of the Who's dilemma.

The song was extremely personal, even though its lyrics were meant to typify what many sixties figures, famous or unknown, had gone through while trying to find some meaning and stability in life. "I'm looking for me, you're looking for you/We're looking at each other and we don't know what to do," the song says.

> They call me the Seeker,
> I been searchin' low and high,
> I won't get to get what I'm after
> Till the day I die

The singer recounts his rejection of such media heroes as Bob Dylan, Timothy Leary and the Beatles against music that is directly descended from the great middle period Who singles, stuff like "Pictures of Lily" and "I'm a Boy."

Too directly descended, in the opinion of such partisan Who watchers as Nik Cohn and *Rolling Stone*'s John Mendelsohn, both of whom gave it curt dismissals. "Musically it's nothing, just a rehash of the traditional Who tear-up, loud and strong and brutal–another 'Call Me Lightning' or 'Magic Bus,' except it's not as good," Cohn said.

Radio programmers and rock fans agreed. "The Seeker" barely crept into the British Top 20, and in America, it stalled out at number 44, an embarrassing occurrence for the Who's first post-*Tommy* release.

Live at Leeds, on the other hand, is the most ferocious, visceral rock the Who have ever recorded. The record is so molten with energy that at times it resembles the heavy metal of Deep Purple and the atomic blues of Led Zeppelin—music derived from ideas implied in much that the Who had previously recorded. From the opening "Young Man Blues," with Daltrey dripping in rampant Zeppelinisms, to the final bars of "Magic Bus," which are Bo Diddley on methedrine *and* nitroglycerine, *Live at Leeds* is absolutely nonstop hard rock.

Of course, *Leeds* is also only an echo of the Who's real stage show. In the first place, it represents only about forty-five minutes out of a show three times as long. Secondly, except for a few passages in the midst of the long "My Generation" sequence, there is nothing from *Tommy*. The improvisations can be as hallucinatory here as in the flesh, though, and much more nuance can be heard (all the words are understandable, each note of the guitar distinct, the bass fat and coherent). *Live at Leeds* is one of the last truly "live" live albums; before long, recording technology would allow bands to overdub all of their mistakes in the studio. At one point during the early part of "My Generation," what sounds like a microphone clunks to the floor. And there's almost no crowd noise; you know this album is live by the heat of the playing, not the rapture of the response. Compared to other live sets released during the same period (The Rolling Stones' *Get Yer Ya-Ya's Out* or Cream's *Wheels of Fire*), *Live at Leeds* is one of the great documents of that rock era.

But it's not in the same league with the record that Nik Cohn and Pete Townshend had been talking about a couple of months before it was released. Cohn had claimed that the Who had also recorded the night before Leeds in Hull, another large Yorkshire city, and that the tapes would be taken from both nights. He had written that the album would omit *Tommy* but include "Happy Jack," "I'm a Boy," "Heaven and Hell," "Tattoo," "Fortune Teller" and "Summertime Blues." Cohn had heard this material, and he was ecstatic about the Who's performance: "Without exception, they are shatteringly loud, crude and vicious, entirely excessive. Without exception, they're marvelous."

In a long interview published in the May 14, 1970, issue of *Rolling Stone*, Townshend told Jonathan Cott that "Heaven and Hell" was left out because it was technically deficient, but he also mentioned "Fortune Teller," and also "I Can't Explain" as part of the set.

There was no explanation of why the album wasn't two discs, at minimum. The Who (or their record labels) may have felt that releasing two consecutive double-disc sets could injure the band commercially.

Live at Leeds was not a true follow-up to *Tommy*. "It's like going back into a position where we were in a decline," Townshend told Colt. "And I prefer that alternative rather than following up *Tommy*. . . . You've got to own up to what's happening, you can't fuck around. It would be very, very difficult to follow up *Tommy*, and I don't think people really want it, anyway."

The Who made *Live at Leeds* to reassert their dedication to the root idea of rock & roll, to remind themselves and their listeners that rock had been profoundly moving and important long before anyone ever mentioned rock opera. But they also were making an image move, trying to steer away the pressure for either a *Tommy* sequel or something to top it.

"In fact, this problem has always existed," Cohn wrote. "Townshend is intelligent, creative, highly complex and much given to mystic ponderings, but the things that he values most in rock are its basic explosions, its noise and flash and image. . . . So he writes stuff like *Tommy*, sophisticated as it is, and he can see that it's good, but at the same time, he feels that it's a cop-out from all the things that rock lives off, almost a betrayal. And he goes out on stage and he smashes his guitar—simple, mindless release. But then he gets his breath back and he knows that's not it, either—to deny his own brain. And so it goes on, round and round with no end."

That state of affairs could not continue. Townshend's dilemma wasn't so much that he had to choose between being serious and being mindless as that he had to come to terms with himself and with his work as the manifestation of a process. Townshend spent the bulk of the seventies establishing rules only he saw, leaping over hurdles he had set up himself, desperately trying to top himself over and over again. Each success was meaningless because it only caused more anxiety over what came next.

So Townshend and the Who became the strangest rock stars: obsessed with their own history to an unprecedented degree, lost in contemplation of their own image and its variations to an extent that only Tommy himself could have understood. It was as if they were trying to retrace the steps that had led them from Shepherd's Bush to Woodstock, because only then would the present make any kind of sense. Townshend went from writing about identity crisis to acting it out.

The very ground beneath their feet was now shaken. The mods had vanished. A few had become the sort of skinheads that Moon had encountered in Hertfordshire, louts more devoted to the terrorization of blacks and Pakistanis than maintaining perpetual cool. The Shepherd's Bush boys had not gone that route, but they were no longer the gang at the Goldhawk, either. Some had taken jobs, some had done a bit of time. Once they acquired families, few were able to maintain themselves as they had been formerly accustomed. Irish Jack moved back to Cork, became a bus conductor, got married, went to work in the post office.

The Who could no longer turn to Kit Lambert for guidance. He was wrapped up in Track Records, distanced from the band because he did not share the touring triumphs and transformations, piqued because, beginning with "The Seeker," they no longer allowed him to produce. Further, he was deeply annoyed—crushed, in fact—by Townshend's announcement that he had lost interest in turning Kit's script into a film. By mid-1971, the Who were often communicating with their managers through intermediaries: Peter Rudge and John Wolff plus lawyers and accountants.

Even when they went back on the road in America that summer, everything was altered. They did not play the Fillmores or the Grande or any of the other ballrooms. They were too big for those now. Instead, they did sports arenas, even playing the baseball stadium in Anaheim, California, across the street from Disneyland. (". . . I see it as a very sophisticated circus act," said Pete of their stage show.) Once the initial plans for a film—"get American money but use an English crew and do it ourselves"—proved impractical, the Who were thrown back onto the most conventional methods of earning ready cash: gigs and record royalties.

Pete still did voluminous, voluble interviews, speaking of his convictions about art and religion and most of all testifying to the awesome power of rock & roll, a witness to his faith.

"I believe rock can do anything; it's the ultimate vehicle for everything," he told Jonathan Cott. "It's the ultimate vehicle for saying anything, for building up anything, for killing and creating. It's the absolute ultimate vehicle for self-destruction, which is the most incredible thing, because there's nothing as effective as that, not in terms of art, anyway, or what we call art. You just can't be as effectively self-destructive if you're a writer, for example, or a painter; you just can't make sure that you're never going to fucking raise your head again: Whereas if you're a rock star, you really can. And of course, all this choice is always there."

Some of the interviews lapsed into even greater contradiction and incoherence. Almost all of them inverted at least a part of whatever had been said the day or hour or week before. Maybe Pete lost track, maybe he was bored, maybe he simply never knew the truth but figured that it was better to *look* certain. That is, he grasped the concept of the interview as a form of communication, understood its ability to make truth of the moment, to leave the past behind and to continually redefine history in terms of *now*. No one checked his facts. He could claim sales of 20 million for *Tommy* and who would know the difference?

"I think there's a kind of contradiction in the Townshend theory of rock. . . ." a *Crawdaddy* interviewer told him.

"Oh, no, there isn't, mate," Townshend snapped back. "That's where you're wrong. I mean, I'm the only person who knows what rock & roll's all about. I'm the only true rock critic. No, I mean, there might be a contradiction in what I've just said. [It literally makes no difference what it was.] I wouldn't go along with all that. . . ."

"Maybe it's a paradox," the interviewer suggested. "[Rock is] reflective of the audience, but you're trying to express something of your own, aren't you?"

"Oh, sure . . . that's how it works. People identify with your frustrations and everybody's frustrated. And the most frustrated people on the planet are always the youngest. The point is, you know things in life aren't right but at the same time you know that rock in itself is an exhilarated enough form to totally wipe all problems away. . . ."

"And this in itself can become a frustration. . . ." suggested the interviewer.

"The same kind as my own now," said Townshend. And carried on, regardless.

If you had wanted to write an essay about the limits of pop stardom, about what money cannot buy, about the dangers associated with success, about pressure and stamina and the need to relax once in a while, Pete Townshend's eyes would have been a great place to start your research. He had grown a beard, his hair was cut in a fashionable shag, his face fit his nose in a way that was almost graceful—he was becoming handsome in his adulthood. But in those blue eyes could be read something else: a bleakness akin to terror, a sadness and desperation that sneered at his constant efforts to dispel it.

Townshend didn't write much in this period, but the songs that did get finished were a reflection of his anxiety. "The Seeker," which even he acknowledged was a message of desperation; "Water," a song about drought at every level; "I Don't Even Know Myself," an angry statement against interpretation but also a confession of total confusion. Then there was "Naked Eye," the one song of these which was integrated into the stage show, the one that sounded like a Who song, the one that *rocked*. And told the truth:

> You hold the gun and I hold the wound
> And we stand looking in each other's eyes;
> Both think we know what's right, both know we know what's wrong. . . .
> It all looks fine to the naked eye
> But it don't really happen that way at all

Those lines are about guilt, the attempt to shirk duty, feelings of deep inadequacy. "Naked Eye" is a great song because the lines are so frank, because they are delivered with such solemn, moody strength, because the music is full of parallel turmoil. It's hard to believe that no one could see that the man who had written them was beginning to crack.

They wrapped up the U.S. tour in mid-July and came home. Except for a few scattered gigs (notably the second Isle of Wight festival at the end of August), they had some time off. The American tour had made it clear to everyone that the Who needed a new stage show. The rock opera had been milked for millions, and everyone was heartily tired of *Tommy* as the focus of the stage show. "If we can't enjoy ourselves playing it," said Townshend, "if we feel we're performing it as a cliché, then the audience can see it, and this is when we say the professionalism has got to stop. We're not going to go on and do a cabaret act."

Once again, Townshend was accurate, but his interpretation was not that of the other members of the band. Townshend hoped to dispel the aura of *Tommy* altogether—he wanted to do something to make people forget it. Roger, Keith and John would be content with a show that shifted the emphasis from *Tommy* but still maintained enough of the rock opera to meet audience expectations. (They had actually tried to run through a set without *Tommy*, but as Moon cheerfully admitted, "We only have two songs left.")

As John Entwistle began writing more songs, with little or no hope of getting the Who to record the bulk of them, he devoted much of his time to creating a solo album. Entwistle had written some of the Who's best material, especially some of its finest stage pieces, including "Heaven and Hell," which became the group's set-opener in many of the post-*Tommy* concerts. John's vignettes and acidic social vision made his material completely distinct from Townshend's. And that's exactly why John's songs would never dominate a Who album—the departure from the band's basic image would be too drastic.

With the inclusion of a couple of atheist-oriented songs, "Heaven and Hell" and "I Believe in Everything," his first solo album, *Smash Your Head Against the Wall* (released in May 1971) functioned as a direct response to some of the Who's recent airy fancies. (In contrast, Daltrey's "Here For More," the B-side of "The Seeker," echoed Pete's spiritual convictions, though from a less sectarian perspective.)

Smash Your Head Against the Wall is a very creditable album, far more substantial than the predictable solo record from a rock band member. Its best songs ("Heaven and Hell," "What Kind of People Are They?" "Ted End," "I Believe in Everything," "My Size") show a genuine stylistic unity. Even the most predictable are craftsmanlike.

"We learned more about John from him making an album than we did in all the years he'd ever played bass with us. Because he *did* it and it spoke to us," said Townshend. "I got a lot of feedback from John's record."

Entwistle did contribute one song, "Postcard," to the next Who recording project. This was a set of five songs done at Townshend's Twickenham sound laboratory for a projected "maxi-single" (the seventies term for an EP). The Who recorded "Water," "Naked Eye," "I Don't Even Know Myself," "Postcard" and a fourth Townshend number, "Now I'm a Farmer," during the late summer of 1970.

The record was never issued. Roger later said they had too much material to fit it onto an EP. In fact, several of the songs were abandoned before being finished, leaking out as B-sides and album filler over the next couple of years. Of them all, only "Naked Eye" was outstanding as a recording, although "Water" also worked well onstage.

The other reason that the disc was never issued was that everyone knew very well that a maxi-single would only mark time without solving any of the basic issues confronting the band.

Townshend claimed that he was "looking for the *natural* thing to do after *Tommy*." But *Tommy* wasn't created as a "natural" follow-up to "My Generation." It had simmered for more than three years. Anyway, inspiration can't be willed into being even at the best of times, which these were not.

Art is like turning corners;
one never knows what is
around the corner until
one has made the turn.
—*Milton Avery*

I n 1970, there was a wave of terrorist airplane hijackings. The United States' invasion of Cambodia was made public, and in the resulting protests, the National Guard murdered four students at Kent State University. The Chicago Eight were still on trial, and there was a variety of politicized activity associated with the issues of feminism, ecology, gay rights, prisoners' rights and the decriminalization of drugs. Many sixties activists grew militaristic in their militance, sensing that the time was passing when the New Left could be effective using its methods of the past few years. Thus arose the part-of-the-problem-or-part-of-the-solution ideology that deliberately polarized society.

At the other end of the scale, some former radicals became involved in Utopian communes and alternate living arrangements of many different kinds. One such group lived on Eel Pie Island, a small island in the middle of the Thames, just across from Townshend's house. "There was like a love affair going on between me and them," Townshend said. "They dug me because I was like a figurehead; I was in a group. And I dug them because I could see what was going on over there."

At one point Townshend felt that the islanders had created a workable alternative lifestyle in a very English context, which he admired. But he soon realized that the commune was riddled with drugs, particularly LSD, and that its energy would never move past a certain level of disorganization. "I got on the end of some psychotic conversations," he said, "and I thought, 'Oh fuck it.' It's not where I'm at. This isn't really what I wanted to be involved in. . . . I'm very old-fashioned. I've seen and done it all in a lot of ways, and I've come back full circle to being right in the middle of the road. And that's not as boring as it sounds. It's terribly exciting, like a revelation, to find that there *is* a middle of the road which is stable. A lot of people find this incredibly frustrating. It makes me angry when people insist that I have a responsibility to do what they think I should do."

Townshend's life was full of commands and commandments, many if not all of them issued by himself. He couldn't stand being lectured by bohemians and radicals any more than he could tolerate the establishment's expectations of him, but Townshend put himself in many similar binds. He had created an archetype of what a Responsible Rock Star should do, and he set out to live up to it, which would have been fine if he hadn't been just contrary enough to keep changing his definition. The result was even more confusion (public and private) over what his role should be than if he had just quietly gone about his business.

Townshend was no hypocrite. He never made any of his pronouncements cynically; whatever he said, he believed—at the time that he said it. The fact that he would believe something else equally as strongly moments later was quite irrelevant to the passion of the particular instant.

Townshend had long believed that rock musicians and their fans had obligations that other entertainers and audiences did not incur. He always modeled his image of the ideal performer/listener relationship upon the intimacy and open criticism of one another he had found among the mods, who worshipped with a sharp, caustic eye. On the other hand, he was not prepared to abandon the privileges of being a famous rock star.

Among his passions was rock criticism. Townshend felt strongly that he was not only an expert rock performer but an expert fan, too. He had believed that ever since he had become a songwriter. One reason Townshend did so many interviews was that he identified with the task of the rock critic/reporter. (Since he had mainly received favorable notices, there was no reason to see the interviewers as adversaries, as many other rock stars did.) In August 1970, Pete joined the ranks of ink-stained scriveners by beginning a monthly column, "The Pete Townshend Page," in *Melody Maker*, the largest and most influential British rock weekly at that time.

Like most such pop columns, "The Pete Townshend Page" was announced with great fanfare and withered away after only a few tries—nine in this case. But Townshend's column was a bit different than the usual fluff that was written by press agents and distributed for innocuous image promulgation. Townshend's writing was often florid and self-aggrandizing, but it could also be insightful, and he often tackled tough questions, writing over and again about the concept of *responsibility*: "Rock can't be held responsible for what it says or does," he wrote in the first installment, "but its audience can." Some of the space was devoted to specific issues (for instance, attacks on the BBC's policies), some to rock history (pirate radio, for instance), some to mere woolgathering (the March 1971 column about touring entitled

"Learning to Walk—The Second Time Around"). It was also during this period that Townshend wrote his essay on Meher Baba for *Rolling Stone*, an excellent piece that clearly spelled out Townshend's convictions (especially regarding drug use) without proselytizing.

Townshend's intentions in writing the column, beyond simply dallying with a form he'd always wanted to try, were diffuse. He obviously wanted to provoke more thought about rock, to challenge readers (he got more than he bargained for when some disparaging remarks about what the Who did *not* have to do brought in a full *Melody Maker* "Mailbag" of anti-Townshend diatribes). And he hoped to prod *himself* into thinking through some issues about which he'd been troubled for a long time.

In a way, "The Pete Townshend Page" columns, even more than the scattered interviews he did in late 1970 and early 1971, were opportunities to pull together loose ideas much as he'd done in the 1968 *Rolling Stone* interview with Jann Wenner. Just as that encounter was a catalyst for *Tommy*, these jottings sparked his next project, a film called *Lifehouse*.

Lifehouse is probably the most frustrating and certainly the most intriguing failure of the Who's checkered career. Townshend has retrospectively termed it a "disaster"; it was the cause (or at least the trigger) of his first nervous breakdown. *Lifehouse* was a watershed between the Who as a band of idealists and the Who as a group of professionals, between the concept of a rock band as an experimental troupe and the idea that it was a profit-generating, creative business. *Lifehouse* was vague and incoherent and at the same time based on the most fully realized plot Townshend had ever concocted. It was completely absurd in the dimensions of its ambition, and it produced the most successfully experimental music the Who had made since "My Generation." All that can be said of *Lifehouse* for certain is that no one except (or maybe including) Townshend ever had much idea of what it was—and that it refuses to die (as late as 1983, Pete was still considering reviving it).

Lifehouse was to be a film of a rock concert but not a documentary; it was a story and a script and forty songs but not a rock opera. It was a spiritual parable but totally enveloped in the latest electronic hardware, from lasers and holograms to synthesizers and quadraphonic sound. In short, it was everything that was on Peter Townshend's mind from the autumn of 1970 through the spring of 1971.

Lifehouse apparently had its genesis in a conversation between Townshend and an executive at Universal Pictures. In this conversation, Pete received (or thought he received) a commitment from Universal for $1 million (about £350,000) to develop a Who film other than *Tommy*.

The story had its origins in Pete's reading in science fiction, in the Sufi music theories of Inayat Khan (particularly *The Mysticism of Sound*), and in his visits with scientists at Cambridge University, where he learned of the latest developments in recording and sound reproduction technology and studied the possibility of computer- and tape-synthesized music making. *Lifehouse* showed the influence of Meher Baba's teachings. But the story also had its origins in Townshend's own observation of rock power, of the way it was used and misused, and of the corruption that had seeped into current modes of presentation.

The basic *Lifehouse* story wasn't particularly complex. It was set in a future world in which rock & roll is unknown, either because it was banned or because no one has yet discovered it. Into this setting comes Bobby, an electronics wizard who was, in some versions, a former rock musician or roadie.

The *Lifehouse* world is troubled by terrible pollution, overpopulation and a fascist government. The privileged and middle classes live below ground, many of them in "experience suits," high-tech outerwear that provides nourishment and every form of mental and sensual stimulation, all controlled by the government. On the surface live "the scum," hippies and other determined individualists and a few farmers.

Bobby is hostile to the government's social controls, dissatisfied with the general lack of soul in society. (Like Tommy, he is also a God-realized personality, with a Divine Mission.) He takes over an abandoned theatre and dubs it the Lifehouse, attracting a core of 300 listener/participants for what emerges as an extravagant, six-month-long rock concert. For each member of the audience, Bobby makes a chart, listing points of physical and psychological data, horoscopes and so forth. From these he arrives at a sound for each: "a single note or a series, a cycle or something electronic."

These charts are programmed into the same equipment used for the experience suits, which Bobby has expropriated from the government. ("Incredible technology which we actually *had*," Townshend claimed, reeling off a list including "cerebrographs," "synthesizers tuned into the heartbeat" and "video feedback.") The programmed music is performed by a rock band (played by the Who) on the Lifehouse stage, inspiring frenzied, orgiastic dancing. But, Townshend said, "the real center is the equipment itself, the amps and tapes and synthesizers, all the machines, because they transmit the sounds: The hardware is the hero." As the various musical personalities are developed and played, first one at a time and then more and more of them together, the listeners undergo a transformation. After six months, they reach a state of mutual harmony, on the road to enlightenment.

"As a last resort, this theatre is set up as a focus for everyone," Townshend told Penny Valentine of *Sounds* in January 1971. "In other words, it's the last hope of humanity. If these people in this theatre can find themselves in the midst of all this chaos, then through very futuristic media things—experience suits, holograms and things—everyone else can. They can get above it and lose the illusion all around them."

Meanwhile, the government has sent in troops to stop the Lifehouse experiments, which are interfering with its social control. The troops are thwarted for a time, because the Lifehouse is surrounded by a force field. While the troops batter at the barrier, the Lifehouse participants are entering a final stage of communal transformation. The dancing becomes more and more ecstatic as the music grows closer and closer to the center of their shared existence. (This is derived from the concept of dervish dancing, of course.)

As this stage begins, the troops have broken through the force field to rush the Lifehouse. "All the sounds merge into one, like a massive, insane square dance. And everyone starts bouncing up and down together, faster and faster, wilder and wilder, closer and closer and closer. Finally the energy gets too much."

As the sound reaches its peak, the soldiers get set for their first shots and nail Bobby, who tumbles from the balcony, where he has been orchestrating the ecstasy. Just as Bobby's body strikes the floor, the Universal Chord is struck and "they actually leave their bodies. They disappear."

The soldiers stand dumbfounded; the government is distraught. Bobby has not only allowed all the Lifehouse participants to escape—in the process, all the wearers of experience suits have died for lack of nourishment and stimulation. The troops and government leaders are left stranded, with no one to bully but one another. "It's just a wasteland sort of thing."

Directly tied into this story were a number of new Townshend songs. "Baba O'Riley," "The Song Is Over," "Behind Blue Eyes," "Pure and Easy," "Won't Get Fooled Again" and even "Goin' Mobile" (as the theme for a pair of surface dwellers who cruise around in a battered old Cadillac limousine), all fitted into the *Lifehouse* plot.

What Townshend was trying to do was nothing new (as he was aware). It was just another version of the legend of the Lost Chord or the Universal Note which when sounded will restore humanity to its original state of harmony with the Creator. "All races, nations, classes and people are like a strain of music based upon one chord, where the key-note, the common interest, holds so many personalities in a single bond of harmony," wrote Inayat Khan.

"I'm trying to do what a lot of people have tried to do before," said Townshend. "To mirror with rock music the creative process—creation, if you like. Dylan's 'Mighty Quinn' will probably come closer to it in the end. But the reason this has to be done is the insinuation I'm making about the audience in the theatre. In other words, they're attempting to find a piece of music which reflects the harmony of mankind, allows them to realize that you end up with a piece of music that is representative of The Note, the thread of life."

In his February 1971 "Pete Townshend Page" column, Townshend quoted from some of Bobby's instructions to the Lifehouse disciples. "Music and vibration are at the basis of all," he said, echoing Khan. "They pervade everything; even human consciousness is reflected by music. Atoms are, at their simplest, vibrations between positive and negative. Even the most subtle vibrations detectable can affect us, as ESP or 'vibes.'

"Man must let go his control over music as art or media fodder and allow it freedom. Allow it to become the mirror of a mass rather than the tool of an individual. 'I will make music that will start off this process,' Bobby vows. 'My compositions will not be my thoughts, however, they will be the thoughts of others, the thoughts of the young and the thoughts of the masses. Each man will become a piece of music; he will hear it for himself and every aspect of his life reflected in terms of those around him. . . . When he becomes aware of the natural harmony that exists between himself as a man and himself as part of creation he will find it simple to adjust and *live* in harmony. . . .' "

Pretty heady stuff for *Melody Maker* or for a movie funded by a Hollywood studio. The column goes on to say that the real necessity is to get into harmony with Nature, that only when one realizes this harmony in his or her own life can one attain any chance of peace or contentment, and that this cannot be given: "It can only be achieved by your own efforts."

That these statements and others like them are pretentious and border on the incoherent is obvious. That they also represent a genuine desire on Townshend's part to participate in the grand process of saving the world is too easily seen cynically. There is a deep and noble innocence in Townshend's conviction that he can change humanity and alter history by constructing the appropriate parable.

"The aim is change," Townshend wrote at the beginning of that column. "A change of lifestyle for the band, a change of focus for the audience and a change in the balance of power that Rock wields. . . . The idea is to make the first real superstar, the first real star who can stand and say that he deserves the name. That star would be us all."

The problem came when Townshend decided that it was necessary to make his dreams come true. "It would be unfair of me to set out looking for that if I didn't know it was possible to find it," he told Valentine. "So that rather than get into another fantasy thing like *Tommy*, I've decided to make every area as practical as possible."

He told Nik Cohn: "I don't mean that I seriously expect people to leave their bodies, but I think we might go further than rock concerts have gone before. I know that when live rock is at its best, which often means the Who, it stops being just a band playing up front and the audience sitting there like dummies. It's an interaction which goes beyond performance. . . . We want to see how far the interaction can be taken."

"We" did not. As Cohn noted, "Not even Townshend's managers have any clear notion of what he's up to. For that matter, neither has Townshend—his plot has been changing day to day, according to his mood."

But Townshend was becoming less concerned with the plot and more involved with the actual equipment needed to create his dream and with the theories behind both sound and audience/performer relationships.

As the winter drew on, Pete delved more and more into other areas, especially the hardware. Among other things, he hoped to develop a workable quadraphonic sound system. (Quadraphonic sound was at the time thought to be the next logical step beyond stereo, a system of sound reproduction that emanated from four separate points surrounding the listener, rather than the two offered by stereo.) He was also working on developing tape players "with very specific logic controls so that as you're playing you can hit a button and get an instant piece of music to play along with you at a given tempo. We went into the production of machines that can alter the tempo of the music but without altering the pitch, so that the music could play along with us at our tempo rather than the other way around."

Inevitably, these experiments crashed. Trying to create a machine that could anticipate the willful genius of Keith Moon was as fruitless as attempting to establish perpetual motion. "The trouble with playing along with a tape is that when it goes into the middle, you've got to follow it; when it finishes, you've got to finish, too," Pete said later. The Who spent eight months, from the fall well into the spring of 1971, fighting the inexorable division between man and technology.

There was yet more to *Lifehouse*'s ambitions. Townshend saw that the typical mode of rock presentation was becoming stale and hackneyed, that in a way, it was even dangerous to everyone concerned.

"There's going to have to be a way of listening to music that doesn't mean that you have to go out to a concert hall between eight and ten in the evening," he insisted. "I've seen Who concerts where the vibrations were becoming so pure that I thought the whole world was just going to stop, the whole thing was becoming so unified. But you could never reach that state, because in the back of their minds everybody knew that the group were going to have to stop soon or they'd got to get home or catch the last bus or something."

Townshend felt that the audience played just as great a role in the making of rock events as the musicians and singers themselves and that this must inevitably be expressed and reckoned with. "Now that the tidal wave is beginning to plane off and cool down a bit, the rock people—the people who are in control of the media—are beginning to realize that they've got a most fantastic responsibility.

"They've got a responsibility because they never got up and said at any time in rock history: 'Look, it's you. It's not me; it's you.'. . . I mean, rock's got to call people out. It's got to come up with an answer—but at the same time, the people come up with an answer." Townshend believed that this would occur through an event; a huge concert like Woodstock came close, but he thought a film could drive the realization home more effectively.

Townshend continued to establish rules for himself, propounding ways in which the world *must* work: "The music we play must be tomorrow's, the things we say have to be today's and the reason for bothering is yesterday"; "There's going to have to be a way of listening to music which doesn't mean that you're going to have to face in a particular direction"; "[Rock's] got to come up with an answer." Unfortunately, while he sincerely believed each of these statements, the rest of the world didn't see things his way.

Most rock musicians had no objection to being placed upon pedestals, given great privileges and mammoth incomes, even though they knew as well as Townshend that without the interaction with their audience their power would be nonexistent. While a number of relative visionaries had suggested that another mode of rock presentation must be created, one which decentralized the performance, there was not enough dissatisfaction with the current modes to create such a change. The fans and the stars were both quite satisfied with rock as it existed. There was no outcry (or not much of one) from the mass of rock listeners to have their contributions recognized, and there was little or no incentive for the performers to spell it out for them. Rock had no intrinsic need to answer any of the social questions it posed.

Townshend predicted calamity if his injunctions were ignored, but neither rock fans nor rock performers perceived this crisis. Left alone, it is true, rock rotted in many ways, and its power was diluted and poisoned—but it did not disintegrate. Pete Townshend had never considered stagnation as an option. Like any true believer, he could not see beyond the boundaries of his faith—a faith in Rock more profound than most men's faith in God.

In the winter of 1970–1971, this passive outcome was anything but obvious. Because rock had witnessed many spectacular changes, it had become difficult to believe that the future would evolve through a slow process, not a new series of cataclysms. Apolitical as the rest of the Who were, even they sensed a change in the wind. As a group that traditionally stayed a step ahead of the trends (and was afraid of the consequences if it didn't), it seemed logical that the Who should pursue Townshend's prophecies and aspirations.

Early in 1971, Townshend did a number of interviews (the most extensive were with Penny Valentine in *Sounds* and with Nik Cohn for the *New York Times*) announcing that beginning in early February the Who would start rehearsals and then perform publicly in a series of experimental shows at the Young Vic Theatre in south London, near Waterloo Station. The Young Vic had been established by the National Arts Council as a venue for experimental theatrical performances. This was the first attempt to present rock there.

The Young Vic shows were to be the realization of Townshend's dreams of a rock revolution. The group planned at least three shows for February, using new material (Townshend had twenty new songs), prerecorded tapes and an elaborate quadraphonic sound system. The original plan had been to take over the Young Vic for a solid six-month booking; the initial shows were to be nothing more than a trial run, during which the Who would begin work on their film. The experiment would continue past the point when filming was concluded, however. "But the Young Vic is a government-sponsored bloody organization," Townshend said later, "and it turned out that we could only have it every Monday and then everybody started to think that it should be every Monday. I could never see it like that. I always figured it would be something where you woke up and went to bed with it. Either that or you came and went every day."

Nevertheless, the Who entered into the Young Vic shows optimistically—at least Townshend did. The rest of the band were just glad to get back to work.

Townshend had been working in relative isolation, without much need to explain his theories and ambitions to everyone. Almost all were mystified when he tried to communicate them. "The more in-depth the features became, the more the listener felt he was falling into a huge hole," Barnes wrote of Townshend's attempted elucidations—and that was the view of a fellow Baba-lover. But everyone felt that Pete would be able to pull the strands of *Lifehouse* together in the process of filming and recording, as he had done with the similarly disparate elements of *Tommy*.

This time, Townshend had simply grabbed more than he could handle. The filming was ready to go, he told Penny Valentine: "We've got the place worked out, the whole military programme is set to go. People are arguing with unions —the whole thing is welding together." But Townshend couldn't get his ideas across to those he would be working with. None of his scripts made complete sense, and his explanations were daft.

"It was explained to me," said Keith Altham, no dummy, "and I really didn't have sufficient intellect to be able to grasp it. Pete explained it once in great detail and I grasped very little of it other than the fact that there is a kind of union of identity which takes place among musicians and an audience, sometimes. And it becomes a kind of creative thing that actually happens at that time. I think Pete was looking for something like that to evolve."

Altham was at the Young Vic performances. "It was a smaller, more contained auditorium—quite small, you could only get a few hundred people in it." But aside from that, the Who's performances there were not much different from what they had done before. Nevertheless, Altham said that after he read the *Lifehouse* script, some months later, he felt that "it preempted things like *Clockwork Orange* and *2001*—for me, anyway. He had ideas contained in *Lifehouse* that were as good as those ideas."

Glyn Johns, whom the Who had asked to join the project as engineer and associate producer, was equally mystified. "Pete gave me a double-album acetate of his demos and a script for *Lifehouse*, and I was told to sort of read and digest it, which I duly did," Johns said. "I don't remember the demos specifically. I know that I found it very difficult to understand the script. I mean, I could not get a grip on it. In fact, I don't think it's possible for anybody to understand it. I was incredibly impressed with the fact that he had written it. I was incredibly impressed with the professional manner in which it was written. But I didn't understand it. And I told him so."

Pete could accept the incomprehension. After all, many of his friends and cohorts had not been able to make sense of *Tommy*, either, and the results had been extraordinary. What crushed Townshend was the reaction of the audience.

These shows were never announced in advance—only the Townshend interviews, done about a month before, indicated that there would be any Who performances in the near future. As a result, the crowd that drifted into the Young Vic was a motley assortment of idlers and freaks, thirteen-year-old skinheads and fixated Who fans.

Townshend's dream included not only an ideal band playing ideal music but also an ideal audience: "The idea was to get two thousand people and keep them for six months in a theatre with us. The group would play and characters would emerge from them, and eventually the group would play a very minor role. Maybe about five hundred of the two thousand people would stay during the six months, and we would have filmed all that happened."

Unfortunately, despite all his theorizing, the composition of his audience was the one aspect of *Lifehouse* that Townshend left to chance. In consequence, the shows were attended by a crowd whose collective attention span might not have totaled sixty minutes, much less six months.

"We went into the Young Vic and it started off really well," he said. "The

Young Vic is a workshop-type theatre, it's in the round, very small and very good. We moved in and started to alter the sound, fitted in a quad system and had billions of toys brought in—videos and recording studios and grand pianos and swings and all kinds of stuff. Then one day we got in an audience as an experiment, and they wanted to see the Who's new act. But it wasn't an act, it was an involving process—a new kind of music. But they wouldn't buy it."

"They wanted us to play 'My Generation' and smash the guitars," said John Entwistle, who wouldn't have been against it.

"The first day about fifty skinheads came in and did a dance which I promptly copied," Townshend remembered. "Which is where two boys dance together and they bop one another's shoulders, you lean forward and the two shoulders bop. I thought that was really amazing. Followed closely by this maniac who ran up to the front of the stage like some drug-crazed hippie and started to yell, 'Capitalist pigs! Bastards! Get off the stage!'

"So I lifted him up onto the stage and beat what shit there was left in him out of him. Whereupon he promptly got up again and got on the drums and said, 'I've always wanted to be in a group!' And then went off again and then came back and started to scream. And I suddenly realized the whole thing about it is you almost need the ritual of starting and finishing. So I thought, 'Fuck it, I'm only fooling myself. It was a dream that was only fiction. It's never going to come true.' "

By this stage, the group was also getting bored. Roger was calling Pete every day, "trying to dissuade me from doing the project," Townshend admitted. And Daltrey had the support of Entwistle and Moon. They wanted to patch together a batch of the *Lifehouse* songs and hit the road. "Basically, every tangent we went off on reinforced Roger's stand, which was that the group was perfectly all right as it was and that I shouldn't tamper with it."

It was all too much. "Every technical bridge we came to was very hard to cross, because we were trying to do everything all at once, trying to make the film, invent the new Who, make incredibly big strides in music, write a whole load of new numbers, I was trying to write a film script, we were trying to service a quadraphonic PA, we were up to our ears in it and getting nowhere very fast," Townshend said.

Given this much overload, it's not surprising that he broke down. "In the end, about halfway through the recording, I just phoned up Chris Stamp, our manager, and said, 'Look we've got to knock it on the head. Let's just put out an album, otherwise I really will go crazy.' And I would have done, no doubt about it," Townshend confessed. "I'd be sitting in a room and everybody in the room would suddenly turn into frogs and the whole room would start to go. It was brought on by problems and none of them ever getting solved—not being able to see anything in the distance."

Townshend never abandoned his faith that he was on the right track. "A lot of the things I was talking about were pretty wild then, but now they're common knowledge," he told Barnes, citing the healing properties of music and the idea that each individual carries a specific electrical charge as examples. "Everybody was just treating me as if I was some kind of loony, and

I think for a while I lost touch with reality. The self-control required to prevent my total nervous disintegration was absolutely unbelievable. I had the first nervous breakdown of my life."

The crash of *Lifehouse* was disorienting to almost everyone involved with the Who. Townshend's guise as the infallible rock maestro was demolished, as was the increasing tendency for the rest of the band to accept him as their de facto leader. "I mean, basically it just wasn't right that Pete should have had all that responsibility. It should have been put into the hands of someone who knew about the process of film making. . . . I mean, okay, we all had our heads with him and the script was very good, but I think it was pretty obvious it wasn't going to work," Roger said.

It would be going too far to say that Daltrey needed Townshend's failure at this stage. But the dismal end of *Lifehouse* worked to his advantage by restoring the spurious "balance" established when Roger had been readmitted to the band in 1965. *Lifehouse* was Pete Townshend's baby, and it's unlikely that the rest of the band had even been consulted much; there were no Entwistle songs in it, there was no major role for Daltrey or Moon, except as members of the group, and the group was peripheral to the main plot.

Townshend never quite recovered from the *Lifehouse* debacle. He lost some of his faith in rock, some of his faith in the Who and a great deal of his self-confidence. "What happened, in a way, is that I think maybe the group isn't capable of doing it now—although I think it was wrong not to try," he said in late 1971. "Basically, the group felt that we were better waving the banner for the Who and the sixties, that we weren't attempting to do anything new because we weren't capable of it. I mean, that's like asking the Who to be the new Beatles. And I thought we were capable of doing that. But then, I think the Who are the Who are the Who and we're pretty much stuck with that. And if we want to do anything different, we're going to have to break up, because we've got too many preconceptions of ourselves and we're too much ingrained in our own sort of history."

Along with the others, Pete opted to keep the band together, not because they were his closest musical companions (they no longer were—for one thing, he was working with other Baba-inspired musicians, notably Ronnie Lane and Billy Nicholls), not for the money alone (*Tommy* would provide him with sufficient income for years), but because he was attached in the most powerful, symbolic and idealistic way to the idea of the Who and the sixties.

That doesn't mean that he had become a self-parodying Chuck Berry figure. The fifties symbolized nothing especially important, at best only nostalgia for lost youth. The sixties represented a set of principles. The Who and its music now stood for those principles. Pete Townshend believed wholeheartedly in that time and in its ideals.

The issue now became what to do with the huge quantity of music that was left over from the *Lifehouse* demos. In March 1971, Kit Lambert and the band went to New York to attempt to remix a few of the songs under Lambert's direction. These sessions were completely unproductive. Not only was Townshend in the midst of his breakdown, but Moon was also uncontrollable. Link Wray, the fifties rock & roll guitarist who had been one of Townshend's idols, dropped by the studio one night and was greeted by a naked Moon who ran up and hugged him, which took Link by surprise, since they were utter strangers.

The failure of this session marked an irrevocable turning point in the band's relationship with Kit Lambert, especially since they immediately turned to Glyn Johns to produce an album. Lambert had never forgiven Glyn for taking Shel Talmy's side during that dispute.

Lambert's hostility to Johns was reciprocated, but on a professional rather than personal basis. As a professional engineer, Glyn Johns thought of Kit as the worst kind of amateur, one who mucked up great music. "I thought they were atrocious. Absolutely atrocious—amateur night," Glyn said of Lambert's Who records. "I think *Tommy* is absolutely atrocious from a sound point of view. Embarrassing. I mean, Kit Lambert didn't have any idea whatsoever about how to make a record—none. The band would dispute that, and more power to 'em. But I mean from an engineering point of view, from a sound point of view. I'm sure he had wonderful ideas and he was a very explosive character. And I know, because Pete's told me on numerous occasions—they all have—that he did come up with great ideas and he was a great influence on the band. But he didn't know how to make records—not from an engineering point of view, at any rate."

Glyn Johns had helped define that perspective. He was the first of the great British engineer/producers, establishing his reputation by working on records as profoundly influential as the Rolling Stones' *Beggars' Banquet*, *Let It Bleed*, *Sticky Fingers*, *Get Yer Ya Ya's Out* and *Exile on Main Street*; the first Led Zeppelin LP; Steve Miller's first four albums, including the brilliant *Sailor* and *Brave New World*; Joe Cocker's first three albums, including his live set, *Mad Dogs and Englishmen*; Traffic's debut LP; and the Beatles' *Let It Be*. These are among the most celebrated recordings of the period, and the live material represents a new dimension of recorded concert sound.

Since *Lifehouse* was basically conceived as a concert project, the Who decided to call Johns in. "We felt that no one else could handle the Who live as well as he could," said Townshend. "Plus the fact that he designed the Stones' mobile studio, which was what we were going to be working in. I talked to him a few times about it, and he got really excited."

"It was done on a very open basis," said Johns. "There was no deal struck, there was no categorization at all. It was not, 'Will you please produce our next album?' It was, 'How about it? How shall we do it?' They weren't going to jump in the deep end and say, 'Please be our producer.' They just wanted to try it.

"So I said, 'Tell you what we'll do—we'll go and do a week's worth of sessions. If you're not pleased at the end, you can have whatever we do free, gratis and for nothing, without any ties, connections or monies or anything else. And if you do like, we'll have a coproduction deal.' " (Glyn got only an associate producer credit on the album, *Who's Next*, though.)

They did the test run at Mick Jagger's country house, Stargroves, where the Rolling Stones' mobile studio was parked. They worked on one song, "Won't Get Fooled Again," one of the numbers Townshend had created around the new ARP 2600 synthesizer, playing his guitar through an "envelope follower." (The synthesizer track on the finished recording is the same one that's on the demo.) "We did a test run, and it was fucking incredible," Townshend recalled. "So Glyn said, 'If you like it here, I really wish you'd let me have a try at Olympic, because it would be amazing at Olympic.' This is where he usually works in England. So we just went in there for four days. Just a casual thing, to try out what we wanted to do. We did six numbers in four days—finished. Went in a week later and did another six. Went in a week later, did another six. We were just churning the stuff out. We had enough for two albums when we were finished."

When *Lifehouse* crashed, it was Glyn's enthusiasm that kept the music alive. "I said, 'There's no problem, why don't we just make an album out of the tunes, because the tunes are *great*,' " Pete said. "So that's what we did."

Johns saw the *Lifehouse* demos as a genuine breakthrough, even if the Who themselves would never quite agree. "Pete came up with sounds—synthesizer basics—for tracks which were just unbelievable. Nobody had done it before in that way, and it was amazing to work with. I mean, like anybody, I have to be inspired by what I'm working with in some way in order to bring out the best in myself. And everything on that record was an incredible inspiration."

The Who turned the song selection over to Johns and decided to have him mix only a single disc. "When we went to listen to the album," Pete said, "we were all in the same room, and we knew we were going to stay together. Everybody had gotten over their hang-ups, and we felt that we'd got over the hump of the hill only to see the same hill there. But at least we were still together on the other side. So Glyn played us the album the way he thought it should be, and we said, 'Great. Put it out.' "

The band felt that *Who's Next* was nothing more than a salvage job: Daltrey said he felt they'd "lost one bollock," and Entwistle was never happy with his bass sound. Glyn Johns knew better. "I think it stands up purely and simply on its musicality. Certainly not on anything to do with concept. You'd never know there was a story involved. It's not necessary."

In terms of establishing a sound and sticking to it, *Who's Next* is by far the most consistent album the Who ever made. Townshend's use of synthesizers was as breath-taking as Glyn Johns claimed, and the power and clarity of its best songs was nothing less than awesome. Moon continued to amaze, especially on the final two songs, "Behind Blue Eyes" and "Won't Get Fooled Again." Daltrey's singing throughout the record again reaches a new peak—more than anyone else in the band, Roger grew better with each record. Entwistle's bass playing is flawless and exciting; his only songwriting contribution, "My Wife," is hilarious, even though it lacks the dynamism of the stage version. Townshend not only contributed the first intelligent use of synthesizers in white rock (Stevie Wonder made a similar breakthrough around the same time), his guitar work seems liberated by his freer use of keyboards (piano as well as the ARP), the vocal arrangements are sometimes beautiful ("Behind Blue Eyes" is majestic) and the best of the lyrics are pointed and poignant.

There seems to have been a conscious effort to keep the album from having any kind of lyrical concept or story line. In a way, it reemphasizes the importance of the link in *sound* among the songs. On the other hand, the inclusion of "Love Ain't For Keeping," "Getting In Tune" and even "Going Mobile" is questionable, especially since much stronger material was available. There is nothing half-hearted or forced on *Who's Next*, as there is on *Tommy*. Each of the weak songs has something to recommend it: the wit of "Going Mobile," Daltrey's vocal in "Getting In Tune," the singing and acoustic guitar on "Love Ain't For Keeping."

Ultimately, it's only knowing what was left off *Who's Next* that makes sense of the band's frustration. Otherwise, the record just feels erratic, nothing uncommon for the Who. But here the lack of consistency reflects a retreat from ambition.

In the three years after *Who's Next* came out, the Who released six songs also written for *Lifehouse*. Of these, "Put the Money Down" and "Too Much of Anything" are basically program numbers (although both are rather amusing expositions of the basic rock star dilemma).

Of the other unused *Lifehouse* numbers, three were issued as singles: "Let's See Action," in November 1971; "Join Together," in June 1972; and "Relay" in November 1972. The fourth, "Pure and Easy," appeared on *Odds and Sods*, the album of Who leftovers assembled by John Entwistle in 1974 (which also included "Put the Money Down" and "Too Much of Anything").

"Let's See Action," "Join Together," "Relay" and "Pure and Easy" are all outstanding Townshend songs, exciting Who performances and major statements of Townshend's thinking about rock, religion, politics and the future. (The personal importance of "Let's See Action" and "Pure and Easy" is emphasized by their inclusion—in altered versions—on Townshend's solo collection, *Who Came First*, released in 1972.)

Townshend has described "Pure and Easy," the most beautiful of these songs, as "the central pivot of Lifehouse." Its importance is so great that the opening lines of the song are actually sung by Daltrey as "Song Is Over" fades out at the end of side one of *Who's Next*.

"Pure and Easy" is a ballad whose lyric concerns the celebrated lost note that symbolizes mankind's loss of harmony with the universe. Many have written about this legend, but few have expressed their longing so beautifully as Townshend:

There once was a note, pure and easy,
Playing so free like a breath rippling by,
The note is eternal, I hear it, it sees me,
Forever we blend and forever we die

If "Naked Eye" is a song about the loss of faith, the inability to live up to the most extreme potential of humanity, "Pure and Easy" is an even more profoundly moving portrait of the constant hope that that possibility will be achieved, of the acceptance of life's horror, of coming to terms with human frailty without wallowing in blame or guilt. It is Peter Townshend's greatest statement of his beliefs; it is perhaps rock's greatest song of faith. And it would have completed *Who's Next* perfectly in terms of its sound, its tempo, its vocals and its message.

"Let's See Action," "Join Together" and "Relay" are all rockers, all concerned with the political subtext of *Lifehouse*. "Let's See Action" is superficially self-explanatory, an exhortatory call-to-arms. But the third verse and coda are a round: "Nothing is/Everything/Everything is/Nothing is," which when repeated as a chant ("Nothing is everything") echoes Meher Baba. (One of the collections of Baba's teachings is entitled *The Everything and the Nothing*, and "Nothing Is Everything" is the title Townshend gives the song on *Who Came First*.)

With its jaunty piano, folkish melody and Daltrey's gritty vocal, plus the confusion of political and religious imagery, "Let's See Action" is reminiscent of nothing so much as a Bob Dylan song. Similarly, "Join Together," with its jawbone synthesizer and incredibly precise ensemble playing, echoes the Band. This music feels alive, the players working off each other with a rare kind of empathy, the sort that may or may not be conscious but certainly can't be communicated in words. The vocals and harmonies snap against one another like synchronized machinery, and the drumming and guitars play tight patterns that are rare in the Who's rather loose repertoire. Once more, the song is a statement of purpose:

It's the singer not the song
That makes the music move along,
It's the biggest band you'll find,
It's as deep as it is wide

One could hardly ask for a better description of what happens at the peak of a great rock concert or for a clearer statement that it is not only the audience who benefits when that state is reached.

"Relay" is not as much of a statement, although it does present an argument against the kind of control represented by experience suits. Again, the sound is incredibly live and is probably the closest to funky the Who ever got; Moon rides the backbeat all the way.

These songs should have been included on *Who's Next*—not because they would have saved it but because they could have perfected it. Even without them, the album contains three Townshend masterpieces—"Baba O'Riley," "Behind Blue Eyes" and "Won't Get Fooled Again"—plus a pair of exceptionally fine songs, "Bargain" and "Song Is Over" and one of Entwistle's most memorable compositions, "My Wife."

With the exception of "My Wife," all these songs tie into the *Lifehouse* story.

"Baba O'Riley" was meant to be the first piece in the movie; "Song Is Over" was the last. "Behind Blue Eyes" was the theme song of a villainous character, Brick, and its mixture of self-righteousness and self-pity is the best Townshend character study since *The Who Sell Out*, so good that it was taken by many to be autobiographical. "Won't Get Fooled Again" ranks with "My Generation," "I Can See For Miles" and "Pinball Wizard" as one of the Who's major anthems of rock & roll power and anger.

Several of the songs have religious subtexts: "Bargain" is nothing less than a prayer, as is the bridge of "Behind Blue Eyes," although that's the most furious prayer ever sent to heaven. The final lines of "Song is Over" ("The song is over, I'm left with only fear/I must remember, even if it takes a million years") are a much more powerful description of Divine Desperation than all of "The Seeker" (they're as good as "Mighty Quinn"). Here, Townshend masters the kind of sentimentality he wanted in "See Me, Feel Me," makes it work for him as an effective statement of his convictions—not an argument for them, but simply an unignorable assertion of what they are.

The most extraordinary music on *Who's Next* comes at the beginning with the very first song, "Baba O'Riley," and at the end with "Behind Blue Eyes" and "Won't Get Fooled Again."

Townshend said that "Baba O'Riley" was the model for most of the music in the film "because we have a prerecorded tape of a synthesizer in the background." Actually, that synthesizer is in the song's foreground, and it carries the first thirty seconds of the song solo, an exceptionally long period in a rock song. The synthesizer is then joined, successively, by piano, drums and voice together with a fat electric bass. The guitar comes in with crushing chords at the end of the first verse. Only at this point does the synthesizer cease to be the center of attention—and then not for long, since Townshend sings the song's bridge ("Don't cry, don't raise your eye/It's only teen-age wasteland") against just the synthesizer riff.

The contrast and tension between Townshend's wistful, high voice and Daltrey's guttural, bitterly angry shout is one of the dominant characteristics of *Who's Next*, and it is never more powerful than in these opening moments, when Daltrey sings "Teenage wasteland/It's only teenage wasteland/ - They're all wasted!" A few seconds later, he sets up an image of himself that goes beyond the *Tommy* characterization. Now he is the definitive macho rock singer, yowling not in complaint or even protest so much as asserting that he feels anguished at the state of his life—or everyone's.

"Baba O'Riley" takes its title from Meher Baba and composer Terry Riley, Townshend's original electronic music inspiration. The synthesizer part used in the album track is a fragment from a much longer synthesizer solo on Townshend's demo; a nine-minute piece of this solo is included on the Meher Baba tribute LP, *I Am*, and it is intoxicating. "Baba O'Riley" gives only a hint of what Townshend could really do with his new instrument, although it's certainly impressive, anyway.

"Behind Blue Eyes" and "Won't Get Fooled Again" are based on staple

315

rock & roll emotions: sanctimonious self-pity and marginally political rage. These songs are high-tech rock a full decade or more before that term gained currency, born and bred from synthesizers ruling the backbeat. But there isn't a thing robotic about either of them—if nothing else made sure of that, Keith Moon would have.

In fact, the drums are absent from the first two verses of "Behind Blue Eyes," more than two minutes, almost certainly the longest period that Keith Moon was ever still in his entire life. But Moon's entrance, when he makes it, is worth any wait—riding right alongside a taut guitar riff, kicking all the props out from under the song's solemnity. Up to this point, the song has been soft, folkish in its plain melodicism and simple statements of suffering and anxiety. Then the drums thunder in, slicing away along with the razor-edge guitar, and the lines Daltrey snarls above that snapping percussion are vows; there is no way to avoid them:

When my fist clenches, crack it open
Before I use it and lose my cool,
When I smile, tell me some bad news
Before I laugh and act like a fool.
If I swallow anything evil,
Put your fingers down my throat,
If I shiver please give me a blanket,
Keep me warm, let me wear your coat

This part of "Behind Blue Eyes" brilliantly unites Townshend's spiritual vision with a topic that had obsessed him since mod days: the crumbling of identity in the face of a loss of cool or control, the importance of maintaining a facade and the terror of not being able to.

"Behind Blue Eyes" ends in shimmering echo, Daltrey's vocal and Townshend's harmony in perfect synch. "Won't Get Fooled Again" picks up in the same mood, with a few bars of synthesizer riffing before a guitar explodes, followed by the thud of Moon's drums and the atomic rumble of Entwistle's bass. Moon serves primarily as a timekeeper here, but he's still one of the crucial elements of the music, making his human and headstrong beat an effective counterpoint to the unchanging, unrelenting waves of synthesizer.

As the song builds to the first bridge, the music becomes almost a competition between the new voice of the Who (the ARP) and its old one (Keith's entire drum kit). Everything else in the song is merely a comment upon this struggle between the human and the mechanical. Even when Daltrey utters his victory yell, it's hard to tell who (or what) has won. The lyric says that nothing has—that everything is still the same. But the music denies that, too.

The second bridge is a different sort of battle—Moon is all over his kit, Townshend is playing tense, surging chords on the guitar and the synthesizer lays back, then charges, shuttling between foreground and background until finally the humans fall away, exhausted. For long seconds, the ARP thrums, monotonous, inexorable, inhumanly hypnotic. Then from Moon, a cascading thump around the kit. Another. A third. And Daltrey comes back with the greatest scream of a career filled with screams, a scream that marks a new era in the music—or at least, the end of an old one.

There is nothing quite like the tension that builds as that synthesizer circles its prey, and there's nothing (or anyway, not very much) to match the triumph of the moment when Keith Moon bashes his way back into the picture. When Roger Daltrey follows his scream with the lyrics Townshend wrote to condemn the revolution ("Meet the new boss/Same as the old boss"), he is also celebrating the triumph of the old values of rock in the new clothes Townshend has cut for them. There's blood in those words and in Daltrey's singing of them, but there's genuine love there, as well.

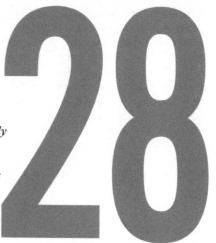

*Chorus had failed miserably
in the East. He had made what
one critic called a "valiant"
attempt to restore the Chorus
to its rightful role. They shut
down his act even though it
was receiving rave reviews. . . .
Of course, there were roles still
open to him, but they were mostly
commercial. Plugging things
he didn't believe in. Puffing
nobodies. . . . But Chorus kept his
optimism, even though nobody
wanted to buy his scripts.*
            —Ishmael Reed,
The Last Days of Louisiana Red

"Won't Get Fooled Again" was issued as a single on June 25, 1971. ("I Don't Know Myself," one of the EP leftovers, was the B-side.) The single version was cut in half, with all the song's drama eviscerated. Yet even this garbled version dominated the airwaves with the freshness of its sound. Cynics who had declared that the synthesizer was too arty-farty ever to find a place in *real* rock & roll boiled down their slogans and swallowed them in a lump.

When *Who's Next* was issued in mid-July, the response was equally enthusiastic. Reviewers, radio programmers and fans were all in awe of the album's mastery of modern technology and rock & roll basics. The record was the most immediate success of the Who's career. It appeared at number 50 in *Billboard*'s August 14 chart, jumped to 12 the next week and then to the Top 10, where it stayed through mid-November (though it never surpassed *Tommy*, also peaking at number 4). *Who's Next* stayed in the Top 40 albums charts through January 1972, in the Top 100 through March. It was certified gold on September 16, only about six weeks after its initial release.

Meantime, the Who had gone back out on tour for the first time in more than a year in the States. They played the biggest halls possible: sports arenas, outdoor festivals and amphitheatres, colleges. There were multiple dates in theatres only when nothing more suitable was available. By now, the Who were touring with a quasi-military setup rather than just a couple of roadies. Many more crewmen were needed to handle the quantities of new equipment.

The sound system had originally been designed by Townshend and Bob Pridden for *Lifehouse*. It was far, far larger than anything anybody else was using at the time, offering about 3,000 watts of total power and providing unprecedented clarity and definition to the sound. (The *Who's Next* tour was the only tour in Who history in which the house sound was consistently faultless.) Pridden wrestled with the equipment nightly, however, especially with the monitors, which didn't always give the band the sound they needed to hear each other. "I was just getting used to the normal mixers and I end up with this huge great board which does things without me touching it," Pridden said. "That was in one way the most harrowing experience I've ever had with a mixer. It was a huge challenge."

The size of the Who's entourage had more than doubled. Peter Rudge was with the band full-time now (in the next year, he would move to New York to establish a management office in America for the group). So were a number of others, including Nancy Lewis, as press liaison, and John Wolff, running the band's intricate lighting display. Everyone had assistants, and moving from town to town became an experience closer to moving an army than the old family circus days of traveling in a bus. Not that the hotel wreckage diminished much or that there was any diminution of the wenching and boozing. If anything, these rituals accelerated. After all, they could afford to pay for minor damages now—but that took the edge off them. More spectacular displays became the order of the day, and Moon got very little sleep.

Within the entourage, the actual band members were coddled like a quartet of demiurges. "I've always handled [Pete] with sort of velvet gloves," said Glyn Johns, not too cuddly himself. "I think a lot of people around him do that. The net result is a bit like the king who wore no clothes."

To be more precise, four naked princelings with no one to say them nay. Townshend, simply by virtue of the fact that he surrounded himself with friends as acerbic as Richard Barnes and Ronnie Lane, probably heard more criticism than most pop stars (though much less than any normal man). The others were even more inclined to have their own way, and for Moon, at least, that meant that indulgence piled upon indulgence to the point of satiation and near-collapse. For those to whom the Who were not celebrities, they were employers, and it is even more difficult to deny a boss than a hero.

This hierarchy was just what Townshend had wanted *Lifehouse* to demolish. If the Who did not pay Pete's predicted toll for being pampered for a very long while, it can be attributed to their bickering and intimacy with one another. Much more than most groups, the individuals in the Who told one another what they thought. Townshend made it no secret that he thought Daltrey a blue-eyed lout out to turn the Who into a band of professionals who ground out rock just for the dough. Daltrey didn't hide his anger at Townshend for squandering time and energy on pretentious attempts to justify the unjustifiable and for failing to walk it like he talked it, nor did he conceal his opinion that Entwistle had cheated the band by making a solo album. Entwistle clearly thought the others morons for bickering so much. He didn't say so, but

John carried himself with a certain attitude that stripped away the need for words. As for Moon, he was a true savant, capable of tottering on the brink of alcoholic idiocy and then turning, with a frighteningly clear gaze, to sum up a situation so perfectly that one had to wonder if all the inebriation had not been just an act to hide the complete penetration of his observations. In short, no one escaped being booked for any offense against the Who, rock & roll, profitability, the Rights of Man or any other mortal or venial sin.

Aside from giving one another lip, the Who had almost no offstage relationship at this point. Townshend might stop by Moon's room to instigate a bit of carnage, but he would retire to sleep or read or write before too long. Keith had the crew and hangers-on to fulfill his requirements for craziness. John kept to himself. Roger needed his rest. From time to time, any single band member might break out of his shell, but rarely would they do so all at once.

The Who's concert set was totally revamped. The new material did not eliminate *Tommy*, but it did place the band and its history in a new perspective. Along with large chunks of the new album, highlighted by "My Wife"—which gained strength onstage—"Behind Blue Eyes," "Won't Get Fooled Again" and "Baba O'Riley," with the band playing in perfect synchronization with the prerecorded synthesizer tapes, there was a sort of twenty-minute mini-opera of the best-known *Tommy* numbers. "I Can't Explain" and "My Generation" stayed, as did "Magic Bus." "Young Man," "Summertime Blues" and "Shakin' All Over" went. They were replaced by Marvin Gaye's "Baby Don't You Do It," revived from the band's Tamla soul period, and a ravishing "Pure and Easy," which fit as well with the *Who's Next* material on stage as it should have on disc.

The playing was tighter, harder, more direct than the more expansive and meandering *Tommy* period shows. Now they opened up a vein and then pounded out the pulse for the rest of the night, closing with "My Generation" and even an occasional pulverized guitar—a gesture not obligatory but heartfelt.

The tour was a triumph, even though it began under bleak conditions that seemed to confirm every dire prediction that Pete Townshend had made. The first show was in New York, at Forest Hills Tennis Stadium, an outdoor amphitheatre seating 7,000. On Thursday, July 30, it poured, and as the drenched crowd huddled beneath the stands or under umbrellas and sopping blankets, they could only shiver as they observed the equipment still being put in place. Outside, a young ticket-scalper was stabbed and killed. Inside, the tension grew so great that John Entwistle actually trashed one of his precious Gibson Thunderbird basses, as everyone, including the rest of the band, looked on in disbelief.

There were no repercussions from the Forest Hills stabbing. The press seemed to accept that the hustler had been the victim of New York violence and not anything especially connected to the perils of rock. The crowd inside was content to sit and soak as long as the Who played, a pattern that was maintained throughout, not just on this tour but for the rest of the decade as well. So the Who toured in continuing comfort, and their audience (like all rock audiences in this time) became increasingly irrelevant, except as a means

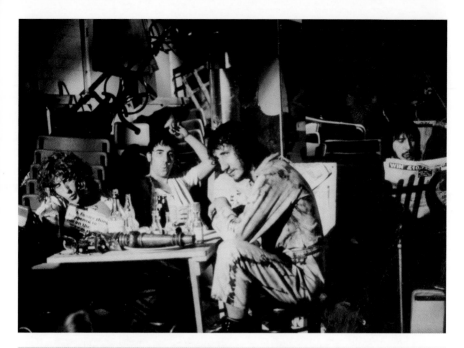

Top: Lifehouse *sessions, 1971. "I think for a while I lost touch with reality. The self-control required to prevent my total nervous disintegration was absolutely unbelievable. I had the first nervous breakdown of my life."*—Pete Townshend. Bottom: *Success at last: collecting gold records for* Who's Next, *1972.* (Trinifold).

Above: *Keith and his daughter, Mandy Moon, 1972. "Keith was unquestionably the funniest man in rock . . . He found life off the road excruciatingly boring and so attempted to carry on as if his life were one long tour."* (London Features International).

Top: *Keith, his wife Kim and daughter Mandy, 1973.* (Trinifold). Bottom: *Roger returns from an American tour in 1976 with his wife Heather and daughters Rosie Lea and Willow Amber.* (Trinifold).

Top: *Backstage, 1974. Left to right: Roger, Bob Pridden, Pete, John, "Wiggy" Wolff and Keith.* (London Features International). Bottom: *During the filming of* Tommy: *Pete Townshend (centre) and Elton John (right) attend a party given by Eric Clapton (left).* (Trinifold).

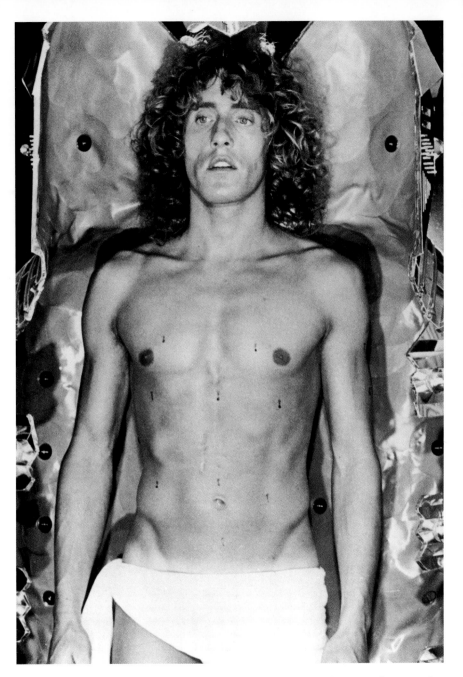

Above: Tommy *reaches the screen, 1975.* "The greatest work of art the twentieth century has produced."—Ken Russell. "Tommy got *even bigger than us:* Tommy *and the Who, then* Tommy. Tommy *comes to town. I've seen that on posters.*"—Pete Townshend. (Trinifold).

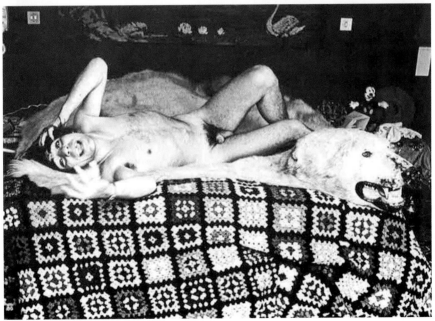

For the Who, Tommy *changed everything. The more conservative Daltrey (top left) and Entwistle (bottom left) saved, living well but within their means. Townshend (top right) felt "embarrassed" to have grown so wealthy and Moon (bottom right) spent everything he could get his hands on. (Trinifold/Pennie Smith/Shepard Sherbell).*

Above: *"Although Keith Moon was the mainspring of the band's style and knew it, he remained unsure of his position—in the band and in life."* (Trinifold).

Top: *UK tour, 1975. "Back to Basics."* Bottom: *US tour, Oakland, California, 1976.* (Trinifold).

Top: *Backstage with the Who's new manager, Bill Curbishley, Oakland, California, 1976.* (Trinifold).
Bottom: *Pete with Ronnie Lane during recording sessions for* Rough Mix, *1977.* (London Features International).

Top: *Punks meet the Godfather. Pete with Sex Pistols Paul Cook and Steve Jones, 1977.* (Trinifold).
Bottom: Who Are You *cover sessions, 1978. Peter Townshend: "I feel maybe we should try to prove
to people and new bands—particularly since the new wave bands are so assertive in their
attitudes—that it is possible to grow within the rock biz; to grow old gracefully and to evolve in a
way that doesn't lose the spirit of things."* (Trinifold).

"By 1978 Moon had become a national celebrity, regarded as an eccentric in the grand British tradition." Top: *With Entwistle and Townshend on the film set for* The Kids Are Alright, *Shepperton, May 25, 1978.* (Dennis O'Regan). Bottom: *Keith's last night out,* September 6, 1978. *After the premiere of* The Buddy Holly Story *Keith and his girlfriend, Annette Walter-Lax, arrive at a party given by Paul McCartney at Peppermint Park, London.*

Above: *Pete, Roger and John (standing behind Keith's mother) attend Keith Moon's funeral on September 14, 1978. "No human being can ever take Keith's place. We love him and he's gone."* —Pete Townshend.

Top: *The 'New Who' performed at Riverfront Coliseum in Cincinnati on December 3, 1979. It was rock's worst concert disaster.* (Popperfoto). Bottom: *The 'New Who' at a launch party for* Face Dances, *March, 1981. Left to right: Kenney Jones, Roger, artist Peter Blake, Pete and John.* (Trinifold).

Top: *On the road again, 1981, Pete entertaining Kenney Jones' son.* (Pennie Smith). Bottom: *The beginning of the American farewell tour, Shea Stadium, New York, Autumn 1982.* (Andy Freeberg/ Retna Ltd).

Above: *The American farewell tour ended in Toronto on December 20, 1982. The last concert? Roger and Pete leave the stage.* (Trinifold).

of footing the bills. The bonds between band and fan were severed now; in a world without true connections, only shallow symbols remained. The moment to replace them had passed. The tour closed in Chicago with Townshend demolishing two guitars at once, battering the ruins of one with another until both shattered into tiny splinters. They had played to more than 700,000 fans.

Back in Britain, the Who took two weeks off and began a tour filled with omens and memories. It opened on September 18 at the Oval, the cricket ground in Kennington, south London, where 35,000 fans turned out to see the Who, the Faces (reformed with Rod Stewart and Ron Wood), Lindisfarne and America play a benefit for the starving masses of Bangladesh. Though it received far less attention than the George Harrison benefits staged at Madison Square Garden earlier that summer, the Who and their comrades raised as much or more money for the cause—and theirs got into the hands of the UNICEF officials and to Bangladesh itself much more swiftly. Aside from that, Kennington was just another rock concert–the performers utterly divorced from the crowd.

The U.K. tour also ended in London, where the Who opened a new rock theatre, the Rainbow, in Finsbury Park, at the north end of town. (The Rainbow's owner was John Morris, the entrepreneur who had conned Townshend into playing Woodstock.)

Two weeks later, they were back in the States, where they played universities and arenas in the south and far west, regions they'd skipped on the summer tour. The tour wound up in Seattle, on December 15. It was the last the Who would see of the concert stage for eight months, the last time they'd play in America for almost two years.

In October 1971, *Meaty, Beaty, Big and Bouncy*, another compilation of singles, was released. *Meaty Beaty* included virtually all the singles from "I Can't Explain" to "The Seeker," a complete collection made possible because Shel Talmy's rights to the material he had produced had finally expired. In that sense, the release was celebratory, a memorial of emancipation. (Talmy must have been more amazed than anyone else at the wealth the Who had brought him.)

The release of *Meaty Beaty* wasn't without turmoil. The album was sent to the pressing plant without Kit Lambert seeing it, and he was away in America when it went into the shops. Upon his return, Lambert attempted to have the record suppressed on the grounds that it was improperly sequenced and because he disagreed with some of the songs selected. Lambert actually succeeded in getting Polydor (Track's distributor) to withdraw the album for two days, but too many copies had been distributed for the changes he wanted to be made, and the original went back on sale.

This incident was indicative of a growing rift between Lambert and the group. Kit had been a great manager at the start of the Who's career, when promotional savvy and sheer guts had been the keys to survival. But he was in no way able to cope with the band's success, and he had little sympathy with Townshend's more serious ambitions. Kit Lambert's sensibility ran to stunts, pranks, in-jokes, the outrageous and the marginal. The kind of mainstream success that Daltrey thirsted for—which Townshend wanted in order to give his music real social power—seemed worthlessly chimerical to their manager. Nor was Lambert particularly interested in the nuts and bolts of running a professional rock band's career. Once the Who grew financially stable, he became more and more bored with the process of grinding out more hits, more tours, more albums, more hype. Unlike Townshend, Kit was not motivated to revolutionize the music industry. He dawdled, began dabbling with drugs, indulged his gay epicurianism to the extreme.

The deepest source of the split between the manager and the group was probably over the issue of production. Lambert felt that the significance of his role in organizing and structuring *Tommy* had never been adequately credited or understood. Pete had always said that he would have been unable to write *Tommy* without Lambert's assistance but that often wound up sounding like Kit's contribution was simply coining the term rock opera. Which was far from the truth. In fact, outside of the basic composition and performance, *Tommy* was in several ways Kit Lambert's work, with its bombastic songs and absurdist story elements. "There are parts of *Tommy* that we don't identify with directly because musically they aren't the way we'd do them, but on the other hand, I'm sure without Kit Lambert's production, it would never have been the triumph it is in terms of record sales and success," Townshend said.

Beyond that, Lambert was annoyed that Townshend had abandoned the idea of making *Tommy* a film, that he had then been bounced as the band's producer and that his replacement had turned out to be his old nemesis, Glyn Johns. "We knew that his pride was going to be hurt by us producing ourselves, but at the same time we knew that it was the only thing that could be done," Townshend said. "Before that we'd been working in my studios trying to get singles and bits and pieces together, and when it didn't work, we called Kit back in again, but he's always known on what basis he was being called in." That apparently meant that the group had been working with Lambert only experimentally. When Lambert proved technically incapable, he was shunted aside. Lambert saw the Who's future as working with film and orchestras, making them more elaborate and baroque than any other rock group. The band (including Townshend, for all his flights of fancy) wanted to get back to the basics. It boiled down to this: The Who liked rock & roll and trusted it. Lambert tolerated rock and looked down upon it.

"It has got to the point where Kit still has bigger ambitions for us," Townshend said when *Who's Next* was finished and he could look around himself again. "We are at the point where the last thing we are thinking about is image. Yet Kit's still talking about concerts on the moon. . . . I think when Kit realized we were unhappy with him, he was hurt and opted out completely rather than take a downward slide. We just generally moved apart. We think completely differently now."

One result of this division of interests was that Lambert began to act more like a manager and recording executive and less as the group's companion and consultant. Another was that the band, especially Roger Daltrey, began a much closer investigation of the Who's business affairs, particularly its finances. The result of that scrutiny was inevitable, though it did not quickly unfold. Lambert was no sharp businessman, and he was not so much dishonest as devil-may-care. But managers—by law, and ethically, as well—take on the responsibilities of other persons' lives at considerable risk and while incurring great obligations. And if these aren't met, a price is paid.

While the Who had never been very prolific, 1972 was nothing less than a lost year. The records released were old material: "Let's See Action" was issued in England in November 1971 and made the British Top 20. "Behind Blue Eyes" came out at the same time in the States but only stumbled into the middle 30s on the *Billboard* chart. In June 1972, the band issued another of the *Lifehouse* leftovers, "Join Together," along with a live version of "Baby Don't You Do It." "Join Together" made the British and American Top 20, though that wasn't especially impressive for a group of the Who's stature. Their records were *expected* to do well, now that they were superstars. When the final *Lifehouse* reject, "Relay" (coupled with Keith Moon's powerful and hilarious "Waspman") failed to make even the Top 20 in England and barely cracked the *Billboard* Top 40, *that* was news. It was also trouble.

The Who had frittered away the year waiting for Townshend to become inspired. They had actually begun recording some new material, among it the *Lifehouse* leftovers, with Glyn Johns at Stargroves in May. The results were basic tracks for a complete album—in fact, enough material for a double set. But it never appeared, because the band felt "it sounded like the shadow of *Who's Next*," as Townshend put it. Five of the tracks were actually completed, and all of them ("Join Together," "Water," "Relay," "Love Reign O'er Me," "Is It In My Head") would eventually be issued.

The rejection of this album reflected the group's continuing uneasiness about *Who's Next*. "It was pretty much an exhausted relationship [with Glyn Johns] at the time," Pete said. There was also Townshend's mental condition to consider. "My problem was severe paranoia. I was very worried about being emotionally and creatively burned by losing so much work in the *Lifehouse* thing." Everyone was holding back to see if Pete could come up with another workable blockbuster. "Our main goal was to produce something which would give us some substance for our stage act, because we'd drained all our material dry," Townshend said.

One part of the unreleased album was a mini-opera, which would occupy a full side of one disc. This was called "Long Live Rock—Rock Is Dead," which Townshend later identified as the germ of what became *Quadrophenia*.

"I went off and started working on that," he told Robin Denselow that autumn, "and really got excited about the idea I had, put about fourteen or fifteen songs together and went rushing back and said, 'Listen, I'm not going to play this stuff, but I can tell you what I've got knocks shit out of what we have already done, so let's shelve all that, put a couple of old songs out as singles and I'll incorporate some others and we could do a new opera.' " That was what everyone wanted to hear, so Pete went to work.

Meantime, Entwistle worked on his second solo album, *Whistle Rymes*, which was released in November to a more lukewarm critical and commercial reception than *Smash Your Head Against the Wall* had received. (The songs were the usual gruesome and belligerent Ox offerings, but the music was stick-in-the-mud heavy rock.)

Keith Moon occupied himself with alcohol, pills and marital strife. He smashed up cars, drank and stripped in pubs and restaurants and on the motorways of Western Europe. He disappeared for days—gone off to Copenhagen, he later confessed—then turned up, remorseful but still drunk.

No one questioned Keith's behavior. They simply marveled that he was able to inflict so much varied abuse upon himself and continue to function. Ups and downs until his eyes crossed, brown ale, champagne, brandy and ginger and no sleep all seemed to leave Moon unscathed no matter how hard he pushed his luck or in what dangerous combinations he combined these vices. Keith Moon seemed indestructible.

He was also miserable and isolated and, more than anything, lonesome. The Who did not fraternize when they weren't working, and Keith preferred hotel life any day to being alone.

"...It's amazing how much you miss them," Keith said wistfully to *Melody Maker*'s Chris Charlesworth that April. Moon came out of his shell only once all year, when he was asked to portray a rock drummer playing behind Billy Fury in the film *That'll Be the Day*, a role he performed with such panache that he nearly stole the show. But that wasn't on until late in the year. Meantime, he roamed lonely.

In East Burwash, near the Kent/Sussex border, where Roger Daltrey now lived, there was pacing and fuming, agitation and upset. Daltrey believed in work. He needed it, and he had no serious ambitions outside of the Who. In his mind, this was the greatest rock band in the world, and being its singer was not only what he did, it was who he was. The concept of solo albums and film careers was not especially appealing to him. But by the end of the year, Roger felt so stir-crazy, he began working on solo material, anyway.

As part of his involvement with the English Meher Baba group he had established in Richmond, Townshend had been involved with two albums of tributes to his spiritual Master. The first of these, *Happy Birthday*, was released in February 1970 on what would have been Baba's seventy-seventh birthday; *I Am*, which contained the nine-minute "Baba O'Riley" track, was issued the next year. Both were pressed in limited initial editions of 2,500 copies each, distributed to Baba-lovers only. But they reached the hands of Who fans and rare record speculators. Soon they were selling in record shops in the States for up to fifteen dollars (about six pounds).

Technically, these albums were bootlegs, and MCA Records (Decca's new name) got upset about them. Townshend wasn't especially concerned, since the Baba message was reaching even more people. However, when MCA offered to release an official limited edition of the record just to undercut the bootleggers, Townshend was naturally attracted. Though the record would appear as a Pete Townshend solo album, all the money generated by it would go to Baba. Pete became wrapped up in the project.

Townshend had not always been the dominant figure on the Baba albums. They included poetry, comic monologues, and all sorts of music, from folkish airs to experimental noises. *Happy Birthday* included a Townshend song called "Day of Silence," his demo for "The Seeker," another song about Baba entitled "The Love Man," and his cracked-voice version of "Begin the Beguine," as well as music by Ronnie Lane and others. *I Am* included only one Townshend song, "Baba O'Riley" in its nine-minute instrumental version, although Townshend did set to music "Parvardigar," a prayer written by Baba, and he played on several more tracks.

Pete could have simply selected from the material here and assembled an interesting sampler that would have served MCA's purpose as well as his own (and presumably Meher Baba's). But nothing in Pete Townshend's life could be so simple. He went back into the studio and spruced up a number of his solo demos, including "Pure and Easy" and "Let's See Action" (retitled "Nothing Is Everything"), wrote two new songs, "Sheraton Gibson" and "Time Is Passing," and held onto the two poems he had set to music, "Parvardigar" and "Content" (the latter based on a poem by Maud Kennedy). He added a version of "There's a Heartache Following Me"—a Jim Reeves song that was (along with "Begin the Beguine") Baba's favorite Western song.

The album also included "Evolution," by Ronnie Lane (which was a different arrangement of "The Stone" by the Faces), and "Forever's No Time At All," with lyrics by Kate McInnerney and music by Billy Nicholls, a Baba-loving cohort of Townshend and the Faces. The package also included a poster of a Mike McInnerney painting, several photos of Baba and a front-cover photo, taken by Graham Hughes (Daltrey's cousin), of Townshend standing on several dozen uncracked eggs wearing a white boiler suit with a grimly serious expression on his bearded face—the very antithesis of "Don't worry, be happy."

Who Came First wasn't a best-seller, but it sold many times what the privately issued Baba LPs would have, and it gave reviewers a new and fascinating picture of Townshend's capacities. In this regard, the album was a complete success. At this juncture, Townshend was the one member of the band with any hope of eventual autonomy from the group. That's a useful option, even if you don't plan to exercise it.

Townshend was still mentally and emotionally exhausted from the *Lifehouse* crisis, determined to prove that the debacle had nothing to do with his abilities as a pop composer, rock theorist or film conceptualizer. In fact, one of the plans afoot during 1972 was to have Nik Cohn write a story called *Guitar Farm*, based on experiences Cohn would have while touring with the band and then living with them at each of their homes for a few days. (However, Cohn declined the opportunity. Instead, Denis Postle wrote a script for the band's tentative deal at Warner Bros.)

"It won't be just about a group on the road," said Daltrey. "We want a film that will reflect what Rock means to the Who and to the general public." Rock was becoming a totemic phrase around the band; invoking the term offered allusions to the whole complex of sixties countercultural values that the surviving bands of that era (particularly the Stones and the Who) came to symbolize. *Rock*, in the sense Daltrey used it, stood for a philosophy that had to do with the milieu around the music more than any specific sound. (Of course, it also offered a convenient way to pay lip service to such values without ever articulating them clearly enough to be pinned down to anything specific.)

"We need a totally new medium to expose the group," Townshend still insisted. "I think the cinema reaches people in a far more intense way, and achieving that end is now top priority." Whether Townshend actually believed this is debatable—but it wasn't true. The Who didn't need a movie to sustain their success, which was now self-perpetuating. And no form of culture reached people more intensely than rock: There was no equivalent of Woodstock in the cinema, and all the closest analogies in terms of the popular power of film were from decades before World War II. The Who may have been desperate to make a movie because it offered prestige (only the biggest pop acts ever got to the screen) or a certain kind of cultural respectability (rock was farce, but cinema was accepted as a *serious* mass art). But cinema had nothing to do with intensifying the relationship of the artist to the audience.

Such issues were at the heart of Townshend's "Long Live Rock" opera. If he could not explicitly connect his attraction of rock to mysticism, Townshend would, then, attempt to define and delineate why the music held so many so powerfully. Gradually, this idea (the "Long Live Rock" opera) began to reshape itself into something else. During the summer, Irish Jack got back in touch, and Townshend found his thoughts turning to mod. By August 26, when Townshend did an interview with *Melody Maker*'s Michael Watts, *Quadrophenia* was already taking shape.

But Townshend was not zeroing in on the opera. It didn't take much to distract him, and through the fall and early winter, as new projects kept presenting themselves, Townshend became wrapped up in each one. Pete made no conscious decision to dabble and explore other avenues. Instinctively, however, he reached for side issues that could alleviate the strain of following *Tommy* and justify the fall of *Lifehouse*.

Pete Townshend was no dilettante. When he got involved, he became immersed. That summer, when American impresario Lou Reizner (who had produced Rod Stewart's first solo album) proposed doing an orchestral LP of *Tommy* with the London Symphony Orchestra and Chamber Choir, Townshend was immediately hooked. (He had avoided becoming involved with the *Tommy* ballet performed by Les Grands Ballets Canadiens in New York that spring, but only because it was almost three thousand miles away.)

About the last thing Townshend needed was to become involved with an orchestra. The Who's reputation and much of his own rested on rock & roll purism, the ability to define all of their ambition within the context of the basic rock quartet. As a composer, though, Townshend could hardly resist. The LSO was 104 pieces, the Chamber Choir 60 voices.

Reizner's plan was to hire well-known pop singers to play each of the characters. The Who's *Tommy* had always been circumscribed by the group's three voices and three instruments. Even though he had rejected Kit Lambert's plan to orchestrate the original, Townshend still burned to know what his music would sound like with a "real" orchestra.

"It brought to life the whole original idea I had for 'Rael,' " Townshend said. "At last I was to hear something I had written played by a grand orchestra." At their second meeting, Townshend brought Reizner copies of the original *Tommy* demos. From then on, Pete stayed in close touch with the development of the project. Although he maintained that he had "no control over anything," he attended all the sessions.

Reizner hired arranger Wil Malone to work up a score (session guitarist Big Jim Sullivan did some of the more blues-based numbers), then went looking for singers. His original idea was to ask Rod Stewart to play Tommy, but Stewart begged off. There were simply too many lyrics to learn.

Townshend suggested asking Roger Daltrey, who immediately agreed. Roger liked doing *Tommy*, he knew the part well and he was totally identified with the Deaf, Dumb and Blind Boy, anyway.

Reizner considered asking some opera singers to fill in some of the other roles, but it was eventually decided that the straight opera angle was amply covered through the orchestral and choral arrangements. Stevie Winwood was signed to play the father, Maggie Bell was the mother, Graham Bell the lover, Merry Clayton the Acid Queen, Sandy Denny the nurse, Stewart accepted the chance to do "Pinball Wizard," and Richard Harris was the doctor. John Entwistle also got involved, as Cousin Kevin. Ringo Starr sang Uncle Ernie as a form of homage to Moon.

Stewart and Daltrey proposed taking the orchestral *Tommy* to the stage. Reizner and Townshend were both eager to pursue that idea, and a show was initially scheduled for the Royal Albert Hall on December 9 as a benefit for the Stars Organisation for Spastics. In late November, the Albert Hall announced a ban on the fete. "They thought the story was unsavory," Reizner told *Melody Maker*. "They don't want these rock artists in Royal Albert Hall." Three years later, after being acclaimed in America and Europe, *Tommy* was still controversial in England.

Reizner then booked the Rainbow for the ninth, and tickets went on sale, at a top price of £200 ($500) each. (Paul McCartney bought five.) The Rainbow stage was redesigned as a giant pinball machine, and a few parts were recast, Peter Sellers stepping in as the doctor and Keith Moon agreeing to appear as Uncle Ernie. The show was a sell-out well in advance, even though these were the highest ticket prices for a theatrical entertainment in British history. (In the end, £10,000 [$25,000] was raised for charity.)

The album was issued to mixed reception. *NME* hailed it as a "milestone in contemporary music," and Chris Charlesworth wrote in *Melody Maker* that Malone's arrangement gave *Tommy* "the treatment it deserves." Others agreed with *MM*'s Barry Fantoni, who compared the elaborate packaging to an advertising brochure and the score to an unholy cross between *West Side Story* and *Handel's Messiah*. "In that it reflects our society, with its pitifully narrow artistic horizons and cultural wasteland, the opera *Tommy* is a supreme triumph," Fantoni concluded.

For Fantoni, and for too many other small minds, *Tommy* wouldn't be truly "cultural" until its presentation as what was conventionally understood as serious culture. Both Townshend's eagerness and reluctance to have *Tommy* orchestrated (and his similar ambivalence toward a filmed version) stemmed from his knowledge that the real power of the piece came from its lack of compromise with cultural stereotypes. Reizner's *Tommy* epitomized non-pop. It was fatuous and bombastic Camp, a betrayal of the spirit of the original— and of the Who. Within weeks of its release, it was also a million-seller.

Between the LP sessions and the benefit concert, Townshend "grew disenchanted with it. It seemed bleak, even though it had much that the original never had and it brought *Tommy* to a whole new audience." In a sense, that was just the problem. Townshend was still looking for a way to eclipse *Tommy* in the eyes of the rock world. Expanding its influence with the general public was counterproductive.

On the night of the event, only Keith Moon seemed eager to be there. "It was great because the four of us shared a dressing room, so there was much the same sort of feeling as before a show," Keith said. And for Moon, the night was a triumph, *Melody Maker* calling his portrayal of Uncle Ernie "the epitome of warped depravity." But even Keith noticed that "Pete was pretty tense."

During the performance, *Tommy*'s limitations as a theatre piece became all too obvious. The plot was still disjointed, and Townshend, who, as narrator, was supposed to help make the story flow, was dead drunk, missed cues, blew lines. Pete was particularly horrible during "Sally Simpson." In the course of the evening, he insulted the audience, Reizner, orchestra conductor David Measham and, at the end, wiped his ass with the libretto and staggered off the stage. Richard Barnes says that Townshend was "frightened," but his behavior only compounded the pomposity of the performance. And despite the flaws, the production retained its appeal. At the end, Townshend told *Rolling Stone* that he felt "the work *Tommy* is now far more in demand than the Who."

Bob Pridden was living in a Berkshire cottage not far from the one in which Eric Clapton had holed up for the past couple of years. Clapton was a mess, addicted to heroin, withdrawn from music, running out of time and money. Pridden proposed that Pete Townshend visit Clapton on the ostensible grounds that he wanted to see the studio facilities in Eric's home.

Townshend went, looked around and asked Clapton where the tapes for his next LP were. Clapton pointed to a mass of dusty reels lying in a corner. He hadn't listened to the partially completed music for months.

Townshend took Clapton along with him to the Who's concert in Paris on

September 9, then began trying to help him restore and complete an album. But this work was wasted—Clapton was simply in no condition to do the job. (Townshend later said that the music was a cross between Ry Cooder and Stevie Wonder, which means it must have been fairly close to the style Clapton had when he did finally begin making studio recordings again eighteen months later.)

Clapton was living with Alice Ormsby-Gore, daughter of Lord Harlech (a Kennedy crony and the head of the British board of film censors). Alice's father was deeply concerned about her addiction, and it was he who proposed doing a charity concert at the Rainbow as a way of beginning to straighten out the couple.

"I just don't know why [Pete] picked on me to do the Rainbow concert," Clapton said to Steve Turner in *Conversations with Eric Clapton*. "It could've been anybody, but I'm grateful he chose me. I was just pleased to be doing it because I wouldn't have made up my mind to do it on my own. It had to be someone dragging me around by the scruff of my collar and making me do this and that."

The concert was booked for January 13. Townshend went to work assembling a band, aided by guitarist Ronnie Wood, of the Faces, who volunteered his new home, the Wick, in Richmond, for rehearsals. Together with Wood and Townshend, the band included Stevie Winwood and Ric Grech, who had been Clapton's bandmates in Blind Faith; Jim Capaldi, Traffic's drummer; Jim Karstein, who had played drums with the Crickets and Delaney and Bonnie; and percussionist Rebop. They worked up a variety of loose arrangements in the week before the gig.

Townshend had idolized Clapton's blues playing ever since the Yardbirds had been the Who's principal competitors on the west London club scene. Townshend and Clapton had never been especially close friends, but they were similar in many ways, both personally and musically. Clapton had had a touch of the mystic about him before his unrequited passion for Pattie Boyd Harrison had led him into the living self-immolation of addiction, and like Townshend, his musical ideas had been radically altered by encounters with Hendrix. But that didn't explain why Pete Townshend decided to help rescue Eric Clapton. Ultimately, Pete did what he did because he couldn't stand so much talent and human energy going to waste. Despite whatever pettiness, hypocrisy and terror might befuddle him, there was not a more decent or compassionate man than Townshend in rock.

On the night of the show, no one was more jittery than Townshend. Eric was still on heroin, and there was no guarantee that he could get himself together to face a crowd again. In the end, Clapton turned up about an hour late because his idleness had caused him to gain weight and Alice had had to let out his trousers.

Everyone was nervous, and it showed throughout the show. Clapton's playing was shaky, and the band remained diffident, not wanting to upstage him. But the gig was completed, and it put Clapton back on the road to health, although he wouldn't be fully functional until well into 1974, after taking Dr. Meg Patterson's electric acupuncture cure.

29

I get accused of being a capitalistic bastard. . . . Well, I enjoy it. I have lots of friends over and we sit up all night, drinking and partying. I enjoy seeing other people enjoy themselves. That's where I get my kicks. I'm kinky that way.
—Keith Moon

After the Clapton concert, Townshend was almost ready to record, but he had to wait while Daltrey and Entwistle finished work on their solo albums. This was John's third and he now had a serious commitment to this aspect of his career. But Roger's was a surprise, since he tended to look askance at Pete's and John's extracurricular activities. It was seemingly born from sheer boredom.

Daltrey had set up recording facilities in his East Burwash barn in mid-1972. One of the first sessions there was the production of Leo Sayer's first album by Adam Faith (a British pop star of the early sixties). Later, Sayer and collaborator David Courtney wrote a batch of songs for Roger to sing. During a five-week stretch in January and February of 1973, Faith and Courtney produced Daltrey's solo album. The result, issued in April, was a collection of light pop songs, no musical threat to the Who.

"I couldn't touch any rock & roll on the record, because I can't do that any better than I can with the Who," Daltrey said. Daltrey's voice proved surprisingly effective for mainstream pop, however, earning him a hit single with the string-drenched but melodic "Giving It All Away." This was followed in August by the release of "I'm Free," sung by Roger, from the orchestral *Tommy* LP. The record was also a hit in England, and suddenly Daltrey had an independent power base for the first time since Townshend had taken over the Who's writing. (*Tommy* had made Roger a star figure but one at the mercy of Townshend, the writer.)

Inevitably, this led to rumors of a split in the Who. Daltrey denied them unequivocal+ly, going so far as to say that he felt that even doing a single live show on his own would "betray" the band. This was a slap at John Entwistle, whose return to fifties rock and R&B styles on his June LP, *Rigor Mortis Sets In*, had led him to think of touring on his own during the Who's fallow periods.

"I play far better on stage," Entwistle said. "I like to do concerts. If the Who don't give me an opportunity to do that, I'll find other ways of getting in front of an audience." This was a threat, but without a hit, Entwistle didn't really have the means to back it up.

Daltrey had hits, and this gave him the clout to make his remarks—clearly directed at Entwistle, since there had been no talk about Daltrey doing live appearances. Yet Roger's driving idea remained the Who itself; even his own solo interests took a back seat.

"My big ambition in life is to keep the Who together, and under the surface it needs a lot of attention," Daltrey said. "I get accused all the time of being a 'breadhead,' but it's just that the other three don't care—and I mean don't *care*."

Daltrey was alluding to his feud with Kit Lambert and Chris Stamp, whose management clients and Track affairs kept them pretty much out of the picture. Although New Action, Ltd., and Track both had capable staff, Daltrey felt—correctly—that as the flagship of the enterprise, the Who deserved more direct consideration from the principals.

In 1972, Daltrey had New Action's books audited and discovered huge sums of money unaccounted for. If Roger had had his way, that would have been the end of their relationship with the managers. But Townshend and Moon both felt that they owed Kit and Chris a debt of loyalty. They accepted Lambert and Stamp's argument that there was no reason for the two of them to be involved with the "minutia of day-to-day management." And Townshend particularly feared losing the creative relationship with Kit Lambert, which had gotten him through *Tommy* and might again prove essential.

Lambert and Stamp had major problems. To Kit, Townshend's recanting on drugs and his seriousness about rock seemed as priggish, as much as a betrayal and letdown, as Daltrey's snooping into the books. As Ray Coleman once wrote, "The ultimate triumph, to Kit Lambert, was to create a magnificent disaster. The only purpose in establishing runaway success was to be able to knock it down." Lambert and Stamp were self-righteous and half-crazed and, by Stamp's own admission, "fucking out to lunch," using cocaine, booze "and everything that was around." In Lambert's case, heroin was around. With those kinds of habits, it wasn't surprising that New Action often seemed to use the Who's money as casually and as cavalierly as they had once used their bankers'.

"There was an office," said Stamp to Richard Barnes. "There was Bill Curbishley, there was Mike Shaw, there was Vernon Brewer, there were accountants, there was anything they needed."

But that was part of the issue. Peter Rudge had been brought into Lambert and Stamp's employ fresh from Cambridge, and within three years, he realized that he was doing as much or more in terms of the Who's live bookings overseas—in that area, he *was* their manager. He demanded—and received—a lump of cash toward starting his own American outfit, Sir Productions, as well as obtaining a percentage of all American income from his first clients, the Who. From late 1971 onward, Rudge handled all of the Who's business in the States as well as other projects, such as the Rolling Stones tour of 1972.

Rudge was an extremely attractive character—especially to the Who. He could talk endlessly, hyping and promoting with an enthusiasm that Kit Lambert had lost. And he was willing to give the band the kind of time and attention that they felt they needed. Rudge was a genuine potential replacement for Lambert and Stamp.

In Lambert's and Stamp's own offices, another star was rising from the ranks. This was Bill Curbishley, an old school chum of Stamp's who had come into the firm in 1971 to work for Track, which was then considering expansion.

Curbishley had no business experience, but he soon showed himself a hard-nosed deal-maker. By 1972, he was making many of the band's touring arrangements in Europe, "showing Kit Lambert, in particular, that there was more money there than he necessarily got in the past," as he put it. On the Who's 1972 tour, in which they played five German cities, Paris, Rome, Zurich, Vienna, Copenhagen and Amsterdam, Curbishley moved the group into the largest available halls, each seating 15,000 to 20,000.

More important, Curbishley drove a different *kind* of bargain. "They [Lambert and Stamp] would go for the easy way out rather than taking the gamble," he said. "Instead of taking guarantees, I struck out with the European promoters for a ninety/ten deal." In this sort of deal, the promoter takes only 10 percent of the profit but puts up less of the expenses and makes no guarantee to the group at all. If the show flops, the group can literally come away with nothing or even a loss. However, with an act that's a sure thing, as the Who were, it is considerably more profitable for the group than the typical 60/40 split.

"I researched it, and I got the feeling that the Who could sell out these halls," Curbishley said. "Kit said to me, 'Don't do that. Do a sixty/forty. Don't do it that way. A bird in the hand is worth two in the bush.' But I did a ninety/ten deal and we came in earning a vast amount more money than they would have."

Curbishley was also getting to know the recording business, signing a Dutch group, Golden Earring, which had some success, and coming close to signing Leo Sayer before Adam Faith decided it would be better not to be with Track, since Curbishley wasn't sure he'd be working there much longer.

By now, Curbishley, like Rudge, had fallen out with Lambert and Stamp. "I'd had a lot of differences with Kit and Chris over the projected *Tommy* movie," he said. In the wake of Lou Reizner's *Tommy* success, the rock opera was once more a viable film property, at least in the opinion of Robert Stigwood, whose experience with *Jesus Christ Superstar* had given him Hollywood clout to go with his intimate knowledge of the English rock world.

"Chris and I had started negotiating with Stigwood," Curbishley said, "and every step of the way we were having problems with Kit. Kit wanted to do the movie, but he also wanted to run everything. He said he wrote the script and it was his idea. He was just running around driving everyone crazy. I would go in one day and shape up negotiations with Stigwood, and the next day you'd go in and everything would be changed, because either Chris had been in or Kit had been in and it's all fucking unmade."

Things became even more complicated because of the cavalier way in which Stamp and Lambert conducted their management business. Stamp has admitted that New Action didn't keep "meticulous accounts." He said that the missing funds had gone to the band for "drugs money, booze money, madness money . . . paid-off chicks, smashed cars and so on. Anyone in rock & roll knew that, but the lawyers had a case."

In fact, once rock acts began to perceive that they had a potential for long careers and interests stretching over a period of many years to protect, such profligacy in the record business was checked as operations were professionalized. Where the kind of behavior of which Stamp speaks wasn't ended, it was put onto the books in some acceptable fashion. At minimum, rock managers were now expected to keep clear accounts.

Stamp and Lambert were almost incapable of thinking in the long term. "All you had to come up with was the one great tour idea, the one great album idea, and that was all that was needed," Stamp told Richard Barnes. "There was no need to be around."

Again, this may have been the idea when Lambert and Stamp had first become rock managers. (It is one explanation of why so many bands, particularly in Britain, wound up either broke or much less well off than they should have been.) But by 1973, the acts were in control. They came up with the plans, and it was up to the managers to coordinate their day-to-day execution, mapping out a developing career, not just a series of one-shot gimmicks. Stamp and Lambert didn't want to do that. Neither were they especially competent deal-makers. They renegotiated the Decca agreement, getting an eight-album pact for $750,000 (300,000) per LP, not bad for the time. But the deal was still with MCA, and there were a number of more efficient companies around. The deal also didn't fully compensate for the terrible conditions under which the Who had been working previously.

Lambert (always the key figure in the management partnership) couldn't bring himself to take seriously the future of a mere pop group, and so New Action, Ltd., didn't function professionally in the seventies' rock environment. As Curbishley put it: "The reason money is a part of it is because there is a certain amount of money there, and if your band isn't getting it, then some other guy is getting it. It isn't going back to the kids. The other side of it is to make sure they get the accolades, the prestige, the plaudits and to make sure they retain their integrity and that they make the right moves." More than any day-to-day rift, it was this lack of long-range management that spurred Daltrey to make a change.

Still, Lambert and Stamp might have survived, what with Townshend and Moon adamantly on the managers' side and Entwistle neutral (though supporting Daltrey when he was pressed). But Lambert and Stamp made two irreparable errors in the first few months of 1973.

The first was rejecting Daltrey's solo album. "I don't know if they thought it would cause a rift in the group or what their reasons were," said Curbishley. "But they told him they didn't like the album; they wanted to change it and they didn't like the fact that he had recorded an entire album of somebody else's songs."

Curbishley couldn't believe it, not only because Lambert and Stamp were flying in the face of Daltrey's desires (he understood well enough that one could not always bow to a performer's wishes). But he also felt that the Daltrey album was not only good but necessary for the Who as well as for Roger. "I felt that Roger needed some affirmation that he wasn't just a puppet up there in front of the Who," Bill said.

Daltrey appointed Curbishley to handle the release of the album; Bill was to receive a percentage of any profits from this record. This was a major move for several reasons. First, it gave Curbishley an independent power base that even Peter Rudge didn't have—a base *within the Who*, which was the fulcrum of all else that New Action and Track Records did. Secondly, Lambert and Stamp's rejection of Daltrey's album would never be forgotten, much less forgiven. Roger considered that Kit and Chris were "pandering to Townshend all the time," as Curbishley put it. (But even Townshend, fed up with Lambert's dissolution, was finding Peter Rudge more companionable now.)

The other blow involved Pete's confidence more directly. In order for the Who to finish their album properly, they felt they must build their own state-of-the-art recording studio. They took over an empty warehouse (originally a church) that John Entwistle had purchased. This became Ramport Studio, in Battersea, just south of the Thames. They began building the studio in November 1972, and five months later, it was sufficiently finished for the Who to come in, do some experimental recordings, determine that the board was inadequate, rip it out and prepare for rewiring. Meantime, they needed cash. Curbishley and the group's accountants went to Lambert and Stamp, in their role as Track Records' owners, to ask for the money, informing the duo that the Who were owed around £100,000 ($250,000) in record royalties. (The Who, despite repeated promises, were still not directors of Track.)

"I told [Lambert and Stamp] what the figure was and they said, 'We won't give them all of that. We'll give them sixty percent or seventy percent,' " Curbishley recalled. "So they wrote the check out. Kit was going to Venice the next day [he'd bought a decrepit *palazzo* there], and unbeknownst to me, he stopped the check before he went. The band went absolutely fucking crazy."

Curbishley quit his job with Lambert and Stamp and took offices in Bond Street, but Chris Stamp continued to send him his pay check, and Stigwood's office insisted that he continue negotiating the *Tommy* film deal. "I found I was being dragged further and further back into it, because the things I had started had to be seen to the finish."

What really broke Townshend was Kit Lambert's inability to function as producer of the new opera. Pete had sacrificed a fine working relationship with Glyn Johns because he wanted the sympathetic and imaginative presence Kit had brought to *Tommy*. He didn't expect Lambert to worry about sounds or songs—he wanted him present as a catalyst for whatever might happen. Pete knew that Lambert would be disruptive, but he expected the disruptions to lead to something better than what could be obtained without them.

Townshend pulled Kit back in primarily to help with the story. But *Quadrophenia*, the opera he'd finally come up with, was more of a sound concept than a story; this time, the plot really wasn't more than a device to contain ideas. There wasn't much for Kit to contribute—not that his contributions to *Tommy* had made its plot lucid in the first place.

Lambert was entering hostile territory. Townshend was upset about the studio money, Daltrey was in the process of dumping him. Kit felt the band had betrayed him, first by refusing to let him orchestrate *Tommy*, and then by choosing to work with his nemesis, Glyn Johns, on the follow-up.

Furthermore, Kit was in an utterly self-destructive end phase. He'd had the success he needed, he had even had independent success (with the Crazy World of Arthur Brown), and it didn't settle well at all. With nothing left to prove, he retired on his feet, spending longer and longer stretches of time drugged or chasing Italian boys in Venice or both. He wouldn't have altered his whimsical schedule very much for the recording sessions, even if he could have.

Lambert would show up in the early evening for a session scheduled for the late afternoon. Then he would have a huge and elaborate dinner sent in or arrange some other form of entertainment after only three or four hours' work. In the old days, this might have been acceptable behavior. But now Lambert was not providing a needed break, he was destroying any hope of continuity and concentration.

Because the studio control room couldn't be put back together for the sessions, the Ramport sessions were run from Ronnie Lane's mobile studio. Engineer Ron Nevison was a relative novice; he had never worked on a project of this scope or with a band of such stature. His only credential was that he had built Lane's studio.

Richard Barnes summed it up perfectly: "Pete was trying to record the most ambitious and complex album of [the Who's] career in a studio that was still being built, without a producer and in quadraphonic sound, a medium that had not yet been perfected." The sessions would inevitably have been difficult. While Kit Lambert was present, they were impossible.

Finally, Roger Daltrey put his foot down. The rest could have their choice. Either the managers went or he did. The stopped check and the disorderly recording sessions settled the question in Daltrey's favor. By mid-1973, Lambert and Stamp weren't managing the Who, although a raft of legal issues remained to be settled among the parties.

Keith Moon was now overtly alcoholic, often unable to maintain any kind of self-control, not even enough to show up at the sessions on time, much less perform capably once he was there. And a drunken Moon in the recording studio was a genuine liability, because when you're just watching, there is no process in the world more boring than record making. And Moon could not endure boredom.

Moon had good reason to drink, not that he ever needed one. His marriage was collapsing, and the reason was his own bizarre behavior. By October 1973, when *Quadrophenia* was released, Kim had left him. (She was soon living with Faces organist Ian McLagan, who she later married.) "We led separate lives under the same roof," she told the press, which seized the news with vulturous enthusiasm. "He'll get up in the morning and decide to be Hitler for the day. And he *is* Hitler."

But Moon still needed some center of stability in his life, even if only as a scarcely visited point of reference. The estrangement of Kim and especially his daughter, Mandy, upon whom he doted, crushed Moon. Insecure as he was, the rejection was devastating. He never recovered.

"If I ever stopped laughing and quit believing in people, then I would get very hurt and totally disillusioned," he told one interviewer. "You have to treat everything as a good experience. There are things that have happened to me that have made me wonder where I went wrong—like my relationship with the wife. . . . Like when I used to go looning off to Copenhagen a couple of years ago and Kim left me for a time. It was then I realized I'd taken the wrong turning, and so I backtracked and learned from my mistakes. You see, I love Kim very much and the group and therefore I wouldn't do anything to hurt them in any way." But Moon couldn't really learn from his mistakes, and this damaged him as much in the eyes of the Who as it did in those of his wife. He was just more indispensable to the band than to Kim.

Keith stumbled through the sessions, but for the first time, he played without the fire and inspiration that had always been the driving force of the Who. His playing was competent but nothing more, and a competent Keith Moon was off the scale of his own expectations, not to mention everyone else's.

The basic tracks came together fairly quickly. Townshend didn't make complete demos for *Quadrophenia*; he left them rougher than usual to give each band member more room to contribute. The original idea of the piece was that each member would write his own theme. When that proved unworkable, Pete tried to write four themes, each reflecting one band member's personality.

Nevertheless, many of the sounds on the demos ended up on the finished album. Townshend's synthesizer tracks and some of his piano work were kept, after the eight-track demos were converted to sixteen-track at Olympic. Some of the record's sound effects were also taken from the demos.

In general, Townshend was tremendously happy with the way the initial recordings turned out. "I've really had more control over this album than any other Who album. I've directed it, if you like, and certainly, people in the band have contributed fantastic amounts in roles that they normally wouldn't play. This is the first album when the Who have used each other's capabilities as musicians to the full."

This was especially true of John Entwistle, who spent several weeks during the summer arranging and conducting the album's horn parts. "On other albums, he's worked off his frustrations by writing a couple of songs," Pete said. "On this, he's done a fantastic piece of arranging work, sitting in the studio writing out and then dubbing on fifty horn parts."

The conclusion of the album, and one of the last things recorded, was "Love Reign O'er Me." Jimmy, the mod hero of *Quadrophenia*, has reached the end of his rope and is moodily sitting on a rock at sea, with the waves crashing in front of him and his thoughts and emotions equally turbulent. To evoke the atmosphere, Nevison and Townshend set Moon up with a full complement of the studio's percussion accessories and let him bang away. At the end, he simply arose and dumped the tubular bells into the rest, looking on joyfully as everything collapsed in a thunderous heap. It was the closest he'd come to a hotel room in his entire studio career, and it was his last great moment on record.

The recording and overdubbing were nothing next to the mixing, for which Townshend and Nevison adjourned to Pete's country cottage. ("I'm a man of many studios now, and I didn't want to leave any of them out," Townshend wrote in the production notes accompanying the disc jockeys' copies of the record.)

There were a number of problems inherent in *Quadrophenia*'s sound scheme. In the first place, quadraphonic sound was an infant technology at the time the record was made. Nobody had conceived a record in terms of that quixotic sound format, which proved to be the music industry's equivalent of the Edsel. Mixing for four speakers rather than two more than doubled the problems of achieving a properly balanced sound.

In addition, Townshend hadn't reckoned with the difficulty of coping with the sound effects, which had to be very precisely integrated with the music. "The effects tapes took days to get right for only a few minutes of use," Townshend noted, adding that at one point during the mix of "I Am the Sea," the album's opening track, they had nine different machines running different bits of information into the master.

In the end, *Quadrophenia* was not released in quadraphonic sound, anyhow. The dominant American record manufacturers, CBS and RCA, adopted competing systems of quadraphonic sound. The CBS system was ineffectual, but unfortunately, that was the one that most record companies—including MCA—went with. As a result, quadraphonic never caught on with consumers, since it required too much rewiring and expensive new equipment without achieving dramatic differences in the listening experience.

"It's all very well on tape, but when you try and get it down onto a record, everything changes and goes completely berserk," Townshend said. As Ron Nevison put it, "Quadraphonic simply wasn't ready for *Quadrophenia*." In the end, the most lasting effect of the quadraphonic sound experiment was probably the title of the Who's seventh album.

Of the fifty songs Townshend claimed to have written for the opera, only sixteen appear on the finished album. (Three more are included on the 1978 soundtrack and a couple of others are on Townshend's 1983 album of demos, *Scoop*.) But even taken together, the *Quadrophenia* demos don't quite add up to a story that tells itself. "It's more a series of impressions," said Townshend. "Of memories. You see a kid on a rock in the middle of the sea, and this whole thing explains how he got there."

The Who didn't have enough voices to give each character in a complex story a distinct role. But this mattered very little in *Quadrophenia*, where almost everything was presented either through the eyes of Jimmy, the mod whose traumas are described, or through the surge of his emotions, which aren't described as much as represented.

When Townshend first broached the idea of such a record to Glyn Johns, the producer thought it "a great idea. But to me, it never came off on the record. It didn't really come to the kind of fruition that it should have."

Johns said that he found it "totally unimaginative from the point of view of sound—every track sounded exactly like the last one, and the last one didn't sound very good.

"I thought it lacked production, as well. Because not only did these tracks sound similar from a literal sound point of view, but there wasn't nearly enough imagination in the arrangements. I'm biased, of course, but I think I'm pretty good at producing, so I'm going to be a bit frustrated with something like *Quadrophenia*."

Quadrophenia frustrated everyone. Moon didn't complain aloud, but over the next couple of years, Townshend disowned much of his own experimentalism, Daltrey made it known that he was hurt and insulted at his voice being buried in the mix and in 1979 Entwistle eagerly remixed most of the tracks.

Townshend's musical concept was never more than partially realized. Many of the songs are little more than compilations of musical fragments, as if they had been artificially condensed—or assembled from odds and ends in the first place. (This is true even of some of the most interesting material, such as "Drowned" and "The Dirty Jobs"). Where Townshend does have a good song idea—"5.15," "The Punk and the Godfather" and "I'm One" are about the best—he overworks it, so that each side seems built around one static and undeveloped idea. There is a great deal of fiery guitar work, some extraordinary synthesizer passages, the bass playing is Entwistle's most fluid and imaginative—but these parts rarely coalesce into a whole song. Townshend has shifted his compositional base from guitar to keyboard, but he compensates by adding guitar fills that are cluttering. The vocal harmonies are rough and patchy, whereas those of all the albums since *Sell Out* are beautifully collaborative. And Daltrey's vocals are slighted, perhaps because, for the first time in years, Roger has retrogressed. But even that retrogression comes out of the writing itself, which asks Daltrey to do things for which his talents aren't suited: "Helpless Dancer" and "Is It In My Head," for instance, require Gilbert and Sullivan recitatives that inevitably seem bombastic, and much of the rest of the album requires a smoother approach than Daltrey can offer.

In the end, only the instrumental passages, "Quadrophenia" and "The Rock," achieve anything like the soaring transcendence of the best of Townshend's other music. The rest of *Quadrophenia* is engaging only in spurts, although some of those spurts—particularly "5.15" and "Had Enough"—rock as hard as anything the Who have ever done.

Much of the problem finally comes down to the mixes, which rob even *Quadrophenia*'s best moments of the precise detail their intricacy demands. Mixing is all about perspective, placing sound elements in the proper relationship to one another. Cooped up for so many months, listening to the album as a series of pieces, Townshend lost his point of view. (The problem is exemplified by the credit to an assistant engineer for "mixing continuity.") The result is a jigsaw in which the proportions keep shifting. These mixes aren't just muddy—like *Tommy*'s—they're a gauze net stretched over the songs, reinforcing the static blandness of which Johns (and so many listeners) complained.

Quadrophenia's sound was especially disappointing since it came on the heels of *Who's Next*, the one Who album that has indisputably great production. Townshend wound up with the opposite of what he intended: Rather than making his music more accessible, he made it almost impossible to hear as anything but a fuzzy ball of noise. Underneath the fuzz, great things are going on, but it's a job to reach them. Since one of the purposes of *Quadrophenia* was to establish a new sound scheme for the Who, Townshend was in effect beaten before he started—and beaten by himself.

Not only that, Townshend was made to seem more self-aggrandizing than he really was when the rest of the Who once more failed to comprehend the best of his ideas. He originally intended to make *Quadrophenia* a truly collaborative composition. "It was a very ambitious cooperative project. I wanted everybody in the group to write their own songs and stuff. Everybody was supposed to engineer their own image, as it were," he told John Swenson.

"I wanted the band to go in and play a piece of music which was completely spontaneous and then give people their respective segment of the track. Let's take, for example, 'Can You See the Real Me.' It's a semi-spontaneous backing track with loose words which I structured later on. So you get that real sort of vital Who backing track sound with some words over the top, and then I'd take the guitar part away and build it into something: Keith, the drum part, that kind of thing. What we could do is take all these individual things down and strip them away and get down to the basic backing track as though that was the result of the stuff instead of the starting point.

"As always, the band just looked at me like I was crazy and walked away. I've explained it to a lot of people, and everybody seems to be able to understand it but them. Then John wrote a song which he wouldn't play for me because he thought it summed up the whole album in one song."

It's one thing for the members of a band to inform their composer that his ideas are counterproductive, dubious or literally unachievable. It is another to reject them out of hand. (That's not to say that the concept outlined above is anything but obtuse, but it isn't as far-fetched as coming up with a chord to make people disappear—not by a long shot—and the band had gone along when Pete had wanted to try *that*.)

The response of most musicians to such a failure would have been to simply quit, strike out on their own, seek out a group of performers who *could* grasp the ideas or who were at least willing to risk toying with them. That Townshend didn't throw over the Who says something about his insecurity and about his own lack of self-confidence. But it also reflects Pete's commitment to the Who as an ideal rock & roll unit and his belief that if he could not communicate his ideas to Daltrey, Moon and Entwistle, he'd have no hope of reaching the average rock listener. There is something tremendously noble and idealistic in this: Townshend was sacrificing his most ambitious artistic ideas to the ability of his audience to grasp them.

"We're not the sort of band that can say, 'We've got to make an album. Let's go in the studio next week and bash out a couple of tunes.' It's not worth recording like that for a band like the Who. It would kill us," said Roger Daltrey. Nevertheless, the group's conservatism was slowly choking it.

"I think we've been far too tight on ourselves," Townshend said. "By that I mean that we've imposed so many rules and regulations on ourselves about what the Who can do and what the Who can't do and what rock & roll is and what rock & roll isn't, what falls into our category and what doesn't." To a degree, Pete Townshend could be blamed for locking himself into those categories, but to a much greater extent, he was painted into a corner by the rest of the band.

Rather than letting the Who break up (which is what his departure would have done), Townshend tried to convert *Quadrophenia* into a statement about where his identity ended and where the band's began, a way of coping with the unique and increasingly difficult problem posed by the fact that the singer and the songwriter were not one.

"Despite the varied themes, Jimmy is seen only through Townshend's eyes, geared through Townshend's perceptions, and the aftermath, as carried through four sides, becomes a crisis of concept, the album straining to back out of its enclosed boundaries and faltering badly," wrote Lenny Kaye in his *Rolling Stone* review.

Townshend had tried and failed to push the Who past its own boundaries. The best he could do now was find a metaphor for the situation. The result of that quest is summarized in a bit of dialogue between Pete and his New York attorney, Ina Meibach. Meibach was trying to get him to concisely synopsize *Quadrophenia*'s plot so that Pete could register the work for dramatic purposes (to prevent unauthorized performances of the entire work).

"Well, I don't know," Pete allowed. "The whole point of it is that the geezer's completely mixed up. He doesn't know and I don't know. I've just adopted this frame of mind in the songs."

We would not willfully obscure a plain matter. The exaggerated pastness of our narrative is due to its taking place before the epoch when a certain crisis shattered its way through life and consciousness and left a deep chasm behind. . . . Yes, it took place before that; yet not so long before. Is not the pastness of the past the profounder, the completer, the more legendary, the more immediately before the present it falls?
 —*Thomas Mann,*
 The Magic Mountain

In *Quadrophenia*, Jimmy, a mod who's out of school but idle, recounts some adventures. He goes to Brighton, to a Who concert, battles rockers, scores pills, seeks and loses women, gets a job and loses that, spends enormous amounts of time doubting his self-worth and sanity. (Of course, he's seeing a shrink.)

Finally, piqued at seeing the girl he desires with one of his mod friends, Jimmy decides to split town and return to the scene of his only moment of triumph, Brighton, the seashore resort where he has felt connected in camaraderie with the other rioting, pilled-up mods.

In Brighton, Jimmy discovers he has made a mistake. The drama is no longer present, and the ace face he worshipped in the battles is revealed as nothing more than a bellboy for one of the hotels. Furious, he discards all the patriotism he has felt toward mod and, empty of hope if not of illusions, swipes a boat and heads out to sea, where he finds a rock and sits on it, contemplating suicide. This introspection leads him to feel more worthwhile: If he has pulled through so far, that means he can continue to win. On the rock, Jimmy achieves a kind of internal peace, though at the end, it's left unclear whether he will have the strength and luck to get back to land without drowning. In a way, the story implies, it doesn't really matter. He has chosen life, and since, for the first time, he'd rather be alive, he *is* fully alive, living not in the past or for a romantic future but in the moment. The album ends on notes of destruction and exhilaration that are inseparable.

That's the story as told in Townshend's recording notes ("specifically intended to be used for reviewer purposes as a guide to your appreciation of *Quadrophenia*"). It isn't necessarily the story that a listener, even one equipped with the album's elaborate photo-book libretto, would garner. But that's all right. As in *Tommy*, Townshend has created an emotional climate that is sufficiently powerful to override the discontinuities of his plot.

Townshend made other claims for the piece. Jimmy has "four distinct sides to his personality," he wrote. "One side of him is violent and determined, aggressive and unshakable. Another side is quiet and romantic, tender and doubting. Another side is insane and devil-may-care, unreasoning and bravado. The last side of him is insecure and spiritually desperate, searching and questioning." Each of these aspects was supposed to be directly linked to the players in the band: Roger is the first, John the second, Moon the third and Townshend the spiritually desperate, searching and questioning part. Each of these sides is represented by a theme: "Helpless Dancer"; "Doctor Jimmy"; "Bell Boy"; "Love Reign O'er Me" are labeled as Roger's theme, John's theme, Keith's theme and Pete's theme respectively.

But these assignments become lost in the details of the action, and they are never developed lyrically. At the end, the singer is not an integrated personality—he's the spiritually desperate seeker (Pete). The only time the four themes are heard together is at the beginning and in a lengthy instrumental section just before "Love Reign O'er Me" called "The Rock." Indeed, it isn't at all clear why Jimmy is termed quadrophenic or even schizophrenic. He has one consistent personality, even though he exhibits fury, sorrow and self-pity. ("Bell Boy" is explicitly sung by a separate character.) Townshend not only doesn't pursue these themes, he never really establishes them in the first place.

Unfortunately, this wasn't the most confusing part of *Quadrophenia*. By making Jimmy a mod, Townshend made him fairly incomprehensible to most people—certainly to most non-Britons and also to the many people in England whose lives had not been touched by mod. Lenny Kaye compared the incomprehensibility of mod in *Quadrophenia* to Americans with the way many English people must have looked at *American Graffiti*, dumbfounded by its rituals and fetishes. But the lifestyle portrayed in *American Graffiti* was exported in all sorts of pop films and pop music. (Anyone who knew the Beach Boys understood its outline.) Secondly, the culture George Lucas's film describes is genuinely pop—it excludes no one except "adults." Mod was a real cult; it defied translation, which is one reason why it was the only important aspect of sixties British pop culture not adopted by Americans.

That needn't have broken *Quadrophenia*'s back. After all, as Townshend wrote in his recording notes, "each facet of his character also represents what I feel to be a particularly marked trait of the 'Rock' generation." Jimmy was a mod because Townshend happened to be one (to some degree). Jimmy is by no means a typical mod. For instance, the political activism expressed in "The Dirty Jobs" is virtually anti-mod. Mods were apolitical, especially at work. If they had any political beliefs at all, they were shaped by the class background that they presumed style would help them escape. The concept of a mod exhorting his fellow workers to remember their history and put up a battle against their bosses (as Jimmy does in "The Dirty Jobs") is ludicrous. But Townshend needed Jimmy to go through a radical stage in order to express that aspect of the sixties idealism which was the philosophy *Quadrophenia* *really* represented. Mod was simply the most convenient vehicle for the Who to use. It also allowed Townshend to use *Quadrophenia* as a device for reassessing the historical importance of the band.

This probably would have been understood more immediately if *Quadrophenia* hadn't been interpreted primarily by rock critics and reviewers whose lives (or at least careers) had been altered by their early encounters with the Who and with mod. (As Charles Shaar Murray wrote in his *New Musical Express* review, "To those of us in the provinces, the Who *were* mod.") Even in America, mod had some following. Among the most rabidly Anglophile fans, it was a quiet cult that included just the sort of person who was liable to become a rock critic. It was largely such critics who wrote about *Quadrophenia*—Chris Charlesworth, Mick Watts and Charles Shaar Murray in the British rock weeklies, all three provincials who had been drawn to London specifically by the magic of mod as expressed by the Who; and the American writers Greg Shaw and Lenny Kaye. These critics interpreted *Quadrophenia* almost exclusively as Townshend's coming to terms with mod. Shaw was savvy enough to see that the mod sensibility had been the driving force behind Townshend's rock & roll perspective all along (though that may have been putting the cart before the horse).

Shaar Murray's *NME* review summed it up best: "Basically, the early Who classics were straightforward expositions of an attitude, while *Quadrophenia* is an investigation of what went into constructing that attitude and of its results." That was exactly right. But Townshend's interpretation of the mod attitude made it virtually synonymous with all the most positive aspects of the sixties counterculture. For Pete, mod was the spirit that led young Englishmen to campaign for nuclear disarmament and young Americans to protest against racial segregation and the atrocity of Vietnam and which prompted youth of both nations on the psychedelic vision quest.

"What I've really tried to do is illustrate that the reason Rock is still around is that it is not youth's music. It's the music of the frustrated and the dissatisfied," Townshend told Shaar Murray.

To an extent, *Quadrophenia* is about mod and about the relationships within the Who. But those topics happen to be excellent metaphors for the problems of transition between the sixties and the seventies. The changes that Jimmy goes through on the rock are (while certainly not autobiographical) very much like the ones that Pete Townshend had gone through in the decade since he first joined Roger Daltrey's schoolboy band. And the changes that Townshend had gone through were similar to those many of his listeners had experienced.

"I think that our album clarifies who the real hero is in this thing," Townshend said, echoing the philosophy of *Lifehouse*. "It's this kid on the front [cover]. He's the hero . . . It's his fuckin' album. Rock & roll's his music."

The Who had now been playing together for a decade. During that time, literally every assumption that they had started out with, about themselves and their audience and their music and the relationships among them, had been turned on its head, challenged or proven naïve. With the exception of the Rolling Stones and the Kinks, the Who were the only band that had survived intact from the days of west London R&B and mod fastidiousness. And the Stones and Kinks had not been present at so many of the most important moments—Monterey and Woodstock, above all—which signaled the changes rock went through. Neither Ray Davies nor Mick Jagger had earned his spurs carving out a niche in America from the back of a bus.

Slogging it out this way, *working* for whatever success he had gained (and as he had written, working harder than he had ever worked before on anything), Townshend found himself, the Who and their audience more and more wrapped up in what had occurred, less and less concerned with what was happening or what was about to happen. "We take our nostalgia seriously," he said to one interviewer, and to another: "It's about growing up. At the end of the album, the hero is in danger of maturing."

Quadrophenia is not a great rock album (though it has great moments). But it is a marvelous piece of social criticism, trying to place the public and private history of the 1960s into a context from which something more productive can be built. Townshend understood the sixties, even as they were going on, as both a Golden Decade and a Giant Drag. On *Quadrophenia* he investigates failure without denying the success, a perspective that has eluded other scholars of the period.

The Rolling Stones could avoid these issues, because irony and ambiguity were their stock in trade; the Beatles didn't have to deal with them because the Beatles had broken up; Bob Dylan retreated from such subjects by indulging himself in pastoralism and in domesticity, which implied that everything had been a hoax; the Kinks were never engaged in a way that allowed them to make broad comments, and anyway, Ray Davies was nostalgic from the start. There was nothing the least bit incongruous to him about looking over one's shoulder at the pop past.

But the Who were moralists. From the very beginning, they assumed the duty of describing what was right and wrong with the world that rock inhabited and helped create. That's what Townshend meant when he said of *Quadrophenia*, "It could have been written in a simple song like 'My Generation,' if I could still write a song like 'My Generation' in 1973." In a way, *Quadrophenia* is that song—or the proof that no one could write it, since the topics Townshend wanted to write about were now too diffuse, complex and contradictory to allow moralistic resolutions. But nothing could stop him from trying.

"There's an incredible set of paradoxes surrounding the whole generation," Pete said. "At one moment they can go on a Ban the Bomb march, and the next moment they're pouring LSD into their heads. We'd stood on stage and watched it go past in the audience. It's an observation made from the stage, as if we were in a cage. You're being looked at, but you're also in the position for observation."

Quadrophenia's two central songs, "The Punk Meets the Godfather" and "Bell Boy," are structured as vocal dialogues between Jimmy and his heroes—in the former, a rock star, and in the latter, the ace face of the beach riots.

"Bell Boy" represents Jimmy's final disillusionment with mod. As incarnated by Keith Moon in a fine bit of cockney swagger, the Bell Boy is a lout, not a rebel, prepared to take what he can get. With his hero revealed as a self-described "boot-licker . . . always running at someone's heel," it's no wonder Jimmy comes up against the nub of suicide. If all that flesh boiled down to nothing more than a pompous fraud, what's left to live for?

But that was specifically a mod's dilemma. There were other currents tugging at the sixties, and "The Punk Meets the Godfather" explores one of the most important of them. Jimmy's confrontation with the rock star represents the anarchist spirit of the sixties, when all power and authority were open to question (although rarely directly challenged and never overthrown). The punk correctly charges the godfather with having done nothing more than sell his audiences their own reflected glory: "You could only repeat what we told you . . . We're the slaves of a phony leader/Breathe the air we have blown you."

The godfather denies none of this, but he isn't about to bow to the bullying. There's something to be said for the view from his side of the cage; whatever slight perspective his distance from the melee has given him mustn't be squandered or buried beneath an onrush of false egalitarianism, which will ultimately only raise more false idols. More than anyone in *Quadrophenia*, the godfather expresses real pity and grief. Only he possesses a sense of how tragic the whole bloody undertaking has been: "And yet I've lived your future out/By pounding stages like a clown," he sings.

Townshend later wrote that *he* was the godfather, which is obvious enough. The song sums up what would happen to the Who as it stumbled into the bleak future no one welcomed or could prevent, and foreshadows the major concerns of Townshend's writing throughout the seventies.

"However far down we go as individuals," Townshend wrote of *Quadrophenia* in 1977, "there will always be rent to pay, so always an audience. When there's an audience, there's salvation. Mixed up in *Quadrophenia* was a study of the divine desperation that is at the root of every punk's scream for blood and vengeance.

"It is really fantastic conceit on the part of the Establishment to imagine that any particular fragment of society is ever the true subject of a rock & roll song. Even in the famous, folk-oriented, political complaining songs of the very early sixties, a thread of upward groping for truth came through strongly. The definition of rock & roll lies here for me. If it screams for truth rather than help, if it commits itself with a courage it can't be sure it really has, if it stands up and admits something is wrong but doesn't insist on blood, then it's rock & roll.

"We shed our own blood. We don't need to shed anyone else's."

Pete Townshend would spend the rest of his career trying to live up to these goals and punishing himself for his inability to do so.

"When the album was completed, it took only a few days for Roger to express his disgust at the result," wrote Townshend. Daltrey felt that the mixes made him look foolish by accenting his worst characteristics, and by burying his best moments and that the music had little or nothing to do with the Who. "We're not robots," he complained.

For his part, Townshend regretted that he had spent so much time and energy, once more depleting his already shaky reserves of inner strength. So he felt he was entitled to some indulgences. "Fundamentally, I had taken on too much, as always, and couldn't handle the strain when things went wrong and people blamed me. I felt I was perfectly entitled to gamble and lose, as no one else seemed prepared to, either with *Quadrophenia* or even the Who's career. So, I felt angry at Roger for not realizing how much work I had done on the album—apart from writing it—and angry that he dismissed my production as garbage. I [now] genuinely feel I was the one who was in the wrong. But it contributed a lot to what happened later."

Townshend and Daltrey were once again warring. The battle lines were drawn precisely around the issue of what the Who should be—onstage and on their records, musically and theatrically. For instance, Townshend wanted to add a keyboard player, Chris Stainton, of Joe Cocker's Grease Band, for the upcoming tour. (Stainton plays on the album.) Daltrey vetoed this idea under the credible premise that adding musicians to the band could escalate for the Who, as it had for the Stones, muddying the waters of a sharply defined image.

Townshend accepted this decision, but blurring the Who's image was exactly what he had in mind. He wanted to escape "the Who myth," by which he meant the whole complex of history and associations and expectations which had been established over the previous ten years. "The thing at present is that the Who—almost against their will—are being extracted from rock and placed somewhere else just by the widening and increasing size of our audience," Pete said. "Why we haven't floundered obviously, is that we have a tradition in the band which no one dares to transgress. If anybody mentions breaking up, they literally have to wash their mouths out with soap and water. It's like swearing in church. It just doesn't come into the picture."

From the vantage point of the rest of the Who, the only mountains standing in the band's way were those which Townshend insisted upon erecting. He was determined that the Who should challenge and disrupt its audiences' preconceptions. Daltrey, supported to a degree by Moon and Entwistle, was determined that those fans should have their expectations met, receiving value for money and a fair bargain.

Superficially at least, the issue was the classic artist-versus-entertainer syndrome. But in rock, the obligation cut both ways. No challenge was worth much if it wasn't amusing to masses of people, and no mass audience was worth much if it only accepted what it came for. (That's the bottom line, even in "The Punk and the Godfather.") This issue was never resolved; maybe it was unresolvable. In a sense, Daltrey and the others were correct: The Who had paid its dues, its appearances were regarded as an affirmation of everything positive about the rock counterculture and there was little to be gained by denying what their shows meant to their audience. To Townshend, however, it was fatuous to think that a band whose members were in their late twenties could continue "going on with that rock & roll adolescent stuff. I don't want to wave the rock & roll flag for the rest of my life. That would be stupid."

The tensions over these and other issues (the music, *Quadrophenia*'s lack of a strong character role for Daltrey, Townshend's paranoia about Daltrey's solo success, Daltrey's loathing of synthesizer backing tapes and Townshend's anger at the band's conservatism) made the two days of rehearsals before going on tour incredibly explosive. To top it all off, the prerecorded tapes that Townshend counted on to expand the group's sound and destroy the old Who malfunctioned continuously, coming in too early, too late, too loud, too soft—anything but right.

During the second day's rehearsal, after a long struggle with "5.15," a song so basic it could easily have been performed by the band without any tape support, Daltrey finally lost his patience and made some exceptionally waspish remarks to Townshend.

Embarrassed at the malfunctioning of his dreams and not about to take any lip from Daltrey anyway, Townshend snapped. He bashed Daltrey on the head with his guitar. Pete was grabbed and held back by John Entwistle, while he spat curses at Daltrey, calling him a "dirty little cunt."

"Don't treat me like one of the crew," Roger snarled.

Townshend broke loose and came at him, throwing punches, landing two, one on either side of Roger's skull, but leaving himself off-balance and unguarded.

It was the kind of schoolyard advantage that the streetwise Daltrey knew how to exploit. He stepped inside of Townshend's reach and threw one perfect punch. It landed on Townshend's chin and poleaxed him. He crashed to the floor, out cold, and lay there long minutes, with Keith Moon weeping over him. Revived but still groggy, Townshend was taken to the hospital and released, suffering with bruises and temporary amnesia.

"Pete should never try to be a fighter," Roger said later. Townshend had had every advantage, and Roger—still Peaceful Perce at heart—had held back for as long as he could before cold-cocking him. Townshend was simply lousy with his fists.

It was a perfect beginning for the tour, which opened to the public on October 28, 1973, at Stoke-on-Trent. In light of what happened later in the States, it's interesting to note that these early English audiences had no more comprehension of the *Quadrophenia* story than the Yanks—though to be fair, the album wasn't out in Britain yet.

The show was an incredibly complex technical challenge. On the first gig, there were twenty changes of guitar for Townshend alone. Furthermore, the tapes still didn't always (or even often) synch properly with the band. Moon had to play through headphones, which meant that he might be keeping perfect time with the click track in his ears while the rest of the band was doing something completely separate. By the second night, five numbers from *Quadrophenia* were already dropped from the show to make it shorter and simpler.

Nor was the Who's sound system adequate to deliver the fine details necessary to properly appreciate the new music, especially not in the barns where the group now played. Reviewing the Who's show later that month at the Lyceum in London, Michael Watts referred to "a huge fist of sound," adding that "the passages of tedium necessary as narrative links are just about vindicated by the excellence of certain songs." To Daltrey, who had traditionally structured the Who's live set to avoid *any* sloping off of energy level, the new material must have represented a huge fist of frustration. He continually punched himself with it.

Yet it was Roger's insistence on explaining the story to the audience between songs that totally shattered any hope of pacing in the stage show. Who concerts once ran on an internal clock that surged and crested but never let up for more than a few seconds. Townshend's sardonic song announcements and Moon's loony routines were part of the flow. Now Roger wanted to stand up and pedantically explain each song for the audience. This unnerved Townshend, who felt, "If you explain the story line too much, it demeans all the other things in the music, makes it too Tanglewood Tales." Daltrey's yakking even got on Entwistle's nerves. He turned to Roger during one of these verbal harangues and said, "Fuck it, let's play." Even the crowd got into the act; in London, when Townshend himself tried to elucidate some plot point, the crowd responded by shouting, "We know it!"

"We bullshitted [the album] up so much that there was no way for the kids to think about it," Daltrey said. "It was done for them." Roger figured he might as well finish the job. He continued his raps. Townshend continued to snap at him. They rowed in public. And all of this only furthered the image of the Who as the one band whose disagreements were always aired, publicly and on the spot.

It wasn't an act. The animosities were real, and they tugged at the band, at everyone, even the irrepressible Moon, until the tour came crashing down around them in a spiraling series of disasters.

It started on the fourth night, in Newcastle. Backstage before the show, Irish Jack walked in covered in badges and with a framed Goldhawk membership button pinned to his coat. The group hadn't seen him in some time. Jack was enthused, as only Jack could be, about Townshend's opera. A celebration of mod was as good as a celebration of himself! (In fact, it had been a letter from Jack that had set Townshend thinking about the mods again in the first place.)

"Well," Jack said with a grin, "I'm thirty."

Townshend was startled. "Incredible," he later told an interviewer. "I couldn't believe it. I always thought he was younger than me, for a start. You always think the audience is younger." (Jack was about eighteen months older than anyone in the Who.) Jack turning thirty reminded Townshend more directly than anything else could have just how long the Who had been playing and with what powerful effect.

Did this incite Townshend? Put his nerves on edge? Or was it just the accumulated anxiety of three nights of dodgy gigs, breakdowns and cock-ups? Fifty minutes into the Newcastle gig, during "5.15," Townshend flipped out completely when the tape synch came in fifteen seconds slow.

He stepped to the side of the stage, grabbed Bobby Pridden by the scruff of his neck and pulled the poor road manager bodily over the mixing desk, then tossed him toward center stage. As Pridden sprawled in front of the crowd, Townshend began pulling at the sound board, yanking out wires, demolishing many of the prerecorded tapes it had taken so many weeks' work to piece together.

The rest of the band watched in a daze. When Townshend finished wrecking the gear, he stalked off the stage. The rest of the band made their apologies, said they'd try to be back and followed him, leaving the audience even more dumbfounded. Pridden was already out the backstage door, walking down the alley, when John Wolff and Bill Curbishley caught up to him. "That's it," Pridden insisted. "I'm finished. Never again." But he let himself be steered back inside.

Meantime, the Who were pacing their dressing room, trying to cool Townshend. After twenty-five minutes, they retook the stage and finished out the show with a medley of oldies. When the set was over, both Townshend and Moon trashed their gear.

Bob Pridden spent the night sitting up in his hotel room repairing the gear, salvaging what he could of the tapes Townshend had ravaged. Townshend called to apologize. The next morning, Bob had to go out-of-pocket for a new guitar.

The following evening, Townshend and Moon appeared on local television to apologize, explain and assure everyone that that night's show would not be canceled. Pridden stuck it out like an old family retainer—that was the truly pathetic part.

For some reason, the American tour had been booked to start in San Francisco, on November 20, rather than on the East Coast, as usual. The difference in jet lag was three more hours, and the band had only one day's rest before their first show, at the Cow Palace, the barn that serves as an arena in San Francisco. The raggedness of that first night's show may be judged by Roger Daltrey's comment when the *Quadrophenia* segment was finished: "And now, for you who've come on the first night of a tour—*'WON'T GET FOOLED AGAIN!'* " The band crashed into the song, but after only a few bars, Keith Moon slumped over his drums.

Band and crew scurried to the drum riser to see what was wrong. Keith was out cold. The roadies carried him backstage into the dressing room, where he was placed in a cold shower and revived. Meantime, Pete made an embarrassed apology to the audience: "We're going to try to revive our drummer by punching him in the stomach and giving him a custard enema." A few moments later, when it became clear that something really serious was wrong with Keith, Townshend again addressed the audience: "The 'orrible truth is that without him, we're not a group. . . . You'll have to wait."

After another half-hour's delay, the Who once more hit the stage. Moon proclaimed himself fit, and the rest of the band tried valiantly to pick up where they'd left off. But Moon was too weak to continue—he didn't even get through the first song. He was taken backstage and then to the hospital, where a doctor pronounced him okay but suffering from the effects of PCP, an animal tranquilizer. (One of the girls who'd been drinking with him nearly died.)

Meanwhile, Townshend was enraged that the beginning of the tour was so disastrous. "Hey," he shouted to the crowd. "Can anybody out there play drums? I mean good. Any takers come up here onstage."

Scot Halpin, a nineteen-year-old who had found himself in the front rows after buying a ticket from a scalper, fought his way over to the security guards and tried to talk his way onstage. He was spotted by promoter Bill Graham, who asked a couple of perfunctory questions, then led him up. "It all happened really quick," Halpin told *Rolling Stone*. "I didn't have time to think about it and get nervous." Townshend introduced him (as "Scot"), called for "Naked Eye," giving Halpin the time signature, and they were off. The Who ran through two other songs, "Magic Bus" and "My Generation," before finishing.

"None of the papers picked it up," Daltrey said, "but he was good." Halpin said it helped that he knew all three songs (even though he hadn't played drums in about six months). "I really admired their stamina," he added. "I only played three numbers and I was dead."

Keith Moon spent the next night, a free date in Los Angeles, sleeping for ten hours and then watching television at a friend's house which wouldn't have been a normal night for him when he wasn't on tour. Between this upset of his system and the confusion of headphones and tape machines, he wouldn't regain his confidence for the rest of this tour.

The Who stumbled eastward for two weeks, Roger still explaining, Pete still trying to shut him up, while Moon grew increasingly depressed over his inability to synchronize with the machines (which weren't able to accommodate him). On December 2, they arrived at the Montreal Forum for a show that wasn't appreciably worse than usual. Later, band and liggers adjourned to a suite in the St. Bonaventure Hotel, where MCA Records was throwing a press reception. (Montreal, Boston and Philadelphia were the closest to New York the Who would come on this tour, possibly because they were uncertain of exposing *Quadrophenia* in all its awkwardness to the full glare of the Manhattan-based media.)

The reception went smoothly enough until Keith Moon took objection to the St. Bonaventure's decor, particularly a painting, the usual blandly offensive thing, which he thereupon removed from the wall. Moon kicked the portrait from its frame, then hung the frame back on the wall and decorated the space left over with catsup in a design he regarded as far more splendid.

Everyone thought this was funny. Townshend then escalated the action, assisting Keith in carrying a heavy marble coffee table to a window from which it was ceremoniously dumped. The roadies and cronies took this as their cue to join in on what became one of the most thorough hotel demolitions in

Who history. Tables, lamps and TV sets were smashed, but that was nothing new. Ripping up bits of the suite's flooring was a novel touch, though. When the carnage ended, MCA publicist Bill Yaryan was shrewd enough to lock the doors to the suite to ensure the band's getaway the next morning.

But Yaryan forgot to turn off the lights. Around 4:00 A.M., a hotel detective used his passkey to make sure the room wasn't still in use. What he saw shocked him. He called the hotel manager, who had everyone in the band's party aroused—a total of sixteen including groupies and Mike Shaw, in his wheelchair—and taken to jail. Among the arrestees was Roger Daltrey, who had retired to bed immediately upon returning from the gig.

Roger and Pete shared one cell, John and Keith another, it was just like the old days of doubling up in hotel rooms.

The Who were used to being able to talk their way out of such scrapes as long as they tossed in a healthy check to pay for repairs. They hadn't reckoned with the Quebecois dislike for anything speaking English, however. The St. Bonaventure's manager was scandalized, and he wanted to punish the band legally. It wasn't until late morning the next day that the group and entourage were finally released on $3,000 (£1,200) bail, reasonably priced since the hotel damages came to $6,000 (£2,500). (These were paid, of course.) The Who were not exactly deported, but they've never played Montreal again.

Peter Townshend attempted to justify such behavior to John Swenson in an interview he gave a few days later in Washington, D.C., just before the tour's last show. "I know it's kind of hard to justify in terms of higher ideals," Townshend said. "I feel the same way towards hotels that our audience feels towards us: I'm kinda grateful they exist, but I hate the prices they charge. . . . It does 'em some good to know that there's still a few bastards left in the world." (Entwistle later wrote a song about the experience, "Cell Number 7," which appears on his *Mad Dog* solo album.)

This was balderdash, an excuse and nothing more. Townshend may have talked a great deal about wanting the Who to overthrow their adolescent image, but when he was on tour, he could not help slipping into old habits. He was drunk and violent and abusive in ways he wouldn't have dreamed of being when he was home. At the same time that Townshend was telling *Melody Maker* that he "didn't get as much out of performing on the stage as [he] used to," he was reveling in every bit of license and privilege touring offered. And feeling tremendously guilty about it afterward.

During and after the *Quadrophenia* tour, the Who was seriously reassessing its status. But all of Townshend's fiercely intellectual logic about abandoning their teen-oriented presentation and growing up with the music were unconvincing as long as his road behavior remained adolescent.

Neither could Townshend make an effective case for turning the Who's superstardom inside out, as "The Punk and the Godfather" suggested he should. The very tapes Townshend believed would change the group's image represented a total divorce from the desires and needs of his listeners. Townshend didn't use synthesizers for their own sake the way that other rock musicians did, so they didn't even acclimate his audience to the presence of new music-making technology. The tapes were not purely an indulgence—Townshend claimed the "contrapuntal" nature of the parts demanded tape effects—but their ineffectiveness made it seem a shame that another solution hadn't been found, even if it meant adding musicians to the group. "Every Who album has been a step forward," Pete mused in *Rolling Stone*. "I wonder whether each step needs to be such a monumental one." No one except Townshend was insisting that it should be.

The route of professionalized entertainment that Daltrey and Entwistle proposed would also prove a disaster for the Who. There was middle ground between the two extremes, but nobody (in the Who or in any of the other bands who had to confront the issue) was finding it.

Once they reached this stage, with the aspirations of one member radically diverging from the others, most bands broke up. There was little to be gained from a continuing collaboration in which all parties seemed hostile to one another's aspirations. But Townshend, the most likely to secede, refused to surrender the flag. And Daltrey and Entwistle, also dissatisfied, hadn't nearly such clear options as Pete. Entwistle's songs had no following outside of a cult of Who fans; that is, he had appeal only to a cult within a cult. And for all of Daltrey's solo success, he still hadn't the musical wherewithal to assemble his own group and certainly wouldn't have found one as uniquely suited to his strengths as the Who if he'd tried.

Only Moon was happy with the band as it was, but then, Keith had arrived a fan and never ceased to be one. With his personal life sinking, Moon had nothing else to anchor him.

So the band stayed together, more from force of habit than for any constructive purpose. They did some shows in London over Christmas and a few in France in the early weeks of the New Year. Then they retired the *Quadrophenia* tapes (without the bonfire they deserved), and prepared, at last, to make a film.

31

The *Quadrophenia* tour taught the Who several important lessons. If nothing else, it convinced even Townshend that prerecorded tapes were not yet usable on stage. As it happens, it was later shown that humans must adapt to the technology (because the technology can't adapt to them), but then, there is nothing especially new about that truth, nor anything at all heroic in it. The Who either refused to adapt, which was virtuous, or could not, which was noble. Anyway, the tapes went down for good.

This was by no means the most significant principle gleaned by the Who from their 1973 tour. What they learned about their audience was far more crucial. Roger Daltrey said it best: "At one time, the kids told the musicians what they wanted. Now they sit back and let the musicians preach to them."

Quadrophenia was the most immediate hit that the Who had ever had. In America, it went gold in a day, Top 10 in two weeks, and got all the way to number 2, the highest-charting Who album ever. Yet this had nothing to do with how well-loved the music was. Both of the singles drawn from *Quadrophenia* stuffed worse than anything since before "Happy Jack"—neither of them even made the Top 40.

The concerts sold out immediately, and though the audiences were often restless, they never went out of their way to express their dissatisfaction (no booing, no walking out, no hostility). At the end of each show, there was always a rousing ovation and the opportunity for an encore. This was the triumph of the Woodstock aesthetic, in which the quality of the music and performance was irrelevant to the real function of the show: the affirmative experience of *being there*. Neither did the record matter much, except as a signal of allegiance through possession.

All of Townshend's efforts to demolish the myth of the Who and recreate a more active relationship with an assertive audience were hopeless, since the Who were already trapped in a process that dictated to *them*. Had the tape effects worked perfectly, it wouldn't have mattered. The Who's audience—like the audience for so many seventies superstar bands—came not to listen or even celebrate but to passively affirm a collective identity. "They want the same thing said again because they still feel it's as important as it was then," Townshend said. "It's not out of nostalgia. They want it in a restorative sense. They want to be able to have music which affirms their selves."

If the rock audience could use its collective energy to build an active group identity, they would have achieved something profoundly important. And in popular culture, it was only rock that offered this opportunity. Townshend knew why. "Most other music sort of comes from on high down toward the listener. Certain rock songs you just take and they're yours."

There was no way this invigoration of rock could take place without the active cooperation of rock musicians. And few musicians were as idealistic and willing to risk their prestige and privileges as Pete Townshend. For a rock band to suggest that the real power in the game came from the audience itself was to suggest the potential overthrow of much of their authority.

There now arose the cult of the semi-popular performer; that is, one who had an audience but remained elitist, whose cachet depended on a series of near-misses with the mass audience but whose lack of any broad base could be considered chic (and profitable). The semi-popular cults (typified by those surrounding Neil Young and David Bowie) were attractive because they allowed insiders to snub other groups of rock fans. The counterparts of those cults were the passive individualists who wanted only to be entertained, to "boogie," to get *down*, and these were the fans who constantly shouted for "Magic Bus" and "Boris the Spider" no matter what else was going on. This part of the rock crowd was less pretentious than the style cultists, but they didn't listen at all. If the snobs on rock's right were obnoxious, these fans were pitiable, for they'd been cheated out of the best part of what the music had to offer—its sense of interaction.

Everyone, no matter where they found themselves in this process, was trapped and diminished by it. Even the musicians didn't really gain, for as they became more popular in a less meaningful sense, it became inevitable that the next generation of listeners would be more fickle and fewer in number. Since rock no longer mattered as much, it no longer kept a firm hold on its fans.

Townshend wanted the Who to abandon its history, but the true danger of rock's current setup could only be understood by reflection upon that history, by using it as a base for growth, not by discarding it. Daltrey (and to lesser degrees, Entwistle and Moon) wanted to give the people what they wanted—even if what they wanted was just more of the same. That grew frustrating, too, since the group was then locked into *Tommy*, "My Generation" and a whole series of performance clichés, from Townshend's knee drops and Daltrey's mike twirling to Entwistle's stolidity and Moon's joke announcements. It's one thing for a band with two years' worth of hits to play them all. But in committing itself to this arrangement, the Who were blocking off an hour or more for what they *must* do and closing down many more productive options. The dilemma was typical of what sixties groups faced in the seventies, since new material was useful only if it accommodated the old, a most unnatural state of affairs.

Thus rock's limits were set. The bands could not break past them; they lacked the will and the incentive. Neither were the kids able to summon up the energy to make a change.

As even Roger Daltrey could see, this situation couldn't last forever. "If they want to bust that frustration bubble, they've got to show their feelings," Daltrey said. "One day they're all going to get so bored, they're gonna go out and smash windows. Then we'll have a whole new rock era."

In the twilight of the old one, the Who once more turned to *Tommy*.

Robert Stigwood became the producer of the *Tommy* film almost by default. Kit Lambert (and his script) were never acceptable to Universal Pictures, which, as owners of MCA Records, had first dibs on the production. Universal dropped its option sometime in 1971, and the Who were then subjected to approaches by various moguls and hustlers. At one stage, the group was so frustrated, it considered a deal with Hammer Films, a British outfit that specialized in low-budget horror films such as *Theatre of Blood* and the Dr. Phibes series.

"We went through a whole thing when what we were really after was a deal which would enable us to control the film," Townshend said. "But we could never get close enough to that. Film companies always wanted somebody else to control it, really.

"What's happened in the past is that an American director has come out and taken me to lunch, sat me down and said, 'You know, Pete, we're talking about a million-dollar movie here, and what we wanna know is your thoughts, we wanna know how you wanna make the movie, Pete.' They were saying, 'Okay, you little English poof, you make the film and please make it gross six times as much as the album did.' And I'd sit there and tell them how to make it. They'd go away and decide, 'Well, maybe we were wrong about wanting to make it.' A week later another mogul comes over and takes me to lunch."

Robert Stigwood had a film business track record as the producer of *Jesus Christ Superstar* and similar conventional entertainments, and he had a long-standing relationship with the Who. Stigwood was sufficiently close to Lambert and Stamp to win them over without being forced to let them run the show. Stigwood managed Eric Clapton, which had put him into frequent contact with Townshend while Clapton's Rainbow gig was being prepared. And he was English (actually, Australian, but he had long been resident in England).

By mid-1973, Stigwood had closed the deal with the Who, arranged a financing and releasing deal with Columbia Pictures, and was ready to begin staffing and casting the project. He proposed Ken Russell as the director; as it turned out, Townshend had hoped for Russell all along.

"In [1969], Russell was a sort of arty film maker," said Townshend. "I thought how amazing it would be if he would do it because he would make it his own and I wouldn't have to sit there and explain it all. . . . I just felt that he was a big enough character to take it and work with it."

Russell was a big character in every way, a huge, burly, grey-bearded Englishman (then in his late forties), who had started out working for the BBC and then graduated to a series of visually bombastic, self-indulgent features including such gross-outs as *The Devils* and *Savage Messiah*. His most successful films were *Women in Love*, a heavy-handed adaptation of the D. H. Lawrence novel, and *The Music Lovers*, a scabrous biography of Tchaikovsky. Russell had an ardent interest in all kinds of music—he would go on to direct biographies of Gustav Mahler and Franz Liszt, and he'd already made *The Boyfriend* in homage to Busby Berkeley's Hollywood musicals. He was a convert to Roman Catholicism, and a religious obsession permeated all his films. Certainly, he was flamboyant enough to tackle rock & roll, coming on like Screamin' Jay Hawkins with an Arriflex. And like Townshend, Russell was torn between his schoolboy image of the high artist and his own vocation as a purveyor of mass entertainment (trash), a contradiction that works its unreconciled way through almost all of his work.

Russell was called in, read "everything Townshend ever said about *Tommy* and his beliefs" and—thus immersed in total contradiction and confusion— sat down and wrote a script. This he showed to Townshend, who made a few suggestions. Russell then wrote a second draft, which became the shooting script (though many changes were made on the set). According to the director, there was "nothing" in this final script that Townshend disagreed with.

Russell radically reorganized the story. Although both he and Townshend have claimed that the changes only clarified some plot points, in fact, they alter the entire focus. Russell has the mother's lover murder the boy's father (rather than the other way around), which eliminates any chance of empathy between father and son and places all the guilt squarely on the parents. The *Tommy* movie wasn't about a deaf, dumb and blind boy's religious enlightenment and his inability to articulate his vision to the world. Instead, it was about the reaction of the boy's parents to his affliction. In the film, Tommy doesn't make a spiritual mistake—his parents *deliberately* cheat the disciples.

Far from objecting to this radical alteration of the meaning of his story, Townshend said that he "didn't care if [Russell] altered all the words. It was just another evolution in the concept."

If that was true, then what Townshend had said about *Tommy* ever since the album's release was a hoax, because the one thing that he had consistently stated was that Tommy had reached genuine enlightenment and that if his instructions could have been followed, they would have worked.

It was Peter Townshend's own inability to cope with the real dimensions of

Tommy's success in moving people that forced him into denying its significance. For someone who was trained to believe that pop was momentary trash and that only Art lasted, *Tommy*'s continued life was a threat. "It challenged our legitimacy as true Rock chroniclers and refused to age," Townshend wrote. Townshend didn't want to be burdened by his own history, but the world refused to release him.

"If I had ever dug in my heels about *Tommy* and said no one has the right to change my conception, it would have killed *Tommy* dead as a concept," said Townshend. In the end, however, he was really seeking something that would sustain *Tommy* as an income-generating property but kill it off as a living story. Thus the *Tommy* film, and thus Ken Russell, of whom Townshend said, "I don't think that rock & roll is something that Ken really cares about or understands." Only by having *Tommy* placed outside the bounds of rock & roll could Townshend be freed of it and of the damnable necessity to do something just as good or better.

So he cut the cord and prepared to stand back, get as far away from the filming as he could. Robert Stigwood immediately upset that applecart by jumping his offer for Pete's participation as musical director from $100,000, which Pete could have spurned, to $250,000.

Pete was probably underpaid. Russell needed Townshend no less than any of the other directors who had considered *Tommy*, perhaps more so, because his script called for the film to be made without a shred of dialogue, not a single spoken word from beginning to end. *Tommy*'s score not only had to be adapted, but new material had to be written to clarify some fuzzy plot points. Townshend wrote four new songs and much incidental music for the film and rerecorded all of the original material.

He faced two mighty obstacles. In the first place, Russell wanted to record the music *before* shooting the film, and secondly, he insisted upon using actors rather than singers for the leading roles. After much persuasion (and a serious audition of David Essex, the star of *That'll Be the Day*), the producers were cajoled into hiring Roger Daltrey as Tommy. But Tommy was a supporting role. The major figures in the film were his mother and her boyfriend, Bernie, and for these Russell insisted on casting Ann-Margret—whose only previous experience in anything resembling rock was playing with Elvis Presley in *Viva Las Vegas* a decade before—and Oliver Reed, English acting's answer to Keith Moon but no singer and certainly no rocker.

"I resisted all the legitimate actors in it," Townshend said. "Because I wanted people that could sing rock. It was Ken who said he had to have those people." So the father (Group Captain Walker) was played by Robert Powell, and the doctor (the Specialist) by Jack Nicholson, whose range was three notes. Even though the remaining roles were padded out by rock vocalists—Elton John as the Pinball Wizard, Tina Turner as the Acid Queen, Eric Clapton as the preacher who sings "Eyesight to the Blind," Arthur Brown as the priest—the film was musically hopeless from the start. *Tommy* may not have been a true opera, but it needed to be sung. This cast couldn't do it.

That was okay with Russell, whose idea seems to have been to travesty rock culture in general. But it sent Townshend off into another of his obsessive, depressive binges. The last straw may have been Russell's rejection of Stevie Wonder as the Pinball Wizard. Wonder had already accepted the producers' offer, and he was quite justifiably outraged that the director had gotten cold feet about a blind black kid being beaten at a game by a deaf, dumb and blind boy. (Later, when Wonder came to England, he refused to speak to Townshend or to Eric Clapton, who was with Pete at the time.) This sort of incident was exactly the reason why the Who should have kept its distance from the film, but with Townshend and Daltrey playing important roles in the production (and with Keith Moon taking another turn as the perverted Uncle Ernie), there wasn't much choice but to implicitly endorse the project.

Anyway, Columbia Pictures wasn't about to serve up $2 million (£800,000) for a twelve-week shoot without any familiar, bankable stars involved. Ann-Margret may have been corny and camp, but the boys in Hollywood knew her name. (Townshend wanted either Cleo Laine or Georgia Brown, both cabaret jazz singers, for that part.)

Townshend began work on the soundtrack in December 1973, right after the Who's U.S. tour ended. He worked at it off and on for the next four months. Pete had four basic tasks: recording the new material (including new vocals for the old tracks), remixing everything, dubbing this onto film stock, and then synching the dub with the print. Since Russell's filming was not completely by the book, there were constant small problems to resolve over the next year, and Townshend worked himself to a frazzle.

He became totally immersed in the remixing of the old Who tracks, eventually scrapping everything and recording new ones. Keith Moon was angry because Uncle Ernie, a major role in the Lambert script, had been whittled down, most of the good bits given to Oliver Reed, and so he made himself unavailable for the rerecording. (Moon was in the midst of selling Tara House for the same £65,000 ($160,000) he'd paid for it and was moving to Malibu, in the California of his dreams, just to get away from the spot where his marriage had disintegrated. He claimed he'd moved to avoid Britain's confiscatory tax rates, but he was never able to stay away long enough to achieve nonresident status.)

Townshend called Moon's absence "a blessing in disguise." Rather than replace Keith with a single drummer, Pete decided that he would rather form a kind of super-session. John Entwistle did most of the bass work and Townshend handled the synthesizers, some of the standard keyboards and many guitar bits. They used drummers Kenney Jones and Tony Newman; keyboardists Nicky Hopkins, Chris Stainton and Jess Roden; the bassist Phil Chen; and guitarists Ronnie Wood, Mick Ralphs, Mike Kellie, Paul Gurvitz and Caleb Quaye. These musicians, in various combinations, recorded the entire album, except for "Pinball Wizard," on which Elton John used his stage band (including Quaye).

There were also a number of singers used, including Billy Nicholls, Pete's younger brother Simon, Liza Strike, Mylon LeFevre, Margo Newman, Sarah

McIntosh, Vicki Brown, Alan Ross and Paul Gurvitz. These background vocals were extraordinarily elaborate, since much of the harmony singing had to compensate for the inadequacies of the actors' voices. "We'd change our voices by sticking a finger down our throats to get a different nuance or blend," said Nicholls, who became Pete's closest collaborator in this phase. "As if there were another person singing, not just the two of us."

Townshend spent up to twenty-three hours a day in the studio. "We'd sing all day," said Nicholls. "I mean, ten o'clock in the morning until two o'clock the next morning. And we'd consume a hell of a lot of Remy Martin just to keep awake. We weren't getting drunk at all, because you're standing behind a mike for so long it burns away." The sessions were held at either Ramport or (for the vocals) at Eel Pie Sound, Townshend's name for his Twickenham home setup.

Ken Russell attended most of these sessions, not often saying much, though Nicholls said that toward their end he became more involved, "walking around the studio with a stick in his hand, beating out rhythms, getting more excited, suggesting more ideas, maybe getting a bit more pissed [drunk] than he would have done earlier on. You could see he was beginning to feel things happening, beginning to see what he'd be doing with the music." It was only for the penultimate number, "We're Not Gonna Take It," that Russell truly drove Townshend, pushing him through two overnight sessions to get the job done *right*.

Townshend didn't take much pushing. He was driven "right over the top trying to improve it and show that some of the compositions were good. Because they had been shortchanged by the original production, I tended to overproduce. There was loads and loads of synthesizer on everything. All those overdubs that we were denied on the first album I was making up for on the film."

The sessions stretched right up to the moment when Russell began shooting in Portsmouth and Southsea, on England's southern coast. Townshend attended the shoot, with increasing degrees of boredom. Filming is hurry-up-and-wait business even when you're involved, and as he had no real role on the set, Pete became stir-crazy quicker than most.

Not that he was idle. The initial rerecording of *Tommy* was sandwiched around Who gigs in France. On April 14, 1974 (Easter Sunday), Townshend played a solo gig—the first of his career—for the Camden Square Community Play Centre. The concert was at the Roundhouse, which was in Camden Town in north London. Meant to be a quiet afternoon's entertainment, the solo show was blown out of all proportion when the press got word of it. Townshend spent a panicky week's preparation, then came out and did a fairly casual show using electric and acoustic guitars, piano, some synthesizer tapes and the original "My Generation" demo as he ran through a set that also included "The Seeker," Jimmy Reed's "Big Boss Man," "Substitute" and "Pinball Wizard." Despite a drunken heckler, the show was well-received and Pete was surprisingly confident.

On May 18, the Who were booked to play a gig at Charlton Athletic Football ground in south London to a crowd of 50,000 who sat in the rain through Lou Reed, Humble Pie, Maggie Bell, Lindisfarne and Bad Company before seeing the Who close the show. It was the first time a British soccer stadium had been used as a rock venue, and the grounds were drastically overcrowded and subject to the hooliganism associated with English football matches: Bottles were thrown, and the crowd wallowed in mud. The BBC filmed the Charlton gig for a fifty-minute TV special, and everyone except Townshend seemed reasonably satisfied that the gig had come off decently despite the weather and the Who's lack of recent work together.

Townshend was still miserable, because the lousy weather and the crowd's passive acceptance of the conditions reminded him too much of Woodstock. His misery was intensified when the Who went to New York in mid-June for four shows at Madison Square Garden. (Both these gigs interrupted the *Tommy* filming, which wound up going on for twenty-two weeks and costing almost $4 million (£360,000), nearly double the twelve-week, $2 million budget. Russell wanted to make up for lost time by shooting at Charlton, where he hoped to build an overhead ramp around the upper rim of the stadium along which Daltrey would run during "I'm Free." This fortunately proved unworkable.)

The Who had skipped playing New York on their tour the previous autumn because of their uncertainty over *Quadrophenia* as a live piece. The group had long avoided playing Madison Square Garden, a 20,000-seat sports arena, preferring to keep their appearances in the American media capital as intimate as possible. But the Who was now too popular to play anything but the biggest halls available; their four shows (80,000 tickets) sold out in just a few hours on the strength of a single announcement on WNEW-FM, the local FM rock station.

Townshend went to New York in the midst of the greatest depression of his life. His drinking had begun to catch up with him. "I gave up drugs and became an alcoholic," he joked to a friend, and if he hadn't been measuring himself against Keith Moon, Townshend would have known it was too true to be funny. He was spending less and less time at home with his family, occupying endless hours with studio work, the film set and hanging out in clubs. He and Nicholls had worked hard enough during the filming to "burn off" the cognac haze, but when he was working at anything less than full intensity, Pete was usually groggy or crazed.

His hair began to fall out (although he later said "only in two one-eighth inch circles at the nape of my neck"), which terrified him. He still wasn't thirty. He had scalp treatments, which restored most of the loss, but these were painful, time-consuming and, while he underwent them, disfiguring. Furthermore, a doctor had recommended that he stop playing live because the constant ringing in his ears signified irreparable damage to his hearing.

"All I know is that I got dragged very low by the fact that I was drinking and by the fact that I was . . . away from home and it was a sort of very low level of existence," Townshend said in *The Story of Tommy*. "That's really one of the things that puts me off touring—what everybody else in the band likes, getting pissed and going out. . . . All that seems to me to be throwing myself into what I regard as not decadent but sort of mucky and nasty. I mean, I do like getting drunk, but it always makes me a wee bit depressed."

In the words of William Burroughs, this is a thin tissue of horseshit. It was not "everybody else in the band" who insisted upon reveling after their gigs—it was Townshend and Moon. Daltrey went to bed; Entwistle could take the hijinks or leave them. Townshend had instigated as much trouble as anyone over the years.

Furthermore, the implication of Pete's complaint is that the Who continued to tour extensively, as they had from 1967 through 1970. But in 1972, they had spent only one month on the road; in 1973, their British tour had lasted only two weeks (and the band was never away from home for more than three or four days running) and their American tour less than a month. So far in 1974, the group had worked for less than three weeks outside of England (two weeks in France, six days in New York) plus whatever time Townshend had *chosen* to spend on the set of *Tommy*. The Who hadn't done anything resembling an "extensive" tour for the better part of three years.

Neither did Townshend become "a wee bit depressed" when he drank. He was subject to raging fits of anger, hostility and irrational violence, both of word and deed, and *then*, as he came to his senses, equally ruthless rounds of painful self-absorption and depression as he tried to come to terms with his drunken behavior. Thus he was dragged down in a spiraling cycle that led to the next round of drink—a classic alcoholic pattern, had he been able to recognize it.

That's no indictment of Pete Townshend. Both depression and alcoholism are diseases, and when they aren't treated, they destroy lives. Sadly, Pete was able to write off the source of every bit of his pain to factors outside himself: the pressure of making the film, the demands of the Who, his shaky marriage. Each of these was a problem only because he made it one. The filming was going well enough, and the rough parts weren't his responsibility; over and over, the Who had proven themselves willing to work at his pace if not around his priorities. When Pete was in reasonable health, his home life was as stable as anyone could ask.

But these problems, manufactured as they were, were again only symptoms of his legitimate illnesses. Because they were cyclical, Townshend could convince himself he was "cured" as each spasm passed; he and those around him would be devastated and shocked when the next cycle began. Had he lived in the States, where depression and alcoholism were virtually chic in their epidemic proportions, Townshend probably would have been helped much sooner. As it was, his grand depression of 1974–75 can only be seen as a link in the chain with his post-*Lifehouse* depression of 1971 and the almost fatal one of 1981–82. It's an odd tribute to his willpower and stamina that Townshend survived these episodes, since so many other rock performers did not get through similar ones.

In the midst of depression, Townshend made vows to change his behavior, and he always did his best to reform. In New York he'd checked into the Pierre Hotel while the rest of the group went to their regular haunt, the Navarro (which had become a home base for them, since its management was perpetually remodeling and therefore simply assigned Keith suites that were designated for demolition). Before the Garden shows, Pete put himself on the wagon, and during rehearsals and through the first night, he stayed thirsty. But when he took the stage, everything went wrong. As John Rockwell noted in his *New York Times* review, the Who were not tight (they'd not played together enough to function at their usual level), and the sound was poor, laden with unwanted feedback and fuzzy in the middle and rear of the room.

Worse, for Townshend, was the sight at his feet: All the old familiar faces from the Murray the K shows, the Fillmore gigs and the Met stared up expectantly. His feelings about these fans had always been pretty ambivalent. "These fans feel they own the Who," he told Chris Charlesworth. "Most of these kids, the ones I've met, seem to have a similar attitude to life. They are the fanatics, and they all seem to be deeply intellectual people who are very worried about life. . . . *Quadrophenia* was for them pretty directly." If Townshend couldn't decide in the space of one paragraph of an interview whether he resented these kids or loved them, imagine his total confusion as he looked down at them in his Garden debut.

Townshend didn't seem to know what to make of their cries. Sometimes all he heard was these kids refusing to stop hollering "Boris the Spider!" and "*Jump, jump, jump!*" At other times he seemed to interpret their shouting as compassionate. "I remember our concerts at Madison Square Garden, having come out of total seclusion in my studio after preparing mind-bending and complex tracks for the *Tommy* film," he wrote in his 1977 *Rolling Stone* article. "When my drunken legs gave way under me, as I tried to do a basic cliché leap and shuffle, a few loving fans got up a chant. *Jump! Jump! Jump!'* "

Either way, Townshend panicked, began to feel that he was forcing himself, entered a terrible state of self-consciousness where nothing he did felt natural. "I had no instinct left," he said. "I had to do it from memory. The other three shows I was terrified. I got smashed or I couldn't have gone on." He stayed drunk until, filled with "disgust, resignation and hope," he flew back to London to complete the *Tommy* score.

Townshend now tackled the exasperating and tricky task of synchronizing the prerecorded music with the action and sound effects. He had to mix as many as fifty tracks of sound, and to top it all off, the initial prints were scheduled to go out using "quintaphonic" sound reproduction, which was quadraphonic sound with an extra speaker directly behind the screen to reinforce vocal clarity. These mixes ate up all of Townshend's time into the summer of 1974 and on through much of the autumn and winter. Every time the film changed through the editing process after shooting finally ceased, Pete had to make changes, too.

The Who needed a Christmas album release, and John Entwistle was assigned to scare up whatever random out-takes were lying around the Track offices and get them in shape.

Odds and Sods, the album Entwistle assembled, showed just how fruitful even many of the Who's failures had been. He came up with enough material for a two-disc collection, although only one was issued. *Odds and Sods* spanned the Who's career, from the High Numbers' 45 "I'm the Face" to "Long Live Rock," the seedbed of *Quadrophenia*. It included "Glow Girl," from which *Tommy*'s plot sprang, several songs from *Lifehouse* and the abortive attempt at a post-*Who's Next* album (detailed above), as well as "Naked Eye" and "Little Billy," familiar from the *Tommy*-era stage shows.

Entwistle initially termed *Odds and Sods* "a collection of old stuff we've always wanted to release but for various reasons never got on albums." But he later told John Swenson that "we thought we'd just have a go at some of these bootlegs. We thought it was about time we released a bootleg of our own."

Odds and Sods was also a sign that the legal situation with Kit Lambert and Chris Stamp had bubbled over into litigation. In the process, the Who were surveying their vaults. (In addition to what's on *Odds and Sods*, Entwistle mentioned locating "Zoot Suit," the other side of the High Numbers disc; "Early Morning Cold Taxi," an out-take from *The Who Sell Out*; a take of "Join Together," three minutes longer than the single; two instrumentals of unspecified vintage; and a couple of out-takes from *Quadrophenia*.)

Lambert and Stamp were sued on grounds of mismanagement, the tactic Daltrey had wanted to use all along. Townshend had capitulated only after discovering that he had not been paid his U.S. song publishing royalties since *Tommy*, leaving him more than $1 million (over £400,000) short. Keith Moon refused to participate in any proceedings against the managers, maintaining that they had all been in it together at the beginning and that everything should be worked out amicably. Nevertheless, in the summer of 1974, Bill Curbishley was officially signed on as the group's manager. (Peter Rudge hung on in America for about another year, until his involvements in New York with the Rolling Stones and with Lynyrd Skynyrd, and with the city's night life, created too great a conflict. But he left in bitterness, feeling that Townshend had betrayed their friendship.) Townshend, however, had been presented with "a *fait accompli*" by Bill Curbishley, who announced that he refused to work any longer with a "dilettante" such as Rudge. "I tried to dissuade him," Pete said, "but he was inflexible. I had no choice, since Rudge was in New York and the Who in London.") The litigation with Lambert and Stamp dragged on for more than two years.

Meantime, *Odds and Sods* did its job with the quiet efficiency one would expect from an album so identified with Entwistle that its only single release was his "Postcard" (the first Who 45 to feature an Entwistle song as the A-side).

"I tried to arrange [the album] like a parallel sort of Who career . . . what singles we might have released and what album tracks we might have released," John said. The album seemed to be accepted in that spirit. "Ironically, the new album accomplishes de facto what *Quadrophenia* strained for—a portrait of rock as a privileged but insular form of life, destined to perish with youth," wrote Jim Miller in *Rolling Stone*.

That was the opposite of the message delivered by the Who's real career, however. There, the moral of the story was that one suffered through into middle age bearing the weight of the past, like it or lump it.

The Who were once more warring, this time about touring. Roger Daltrey felt that the Who needed to work out their new material on the road (as they and most other bands had originally done). Townshend, however, was most comfortable in the studio, and he blamed much of his anxiety, depression and drinking to the long spells of road work the band had undertaken in the past.

Keith Moon was in California, eager to tour. He was in pretty sorry shape. Keith needed the Who to get back together more than anyone, but he was probably the least prepared to make the changes necessary that would allow them to develop into a mature organization. Frustrated, Moon turned to recording a solo album. In March 1975, *Two Sides of the Moon* was issued, a predictable amalgam of Beach Boys tributes—"Don't Worry Baby" was the inevitable single—and noisome madness. (Moon had also appeared as a nun in Frank Zappa's 1972 film, *200 Motels*.)

John Entwistle was eager to resume playing concerts. He felt cooped up with his wife and son, Christopher, and studio work bored him. If the rest of the Who wanted to bow to Townshend's wishes and become a part-time band, Entwistle would lead his own band as writer, guitarist and singer. In early 1975, he made good on his threat and embarked on a solo tour of England and America with his band, Ox. The tour coincided with the release of his fourth solo album, *Mad Dog*.

Quiet and seemingly stable as he was, Entwistle was by far the most peculiar of the Who. Even to the conservative Daltrey, Entwistle seemed to have "a very strange, narrow set of ideas." Even more than Roger, John thought that rock bands worked, just like everybody else in the world. He refused to relax into luxury. Yet Entwistle was the most possession-oriented of the band. He had amassed a huge collection of electric basses, a substantial assortment of medieval armor, a pleasant city home in Acton, a lavish country estate, outlandishly equipped automobiles and fully stocked bars.

Entwistle formed Ox as a twelve-piece group in late 1974; he claimed it cost him $5,000 (£2,100) a week just to rehearse. Though he made *Mad Dog* with the large band, there was no way he could justify the huge expense of taking such an ensemble on the road. So he settled for touring with only a five-piece group.

Entwistle had now written enough material to feel that he had established himself as a separate entity from Townshend. As John Swenson wrote, "He developed exactly in opposition to Townshend. . . . Townshend was a classicist . . . Entwistle, on the other hand, was an absurdist; he had none of Townshend's aesthetic purity." John's songs were basic and simple. The lyrics were devilishly funny. He felt that there was a ready market for such music. Entwistle had to take the chance; he knew that only by breaking outside the Who could he ever hope to escape Pete Townshend's shadow.

Roger Daltrey, who had taken just this step with his solo LP and film role, should have been the most understanding about Entwistle's need to stand alone. Instead, Roger threatened John, warned him against doing a solo tour.

"I don't know what Roger's got in the back of his mind, but he told me to just put out an album and then not actually appear with the group," Entwistle said during the tour. "I've had a very hard time with Roger about it. I don't know whether he's got something about me singing, trying to take his job away. The story about me being the quiet one of the Who is not quite true. Roger is the hermit. When we're on tour, we never see him, except on stage."

Even in the context of the Who, these were warlike statements. Entwistle and Daltrey had been antagonists for a long while, especially since Entwistle preferred to sing his own material as he did on "My Wife" and "Boris the Spider." Daltrey and Entwistle should have been allies, since they were both determined to get the Who back on the road. But Roger put the Who above all other goals, while Entwistle set out to carve out a safe future for himself in case he couldn't revive the band.

Unfortunately, Roger's advice was correct. Entwistle's name was familiar only to Who fans, and like most spin-off performers, he found his cult was a minor fraction of the band's audience. Further, John lacked strong stage presence, and with Ox he was thrust into the spotlight full time. The five-piece band with which he traveled was plagued by internal dissension, much of it originating with Memphis guitarist Robert Johnson, who tried to steal the show by aping Townshend; and Entwistle often felt that he was being upstaged in his own act, no better off than he was in the Who.

In the end, *Mad Dog* didn't sell much more than his others; for the fourth time in a row, one of John's solo LPs failed to make *Billboard*'s Top 100 album chart. The Ox tour didn't draw, and the American leg was cut short, ending in St. Louis on March 23, just three days before *Tommy*'s premiere at the Ziegfeld Theatre in New York. Entwistle's losses totaled $75,000 (£32,000).

Columbia Pictures began rolling out the hype for Ken Russell's *Tommy* at the beginning of March. The increase in budget had taken the picture out of the safe bet category, and it needed some high-powered press attention in order to do well. So the slick Hollywood PR man, Alan Carr, and his New York alter ego, Bobby Zarem, were hired to handle the film. This proved counterproductive, since Carr and Zarem both understood the film only as a Camp spectacular and alienated that part of the U.S. rock press that wasn't already turned off by the movie itself.

Carr and Zarem didn't misunderstand the picture. Ann-Margret is one of the contemporary queens of Camp, an actress who has played so many blowzy roles that she is now identified with gay desperation in much the same way as Judy Garland once was. The very concept of a rock musical in which *all* the dialogue was sung struck many as fatuous to the point of satire, and Russell's script and direction reinforced this idea.

"*Tommy* is the greatest work of art the twentieth century has produced," Russell declared. "*Tommy* is greater than any painting, opera, piece of music, ballet, dramatic work or what you will of the century." ("Gee, wait'll he hears 'My Generation,'" mused one rock writer.)

For Ken Russell, *Tommy*'s story had nothing to do with rock. "It deals with a pretty big thing," he said. "False messiahs, true messiahs, man being God,

God being man, whatever. That's what interests me." Clearly, the music did not. By casting the film with so many non-singers, Russell effectively sabotaged whatever was potentially serious about it. Oliver Reed was somewhat humorous as the tuneless Frank, but Ann-Margret's singing was insipid, weak and emotionless, while Jack Nicholson's cameo was half-hearted and cynical.

The best film critics understood Russell's message immediately. Andrew Sarris, of the *Village Voice*, who didn't like Russell's work in general but enjoyed *Tommy*, put his finger on it. "We [non-rock fans] like what we see in *Tommy* because it confirms our belief that Rock has entered its mindlessly decadent phase, all noise and glitter and self-congratulation. It no longer comments on US: We comment on it." In *Time*, Jay Cocks, much younger and a rock fan himself, noted "the daffy banality of *Tommy* itself." Cocks praised "Ken Russell's attempt to comment upon and satirize a culture where a shaky totem like *Tommy* could attract such worshipful respect . . . Russell mocks the very seriousness of the piece by focusing on, then extending it."

In a society where rock was still disreputable and threatening, Ken Russell's version of *Tommy* was looked upon as a handy club against the uprising of barbarian culture, which the music represented. It is not surprising that every rock critic who wrote about the film despised it (led by a scathing attack by Jon Landau in *Rolling Stone*). Of course, *Tommy* never was a manifestation of rock's truest seriousness: It was a fairy tale for new initiates. But the Who's deep involvement made Russell's farcical production seem like the best that rock itself imagined it could offer.

If anything redeemed Russell's *Tommy*, it was Roger Daltrey, who, as Landau wrote, made "a sensational screen debut. He comes off as a natural, at ease in front of the camera, remarkably unselfconscious." But Daltrey worked uphill all the way, fighting Russell's bombastic and heavy-handed conceptions and the mediocrity of the other performances. (Only Reed's and Tina Turner's are less than jive.)

Pete Townshend would be nominated for an Oscar for best score adaptation, but his new songs were far less than classic, and his arrangements succumbed to every fault of *Quadrophenia*'s electronics, cubed. "Just for the record," wrote avid Who fan John Mendelsohn in his *Rolling Stone* review of the soundtrack album, "the four tunes that were written especially for this version scarcely justify its purchase, largely because of the extent to which they feature Ann-Margret." Pete had buried himself in intention and aspiration and ended up with music that lacked all of the ease and grace of his best work.

For the band, who still needed to keep their street credentials intact, the most mortifying aspects of the experience were the parties arranged by Carr and Zarem for the New York and Los Angeles premieres. The New York event was held in the Fifty-seventh Street IND subway station, the newest, most modern and least funky in the city. It featured huge centerpieces made of fresh fruits and vegetables, enormous quantities of food and liquor and such pseudo-celebrities as Angela Lansbury, Halston, Anthony Perkins, Marion Javits, Andy Warhol, Anjelica Huston, Prince Egon Von Furstenburg and whatever rock & roll trash could elbow their way past the drag queens. Of the cast, Ann-Margret, Elton John, Tina Turner and the Who turned up. The fiasco cost $35,000 (£15,000) and a good deal of self-respect, particularly when it was repeated with the same extravagance in Los Angeles the following week.

For Pete Townshend, the entire *Tommy* film experience was shattering. "Those premieres did Pete a lot of harm," said Daltrey. "He got all these paranoias about who the hell is going to like the Who now. I mean, our fans still like us. The film ain't important at all. It's the Who that's important."

But that only made it worse for Townshend. Daltrey was a realist, even though he subscribed to many of Pete's basic ideals. Townshend was a romantic who could not bear to see what his naïveté about moviemaking had wrought: a betrayal of the very rock sensibility he had been championing. The fact that his fans accepted the gaffe and forgave him, agreeing with Roger about what was important, merely made Pete feel worse.

That evening they considered
how best they might proceed
and agreed to separate and
go their several ways, for
it would redound to their
shame if they rode in a band
together. . . . Then they rode out from
the castle and separated as they
had decided amongst themselves,
striking out into the forest, one here,
one there, wherever they saw
it thickest and wherever path
or track was absent. And
even those men who fancied
themselves hard and proud
shed tears at this leave-taking.
—The Quest of the Holy Grail

32

Unable to unlock his cycle of misery, Pete Townshend continued on in despair. Each new event seemed to skid him further into utter self-loathing. The *Tommy* premieres were only a public version of the rootless extravagances that both repelled and attracted him on tour.

"I felt part of rock & roll was going on the road, getting drunk, having a good time and screwing birds," he said. "I was going slightly barmy. I was hallucinating, forgetting big chunks of time—only because I was drinking so much, I think. Like I was waking up in bed with somebody and I wouldn't know what had led up to that particular point. Then I was going home and trying to face me old lady."

On the surface, Townshend's home life should have been a pillar of stability. As a fellow art student and as a waitress at the UFO Club, Karen had watched Pete go through the process of transformation from art student to rock star, from pot head to Baba-lover. She was sympathetic, having gone through many of the same changes on a different scale. (Karen was also a Baba-lover, and she was now studying for a teaching certificate.) The couple had two daughters, Emma (born in 1969) and Aminta (born in 1971). Their home was lovely and comfortable. When he was in the swing of domesticity, Pete doted on his family. But the Who—particularly during American tours—kept disrupting this environment, and each time he came home, he could barely find the energy to restabilize.

"The worst thing is when you actually get back after a lengthy tour feeling that you can then stop living, saying, 'Well, I can't really give, because I've done my gig.' But how does any guy feel when he comes home at the end of his working day? He's expected to come home and be the father and be the husband and be the lover and be everything else," Townshend said. "I demanded a whole lot more of my fuckin' parents in terms of their realness. I wanted them to be more real than they were capable of being, to a great extent.

"To then take all those things that we demand and want today—all of us—and say that you're excused all that because you happened to go on the road for fifteen or sixteen weeks at a stretch, it's like being a big having-your-nappies-changed kid."

Of course, Townshend hadn't been on the road for "fifteen or sixteen weeks at a stretch" in five years. As in any relationship, the tensions between the Townshends were cumulative, and going away seemed to accelerate them. Anyway, the stress Pete felt was not only lurking on the Who's road trips; the temptations were no further away than Soho.

So Townshend threw himself into the other aspect of his work, immersing himself for long days and months in those rooms without windows where records are made. In the studio, Pete Townshend became an altogether different sort of rock star: idealist, coherent, mature, principled, thoughtful, confident, articulate, a perfect specimen of what was right with rock as music and as a social institution. "Basically, I want everything I do to count, honestly and directly, in a way that can get as much feedback as possible," he said. In the studio, Pete acted out his most positive fantasies of adulthood and maturity. But when he emerged from the isolation he found an unchanged world that taunted, tormented and further tempted him. His best ideas were misunderstood by the band and his business associates, though much of the reason may have been Pete's own intense periods of isolation, which made it hard for him to make others see what he had thought out in detail long before. He felt incredible pressure to make each album a giant step, to live up to the ballyhoo, to act out what was Expected of a Rock Star—though he had created much of the pressure and almost all of the ballyhoo himself and though he was fully capable of changing the definition of what was Expected any time he chose. Pete was incapable of resisting the opportunities to tour and, once on tour, the chances to carouse. Over and over, Townshend found himself drawn to the gutter, where he acted as though he'd mistaken it for a trough.

Townshend's lack of hope had another source. In the mid-seventies, rock was at war with itself. Or rather, the war rock had always fought was becoming better understood by both observers and participants. It's too simple to say that the struggle was between the rebel recklessness of the fifties and the self-serious counterculturism of the sixties. For within every seemingly primitive wildman, from Elvis Presley and Jerry Lee Lewis to Little Richard and Link Wray, came a screaming plea not only for attention but dignity as well; the wildness and rebellion were just ways of asserting one's right to those things, the hedonism that was taken in compensation when the higher rewards were not forthcoming. In the same way, the sixties were divided between nihilism and self-indulgence and the most politically conscious, principled, optimistic behavior imaginable. Often, these aspects were intertwined—there were principled optimistic dope-dealers, political idealists who chose nihilism—but both were always there.

The sneering spectre of the seventies was everyone's willingness to settle for one side or the other: to adopt such pseudo-dignified poses that one lost one's rebellion and wildness or become such a self-indulgent nihilist that principles and hope were abandoned. The Rolling Stones put a name to this danger with their great 1974 album, *It's Only Rock 'n Roll*. That, of course, was the one thing rock could never be—if it were to remain meaningful in anyone's life.

"It's only rock & roll" was the excuse for rock developing as a big business, for rock turning its back on the goals and dedication of its early days, for the increasingly complete alienation of listener from musician, in short, for rock becoming just another form of show business entertainment. Having sown the seeds of professionalism, rock reaped cynicism.

This could happen, of course, because rock had no firm boundaries or definitions, because even the best people in the field—Townshend first among them—were contradictory when they talked about what it meant. Pete, for instance, continually implied that rock was a young man's game, that the music was just teenage fodder, important primarily because it helped people mature. In the persona he developed in the studio and in interviews, Pete Townshend himself was living proof that something more was true, that rock could help anchor adulthood as well as adolescence. But as long as Townshend, for whatever murky reasons of chic or habit, continued to promulgate the false doctrine of rock as child's play, he played into the hands of middlebrow dismissals of rock—and of the Who. When Derek Jewell wrote in the Sunday *Times* of London that "the Who are trapped playing aging music for the aging young," the tragedy was that it sounded like a line Townshend could have uttered himself.

But Pete wouldn't have meant it. Townshend was struggling to create a form of rock that contained the best of the old but enabled him to live with himself as an adult. He was held back by only two things: his own contradictory sense that rock was kid stuff and the fact that the Who continued to symbolize the unquenchable fire of the earlier time.

There was no one around to better symbolize that era, and the Who, Daltrey in particular but Townshend included, still felt a genuine commitment to the feelings expressed in "My Generation," "Substitute," and their other early hits. As a result, the Who *were* stifled by being locked into their history, and the age of the band's audience grew younger throughout the seventies. That is, the sixteen-year-olds who had gone to the Fillmore may have moved away from rock, but their younger cousins went to see the Who at the hockey arenas. For better or worse, Townshend's genius so far had been to explicate and refine rage, lust, betrayal, isolation and fear—the staple emotions of teenagers. There was no way to turn back from this part of their history; it would have been both unfair to those who still listened (and even to older fans who still valued their expressions in this area) and completely unprofitable, anyhow.

Two things happened. The Who made the turn toward more "mature" music in the studio (and sold less records), and they kept on doing the same old stage show (and sold more tickets).

Meantime, Pete Townshend was gaunt, haunted, balding. On May 19, 1975, he turned thirty.

That week, Townshend sat down with Roy Carr of *New Musical Express* for a lengthy interview. There was no particular purpose for the story, since the Who had no records due for release. (In fact, they were still preparing to go in and make one.) Given the relationship that had grown up between the music press and musicians, in which stars did interviews only when they had product to promote, the timing was strange. But then, the Who had grown up accommodating the press, and besides, the band had developed a close relationship with a few select reporters on the weeklies—Carr, Keith Altham (until he became a publicist, with the Who among his clients), Penny Valentine of *Sounds*, Chris Welch of *Melody Maker*.

It quickly became clear that Townshend knew exactly what he wanted to say. "If you're in a group, you can behave like a kid, and not only get away with it, but be encouraged," he began. And Townshend came prepared to finish what he'd started: He poured out all the rage and humiliation and frustration he'd been caused by rock in general and the Who in particular. He attacked the privileges of rock musicians, "pretenders" (rock stars who had "adopted false poses"), the passivity of the rock audience and the groups' willingness to exploit it. He criticized rock for becoming too self-important and slammed the idea that rock "is just making records, pullin' birds, gettin' pissed and having a good time." He was scathing about Steve Marriott, Mick Jagger, Chuck Berry, Jeff Beck, Jimmy Page, and Yes. He explained bitterly but eloquently his hatred of what he and the Who were becoming, his repugnance at the stale stage show and what he saw as the rest of the band's refusal to follow him into deeper water. Townshend painted a devastating, mercilessly accurate portrait of a rock scene in splinters, a rock band in decline and, ultimately, of his own confused determination.

Needless to say, the interview was filled with inaccuracies and distortions: He claimed not to have seen Moon since the previous August, although he and Keith had both attended the *Tommy* premieres in March; he claimed to have written "My Generation" at "twenty-two or twenty-three," while the song had been a hit months before he had turned twenty-one; he alleged that all the pressure on him came from the other members of the band and let up only when they were engaged, as at present, in solo projects; he once more claimed that "I Can See For Miles" had bombed out in Britain. It was as though he were serving notice to the rest of the group.

"Roger speaks out about 'we'll all be rockin' in our wheelchairs' . . . but you won't catch me rockin' in no wheelchair," Townshend snarled. "I might be making music in a wheelchair—maybe even with the Who—but I feel that the Who have got to realize that the things we're gonna be writing and singing about are rapidly changing.

"There's one very important thing that's got to be settled . . . The group as a whole have got to realize that the Who are *not* the same group as they used to be. They never ever will be. . . . Everybody has a hump, and you have to admit that you've got to go over that hump."

Townshend stressed his commitment to rock, and, ultimately, to the group, but as the tirade wore on, one had to wonder why he wasn't simply announcing the breakup of the band. "I've been working on tracks for my next solo album," he said. "Invariably, what will happen is that once we all get into the studio, I'll think, 'Oh fuck it,' and I'll play Roger, John and Keith the tracks I've been keeping for my own album and they'll pick the best. So long as the Who exists, I'll never get the pick of my own material . . . that's what I dream of."

Townshend hedged all his bets. After his whining about material, he was quick to say, "But if the Who ever broke up because the material was substandard, then I'd really kick myself." And the interview ended with his proclamation that "track by track, the new album that the Who are making is going to be the best thing we've ever done."

The net effect of the interview was to confuse everyone who read it, including Roy Carr, who signed off by saying that judging from the material at hand, Pete was either past it or "just after a bit of public feedback." But Townshend's message was delivered not to the public so much as to the other members of the Who, Roger Daltrey in particular.

In May, Roger was off starring in *Lisztomania*, a second film with Ken Russell, and completing his second solo album, *Ride a Rock Horse*, a rather forced slab of soul music that was issued in June. (It didn't sell as well as his first.) In early August, Daltrey was finally free to speak his mind, which he did, very pointedly, to *NME*'s Tony Stewart.

Typically, Roger's counterattack was even more frontal than Pete's original assault. "I never read such a load of bullshit in my life," the singer said. "I don't feel that way about the Who, about our audiences or anything." Daltrey claimed that Townshend's behavior and statements had cost him the respect not only of Roger and the band but also of Who fans.

Daltrey's wrath centered not on Townshend's queasiness about aging—Roger was a year older, and he must have had some sense of what Pete meant—but on the guitarist's assertion that the Who had played badly in recent gigs. "The Who *weren't* bad. I think we've had a few gigs where Townshend was bad—and I'll go on record as saying that. I think we had a few gigs where under normal circumstances we could have waltzed it. We could have done Madison Square Garden with our eyes closed, only the group was running on three cylinders. Especially the last night.

"You *don't* generalize and say the Who was bad. Because the Who wasn't bad. Wasn't quite as good as we could have been, but it was because Townshend was in a bad frame of mind about what he wanted to do. And *he* didn't play well."

Roger Daltrey was now a consummate rock professional. He believed in approaching each gig and recording as a job, a task to be performed, not as a mystical moment of inspiration. Naturally, this left him much more content with the Who's current image.

Daltrey was immune to many of the sore spots that bothered Townshend most. For Roger, doing his job was what sustained rock—and he believed as deeply as anyone that rock must be sustained, for it had saved his life by dragging him out of Acton and the Bush. That was an aspect of rock that Pete Townshend, who had never been threatened with anything as demeaning as a life of sheet-metal work, would never fully comprehend.

Roger was justifiably irked by the cavalier attitude Townshend had displayed in fighting Lambert and Stamp. (Their conflict over the lawsuit was one of the things that provoked Pete's original interview.) Daltrey had never had much sympathy for the group's antics on the road, either. Chances are, Roger also considered Townshend's attack on him outside the bounds of professional protocol (as it was), not to mention being personally hurt by what Pete had said. So Roger took the gloves off, and he won, hands down, by simply laying out the vicious truth.

Daltrey pointed out that if Townshend was as frustrated as he claimed, then Pete should find a new vehicle, rather than just blaming the band. He criticized Pete's dominance of the Who, which squeezed everybody else out of the creative picture, made hash of Townshend's suggestion that he was under any more pressure than anyone else when it came to touring, recounted the story of their fistfight at the *Quadrophenia* rehearsal, referred to the management lawsuit, and virtually accused Pete of being a liar. ("You can't live on lies forever.")

From moment to moment, Roger was conciliatory, saying that he liked some of the material on the next album, that he regretted that he and Townshend seemed unable to communicate, that he understood Pete's difficulties. But in the end, he couldn't resist having one last good rip.

"I'm just thinking about what he said. That I'd like to believe that rock & roll was birds, booze and fun. The naïveté of that is that the last few bad gigs the Who did were, in my opinion—apart from his head trip—bad because they were physically out boozing and balling all night. And by the time it got to the show at night, they were *physically incapable of doing a good show*."

"Was that all of you?" asked Stewart.

"No. That was Townshend. Moon does it, but he can control it. On a few of the last gigs, Townshend was pissed and incapable.

"So don't talk to me about booze, because I've never been onstage drunk in the last seven years, Mr. Townshend! I'm just getting a bit fed up with these left-handed attacks."

Roger concluded with the suggestion that he should perhaps write the group a letter "because there's no way of ever speaking to them about it." Unbelievable as it seems, in the ten weeks between Townshend's interview and Daltrey's (which ran in the August 9 issue of *NME*), he and Townshend had not only been attending meetings about the lawsuit against Lambert and Stamp but had actually recorded a whole album together. The atmosphere during the recording was tense, but there's absolutely no evidence that Roger and Pete ever confronted one another directly—they seem to have talked about these matters only with reporters!

Soon after his *NME* interview, Townshend presented the rest of the Who with a collection of demos from which the material for their next record was chosen. It was easy to imagine that these songs were intended for a Townshend solo album: They were personal, confessional, a reflection of all the gall and bile on which Pete had been choking over the past few months.

Glyn Johns remembers those demos as not being especially suited to the Who's style; they were quirky, oriented to ukulele and banjo and piano, without much guitar or any synthesizer. (Much to Townshend's chagrin, Johns himself chose a self-mocking ukulele piece, "Blue Red and Grey," for the album.)

Roger Daltrey had told Pete that there was no chance of him going ahead with a recording project as long as it was likely to be issued on Track. Entwistle was also incensed, because during his solo tour, Kit Lambert had phoned Alison Entwistle threatening a lawsuit if John signed a solo record deal with anybody but Track. (John had considered doing this to bail himself out financially.) Roger's *Ride a Rock Horse* had been issued that June on Polydor, not Track.

Daltrey was no longer personally managed by Kit and Chris but by Bill Curbishley. (Curbishley was executive producer of *Lisztomania*, with Brian Lane, manager of Rick Wakeman, who had composed the film's soundtrack.) Now Roger and Bill wanted Lambert and Stamp gone altogether, but only Townshend could finish them off.

Townshend considered the management dispute a personal problem between Roger and himself; it wasn't until after the LP sessions, when he spent some time in New York, that a friend gave him the proper advice: "Let Roger win."

"We've been to a solicitor now, and we found out that we've been screwed up the fucking alley, like most groups do. . . . It's a nasty situation. Townshend wants out of it, but he doesn't want to be the one to do it because he feels he owes them something," said Daltrey that autumn. Roger realized that since Lambert and Stamp were still getting 30 percent of the Who (15 percent more than most managers of superstars), the Who owed them little or nothing.

Townshend had to acquiesce, because in addition to the missing sums, Lambert and Stamp's casual bookkeeping had led to tax trouble so deep that if it had continued the Who would have been forced to leave England.

Townshend agreed to let the attorneys begin preparing lawsuits while the band recorded. Kit Lambert struck first, going public with the disagreement in a press release that appeared in the July 19 *NME* under the headline, "TOMMY: LEGAL BUSTUP FLARES."

Lambert announced that he was preparing "final documents for 'drastic and far-reaching' legal action" not against the Who but against Robert Stigwood and his associates in connection with the film and soundtrack of *Tommy*. He alleged that money due himself and Track Records had been withheld.

Lambert claimed he owned the "world copyright" to the piece and that he had written the original screenplay. He also charged that Stigwood "alienated the affections of my former partner, Chris Stamp, whose resignation I am now demanding from the board of all companies associated with the Who." Kit further said he'd fired Bill Curbishley as Track's managing director and was throwing him off the company's board. (Curbishley had in fact resigned his directorship months before.)

Lambert had now cracked up completely, even throwing out charges against his only firm ally, Stamp. (There's no question that Kit's management of the Who had been consistently negligent and had recently been incompetent, but he was being treated as though his earlier work for the group was immaterial.) Most bizarrely, Lambert ended by emphasizing that he considered *Tommy* "a superb film."

This contentious atmosphere was an important undercurrent of the songs that the Who recorded in mid-1975. In one of them, "However Much I Booze," Townshend actually alludes to the battling between Roger and himself: "Are the problems that screw me up really down to him or me?" he wonders. Townshend's worst nightmare had been that the Who would become enmeshed in the affairs of tax accountants, lawyers, and money issues. "I really felt like crawling off and dying," he said later. "I felt the band was finished and I was finished and the music was dying. . . . I started to get disenchanted not only with what we were doing and everything around the band but because nobody else seemed to be pushing, either."

Working with Glyn Johns once again, Townshend was freed from some pressure. As producer of *Quadrophenia*, Pete felt that he'd taken more heat than a band member could handle. "If somebody wasn't happy with the bass sound, it was my fault; or if the mix wasn't right, it was my fault," he said. He never wanted the responsibility that came with positions of real leadership.

Though there were some patchy spots at the beginning of the sessions— John, Keith and Pete eventually skipping out to rehearse for three days to regain their ensemble feel—Glyn Johns kept the project moving, with none of the delays and technical crises which had plagued the Who's recent recording attempts without him. Producing them was a formidable task, especially since both Moon and Townshend were still drinking heavily.

The resulting album was, for Townshend, "an extremely effective record in putting across what was in my head at the time, and I think to some extent what was really happening to the band at the time." The others found it considerably more frustrating. Roger had reservations about the material. That was predictable. But when Moon went on John Peel's radio program in early October to preview side one of the record a few days before its release, he claimed that he hadn't even heard most of Daltrey's vocals. "This is as new to me as it is to you," Keith said, and he wasn't joking.

Neither was Entwistle, who appeared on the show the following evening. John said that he wasn't exactly sure what they'd be hearing, since Pete had changed several song titles. He added that in his opinion Townshend's new songs were so personal that no one else could really discuss them.

Nevertheless, *The Who By Numbers* made the *Billboard* Top 10, although it peaked at number 8 and stayed there for fewer weeks than the past three LPs, despite a hit single, "Squeeze Box," which gave the Who its first Top 20 single since "Won't Get Fooled Again." The Who's audience was now a hardcore cult that rushed to buy each new product, so that the album would sell almost a million copies in the first few weeks, then taper off as new listeners trickled in, drawn by a hit single or a concert tour, if at all. (This pattern was also associated with many of the other top hard rock acts of the seventies, from Led Zeppelin and the Rolling Stones to Aerosmith and the entire range of heavy metal bands. All of these acts also tended to sell concert tickets in far greater numbers than records.)

What most distinguished *The Who By Numbers* was its spare sound. Without any synthesizer, and with Townshend playing frenzied bursts of guitar rather than his usual sustained chords, the album seemed stark and modest. The LP was presented as ten unconnected songs, but in both sound and substance, certain themes were immediately apparent—mostly age and disillusionment, the nature of commitment and the idea of rock & roll as balm and salvation. What primarily came across was a resounding mixture of anger and anguish. Roy Carr described it as "Pete Townshend's suicide note." Simon Frith wrote that Townshend now seemed cynical on record: "Like any other rock fan, he won't get fooled again; rock ain't going to save *his* life, and sometimes . . . he can't remember why his band seemed so *necessary*, what part they played for him."

In fact, what Townshend had created was a rock & roll version of F. Scott Fitzgerald's "The Crack-Up," that chronicle of time spent "in a real dark night of the soul [where] it is always three o'clock in the morning, day after day. At that hour the tendency is to refuse to face things as long as possible by retiring into an infantile dream. . . ." And on the first track of *The Who By Numbers*, that's just what Townshend did: "Slip Kid" was a story of the archetypal rock & roll brat, the sort of character Townshend swore he'd abandoned after *Quadrophenia*.

But midway through the song—in its second verse—the perspective changes from sixteen to sixty-three, still confronting the same old dilemma: "There's no easy way to be free." By the end of "Slip Kid," as Townshend leans into a gut-churning solo, it becomes apparent how uneasy he was.

"However Much I Booze," which follows, sets the stage not only for the rest of *The Who By Numbers*, but for all of Townshend's writing over the next few years. The song is extraordinarily personal, confessional in the most condemnatory sense, full of jibes at his own self-seriousness and vanity, the full blast of Townshend's scorching sarcasm turned upon its ultimate target—himself.

This song and those that follow seem to have been written from within Fitzgerald's dark night of the soul, in a dishevelled room, illuminated dimly by a TV set that shows only rock videos, sung by an aging, still successful rock star who stares drunkenly at the tube with a bottle of gin in one hand and a pistol-shaped guitar in the other.

Townshend had always written about how and why one doesn't fit into the world, the consequences of failure and success. He had always worried about the context in which his music was heard. From the start, he had hungered to create some readily definable role and a clear set of responsibilities for the rocker. But he'd never been so unremittingly morbid about the possibilities, had never taken his inability to answer the deepest, most difficult questions as such a curse. And it showed in the music: Where the Who had always escaped their contradictions with big blustering power chords, the sound now grew tense and edgy, on the verge of explosions that never arrived.

Religion offered no succor. "Imagine a Man" painted a picture of apocalypse brought about by hypocrisy and boredom. Friendship is no refuge, nor rock a solace. Even Entwistle, who at least seemed to have maintained his sense of humor amidst the contagious gloom, painted a "Success Story" in which the hero, a chart-bound rocker, can only groan, "Take two-seventy-six/You know, this used to be fun."

With "In a Hand or a Face" Townshend's self-pity becomes so complete, it really is a suicide note: "Ain't it funny how they all fire the pistol/At the wrong end of the race." (Daltrey is at his most vicious in this song.) But if anyone wants to know what Doug Sandom meant when he marveled at how sarcastic Townshend could be, they only need to hear "They Are All in Love" and "Blue Red and Grey," in which Townshend tortures himself and everything he loves until it bleeds.

Both songs have gay and innocent melodies undercut by lyrics that suggest that the singer is an idiot who is at best oblivious to his own pain, at worst, guilty of extending everyone else's agonies.

Goodbye all you punks, stay young and stay high,
Just hand me my checkbook while I crawl off and die,
Like a woman in childbirth, grown ugly in a flash,
I see magic and pain, now I'm recyclin' trash

Those lines are the conclusion of "They Are All in Love," a title unmatched in irony. "Blue Red and Grey," which follows immediately, is Townshend's ukulele, a bit of brass and his voice prattling on like Tiny Tim about holidays, middle-class privilege, the struggle of trying to fit into family life as a night person and other non-crises.

The net effect of *The Who By Numbers* was to create a new image of Pete Townshend as a rock star who regretted much of his past and was struggling to learn to live with it. If the album had an historic antecedent in its bitterness and sheer emotional power, it was certainly *My Generation*.

But then again, what Townshend was really fighting was his own recognition that he *didn't* hope to die before he got old—instead, he hoped to live without ever aging.

For the Who, *The Who By Numbers* represented a coming of age as a band, a willingness to stop fiddling and get on with a purely professional presentation of themselves. For Townshend, it represented just another stage in the development of the central issue of his career, the struggle between maturity and immaturity, the question of whether he could fashion something legitimate from the trashy culture form he loved. With *The Who By Numbers*, Townshend finally understood that there was no way out, that he could resolve these contradictions only by the process of living through them. Which, of course, only left him more despondent.

It would be foolish to say that *The Who By Numbers*, through its expiation of Townshend's guilt and pain, solved any of his problems or that as a result of baring his soul he regained his health. As Fitzgerald wrote, "A man does not recover from such jolts—he becomes a different person and, eventually, the new person finds new things to care about."

Richard Barnes later wrote that Townshend told him that he wished he'd broken up the Who then, "when he first felt he should." Barnes added that he believes that the only reason that the group stayed together was money. Certainly, that was a big part of it. Yet it does Townshend an injustice, as a man and as an artist, to think that he kept the group together for only such a crass purpose. In truth, Townshend does not care very much about wealth; he has spent nearly as profligately as Moon (though on more purposeful projects).

A rock band also offers other forms of security. Consider John Entwistle's description of why the Who did not include more selections from *Quadrophenia* in their post-1974 stage shows: "We had to play it perfectly to make it work each time, we had to play it with an incredible amount of energy, or it sounded bad, whereas our normal act is set up [so] that even if we play badly, we'll still sound good, so we can afford to have a bad night and get away with it." It was not only lack of economic risk that held the Who together, it was lack of chance-taking in performance, in their entire manner of dealing with the public onstage and on record.

Artistically, of course, the failure to gamble is death. But except for Townshend, the other members of the Who did not think of themselves as artists. Daltrey, Entwistle and Moon were now show biz professionals: Roger had become a multiply talented stage and screen performer; Keith was both a genius musician and a true Star; John was a gifted musician and a songwriter.

Only Townshend had the scope of ambition and the intellectual frame of reference associated with the artist. It was not he alone who had made the Who a great musical group, but it was Pete Townshend, and only Townshend, who conceived of this rock group as a repository of idealism and integrity. It was he who envisioned a rock band that would deliver work of high quality not only because that was the smartest thing to do but because to offer anything less would be wrong.

The rest of the Who subscribed to these ideals. Daltrey, for one, believed in them more completely at this stage than Townshend, in his cynicism, could any longer hope to. But only Pete Townshend could have conceived and articulated those ideas in the first place. Only he could have shown the Who how to tap into the spiritual and artistic traditions which suggested how best to make sense of their idealism about rock.

The Who's success in carrying those ideals to a mass audience was the entire source of its success in every other way: The crowds turned out, season after season, to witness the reaffirmation of a dream, for the chance to observe the highest rites of human possibility enacted in a language to which anyone could have access.

Having reached their version of this pinnacle, the Beatles folded, splitting up to explore other paths. But Townshend was before all else an apostle of rock & roll, and if he could not strike the lost chord that would raise him and his audience to Nirvana, he still refused to abandon the crowd. The strength of rock was collective, despite the music industry's continual glorification of individuals. By 1975, that united strength was refuted and subverted in almost every quarter. Recognizing rock as a music of community could never be as profitable as selling the music as the product of single heroes who accomplished everything by themselves and were thus entitled to lord it over their listeners. That this was a lie—that no performer could achieve *anything* by himself—Townshend understood very clearly. And for just this reason, he could not turn his back on the ultimate metaphor for rock's sense of community, the rock band.

"I was a standing corpse, working for a machine," he said. "I felt old, dead, finished. I thought, 'This is it. The end. I don't want to go on.'

"And we looked around. There was absolutely no one else. So we went on for a little while longer. . . ."

33

*I'm really glad that Pete said
what he said and I said what I
did, because it finally brought
all our problems out in the open.
. . . There's no excuses any of us can
make. If someone throws a tantrum
on stage now, it's them throwing a
tantrum and it's their bleedin'
problem. If anyone creates a
stink, it's all down to them.
Nobody's gonna hide
behind the Who.*

—Roger Daltrey

In August 1975, while Glyn Johns mixed *The Who By Numbers*, the Townshend family took a holiday in America, visiting New York; the Meher Baba center in Myrtle Beach, South Carolina, a bit of serene wilderness near one of the most honky-tonk towns on the midatlantic seacoast; and northern California, where they stayed with the Baba-oriented Sufi group headed by Murshida Ivy O. Duce.

When they left Britain, Pete was shattered, his faith still in shreds. In one of his "Pete Townshend Page" columns, he had quoted one of the musical theories from *Lifehouse* in a way that made it clear that he believed it to be true: "We can live in harmony only when Nature is allowed to incorporate us into her symphony. Listen hard, for your note is here. It might be a chord, or a dischord. Maybe a hiss or a pulse. High or low; sharp or soft, fast or slow. One thing is certain. If it is truly your own note, your own song, it will fit into the scheme. Mine will fit yours and yours will fit his, his will fit others. . . . To realise the harmony, that *rightness* about your own note, even your own life, however you feel it could be improved by change, it has to be revealed. It can only be revealed by your own efforts."

Townshend was now living through a mad satire of his own tenets. In a *Rolling Stone* article he wrote about his spiritual crisis (in 1977, after it seemed to have passed), Townshend recounted a dream in which he heard an entrancing noise that "sounded like a breath being gently sighed away, but the listener's ear seemed inside the mouth of a lion." This sound drove Pete to previously unimagined heights of ecstasy, and he determined to capture it and discover its source. "If I could only break down this sound, I could remake it for the whole world to hear. I could make a reality of this outer limit of my unleashed and unfettered musical imagination: glorious, celestial music of only dreams. . . .

"Recklessly, I plunged deeply into the music. As I became submerged, it became slightly more coarse; it was, indeed, like diving into the sea. The feeling of the sharp, cool water is always a shock when one has spent an hour gazing languidly at the sunny surface of the waves. I could still hear the rippling and soaring of the incomparable sigh, and I was now in it, of it. I delved even more deeply into the secret. . . .

"For a few minutes, I was lost in my search. I forgot to listen quite so intently and began turning over in my mind the various possibilities and alternatives. Was it a million pianos? Perhaps the sound of a heavenly choir?

"That was it! The heart of this sound was the human voice; there could be no question. I plunged headlong, further into the chasm of this incorporeal symphony. As I thrust inward, it was apparently simplifying.

"Then in a second, the whole world seemed to turn inside out. My skin crawled as I recognized the unit elements of that superficially wonderful noise. I could not believe what I heard. As I tore myself away, I felt I was leaving sections of myself behind, caught up in the cacophonous dirge. I tried to wake myself but only succeeded in breaking through a superficial level—no longer a dream within a dream, merely a nightmare. A game, a ghastly trick perpetrated on me by my own mind. A vitiated and distorted ploy of my ego to stunt my trust in nature's beauty, kill my appetite for the constant, for the One within the many, the many within the One.

"For the sound that I was hearing was the Niagran roar of a billion humans screaming. . . . I now know that of all things on earth nothing is so inherently evil, so contemptuous, so vile, so conniving, so worthless—as my own imagination."

Pete Townshend must have felt that the best parts of his own mind were arrayed against him.

Despite the reassuring company of his family, Townshend was still shaken when he arrived at Myrtle Beach. But he was soothed enough to be able to make the further journey to California, where the Townshends were to spend an entire month with the Sufis.

Townshend was hoping to open a London center for Baba-followers in the coming year; he wanted Murshida Duce's counsel and guidance in this project. Pete was worried that he might not be able to cope adequately with the human needs of the staff and that he was living such a hypocritical life that he might endanger himself, the center or Baba's work in England. The Myrtle Beach devotees had encouraged him, but Murshida Duce was a more commanding, authoritative figure—Baba had personally rewritten the charter of her Sufi group, and she worked in ways that were nearly as mysterious and as oblique as the Master's.

In California, the Townshends stayed away from rock & roll. They spent the early days of their visit swimming, picnicking, camping, relaxing. If the punishment fits the crime, then surely this was a cure cut to measure for the disease. Pete would have ignored any injunction to rest and take it easy, but he could handle the recuperation if it was presented as spiritual treatment (which it was, after all).

Early in his visit, Pete was invited to the Murshida's home, ostensibly just for a chat. Murshida Duce was then about eighty years old, a polished woman who had been a nurse, a classical musician and the wife of an oil executive, as well as a spiritual seeker. Her methods were, as stated, often subtle and indirect. Planning only to fill Murshida Duce in on news of the Baba community in London and to get her thoughts on the proposed Baba center there, Townshend was surprised to find himself breaking down and confessing all the sundry and sordid grotesqueries of his existence in the rock world over the previous few years: "the paranoia, the drunken orgies, the financial chaos, the indulgent self-analysis . . . and, of course, the dreamy hopes for the future.

"Without batting an eyelid," wrote Townshend, "she listened to stuff that was making me recoil myself, then went on to talk a little about her own youth, her life with her husband, the trouble some of her students were having at the time. In short, she got me right in perspective."

It was a different Pete Townshend who showed up for the Who's late September 1975 rehearsals for their tour, which would begin the first week in October. Keith Moon told Townshend that the really remarkable thing was that Pete walked into the room with a smile on his face. (He was pretty much obliged to. In the *Rolling Stone* story, Townshend tells an ambiguous tale in which he receives orders direct from the Great Beyond to "keep playing guitar with the Who until further notice.")

Pete had slowly but surely been getting better. Keith Moon's progress was just as inexorably downhill. His life in Los Angeles, although frequently interrupted by Who business—the film, the album, the tour—was one long revel. In his way, though, Moon wasn't any less desperate than Townshend; it was just that he centered on the comic and upbeat side of tragedy, while Pete saw only the dire face of the coin. Every one of Moon's antics had an undercurrent of anguish. His carousing with Harry Nilsson, Ringo Starr and other members of Hollywood's Anglo-American Rat Pack was the product of wealth, boredom and above all, loneliness. (John Lennon participated but only during the spell when Yoko Ono had sent him packing.) Whenever one of the gang had a steady relationship, he dropped from sight. Mostly, though, the boozing, pills and hearty, hollow, all-night camaraderie ensured that no relationship was steady for long.

During the early days of recording *The Who By Numbers*, Keith had actually gone on the water wagon, a gesture that so impressed Pete Townshend that he, too, climbed aboard. But both soon fell off, Pete, using the excuse that his hair had started to fall out once more, Keith because drinking had become his way of life, not just a pick-me-up and a way of staying chipper but a reason for climbing out from under the covers in the first place.

No less than Townshend, Moon was ill. But because those around him didn't view his alcoholism as a disease—because it was understood as "Moonie's nature"—no treatment was tendered. After all, you can't change a man's nature. By definition, then, Keith Moon's condition was always pretty much the same. Townshend later said he did introduce Moon to a fellow musician who was a member of Alcoholics Anonymous. According to Pete, "He told me Keith was not an alcoholic. He told me that I possibly was. Later, I persuaded Keith to see Meg Patterson and George Patterson did help Keith—he travelled with us in Europe. Eventually Keith's drinking was seen to be disguising a wild addiction to cocaine in its eighth or ninth year. I don't think he ever stopped using it."

Yet as the Who began their first tour in nearly two years, the focus of attention wasn't Keith but the fact that the Who, after all their public squabbles, had managed to get back onstage together at all.

Daltrey described the tour as "back to basics." Moon put a finer point on it with an introduction one night. "We'd like to do something that Pete wrote several years ago," he proclaimed in his thickest mock-public-school accent. "Since then it's been made into lots of things—sterling, dollars, pounds, yen. This is something called . . . *Tommy*." Well that was about as back to basic as you could get for the Who. They did five numbers from the opera, a full half-hour of a show that ran close to two and a half hours. The set included only two songs from *The Who By Numbers*, "Dreaming From the Waist" and "Squeeze Box." There were four songs from *Who's Next*, a selection of the early singles ("I Can't Explain," "Substitute," "Magic Bus," and "My Generation" in an extended version that included bits of Bo Diddley's "Road Runner"). Chris Charlesworth wrote that the show indicated that they had learned to "celebrate rather than fear" Who history.

John Entwistle seemed to agree, telling John Swenson a bit later in the tour: "We're in a unique situation. We're the only group to have been around for eleven years and to have to include songs from all the different parts of our history. Our audiences are made up of young kids who still haven't heard the *Who's Next* songs live, so we're in a position of having to introduce our new fans to songs the old ones are already familiar with." The fans did not seem to mind; old and new, they flocked to the shows, hooked on one more recitation of a litany of rock & roll faith, persuaded by the perennial promise with which Entwistle concluded: "By this time next year our stage act will probably be different." The Who made this vow regularly for the better part of the next decade; it never happened.

There was one significant addition to the program: John Wolff had acquired, through the Who's holding company, a lavish £30,000 ($66,000) laser display, which lit up the stage with a beautiful array of effects, primarily during the *Tommy* episode. (Wolff would go on to become one of Europe's leading experts in laser technology, giving formal lectures on the subject and staging exhibitions in art galleries.)

For the fans, this wasn't much to offer, but there were no complaints. If anything, the fanaticism of the group's following grew. Still it was a remote relationship between the Who and its die-hards now, a bond of passive consumerism. The seventies version of rock activism was the tour-follower, the kid who saved all his money in order to be able to hitchhike to all the gigs. This was made possible by the increasing rarity of such tours: Two years between extensive concert tours became standard practice for groups of the stature of the Who and the Rolling Stones around this time. Many of these fans were "involved" only to the extent that they had the wherewithal to buy the official T-shirt, poster, scarf and cap, to hitchhike and sleep in a bedroll in pursuit of tickets in distant cities, to buy all of the official records and as many bootlegs as could be scoured up. Anyone with less leisure or income was, by definition, shut out from this form of "involvement." There was no movement to push the performers to inspire their audience to look more critically at the world, or even more introspectively at their own lives. Hints that the princelings of rock were merely paying lip service to their more exalted ideals were simply sneered away: "It's only rock & roll," indeed. Townshend wasn't the only one who was depressed and tempted to give up—so was anybody else with a memory and a conscience.

So the Who's tour went on, with its heaps of sound and light and laser gear, its militia of managers, accountants, agents and crewmen. The shows were guaranteed sellouts virtually everywhere; the question was now how quickly the tickets would be gone, not whether they'd sell. In the bigger towns, the real issues became how many shows the Who would play and in what size halls. For the most part, they played the biggest indoor arenas available, including three nights at 10,000-seat Wembley Pool in London.

The U.K. leg of the tour began on October 3, 1975. A week later, a previously scheduled break scattered the band. Daltrey went on a PR junket to New York, where *Lisztomania* was just opening to unanimous critical negativity. John Entwistle stayed in Manchester (where the Who had last played) to tape a course on bass playing for the BBC. Keith went to London to begin making a never-completed comedy album. Pete went to India, where he visited Meher Baba's surviving Mandali and the shrine at his Master's tomb.

When they rejoined, Moon's composure was shattered, for no particular reason. Always erratic, he'd simply lost his bearings.

The first gigs after the break were in Glasgow on October 15 and 16. After the second show, the Who headed for its British Airways flight to Leicester in the Midlands, a short hop. But the plane was put down by fog, landing at Prestwick Airport, not far from Glasgow.

Moon was enraged by the delay, primarily because he hated airports and hadn't the patience to wait for the weather to lift, especially after the pubs were shut. Walking by a computerized ticket terminal, he bashed and kicked it, inflicting serious though not irreparable damage.

The British Airways agent was incensed. He called the cops, and Moon was hauled off to the local jail, where he occupied himself by having an elaborate meal sent in. The next day, Keith was taken to court, where he was charged with breach of peace, told by the high sheriff that his conduct was "disgraceful," and fined. After offering to help the airline out by buying one of its surplus aircraft, ("Unlike me, they have a cash crisis on their hands"), Moon was released and met up with the band in time for their scheduled show in Leicester. It was a minor incident but not without its ominous implications, which were shortly confirmed.

The Who got through the first leg of their American tour without further incident. (This tour included a sold-out show at the 78,000-seat Pontiac, Michigan, Silverdome.) *Variety* reported that the three-week junket had pulled in $3,005,097 (£1,353,647), including $600,000 (£270,270) at Pontiac. The band's take, according to the reliable show biz trade journal, was $1,589,097 (£715,809), or about $350,000 (£157,000) per man, before taxes. This more than made up for the (as always, unprofitable) British tour, on which Moon claimed his total profit—after damages—was £46.70 ($103.67). The Who played three nights at the Hammersmith Odeon, just before Christmas, then took the next two months off.

On March 1 and 2, 1976, the Who played two nights at the Parc des Expositions in Paris. A week later, they flew to America for the beginning of another three-week tour, this one covering the length of the country, from New York's Madison Square Garden to Anaheim Stadium in southern California.

Two numbers into the opening gig, at Boston Gardens, Moon slumped over his drums in collapse. He was taken backstage and treated but simply couldn't continue. The official diagnosis was influenza. But something more was going on. The Boston show was moved to the end of the tour, April 1, and the show slated for the next night in Madison Square Garden was pushed back a day, to March 11.

The next night, Bill Curbishley and his wife, Jackie, who assisted him in managing the band, were in bed in their room at the Navarro Hotel in Manhattan. The phone rang. It was Moon. "I'm going to throw all the furniture out the window," he said.

"Well, throw it out the window, then," replied Curbishley. "Fuck it. I'm going to sleep." Bill hung up, but Jackie insisted that he go down to Moon's room. Curbishley resisted, familiar with Moon's shenanigans and confident that the drummer would wake someone else if his manager didn't respond. Keith probably just wanted someone to drink with. Jackie persisted, and since she wouldn't let him sleep, anyway, Bill finally threw on his clothes and got in the elevator. He arrived at Moon's door, which was slightly ajar.

"I tried to open it and I couldn't; there was something in the way," he recalled. "I managed eventually to get it open and went into the bedroom and there was Moon. The whole of the apartment was fucking saturated with blood. I've never seen as much blood in my life.

"He was lying on the floor; he had cut his foot. He had kicked a painting and the glass had broken and he had cut his foot right in the instep, in the vein. With every heartbeat it was spurting out black blood. He'd lost fucking pints.

"I got a towel and put a tourniquet on his leg, then phoned Jim Callaghan, our security guy. I told him to get down to the lobby and get a cab to take us to the nearest hospital. I picked Moon up and put him over my shoulder. All I had on was a pair of jeans, no shirt and no socks, and the blood was pissing over me. I was covered in blood.

"I got him in the elevator, got him downstairs and the bottom of the elevator was covered in blood. We got him into a cab and got him to the nearest hospital, which was a real flaky fucking hospital. There were all these druggies and alcoholics on the fucking floor.

"As we were going in to the doctor, Moon came around slightly. I said to him, 'Don't worry. We'll get you taken care of. I'm gonna get the doctor to get you nice and fit, so you're back within two days. Because I want to break your fucking jaw. Because you have fucked this band around so many times and I'm not having it any more.' "

The next morning Curbishley phoned the hospital, but Keith had already checked himself out and was back in the Navarro. "That was one time he definitely would have died," Curbishley claimed, "because there was no one there, he had lost so much blood, he was too weak even to get to a phone. There had been other times when he had been near death. But that was Moon." It's impossible not to wonder whether it need have been—but once more, the attitude was not that Keith needed help but that his difficulties were innate. (Remember, you can't change a person's nature.)

Roger and John were now ready to throw Moon out of the band. They had seen enough of his self-destruction and its disruption of the Who's schedule. Daltrey was somewhat sympathetic, thinking that Keith was simply grieving over the breakup of his marriage. The drummer's problems ran a good deal deeper than that, though. Keith Moon had been overindulging in alcohol and downing pills in vast quantities since he was sixteen. He didn't always seem to enjoy his escapades, but he was powerless to control himself; there was an utter absence of self-discipline in Keith's makeup. At least when it came to some things. At other times—"if there was something at the end of it for him," said Curbishley—he was totally aware. Moon was smart, wily, generous; he was also the opposite of each of these things. Like Townshend, he was trapped in a perpetual cycle of adolescent behavior and adult recrimination. Where Townshend struggled to break the pattern and come to terms with adulthood, though, Keith applied his willpower to avoiding solutions to his real problems, as if he feared that growing up would cost him his incredible wit, his sweet impulses of generosity and affection, his friends and his talent itself. It was as if Moon feared that looking at himself coldly and soberly would have revealed something too ugly to withstand.

Anyone could have told him this wasn't true, that he was extraordinary stoned or straight.

"Moon has a presence—the closest thing I've ever witnessed to a true Star quality—which takes control of everyone present the moment he enters the room, arms flailing out mock royal greetings to friends and strangers alike," wrote John Swenson upon first meeting him in the mid-seventies. "The master of the put-on, Keith is still the nice guy who buys drinks for everyone and enjoys being the life of the party. His nonstop banter only approximates conversation; sequentially, his thoughts make little or no sense, with the only ground rule being that every sentence will end in a punch line. . . ."

This was everything beautiful about Moon, but only those who saw him enact this ritual, over and again, could grasp the way each lovely action masked a darker side. Keith's jollity concealed his fear of not being liked; his generosity was insurance against being left alone or ignored; his humor hid myriad fears; his lack of logic was his final statement that he would remain a child or die trying. As Simon Frith wrote, it was Keith Moon, not Pete Townshend, who lived out the lyrics of "My Generation."

In the end, the rest of the band couldn't dump Moon. Townshend didn't want to be without him, but more than that, the Who were all too aware of what might happen to Moon if they tossed him out. As John Entwistle said, "What would Keith Moon do without the Who?" Finally, there was also the fact that the Who's magic was itself collective. No one asked what the Who would do without Keith Moon. Even so, the question wouldn't go away.

Despite Moon's deterioration, which began to tell on his playing, the Who toured more in 1976 than they had since 1971. The reason was simple: They had to, because Lambert and Stamp still had much of their money tied up. So touring was their only way of getting hold of much cash (except for royalties from *The Who By Numbers*, which had been made under a new agreement with Polydor). As a result, a tour of France in late May was followed by three outdoor dates, in England, Scotland and Wales. This was "The Who Put the Boot In," a tour of football stadiums that was considerably more lucrative than their similar tour of opera houses after *Tommy*. They played Charlton again (and it rained and was overcrowded and nasty again); Celtic Football Ground in Glasgow; and Swansea City Football Ground in Swansea, Wales. (At the Charlton show, *The Guinness Book of Records* measured the volume at 120 decibels, close to a jet plane's roar and a world record. No wonder Townshend was complaining of a constant ringing in his ears.)

They took a couple of months off after the June 12 Swansea gig. Moon went back to Los Angeles, where he had a celebrated run-in with his next door neighbor, actor Steve McQueen. McQueen loathed the chaos and noise that Keith brought to the chic Malibu colony. Knowing this, Moon never stopped badgering the movie star, eventually forcing McQueen to build a fence between their properties. Moon was overspending, as usual. His chauffeur and aide de camp, Dougal Butler, recalled Keith indulging his passion for cars by blowing a whole royalty check on a vintage Rolls-Royce. After a few months, Moon had to quit the Malibu house; its owner, television personality Robert Q. Lewis, later sued him for back rent and damages.

Because they'd been playing together so often, the Who were again reaching the kind of performance peak they'd attained after *Who's Next*.

Their prowess went to waste when three August dates in the American South flopped. The initial shows, indoors at the Capitol Centre near Washington, D.C., went smoothly, both musically and financially. But playing in a football stadium in Jacksonville, Florida, during hurricane season wasn't a brilliant move, especially since the South had always been the Who's weakest American market, as it was for most British groups. The Who drew 15,000 fans, which would have been a success in any arena, but only half-filled the stadium. "We were playing for the kids who weren't there," Townshend said afterwards. The final show, in Miami's soggy baseball stadium, was uncomfortably humid but packed. The Who's music was as powerful and focused that evening as it had ever been, earning them a rave write-up in *Rolling Stone*. For a few hours, it was possible to forget that the band had any problems.

But after the gigs, they lingered at the posh Fountainbleau Hotel in Miami Beach, and after two inactive days, Moon went berserk. He was walking through the hall with a portable tape deck, blasting one of his own records at top volume, when an assistant manager walked up and told him firmly to stop making so much noise. Moon turned down the volume. "Wait here a minute," said Moon, and entered his room, locking the door behind him. In the hallway, the manager trembled at the crashes, bangs and shrieks that followed.

Moon flung open his door, and with a wave of his arm, ushered the manager into his demolished suite. "*That* was noise," he proclaimed, reaching over to turn his tape deck back on. "THIS [he shouted over the cacophony] is the Who!"

Not sharing Keith's sense of humor, the hotel management called the cops. Bill Curbishley bailed him out, then had the drummer committed to Hollywood (Florida) Memorial Hospital for "psychiatric observation," presumably a euphemism for "alcoholic dry-out." Keith was released three days later. The diagnosis was "extreme exhaustion."

Another tour was booked to begin in San Diego on October 7, a two-week stint covering the West Coast and Canada. Keith was in no shape to make the trip. But his new girlfriend, a Swedish model named Annette Walter-Lax (a ringer for Kim), convinced him to enter an L.A. clinic to dry out. Moon came out in better shape than he went in but soon went about methodically reversing the improvement. At least he was in presentable shape for the final leg of the 1976 tour. It ended in Toronto, at Maple Leaf Gardens, on October 21. At the end of the show, which concluded with the band's now traditional set-closer, "Won't Get Fooled Again," Townshend beat a Les Paul to bits. Keith put his foot through his bass drum. It was his last show in North America.

34

Rock & roll doesn't age you in time. It ages you quicker than time.
　—*Pete Townshend*

A t the end of November 1976, the release of "Anarchy in the U.K.," the first single by the Sex Pistols, cracked rock & roll in half. It split the music historically, the scene musically, the audience into hostile camps. For the Sex Pistols and the punk rockers who followed them, "rock and roll had become simply the shiniest cog in the established order," as Greil Marcus wrote. "The Sex Pistols damned rock & roll as a rotting corpse—as a monster of moneyed reaction, a sentimentalized corruption that no longer served as more than a mechanism of glamorized oppression, self-exploitation and false consciousness." Yet, as Marcus also pointed out, they also *played* rock & roll—not the glossy surface of the sound, but its raw, naked guts, music much like the early Who singles but angrier, more bitter, less orderly. The punk rock groups who followed the Sex Pistols didn't have faith in anything at all, certainly not in music. They were responding to a betrayal that cut to the heart of the social world that rock had created; they owned no optimism, because optimism requires a future, and "no future for you" (the chorus of "Anarchy in the U.K.") was punk's first axiom.

The punks were the children of contemporary England, people in their late teens or early twenties who had grown up facing permanent unemployment while rock stars grew rich and fiddled with purely aesthetic issues. The new wave of bands lived in a polarized England: fascist youth groups combatted socialists in the same streets where whites battled blacks (West Indians, Africans) and browns (Pakistanis and Indians)—racial groups who had become an increasingly important and visible part of post-imperial English life. Added to the innate hostility between old and young, privileged and oppressed, cops and kids, was a loathing of anyone who pretended that there was hope. On top of everything else, punk was a war between optimism and pessimism.

If this sounds like France or America in the 1960s, the analogy is close enough. The punks would certainly have despised the comparison, for as Marcus noted, "they denounced all their forebears," especially their youth culture and rock & roll ancestors. Punks were *outré*, indecent, ugly, sexless, bored (not even jaded), nihilistic, mutilated, sadistic, perverted and unmusical. And they pronounced all these epithets virtues.

There was nothing reasonable about the punks. They did not come to stage a revolt that would replace the established order with something more positive. They came to smash, loot and burn a culture they despised, largely because they knew it despised them. In the wake of the Sex Pistols, dozens of bands bloomed. But these bands did not resemble the careful harmonic craftsmen of Liverpool or even the upwardly mobile mods and bohemian aesthetes of the London R&B world. The range of the punk bands was enormous, from great (the Clash) to horrid (the Damned), from the authentically dangerous (the Pistols, X Ray Spex) to grasping posers (the Stranglers), from the genuinely inept (the Pork Dukes) to the willfully amateurish (Chelsea). Along with them arose a new breed of independent record entrepreneurs determined to break the hegemony of Britain's traditional rock economy (controlled by corporations, which, in the wake of the Beatles, had simply substituted a few new figureheads and carried on as before). And just behind the entrepreneurs came a new squadron of more pop-oriented bands (Graham Parker and the Rumour, Elvis Costello and the Attractions, the Buzzcocks, the Vibrators, the Jam, the Boomtown Rats, Wire and a chain of others) that were the most prolific and creative since the mid-sixties.

The aim was to eradicate the hierarchy that ran rock—ultimately, to eradicate hierarchy, period. In the end, punk did no more than disrupt it, but that disruption proved to have exceedingly useful consequences. More than anything, the Sex Pistols, the punks who succeeded them and the best of the new wavers who followed created a new music-based community in which the bands were once more in close touch with their audience, in which the music was conceived as something that must meet human needs—for political discourse or dance action or anything in between.

The reaction to punk among rock's Boring Old Farts, as someone labeled everybody from John Lennon to Peter Frampton, was diverse. The dumbest soon exposed their narrowness: Caviling about punk's "lack of musicality" and its "violence," they wound up sounding like nothing so much as the squarest parents on the block. Others were shrewder than that, either biding their time while waiting for a chance to cash in on whatever more manipulable trend next appeared or expressing various degrees of support.

To the punks themselves, the response of the Boring Old Farts did not matter much, since to them, such performers were already has-beens. But the punks never represented a majority of listeners in England or anywhere else—they weren't even a majority of the people who responded to rock intensely or took it seriously. But committed older rock fans welcomed the punks because they smashed rock's boring tendency to become "respectable" and because they made rock responsible, if not idealistic, once again.

For the most part, the Who responded positively to punk. Moon and Entwistle were moderately enthusiastic, but both seemed to see punk's arrival mostly as a purely musical development and discussed it largely in terms of the Who's influence. (Hardcore punk sounded like Keith Moon was the only previous drummer in the history of the world.)

Roger Daltrey said that he identified with the punks, at least to the extent of perceiving them as "just kids off the streets [whose] music is exactly the same as we were doing—good rock & roll energy." Daltrey was right. By early 1977, "Substitute" was back in the British Top 10, and a mod revival was in the bud. Roger also appreciated the working-class anger of the punks. He saw other connections with the Who, too, claiming that Malcolm McLaren, the provocateur behind the Sex Pistols, had gotten many of his ideas from talks with Chris Stamp.

Punk's arrival left Pete Townshend profoundly moved and even relieved. Though he took some of what the new bands said about Boring Old Farts to heart (they were only expressing his own worries), Pete also identified with the punks completely. In the *Rolling Stone* article about his crack-up, Townshend wrote: "I spent the last three days of March talking about punk rock with Chris Stamp. I'm sure I invented it, and yet it's left me behind. If anything was ever a refutation of time, my constant self-inflicted adolescence must be.

"Chris told me the punk crowds banged their heads through ceilings, swore at one another, and if a fight broke out, one became the aggressor, one the victim. The crowd was one, the fighters played out roles.

"Damage, damage, damage. It's a great way to shake society's value system. It makes mothers disown their children. It makes teachers puke.

"I am with them. I want nothing more than to go with them to their desperate hell, because that loneliness they suffer is soon to be over. Deep inside, they know.

"I prayed for it, and yet it's too late for me to truly participate. I feel like an engineer.

"Just let me . . . watch."

Townshend was doing more than learning about punk rock from Chris Stamp in those early weeks of March 1977. The two were in the final stages of negotiating a settlement of all the litigation between the Who and their former managers.

Lambert and Stamp had held out for so many months by obtaining a £56,000 ($97,000) bank loan that Lambert had arranged as slyly as in the early days. Lambert and Stamp were ultimately stymied by the Who's refusal to sign any papers involving New Action or Track, just as the band were by the managers' refusal to release their money. Track had never developed any other lasting successes: Hendrix had died, Arthur Brown had dropped out, Thunderclap Newman had broken up, the rest of the label's talent roster never sold. One reason the label often avoided paying the Who's royalties was because it was always short of cash.

The final six months of the litigation were spent tussling over Townshend's American publishing royalties. Ironically, a key intermediary in the dispute turned out to be Allen Klein. In a series of March meetings that often lasted ten to twelve hours, Klein produced sheets of figures and rafts of statistics, marshaled a mountain of evidence and succeeded in thoroughly muddling the issues for both sides, who did not so much settle as give up. They arrived at a figure: Townshend would receive $1 million (around £575,000) in full settlement of his U.S. copyrights to date, the rights to the recordings would revert to the Who's companies and both sides would drop their litigation. They'd go their separate ways from then on. They arrived at an agreement, giving Pete more control of his songs, Klein a cut in his publishing, and Chris Stamp almost nothing. Pete also received several hundred thousand dollars in back royalties. The agreement ended the litigation; they'd go their separate ways from then on. At the end of the process, Townshend was handed a check for seven figures.

He left the meeting with Chris Stamp. They headed toward the Speakeasy, a Soho club where John Otway and Wild Willy Barrett, a pair of Midlands oddballs whom Townshend had helped get started, were playing. Townshend was in an uproar.

"I don't fucking believe all that!" he shouted. "I don't believe that after all these years in the rock business that I've sat through all that shit and gone through all that for six months just to get a fucking check. I feel like a piece of shit. And Allen Klein!"

"Look, Pete," Stamp said, "Allen Klein has been involved with the Who in ways you'll never know. Just be happy it's finished."

Down in the dark of the Speakeasy, Otway and Barrett were doing their final number. Townshend wasn't listening; he wanted to get drunk, and he did, on only two shots of whiskey. He began ranting, preaching, punching friends, smashing glasses, generally going berserk.

At the bar, he spotted two punks. Townshend peered through the dim smoky haze.

"Who are those guys?" he asked Stamp.

"They're in the Sex Pistols," Chris replied.

Townshend raced to the bar and pinned the hapless punks against it. "What the fuck are you doing in a piss 'ole like this?" he sneered. At last, he thought, he'd gotten his hands on Johnny Rotten, the Sex Pistols' spokesman and singer.

"Well, what the fuck are you doing here?" one of them replied. Townshend lifted him off the ground by the collar. "Uh, hello, Pete. Nice to meet you."

"Look, Johnny . . . " Pete began to snarl.

"No, no, I'm Paul Cook," said his victim, the band's drummer. "This [he gestured at his companion] is Steve Jones." Jones was the guitarist.

Townshend sat Cook down, but his raving didn't cease, it was only ignited further by the ignominy of having made the touristy mistake of presuming that any old Sex Pistol must be Johnny Rotten.

"Rock & roll's going down the fucking pan!" he shouted. "You've got to take over where the Who left off—and this time, you've got to finish the fucking job!" For long minutes, he ranted. At the pinnacle of his tirade, Pete took out his check and ripped it to bits, threw the pieces on the floor, spat upon them, ground them beneath his heel, all the while spouting more invective, riddled with allusions to decadence, disgraces and disagreements that his listeners (which now included almost everybody in the joint) could have known nothing about. After a few minutes, he ran out of steam and slowed down enough for Cook to cut in with a question.

"Uh, Pete," he said cautiously, "the Who aren't going to break up, are they?"

"What does it matter if the Who break up? We're fucking finished! It's a disaster! We've compromised everything to bits, anyway. We're prostitutes."

"'Cause we really like the Who, don't we, Steve? They're our favorite group. Be a drag if they broke up."

Townshend groaned and cursed, let out a mighty "*Arrrgggh!*"

"I'm disappointed in you," he said, and left the club. He walked only a few paces beyond the exit, then slumped into a nearby shop doorway, out cold.

He awoke with a policeman's boot in his midsection. Townshend's celebrated blue eyes fluttered open, fighting off the sun and a bitter headache. "Wake up, Pete," said the cop. "As a special treat, if you can get up and walk away, you can sleep in your own bed tonight."

Townshend climbed to his feet and staggered away, a disheveled, slouching, humiliated and exhausted figure. He made it to the nearest tube station, bought a ticket to Richmond, took a cab from the station and dumped himself on his own doorstep. When he entered the house, Karen was waiting, annoyed and worried.

"Where have you been?" she asked.

"I've been to hell," groaned Pete, and went to bed. He wrote about it when he woke up, in a song called "Who Are You," which captured the strain and humor of the period, the fundamentally ludicrous experiences of the evening. Townshend never needed much excuse to wallow in self-loathing, and the legal settlement, which ensured his wealth and killed his relationship with Kit Lambert, was better than most. Pete also felt that too much involvement in legal and business affairs was unartistic.

"I felt I was spending all my time behind a desk and the Sex Pistols were out enjoying the dream," he said. But the Who, his vehicle for the pursuit of that dream, did precisely nothing together in 1977. For the first time in more than ten years, there wasn't even an album released at Christmas. Instead, they worked alone. John Entwistle dabbled with a science fiction story he was attempting to write as a rock opera—a tale of clones, some aspects of which would shortly cease to be fictional. Roger Daltrey made a third solo album, *One of the Boys*, the best he'd done, even though it didn't come close to being a hit. Pete Townshend finally opened his Meher Baba center and laid plans for a bookstore (Magic Bus, in Richmond) and a publishing company (Eel Pie Publishing). Like John and Roger, Pete spent a great deal more time attending to domestic duties. Unlike them, he wedged in fairly frequent rounds of club-hopping, staying in touch with whatever musical commodity was currently recognized as being liked.

Keith Moon remained exiled in California without any particular domestic life to speak of. He was still seeing Annette Walter-Lax but also still pining for Kim and Mandy. Mostly, he was answering Entwistle's question—"What would Keith Moon do without the Who?"—in all the worst possible ways.

As the Who, they invested over £1 million (around $1,750,000) in acquiring a portion of Shepperton Film Studios, in the London suburbs. There they had rehearsal space, access to sound stages and space to store and experiment with their own recording, lighting and laser equipment. Bob Pridden and John Wolff had virtual laboratories on the grounds. The Who also moved into the movie business, putting up an eventual £300,000 ($525,000) to enable Jeff Stein (an American Who fan still in his early twenties) to acquire old footage of the band for a career retrospective film. Curbishley made a financing deal with Polytel, the Polydor film wing, to shoot *Quadrophenia*, working with Franc Roddam, a young writer/director who'd never done a feature but who had made an impressive film for the BBC, *Dummy*, about a deaf teenage whore. There was serious talk of reviving *Lifehouse*; scripts were redrafted, directors sounded out, Townshend wrote some new songs in hope that they would fit a more realistically crafted version of the film. (He was now willing to concede the acceptability of merely creating the *illusion* that Bobby and the audience disappeared.)

Townshend still felt that he had betrayed Kit Lambert and Chris Stamp, even though he understood intellectually that they had been counterproductive and worse as his business representatives. And he was now managed by someone with whom he did not share as much (and, in fact, may even have felt threatened by). At least on the surface, Bill Curbishley was Roger Daltrey's man. Bill's style had more in common with Roger's street-level suss; he was without the social sensitivity and grace of Kit Lambert. Yet Curbishley delivered more of Townshend's dream than Kit and Chris had ever been able to. The Who had their own films in production at last. For the first time, someone rational was in charge of the band's business.

Townshend and Curbishley's relationship never lost its undercurrent of antagonism. There was never much warmth between them. As late as 1982, Curbishley could say, "Pete Townshend will always be dishonest. It's in his nature."

In the words of Little Richard, Pete Townshend "got what he wanted and he lost what he had."

In late 1976, Ronnie Lane came to Pete to ask for help in making his next solo album. Since leaving the Faces in 1973, Lane had fallen on hard times.

Having left the band because he was sick of big-time rock, Ronnie had become a sort of wandering gypsy musician, actually traveling for a time in wagons and playing outdoors under a tent. Glyn Johns had helped him score a quick hit in 1974, with "How Come," but that record was only successful in England, and it was no more possible to successfully sustain a band at more than subsistence level without U.S. hits in 1974 than it had been in 1964 (or would be in 1984). Eventually, even Lane's mobile studio (which served as the control room for *Quadrophenia*) was lost because his managers had not left him enough cushion to handle his tax bills after the successful years with the Faces.

In early 1976, shortly after an abortive attempt to re-form the Small Faces, Lane contacted Townshend. "Basically, the album came about because I was in financial trouble, and I went to see Pete, not to ask for anything, just to see him socially," said Lane. "Obviously, we talked about each other's state. Mine came up and he said, 'Well, we've talked about working together in the past. Why don't we get an album together?' I said, 'That would solve my problem.' It did."

Townshend said that he was "keen to do something with Ronnie, as I knew he would stir me up from my veritable complacency." They approached Glyn Johns—another person with whom Townshend was eager to work "without the heavy pressure of a Who gig." Glyn said that he was "dog tired, overworked" but agreed. At the producer's suggestion, an all-star lineup of musicians was assembled, including Eric Clapton, Charlie Watts of the Rolling Stones, Rabbit Bundrick, John Entwistle, sub-Stone Ian Stewart, Mel Collins, Henry Spinetti, Benny Gallagher, Graham Lyle, Billy Nicholls and Peter Hope-Evans.

Townshend and Lane had a quixotic relationship, and Sancho Panza resented his role. Lane had about half an album's worth of material already composed; Townshend had a few songs of his own ready. In the course of production, Ronnie wrote one more, a lovely folkish air, "Annie," while Townshend contrived "Street in the City," an elaborate orchestral arrangement conducted by his father-in-law, Edwin Astley. (Jon Astley, Karen Townshend's brother, had become Glyn Johns' assistant engineer, as well.) Lane and Townshend played and sang together on only three numbers, "Rough Mix," "Heart to Hang on To," and a version of Don Williams' country hit, "Till the Rivers All Run Dry."

According to Lane, the sessions were "quite funny. A lot of rowing. Me and Pete, we love each other a lot, but we rub each other up the wrong way, as well. He's a much bigger fellow than me, as well—he's got a longer reach than I have." Townshend wrote production notes for the project which capture the flavor of the occasion:

"Sometimes Ronnie and I would talk about life. That would mean Ronnie insulting me and me hitting him. Sometimes Eric Clapton would come to play. That would mean Ronnie insulting him, Eric hitting him, and then falling over. Glyn and Ronnie often discussed Ronnie's songs. That consisted of Ronnie trying to keep Glyn in the studio till three or four in the morning while he insulted him."

Lane thought Townshend next to impossible to truly collaborate with. "I couldn't make out why we didn't spend an hour or two or an evening or two to write a song together. I've got a few ideas. Pete had a few ideas. My ideas weren't finished, and with his help they could have been finished—things like that. And vice versa. So I said, 'Why don't we get together and write some things?' He turned around and said, 'What? And split the publishing?' I was floored. I never brought it up to him again."

That sort of rough humor, so abusive when it hits the listener the wrong way, is probably the reason Pete and Ronnie bickered and battled so much. For his part, Townshend confessed to being stubborn. "My material is always somehow dead set in my head. It takes a hard man to change my ideas and preconceptions," he wrote. Lane was not about to indulge in the kind of protracted struggles that the other members of the Who sometimes did in order to modify Townshend's original plans. The only song on which Lane and Townshend receive joint credit is "Rough Mix," a blues-based instrumental that features neither of them, just Eric Clapton's guitar and Rabbit Bundrick on organ loping side by side, effortless but aimless.

Townshend did feel that he and Lane influenced each other's music. "I was able to gently contribute to Ronnie's stuff, getting to play in a way I hadn't done for years, without tension or pressure," he said. "Ronnie's contribution to my stuff came in a much deeper way. Not only would I not have produced the tracks I did with him on the album were it not for him, but his encouragement and enthusiasm made me try more as a musician than as a sensationalist. When I finished a number, it was Ronnie who looked proud. When I did a good vocal, it was Ronnie who got the kick. It's hard to explain, but in a word, friendship says it."

Townshend's songs here suggest that for once his rhetoric jibed with reality. With the exception of "Street in the City," a rather formal experiment, Townshend's music on *Rough Mix* has an ease and naturalness long missing from his work with the Who. Pete had never displayed so much knowledge of and ability to work with folk-based music, and his rock & roll had rarely been so graceful. And for once, Townshend's lyrics lived up to their archetype: honest, clear and convincing, not afraid to be sentimental and self-mocking. To put it simply, Pete sounds as though he's enjoying himself for the first time since *The Who Sell Out*. Freed of the need to prove something to the Who, Townshend made music that was captivating in its maturity and, as a bizarre by-product, seemed much more innocent than anything he'd essayed in ages.

The three tracks on which he takes solo vocals are the best. "My Baby Gives It Away" is a straight-ahead rock number with a solid groove established by the drumming of Charlie Watts. Singing against the funkiest backbeat he'd ever been given, Townshend created the sort of vignette and characterization he had abandoned during his opera years. The story of a girl who is the ultimate in free love, "My Baby Gives It Away" careens from punch line to punch line, and even on the bridge, when Townshend adds lines that enjoin all listeners to get an electric guitar because "there's no other way to beat the blues," he is distanced enough from his own intensity to wryly comment, in a voice somewhere between Randy Newman and Roy Orbison: "*Ah* beat 'em."

In "Keep Me Turning," Townshend learns to laugh at his spiritual ambition, too. Among lines about planetary overcrowding and apocalypse, Townshend interweaves a story of cosmic futility that would not have been out of place on *The Who By Numbers* (or in *Lifehouse*): "They saw the Messiah/But I guess I missed him again/That brings my score to a hundred and ten." Townshend uses the backstage passes used at rock concerts as a metaphor for getting into heaven (or reaching Nirvana). In the end, he's able to smile even at his hope of ever reaching his heart's desire. But the song's real force lies in the gentleness with which Townshend delivers the chorus, which prays for deliverance from the repetitious cycle of life (or lives). Because it's not burdened with the hostility of his Who songs, "Keep Me Turning" is a much clearer indication of the real nature of Townshend's spiritual vision.

There is a temptation to see "Misunderstood" as a parody of punks ("Just wanna be a moody man/Say things that nobody can understand") or of the kind of street toughs who made up more and more of the Who's American audience, belligerent males with nothing more on their minds than; "Just wanna be misunderstood/Wanna be feared in my neighborhood." Yet in the end, this song is even more autobiographical than "Keep Me Turning," and it seems merely accidental that it was not included on *The Who By Numbers*. Townshend sings the song so slyly and the accompaniment is so slight and silly that it's hard to take it seriously. Yet no one but Pete Townshend better fits the character "Misunderstood" describes:

I wanna be either old or young,
Don't like where I've ended up or where I've begun,
I always feel I must get things in the can,
I just can't handle it the way I am

At such times, Pete seemed far from the identity crisis of the year before.

When *One of the Boys* was issued in the spring of 1976, Roger Daltrey did several prominent interviews designed to goad Townshend into renewed action or at least to express his own determination to get the Who working once again. "It's more important now than ever that the Who survive, because they're the only group left that really said and did a lot from the old days," Daltrey said. And although he admitted that being locked into their old material was a problem, he added: "The only thing that still matters to me in life is getting on that stage in front of an audience. Nothing else is as important. I still get a thrill out of it."

In the interviews he did following the release of *Rough Mix* in September, Townshend skillfully repositioned himself in relation to the changes wrought by punk, as an individual within the Who and as a member of rock's old guard. Although Pete said that the spirit of the new music evoked memories of his own salad days, he was as snide as ever about his competitors.

"Well, they can't ever pull down the Great Temple of rock, unfortunately. It's never been there, so how can they pull it down?" he sneered. "I used to wake up in the night praying to be destroyed: 'Get me out of this bloody whirlpool.' I thought the hypocrisy of the position the Who was in was just unbelievable. In the end, I actually thought of inventing a new form of music which would take over from where the Who left off. In my imagination, I invented punk rock a thousand times.

"There is a great humanity in the punk scene, a great moral social conscience. It's making it work that is difficult."

Townshend said that the only reason he hadn't quit the Who was because of "an unwillingness to change" and because of a lingering loyalty to the other members and the Who's "diehard" fans. There could be no more Who tours, however. Pete had hearing problems, he felt obliged to spend more time with his children and he had questions about the basic listener-performer relationship in the kind of shows the Who now played. "Are we really making fans happy?" he asked. "Every time we go into a town, we get complaints we're not playing enough shows. If we play at a big stadium, we get complaints it's too big and they can't see us. The only answer is to play small halls for years at a time. I've got other things to do."

During one of their periodic meetings with their business advisers, Townshend informed the band of his decision not to do any more touring. As he expected, John's face clouded over. Keith seemed fairly noncommittal, but then, Moon wasn't in shape to challenge anyone effectively (or to tour, for that matter). To Pete's amazement, Roger said he agreed.

Well, Daltrey had other irons in the fire. He had accepted a part in *The Legacy*, a trashy horror film, playing a pop singer who gets his throat cut, a role that appealed to his sense of irony. And Roger was developing a movie project of his own based upon the book *McVicar*, the autobiography of John McVicar, the British escaped convict who had become public enemy number one by using the tabloids to taunt the cops while he was on the loose and then became a formidable leftwing sociologist when he was recaptured. McVicar's book about his incarceration, which incorporated his own dramatic story as well as harsh, well-reasoned criticism of the British penal system, had made him a national celebrity and earned him his early release from jail. Roger identified wholeheartedly with this smart, wily character because McVicar seemed like someone Roger Daltrey might have become if his music hadn't paid off. Daltrey also worked his farm seriously, even stocking the ponds with trout for commercial sport fishing.

In 1976 and 1977, the band probably could not have made any road plans anyhow, since Keith Moon was in genuinely dire physical as well as emotional condition. The drinking had begun to take a visible toll: Keith's weight had ballooned, and the cheeks that had once seemed perpetually rosy now had the ruddy false heartiness of alcoholism. There was no possibility of mounting a tour as long as Moon was in such straits.

Nevertheless Townshend had enough demos for another Who album. Sessions were booked for Ramport beginning in early December. Glyn Johns would again produce. But the early days of recording went nowhere. Keith, Pete and John spent much of their time sipping cognac and ginger or vintage port, swapping yarns and ignoring the studio technicians. Several times, Glyn went home early in disgust. Roger often didn't bother coming in at all; he lived two hours away from the studio and figured there was no sense in spending all that time traveling if the others were going to waste more of it in the studio.

Little or nothing was accomplished the few times they did buckle down. "The demos were not really reproducible by the band," said Johns. "In other words, he'd written grooves and certain sound ideas which were not really the Who—not with Keith Moon in 'em, anyway.

"Pete's preparation was as good, the amount of material was as much. But he'd gone into a different musical thing—which I, for one, was tremendously impressed with. Unfortunately, a lot of it didn't really suit the Who as the Who saw themselves."

In the wake of the punk upheaval, Townshend felt liberated from having to fly the flag of rock & roll. He wanted to turn once again to extended and more "mature" forms of music. "At the moment, I'm really keen on trying to steer the Who in the direction of doing grandiose projects of some sort—films, musicals, concept albums," he said just after the release of *Rough Mix*. "It would be easy pickings to stick out an album—'a hard-edged rock album'—which would sell a couple million in the States. But frankly, I'd prefer to make a film, despite the fact that my hair fell out when we did *Tommy*."

So Pete's demos incorporated more elements derived from jazz and *musique concrète*. He revived many of the synthesizer ideas suggested by *Quadrophenia*, introduced more elaborate guitar figures (for the first time emphasizing notes rather than chords), created more elastic and diffuse structures, used eccentric time signatures. This material was a radical departure from both the brittle hard rock of *The Who By Numbers* and the folkish ease of *Rough Mix*. Although the compositions still had verses and choruses, they had much more in common with the "art rock" of such post-*Sgt. Pepper's* groups as Genesis and King Crimson than with the Who's traditional hard rock. And of course, art rock was music associated with the studio, not the stage. Townshend's ambitions had taken a truly decisive turn.

Not necessarily one that the rest of the band could or would go along with. The new material didn't ask much more of Roger Daltrey—many of the vocals were either highly theatrical, resembling Gilbert and Sullivan in their cadences, or else variations on the drones and chants that interested Townshend in Indian and Middle Eastern music. But Roger would rather sing rock, and he was convinced the world would rather hear it. Entwistle was more than capable of playing whatever was required, but John also regarded anything that didn't kick ass directly as a step in the wrong direction. As for Moon, whatever flexibility he had ever had was now pickled, only a memory.

"I would have loved to see the Who go in the direction those demos went. They certainly, all of them with the exception of Moonie, had the ability, and I liked the idea of a slight change," said Johns. "But it wasn't to be."

By the middle of December, everyone was sufficiently frustrated to simply drop the sessions for a long holiday break and the band's only stage performance of 1977, a gig at Kilburn Gaumont, with 1,500 guests invited by the band and Capital Radio (London's first legal commercial radio station, which had begun broadcasting in 1973). The gig was arranged because in the course of researching his retrospective film, Jeff Stein had been able to locate almost nothing of quality from the band's post-*Who's Next* stage performances. (Entwistle said that was because the band had banned cameras from their gigs as soon as they had the clout to do so.)

The Kilburn show was a disaster. Moon hadn't practiced "in three years" (in John's words), and he was a nervous wreck, distraught at having to face a public appearance in such gruesome physical condition. For the first time, there was no way to conceal his weaknesses: They showed in his potbelly and in his playing.

The rest of the band was almost as nervous—it had been fourteen months since Toronto. "That was the first time I can remember being drunk before a show," said Entwistle. Between their ragged playing and the necessity of stopping and starting while camera angles and lenses were changed, the show was such a negative experience that no one could have blamed them if none of the Who ever took a stage again.

The album sessions were scheduled to start afresh in mid-January but accidents delayed them once more. First, Rabbit Bundrick, who was playing keyboards on the record, slipped getting out of a taxi at the studio door and broke his arm. Then Townshend, while visiting his parents, put his fist through a window in frustration at his inability to get them to stop bickering; when they didn't listen, he rubbed his fingers in the glass and was taken, bleeding, to the hospital for stitches. There wasn't any permanent damage, but he couldn't play until mid-February.

Keith Moon had returned to England permanently. He took over Harry Nilsson's flat in Park Street, Mayfair, not far from where Kit Lambert and Chris Stamp had been staying when the Who had first started recording. During the break in recording, Moon went off to a health farm without even Annette for company. He looked better on his return, having taken off a bit of weight. "At one point, we thought this was it," said Entwistle. "Then he went into the health farm and reappeared totally revitalized." Moon's health had always seemed as indescribably subject to regeneration as if he were a character from a cartoon. But Keith's return to health was either temporary or completely illusory. He had not regained his touch at the drum stool, and this upset him so much that he fell back off the wagon. Sometimes he didn't show up for sessions at all.

"Moonie played games," said Glyn Johns. "You never knew if he was drunk or not drunk, why he was pretending to be drunk or why he was drunk, if he was. But you can guarantee that there was an extremely good reason for it, which he wasn't going to own up to. It could have been insecurity, it could have been anything."

"Pete was really worried about the fact that he was drinking as much as he was. We all were. Pete was instrumental in trying to get Moonie to stop drinking. I remember he did for a while. But there was always the overriding thing, it seemed, that everybody believed he was totally indestructible, that the guy was made of concrete, because he abused himself far more than any other human being I ever met. We all believed he was invincible because he held himself together so well until the end."

Moon's playing had always been eccentric and erratic, but now, according to Glyn, even what minimal attention span he had began to disintegrate. "I think personally that he'd lost confidence in his own ability. So he covered up, because of the manner in which he played. If he was ever called on to do anything that had to be in any way rigid, he always found it very difficult. If there was an arrangement and he had to change his rhythm pattern for the bridge or whatever, he never knew where he was in the song. He just hit things as fast and as hard as he could, and that was it.

"If there was a stop, he'd feel that coming and he'd stop. But if you said to him, 'Okay, I want you to go to a ride cymbal in the choruses,' he wouldn't even know what a fucking chorus was. Or 'Don't play the ride cymbal.' Because that was his big thing, hitting the ride cymbal all the time—which is just like a big wash all over everything, so if you were trying to do anything with any degree of subtlety in it, you'd had it. You had to take his cymbals away from him—you had to remove them from the kit so he couldn't hit 'em.

"If you said to him, 'At the end of the intro, change to half-time,' he wouldn't know what the fuck you were talking about. He'd go, 'Yeah, okay.' He'd never do it. He didn't want to have to think like that. In earlier days, he would have known what I was talking about and he would have got through it. He would have sat and watched me—I always set him up where I could see him, and I'd wave at him, you know, I'd give him signals through the window, exactly what he was supposed to do.

"In a way it became a joke, it became a sort of ritual with he and I. It was always a battle. He'd always try and make me feel awful about trying to get him to do something different—like suddenly taking half his kit away. It was all game-playing with him.

"But by that time, he'd lost the ability to do it. And of course, the more it went on, the more he kept fucking up takes and so on, the more insecure he got, like anybody would get. And of course, then it just got worse and worse."

Entwistle and Daltrey were ready to dump Moon from the band. But after what he'd gone through with Lambert and Stamp's departure, Townshend simply could not bear the thought of losing Moon, too. Pete took Moon aside and firmly warned him that if his playing didn't shape up, he would be out of the Who. Moon made some adjustments, and when he did, they began to make some progress again, but it was still hard going, and on one song, "Music Must Change," which was in 6/8 time (always a nemesis for Keith), they simply used the percussion from Pete's demos: his footsteps on the hardwood floors of his country house.

It wasn't only Keith with whom Glyn Johns found himself in dispute. Indeed, Glyn's problem with Keith didn't amount to a spat so much as mutual frustration. But Glyn's prodding of Roger Daltrey, trying to get the singer to sing differently, in the style of the new numbers, met stiff and constant resistance, until Roger finally threatened to hit Johns, who also lost his normally unruffled, haughty cool. They made up, but the tension lingered.

In retrospect, Johns understood Roger's feelings. Like any band who had become superstars, the Who tended to ape itself whenever in doubt. "I think it's quite a normal subconscious reaction," Johns said. "I think it's something about any band that's been around that long and is renowned for one thing. You know that 'chigga chum' works for you. You think, 'I've made a lot of money out of 'chigga chum.' You don't even think about it. You just do it." Glyn figured his job was to make the musicians think about their reflexive habits. But Daltrey, especially, wanted to maintain a base of familiarity within the stylistic changes the band was making. Although he eventually succumbed to a few of the producer's ideas (and wound up very proud of his performances on the record), Roger would never feel totally comfortable with any technique more elaborate than a growl and a scream.

As the sessions waffled into the spring, Johns was faced with a conflict between the Who project and making the next record by Joan Armatrading, a singer with whom he'd made several recent hits. "In the end, I ran out of time; I had to move on to something else," he said. "Obviously, they'd got a time problem as well, so they couldn't wait for me, and they chose not to. Which was quite acceptable. They used my assistant at the time, Jon Astley, to finish it, and I think he did a very good job. I have no complaints at all.

"But by the time we'd got to that point, I wasn't keen on finishing the record, anyway. I was bored rotten. I mean I was ab-so-lute-ly bored."

Jon Astley recorded various bits and pieces of many of the songs on the album, which was to be called *Who Are You*, after the song Townshend wrote about his night of madness at the Speakeasy. Astley recorded all of "New Song," "Guitar and Pen" and "Sister Disco," which were perhaps the least orthodox compositions on the record, an indication of how difficult Johns's problems with Moon must have been. The sessions stumbled to a finish just as summer was beginning, then Pete and Astley spent the next few weeks mixing.

Woe to the stragglers!
We exist only in so far as
we hang together. He had
straggled in a way; he had not
hung on; but he was aware of it
with an intensity that made him
touching, just as a man's more
intense life makes his death more
touching than the death of a
tree. I happened to be handy,
and I happened to be touched.
That's all there is to it.
          —*Joseph Conrad,*
             Lord Jim

The Kilburn gig was so poor that Jeff Stein was left with the same gaping holes in his film. Stein was young enough to be brazen, and he pushed all through the *Who Are You* sessions for the band to do another performance for his movie. His argument was that the Who themselves would be disappointed if he had to use only the contemporary footage he already had. Eventually, Stein wore the band down, and in late May 1978, the band arranged another show, this one on a soundstage at Shepperton. This time, they preceded the gig with an afternoon's rehearsal, which Stein also filmed. It was a lark, the band running through such numbers as "Barbara Ann" and "I Want to Hold Your Hand." (A bit of the former was included in the movie.)

The actual show was much stronger than the one at Kilburn, largely because the Who decided to do it as a concert. The audience was hand-picked because the group wanted listeners who would be receptive to long waits between shots. But in the end, they realized that they wouldn't give a proper performance unless they went through their act from top to bottom. And they did, turning in a delirious "Baba O'Riley" and some other strong songs.

When the show was over, the band trudged sweating backstage, exhausted. Stein once more decided to brave their wrath. He went to Townshend and said, "Look, Pete, I still don't have a definitive 'Won't Get Fooled Again.' You've gotta go out and do it one more time." Stein was also thinking of the Who fans out front, who were still chanting and hooting for more.

Townshend thundered curses and imprecations, swore that Stein was incompetent and downright evil. Then he and the band looked at one another and trooped back to the stage. They were met with hosannas and calls for all the favorite songs they'd not yet done that night.

Townshend stepped to the lip of the stage, and a sneer curled his lip. "There's a guitar up here if any big-mouthed little git wants to fuckin' take it off me," he snarled, and was met with cheers. He stepped to the rear of the stage, twiddled an amplifier dial, zipped up his waist-length brown jacket and signaled Bob Pridden to begin the synthesizer tape for "Won't Get Fooled Again."

Knowingly or not, Stein had provoked the Who. They went through the motions, giving him just what he wanted in the most grudging way. But their resentment just added an edge to their performance; try as they might to shrug this one off, every bit of strain that was added to the song only improved it. They came out of the synthesizer break, and Moon lunged for his tom-toms, the headphones slipping forward on his sweaty head, and Daltrey screamed and Townshend did a skidding knee drop across the breadth of the stage. Stein had what he needed, a breath-takingly brutal version of the band's set-closer. Townshend banged his guitar again and again upon the stage; it did not shatter. Moon tried to kick over his drums, but the kit was nailed down. So he stood on his toms, and Townshend reached out a hand and helped him step over.

Keith stepped down hard, a bit staggered, and fell into Pete's arms. They hugged each other tight, and then the fans began to leap on the stage, only a few of them, but it felt like an army, they grasped their heroes so tightly. The musicians pulled away, took one final bow. Pete waved and led Keith off the stage.

It was the last time Keith Moon ever faced an audience.

Trouser Press, the American Anglophile rock magazine, sent editor Dave Schulps to England around the time of the Kilburn show. He thought he was going to be conducted on a guided tour of the famous stash of Pete Townshend demos by the *auteur* himself. What happened, however, was that Townshend and Schulps sat down for Pete's latest interview-confession.

Townshend had a specific purpose in doing the interview. He wanted to make it explicitly clear to his American fans that the Who would *not* be playing live any longer, that he felt the band had "created a straitjacket" and that there was no chance he would be changing his mind. "It's like being the Queen. People wave and shout just because you're there," he said.

"Different people want different things," Townshend went on. "I hear that Jagger said the Stones would be onstage until they're fifty, and look at the human wreckage they've already left behind them. I don't want to be responsible for that for the rest of my life. I can excuse a lot of the wreckage the Who have created, put it down to experience. But now, I can't do it."

He added that the damage to his ears had a great deal to do with his decision. "Electric guitar hurts my ears. It's bad to the extent that if I'm subjected to really loud noise for a long time, I get a lot of pain. And apparently, pain is the indication of further damage." He'd done recent Who gigs with earplugs, which bothered him only when he tried to sing and couldn't hear himself properly. But he also admitted that "to some extent, the thing about that sound is the pain of it. The thing I used to adore was the fact that it *hurt*." This may have been one more reason for his turn to more complex but less physical music.

Pete's biggest fear about the Who continuing was that they would just "crash on and on and on until they became seedy and plastic." He claimed that the Who were really the only band "that's lasted with any kind of integrity whatsoever." Schulps asked him how he defined integrity.

"We haven't made too many of the obvious mistakes," he replied. "Nobody has killed themselves off with dope, nobody has done anything wildly dishonest, nobody has killed anybody. We've never put out what I feel was a dishonest record, we've never deliberately gone out to exploit large numbers of people, we've toured and worked hard whenever we could. . . .

"I feel maybe we should try to prove to people and new bands—particularly since the new wave bands are so assertive in their attitudes—that it is possible to grow within the rock biz; to grow old gracefully and to evolve in a way that doesn't lose the spirit of things." But he knew that the band had "come through on a razor's edge. . . . We've been very lucky."

The oddest thing about the Schulps story was a sidebar interview with Roger Daltrey in which the singer contradicted Pete completely. Whether they had had a disagreement after the band meeting, whether they had misunderstood each other at the meeting or whether Roger had just been humoring Pete is hard to tell. But what Daltrey told Schulps was direct and explicit: "I can't wait to get back onstage again. . . . Oh, I mean, Pete has bad problems with his ears, it's true, but we all want to go back. We'll work on him."

In July, Keith and Annette took a holiday trip to Mauritius, a small island in the Indian Ocean. When he left, Moon seemed to be making progress. He hadn't quit drinking entirely, but he was looking a bit more fit, and his really radical episodes of being out of it were less frequent.

Moon was never one to endure boredom, though, and Mauritius was far enough away to make the plane flight exceedingly tedious. On his way back home, Moon began drinking and lost control, assaulting the stewardesses and the crew. When the plane made an intermediate stop in the Seychelle Islands, Moon was tossed off and taken to a local hospital, where he was pronounced unfit to travel. He made it home the next day—on Air Kenya, not British Airways, which had had enough of him.

The incident merely reconfirmed what the rest of the band already knew about his chances for getting well. The ground was laid for Keith's removal from the Who. John and Roger were ready to make a move, but Pete held back, out of loyalty if nothing else.

A few weeks later, it was announced that Keith Moon had been appointed director of public relations and publicity for the Who Group Ltd's interests at Shepperton Film Studio. It was a task for which Keith was well-suited, and he took his duties seriously, actually doing interviews to boost the place. Yet as many suspected (and as Keith must also have divined), this new job was preparatory to his departure from the Who.

The timing wasn't right. *Who Are You*, the Who's ninth album of original material, was released in late August 1978. It was preceded by a single, "Who Are You" (with another Entwistle B-side, "Had Enough"). This was the song that told of Townshend's Speakeasy demolition derby and encounter with the Sex Pistols, and the lyric was both funny and oblique. The chorus was a different story, though. The song began and ended and had an extensive middle section composed solely of this chorus, a circular chant of the title: "Who are you? Who, who . . . who, who?" Townshend based it on the chanting of the Sufi dervish dancers of Turkey and the Near East, who uttered similar syllables as they whirled. He structured the number around a schematic developed with "Won't Get Fooled Again" and "Behind Blue Eyes" which now became one of the central devices of his writing: an up-tempo opening verse/chorus section leading to a central section where the rhythmic and melodic material was slowed down and elaborated, returning to the opening section for the conclusion. This was especially effective on "Who Are You" because the lyric was basically a chant, anyway. The result was the Who's first really classic single in years. The group's characteristic energy and drive was propelled by unison riffing between guitar, bass and synthesizer and accelerated by the tension between Daltrey's lead vocal and the chorus.

"Who Are You" closed the album with more than six minutes of classic Who music, which made the rest of the record an anomaly. The album's theme was expressed in the titles of the first and last songs on side one, "New Song" and "Music Must Change," and it is directly or indirectly a concern of two of Townshend's other three songs, "Guitar and Pen" and "Sister Disco."

Who Are You is not nearly as unified as *The Who By Numbers*, since the theme of Townshend's songs has almost nothing to do with that of Entwistle's. And the music doesn't reinforce the message: There is nothing truly new here, no real departures. The synthesizer work is arresting, but it is only a development of the playing on *Quadrophenia*. "Music Must Change," without any drumming and with very jazzy licks from Townshend, is a genuinely different sound for the Who, but it's not necessarily successful. "Sister Disco" has nothing to do with disco music, and as a song about music fans, takes a back seat to any number of Townshend's other pieces on the same subject.

John Entwistle's songs are the most basic rock on the album. If Townshend playing a few Kenny Burrell licks was supposed to represent progress for the Who (a false assumption), then Entwistle's introduction of the thunderously loud and melodic nine-string bass on "Trick of the Light" must have been the millennium, since it obliterated the need for another guitar of any kind. In fact, the heavy impasto with which the rumbling nine-string overlaid the sound prevented anything but a hint of other sounds in the same range coming through—Entwistle was playing like the Panzer Korps. "Trick of the Light" was about an encounter with a prostitute and seemed unlinked to anything but

Entwistle's traditionally kinky vision. But "905" and "Had Enough" were both taken from the science fiction rock opera on which John had been working since the release of his *Mad Dog* solo album. He had now scuttled that idea in favor of incorporating some of his songs into the revived *Lifehouse*.

What also aided Entwistle's material and made it fit into the album much more naturally than usual was his willingness to let Roger Daltrey take lead vocals on "Had Enough" and supply prominent backup on "905." Daltrey's vocals were generally confident throughout the record; he had finally learned to sing the songs without feeling intimidated by Pete's demos, or so he said.

Unfortunately, the songs boasted too much about breaking new ground to get away so easily. They hadn't really spaded up anything. Without a really inventive drummer, the Who were sunk—and Keith's drumming was unacceptably sluggish everywhere, except on "Who Are You," where it tagged along behind the inspiration of the rest of the number rather than leading the way, as Moon would have forced it to do in the past.

But all the blame doesn't belong to Moon. Townshend wanted to do a grand, unified project, and he hadn't come close. Even the experiments he did make were far more conventional than anything he would have tried to pass off as innovations in his heyday. "Music Must Change" was so weighted with allusions to other forms of art and music that it sank under its own pretensions, and the mocking use of synthesizer as a semi-classical string section in "Sister Disco" was an all-too-obvious conceit.

The worst offender may have been "Guitar and Pen," which was as frank and passionate as the songs on *The Who By Numbers* and *Rough Mix* but had an absurd Gilbert and Sullivan arrangement that reduced Townshend's confessional sincerity to absurd overemotionalism. Ultimately, what Pete has to say is overwhelmed by the stiff and formal way in which it's said: the guitar and piano solos in "Guitar and Pen" are so self-consciously "musical" that they're laughable. Only Daltrey's vocal, which is so bloodthirsty and aggressive that it takes the song well beyond any true seriousness, redeems "Guitar and Pen"—and then only by suggesting that maybe the Who still remembered that the truest response to outrageous fortune was laughing at yourself.

Nevertheless, Entwistle's songs and the success of the edited version of "Who Are You" as a single gave the album enough energy and true rock grit to put it over with more than just Who fans: The album peaked at number 2, the highest any Who album ever got.

Who Are You was released near the end of August. In lieu of a tour, the band came to America two weeks earlier for a series of interviews with press, radio and television. There was much to explain. The band hadn't been to America for nearly two years, there were rumors of breakups, Townshend's declaration that he'd retired from touring had appeared in *Trouser Press* (alongside Roger's assurance that he would change Pete's mind), Moon's condition was subject to widespread speculation.

Only Keith, Pete and Roger went to the States. John stayed behind, working on the soundtrack of *The Kids Are Alright*, the title given to Jeff Stein's movie about the band. Daltrey, traveling with his family, spent the first two days in Connecticut visiting his in-laws. That left Pete and Keith to do the bulk of the East Coast interviews, beginning with an early morning appearance on the nationally televised *Good Morning America*. There they talked about their new record, showed a short clip from *Kids* that featured Roger singing "I Can't Explain" at the Marquee, explained why Townshend no longer wished to tour (which boiled down to the trouble with his hearing and a desire to be more of a family man) and generally went over the head of host David Hartman. Like most TV interviewers, Hartman was a complete foreigner in the rock & roll world. His questions were about Entertainment; their answers came from rock & roll. For Townshend (who admitted in *Rolling Stone* that he saw even Meher Baba "through two slits, labeled *R* and *R*"), the interview eventually became unbearable.

Finally, Pete spoke his piece. "We're not perfectionists," he said. "We're idealists. We think that rock & roll is more than just music for kids. Rock music is important to people because in this crazy world it allows you to face up to problems. But at the same time, to sort of dance all over 'em." Moon looked like he wanted to applaud. Even Hartman seemed impressed, though the true content of what Townshend said probably eluded him.

Keith was theoretically on the wagon, but he broke out champagne that morning and raved on through the several other days and nights in the States. As always, Moon's interviews were entertaining and oblique. Yet there was an element of sadness in his demeanor; he seemed a little weary and a lot slower. Still Keith maintained that he was committed to the Who, to music, to health. He claimed that his physical and mental illnesses had been "amazingly exaggerated."

"I feel I've got a sense of purpose," he told *Rolling Stone*. "In the two years off, I was really drifting away with no direction, no nothing. I'd try to do things and get involved in projects, but nothing ever came close to the feeling I get when I'm working with the guys. Because it's fun, but at the same time I know I've gotta discipline myself again.

"I accept that. And also, it teaches me to take it as well as dish it out—that's rock. It's something you learn very quickly in the Who." Moon clearly felt more secure whenever he traveled with the other band members than he ever could when he was isolated from them. Yet the chances of Keith maintaining that closeness seemed slender then and look even slimmer in retrospect. Even if Townshend had backed down from his vow never to tour again, there was little doubt that Moon would have been replaced. John and Roger had little hope that Keith would ever lick his alcoholism, and even Pete knew how poorly Keith had played on *Who Are You*.

So the interviews went on, round after round, Townshend saying that while he'd love to find a way to do what the Who was clearly best at doing, he simply didn't feel it was worth the risk to his health and marriage, Daltrey claiming that he'd "find a way" to get the band on the road, Moon staying out of the argument but clearly praying for togetherness. Meantime, John signaled from London that "it's just not in me" to stop touring. He maintained that being at home was as hard on his marriage as being away was on Pete's. (This may or may not have been an example of John's legendary wit, but it is true that before three more years were out, he and Alison were divorced.)

On August 7, just as the group arrived in the States, word came of a death in the family. Pete Meaden, who had been managing the Steve Gibbons Band with Bill Curbishley and had been an occasional patron of Baba meetings, died in London. The official verdict was suicide; the cause was a drug overdose. Townshend seemed especially saddened.

Back in England, there were major rows about *The Kids Are Alright*, which was late and drastically over budget. *Quadrophenia* was almost ready for production. *McVicar* was being scripted, then cast. Townshend was preoccupied with his book publishing venture, planning a solo album, writing a film script, trying to finance a *Lifehouse* revival, working on various Meher Baba projects. Roger had his fourth solo album in the works. John was remixing *Quadrophenia* for that movie's soundtrack, as well as the music in the *Kids* film. Keith was at Shepperton.

The Who still traveled in separate circles. Pete had his Meher Baba friends and a few in the world of art outside rock. From time to time, he would go slumming, hitting the clubs to look at new young bands. With London abuzz with post-punk energy, he never had trouble finding something at least marginally amusing. John's clubbing tended to be more straightforward, looking for booze or some basic rock. Roger was holed up in Kent; he ventured into London only rarely, and then usually on business.

Keith and Annette went out almost every night. Moon was overjoyed to be back in England, where he was a national celebrity, taken to heart after all these years by the nation, regarded as an eccentric in Great Britain's grand tradition.

On September 6, 1978, Paul McCartney held a midnight screening of *The Buddy Holly Story*, a new American film about the life of the great rock star. McCartney now owned all of Holly's song copyrights, and he celebrated Buddy's birthday (September 7) with a week of festivities each year. *The Buddy Holly Story* screening was preceded by a party and meal at Peppermint Park, a London restaurant. Keith was invited, of course, and was one of the evening's most noted guests, sitting at the head table with Paul, his wife, Linda, TV celebrity David Frost and Frost's date. The party was full of old music business friends of Moonie's. Because he had spent so much time in the studio, then on holiday, many hadn't greeted him since he'd returned. The former Faces drummer, Kenney Jones, was impressed with how sober his old chum seemed. Keith also ran into his old mate Roy Carr, who was sufficiently concerned by how pallid Moon looked to invite him to spend some time in the country with his family in order to recuperate and dry out.

Moon came home around 4:30 A.M. and took a handful of sleeping pills, a sedative called Heminevrin, a muscle relaxant and hypnotic of some power used to curb alcoholism and epilepsy. (Keith had shown symptoms of the latter illness during one of his dry-outs.) After putting on a videotape of the Vincent Price horror film, *The Abominable Dr. Phibes*, a camp classic, he drifted off to sleep with Annette at his side.

Around 7:30 that morning, Moon came wide awake. He was starving. He prodded Annette, trying to convince her to get up and make him a meal. Failing to arouse her, he padded into the kitchen and grilled himself a steak, ate it, washed it down with some champagne, took another handful of Heminevrin and drifted off again. This time, he didn't wake up.

Annette Walter-Lax found the body at 4:30 P.M. She called Dr. Geoffrey Dymond, the physician who had prescribed Moon's medication, and he phoned an ambulance. Around that time, Bill Curbishley phoned, and Dymond gave him the news, suggesting that he notify the band and relations as soon as possible, since the ambulance men would surely tell the press.

Curbishley called Townshend. Pete began to weep but said that he would call the others. He rang Roger first.

In Burwash, Daltrey answered the phone himself. "He's done it," Pete said in a choked voice. "Who?" said Roger. "Keith." There was little more to add.

In Ealing, John Entwistle was talking with a group of Irish journalists when he was summoned to the telephone. Pete gave him the news, which greatly shook John, the most reserved of the band but also the one who was in many ways closest to Keith, playing with him in the intimate way that bassists and drummers must share, his roommate in the beginning. Pete was understanding but asked that John avoid telling the interviewers, if possible. Keith's mother had not yet been informed. (His father had died only a few weeks before.) Kim and Mandy Moon also hadn't been told.

John went back to the interviewers and sat down, resuming the conversation as calmly as he could. But when one of them asked him about the group's future plans, he couldn't hold back any longer. Entwistle, the stolid ox, burst into tears, confessing that the Who could not know their future because Keith Moon was dead.

36

Here ends the story of the Who. In its wake, a new one began, and even though it involved all but one of the central figures in the other, it is a very different story indeed—ultimately, it's the story of a different band.

As it developed, Pete Townshend and Roger Daltrey each got what they wanted from the new Who. Roger and Pete both described Keith's death, soon after it occurred, as an opportunity, almost a parting gift from the drummer, and they weren't far wrong. Which is not to suggest that Moon died deliberately that night. The irony of the fateful link between pure, doomed Buddy Holly and anarchic, doomed Keith is too perfect to need such melodramatic sweetening. Still, without Moon, much of what the band had demanded of itself became easier to obtain.

Townshend's prayers were answered in that the group was liberated from the most onerous part of its history. The Who was symbolically important as a true *group*—not as an assembly of key players who worked with whomever else happened to turn up (which is what the Rolling Stones had become and how some seventies bands—Steely Dan, for instance—were designed). When Moon died, the band's history felt complete. What remained was still an exceptional rock band but not anybody's standard-bearer. That role moved on into other hands.

Roger Daltrey got his wish. Pete Townshend felt there was something to prove again. It was Pete's idea to recruit another drummer. He suggested Kenney Jones, an old friend, a familiar face (he'd been the principal drummer on the *Tommy* soundtrack), a rock & roller. In November, Townshend offered Jones a role as a full partner in the band. He took them up on it.

411

A few die-hards were outraged. The Who, to them, was an inviolate concept, and Keith Moon was an irreplaceable part of it. Yet the survivors had to take the chance of going on. It was the one risk the Who had left. So by May 2, 1979, the Who were back onstage at the Rainbow in London sounding as good as ever—well, maybe not up to their early seventies peak, but certainly better than they had with Moon toward the end.

The new Who was next put on display at the 1979 Cannes Film Festival, where the group played at an outdoor amphitheatre in nearby Frejus, France, on May 12 and 13. The show was part of the festivities surrounding the release of the first two movies backed by the Who Group Ltd., *The Kids Are Alright* and *Quadrophenia*.

Kids is one of the most anarchic documentaries ever assembled, running two hours without a shred of narration and with not so much as a subtitle identifying characters or dates. *Kids* was the perfect cult item, and Who fans flocked to it. Hardly anyone else did, however, so even though it remained a staple on the midnight movie circuit, part of every kid's introduction to the verities of the Rock of Ages, the film had little impact outside the Who's cult. *The Kids Are Alright* is, nevertheless, one of the great rock & roll movies, capturing all of the Who's sass and humor and taking the wind out of the band's pomposities at each and every opportunity.

Quadrophenia, well-directed by Franc Roddam, was a surprise, turning Townshend's diffuse story into a tight tale of rockers versus mods, Brighton beach riots, teenage existentialism and young lust. The film got much of the period detail wrong—overemphasizing the role of sex, playing the wrong records, missing the dances and making the flash seem drab. Yet somehow, Roddam caught the spirit of both the time and Townshend's opera. Roddam's *Quadrophenia* was exciting in just the way Ken Russell's *Tommy* hadn't been—the script even made sense of the plot. And John Entwistle's remix of the original album added a new sense of detail and excitement.

The Who were obviously hoping that these two films would simultaneously kill off interest in their history and initiate a future in feature films. In an odd way, the films did achieve the former goal, but only for the group's older fans, who could appreciate both the intimacies and in-jokes of *Kids* and recall their own version of the yarns spun in *Quadrophenia*. For non-initiates, *Kids* was opaque, and *Quadrophenia* meant nothing outside of England and Australia. The rest of the world was left wondering what the riots were all about—for that matter, what a mod was. Without an American hit, the Who's film career was stalled—not dead, but not prospering, either. After the 1981 release of *McVicar*, another film whose English subject matter was largely impenetrable to American audiences, the film division of the Who Group Ltd. released nothing for the next two years.

In England, *Quadrophenia* was an almost immediate hit, its success coinciding with a mod resurgence. Soon, teenagers were sporting anoraks and French crew cuts, riding around town on Vespas. There were even new incidents of beach hooliganism. The new mods paid lip service to the Who, but they had their own bands, especially the Jam, led by Paul Weller, who based his considerable arsenal of musical and image-molding ideas on patterns established by the Who. (Weller even shared Townshend's perpetual identity crisis.)

Emotionally, Townshend was now free from forever protecting the sacred carcass of mod. But that also meant that Pete was a bit at sea about what to do next.

Almost immediately, their new mobility sent the Who back to America. (They played a number of gigs in Europe and England that summer. Pete also did solo appearances in support of Rock Against Racism and Amnesty International.) The Who hit the States in early September 1979 for dates in and around New York City which were generally well-received both by older fans and by the tough, long-haired, beer-swilling teenagers who were the bulk of the Who's recent converts. In New York, they played a week's worth of shows (seven in nine days), and Townshend seemed to cruise through them, even after he badly cut his hand one night at Madison Square Garden.

In late November, the Who returned to America for another tour, this time, a month of dates that opened at a small hall in Detroit. They appeared at a variety of venues, from the Silverdome in Pontiac to large hockey arenas and even a few 3,000- to 5,000-seat auditoriums.

This tour was planned as a typical superstar tour of the late seventies. In general, the Who played modern facilities with poor but serviceable acoustics and elaborate security and ticket-taking precautions. In these halls, the management was oriented to the sports world and resented the intrusion of the long-haired young people, whose enthusiasm was misunderstood as rowdiness. Sometimes the adolescent belligerence of rock fans was provoked into something nastier, just so that the staff could have the pleasure of bullying the crowd. (It was much harder to harass the bands, since the economic fate of the sports arenas was determined by how many functions were held there, and rock was their surest draw.)

The rock audience was not only shafted by the staff at the hall but also by the ticket setup. Scalping and the siphoning off of the best seats in the house for insiders was widespread, and in some halls, the practice of "festival seating," which ostensibly made all ticket-holders equal, simply played into the greediest tendencies of the fans themselves.

Festival seating is a general admission ticket policy in which there are no chairs or benches placed on the floor in the front of the stage. Into this empty space, listeners crowd on a first-come, first-served basis. Theoretically, festival seating equalizes the pressure for good seats, since those who line up first can have their pick of the place. But in fact, festival seating was an excuse to pack more people onto the floor—in some buildings, an additional two thousand or more people could be jammed in if there were no chairs. And in the end, the practice merely transferred the inequities of ticket-buying, taking the advantage from those with the money to pay scalpers (or with inside connections) and giving it to those with the leisure or patience to waste long hours queuing. Festival seating also ensured a mob scene, as early arrivals jostled for good position and latecomers tried to crash their way to better vantage points.

For the Who's show at Riverfront Coliseum in Cincinnati on December 3, 1979, the crowd began lining up in the bitterly cold wind many hours before the scheduled starting time of 8 P.M. By 2:15, there was a crush of bodies around the single set of doors through which Riverfront's staff would allow patrons to pass. And by 6:15, thousands of people were lined up, shaking with cold, many pushing and slamming into those in front of them, jostling for position.

The crowd thrust at each other with unbelievable force, magnified by their numbers and lack of space.

Those in the middle were constantly in danger of being swept underfoot and trampled; those in front were pressed so hard that they feared the plate-glass doors would shatter.

The crowd was now growing steadily. A good share of the 18,000 patrons had arrived early, and still they were herded into the small plaza in front of that single rank of doors. Although there were warnings from the police outside, the Coliseum staff and the concert promoters, Electric Factory Concerts of Philadelphia, refused to open the doors before 7:00 P.M., even when the crowd started shoving furiously as the Who went through its soundcheck just after six o'clock.

When the doors were opened, the crowd rushed in, ignoring the pleas of those caught in the middle and thrust forward rapidly against their will. Some of the glass in the doorways shattered. In the wake of the stampede for the seats, many were injured. Eleven died: Walter Adams, Jr., age seventeen; Peter Bowes, eighteen; Connie Burns, twenty-one; Jacqueline Eckerle, fifteen; David J. Heck, nineteen; Teva Ladd, twenty-seven; Karen Morrison, fifteen; Stephen Preston, nineteen; Philip K. Snyder, twenty; Bryan Wagner, seventeen; and James Warmoth, twenty-one. Most were trampled; some suffocated. The dead included seven teens, four adults; seven men, four women—a representative ratio of Who fans. It could have been anybody.

Inside, most of the crowd did not know what had happened. Many of the early arrivals stepped over bodies but never knew it, so quickly were they swept along. Some of the fans had been badly frightened at being hemmed in, but even they weren't aware that anyone had been seriously injured, much less killed. Latecomers saw that there had been trouble but had no idea how bad. The Who played their full show, unaware of the deaths. Bill Curbishley informed them after the show, as was proper. If an announcement had been made from the stage about what had really happened—or if the Who had stopped the show—an even worse stampede could have ensued.

The Who was in shock. How great was their responsibility? Obviously, even the uninvolved could ponder that question for decades without reaching any sure answers. Still, the blame had to be parceled out, and it was. Quite correctly, some of it went to the police, who had not forcefully exercised their authority once they'd spotted a potential problem. A good deal more went to the Coliseum staff and to the promoters, who had ignored not only past experiences at Riverfront and the police warnings but also their own senses, as they let the situation grow more and more dangerous without altering their prearranged plans. (Since no one could reach the plaza where the crowd was formed without having shown a ticket at a lower level, there was little chance of gate-crashers being admitted—not that the need to protect the show against crashers was any excuse.) Too little blame was directed at the crowd itself, which had behaved selfishly, exhibiting a greed for entertainment that was the antithesis of the principled idealism of which Who fans often liked to boast.

The blame remaining belonged to the Who itself. Not because the Riverfront deaths happened but because the Who had finally become so divorced from their listeners that they had allowed themselves to participate in the greedy scheme—festival seating, one essential precondition for such a disaster to occur.

That doesn't mean that the Who had behaved badly that night. Certainly, if the promoter or hall staff had asked the band or its representatives if the doors could be opened early, the band would have understood the situation and agreed. But the Who's understanding of their function as a group was imbedded with the notion of a basic identification between themselves and the audience. They were especially shaken not just by the fact that something like this could happen at a rock gig but by the fact that it had happened at *theirs*.

What had occurred at Riverfront Coliseum could have happened to almost any rock band. In itself, that's one measure of how drastically the Who had changed since 1963, when they had been at one with their crowd. But it has little do with the Who's changes since Moon died. In a way, given the band's rowdy image, it's surprising that some haunting catastrophe hadn't occurred earlier.

The real difference between the old Who and the new one was in what happened after the incident. Cincinnati was a ten-days wonder in the press but soon forgotten, dredged up only in passing in press accounts of the band's career. The Who played out the rest of their tour and spent most of the spring and early summer of 1980 touring the United States. Since no one asked about "the incident," after a time, it ceased to be a factor in their public image. Daltrey said that the band would do "anything we can do to stop it from ever happening again." But on succeeding tours the band took only minimal steps to protect their fans. They still played shows with festival seating. In the interviews the band did in 1981 and 1982, Cincinnati was not a major issue; often, it didn't come up at all.

But the Cincinnati deaths seemed to send Pete Townshend into another spiral of depression, anxiety, alcoholism and worse. In a way, he seemed to accept the eleven corpses as proof that the Who should not have continued without Keith Moon. And in another way, he simply didn't want to think about it. Pete said as much to disc jockey Tom Bender in Detroit only a few days after the disaster: "I just want to work and be happy. We didn't know anything about the accident. But everything in my life tells me to stop—my two little girls, my brain, body, everything tells me to stop. I'm not going to stop. I just don't *care*, really. I really don't *care* what happens anymore."

That didn't mean that Townshend didn't feel badly about those who died. He did. But Pete's comments indicate his acceptance that his time as a rock idealist was past. Townshend now wanted to become nothing more than a music professional. Roger Daltrey had won, all right. The Who were entertainers now, and except to the fanatic and the naïve, that's what the new version of the band stood for.

Often enough, Townshend seemed to have to work extra hard in his new role, which certainly didn't come naturally to him. Of the Who, Pete alone would sometimes raise the spectre of Cincinnati, even when an interviewer had not. Once again, he grew gaunt and spooky.

Along with the concert promoter, the Coliseum and the city of Cincinnati, the Who were sued by the relatives of the dead, and even though the band was insured, the liabilities were extreme. Inevitably, Townshend's penchant for making confusing and contradictory remarks (reflecting his own confusions and contradictions) got him into trouble. In the spring of 1980, a settlement was nearly reached between the band and the families. The group was willing to do something to indemnify the bereaved against their loss. The families were willing to be a bit understanding.

Then Townshend did an interview with Greil Marcus of *Rolling Stone*. Marcus was a rock critic of the old school, and he pressed for Townshend's answers on what had happened and, more importantly, pushed Pete to spell out his emotions about the Riverfront deaths. Townshend poured it all out.

"The amazing thing, for us, was the fact that when we were told about what happened at that gig, that eleven kids had died, for a second, our guard dropped. Just for a second. Then it was back up again.

"It was, 'Fuck it! We're not gonna let a *little thing* like this stop us.' That was the way we *had* to think. We had to reduce it. We had to reduce it, because if we'd actually *admitted* to ourselves the *true* significance of the event, the *true* tragedy of the event—not just in terms of 'rock' but the fact that it happened at one of our concerts—the tragedy to us, in particular, if we'd admitted that, we could not have gone on and worked. And we had a tour to do. We're a rock & roll band. You know, we *don't fuck around* worrying about eleven people dying. We *care* about it, but there is a particular attitude I call the 'tour armor': When you go on the road, you throw up an armor around yourself, you almost go into a trance. I don't think you lose your humanity, but think: For ten, maybe fifteen years, the Who smashed up hotel rooms—why? Where's the pleasure in it? We actually quite relished general violence. I don't understand why it happened. . . . It doesn't happen now, but it did happen, for a long time. I think that for me, tours were like a dream. . . .

"Immediately after the Cincinnati gig, to protect ourselves partly from *legal* recriminations, we doubled, trebled and quadrupled external security at halls. . . . But a lot of kids complained: Everywhere they'd look there was a cop. It spoiled their evening for them. They felt, 'Okay, it happened in Cincinnati, *but we don't need that. . . .* ' "

Pete's logic was not satisfactory. (The fact that people liked festival seating was irrelevant to its causal relationship in Cincinnati or to the question of banning it.) His tirade tried to fend off the depth of the question by dealing with its most pungent superficialities. And Marcus called him on it, and Townshend responded by talking about how the Who had responded personally.

"The other side of it is worth mentioning," he said. "The fact that the Who don't just get their strength from wearing armor. We did go home and we did think about it and we talked about it with our families and our friends. I went home to about ten letters from the families of the kids who'd died: letters full of deep, deep affection and support and encouragement. It wasn't like these people were being recriminatory. The father of the girl who died who had two children was writing to say that it would hurt *him*, the family, the friends of the family and friends of the girl if they knew that because of what happened, because of her death, we changed our feelings about rock. They understood her feelings about the band and about the music—you know what I'm saying?

"I think only time will tell. If I could dare say it, I'd say that Cincinnati was a very, very positive event for the Who. I think it changed the way we feel about people. It's changed the way we feel about our audience . . . in terms of affection and also remembering constantly that they are human beings—and not just people in rows. And I hope the reverse: that people who come to see the band will know that we're human beings, too, and not this *myth*. . . .

"I mean, I watched Roger Daltrey cry his eyes out after that show. I didn't, but he did. But now, whenever a fucking journalist—sorry—asks you about Cincinnati, they expect you to come up with a fucking theatrical tear in your eye! You know: 'Have you got anything to say about Cincinnati?' 'Oh, we were *deeply* moved, terrible tragedy, the horror, loss of life.' *Arrrrghh*! What do you do? We did all the things we thought were right to do at the time: sent flowers to the fucking funerals. All . . . *wasted*. I think when people are dead they're dead."

That did it. Townshend's sarcasm sank him. The problem wasn't that he was wrong; the sanctimonious show business attitude that uses all tragedy as an excuse to exhibit dramatic emotion is a real issue in the response to events like Cincinnati. But Pete had suggested (whether or not he knew it) that his own remorse was less than sincere.

(Townshend said just before this book went to press that he found the entire *Rolling Stone* episode "unfortunate," because the quotations were "sensationally framed, without vocal inflections; it actually looks like I actually mean what I'm saying or at least, that I believe what I'm saying is worth saying. When I spoke to Greil Marcus, I was sarcastic and—I thought—self-detrimental about the group's bloodyminded determination to carry on after the tragedy. I was simply trying to illustrate how absurd show-business thinking is. It didn't come off and hurt the feelings of the relatives." He clearly regrets the entire statement.)

After the story appeared, the families stopped talking about a settlement; by mid-1983, the Who still hadn't been able to settle the case. Given the way that American justice grinds—so exceedingly slowly that it might well grind finer than that of the Lord—it may be many more years before Cincinnati is out of the courts.

Greil Marcus defined the tragedy that remained. "What strikes me most about what happened in Cincinnati is that it seems, now, not to have happened at all," he told Townshend. "It has not become part of the rock & roll frame of reference, as Altamont instantly and permanently did. It seems to me that it was an event that should have signified that something new about the relationship between bands and their audiences, or about rock & roll as mass culture, was taking place. It ought to have forced people to reexamine a lot of assumptions, a lot of what they took for granted. That hasn't happened."

Nor would the new Who ever encourage it to happen. That was perhaps the biggest tragedy of all.

Not only was the Who split between its two incarnations—with Moon and without him, with ideals and without them—the new version of the band was itself musically schizoid, presenting one sound onstage, where the old repertoire dominated, but quite another on records.

The nature of this split in the band's work reflected the deeper split in objectives among Townshend, Daltrey and Entwistle. (Jones was a full partner, but he was not a major factor in the internal politicking, forming a series of alliances that did no more than temporarily reinforce whichever faction held the upper hand. For a time, Jones was subject to public and private abuse from Roger Daltrey. Then they became allies. So it went. So it goes.)

Roger and John were quite content to grind out the old hits onstage, leaving a bit of space for Pete to try new songs at the end of the shows. Very little of the live material came from any album after *Who's Next*—only two or three songs from *Who Are You* and almost nothing from the Who's studio albums of 1981 and 1982, *Face Dances* and *It's Hard*. Nor was any new material from pre-*Tommy* albums recycled. An occasional rendition of "Naked Eye," "Tattoo" or "Young Man Blues" was all that broke the formula—old singles like "Substitute" and "I Can't Explain," bits of *Tommy* and *Who's Next* alternated and interspersed with a few seventies hits ("5.15"), maybe a smattering of "Road Runner" or some other riff that could be extended into a jam, plus a couple of tracks from whatever the most recent album was.

Because Jones was as consistent as Moon was erratic, the texture of the Who's two-and-a-half-hour performance was much more precise. There were still soaring moments when the Who were as exciting as any band in the world, but they always were predictable peaks, precisely placed in a set that was professionally and reliably paced at last. Very entertaining and very meaningless.

The stage show was still the thunder of the past, however regulated and cautiously doled out. *Face Dances* and *It's Hard* barely seem to have been made by the same band; they are lackluster, without any sort of spark, and they are much lighter in tone than any previous Who albums. There is not much guitar playing, and there is not much of the chordal density of the most famous and successful earlier Who music, either. The exceptions were always John Entwistle songs, which overcompensated by relying on lumbering bass lines and heavy metal murkiness. On Townshend's new songs the Who toyed so gently with its music that it never stung you at all. On the Entwistle numbers the listener was clobbered with music from which all subtlety had been extracted, leaving only the crudest denominator of rock, a sodden beat.

It was easy to blame Kenney Jones for this—and it was also incorrect and unfair. True, Jones couldn't match Moon's imagination—but in the end, Keith himself hadn't been able to match his own earlier flights. Onstage, Jones was fine, for there he was mostly required to replicate ideas Keith had developed in his prime. In the studio, however, trying to come up with something new, the lack of a truly inventive, risk-taking drummer hamstrung the Who. But if Jones was not a solution to the problem posed by the creative disintegration of Moon, it must be said that he never presented himself as one. Jones was hired because he would fit in—the one thing that Moon hadn't ever done.

It was also a mistake to blame producer Bill Szymczyk for *Face Dances*. That was probably the least effective Who recording since they dumped Lambert as producer, and certainly, the album's sound isn't even up to the standard of the best stuff on *Who Are You*—but the same could be said of *It's Hard*, and nobody tried to pin the blame for that on producer Glyn Johns. The Who's recorded sound had simply become dull and fundamentally unimaginative. The reason lay more in the very conception of these records than in any specific detail of production or playing.

Townshend had complained for years that the Who soaked up all his good material. He felt, quite correctly, that as long as his best songs belonged to the band, there was little or no point in making solo albums. By 1980, he was sufficiently fed up to turn the tables; from the next batch of songs he wrote he took the first ten good ones for his first true solo LP, *Empty Glass*. Almost any of these would have been appropriate for the Who, and the inclusion of just one or two of the best might have lent *Face Dances* some artistic life. (Of course, part of the problem was that the rest of the Who made lousy decisions about what songs to leave off their albums—neither the song "Face Dances" nor "Dance It Away," which were featured in the band's 1979 and 1980 shows as encores, was used, and each of those was better than anything the Who eventually released.)

The other problem was intrinsic to Townshend's ambition. *Empty Glass* is assembled as a song cycle—a concept album in the same sense as *The Who By Numbers*. The songs are very personal, but they reflect a unified set of emotions (rage, frustration, fear of getting old, fear of failure, hostility toward the media—all the Townshend staples). The love songs are clear interminglings of romantic love, physical lust and Pete's passion for Meher Baba. Most of all, *Empty Glass* (which was produced by Chris Thomas) has a cohesive, brittle, abrasive, straightforward rock sound, balanced by a few lighter pop tunes. (One of the latter, "Let My Love Open the Door" became a number 9 hit in the States.) The album stands with *The Who By Numbers*, *Rough Mix* and "Who Are You" as the most exciting and effective music Pete Townshend made in his second decade of stardom.

Townshend's second solo album, the Chris Thomas-produced *All the Best Cowboys Have Chinese Eyes*, was released in mid-1982, only a few months before *It's Hard*. Again, Thomas provided crisp, clear sound, and the best songs—"The Sea Refuses No River," "Slit Skirts," "Uniforms," "Stop Hurting People"—had real bite and the most ambitious structures of anything Pete had composed in years. But the lyrics were often oblique, befuddled and pretentiously experimental. The exceptions ("The Sea Refuses No River," "Stop Hurting People") were spiritual apologies, although "Uniforms" comes close to summing up in a single lyric what *Quadrophenia* had evaded for an hour. In the end, however, what makes *All the Best Cowboys* interesting is its consistent sound and subject matter.

Lyrical and musical unity is exactly what the Who albums of the early eighties lacked. On both *Face Dances* and *It's Hard*, the songs were diffuse, the arrangements oblique, the lyrics too personal. The arrangements relied too much on synthesizers, as if Townshend was trying to equate elaborate technique with the band's stature as one of the last citadels of the first British rock era. In this context, Entwistle's heavy metal just added to the already rampant confusion; John's songs had about as much relationship to Townshend's contributions as they did to Stockhausen.

These were the first Who albums without a conscious theme, or at least an overriding focus, since *A Quick One*. Townshend was now simply delivering product on a schedule; there were no more lengthy delays while he schemed and plotted to establish a larger picture into which his tunes could be fitted.

Instead, the lyrics made sense only in the context of Pete's personal concerns: "Don't Let Go the Coat" is a nice tribute to Meher Baba (who instructed his disciples to "hold fast to the hem of my robe"). But in Roger Daltrey's mouth the song was one-dimensional. It wasn't Roger's fault, since Townshend didn't really try to give "Don't Let Go the Coat" a substantial subtext that the singer could plug into. The heartless music would have rendered *Face Dances* and *It's Hard* ineffectual anyhow, but by delivering random thoughts not connected to one another or (in the end) to any of the band's historical concerns, Townshend was clearly signifying his basic lack of interest in the Who except as a business proposition. Pete was now saving his best songs for himself, and whatever their flaws, *Empty Glass* and *All the Best Cowboys Have Chinese Eyes* are the only two LPs of the eighties in which Townshend's music displays the energy and sensibility one expected to find in the Who's work.

By early 1981, Pete Townshend was swamped in projects and responsibility. In addition to his solo career and the Who, he had formed Eel Pie, the book publishing company, a Thames River barge fleet, opened a bookstore, helped run a Meher Baba center called Oceanic and run several recording studios. On top of this, there was his family life, which was not going well, largely because he devoted so much time to everything else, causing Karen and the kids to justifiably feel ignored.

Once again, Pete slid into the cycle of alcoholism and depression. This time, the booze and depression ripped his entire life apart; before he snapped out of it, Townshend came very close to the naked edge itself.

The trouble started with money. Townshend had entrusted his non-musical ventures to cronies and amateurs. Some were well-intentioned, some were on the fiddle from the start. At the beginning of 1981, Townshend's bankers informed him that he was £500,000 ($1,085,000) in debt.

"In the past, my answer to financial problems always has been to go out on the road with the Who or to sign a music publishing deal or to get another record advance," Townshend told Chris Salewicz of *Time Out*. "Which basically accounts for the problem I've had for a long time with overwork and over-commitment. It's not altruism. It's fucking stupidity." This time, the hole that had been dug for him was too deep to quickly climb out of. The barge company went down immediately and the bookstore was soon sold. The Baba center's activities withered away. Eighteen months later, Pete sold the publishing company, too.

The Who were in the midst of their longest British tour in ten years, which had begun on January 20, in Sheffield, and extended off and on through mid-March. When the Who played the Rainbow in London, on February 4 and 5, Townshend was absolutely desperate; he drank four pints of brandy onstage, tried to talk his way through the set and wound up in a public fight with Daltrey. The rest of the tour wasn't nearly so bad (Pete and Roger even golfed together in Scotland). But the latest cycle had its hooks in.

"Like every arsehole writer," Townshend told Salewicz, "I felt that drinking was helping me to work or at least helping with some of the pressure I was going through. . . . I was drinking myself into oblivion in order not to face up to the fact that there were certain things I couldn't do and certain things I just didn't *want* to do. I wasn't running away from life but from particular issues."

Some of these had to do with the Who, which had increasingly come to seem a purely financial proposition. But the more important things Townshend avoided were personal and revolved around his marriage. "Drinking took me back to being adolescent and loathsome and all the things that come up like natural armor," he told Pete Hamill. "I realized that I wasn't dealing with anything. *Anything*. I wasn't capable of sitting down with my wife. I didn't see the problem. I talked about other things. The booze. The band. But I never got around to straightening myself out and sitting down and looking her in the eye and saying, '*What has gone wrong?*' "

He moved out of the Twickenham house, taking up residence in the country, spending some time in a King's Road flat in central London, making pleasure trips to New York, Los Angeles and Paris. He drank more and more heavily. It was one long round of wine, women and song—a schoolboy fantasy come to life. He still had enough money left for a final plunge.

The depression was given another boost when Kit Lambert died in mid-April. Lambert had been traveling in his own tight spiral of desperation ever since losing the Who. He went broke and lost his Venetian palazzo; at one point, Chris Stamp tried to have him committed for his own good. When Kit died, he was living with his mother. Lambert died of a fall down the stairs at her home—but a contributing factor may have been a beating he was supposedly given at a gay club a few hours earlier.

Now all the great loons were gone: Moon, Meaden, Lambert. Townshend, who had done the rounds with those men so often, who had put their philosophy into one succinct maxim ("Hope I die before I get old"), felt abandoned. "I had an intuition that I was going to burn out," he told Salewicz.

He began to traffic with the androgynous crowd called new romantics, slickly dressed unisexual dance-beat fanatics such as Steve Strange, who ran the Club for Heroes. In addition, he hung around the all-purpose London rock joint, the Venue, and the posh private club, the Embassy. And he began to take drugs for the first time in a decade.

"Meher Baba came down very heavily against drugs, so for a while I pushed him out of my life because I couldn't live within those principles," Townshend said. "But in a way, I did it almost deliberately." The first time he went to the Club for Heroes, he was carried out after turning blue from an overdose.

In November, Townshend took himself to a doctor and asked to be committed to an alcoholism clinic. (Betty Townshend had also taken the cure recently, and Pete was partially inspired by his mother's example.) He was sent to a clinic, given hypnotherapy and a tranquilizer called Ativan.

Ativan is itself an addictive drug, and Townshend was soon hooked. "I just took anything I could lay my hands on as a way of passing the time, really, because I *hated* the sensation of not being drunk," Pete said. He began free-basing cocaine—smoking it in a waterpipe. Unbeknownst to him, the coke was often cut with heroin. The result, he said, was "instant" addiction.

Townshend had crashed as deeply as he could and still survive; had he reached the hospital a few minutes later when he'd o.d.'d at the Club for Heroes, he surely would have died. The question now was whether Pete had the will to pull through. In some ways, regaining his health would be even more difficult for Townshend than for most addicts and alcoholics. Many people had placed him on a pedestal, almost worshipping him as the perfect rock star, the one who had avoided the most obvious traps of fame. Now he had succumbed to them all: the trendy night club dinge, the drugs, the wantonness, the rootlessness and abandonment of his family. Close friends were shocked and worried. Roger Daltrey seriously considered calling it a day with the Who, both because he was frightened of what Townshend was doing to himself and because he sincerely believed that the band might be part of what was dragging Townshend down. Even Roger didn't want the Who to continue that badly.

Townshend did have the willpower and the humility to come through the experience. He went to California at the beginning of 1982. Meg Patterson had moved her clinic, with the electroacupuncture cure that had worked for Eric Clapton, to San Diego. Townshend spent a month there, not only getting the poison out of his system but also coming to some difficult conclusions about himself and his life. He wanted to put his marriage back together, give the Who a final try (so that the band might go out on a high note), return to the life he had abandoned, try to become an adult.

He did not want to die, and this was in itself a bit of a revelation. Pete must always have wondered if he'd meant to take his famous phrase all the way. Now he knew he wouldn't. (Most encouragingly, the healing process didn't stop when he came home—he continued psychotherapy back in London.)

The afternoon before he was to leave the California clinic, Townshend and a friend were out walking along the beach. Pete spied a jar of white powder in the sand. He picked it up, dipped a finger inside and put it to his tongue. As the nerve endings froze, he knew he was holding in his hand enough cocaine to sustain any habit for months. (The jar had probably washed ashore after being abandoned by smugglers pursued by the coast guard.)

Townshend looked at the jar and was tempted.

He picked it up and threw it onto the rocks at the edge of the sea, where it smashed, and every grain of the powder dissolved, mingling with the pure Pacific waters, salts among salt.

That's not quite the end of the story—not that it has an end yet. The Who regrouped and recorded *It's Hard* in the summer of 1982. That fall, they returned to America for what was billed as the Who's First Farewell Tour. It was (maybe, perhaps, almost) their last go around. If they wanted it to be. They hedged every bet.

If there remained any doubt that the Who had become a purely commercial proposition, that tour should have settled it. In the process of playing the largest arenas and stadiums available, often in beastly weather, under the banner of the beer company that had bought rights to their name, the Who were almost visibly burning the bridges to their past, severing the final links with their rhetorical idealism.

This might have been fitting, if the first farewell tour was indeed guaranteed to be their last. The Who had served rock & roll long and for the most part honorably, and if they'd come to the end, they had a right to a bit of profit-taking. But no one would say for certain that it *was* over. Townshend did his usual waffling: There would be no more tours, but the band would continue recording and from time to time might do isolated live gigs. Daltrey's position was that they could do whatever they wished—many other stars, from Frank Sinatra to David Bowie, had announced multiple "retirements." John Entwistle listened to the others speak and got angry; he wished to continue with the Who as a full-scale proposition, and he gave every indication of preparing to bolt the group if that didn't happen. Kenney Jones said nothing.

As professionals, the Who still had obligations. They had signed a recording contract with Warner Bros. Records in 1980, with total guarantees of $12 million (almost £6 million). They still owed Warner's one more studio album. There was talk of a live album from the American tour, of doing extensive farewell tours of Britain and Europe—even of braving Australia again. Rumors of a *Lifehouse* revival resurfaced. But no one said for sure.

The American farewell tour ended in Toronto. The show was broadcast live on pay television all over North America. The final concert varied not at all from the band's usual set. At the end, no one broke a guitar or tipped over a drum. All eyes were dry. Before the applause faded, they took their bows and walked offstage.

SELECTED BIBLIOGRAPHY

NEWSPAPER AND MAGAZINE ARTICLES

Altham, Keith. "Air Crash Lyric May Be Who's Next Single." *New Musical Express*, n.d.
———. "Moon Talks Tommy." *Top Pops*, May 17, 1969.
———. "Where Townshend's Head Is At!" *Record Mirror*, November 7, 1970.
———. "Talking to Pete Townshend." *Record Mirror*, February 13, 1971.
Anzar, Naosherwan. "Pete Townshend Superstar." *The Glow*, n.d. "At the Where?" *Time*, June 22, 1970.
Bailey, Andrew. "A Who Sings His Heart Out in the Country." *Rolling Stone*, April 26, 1973.
Brooks, Michael. "Pete Townshend Interview." *Guitar Player*, May/June 1972.
Brown, Mick. "Who's Still Angry? Roger Daltrey Is." *Rolling Stone*, June 2, 1977.
Campbell, Mary. "He Holds the Who Together." *Associated Press*, August 11, 1974.
Carr, Roy. "Keith Moon Interview." *New Musical Express*, n.d.
———. "The Punk as Godfather." *New Musical Express*, May 31, 1975.
———. "The Best Part of Almost But Not Quite Breaking Up . . . Is Staying Together And Having a Wonderful Time." *New Musical Express*, October 18, 1975.
———. "The March of the Mods Re-Visited." *New Musical Express*, July 17, 1976.
———. "Which Way to the Cannes Film Festival." *New Musical Express*, May 26, 1979.
Charlesworth, Chris. "I See a Mad Moon Rising!" *Melody Maker*, November 7, 1970.
———. "Where to Now, Who?" *Melody Maker*, July 17, 1971.
———. "Thumbs Down in Rome." *Melody Maker*. September 23, 1972.
———. "A Nasty Case of Rigor Mortis." *Melody Maker*, December 23, 1972.
———. "Giving It All Away." *Melody Maker*, April 7, 1973.
———. "Entwistle's £25,000 Hobby." *Melody Maker*, December 14, 1974.
———. "Anyway, Anyhow, Anywhere." *Melody Maker*, September 16, 1978.
Charone, Barbara. "The Celluloid Passion of Roger Daltrey." *Crawdaddy*, April 1975.

——. "Roger Rides a Rock Horse." *Sounds*, June 28, 1975.

Clark, Al. "The Who Put Their Balls on the Rails." *Time Out*, August 1971.

Cocks, Jay. Review of *Tommy* (film). *Time*, March 31, 1975.

——. "Rock's Outer Limits." *Time*, December 17, 1979.

Cohen, Marc. "A Conversation with the Ox." *Who's News*, n.d.

——. "A Candid Conversation with John Entwistle." *Who's News*, n.d.

Cohn, Nik. "The Who: The Last of the Pop Groups." *Eye*, n.d.

——. "Pop Scene: *The Who Sell Out*." *Queen*, n.d.

——. "Finally, The Full Force of the Who." New York *Times*, March 8, 1970.

——. "The Who, From Tommy to Bobby." New York *Times*, n.d.

——. "Whoop-De-Do." *New York*, December 15, 1975.

Collins, Michael. "Pete Townshend: Busy Days." *Rolling Stone*, June 20, 1974.

Cott, Jonathan, and Dalton, David. "Interview with Pete Townshend." *Rolling Stone*, May 14, 1970.

Creeden, Larry. "Keith Moon's Lust for Life." *Trouser Press*, June/July 1976.

Crescenti, Peter. "Who's Wallflower Branches Out." *Zoo World*, January 2, 1975.

Crowe, Cameron. "*Penthouse* Interview: Pete Townshend." *Penthouse*, December 1974.

Dawbarn, Bob. "The Economy Size Family Pack Who—For U.S. Consumption." *Melody Maker*, May 20, 1967.

Denselow, Robin. "Townshend Prays, Writes New Opera." *Rolling Stone*, October 26, 1972.

du Noyer, Paul. "Pete Townshend: Forever's No Time At All." *New Musical Express*, June 12, 1982.

"Every So Often a Group Is Poised on the Brink of a Breakthrough . . . Word Has It. It's the Who." *Melody Maker*, June 5, 1965.

Flippo, Chet. "Who's Quiet Now." *Rolling Stone*, December 5, 1974.

——. "Rock and Roll Tragedy." *Rolling Stone*, January 24, 1980.

Frampton, Peter. "On Tour with the Who." *Melody Maker*, November 4, 1967.

Frith, Simon. Review of *The Who By Numbers*, *Let It Rock*. November/December 1975.

——. "Keith Moon Dies Before He Gets Old." *Village Voice*, September 18, 1978.

——. "The Kids Are All Wrong." *Melody Maker*, July 21, 1979.

Gambaccini, Paul. "Quadromania: The Who Fuss, Fight and Hit the Road." *Rolling Stone*, December 4, 1975.

Garbarini, Vic. "Pete Townshend: Behind Chinese Eyes*.*" *Musician: Player and Listener*, August and September 1982.

Gardiner, Diane. "The Who See America." *Hit Parader*, December 1968.

Gidion, Pete. "Who's Peter Townshend Explains Their Tommy." Detroit *Free Press/Up Beat*, n.d.

Goldstein, Richard. "Rock 'n' Wreck." *Village Voice*, April 6, 1967.

Green, Richard. "I Had to Do a Solo Album or I'd Go Out of My Mind." *New Musical Express*, April 24, 1971.

Hamill, Pete. "Rock of Ages." *New York*, October 18, 1982.

Hanel, Ed, and Carlson, Jon. "John Entwistle Pours It All Out." *Trouser Press*, February/March 1977.

Hayman, Martin. "John Entwistle Interview." *Sounds*, n.d.

Heilpern, Jon. "The Why and How of the Who." *Observer Sunday Magazine*, n.d.

Henahan, Donal. " 'Tommy' Is Poignantly Sentimental." New York *Times*, June 8, 1970.

Hopkins, Jerry. "Keith Moon Bites Back." *Rolling Stone*, December 21, 1972.

Johnson, James. "Pete Townshend Interview." *New Musical Express*, July 20, 1974.

Jones, Nick. "Caught in the Act." *Melody Maker*, January 9, 1965.

——. "Well, What Is Pop Art?" *Melody Maker*, July 3, 1965.

——. "The Price of Pop Art." *Melody Maker*, August 28, 1965.

——. "Pictures of the Who." *Melody Maker*, April 29, 1967.

——. "I Became a Hero—Smashing Guitars." *Melody Maker*, October 14, 1967.

Kaye, Lenny. "Quadrophenia: Who's Essay on Mod Era." *Rolling Stone*, December 20, 1973.

Kinnersley, Simon. "Terminal Maturity." *Time Out*, February 2, 1979.

Landau, Jon. Review of *Happy Jack*. *Crawdaddy*, August 1967.

Leigh, Wendy. "Who's Hot? Roger Daltrey, That's Who!" *High Society*, May 1979.

Lippincott, Proctor. "The Who." *Blast*, August 1978.

Loder, Kurt. "*The Rolling Stone* Interview: Pete Townshend." *Rolling Stone*, June 24, 1982.

Logan, Nick. "Who Enter Period of Self-Examination." *New Musical Express*, July 17, 1971.

Lopez, Sonya. "Who Is Tommy." *Radio Times*, October 3, 1974.

McConnell, Andy. "The Mooning of America." *Crawdaddy*, May 1975.

Mackie, Rob. "Rising Like a Dinosaur." *Sounds*, October 27, 1973.

Mamis, Toby. "Growing Pains." *Penthouse*, n.d.

Marcus, Greil. Review of *The Who on Tour/Magic Bus*. *Rolling Stone*, November 9, 1968.

——. "The Different Drummer." *Rolling Stone*, October 19, 1978.

——. "The *Rolling Stone* Interview: Pete Townshend." *Rolling Stone*, 1980.

Mendelsohn, John. Review of "The Seeker." *Rolling Stone*, n.d.

——. Review of *Tommy* (soundtrack album). *Rolling Stone*, n.d.

Miles. "Miles Interviews Pete Townshend." *International Times*, February 13-26,1967.

Miller, Jim. Review of *Odds and Sods*. *Rolling Stone*, December 5, 1974.

Mills, Bart. "The *Gig* Interview: Pete Townshend." *Gig*, December 1977.

Moon, Keith. "America by the Who." *Rave*, September 1968.

Nelson, Paul. "Who? A Conversation with Peter Townshend—of the Who, That's Who." *Hullabaloo*, March 1968.

——. "Peter Townshend of the Who Talks! We Listen!" *Hullabaloo*, May 1968.

——. " 'Rock Is Too Serious,' Say the Who." New York *Times*, June 2, 1968.

——. "More of the Peter Townshend Interview." *Hullabaloo*, October 1968.

——. "What? More of the Peter Townshend Interview? Who?" *Hullabaloo*, December 1968.

——. "Peter Townshend on 'The Deaf, Dumb and Blind Boy.' " *Circus*, May 1969.

Nicholson, Jacquelyn R. "Tommy's Star Talks About His Climb from Rebel Bastard to Millionaire Rock Idol." *Playgirl*, December 1975.

Nightingale, Anne. "Moon the Loon." *19 Magazine*, n.d.

Nolan, Hugh. "Who: Cattiest Group in the Business." *Disc and Music Echo*, November 30, 1968.

Norman, Tony. "Roger Daltrey Interview." *New Musical Express*, n.d.

Palmer, Tony. "A Freakish Parable." *The Observer*, May 12, 1969.

Peacock, Steve. "Pete Townshend Interview." *Sounds*, July, 17, 24, 1971.

——. "Baptism by Pond Water." *Sounds*, May 11, 1974.

Perry, Charles, and Bailey, Andrew. "Who's Spooky Tour: Awe and Hassles." *Rolling Stone*, January 3, 1974.

"Pete Townshend Interview." *Crawdaddy*, n.d.

"The Pop Think-In: Roger Daltrey." *Melody Maker*, September 24, 1966.

"The Pop Think-In: Keith Moon." *Melody Maker*, December 31, 1966.

"The Pop Think-In: Pete Townshend." *Melody Maker*, March 26, 1966.

"The Pop Think-In: Pete Townshend." *Melody Maker*, January 14, 1967.

Robbins, Ira. "The Who Movie: 'Kids' Director Jeff Stein Tells *TP* All About It." *Trouser Press*, April 1979.

——. "The Who: An Ideal Compilation." *Trouser Press*, January 1982.

Robinson, Richard. "The Hit Parader Interview." *Hit Parader*, May 1974.

Rose, Joseph. "The Spiritual Responsibility of Pete Townshend." *Hit Parader*, June 1975.

——. "Roger Daltrey Speaks Out on Fighting, Wealth, Politics and the Who." *Hit Parader*, May 1976.

Rosen, Steve. "John Entwistle: The Who's Great Bass Guitarist." *Guitar Player*, November 1975.

——. "Interview." *Record Review*, December 1979.

Ross, Ron. "Townshend's Vision: Technologized Rock." *Circus*, n.d.

Rudis, Al. "Daltrey: 'When We Fight It Can Get Vicious.' " *Melody Maker*, February 9, 1974.

——. "The Who." *FM Guide*, May 1974.

Ruffell, David. "The Who Official Fan Club Newsletter." May/June, 1967; July/August 1967; September/October 1967; November/December 1967; January/February 1968; September 1968; October/November 1968; November /December 1968; no. 1, 1969; no. 2, 1969; no. 3, 1969.

Salewicz, Chris. "Pete Townshend: True Confessions." *Time Out*, June 4-10, 1982.

Sanders, Rick, and Dalton, David. "Pete and Tommy, Among Others." *Rolling Stone*, July 12, 1969.

Sarris, Andrew. "Films in Focus." *The Village Voice*, March 31, 1975.

Schulps, Dave. "Ox Tales." *Trouser Press*, June/August 1975.

——. "Who in Action!" *Trouser Press*, March 1978.

——. "Pete." *Trouser Press*, April and May 1978.

——. "J. A. Entwistle, M.D." *Trouser Press*, November 1978.

"Second Thoughts on Monterey." *Melody Maker*, July 1, 1967.

Shaar Murray, Charles. "Four Way Pete." *New Musical Express*, October 27, 1973.

——. "See Me, Feel Me, Buy Me." *New Musical Express*, March 29, 1975.

Shaar Murray, Charles, and Carr, Roy. "Who Consumer Guide." *New Musical Express*, November 10, 1973.

Shaw, Greg. "The Who's Mod Generation." *Phonograph Record*, n.d.

"Smash-Up TV Show for Who." *Melody Maker*, October 1, 1966.

"So I Said to John Entwistle's Dog . . ." *Disc and Music Echo*, July 6, 1968.

Stein, Bruno. "The Who Punch Out." *Creem*, March 1975.

——. "Roger Daltrey: Talkin' 'Bout My D-D-Dedication." *Creem*, January 1975.

Stewart, Tony. "Who's Last." *New Musical Express*, August 9, 1975.

Stokes, Geoffrey. "A Fusion of Rage and Boogie." *Village Voice*, June 20, 1974.

Swenson, John. "The Who Puts the Bomp." *Crawdaddy*, December 5, 1971.

——. "QuadroWho: The Whole Truth." *Crawdaddy*, January 1974.

——. "The Who Plunge Into Madness with *Quadrophenia*." *Circus Raves*, March 1974.

——. "Who Interview." *Modern Hi-Fi and Stereo Guide*, August 1974.

——. "Strange Stagefellows." *Rush*, n.d.

Swenson, John, ed. "A Salute to the Who." *Record World* (special issue), November 23, 1974.

Tiven, Jon. "An Interview with Roger Daltrey." *New Haven Rock Press*, no. 16.

Tobler, John. "Chatting with Pete Townshend." *Zig Zag*, May and June 1974.

Tolliday, Ray. "Well, What Would You Have Done After *Tommy*?" *Creem*, October 1971.

Townshend, Pete. "Dear *Melody Maker*." *Melody Maker*, August 12, 1967.

——. "The Pete Townshend Page." *Melody Maker*, August 22, 1970; September 19, 1970; October 17, 1970; November 14, 1970; December 12, 1970; January 16, 1971; February 13, 1971; March 13, 1971; April 17, 1971.

——. "In Love With Meher Baba." *Rolling Stone*, November 26, 1970.

——. Review of *Meaty, Beaty, Big and Bouncy*. *Rolling Stone*, December 9, 1971.

——. "Pete Townshend Writes for *Sounds*." *Sounds*, June 24, 1972.

——. Advertisement for *Who Came First*. *Crawdaddy*, January 1973.

——. "Rock Recording." *Hit Parader*, May 1974.

——. "The Punk Meets the Godmother." *Rolling Stone*, November 17, 1977.

———. "Coming On Nicely." *The Image*, December 1973.

Townshend, Pete, as told to Smith, Debbie. "The Who Have Arrived!" *Go!*, April 14, 1967.

Townshend, Pete; with Melly, George; and Muggeridge, Douglas. "Pop and Light Music: A New Plan for Radio." *Radio Times*, March 19, 1970.

Valentine, Penny. "Who Are the Who Birds?" *Disc and Music Echo*, May 17, 1969.

———. "The *Sounds* Talk-In: Pete Townshend." *Sounds*, January 2, 1971.

———. "Daltrey's Utopia in the Wilds of Sussex." *Sounds*, November 20, 1971.

———. "Let's See Action." *Sounds*, December 2, 1972.

———. "The *Sounds* Talk-In: Roger Daltrey." *Sounds*, March 17, 1973.

———. "Heroes and Villains and Fools." *Street Life*, November 1, 1975.

Van Ness, Chris. "An Interview with Pete Townshend and the Who." Los Angeles *Free Press*, December 1971.

Vitka, Bill. "The Man Behind the Who Concert." *SoHo Weekly News*, January 10, 1980.

Wale, Michael. "Townshend Explains *Quadrophenia*." *Zoo World*, December 20, 1973.

Watts, Michael. "The Eternal Mod." *Melody Maker*, August 26, 1970.

———. "Townshend: Picking Up the Pieces." *Melody Maker*, October 14, 1978.

Welch, Chris. Review of *A Quick One*. *Melody Maker*, December 10, 1966.

———. "Would You Let Your Daughter Marry A Venusian?" *Melody Maker*, May 4, 1968.

———. "Bus Ride Back to the Pop 30 for the Who." *Melody Maker*, September 21, 1968.

———. "Tackling the Most Serious Projects of Their Lives." *Melody Maker*, November 9, 1968.

———. "Why the Who Aren't 'Pop' Anymore." *Melody Maker*, April 19, 1968.

———. "The Renaissance of the Who." *Melody Maker*, May 10, 1968.

———. "Where Now for *Tommy*?" *Melody Maker*, January 10, 1970.

———. "Squire Daltrey." *Melody Maker*, October 23, 1971.

———. "Talking 'Bout My Generation." *Melody Maker*, October 27, 1973.

———. "Daltrey: Grandfather of Punk Rock." *Melody Maker*, April 30, 1977.

———. "The Return of You Know Who." *Melody Maker*, September 17, 1977.

———. "Amazing Journey." *Melody Maker*, August 12, 1978.

———. "The Who Sell In." *Melody Maker*, January 27, 1979.

———. "What's Next for the Who." *Melody Maker*, May 26, 1979.

Wenner, Jann. "The Who: Getting Away from Car Accidents." *Rolling Stone*, January 20, 1968.

———. "The *Rolling Stone* Interview: Pete Townshend." *Rolling Stone*, September 14 and September 28, 1968.

"The What and Why of the Who." *Time*, September 20, 1968.

"Who—Finally Reaching the Sounds They All Search For." *Melody Maker*, November 19, 1966.

"Who Make Drastic Policy Changes." *Melody Maker*, July 17, 1965.

"The Who Split Mystery." *Melody Maker*, November 20, 1965.

"Who's Farewell to *Tommy* Pulls 55G at Met." *Variety*, n.d.

Willis, Ellen. "Musical Events: Rock, Etc." *The New Yorker*, July 12, 1969.

BOOKS

Ashley, Brian, and Monnery, Steve. *Whose Who? A Who Retrospective*. London: New English Library, 1978.

Barnes, Richard. *Mods!* London: Eel Pie, 1979.

———. *The Who: Maximum R&B*. New York: St. Martin's Press, 1982.

Butler, Dougal; with Trengove, Chris; and Lawrence, Peter. *Moon the Loon*. London: Star Books, 1981.

Charlesworth, Chris. *The Who*. London: Omnibus, 1982.

Clarke, Steve. *The Who in Their Own Words*. New York: Quick Fox, 1979.

Cohen, Stanley. *Folk Devils and Moral Panics: The Creation of Mods and Rockers*. London: MacGibbon and Kee, 1972.

Fitzgerald, F. Scott. *"The Crack-Up" with Other Pieces and Stories*. Harmondsworth, Middlesex: Penguin, 1965.

Frith, Simon. *Sound Effects: Youth, Leisure and the Politics of Rock 'n' Roll*. New York: Pantheon, 1981.

Fuller, John G. *Are the Kids All Right?* New York: Times Books, 1981.

Hamblett, Charles, and Deverson, Jane. *Generation X*. London: Tandem, 1964.

Hanel, Ed. *The Who: The Illustrated Discography*. London: Omnibus, 1981.

Herman, Gary. *The Who*. London: November Books, 1971.

Hounsome, Terry, and Cambre, Tim. *New Rock Record*. Poole, Dorset: Blandford Press, 1981.

Kooper, Al; and Edmonds. *Backstage Passes* (Briarcliff Manor, N.Y.: Stein and Day), 1977.

Laing, Dave, and Hardy, Phil, eds. *Encyclopedia of Rock, 1955–1975*. London: Aquarius, 1977.

Lippard, Lucy R. *Pop Art*. London: Thames and Hudson, 1970.

Marchbank, Pearce, ed. *The Who File*. London: Wise Publications/ Fabulous Music Ltd., 1979.

Miller, Jim, ed. *The Rolling Stone Illustrated History of Rock & Roll* (revised edition). New York: Rolling Stone Press/Random House, 1980.

Mungham, Geoff, and Parson, Geoff, eds. *Working Class Youth Culture*. London: Routledge and Kegan Paul, 1976.

Poggioli, Renato. *The Theory of the Avant-Garde*. Cambridge, Mass.. Belknap/Harvard, 1968.

Pollock, Bruce. *In Their Own Words*. New York: Collier, 1975.

Reed, Oliver. *Reed All About It!* London: Coronet, 1979.

Rolling Stone, ed. *The Rolling Stone Record Review*. New York: Pocket Books, 1971.

——. *The Rolling Stone Record Review, Vol. II*. New York: Pocket Books, 1974.

——. *The Who: Ten Great Years*. San Francisco: Straight Arrow, 1975.

Russell, John. *The Meanings of Modern Art*. New York: The Museum of Modern Art/ Harper & Row, 1981.

Santelli, Robert. *Aquarius Rising*. New York: Delta, 1980.

Solomon, Clive; Pizzey, Howard; Watson, Martin. *Record Hits: The British Top 50 Charts, 1952–1977*. London: Omnibus, 1979.

Spitz, Robert Stephen. *The Making of Superstars*. New York: Anchor Press, 1978.

——. *Barefoot in Babylon*. New York: Viking, 1979.

Swenson, John. *The Who*. London: Star Books, 1981.

Thomson, David. *England in the Twentieth Century*. Harmondsworth, Middlesex: Pelican, 1981.

Tobler, John, and Grundy, Stewart. *The Record Producers*. New York: St. Martin's Press, 1982.

Townshend, Pete, and Barnes, Richard. *The Story of Tommy*. London: Eel Pie, 1977.

Turner, Steve. *Conversations with Eric Clapton*. London: Abacus, 1976.

——, ed. *A Decade of the Who*. London: Fabulous Music Ltd., 1977.

Waterman, Ivan. *Keith Moon: The Life and Death of a Rock Legend*. London: Arrow, 1979.

Whitburn, Joel. *Top LP's, 1945–1972*. Menomonee Falls, Wisconsin: Record Research, Inc., 1973. *See also annual supplements.*

——. *Top Pop Artists and Singles 1955–1978*. Menomonee Falls, Wisconsin: Record Research, Inc., 1979. *See also annual supplements.*

All U.S. chart positions cited in this book are based on Joel Whitburn's *Record Research* and its various supplements. All U.K. chart positions through 1975 are based on Clive Solomon's *Record Hits*. Thereafter, the primary, though not sole, source is Ed Hanel's *The Who: The Illustrated Discography*.

INDEX

430

"The career of England's biggest group after the Beatles and the Rolling Stones, a remorselessly detailed, cumulatively depressing succession of wanton mismanagement. The surprise is that they managed to make any records or money at all."
—*The Sunday Times*

"Originally invited by Pete Townshend to write the definitive book of the band, this is a well written and thoroughly researched overview of the Who. Neat, sturdy and workmanlike"
—Ross Fortune, *Time Out*

"*Before I Get Old: The Story of The Who* is certainly the most exhaustive and informed book ever written on the group."
—Mick Brown, the *Guardian*

"One of the most detailed and provocative biographies yet written about any rock band—definitely not fan magazine stuff, but intelligent, literate material for adult rock lovers."
—Joel Selvin, *The San Francisco Sunday Examiner and Chronicle*

"*Before I Get Old* is not a breezy chronology; it demands the reader's attention. It may also be the best rock biography ever."
—David Hinckley, *Daily News*

"Everything you have ever wanted to know about the rock band the Who. Marsh's history is well researched and comprehensive"
—*Booklist*

"Marsh's perceptive study should be read by anyone who cares to understand rock's decline as meaningful pop art. Highly recommended."
—Thomas Jewell, *Library Journal*

"More than simply a biography of one of rock's most interesting bands, this is the social history of an era . . . Marsh is the author of a number of books on rock and roll . . . this is his best yet."
—*Publishers Weekly*

"I highly recommend picking up a copy of *Before I Get Old*
anyway, anyhow, anywhere you can. Marsh takes his readers
on an amazing journey that should not be missed
by any listener of rock and roll."
—David Lupin, *The Tickler*

"*Before I Get Old* is written in a caring and thorough manner
that could only be generated from a first-rate Who fan . . .
the essential work on rock's essential band."
—*Illinois Entertainer*

"Marsh goes beyond creating a documentary by including
his own opinionated analysis. His clear, thought-provoking prose
paints cultural landscapes chronicling a sequence of era
phenomena always intertwined with the music."
—Keith Brown, *The Oakland Press*

"*Before I Get Old* is one of the most impressive and original books
written about rock music . . . scholarly, informative and entertaining."
—Van Nuys, *CA. News*

"This 524-page masterwork contains everything you'd want
to know about the world's most enigmatic rock band"
—Raj Bahadur, *Scene*